DUNNAN'S

Guide to
YOUR INVESTMENT$®
2000

DUNNAN'S

Guide to
YOUR INVESTMENT$®
2000

NANCY DUNNAN

A HarperResource Book
from HarperPerennial

GRATEFUL ACKNOWLEDGMENT IS MADE FOR PERMISSION TO REPRINT:

"How to Calculate the Effect of Inflation" table reprinted with permission from *Encyclopedia of Banking and Financial Tables,* copyright © 1980, 1986, Warren, Gorham & Lamont, Inc., Boston, Mass. All rights reserved.

"The Power of Compound Interest" table reprinted with permission from *Encyclopedia of Banking and Financial Tables,* copyright © 1980, 1986, Warren, Gorham & Lamont, Inc., Boston, Mass. All rights reserved.

"Calculating Growth Rates" table from *Security Analysis,* Fourth Edition, by Benjamin Graham et al. Copyright © 1962 by McGraw-Hill, Inc. Reprinted by permission of McGraw-Hill, Inc.

Designed by Gayle Jaeger

ISSN–1526–5919
ISBN 0-06-273691-4

99 00 01 02 03 ◆/RRD 10 9 8 7 6 5 4 3 2 1

To Dr. Bruce Valauri, whose kindness,
expertise, and care is much appreciated.

CONTENTS

PART THREE
When the Bulls Are Running

PART FOUR
High Risk for High Returns

PART FIVE
You and Your Account

PART SIX
Financing Your Lifestyle

PART SEVEN
Taxes and Your Investments

PART EIGHT
Your Customized Portfolio for 2000

APPENDIXES
Investment Analysis and Information Sources

Acknowledgments

I wish to thank the following people for their expertise and willingness to provide valuable, accurate information:

American Association of Homes & Services for the Aging	Washington, DC	Robert Greenwood
Bureau of Public Debt	Washington, DC	Peter Hollenbach
Burnham Securities, Inc.	New York, NY	Jay J. Pack, David Anderson
Comparative Annuity Reports	Fair Oaks, CA	Joe Rosanswank
Credit Union National Association	Madison, WI	Steve Bosack
Dow Theory Forecasts	Hammond, IN	Charles B. Carlson
Dow Theory Letters	La Jolla, CA	Richard Russell
Gabriele, Hueglin & Cashman	New York, NY	Janet Dugo
Health Insurance Association of America	Washington, DC	Susan Cornell
International Strategy & Investment Group	New York, NY	Joel Fein
Investment Company Institute	Washington, DC	Michelle Worthy
National Association of Investors Corp.	Madison Heights, WI	Kenneth S. Janke, Robert O'Hara
No-Load Fund Investor	Irvington-on-Hudson, NY	Sheldon Jacobs
Schroder & Company, Inc.	New York, NY	John Murray
Securities Investor Protection Corp.	Washington, DC	Michael Don
Social Investment Forum	Washington, DC	Ross Gaskin
Social Security Administration	Baltimore, MD	Carolyn Cheezum
Standard & Poor's Corp.	New York, NY	Arnold Kaufman
T. Rowe Price Associates	Baltimore, MD	Steven E. Norwitz
Thomas Heller Tax Services	New York, NY	Thomas Heller

And, with special appreciation to:
Robert Wilson, HarperCollins
Tim Hays
Marcy Ross

Your Personal Financial Calendar for 2000

"Remember that time is money."

Benjamin Franklin

You don't want to overlook key dates during 2000. If you do, you could lose money—by missing important opportunities and by having to pay tax penalties. That's why we've prepared a financial calendar for the year. . . so you'll know when your estimated taxes and other tax returns are due. We've also tossed in some seasonal money-saving tips so that the year 2000 will be a winner—for you and your family.

YOUR PERSONAL FINANCIAL CALENDAR FOR 2000

Clip and save this calendar and consult it all year round to avoid incurring tax penalties, wasting your hard-earned money, and generally being financially foolish. *NOTE:* Those marked with an asterisk (*) are tax-related actions that must be taken by that date.

SECTION 1

January

- Do your annual Net Worth Statement.
- Determine your financial goals for the year; write them down.
- Set up file folders for 1099s, W–2 form, tax-related documents; give up the old shoe box or shopping bag you've been using.
- Put business-related receipts in a separate folder used to document tax-deductible business expenses when you file next year's returns. Include: receipts for taxis, tolls, gas, telephone and fax charges, rent, stationery, equipment, books, professional dues, etc. Read IRS publications 535, *Business Expenses,* and 463, *Travel, Entertainment, Gift & Car Expenses;* both are free by calling 800–829–3676.
- Buy holiday cards and wrapping paper on sale.
- Pay off holiday credit card debt.
- **** January 15: Your final estimated tax payment for 1999 is due if you did not pay your income tax (or enough of your tax) for that year through withholding.

    Use Form 1040ES.
- **** January 31: If you did not pay your last installment of your estimated tax by January 15, file your income tax return for 1999 by February 2 to avoid late payment penalty for the last installment.

    Use Form 1040 or 1040A.

Notes _____

_____

_____

_____

_____

_____

SECTION 2

FEBRUARY

- Call any banks, brokerage firms, mutual funds, or employers that have not sent you their IRS records by the end of the month.

- Make an appointment with your accountant to discuss taxes. The earlier, the less stressed out he/she will be, and the more attention your return will receive.

- File income tax early and use any refund to reduce credit card debt and/or your car or any other loan that doesn't have a prepayment penalty.

- Visit or call your local IRS office for copies of free booklets on preparing your tax return; avoid the March and April rush.

  To order by phone, call 800–829–3676.

- Shop Presidents' Day sales for winter clothes.

- For a list of outlets in your area where prices are 25% to 70% less, call Outlet Bound, 800–336–8853.

  Get organized to swap your house or apartment for this summer's vacation and thus eliminate hotel bills. Contact: Homelink, 800–638–3841; Intervac, 800–756–HOME; or if you're a teacher, Teacher Swap, 516–244–2845.

**** February 15. If your child/student is working but will not earn enough to owe any tax, this is the last date to file a Form W–4 with his/her employer so that taxes will not be withheld.

NOTE: You can file a new Form W–4 to adjust your withholding allowance any time of the year. Check with your accountant or benefits officer.

Notes

_____

_____

_____

_____

_____

_____

_____

SECTION 3
MARCH

- Challenge your property tax bill. Most states allow appeals in early spring. About half the home owners who question their assessments through official appeals win reductions of 10%.
- Read *How to Fight Property Taxes,* from National Taxpayers Union; $6.95; 703–683–5700.
- Finish preparing your tax return. If you're doing your own return but need last-minute help, call the National Association of Enrolled Agents, 800–424–4339, for the names of those in your area; certified by the IRS, they are less expensive than CPAs.
- **See** Chapters 34 and 35 on taxes and investments.
  Buy air conditioner and fan before prices go up; you'll save anywhere from $50 to $250 per appliance.
- ******** March 2. If you're a farmer or fisherman, file your last year's tax return to avoid an underpayment penalty for the last quarter of 1999 if you were required to pay estimated taxes on January 15.

  Use Form 1040.

Notes

_____

_____

_____

_____

_____

_____

_____

_____

_____

_____

_____

_____

_____

_____

SECTION 4

APRIL

■ Move this month if it's part of your plan. Costs are 40% to 50% cheaper between October 1 and May 1 and highest during the summer months when kids are out of school.

■ Insist your mover give you the booklet *Your Rights and Responsibilities When You Move,* by the Interstate Commerce Commission. Read it before signing a contract.

■ Save all receipts if your move is job related; some expenses may be tax-deductible.

■ Read IRS publication 521, *Moving Expenses;* free by calling 800–829–3676.

■ Support Earth Day, April 22. Reduce cost of garbage pickup and recycling by contacting Mail Preference Service Direct Marketing Association, Box 9008, Farmingdale, NY 11735; 212–768–7277. They will remove your name from most mailing lists. To get off all lists, consult *Stop Junk Mail Forever,* an excellent, $4.50 booklet from Good Advice Press, Box 78, Elizaville, NY 12523, 914–758–1400.

**** April 15. File your income tax return for 1999.

        Use Form 1040, 1040A, or 1040 EZ, and pay any tax that is due.

**** April 15. This is the last day you can fund your IRA.

        See: Chapter 32 for investment suggestions.

**** April 15. Fund your Keogh or SEP if you have self-employment income and are not filing for an extension.

**** April 15. If you are not filing your taxes, get an automatic four-month extension by filing Form 4868. And pay any tax you estimate will be due.

        NOTE: If you get an extension, you can't file Form 1040EZ.

An extension applies to the filing time but not to the time for paying any taxes due. You'll be penalized if the total tax you've paid including withholding, estimated payments, and the check you send on April 15 does not equal at least 90% of the tax you owe for 1999.

**** April 15. If you made any taxable gifts during 1999 (those that were more than $10,000 per donee), file a gift tax return for that year.

        Use Form 709 or 709(A) and pay any tax due. Or for an automatic four-month extension, file Form 4868.

**** April 15. Pay the first quarterly installment of your 2000 estimated tax if you're not paying your 2000 income tax (or enough of it) through withholding tax.

  ■ Use Form 1040ES.

  ■ Pay your IRS trustee or custodial fee with a separate check, so it is tax deductible.

■ Call 800–829–1040 for last-minute help in filing your return. To hear tax recorded info on 140+ topics, call TeleTax at 800–829–4477.

Notes

SECTION 5

MAY

- Get your air conditioner overhauled, clean and/or replace the filter to increase efficiency.
- Make spring-cleaning pay off. If your power company has two-tier pricing, run the dishwasher and wash and dry curtains, bedspreads, and cotton rugs in the evening when rates are lower.
- Do some spring financial cleaning. Take an inventory of your household possessions and check insurance coverage. Items should be covered at their replacement value, not what they cost initially. Make a written or videotaped inventory of your possessions; for jewelry, antiques, collections, and other valuables, get an appraisal. For the name of a local appraiser, call the American Society of Appraisers, 703–478–2228, or click on: www.appraisers.org

  ☑ *HINT: Keep a copy of your inventory at work or in your safe-deposit box.*
- Book summer vacation hotel/resort and airline tickets now to avoid last-minute, outrageously high rates.
- Cut vacation costs by reserving space early in a national park.
- Call The National Park Reservation System, 800–365–2267; and for literature, The National Park Service, 18 C Street NW, Washington, DC 20240; 202–208–4747.
- Check your frequent flier miles now and use them to get limited space on planes for the summer months.

Notes

_____

_____

_____

_____

_____

_____

_____

_____

_____

_____

SECTION 6

JUNE

- Do a semiannual review of your investments. Note the total return figures and yields and compare them with those of January 1 and of one year ago. Then:

- Meet with your stockbroker and/or financial adviser to review your account; decide what securities to hold or to sell.

- **See** Part 8 in this book for specific portfolio suggestions.

- Give a garage or yard sale. Invest the cash you take in.

- **See:** Chapters 3 and 5 on where to invest small amounts of money and get high, safe yields.

- Donate what you don't sell to charity for a tax deduction. Get a receipt.

- Read IRS Publication 526, *Charitable Contributions;* free; 800–829–3676.

- Discuss finances and house rules with any adult children returning home to live with you after graduation (or for any other reasons).

- Read *Never Call Your Broker on Monday,* by Nancy Dunnan (New York: HarperCollins, 1997).

- **See:** Chapter 29 for suggestions on handling family finances.

- Rent, don't buy, wedding dress, bridesmaid clothes, or tuxedos; you'll save at least 50%.

- Get a tune-up for your car; check air-conditioning, water, coolant, and tires, especially if you're driving on a trip.

**** June 15. Pay the second installment of your 1999 estimated tax.

                Use Form 1040ES.

**** June 30. If you have a bank, securities, or other financial accounts in a foreign country that's worth more than $10,000, you must file Form TDF 90–22–1 with the Department of Treasury by this date.

Notes

_____

_____

_____

_____

_____

_____

SECTION 7

JULY

- Read a good investment book on the beach or in the mountains.

  ☑ *HINT: Keep the receipt; it may be tax deductible.*

- Save patriotically. EE Savings Bonds, tops in safety, cost as little as $25, and there's no sales fee.

- For info and current yields, call 800–US–BONDS.

    See: Chapter 10 for more details on bonds.

- Call your nearest Federal Reserve Bank or branch to find out how to purchase U.S. Treasuries without a fee.

    See: Chapter 10 for telephone numbers.

- Talk to colleagues or friends about starting an investment club in the fall. During the summer read the information published by the National Association of Investment Clubs.

    Call 877–275–6242 for material.
    See: Chapter 5.

- Study your cash flow situation during this lazy month.
- Use the worksheet on page 13 to see just where your money is going and then resolve to cut back by September if you need to do so.

Notes

_____

_____

_____

_____

_____

_____

_____

_____

_____

_____

SECTION 8

AUGUST

- Go for good deals on lawn and patio furniture, bathing suits, lawnmowers, barbecues, and camping and ski equipment.

- Prepare your child or grandchild going off to college. Discuss checking accounts, credit cards, and budgeting for the school year.

- Visit a stock exchange or Federal Reserve Bank/branch while traveling in the United States or abroad. **See:** Appendix D and Chapter 10 for addresses and phone numbers. Most have excellent books and pamphlets in their gift shops.

  ☑ *HINT: Good place to take kids and grandchildren and introduce them to "live investing."*

- Take steps to get last-minute money for your child's college tuition payments.
  > **See:** Chapter 29 for a list of loan sources and ideas for meeting educational expenses.

**** August 17. If you filed for an automatic four-month extension, your 1999 income tax return is now due.
  > Use Form 1040 or 1040A, and pay any tax, interest, and penalties due.

**** August 17. Last date to file for a further two-month extension.
  > Use Form 2688.

**** August 17. If you filed for an automatic four-month extension on your gift tax return for 1999, file the return by this date and pay any tax, interest, and penalties due.
  > Use Form 709 or 709A.

  Or if you need an additional extension, check the "Gift Tax" box on Form 2688.

Notes

_____

_____

_____

_____

_____

_____

_____

_____

_____

SECTION 9
SEPTEMBER

- Go back to school. Take a class in financial planning, investing, or money management.
- Figure out what your child earned from a summer job. Ask your accountant if he/she needs to file a return.
- Read IRS Publication 4, *Student's Guide to Federal Income Tax;* free by calling 800–829–3676.
- Weatherize your home. Call your local power company for a free (or inexpensive) winter energy audit.
- Read *How to Weatherize Your Home or Apartment,* $4.75, from Massachusetts Audubon Society, Educational Resources, 208 South Great Road, Lincoln, MA 01773; 781–259–9500.
- Begin your investment club, as discussed in the month of July.
    See: Chapters 14 and 15 on picking stocks.
**** September 15. Pay the third installment of your quarterly 2000 estimated tax.
    Use Form 1040ES.

Notes

_____

_____

_____

_____

_____

_____

_____

_____

_____

_____

_____

_____

_____

SECTION 10

OCTOBER

- Review your will. Since this is a slow month regarding taxes, take time to reread (or make) your will.
- Update if: you've gotten married, separated, or divorced; if you've had a child or grand-child; if your income has changed significantly; if you've moved to a new state; if a close relative or someone named in your will has died; if the tax laws have changed.
- Service your furnace. Replace disposable filters or clean permanent ones.
- Caulk around windows and doors to reduce heating costs.
- Get your flu shot or checkup before cold season; good health is one way to cut medical costs. If your doctor prescribes medication, buy your drugs at a discount through a mail-order pharmacy, such as the one operated by the American Association of Retired Persons.

  ☑ *HINT: You don't have to be retired or a member to participate. Call 800–456–2277 for prices.*

**** October 15. If you received both a four-month and additional two-month extension for your 1999 income tax return, file now and pay any tax, interest, and penalty due. Use Form 1040 or 1040A.

**** October 15. This is the last day to make a Keogh or SEP contribution for calendar year 1999 if you were granted an additional extension of time to file your return.

Notes

_____

_____

_____

_____

_____

_____

_____

_____

_____

_____

_____

_____

SECTION 11

NOVEMBER

■   Talk with your broker about year-end tax swaps and what securities you may want to sell
    before the year end.

        See: Chapters 34 and 35 on taxes.

■   Make charitable contributions for tax deduction.

■   To find out whether a charity is approved by the National Charities Information Bureau,
    call 212–929–6300, or click on: www.ncib.org

    ☑ *HINT: If your gift is more than $250, a canceled check is no longer adequate proof.
    You must possess a written acknowledgment of your donation from the charity to be
    able to deduct it. If your gift is property, not cash, it must include a description of the
    property.*

■   Buy a car this month. Dealers, forced to clear their showrooms for next year's models,
    start offering reduced prices, rebates, and good financing deals. Or buy a used car.

■   To find the current value of a new or used car, call The Consumer Reports Used Car Price
    Service, 800–232–3470; $12/new car and $10/used car.

■   Quit smoking during the American Cancer Society's "Great American Smokeout Week"
    this month. At $3.50/pack, one pack a day is $1,277.50 a year. And you'll cut the cost of
    your life insurance premiums.

■   Begin making Christmas and Hanukkah cards and gifts.

■   Get free firewood. If you live in one of the 155 national forests, you may be able to pick up
    several cords of firewood free, or for a small fee. (A cord of wood regularly runs $85 to
    $125, depending upon where you live.) Check with your regional office of the U.S. Forest
    Service, or call the Federal Information Number, 800–688–9889, for your area number.

Notes

_____

_____

_____

_____

_____

_____

SECTION 12

DECEMBER

- Empty closets and cupboards and give away items to charity for an end-of-the-year tax deduction.
- Review last year's tax return; it will remind you of the tax-deductible expenses you took and can probably take again.

    See: Chapter 34 for a list of deductions.

- Review financial documents. This is the best way to avoid automatically renewing policies, especially life insurance.

    See: Chapter 33 on insurance.

- Play Santa Claus. You can give up to $10,000 to any number of people and not pay a gift tax.

    ☑ *HINT: Checks should be cashed before the end of the year.*

- Push investment income, bonuses, and freelance earnings into next year to delay paying income taxes; you'll also have use of the money for a year. Implement stock or bond swapping for tax purposes.

    See: Chapters 9 and 34 for instructions on how to do swaps.

    ☑ *HINT: For other last-minute tax-savers, see: Chapter 34.*

**** December 31. This is the last day to set up a Keogh Plan for 2000, if you're self-employed. You have until April 15, 2001, to put money in the plan, but you must do the official paperwork now.

    See: Chapter 32 for everything you need to know about Keoghs.

**** December 31. This is also the last day to pay deductible items, such as state estimated taxes, and still get a deduction.

Notes

_____

_____

_____

DUNNAN'S
Guide to
YOUR INVESTMENT$®
2000

This book is intended and written to provide the author's opinions in regard to the subject matter covered. This book is prepared solely by Nancy Dunnan. The author and the publisher are not engaged in rendering legal, accounting, or other professional advice, and the reader should seek the services of a qualified professional for such advice.

The author and the publisher cannot be held responsible for any loss incurred as a result of the application of any of the information in this publication.

Every attempt has been made to assure the accuracy of the statistics that appear throughout *Your Investment$®*. In some cases, data may vary from your reports because of interpretations or accounting changes made after the original publication. In others, there may be errors—for which we apologize. Please remember that *Your Investment$®* is a *guide,* not a definitive source of financial information. When you have a question, check with your broker's research department.

Getting Started Investing

"I've been rich and I've been poor, and believe me, rich is better."

Sophie Tucker

DUNNAN'S THOUGHTS ON THE YEAR 2000

You, too, can start on the road to riches or increase the riches you already have during 2000 by heeding the suggestions and advice in this year's edition of *Dunnan's Guide to Your Investment$®* *2000*. It doesn't matter whether you have $5,000, $50,000, or $550,000. At all three levels and those in between, there are many investment choices—so many, in fact, you may have difficulty deciding where to put your money.

That is what this section, Part One, will help you sort out. It will simplify what can otherwise be a tough decision-making process. Gathering and understanding the information needed to make those decisions is your first step in building up your riches and becoming at ease in the world of finances.

IF YOU ARE A BEGINNING INVESTOR:

Please start by reading all of Part One, Getting Started Investing. Here you will find information on basic, time-tested choices, as well as on:

- How to pick a money market fund
- How to get the best deal at your bank
- The advantages of a credit union
- When to move into mutual funds, and which ones to choose
- How to protect and insure your money

IF YOU ARE A SEASONED INVESTOR:

You should begin by reading Chapter 1, which contains new and timely advice on special investments for 2000. Then move on to the Investor's Almanac where we discuss this year's hot collectibles, and Part Two to size up the risks and rewards of more sophisticated investments.

DUNNAN'S NINE RULES FOR IMPROVING YOUR FINANCIAL LIFE

1. **Be heads up.** Take time to learn how to handle your money. You know perfectly well that the stock market goes up and down, that interest rates change, that unemployment and generally hard times are unfortunately part of our lives. So be smart: Don't passively put your financial matters in the hands of your spouse or your parents, a stockbroker or financial planner, or even the corporation you work for. To do so, I warn you, is childlike and courting disaster.

    If you choose to remain uninvolved or ignorant about the stock market, the direction of the economy, and the workings of the financial world, I guarantee one thing: It will cost you money.

2. **Be informed.** The two best defenses you have against trouble are relatively simple: The first is *information,* and the second is *diversification.* After taking time to learn how the economy, individual companies, the banks, interest rates, the dollar, and inflation affect your investments,

---

Your Personal Financial Library

Read one of these 15 publications each week or month. I've arranged them by approximate level of sophistication, beginning with the most elementary. Subscriptions are available for each, and many are available over the newsstand.

1. *USA Today*	8. *Smart Money*
2. Your local newspaper	9. *Money*
3. *Bottom Line Personal*	10. *The New York Times*
4. *U.S. News & World Report*	11. Standard & Poor's *The Outlook*
5. *Better Investing* (National Assn. of Investment Clubs)	12. *BusinessWeek*
6. *Newsweek*	13. *Barron's*
7. *Your Money*	14. *Value Line Investment Survey*
	15. *Investor's Business Daily*

---

you may still lose money some of the time, but you will win far more often—if you are both diversified and informed.

Begin by reading at least one intelligent financial publication each week. Select one that matches your level of sophistication. Carry it with you (**See:** the box above). Watch the market news on CNN, CNN-FN, CNBC, or PBS television, or listen to broadcasts on public radio. Know what's happening, in this country and abroad.

3. **Be diversified** among types of investments and risk levels. Check your holdings against the Investment Pyramid on page 14. Make certain you have dollars invested in several different levels of the pyramid.

4. **Don't be tempted by those special "hot opportunities"** until you've developed a balanced portfolio. Stay away from futures, commodities, unknown issues, and other complicated investments. These are dominated by the professionals, who have more skill, knowledge, and money than most individuals—and even they get hurt.

5. **Don't follow the crowd.** This is more often than not a mistake. Keep in mind that every major market advance has begun when pessimism was loudest and prices lowest.

6. **Don't dash in and out of the market.** That's simply asking to have your profits eaten up by commissions.

7. **Don't be in a hurry to invest your money.** If you miss one opportunity, there will be another one just as good and perhaps even better coming along tomorrow or the next day.

8. **Don't fall in love with your investments.** If you do, you'll never sell and take your profits. And you'll never sell to cut losses.

9. **Don't be greedy.** Keep in mind that most investments eventually become overpriced, and no tree ever grows to the sky.

LISTENING TO THE PROS

Often it's easier to remember short, savvy soundbites than it is to read pages and pages of intensely detailed economic stuff from Wall Street. You won't go wrong if you follow these words of wisdom:

- *Einstein:* The great Albert once noted that "compound interest was the greatest idea ever conceived by the mind of man." I think his own theory of relativity runs a close second. The investment strategist for Liberty Financial Companies, Porter Morgan, made even greater sense of out Einstein's point in his essay "Three Ways to Become a Millionaire." Morgan calculated

---

Financial Resolutions for 2000

I resolve to:

- *Pay* myself every month—to make savings the first check/deposit I make after my mortgage or rent
- *Set up* a realistic, automatic savings plan
- *Live* within my income
- *Organize* my financial papers
- *Review or write* my will and health care proxy
- *Subscribe* to a financial publication . . . and then actually read it
- *Aim to be an* informed investor, not a timid one or a speculator
- *Spend* half an hour each day listening to or reading about financial matters
- *Invest* only in things I understand, and learn about those I don't
- *Keep* a financial notebook handy in which to write down ideas, questions

And finally,

- *Read* most of this book and deduct the cost from my taxes.

that if, when Christopher Columbus got off the boat in the New World, he'd invested just $1 in a savings account paying 5%, that account today would be worth over $47 billion. Of course, this was over the course of 500 years . . . but you get the point.

■ *Rockefeller:* John Kenneth Galbraith, in his book *The Great Crash,* reminds us that John D. Rockefeller told the press after the crash of October 29, 1929, "Believing that fundamental conditions of the country are sound, my son and I have for some days been purchasing sound common stocks." To this Eddie Cantor replied, "Sure, who else had any money left?"

■ *Mark Twain:* After reading the *Dunnan's Guide to Your Investment$®* and becoming an informed investor, you, too, will be able to decide whether you wish to follow Rockefeller's notion or side with Mark Twain, who said, "October. This is one of the peculiarly dangerous months to speculate in stocks. The others are July, January, September, April, November, May, March, June, December, August, and February."

■ *Warren Buffett:* If you follow Rockefeller's path, I urge you to keep in mind that it's terribly important to cut your losses—when and if you have any. As Warren Buffett, the chairman of Berkshire Hathaway, Inc., said in one of his annual reports, "Should you find yourself in a chronically leaking boat, energy devoted to changing vessels is likely to be more productive than energy devoted to patching leaks."

■ *Mae West:* Personally, I like Mae West's attitude best: "Too much of a good thing can be wonderful." May 2000 be a wonderful year for you and your investments.

1

Special Advice for 2000

Behold the turtle. He makes progress only when he sticks his neck out.

James Bryant Conant

"The safest way to double your money is to fold it over once and put it in your pocket."

There's some debate about which great wit first offered this advice. Most say it was Frank McKinney Hubbard, who worked on the *Indianapolis News* in the 1930s, where, under the name Kim Hubbard, he wrote and illustrated amusing stories about the rustic philosopher Abe Martin.

However, there's absolutely no debate over the fact that it's never easy to double your money, whether it was in 1930 or in 2000. Yet there are a number of steps you can take to increase your personal wealth during 2000 in addition to folding over any spare bills you might have on hand.

AN INVESTOR'S ROAD MAP FOR 2000

Although it's impossible to predict precisely what will happen in the financial world during 2000, there are eight possibilities you should seriously consider.

1. The U.S. stock market will continue to rise, interrupted by occasional corrections.
2. Interest rates will continue to move up slightly to counteract any rise in inflation.
3. We will do more trading of securities and more purchasing of products and services via the Internet.
4. More and more Americans will work at home and/or find work through temp services and placement companies.
5. Major publicly traded companies will offer their shares directly to individual investors, bypassing the need to use a stockbroker.
6. The new, lower capital gains tax (20%) on investments held over 12 months, will add to the appeal of growth stocks.
7. For all taxpayers, except those in the 15% tax bracket, the fact that interest and dividend income are taxed at regular rates makes bank CDs, savings accounts, and Treasuries investments less attractive unless rates rise.

And of course . . .

8. We will all grow one year older.

These trends create unique and interesting investment opportunities for 2000. Bear them in mind as you save, invest, and adjust your personal portfolio over the next twelve months. Begin by implementing the following twelve suggestions.

DUNNAN'S DOZEN—FINANCIAL STEPS FOR 2000

Action Step #1

Don't let greed dictate. Re-evaluate your portfolio.

Sell any mutual funds or stocks that were dogs or mistakes to begin with, and take profits where you've done well. Add solid blue chips on dips. Hold for at least twelve months to take advantage of the favorable long-term capital gains tax rate. Those marked with an asterisk (*) have paid dividends for 50 years and have increased their dividends in each of the last ten years.

Ten to consider:

- Abbott Laboratories*
- Coca-Cola*
- Exxon Corp.
- General Electric
- Johnson & Johnson*
- Merck & Co.*
- Pfizer*
- Procter & Gamble
- Royal Dutch Petroleum
- Walgreen Co.*

Action Step #2

Add long-time dividend payers to your portfolio.

Stocks that have strong and growing dividends provide protection on the downside as well as a modest amount of income. These fifteen have paid dividends for 50 years and have increased their dividends in each of the last ten years.

- Banc One
- Becton, Dickinson
- Bristol-Myers Squibb
- Campbell Soup
- Duke Energy
- First Union
- Gillette Co.
- Kimberly-Clark
- Marshall & Ilsley
- PPG Industries
- Rubbermaid, Inc.
- South Trust Corp.
- State Street Corp.
- Universal Foods
- Warner-Lambert

Action Step #3

Invest in Internet and technology stocks, but carefully.

Unless you've done a Rip van Winkle, you know that the Internet is *the* booming industry in this country. The problem: Many companies in the field have yet to turn a profit or even come close. So earmark a portion of your portfolio for this sector, realizing that although you may realize impressive gains it's still risky business. Begin by looking into QQQ, a stock that replicates the Nasdaq 100 and therefore participates in the Internet/technology sectors. (**See:** pages 155–156 for details) Thirteen additional suggestions:

- Black Box Corp.
- Cisco Systems
- Convergys Corp.
- EMB Corp.
- Earthlink Network
- Nokia Corp.
- Qualcomm, Inc.
- Siebel Systems
- Sterling Software
- Tellabs, Inc.
- Unisys
- Visx, Inc.
- Vodafone AirTouch

Action Step #4

Invest in companies that help people find work or relocate.

More and more Americans are finding work through placement agencies and/or are working as temps or permanent temps. These four companies are likely to see increased revenues during 1999–2000.

- Kelly Services
- Korn/Ferry Int'l.
- Manpower
- Olsten Corp.
- Robert Half International

Action Step #5

Invest in companies that are involved in the graying of America.

As the baby boomers and the rest of the nation age, a growing number of products and services are necessary to take care of this segment of our population. These companies, in addition to the drug manufacturers, do just that.

- Ameripath, Inc.
- Biogen Inc.
- Cardinal Health
- Elan Corp.
- Express Scripts
- General Nutrition
- Health & Retirement Properties
- Healthcare Services Group
- Immunex Corp.
- Lincare Holdings
- Sepracor Inc.
- Visx
- Wellpoint Health Networks

Action Step #6

Invest in companies with low debt.

These ten companies are well positioned to weather economic downturns, to cover their dividends, to purchase other companies, to expand.

- Bob Evans
- Dollar General
- Dun & Bradstreet
- A.G. Edwards
- Family Dollar Stores
- Smucker (JM)
- Stride Rite Corp.
- Tootsie Roll Industries
- Walgreen Co.
- Weis Markets

Action Step #7

Invest in regional banks.

This group is ripe for longterm profits and takeovers. Eleven considerations:

- American Bank of Connecticut
- Bancwest Corp.
- Bank of New York
- Fifth Third Bancorp
- First Tennessee National
- Marshall & Ilsley
- North Fork Bancorp
- Old Kent Financial
- People's Bancshares
- Unionbancal
- Wilmington Trust Corp.

Action Step #8

Consider refinancing your mortgage.

As we go to press, interest rates on 30-year, fixed rate home mortgages are starting to creep up. Don't delay. Refinance your mortgage or, if you're thinking of buying, do so. Ask your current lender to figure out what your new payments would be with a lower rate, or run the numbers yourself, using a mortgage calculator posted on the Internet or by calling the numbers given below.

- Fannie Mae: www.homepath.com or call: 800–732–6643
- HSH Associates: www.hsh.com or call: 800–873–2837
- Mortgage Bankers Association: www.mbaa.org
- Bank Rate Monitor: www.bankrate.com
- Best Rate: www.bestrate.com

Then, figure how many months it will take you to make up the costs of refinancing. If you think you'll move before that date, it probably doesn't make sense to refinance.

Action Step #9

Check your credit report.

If you think you want to refinance, get a mortgage, or take out a business loan, you will need a clean credit record. Even one or two late payments on your credit card can stall or even nix getting a mortgage. If there are mistakes, you want to get them fixed. You can get a copy of your credit report for a small fee by calling the three major credit agencies.

- Equifax: 800–685–1111
- Experian: 888–397–3742
- Trans Union: 800–888–4213

Action Step #10

Be aware of key tax rulings.
Discuss them with your tax account, stockbroker, and financial planner.

- The favorable capital gains tax rate of 20% kicks in when you've held a stock twelve months.

- You can convert your older IRA into the new Roth IRA even if you discover later on in the year that your income exceeds the $100,000 minimum. You may revoke the conversion by April 15, when your tax return is due.
- When you sell a home you've lived in for at least two out of the prior five years, you can take a tax-free gain of $500,000 on a joint return or $250,000 on a single return.
- If you live in your primary residence for less than two years, you can still take the tax-free gain if you sell it because of a job move, for medical reasons or for other "unforseen circumstances."
- If you are divorced, legally separated or have lived apart for at least 12 months, you can limit your liability for unpaid taxes on a joint return. You'll need to consult your accountant for details.
- Student loan interest is deductible for up to 60 months of interest. The maximum deduction is $1,500 on your 1999 tax return and rises gradually to $2,500 in 2001. It is available for refinancing of old loans as well as for new loans, and can be deducted only by the person paying the interest; and that person cannot be a dependent.
- You can take money out of your IRA before age 59½ without a penalty if it's: to pay for higher education costs for yourself, a spouse, child, or grandchild; to meet medical expenses that exceed 7.5% of AGI; to pay health insurance premiums if you are unemployed for more than 12 weeks; to help buy a first home for yourself, a child, a grandchild, or a parent, with a lifetime limit of $10,000.
- Amounts contributed to a Roth IRA can be withdrawn tax-free and penalty-free after five years. That means you can tap this money before age 59½ for tax-free funds.
- Retirement distributions from a Roth IRA will be totally tax free, providing the five-

year holding period is met and the owner is over 59½

- Mandatory distributions at age 70½ from a Roth IRA are not required.

Action Step #11

Buy U.S. Treasuries.

I recommend this as one of your action steps every year. . . and recently it's become even more appealing because the government reduced the minimums on all Treasuries to just $1,000. You'll find details for how to purchase Treasuries without a broker's fee in Chapter 10. Remember, you pay no state or local income tax on the interest earned. This is a good year to also consider the relatively new Inflation Indexed Treasury.

Action Step #12

Move money out of your bank savings account.

I repeat this action step as well. I am always amazed at how many people have money parked at their bank where it's earning a paltry 2–3%. Don't wait another day to make this change. Move it to a money market fund; you'll double your interest and get free checks for those you write in amounts of $500 or more.

Call: The Strong Funds at 800–368–1030 or click on: www.strongfunds.com for details. This Milwaukee-based mutual fund company has consistently had two of the highest yielding money market funds. As we go to press, the regular money market fund is yielding 4.56% and the Investors Money Market Fund, 5.22%.

2

Building Your Personal
Investment Pyramid

One of the questions I am asked most frequently is, "How do I get started investing? I don't know where to begin." It's a very valid question, and one you should not be embarrassed to ask.

There are hundreds of choices out there, and many more people willing to sell them to you. How do you choose between stocks and bonds, mutual funds and bank CDs, Spiders and LEAPS, zeros and Diamonds, options and commodities, foreign stocks or foreign currencies? Real estate or gold?

An easy way to get started is to envision your financial world literally as an *investment pyramid*—it works whether you are a new investor or a sophisticated money manager who has weathered numerous bull and bear cycles.

The pyramid is a visual way in which to see how much risk accompanies each type of investment . . . and exactly when it's appropriate to add each as you build your portfolio.

YOUR HOMEWORK ASSIGNMENTS

To make the most money, you need to be prepared, like the Boy and Girl Scouts—and to do your homework. Here are your four assignments.

Lesson #1: Know Thy Worth

Before making any type of investment expenditure, whether it's buying a stock, a bond, or a house, you need to know your approximate net worth—not down to the last penny, but within

several thousand dollars or so. This is one of the first questions any reliable stockbroker, money manager, and bank mortgage officer asks potential clients. If, like most people, you're not sure, don't panic. Figuring it out is easy—all you need is a free evening, a calculator, your checkbook, bills, and a record of your income. Then follow these two easy steps:

1. Add up the value of everything you own (your assets).
2. Subtract the total of all you owe (your liabilities).

The amount left over is your net worth. You can use the worksheet on page 11 as a guide for arriving at the correct amount. When figuring your assets, list the amount they will bring in today's market, which could be more or less than you paid for them originally.

Assets include cash on hand, your checking and savings account balances, the cash value of any insurance policies, personal property (car, boat, jewelry, real estate, investments), and any vested interest in a pension or retirement plan.

Your liabilities include money you owe, charge account debts, mortgages, auto payments, education or other loans, and any taxes due.

Lesson #2: Know Where Thy Worth Is Going—a.k.a. Budgeting

Unless you like number crunching, you're probably not exactly thrilled with the idea of doing a budget,

10

Finding Your Net Worth

ASSETS as of _____(date)		LIABILITIES as of _____(date)	
Cash on hand	$_____	Unpaid bills	
Cash in checking accounts	_____	Charge accounts	$_____
Savings accounts	_____	Taxes, property taxes, and	
Money market fund	_____	quarterly income taxes	_____
Life insurance, cash value	_____	Insurance premiums	_____
Annuities	_____	Rent or monthly mortgage payment	_____
Retirement funds		Utilities	_____
IRA or Keogh	_____	Balance due on:	
401(k) plan	_____	Mortgage	_____
Vested interest in pension		Automobile loans	_____
or profit-sharing plan	_____	Personal loans	_____
U.S. savings bonds, current value	_____	Installment loans	_____
Investments		**Total liabilities**	$_____
Market value of stocks, bonds,			
mutual fund shares, etc.	_____		
Real estate, market value of real property			
minus mortgage	_____	Assets	$_____
Property		Minus liabilities	–_____
Automobile	_____	**Your net worth**	$_____
Furniture	_____		
Jewelry, furs	_____		
Sports and hobby equipment	_____		
Equity interest in your business	_____		
Total assets	$_____		

but if you're serious about taking good care of your net worth, then a little budgeting is part of the deal. In fact, it's really the only accurate way to know how much you're spending and on what, and it's also a way to set aside money for investing, which is probably the reason you bought this book in the first place.

If you need help in establishing a budget for saving and investing, use the fill-in Cash Flow worksheet on page 13. And set aside a certain dollar amount every week, on a regular basis—no matter the amount. Saving is a habit, not an art form, and you can do it with any dollar amount, large or small.

Ideally you should try to save 5% to 10% of your annual income; if you make more than $75,000 a year, aim for 15%.

☑ HINT: *Here's my favorite gimmick for those of you who need one to get you going: Begin by saving 1% of your take-home pay this month and increase it by 1% each month for a year, so that at the end of 12 months you'll be saving 12%.*

In the meantime, take a look at the table on page 12, which shows what happens to $1,000 over 20 years when you put it in an investment yielding 5¼% and the income earned is reinvested or compounded.

What Happens to a $1,000 Investment at 5¼% Compounding

Frequency of Compounding	1 Year	5 Years	10 Years	20 Years
Continuous	$1,054.67	$1,304.93	$1,702.83	$2,899.63
Daily	1,054.67	1,304.90	1,702.76	2,899.41
Quarterly	1,053.54	1,297.96	1,684.70	2,838.20
Semiannually	1,053.19	1,295.78	1,679.05	2,819.21
Annually	1,052.50	1,291.55	1,668.10	2,782.54

Lesson #3: Know Thy Goals and Priorities

After you've accumulated money to invest, your next homework assignment is to decide what you want to accomplish by investing. If you were to take a trip to Europe or travel by car across the country, you would take along a good road map. So, too, it is with saving and investing. The road map, however, consists of financial, not geographic, destinations. When you travel through Italy, you decide what towns, cathedrals, or monuments you want most to visit; how long it will take you to get from one to the next; and approximately what it will cost. Just do the same as you plot out your financial journey through life.

Your highlights or destination points may include some of these:

- Building a nest egg for emergencies
- Establishing an investment portfolio
- Paying off college loans
- Preparing for retirement
- Paying for your child's education
- Buying a house, car, motorcycle, or boat
- Traveling or taking a cruise
- Investing in art or antiques
- Adding on a room or installing a swimming pool or tennis court
- Setting up your own business

WRITING DOWN YOUR GOALS

Goal-setting, you will discover, enables you to take firm control of your financial life, especially if you actually write down your goals. The process of listing goals on paper, perhaps awkward at first, forces you to focus on how you handle money and how you feel about risk versus safety. I think it's best to divide your goals into two sections: immediate goals (those that can be accomplished in a year or less) and long-range goals.

You'll find it a lot easier to put aside 5% to 15% every month when you know that it's going to pay down your mortgage, take the family to Paris, send you back to school.

If You're Single

Those of you who are living on your own could have as some of your immediate goals:

- Get a graduate degree
- Join a health club
- Save for summer vacation
- Start to pay off college loans

Longer-term goals:

- Buy a car
- Set up a brokerage account or buy shares in a mutual fund
- Purchase a co-op or condo with a friend

If You're Married

Those of you who have tied the knot, and may even be raising a family, should shift your goals somewhat to include:

Your Cash Flow
Where It Comes From

Where It Goes

	Annual Amount		Annual Amount
Take-home pay	$_____	Mortgage or rent	$_____
Bonus and commissions	_____	Income taxes	_____
Freelance consulting	_____	Property taxes	_____
Interest	_____	Utilities	_____
Dividends	_____	Automobile	
Capital gains	_____	Maintenance	_____
Rent	_____	Insurance	_____
Pensions	_____	Commuting or other transportation	_____
Social Security	_____	Insurance	
Annuities	_____	Homeowner's or renter's	_____
Tax refunds	_____	Life	_____
Alimony	_____	Health	_____
Other	_____	Disability	_____
Total	$_____	Child care	_____
		Education	_____
		Food	_____
		Medical expenses	_____
		Clothing	_____
		Household items	_____
		Home improvements, upkeep	_____
		Entertainment	_____
		Vacations, travel	_____
		Books, magazines, club dues	_____
		Contributions to charities or organizations	_____
		Total	$_____
		Surplus or deficit	_____

- Buying a house
- Setting up a college fund for your children
- Building a growth portfolio
- Travel with the family

If You're Heading toward Retirement

Whether you're single or married, at this point you should:

- Shift part of your portfolio to safe, income-producing vehicles
- Increase the amount you contribute to all retirement plans

- Find appropriate short-term tax shelters
- Set up a consulting or moonlighting business; incorporate
- Pay off mortgage
- Be debt-free the year before you retire

Lesson #4: Building Your Investment Pyramid

Once you know why you want to save and invest, you're ready to be like the Egyptians and build your own financial pyramid—one in which each level builds on the strength of the earlier ones.

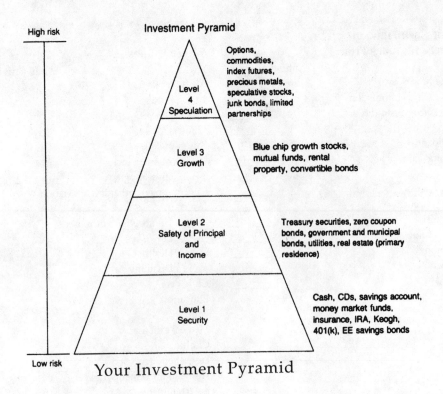

Your Investment Pyramid

This approach to investing is about as safe as you can make it. You'll wind up with an automatically designed money system that will provide for real financial growth and lots of protection regardless of your age, marital status, income, or level of financial sophistication.

As you can see by looking at the illustration, you obviously begin at the beginning, on **Level 1**, the comfort level. It is the lowest in terms of risk and the highest in safety. As your net worth grows, you automatically move up to the next level, increasing both the amount of risk involved and the potential for financial gain.

Level 1 covers life's basic financial requirements and includes:

- An emergency nest egg consisting of cash or cash equivalents, such as a savings account, CDs, money market funds
- Health, life, and disability insurance

- A solid retirement plan, including an IRA, Keogh, or 401(k)

Before leaving this level, you will have saved enough cash or cash equivalents to cover a minimum of six to nine months' worth of living expenses. This minimum is your emergency reserve, and when you've achieved this goal, you're financially solid enough to advance to Level 2.

Level 2 is devoted entirely to safe income-producing investments, such as corporate or municipal bonds; Treasury securities; longer-term CDs; zero coupon bonds; and real estate (your primary residence)—all of which are described in this book.

Although safety is key at this step, the liquidity factor emphasized in Level 1 is now traded off for a higher return or yield. And because some of these items, notably zero coupon bonds and CDs, are timed to mature at a definite date, they provide ideal means to meet staggering college tuition bills and retirement costs.

Money to buy real estate is also included, not only because it gives you a place to live, but also because historically real estate has appreciated significantly in value. At the same time, it offers tax benefits in the form of deductions for mortgage and home equity interest payments and for real-estate taxes.

Level 3 involves investing for growth. At this point you can afford to be more adventuresome, more risk-oriented, and less conservative; and this book shows you how to turn away from liquidity and assured income and toward growth and blue-chip stocks, mutual funds, convertible bonds, and rentable property.

☑ *HINT: If you find you're interested in the stock market, this is the ideal time to join an investment club and learn by doing.*

Level 4, the pinnacle of the pyramid, is given over to the riskiest investments, which may or may not yield spectacular returns. These include speculative stocks, stocks in new companies, takeover candidates, options, commodities, index futures, gold and precious metals, junk bonds, and limited partnerships, all vehicles discussed in detail in the following chapters.

FOUR DUMB INVESTMENT MISTAKES YOU CAN ACTUALLY AVOID

You may think that only novices make investment mistakes—not true. Here are four common traps into which the pros as well as new investors fall, along with practical solutions for each. Chapter references are to further material in this book.

1. *Chasing yields.* When CD and money market funds pay attractive yields, it's easy to park our money in one or the other or both. This is perfectly okay with some of your money, but it's

no way to keep up with inflation, let alone beat inflation.

Solutions: (1) Stagger bond and CD maturities so that you continually have money coming in for reinvestment should rates go up. (2) Put only one-quarter of your income portfolio in risky, high-yield bonds or bond mutual funds (**see:** Chapter 6).

2. *Failing to diversify.* It's easy to be lazy, keep doing what works, and overlook the importance of dividing your portfolio into different investments—ones that work in different ways so that you are protected when interest rates move up or down or when the market is bullish or bearish.

Solutions: Divide your money among these categories: (a) money funds, CDs, and Treasury bills; (b) domestic stocks; (c) foreign stocks; (d) domestic bonds; (e) international bonds; and (f) real estate. Then, within each category, you can diversify even further. With stocks, divide your money among blue chips, small-caps, utilities, growth stocks, and some new issues, for example.

Within the bond category, you can further divide your investments into different maturities (ranging from short- to long-term); into tax-free municipals; and into different risk levels: government bonds, AAA-rated corporate bonds, and higher-risk junk bonds (**see:** Chapters 10 and 13).

3. *Not taking advantage of dollar cost averaging.* Most investors either put too much or too little into stocks or mutual funds at one time.

Solution: Instead, invest a set amount on a regular basis, say, once a month, to smooth out market fluctuations. You'll generally wind up making purchases at a lower cost per share than if you bought all at once (**see:** page 258).

☑ *HINT: Need a little arm-twisting to get going on a regular savings plan? Set aside a certain amount weekly or monthly and look at what can happen.*

What Happens When You Save at 5¼%

Monthly Amount	Number of Years				
	5	10	15	20	25
$100	$7,348	$18,295	$34,604	$58,902	$85,103
$300	22,043	54,884	103,811	176,706	285,308
$500	36,738	91,473	173,019	294,510	475,513

The accumulation of interest and/or dividends is impressive. Here's what happens when you invest $100, $300, and $500 every month, assuming a fixed rate of 5¼%.

4. *Hanging onto a losing investment.* Too often we are taken with a stock or other investment, so it's hard to admit we made a mistake.

Solution: Set a percentage loss figure and stick to it. Write it down in your investment book or on your computer disk. When you sell, note why the investment turned out to be a loser, so you can avoid repeating your error.

ASSET ALLOCATION

Before we move on, it's important to take a moment to explain asset allocation. This phrase refers to the way you divide your investment portfolio among the three basic investment categories or asset classes: 1) growth (e.g., stocks), 2) fixed-income (e.g., bonds), and 3) cash. What percentage you have in each category depends on the degree of risk you want to take, how old you are, what your goals are, and your personal wealth.

Putting these three together—cash, stocks, and bonds—in a combination that works specifically for you is what asset allocation is all about.

Why have money in all three categories? Because, at any given time, each one performs differently from the others. For example, when interest rates are high, cash assets such as money market funds, Treasuries, and bank CDs offer high yields, but stocks tend to perform less spectacularly. The bottom line is that you benefit from the asset classes that are doing well while minimizing your exposure to those that are not. In other words, a good mix will offer you smoother sailing and a better total long-term return.

Aggressive investors with long-term goals will want to have more stocks in their portfolio, while more conservative investors will want more in bonds. Both will need some money in cash to meet short-term needs and to provide an emergency nest egg.

If you are seeking maximum growth, are willing to accept risk, and are seeking to meet long-term goals, such as paying for a child's education or saving for retirement, your asset allocation might be:

- 85% in stocks
- 10% in bonds
- 5% in cash

A more conservative allocation would be:

- 55% in stocks
- 40% in bonds
- 25% in cash

WHAT TO DO WHEN: A MONEY STRATEGY CHECKLIST

In Your 20s and 30s

- *Write* your will
- *Set* up a savings plan
- *Buy* a house
- *Invest* in at least one growth mutual fund

13 Tips for the Beginning Investor

1. *Don't think you'll get rich overnight.* Few people do.
2. *Don't rush into stocks or bonds* until you've saved the equivalent of six to nine months of living expenses in a money market fund, CDs, or treasuries.
3. *Know whether you're investing for income or growth.* Many people never bother to figure this out and are disappointed with their returns.
4. *Pick stocks and bonds of leading companies* at the beginning. They have proven track records, a lot of research is available for them, and there will always be a buyer should you wish to sell.
5. *Buy a stock* only if you can state at least two reasons why it will appreciate in price or continue to pay high dividends.
6. *Resist churning your own account* so that commissions won't eat up your profits.
7. *Spread out your risks.* Every company and mutual fund has the potential to be a loser some of the time. Therefore, never put all your eggs in one basket.
8. *Decide on the maximum amount* that you're willing to lose and stick to it.
9. *When you lose money,* if you do, try to determine why your choice was a poor one.
10. *Study investing* and investments on a regular basis.
11. *Never invest in something you don't understand.*
12. *Don't listen to hot tips* from people who think they're hot.
13. *Sell when you double your money* and go out for dinner.

- *Get* disability insurance, and life insurance if you have kids
- *Begin* contributing to a retirement plan
- *Start* your IRA

In Your 40s and 50s

- *Do* all of the above if you haven't already
- *Invest* for income as well as growth
- *Put* part of your portfolio into tax-exempt investments
- *Fund* your retirement plan to the max
- *Think* carefully about buying a nursing home insurance plan
- *Draw up* a durable power of attorney or living trust, and a living will

- *Consult* an attorney if your estate is over $675,000 this year
- *Pay* off your mortgage before you retire

In Your 60s or at Retirement

- *Invest* more for income, but keep some growth stocks
- *Aim* to reinvest income and gains to beat inflation
- *Review* your will and estate plan
- *Investigate* retirement housing; actually visit several choices
- *Talk* to your family about your estate plans and funeral wishes
- *Revise* your will if it's out of date

3

Finding Safe Places for Your Money: Banks, Money Market Funds, CDs, and Credit Unions

*T*hroughout your investment life there will be many times when some of your assets should be kept liquid—liquid meaning almost instantly available. But don't confuse instant with meaning in a bank savings account. You should *absolutely not* have money in this type of account—the interest rate is always way, way too low.

So what can you do? You have six other options:

1. Interest-bearing checking accounts (sometimes called NOW accounts)
2. Bank or credit union money market deposit accounts
3. Bank or credit union certificates of deposits (CDs)
4. Money market mutual funds
5. U.S. savings bonds
6. U.S. Treasuries

(The latter two are discussed in Chapter 10.)

Check the table on page 19 to compare the current yields for each one (as we went to press), as well as their average minimum dollar requirements and the amount of time you can have your money invested in each one.

I don't by any means suggest you put all your money in these safe havens—even their yields are too low—but you should certainly earmark about one-quarter of your assets for this Level 1 category.

Investors—amateurs and pros—have come to realize that even the bluest of the blue chips can fall in price and thus diversification is not just mumbo jumbo from the mouths of conservative financial advisers and writers such as myself:

It is the basis of protecting one's investments in economic climates of all kinds.

☑ *HINT: Be sure you know the difference between interest rate and yield. Interest rate is the annual return without compounding. The effective yield reflects compounding—daily, monthly, quarterly, annually. Compare the same figure when shopping around.*

PROTECTING MONEY AT YOUR BANK

In late 1992, the Federal Insurance Deposit Corporation (FDIC) limited the interest rates that our weaker banks can give customers, while at the same time permitting well-capitalized banks to determine their own interest rates. So, undercapitalized banks can no longer pay extremely high rates to get you in the door; however, it still pays to shop around, because rates, fees, products, and services continue to vary from bank to bank. Although it's time consuming to get on the phone, do. It could mean you're landing as much as 2% more.

☑ *HINT: All things being equal, however, there's something to be said for having all or most of*

Safe Havens

INVESTMENT	YIELD (SEPTEMBER 1999)	AVERAGE MINIMUM INVESTMENT
■ **1 to 3 Months**		
Money market mutual funds	4.53%	$1,000
Bank money market accounts	2.15	1,000
6-month CDs	4.30	500
3-month Treasury bills	4.78	1,000
Passbook savings account	2.05	50
Credit union savings	3.98	50
■ **3 Months or Longer**		
12-month CD	4.66	500
1-year Treasury bills	5.12	1,000
10-year Treasury bonds	5.76	1,000
30-year Treasury bonds	5.90	1,000
I bonds	5.05	1,000
EE savings bonds	4.31	25

your banking done at one institution. Called "relationship banking," it may mean you can get higher interest on your savings, lower fees on your checking, and better terms on your loans. That's because when all your banking is lumped together, you become a more important customer. But find out.

☞ *CAUTION: Unless you have a very small amount to save or are opening an account for a child, skip savings accounts; better interest rates are available through the accounts described in the rest of this chapter.*

To get the most out of your bank:

1. Ask for overdraft checking privileges—that is, a permanent line of credit that prevents you from bouncing a check. The bank will automatically cover your check even if you don't have enough money in the account, for up to a predetermined dollar amount. You will have to pay back the loan plus interest.

2. Once you have more than $2,500 in your NOW account (or whatever the minimum balance required is), move the excess into a money market deposit account at the bank or to a money market mutual fund—whichever has better rates.

3. Don't buy bank-printed checks. You can save money by ordering checks from Checks in the Mail (800–733–4443) or Current, Inc. (800–426–0822).

4. Don't withdraw money from an ATM at a bank other than yours; it will cost you $2 or more a visit. Take out what you need once a week from your own bank.

5. Banks love mortgages—they make money on them, because you actually pay about $2 to $3 for every dollar you borrow on a long-term mortgage. Cut this by making an additional principal payment every month.

$TIP: Pay an extra $50 a month on a 30-year, $100,000 mortgage at 9% and these additional payments of around $14,000 will save you almost $50,000.

6. Ask for free checking—you may get it if you're a senior citizen, disabled, a student, or a big customer. If you have a mortgage, car loan, or CD at the bank, mention it in connection with getting noticed.

7. Ask for a free safe-deposit box.

Bank Money Market Deposit Accounts

The counterpart of a money market mutual fund at a bank is a money market deposit account. They pay relatively competitive interest rates, offer liquidity, and your money is insured up to $100,000 by the FDIC or, at a savings and loan, by the FSLIC.

CAUTION: They tend to pay slightly lower yields than money market mutual funds and Treasury bills, and their rates change periodically with fluctuations in overall short-term rates, which is also true of money market mutual funds. The minimum to open ranges from $100 to $10,000.

■ *Advantages:* These accounts also offer convenience; most banks let you write checks on them for any dollar amount, although they limit the number of checks you can write to third parties (anyone but yourself)—typically to three checks per month to a third party and three preauthorized transactions (as might occur when you arrange in advance to pay a specific bill, such as a mortgage payment).

Generally, you may withdraw cash in person as often as you like. On the other hand, money market mutual funds let you write as many checks as you like, but you must write them for a minimum amount—usually $250 or $500.

■ *Disadvantages:* Yields and penalties for falling below the required minimum vary from bank to bank. Find out whether your bank avoids paying interest on a money market deposit account if the balance drops below a certain minimum.

Certificates of Deposit (CDs)

CDs, also known as time certificates of deposit, are safe, reliable savings instruments available at most every local bank. The certificate indicates that you have deposited a sum of money for a specified period of time (six months, one year, etc.), at a specified rate of interest.

■ *Advantages:* The fact that CDs are insured up to $100,000 has made them popular with savers seeking a high level of safety. Banks are free to set their own minimum amounts, but they tend to range from $500 to $5,000 and more. Those that are $100,000 or over are called jumbo CDs and pay a slightly higher yield.

Determining how long to tie up your money is not always easy. If you've invested in a three-year CD and interest rates rise, you'll be stuck with the old lower rate. On the other hand, if rates fall, you'll be glad to have locked in the high yield. In general, if rates are falling, buy longer-term CDs, and if they are rising, keep the maturities short.

You should also ask the bank how you will find out when your CD is due. The bank should either send you a reminder or call you a few weeks beforehand, so you can decide whether to withdraw your certificate or roll it over into a new CD.

☑ *HINT: To maximize your return, buy a CD in which the interest is not actually paid out until maturity. This gives you the benefit of compounded interest.*

■ *Disadvantages:* If you take out your CD before it matures, you will be penalized. The typical penalty is three months of interest on a CD of less than one year, and six months of interest on one that's longer than a year.

EXAMPLE: If you bought a two-year CD for $10,000 earning 5% and an emergency comes along and you have to take some of the money out, you'll be hit with a charge of $250.

Exceptions to the rule: Early withdrawal penalties are usually waived in three instances:

- If the owner dies or is found to be mentally incompetent
- If the CD is in a Keogh or IRA retirement plan and the depositor is over 59½ years old
- If the bank offers penalty-free early withdrawals

 HINT: *If you have $50,000 to $100,000 to invest in a CD, negotiate your rate. Banks may pay between ¼% and 1% more on large CDs.*

Zero CDs

Some brokerage firms offer zero coupon CDs in a variety of maturities. This type of CD does not pay interest on a regular basis. Instead, it is sold at a discount from face value. The interest accrues annually until the CD matures. You must report the income for tax purposes each year as it accrues.

Retirement CDs

This new product, available from a relatively small number of banks, is aimed at those who want safety rather than growth. Also known as an annuity CD, it combines a bank deposit with an annuity. As with the standard CD, your principal and interest are insured by the FDIC, up to $100,000. And, as with an annuity, all earnings are tax-deferred until you withdraw them. At that time you receive a monthly income for life.

 CAUTION: *The FDIC does not insure your lifetime payments; if the bank fails and is liquidated, you would get back your principal and interest, minus whatever payouts you'd already received.*

In general, however, it's a safer investment than the straight insurance company annuity, because when insurance companies go belly-up, part of your money can be lost. The tradeoff: Retirement CDs have a lower yield.

Finding Out the True Rate

Bank CD ads are often very confusing, with two rates given: fixed rate and yield. The yield figure is always higher, but to earn it, you must have your CD at the bank for one full year at the same annual rate.

EXAMPLE: If your bank advertises a fixed rate of 6.5% and a yield of 6.75%, and you buy a six-month CD and take it out at maturity, you will earn only the 6.5% fixed rate.

 HINT: *Roll over your six-month CD so that it is on deposit the full year in order to earn the effective annual yield. In most institutions, the original yield is applicable even if the yield falls.*

Advantages of Buying CDs from a Stockbroker

Buying a CD through your stockbroker is often a better deal than buying it through a bank because yields tend to be higher. That's because brokers have access to CDs from banks across the nation and are not limited to just one institution. Merrill

CDs with a Twist

Bank		Special Feature
Security First Network, NY	(800–736–2321)	Preferred rates
College Savings Bank, Princeton, NJ	(800–888–2723)	Rises with college tuition
BB&T, Baltimore, MD	(800–220–2080)	Automatic homesaver's CD
Wells Fargo Bank, San Francisco, CA	(800–869–3557)	Continual deposits; expandable CDs

Lynch, for example, can tap about 160 banks, which gives investors more choices in terms of maturity, yield, and risk factor. And because brokered CDs are still bank CDs, they are insured up to $100,000.

Stockbrokers usually do not charge fees for CDs, because they receive their commission from the issuing bank. Brokered CDs are also more liquid than those available at banks, because they can be sold by your broker in a "secondary market." And there's no penalty for selling prior to maturity as there is when you cash in a bank CD.

A Word about Interest Rates

Even though CDs are regarded as a very safe investment, their value, just like bonds, rises and falls in direct relationship to interest rates: If interest rates rise, the price of your CD will fall and you'll receive less than face value if you sell. If interest rates fall, you may be able to sell your brokered CD at a premium, because it's worth more, because its rate is higher than that being paid on newly issued certificates.

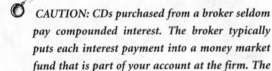 *CAUTION: CDs purchased from a broker seldom pay compounded interest. The broker typically puts each interest payment into a money market fund that is part of your account at the firm. The interest is often lower than that being paid on your CD. Check with the broker first, so you understand exactly how your interest will be handled.*

Out-of-State CDs

If you're seduced by ads for higher yields at out-of-state banks, remember that the grass isn't always greener. Proceed with caution, and steer clear of troubled banks and S&Ls. Even though your money is insured up to $100,000, if the institution is closed, there may be a delay in getting your money out, and there have even been cases where high yields have been reduced.

To find the nation's best CDs, check:

- *USA Today* and *Investor's Business Daily,* which have very easy-to-read listings
- The Wednesday issue of the *Wall Street Journal,* which lists the top-yielding CDs for one-, two-, three-, and six-month, and one-, two-, and five-year maturities.
- Personal finance magazines, such as *Money* and *Your Money,* which run lists of high-yielding CDs and bank money market deposit accounts.

BANKING ON-LINE

In order to stay competitive, some banks are matching rates being paid by money market mutual funds. Best bets: branchless banks that do business by mail, phone, and the Internet such as:

- Key Bank, USA: 800–872–5553
- Bankfirst: 800–328–2411
- Advanta National Bank: 800–441–7306
- TeleBank: 800–638–2265

Best Bank CDs

FINANCIAL INSTITUTIONS, CONTINUALLY BATTLING FOR MORE DEPOSITORS, OFTEN HAVE INTEREST RATE WARS. THESE BANKS ARE TYPICALLY AMONG THOSE OFFERING THE HIGHEST RATES ON CDs.

Providian Bank	800–821–9049
Key Bank USA	800–872–5553
M&T Bank NA	800–724–2440
MBNA America	800–577–3556

Brokered CDs

Firm	Telephone	Minimum
A. G. Edwards	800–999–4448	$1,000
Fidelity	800–544–8888	5,000
Edward D. Jones	314–515–2000	5,000
Merrill Lynch	local office	1,000
US Bankcorp Piper Jaffray	800–333–6000	1,000
Prudential Securities	local office	1,000
Charles Schwab	800–435–4000	5,000
Soloman Smith Barney	local office	1,000

(Data current as of Fall 1999.)

 CAUTION: Money market depositors at banks can make only six withdrawals per month and only three of those can be checks.

MONEY MARKET MUTUAL FUNDS

These funds are pooled investments sold by mutual funds, insurance companies, and brokerage firms. They take your cash and invest in something called the money market—a term that describes the way in which the government, banks, corporations, and securities dealers borrow and lend money for short time periods.

Money market mutual funds actually buy such short-term financial instruments as Treasury bills and notes (government IOUs), CDs (bank IOUs), and commercial paper (corporate IOUs). Many also invest in repurchase agreements, bankers' acceptances, federal agency securities, Eurodollar CDs, and Yankee-dollar CDs.

Money market funds are an excellent parking place for your money while you try to decide where to invest. They are not a true investment

---

Four Ways to Make More Money at Your Bank

1. *Stagger your CD maturities* by purchasing a variety of maturity dates, say, for 6 months, 12 months, and 15 months. If interest rates rise, you can reinvest CDs that mature at the new rate. If rates fall, your longer-term CDs will be earning the old, higher rate.

2. *Invest your CD interest.* Ask your bank to invest your CD interest automatically in a money market deposit account. You'll earn interest on your interest yet have access to the money without incurring a withdrawal penalty.

3. *Snowball your CD.* If your bank offers higher rates on larger CDs, it may pay to roll over several small CDs into one big one. Select a target date, say one month after your longest-term CD matures. When you renew your smaller CDs, have them mature on that date. Then all your CDs will mature on the same day, and you can reinvest in one large CD with a high rate.

4. *Establish* your own interest-bearing checking account. Instead of depositing your paycheck into your checking account, put it in your money market deposit account. Several times during the month, transfer money to cover your checks. You will earn money market rates and be less tempted to spend without thinking about it first.

The Eight Advantages of Money Market Funds

1. *Daily income.* Dividends are credited to your account each day, which means that your money is always working for you.

2. *Liquidity.* There is no minimum investment period, and there are no early withdrawal penalties. Money can be withdrawn quickly by telephone, mail, wire, or check.

3. *Stability of principal.* Most money market funds have a constant share price of $1. This makes it easy to determine the value of your investment at any time. Earnings are also paid in shares, so the value of a share never increases above $1. For example, if your interest in a money market mutual fund averaged 5% and you invested $1,000, at the end of one year you would have 1,050 shares worth $1,050.

4. *No fees or commissions.* When you buy shares, all your money goes to work immediately.

5. *Small minimum investment.* Some funds require as little as $500 initial investment; most minimums are between $1,000 and $2,000. In general, funds do not require shareholders to maintain a minimum investment.

6. *Safety.* Your money is used to buy prime debt of well-rated corporations or the U.S. government and its agencies. If you choose a fund that invests only in U.S. government securities, your yield will be $1/2$% or so lower, but you can count on Uncle Sam's guarantee. Money market funds bought through your stockbroker are protected by the SIPC. (See page 35 for details on SIPC.)

7. *Check-writing.* Most funds offer this service free, although some require that checks written be for at least $250 or $500.

8. *Continual high yields.* If rates drop, you will receive the higher interest rate for about a month afterward until the high-yielding securities are redeemed. With a bank, the yield changes more frequently, usually on a weekly basis.

except when rates are high. Their rates are almost always slightly higher than the bank equivalent, a money market deposit account. Your shares are always valued at $1/share.

How to Find a Money Market Fund

To buy shares in a money market fund, you simply call the fund directly or your stockbroker. You can get your money out at any time, either by writing a check (the fund provides the checks) or by wire.

You can find a list of money market funds in the financial pages of most newspapers, and several financial magazines list those with the highest yields. See: box on page 25 for Dunnan's recommendations.

How to Select the Right Money Market Fund

There are hundreds of money market mutual funds out there. They fall into four basic cate-

gories—knowing which one is best for meeting your investment goals will help narrow the search.

- *General funds.* Available from your stockbroker or directly from the fund itself by calling its toll-free number, general funds invest in nongovernment money market securities.

- *Government-only funds.* Limit their investments to U.S. government or federal agency securities. Because their portfolios are backed by the "full faith and credit" of the U.S. government, they are regarded as less risky; consequently, they have lower yields than general funds.

- *Federal tax-free money market funds.* These restrict their portfolios to short-term tax-exempt municipal bonds. Their income is free from federal tax but not necessarily from state and local taxes. Advisable only for investors in the 28% tax bracket or higher. Their yields are,

Best of the Money Market Funds   Yields, Fall 1999

Alger Fund	4.35%	800–992–3863
Dreyfus Liquid Assets	4.43	800–645–6561
Dreyfus Worldwide Dollar Fund	4.45	800–645–6561
Evergreen Fund	4.53	800–235–0064
Fidelity Spartan*	4.34	800–544–8888
Strong Money Market Fund	4.58	800–368–1030
Vanguard Prime Portfolio	4.47	800–662–7447

*Fidelity Spartan charges $2 per check if there's less than $50,000 in the account.

of course, much lower, sometimes about half those of a regular money market fund.

■ *Double or triple tax-exempt money funds.* Designed for residents of high income-tax states, such as New York, California, Massachusetts, and Connecticut, these invest in short-term tax-exempt municipals and are free from federal, state, and often local taxes for residents of the states and localities that issue them.

By shopping around you will find that some funds have higher yields than others (see the lists in this chapter). At various times the yield discrepancy has been as much as 3% to 3½% on taxable funds, but the current yield is not the only factor to consider; look also at the 12-month yield and the character of the fund's holdings.

☑ *HINT: To determine how you would fare in a taxable versus a tax-exempt fund:*

1. *Subtract your tax bracket from 1*
2. *Divide that number into the tax exempt yield times 100*

Understanding the Risk Factor

The risk factor—even though it's quite minimal with money market funds—rises with the portfolio's maturity. By law, any money market fund that says it keeps its net asset value at $1 per share is required to limit its average portfolio maturity to 90 days. If you're a conservative investor, select a fund with maturities of 90 days or less. If you're willing to assume more risk, you may get a slightly higher yield.

How Steady Savings Pays Off

IF YOU MAKE MONTHLY PAYMENTS INTO YOUR MONEY MARKET FUND AT THE BEGINNING OF THE MONTH, HERE'S HOW YOUR ACCOUNT WILL GROW:

Monthly Payment	Rate of Return	1 Year	5 Years	10 Years
$50	4%	$613.16	$3,326.00	$7,387.03
$100	4%	1,226.32	6,652.00	14,774.06
$100	4%	1,839.48	9,978.00	22,161.10

NOTE: Amounts are slightly less if payments are made at the end of the month.
SOURCE: Strong Funds, Milwaukee, WI.

Lower-quality portfolios lead to higher yields but also higher risk.

CREDIT UNIONS

A credit union is a cooperative, not-for-profit financial institution organized to provide checking, savings, loans, and other financial services for members. Membership is limited to those having a common bond—occupation, association, etc.—and to groups within a community or neighborhood. Many credit unions allow members to remain members even if they move away or change jobs.

Credit unions are member owned and controlled, with each member having an equal vote and the opportunity to serve on the board of directors. The board, elected by the membership, sets dividend and interest rates. Board members are volunteers, except for the treasurer, and they may not receive payment for their services.

Credit unions are either state or federally chartered. State chartered unions are supervised by a state regulatory agency. Federally chartered ones are supervised by the National Credit Union Administration, an independent agency in the executive branch of the federal government. Member share accounts are insured up to $100,000 per account by the National Credit Union Share Insurance Fund.

There are approximately 11,400 credit unions representing more than $400 billion in assets and over 76 million individual member-owners.

Credit union CDs, sharedraft accounts (interest-bearing checking accounts), and money market deposit accounts pay extremely competitive rates, often $1/2$% higher than banks. Loans may be $1/2$% to 1% lower.

Credit union credit cards are often a great bargain, charging on average 2% less on unpaid balances than other credit card issuers.

Credit unions can afford to undercut their competitors because they are nonprofit corporations, don't pay federal taxes, and are essentially volunteer directed. Credit unions are also available for students.

What the Money Market Mutual Funds Buy

- *Bankers acceptances:* drafts issued and sold by banks with a promise to pay upon maturity, generally within no more than 180 days
- *Certificates of deposit:* large-denomination CDs sold by banks for money deposited for a minimum time period (14 days, 91 days, etc.)
- *Commercial paper:* unsecured IOUs issued by large institutions and corporations to the public to finance day-to-day operations, usually in amounts of $100,000 for up to 91 days
- *Eurodollar CDs:* dollar-denominated certificates of deposit sold by foreign branches of U.S. banks or by foreign banks; payable outside the United States, the minimum is generally $1 million, with maturities of 14 days or more
- *Government-agency obligations:* short-term securities issued by U.S. government agencies
- *Repurchase agreements ("repos"):* short-term buy/sell deals involving any money market instrument in which there is an agreement that the security will be resold to the seller on an agreed-upon date, often the next day. The money market fund holds the security as collateral and charges interest for the loan. Repos are usually issued as a means for commercial banks and U.S. government securities dealers to raise temporary funds.
- *U.S. Treasury bills and notes*

Ultrasafe Money Market Funds

MUTUAL FUNDS SPECIALIZING IN U.S. TREASURY SECURITIES YIELD

Capital Preservation Fund	800–345–2021	4.33%
Fidelity Government Reserves	800–544–8888	4.26
Fidelity U.S. Treasury Money Market	800–544–8888	4.31
Vanguard U.S. Treasury Money Market	800–662–7447	04.45*

FEDERAL TAX-FREE MONEY MARKET FUNDS

Franklin Tax-exempt Money Fund	800–342–5236	2.44
Lexington Tax-free Money Market	800–526–0056	2.43
USAA Tax-exempt Money Market	800–531–8181	2.44

HIGH-INCOME STATES: TRIPLE TAX-EXEMPT

Dreyfus Tax-exempt Money Market	800–645–6561	2.45
Fidelity Mass Tax-free MM Portfolio*	800–544–8888	2.51
Vanguard Tax-free Calif Money Market	800–662–7447	2.75

*Double tax-exempt.
(Yields as of Fall 1999.)

FOR FURTHER INFORMATION

Material on Credit Unions

Credit Union National Association
P.O. Box 431
Madison, WI 53701
800–358–5710
website: www.cuna.org

Material on Banking

Consumer Federation of America and the AARP, *Money in the Bank: How to Get the Most for Your Dollar* (New York: Perigee Books, 1998).

How to Take Advantage of Interest Rate Changes

1. *When rates are low:* Buy short-term CDs.
2. *When rates begin to rise:* Put more money into your money market account, so you can ride up with the rates.
3. *When rates are high:* Lock in yields with long-term CDs. Move money out of money market accounts into higher-yielding CDs.
4. *When rates are falling:* Immediately lock in with a CD before they fall further.
5. *When rates are low:* Invest over the short term and add to your money market account so that your cash will be available for reinvesting when rates begin to rise.

4

Protecting Your Cash and Your Investments

*T*umultuous markets, changing interest rates, bank failures, mergers of financial institutions, on-line banking and trading, and the occasional dishonest broker cause even the most trusting of us to worry about how safe our money is—and rightly so.

Here's what you need to know.

IS YOUR BANK SAFE?

The Nitty Gritty

Most of the country's commercial banks are insured by the Federal Deposit Insurance Corporation (FDIC), an independent government agency. To be eligible for membership in the FDIC, a bank must meet certain standards and be regularly examined by both federal and state agencies. Member banks pay insurance fees, which are in turn invested in federal government securities. These securities constitute the FDIC's Bank Insurance Fund. In addition, the FDIC may borrow several billion dollars from the U.S. Treasury if it needs to.

Most savings and loan associations (also known as thrifts) are insured by the FDIC through the Savings Association Insurance Fund (SAIF). Some savings and loan associations are insured by state insurance, a very few are privately insured, and a handful have absolutely no insurance at all.

☝ CAUTION: *Make certain you are with an insured S&L.*

Most credit unions (97%) are insured by the National Credit Union Administration (NCUA); others, by state agencies.

The FDIC and NCUA are backed by the federal government, and money insured by them is considered safe, because the government would presumably come to their rescue. Banks that are insured by a state or privately, however, do *not* have the backing of the federal government.

KNOW THE FDIC RULES—BANKS PROTECT ONLY SOME OF YOUR MONEY

The solution is not to tuck your money under the mattress, but to bank only at federally insured institutions and to know the facts about insurance coverage. Here they are:

Rules for Existing Accounts

■ Contrary to popular opinion, or wishful thinking, the government does not insure $100,000 per account. Instead, it insures $100,000 per person at any one bank or savings and loan in any "one right and capacity." If you have several savings accounts, even at different branches of the same institution, and they are all in the same name, they are lumped together for insurance coverage. In other words, if you have four accounts in the same name in one institution, you are insured only for a total of $100,000, not $400,000.

Government Protection

Federal Deposit Insurance Corporation Bank Insurance Fund

- Insures depositors for up to $100,000
- Consumer hotline: 800–934–3342
- Address for more information on deposit insurance: 550 17th Street NW, Washington, DC 20429
- website: www.fdic.gov

Savings Association Insurance Fund

- Insures depositors for up to $100,000
- Consumer affairs: 800–934–3342
- Address for more information on evaluating SAIF: 550 17th Street NW, Washington, DC 20429

National Credit Union Share Insurance Fund

- Insures depositors for up to $100,000
- Telephone: 703–518–6300
- Address for more information on your credit union: 1775 Duke Street, Alexandria, VA 22314

- The $100,000 figure applies to both principal and interest. So, if you have $98,000 in an account and you then earn $5,000 in interest, your account will be insured for $100,000, leaving $3,000 uninsured.

- If you have money in a checking account, a savings account, and a CD at one bank, in your name, you do not get $100,000 of insurance for each account—you get a total coverage of only $100,000. And changing your name on different accounts, by using a middle initial, for example, will not boost your coverage.

- If you are married, you can get coverage for more than one account: You and your spouse can each have an individual savings account. You may also have one joint account. In addition, you can set up two trust accounts, known as revocable testamentary accounts: one in trust for your spouse; the other being your spouse's, in trust for you. This type of account pays the balance to the beneficiary upon the death of the grantor of the trust. And you could each have an IRA account. That's a total of seven accounts. With $100,000 in each, all

$700,000 would be insured even though it's all in the same bank.

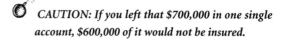 **CAUTION: If you left that $700,000 in one single account, $600,000 of it would not be insured.**

- Some other types of testamentary accounts are insured separately if the beneficiary or beneficiaries are qualified as kinship—a child, stepchild, grandchild, step-grandchild, or spouse. An account in trust for a parent, niece, or friend is treated as another account in your name and does not get separate coverage. Note that these types of accounts are insured to $100,000 per qualifying beneficiary. Thus, an account in trust for your three children is insured to $300,000.

- Joint accounts are insured separately from individual accounts, but with certain limitations—you are insured for up to $100,000 on the money you have in all joint accounts at any one bank. If, for instance, you have $100,000 in three joint accounts at the same bank—one with your wife and one with each of your two

Help from Regulators

If you're having a problem with your bank, call one of the regulatory authorities listed below. They are surprisingly accessible, often more so than your local bank official. If you need to file a written complaint, include a brief statement describing the problem and a list of the steps you've taken to try to resolve it. Include your bank account number and copies of all documents. Keep a copy for your files.

Ask the customer service department which regulator oversees your bank—they are legally obligated to tell you.

FDIC
Office of Consumer Affairs
550 17th Street NW
Washington, DC 20429
800–934–3342
website: www.fdic.gov

Federal Reserve Board
Consumer Affairs
Mail Stop 800
20th and C Streets NW
Washington, DC 20551
202–452–3946
website: www.bog.frb.fed.us

Office of Thrift Supervision
Consumer Affairs Division
1700 G Street NW
Washington, DC 20552
202–906–6237 or
800–842–6929
website: www.ots.treas.gov

U.S. Comptroller of the Currency
Customer Assistance
250 E Street SW
Washington, DC 20219
800–613–6743
website: www.occ.treas.gov

daughters—your share of each would be $50,000, or half, for a total of $150,000. Of that only $100,000 will be insured.

- *POD Accounts.* In this type of account, a depositor indicates that upon his or her death, the money goes to a named beneficiary. POD accounts are insured for up to $100,000 for each beneficiary, who could be a parent, sibling, spouse, child, or grandchild.

☑ *HINT: For more details, check with the FDIC at: 800–934–3342 or: www.fdic.gov and then click on "Consumer News & EDIE."*

- The FDIC treats all joint accounts owned by the same combination of people at the same bank as being one account. So, if you and your spouse have a joint checking and a joint savings account, the two together are insured for

up to $100,000. And don't try reversing the order of your names or using your Social Security number on one and your spouse's on another—it doesn't work.

☑ *HINT: If you have a loan or home-equity line of credit at your bank, check its financial condition (see "How to Check Up on Your Bank" below). If your bank should fail, you could lose access to your credit line—a real problem if you need the money.*

Remember, too, that changes in your life can affect your FDIC coverage. For example, death could convert your joint account to an individual account and thus put you over the $100,000 limit. Or your interest accrual or a large cash payment, say, from the sale of a home, insurance proceeds, inheritance, or a lump sum pension distribution, could likewise toss your balance above the insurance limit.

Choose Only Insured Bank Products

Banks offer both insured and uninsured products. If you are uncertain about a particular product, ask the bank to give you written assurance regarding its coverage.

Products that are typically insured include checking accounts, savings accounts, NOW accounts, Christmas club accounts, certificates of deposit, money market deposit accounts, and trust fund accounts.

Banking products that are not typically insured include annuities, mutual funds, life insurance, stocks, bonds, government securities (Treasury bills, bonds, notes), repurchase agreements, and commercial paper, which includes shares of the bank's stock.

HOW TO CHECK UP ON YOUR BANK

You can protect your money by banking only at financially solid institutions. It is not difficult to find out whether your bank is solid—these two private rating companies provide in-depth studies of the banks, savings and loans, and credit unions:

Veribanc, Inc.
PO Box 461
Wakefield, MA 01880
781–245–8370; 800–442–2657

Bauer Financial Reports
Box 145510
Coral Gables, FL 33114–5510
800–388–6686

And also, request and read the "Report of Condition" on your bank (not available for branches, only main banks). It will tell you how much the bank is making, what its loan portfolio is made up of, and what percentage of loans is non-performing. Send a check for $10 to:

FDIC
Disclosure Group, Room F–518
550 17th Street NW
Washington, DC 20429
800–945–2186

If Your Bank or Savings and Loan Fails

Should the unthinkable happen and a federally insured bank or savings and loan fail, the FDIC or the Savings Association Insurance Fund (SAIF) will either liquidate the institution's assets to pay off depositors or transfer assets to a healthy institution. You may have to wait, but you will receive your principal and interest, up to $100,000.

In most cases, in fact, a solvent institution takes over the failed institution's assets and liabilities. For example, the April 1990 collapse of Seamen's Bank for Savings in New York, the largest bank failure of the year, was estimated to cost the FDIC $2.8 billion. Seamen's 13 branches, valued at $2.1 billion, were sold to Chase Manhattan Bank for $5 million.

CAUTION: When accounts of a failed institution are transferred, the new management can lower the interest rate being paid on CDs or increase the rate you pay on a home-equity loan or other credit line. However, you must be given prior notice and time to make penalty-free switches to another institution that has more favorable rates. If bank officials won't let you know whether they are honoring your existing terms, take it as a warning and begin looking for a new bank or savings and loan.

If you have a loan, the loan cannot be called in by the new bank under any conditions not spelled out by the original loan agreement. Check your agreement for loopholes. If you don't understand it, ask your lawyer.

CAUTION: If a federally insured institution fails, regulators will liquidate the assets, and insured depositors will be paid usually within five business days. If you have money in excess of the $100,000 insured limit, however, you will have a pro rata stake for that portion in excess of $100,000, along with other creditors, and you may or may not get that portion of your money back.

How Safe Is Your Safe-Deposit Box?

If your bank fails, the acquiring institution will take over the safe-deposit boxes and you will be notified. If there is no acquirer, you will receive written instructions about coming in and removing the contents.

Even under normal circumstances your safe-deposit box may not be so safe. The contents are not insured by FDIC nor by the bank that rents you the box. Take time to read the rental contract to see whether there's any insurance coverage.

I suggest that you purchase fire or theft insurance if you do not have safe-deposit box coverage as part of your home-owner's or tenant's insurance policy; check with your agent.

Stolen funds may be covered at the bank by a blanket bond, which is a multipurpose insurance policy banks buy to protect the institution from fire, flood, earthquake, embezzlement, and just plain old-fashioned robberies and stickups. If a bank employee messes around with a customer's account, the blanket bond insurance will probably cover your loss. On the other hand, if a third party gains access to your account and transacts business using your checks or ATM number, you must notify both the bank and the police.

HOW SAFE IS YOUR MUTUAL FUND?

The mutual fund industry is governed by the Investment Company Act of 1940—but that does not guarantee total protection. Here are the facts:

■ *Bankruptcy.* The assets of a mutual fund belong to the shareholders, and all securities are held in trust by a third party. A fund's directors can theoretically ask shareholders to allow the fund to close down if its assets have dwindled and it's no longer profitable to operate, for example. To date, this has never happened.

It's far more likely that a troubled fund will merge into a larger, healthier one; this often happens when a bank, S&L, or brokerage firm goes bankrupt. However, a very small fund that is poorly managed might be unable to attract a merger candidate.

If a fund were to liquidate, the shareholders' fortunes would depend on market conditions and the quality of the fund's holdings. The SEC would oversee the sale and subsequent distribution of assets. A small fund with large holdings of thinly traded securities or little cash on hand could be in for losses if the market were down.

■ *Suspension of trading.* Trading can be suspended only in the case of a national emergency—if the New York Stock Exchange closes, there's a presidential assassination, war, etc. Yet, even in these situations, you can place a redemption order, and it will lock in the fund price at the close of the trading day.

■ *Importance of cash reserves.* The fund managers almost always hold cash and Treasury securities in their reserves, plus proceeds from security sales. Funds also have bank credit available to them: They can borrow $1 for every $3 of assets. Yet, a heavily invested fund, when faced with a barrage of redemption requests, might have to sell stocks even when it would prefer not to.

HINT: Invest only in a fund that has at least 10% or more in cash reserves.

HINT: It doesn't matter what time of day you put in your mutual fund buy or sell order; as long as it's in before 4 P.M., Eastern time, you're guaranteed the closing share price that day. Phones are busiest in the morning.

HOW SAFE IS YOUR MONEY MARKET FUND?

Everyone wants to know how safe their money market fund or account is. It's very safe. But every investment has some degree of risk. Money market funds have an excellent safety record, primarily because they invest in short-term securities of the government, large institutions, and corporations.

The basic principle to keep in mind is: The shorter the maturity of an investment, the lower the risk. Why?

Short portfolio maturities keep a fund's risk level to a minimum, because a bank or corporation whose securities are sold in the money markets is not very likely to default in such a short time. In addition, securities that mature so quickly seldom fluctuate in value. A money market mutual fund's securities must mature in one year or less, and no one individual security may make up more than 5% of a fund's assets.

☑ *HINT: The average maturity is about 40 days. You can check maturities in the financial section of your newspaper.*

For the ultimate in safety, select a fund that invests only in Treasury issues (**See:** list on page 27). These are backed by the full faith and credit of the U.S. government. They are called government or Treasury-only funds. The yields are about 1% lower than nongovernment money market funds.

Money market funds must have:

- Ninety-five percent of their assets in short-term debt, such as the highest-grade commercial paper. The other 5% can be held in second-tier paper, such as A–2 or P–2, but no more than 1% of this can come from the same issuer.
- No more than 5% of a fund's total assets can

be invested in the securities of a single issuer, except for those of the U.S. government.

- The average maturity of a fund's portfolio can be no more than 90 days.

☑ *HINT: Invest in a large money market fund, one with at least $1 billion in assets. It's more likely to protect shareholders than a small fund.*

EVERYTHING YOU EVER WANTED TO KNOW ABOUT DERIVATIVES

Back in 1994, the "D" word entered our world—at that time some leading corporations such as Procter & Gamble and Gibson Greeting suffered losses on investments and Orange County, California, one of the richest counties in the country, filed for bankruptcy because of investments in derivatives.

Most mutual funds have derivatives, and for that reason, Morningstar Mutual Funds, the Chicago research and rating service, has information on how funds use derivatives. For each fund it lists the four basic categories of derivatives:

- Options and futures
- Illiquid securities
- Exotic mortgages
- Structured notes

It then gives the percentage of assets the fund invests in each type.

Just What Are Derivatives?

A derivative is a financial instrument whose price is derived from other prices—prices typically of an underlying security, asset, or index.

The most familiar and oldest of derivatives are found in the commodities markets where farmers and those who purchase farm products used *options* and *futures contracts* to protect themselves in the price they either pay or receive for wheat, cattle, corn, coffee, etc.

They are also used to control the risk of

volatile interest rates and exchange rates as well as for purely speculative purposes. Some of them have fairly complex features that make them particularly sensitive to any changes in the underlying security's price.

In addition to basic options, forwards, and futures, there's a more complicated type known as a synthetic security. These include indexed securities whose values are tied to the movement of what is known on Wall Street as an unmanaged market index, such as the Standard & Poor's 500 floating rate notes (which reset their interest rates periodically to reflect changes in other rates), and mortgage-backed securities in which the interest and principal payments from the underlying mortgages are sold as separate securities.

Pools of home mortgages cut up and packaged as collateralized mortgage obligations, or CMOs, are technically derivatives.

All types of derivatives come with risks. Market risk is a key one—the risk of loss due to changes in the prices of securities underlying the derivatives. There's also income risk—risk that the stream of income will change. This is particularly applicable to derivatives based on a security or index. Another risk is called valuation risk—that the instrument has not been priced accurately. Two other risks: liquidity risk—that the security cannot be sold at a good price; and finally, counter-party risk—the risk that one party to an agreement cannot meet its obligation.

The Advantages of Derivatives

If your mutual fund owns index futures or options (two of the more common types of derivatives), don't panic. In fact, if they are used intelligently and carefully they may even reduce your risks.

Many sound portfolio managers use derivatives to counterbalance the movements of stocks, bonds, commodities, and currencies, by creating separate but related deals to the actual markets for these investments. Strategies involving derivatives to offset market activity are known as hedges.

Managers of international stock and bond portfolios very often use currency forwards and options to keep the portfolio stable, because the value of the portfolio's international investments fluctuate with changes in the value of currencies.

In another situation, a portfolio manager might buy a futures contract on the S&P 500 index in order to put new cash to work while seeking more suitable stocks.

How Derivatives Work

Let's look at options, a common type of derivative. Its value depends on the movements in a stock's price. It has a specific shelf life—often three months. There are two types of options: calls and puts. Call options let the holder buy shares at a specified price (known as the strike price), whereas put options let the holder sell shares at a specified price. The value of a call increases when the stock goes up; the value of a put increases when the stock price falls.

You might want to write a call on your stock as a way to make money. If your stock is trading at $50, you write an option and sell it to another investor to purchase shares at $60 for $2 a share. If the stock doesn't reach $60 before the option expires, you gain $2 per share in income and also collect any dividends the stock pays out.

Options are explained in detail in Chapter 17.

The Disadvantages

The trouble, however, arises when the portfolio manager uses borrowed money or invests only a fraction of the cost of the securities underlying the derivatives. Known as leveraged investing, it backfires completely if the manager guesses wrong.

What Derivatives Mean to You

Although some derivatives are relatively safe and liquid, others have been deemed inappropriate, especially for money market mutual funds. To make this point clear, the SEC has stated that these derivatives are unsuitable for money funds:

- Inverse floaters
- Leveraged floaters
- CMT floaters
- Capped floaters
- Dual-index floaters
- COFI floaters

☑ *HINT: You should feel free to call your mutual fund and ask its policy on derivatives. To avoid derivatives altogether, stick with funds that are 100% invested in U.S. Treasuries.*

If you'd like a slightly higher yield (accompanied by a bit more risk), look into money funds that invest in Treasuries and repurchase agreements, a.k.a. repos. A standard repo agreement works like this: The fund manager buys a position in government agency securities from a bond dealer, agreeing to sell them back the next day at the same price plus a little interest. Although the fund has taken on a degree of risk, it also has the securities as collateral in the event that the bond dealer can't make good on the repurchase agreement.

HOW SAFE IS YOUR BROKERAGE ACCOUNT?

Your money, or at least much of it, is protected at your broker's firm by the Securities Investor Protection Corp. SIPC, as it's called, consists of a $1-billion plus fund supported by some 7,500 member brokerage firms. It also has a $1 billion credit line with the government that can be activated only by the SEC, as well as a $1 billion credit line with banks.

SIPC is neither a government agency nor a regulatory agency. Rather, it is funded through assessment of dealer members. All brokers and dealers registered with the SEC and national stock exchanges must contribute, except those dealing exclusively with mutual funds.

If a Brokerage Firm Fails

When this happens to a firm that's an SIPC member, SIPC then applies to a court, which appoints a trustee to liquidate the firm and perhaps transfer customer accounts to another broker. (If the firm is small, the SIPC may decide to cover losses from its funds directly.)

If it has the securities on hand, the liquidating firm will send the securities registered in customers' names directly to them. If it does not have enough securities to meet all customer claims, they would be secured on the open market. Any remaining claims will be settled in cash. However, this ties up your money for several months.

If the brokerage house in liquidation does not have enough securities or funds to settle all claims, the rest will be met by the SIPC—up to $500,000 per customer, including $100,000 for any cash held in the brokerage account.

Your Account

If you have investments in a brokerage account, SIPC will cover the market value of your stocks, bonds, CDs, mutual funds, notes, and warrants on securities. Commodities and commodity options, gold, and silver are *not* covered. Coverage is up to $500,000, including $100,000 in cash.

☑ *HINT: Extend your coverage by opening a second account as a joint account with your spouse, as a trustee for a child, or as a business account. Each account receives full protection—$500,000.*

Keep in mind that the SIPC covers losses due to the failure of the firm, not losses because investments turned out to be of poor quality or because securities fell in price. And many brokerage firms carry additional insurance, about which you can ask your broker. In the past 28 years, SIPC has liquidated 277 firms. In 1998, only 6 were liquidated.

Questions to Ask Your Broker

Ask your broker or financial planner these questions when you're faced with an investment you're uncertain about:

- How much of my money is being invested in the primary product? Where will the rest be invested?
- How long is the guarantee or insurance good for?
- Am I protected against market loss?
- If the project or investment fails, who is responsible for covering the losses?
- Who backs the insurance or guarantee?

HOW SAFE IS YOUR PENSION PLAN?

Think of pension plans like any other investment—one that requires safeguarding. Never ever assume your retirement money is 100% safe. Review the following facts and then talk to your pension fund manager.

- Defined benefit plans promise a set amount upon retirement, usually based on factors such as age, earnings, and years of service. Most are insured by the Pension Benefit Guaranty Corporation (PBGC), an FDIC-like agency that will pay each employee a certain amount determined by law. For example, if a plan closed down or the company failed in 1997, those retiring at age 65 would receive about $33,000 per year.

  However, PBGC does not insure all types of plans. Among those not covered: those that do not promise specific benefits, such as 401(k) plans, profit sharing, and defined contribution plans.

- A company can terminate a fully funded pension plan at any time and pay benefits in a lump sum or buy annuities from insurance companies to take over monthly benefit payments. When that happens, you have lost your protection.

- Defined contribution plans, which include 401(k)s, profit-sharing plans, and employee stock option plans, include more than 80% of all private pensions. The amount contributed to the plan by you and by your employer is typically a percentage of your pay or the company's profits.

  You are not guaranteed a specific amount upon retirement. You get the contributions made plus any earnings. And this type of plan is *not insured* by the Pension Benefit Guaranty Corporation.

- About one-third of the money in defined contribution plans is invested in a Guaranteed Investment Contract (GIC), which, like bank CDs, pay a guaranteed interest rate for a set time. GICs are sold by insurance companies; if you do not live in one of the states that insures these plans, your money is backed by the insurer only. If the insurance company is in bad shape, then so is the GIC it sells.

- Ask your company's plan administrator for a copy of Form 5500, the financial report the plan is required to file with the Labor Department.

- If your pension money is invested with an insurance company, read the section that follows for safety tips.

HOW SAFE IS YOUR INSURANCE COMPANY?

In recent years several life insurance giants became insolvent. And consumers have less protection when life insurers fail than they do when banks tumble. Insurance companies are regulated by state commissioners, not by federal authorities, and there is no national fund to cover losses. Each state has a life and health insurance guarantee association insurance fund. These nonprofit organizations were created by state law to provide money to policyholders.

Typically they cover individual policies up to $100,000 of cash value or $300,000 of life insurance and death benefits. Each insurance company is assessed 2% of premiums received in the state for policies and contracts covered by the guarantee association. This money is in effect turned into an insurance pool.

Depending upon how well funded the insurance pool is and how large the losses, you might have to wait for your money. A state regulator can intervene if a major insurer runs into trouble. This was the case when the failed Executive Life Insurance lost some $900 million in the 1990 market. Its assets, valued at $13 billion, plunged; then policyholders, hearing about the problem, began to cash out and Executive Life had to pay about $4 billion in policy redemptions.

Until policies can be transferred to another company or some other arrangements are made, insurers typically lose access to the cash value of their contracts, sometimes for periods of a year or more. It is possible that, in the final analysis, they may get less than the contract's full value.

☑ *HINT: Call your state insurance commission to make certain you would be covered under the state guaranty system if your insurer became insolvent. Some state plans cover contract holders of companies headquartered in that state regardless of where they live; others guarantee only their own residents and only if they are insured by companies licensed in that state.*

How to Protect Your Insurance Coverage

The best way to avoid problems is to do business with financially sound life insurance companies— those that have A+ or A++ ratings by A. M. Best or AA or AAA by Standard & Poor's and Moody's.

Firms rated B+ or better by Weiss Research are regarded as solid. All are independent services that rate the financial conditions of companies, including insurance companies.

> Standard & Poor's
> 212–208–1527
> free
>
> Moody's
> 212–553–0377
> free
>
> Duff & Phelps
> 312–368–3157
> free
>
> Weiss Research
> 800–289–9222
> $15/verbal report
> $25/written report
>
> A. M. Best
> www.ambest.com
> $4.95 per rating

WITH THE GOVERNMENT

You often hear the phrase "protected by the full faith and credit obligation of the U.S. Government." It applies to investments in EE Savings Bonds, Treasury bills, notes and bonds, and Ginnie Maes (Government National Mortgage Association bonds). It means you don't have to worry about default of principal and interest when you invest with our government.

However, it does not protect you if the price of your Treasury or Ginnie Mae fluctuates due to changes in interest rates.

Government agencies that issue bonds carry what is known as a moral obligation against default and timely payment of principal and interest by the U.S. government. That means you're protected if you invest in bonds issued by the Small Business Administration, Federal National Mortgage Association, and other agency bonds.

Ponzi Schemes

Last year Americans reportedly lost at least $8.3 million in a Ponzi scheme operated by a man named Hugh Rollins. He built a classic scheme around the idea of financing government contractors with promissory notes underwritten by individuals. He told investors their annual returns would be as high as 84%. Rollins, however, never once made the loans to the contractors and the so-called "interest" payments to investors actually came from money he took in from new investors.

The telltale sign of a Ponzi scheme is simple—guaranteed, extremely high profits. However, there is no such thing; profits cannot be guaranteed. If you're ever tempted by a fast-talking money maker:

1. Get details in writing. Show the material to both your accountant and your lawyer.

2. Check with your state attorney general's office, your state securities agency, and the Better Business Bureau where the promoter is headquartered to find out if complaints have been filed.

3. Ask the promoter for names of at least three investors who are not relatives. Contact each and ask what, if any, return they received on their investment.

4. Make an appointment with the promoter. Visit his office. Take your lawyer or accountant with you.

The old cliché—if it sounds too good to be true, it probably is—definitely applies.

HOW SAFE ARE YOUR MUNICIPAL BONDS?

Many municipal bonds carry insurance against default. These bond issuers have to be financially sound to get the coverage in the first place. Insured bonds yield about $1/4$ of 1 percent less than uninsured bonds.

Most are insured by either the American Municipal Bond Assurance Corp. (AMBAC) and by the Municipal Bond Insurance Association (MBIA). Both are well capitalized for covering defaults. In addition, at least one-third of bonds covered by insurers are also backed by tax revenue.

PROTECTING YOURSELF AGAINST SCAMS

A surprising number of intelligent people are taken in by scam artists, who seem to know just how to swindle money out of investors and savers alike. The best of the scam artists tie their pitch to current events, thereby improving their credibility and creating a sense of urgency. They do best among the elderly, who tend to be more passive (or kindly) when it comes to dealing with strangers.

As the American public becomes increasingly tired of telephone solicitations, scam artists are switching to other means, primarily church groups, professional societies, and group-help organizations. Some have even managed to infiltrate organizations that help families of AIDS victims. Once the swindler has made (or says he has) a substantial amount of money for one member, he then tries, often with success, to work the whole group.

"An Investor Alert," published by The North American Securites Administrators Association (NASAA) and the Council of Better Business Bureaus, warns that banks, in an effort to keep depositor's money, are offering investments, mutual funds, and annuities that may not be covered by federal deposit insurance.

☑ *HINT: To protect yourself, never give a cold caller your credit card number, your bank account number, your Social Security number, or write him a check.*

IF YOU ARE ELDERLY OR HAVE ELDERLY FRIENDS, YOU SHOULD KNOW THAT:

- Con artists study obituaries, notices of probate proceedings, and real estate transactions to find elderly victims.
- Con artists know that the elderly often have substantial savings or proceeds from pension and insurance policies.
- Widowed men and women often lack experience in managing finances if their spouse took care of such matters.
- The elderly are often home alone with no one to ask them to think twice about an impulsive investment.
- Elderly people tend to be less suspicious of strangers and more willing to talk to them, even to invite them into their homes.
- Today's older people grew up thinking a handshake was the right way to make a business deal.

FOR FURTHER INFORMATION

About the SIPC and What It Covers

SIPC
805 15th Street NW, Suite 800
Washington, DC 20005
202–371–8300
website: www.sipc.org

About Your Bank

If you have a complaint or a question about your bank, write to the Consumer Services Division of your State Banking Commission or Department in your state capital.

If you live in New York, write to:

Consumer Services Division
New York State Banking Department
2 Rector Street
New York, NY 10006
212–618–6445

About a Brokerage Firm and Its Insurance

Office of Investor Education
Securities & Exchange Commission
450 Fifth Street NW
Washington, DC 20549
202–942–7040
website: www.sec.gov

About Pension Plan Protection

Pension Benefit Guaranty Corp.
1200 K Street, NW
Washington, DC 20005
202–326–4000
website: www.pbgc.gov

Ask for its two free brochures:

Your Pension: Things You Should Know About Your Pension Plan
Your Guaranteed Pension

About Scams

The Consumer's Resource Handbook is free from:

Consumer Information Catalog
888-878-3256
website: www.pueblo.gsa.gov

It tells you what steps to follow if you've been taken and includes sample complaint letters, addresses, telephone hot lines, government agencies, etc.

The National Financial Fraud Exchange (800–822–0416) collects public information about financial and real estate frauds from some 100 government and private watchdog groups.

You can run a name through the system for $39; each additional check is $20. If the person you're checking up on has had a complaint filed and is in the system, you'll be told on the telephone; a written report is free; a faxed report is an additional $5.

An individual is in the system if he or she has SEC violations or infractions, fines, sanctions, or other official complaints.

5

Moving from Saver to Investor

Now that you have set aside money in several safe places where it is earning well above the savings account rate, you are ready to stretch your wings and move into the arena of the true investor.

$TIP: Incidentally, before you leap from saver to investor, let me remind you once more that you should have a minimum of six months' worth of living expenses in one of the safe havens discussed in the previous chapters. That means if you need $4,000 per month to operate comfortably, set aside $24,000 in a combination of CDs, Treasuries, and money funds. Then if you are hit with a financial emergency, such as losing your job or becoming ill, you will have immediate liquid resources to draw upon.

☑ *HINT: If you feel your job may be in jeopardy, set aside at least nine months of expenses—it often takes that long to find a new position.*

Moving from saver to investor is a step many people, especially those with a conservative bent, find difficult to take. Some, in fact, never manage to make the move at all. Although there's nothing inherently wrong with leaving your money in a safe haven, during inflationary periods you may actually lose money, and during a bull market, even a mini one, you'll be on the sidelines. And if you're facing high taxes, these safe investments are not truly safe at all; for instead of reducing your federal income tax bite, they add to it.

Of course, no investment is for all seasons. Review the boxes on page 45 to help you determine which vehicles are best during various economic periods. Keep in mind that the greater the risk you take, the greater the potential return.

MUTUAL FUNDS VERSUS INDIVIDUAL SECURITIES

One of the first key decisions you will have to make as you move from saver to investor is whether to select your own stocks and bonds or to buy shares in a mutual fund. Mutual funds, in which professional portfolio managers make all the buy and sell decisions, are described fully in Chapter 6.

There's no reason, however, to shy away from picking individual stocks, especially if you're willing to spend some time researching them.

Begin in Your Own Backyard

Why not start with what you know? Investigate your local utility company or a corporation headquartered nearby.

For additional research information:
1. Call for the annual report
2. Ask a local broker for his/her opinion
3. Visit the company in person; take a tour; attend the annual meeting

Moving from Saver to Investor

INVESTMENT	WHERE TO FIND	FACTS TO KNOW
Savings account	Bank, credit union	What is the interest rate? How often is it compounded? Is it federally insured?
Money market deposit account	Bank, credit union	What is the interest rate? How often does it change? Are there withdrawal penalties/limitations?
Certificate of deposit (CD)	Bank, credit union	How much money will I have at maturity? Can I roll it over at the same or a higher rate? Are there withdrawal penalties?
Brokered CD	Stockbroker	Will my interest compound? If I sell my CD back to you before maturity, will I lose money? Is the originating bank sound?
Money market mutual fund	Brokerage firm, mutual fund	What is the yield? What is the portfolio's average maturity?
EE and I savings bonds	Bank, Federal Reserve, Bureau of Public Debt	What is the current rate? When do the bonds mature?
Treasury issues	Federal Reserve, Bureau of Public Debt, stockbroker	What is the current rate? Is there a purchase/sales fee? When do they mature?
Stocks	Brokerage firm, investment club dividend reinvestment plan	What is the commission? What is the Value Line rating? Is there a dividend?
Bonds	Brokerage firm	What is the commission? Can the bond be called? What is the yield? What is the rating?
Mutual funds	Mutual fund, brokerage firm	What is the total return for six months, one and five years? Are there fees?

Another easy way to dip into the market is by purchasing shares in the company you work for or one whose products or services you use and like. If you are wedded to your Nikes or if you love Snapple, you might like to start down the investor's path by purchasing stocks in those familiar companies.

Eight Ways Beginners Can Win in the Stock Market

If you're the type that worries about money or just wants to keep the risk quotient manageable, here are seven easy techniques that will enable you to maintain a healthy portfolio and weather declines in the market.

When Investments Perform Best

INVESTMENT	ADD TO YOUR PORTFOLIO	RISK LEVEL
Growth stocks	When economy is growing at above average rate; when interest rates are stable	Medium to high
Blue-chip stocks	During slow to moderate growth periods; when interest rates are falling	Medium
Utility stocks	When interest rates are falling; when energy costs are falling	Low to medium
Long-term bonds	When interest rates are falling	Low to medium
Short-term notes and bills	When interest rates are stable or falling	Low
Money market funds and CDs	When interest rates are rising	Low

- *Diversify.* To some extent you can protect yourself from market swings by owning a mixture of stocks, bonds, precious metals, real estate, and other investments, because rarely does everything decline at the same time.
- *Buy for the long haul.* Plan in general to hold your stocks one to three years, then, hour-by-hour, day-to-day, and month-to-month fluctuations can largely be ignored.
- *Select investments on the basis of quality.* Buy stocks of financially sound companies. *Ignore rumors.*
- *Own high-yield investments.* Common stocks with high dividends, preferred stock, good quality high-yielding bonds, and closed-end bond funds all help cushion stock market dips.
- *Protect yourself with convertibles.* Their yields are higher than the underlying stock of the same company, and should the stock fall in price, the convertible (CV) will fall less (**see:** Chapter 11).
- *Use dollar cost averaging.* With both mutual funds and stocks, this approach enables you to buy more shares at lower prices and fewer

shares at higher prices, as well as to ignore short-term market gyrations. (**See:** page 258 for more on dollar cost averaging.)
- *Don't buy on margin.* You will be able to hold your stock through all kinds of economic weather if you pay cash. With a margin account, you are subject to margin calls from your broker—a demand for more money, often when you can least afford it (**see:** Chapter 26).

The Perils of Being Too Cautious

Even though it's important to sleep at night, you should also avoid taking the path of least resistance—that of being an ultraconservative investor who stashes large amounts of money in savings accounts or money market funds or, even worse, buys stocks and holds them until forced to sell because of the need for cash or money to live on.

The conservative approach provides peace of mind, but it's very poor protection against inflation and low interest rates. If, for instance, the cost of living rises 4% a year, and your conservative investments don't keep pace, you will actually lose money. With a 4% rise, the real purchasing power of every $1,000 is cut to $822 in five years and to $703 in ten years.

FINDING MONEY TO INVEST

Obviously, you need money to invest, to achieve your financial goals and to lead a stress-free life. You won't accomplish any of these if you set aside money sporadically—you need to save on a regular basis.

Painless sources of money to invest:

- Dividend checks
- Gifts
- Bonuses
- A raise
- Tips
- Automatic payroll deduction plan
- Inheritance
- Freelance and consulting activities
- Company savings plans
- Tax refunds
- Lottery winnings
- Return of a loan

☑ HINT: *Another "automatic" technique for saving money to invest: Once you've paid off your mortgage, college loan, car loan, etc., save that amount. You have been living without the cash all these years; now stash it in your money market fund until you're ready to invest it in stocks, bonds, or mutual funds.*

SPOTTING ECONOMIC TRENDS

To build and maintain a profitable portfolio, you must develop a sense of the country's economic strength or weakness. By following these key short-term market indicators, all of which are reported in the media, you can take the pulse of the nation.

- *Capacity utilization.* Measures the activity of U.S. manufacturers and the percentage rate at which factories are operating. A healthy rate is about 85%. When it drops, unemployment is high.

- *Consumer price index.* Also known as the cost-of-living index (COLA), it measures price changes for goods and services. Its components include housing, food, transportation, clothing, medical care, and electricity.

- *Gross domestic product.* The GDP measures the total value of all goods and services produced and sold in the United States over a particular time period. It tells whether the U.S. economy is expanding or contracting. Less than 2% is regarded as slow growth; over 5% is a boom. When the GDP declines two quarters in a row, it indicates that a recession has begun.

- *Index of leading economic indicators.* This index represents 11 components of economic growth, ranging from stock prices to housing permits. If it falls for three or four consecutive months, an economic downturn is likely.

- *New car sales.* Consumer buying trends are reflected in this purchase pattern, reported every ten days. Keep track over a minimum of two months.

- *Retail sales.* Compares monthly sales with those of the previous month, six months, and one year.

- *Department store sales.* These reflect both regional and seasonal trends but can be an accurate indicator if they confirm other trends.

- *Housing starts.* Any improvement indicates optimistic consumer attitudes and, quite often, lower interest rates.

- *Unemployment.* This statistic reflects the overall status of the country's economy. Watch it regularly.

- *Federal funds rate.* This figure, which fluctuates daily, tracks the interest rate banks charge each other overnight.

- *Prime rate.* Interest rate banks charge their creditworthy customers. Follow at least three months.

- *Broker loan rate.* Interest rate for brokers borrowing money from banks.

☑ *HINT: For more information on how to use eco-nomic trends, read* Market Movers, *by Nancy Dun-nan and Jay J. Pack (New York: Time-Warner Books, 1993).*

MAKING MONEY WHEN INTEREST RATES CHANGE

Interest rates continually move up and down, and as they do, they impact directly on the appeal of many investment choices that are popular with those of you who are conservative investors, such as Treasury bills and notes, money market funds, and CDs. And so . . .

1. When rates peak and start to head down, high yields suddenly become history. When that happens, you want to be locked in with high-yielding CDs and Treasuries, not only to profit from high rates but also to benefit from rising bond prices that always accompany falling rates.
2. On the other hand, when rates are low, you want to be in short maturities, so you can reinvest as rates rise. Use the boxes on page 45 as a guideline for timing your investments with changing rates.

To help you decide when to purchase long-term bonds, CDs, and Treasuries, use these three basic indicators:

■ *Money market maturities.* The average maturity of money market fund portfolios indicates what direction the professional fund managers think interest rates will take. This maturity statistic, available by calling a fund, gives the average maturity of Treasury bills, CDs, and other short-term securities in the fund's portfolio. A fund with short maturities indicates that the manager thinks rates will climb even higher. Rates tend to turn downward when maturities reach 39 or 40 days.

■ *Prime rate.* A drop in prime usually occurs after other short-term rates have fallen, indicating that banks anticipate the downward interest rate spiral to continue. When prime drops, investors should lock in the highest yields available.
■ *Yield curve.* This illustrates the relationship between short- and long-term interest rates. Usually long-term rates are higher than short-term rates to reward investors for tying up their money for many years. When short-term rates are higher, the yield curve is inverted. An inverted yield curve generally indicates that interest rates have not yet peaked.

AVOID SALES FEES AND COMMISSIONS

There are two types of investing expenses, both of which can be controlled: (1) sales commission which you pay when you buy stocks, bonds, Treasuries, and load mutual funds, and (2) mutual fund expenses. Some useful tips on reducing fees and commissions follow.

Cutting the Cost of Buying U.S. Treasuries

Banks and brokerage firms charge sales commissions for buying and selling Treasury securities, which range from $25 to $75+ for up to $10,000 worth of securities. The discount broker Charles Schwab (800–442–5111) charges a flat fee of $49 whether you purchase one Treasury or hundreds of them. Check out fees with other brokers before making a Treasury purchase.

☑ *HINT: Avoid commissions entirely by purchasing directly from the Treasury through its Treasury Direct system. For a free brochure, call your Federal Reserve Bank. (See: pages 99–100 for the telephone number and address of the one in your area.)*

Review Your Portfolio When . . .

- There's a significant move up or down in the stock market
- Prime and other bank interest rates change
- A new tax law is passed
- The dollar becomes substantially stronger or weaker in the international market
- There's been a major scientific breakthrough
- Regulatory agencies adopt a new policy
- The inflation rate changes
- There's a change in political leadership
- Foreign-trade restrictions are put into effect
- A new international trade agreement is reached
- New rules are passed on margin accounts
- War begins or ends
- The economy changes from boom times to recessionary times, or vice versa
- Bond interest rates move up or down two points or more

And Then Take These Steps . . .

- Buy more stock of a proven company when the market falls and prune out losers when it rises.
- As rates move up, lock in higher yields in CDs and longer-term bonds; as rates fall, invest short-term—under two years—and look to stocks.
- Talk to your accountant about ways to cut taxes and take advantage of new rulings.
- When the dollar is stronger, go to Europe on vacation; when it weakens, buy foreign currencies.
- Select one or two stocks within the industry to buy.
- Look for investments that will benefit from new attitudes and legislation, such as environmental mutual funds, waste and hazardous waste removal stocks, engineering companies, and water purification stocks.
- If inflation increases, interest rates will rise, so turn to money market funds and high-yielding CDs. If inflation decreases, stocks will do well.
- Read the newspaper to determine the current administration's priorities—military buildup or reduction; concern about education, the environment, or health care; protection of the rich—and position on taxes. Invest in areas where there's likely to be increased spending.
- Reduce holdings in companies or mutual funds heavily dependent on foreign sales.
- Look for corporations already operating or prepared to operate in that country.
- Call your broker to discuss implications for your account.
- If war starts, buy military stocks or investigate which commodities may be in short supply, depending on location of the conflict—copper, gold, wheat, oil.
- If war ends, decrease military holdings.
- If the economy is booming, take profits. If a recession starts, build up cash reserves and buy stocks at their lows.
- If rates go up, buy longer-term bonds. If rates decline, keep shorter-term bonds.

Cutting Costs When Buying Mutual Fund Shares

Funds sold by brokers, called load funds, charge front-end loads or fees of as high as 8.5%. Many funds have back-end loads of up to 1.5%, which go into effect when you sell your shares. Still others have 12b–1 fees—an annual fee of up to 1% to cover marketing costs to bring in new shareholders. These 12b–1 fees are on top of annual management fees, which range from 0.3% to 1.5%. (Management fees are highest for international stock funds, which must be actively managed.)

The SEC passed a ruling in the spring of 1988 that all sales charges and fees must be listed in the fund's prospectus, accompanied by a table showing their precise effect on a $1,000 investment after one, three, five, and ten years.

☑ *HINT: Buy no-load funds directly from the mutual fund company and you'll have no sales fees, unless it's a low-load fund. Most of the funds recommended in this book are no-loads.*

Cutting the Cost When Buying Individual Stocks

The smaller the number of stocks you buy and sell, the more costly it is.

✐ *CAUTION: If you buy fewer than 100 shares of any stock (100 shares being a round lot), you wind up paying the same commission as though you'd purchased 100 shares. So, buy in round lots.*

Use a Discount Broker

You can cut sales commissions significantly by purchasing stocks through discount brokerage firms, although you have to give up the research and personal feeding and care you get from a full-service firm. However, you'll save as much as 50% to 80%.

Discounters also relieve you of another fairly new expense: annual fees for customers who do not actively trade their accounts. The leader of this charge, Merrill Lynch, charges $40 annual fee; other full-service firms have similar charges, while Charles Schwab charges $20 for inactive accounts under $10,000. **See:** Chapter 25 for more on discount brokers.

Buy Stocks On-Line

Reliable on-line brokers offer terrific discounts. A New York–based company, Datek Online, was among the first, followed by Schwab, J. B. Oxford, Waterhouse, DLJ Direct, and E-Trade.

Click on their home pages for info on prices and services:

- www.datek.com
- www.schwab.com
- www.etrade.com

(**See:** Chapter 27 for more about on-line investing.)

BUY STOCKS DIRECTLY

Over 150 companies let investors buy even their first share directly, thus bypassing a stockbroker. In addition, more than 50 foreign stocks can be bought directly. With most, you must agree to join their Dividend Reinvestment Plan. In addition, the companies also allow you to make optional cash purchases of additional shares. Most don't charge fees, but when they do, they are small, especially compared to brokerage commissions.

☑ *HINT: For more information on this inexpensive way to build your portfolio, read: Standard & Poor's* **Directory of Dividend Reinvestment Plans** *($42; 800–221–5277.)*

And remember, reinvested dividends are taxable income in the year of distribution even though you don't receive a dividend check.

Twenty-one Companies That Will Sell You Shares via the Phone

COMPANY	TELEPHONE
Allstate	800–448–7007
American Electric Power	800–955–4740
American Express	800–463–5911
Ameritech	888–752–6248
Avery Dennison	800–649–2291
Bell Atlantic	800–631–2355
Bob Evans Farms	800–272–7675
Campbell Soup	800–649–2160
Disney (Walt)	800–948–2222
Exxon	800–252–1800
Ford Motor	800–279–1237
Gillette Co.	800–730–4001
Home Depot	800–716–3607
IBM	888–426–6700
McDonald's	800–621–7825
Merck & Co.	800–522–9114
Owings Corning	800–472–2210
Peoples Energy	800–228–6888
Wal-Mart Stores	800–438–6278
Weingarten Realty	800–550–4689

You can also purchase stock directly from a number of public utility companies if you live in an area serviced by them. These include:

Carolina Power & Light
Duke Power
Hawaiian Electric Industries
Minnesota Power & Light
Philadelphia Suburban
San Diego Gas & Electric
Wisconsin Energy

Some direct purchase plans, including those offered by Allstate, Campbell Soup, Exxon, and Ford Motor, now include the Roth IRA. Look for more to follow suit during the year.

$TIP: Home Depot recently became the first company to allow investors to purchase shares directly on the Internet. Check it out at: www.homedepot.com

Protective Measures

- *Start small.* Don't race out and buy 10 or 12 stocks at once. Begin with one or two and get the feel of the process.
- *Set up a record-keeping system.* You'll need to track the number of shares purchased directly, the number purchased through dividend reinvestment, the price and the dates of all shares purchased.
- *Keep your year-end statements.* They contain information you need to determine how much you owe the IRS. And equally important, when you sell shares you will need this statement to figure out the original price you paid, known as the "cost basis."
- *Pick stocks for the long haul.* If you hold your shares at least a year, you'll reduce your capital gains tax. (Capital gains on shares held at least 12 months are taxed at 20%. Gains on shares

held less than 12 months are taxed at your or-dinary income tax rate, which could be as high as 39.6%.)

■ *Sell all.* If you can, sell all your shares in one company at one time. Doing so makes it possible to use the average cost basis of all the shares. This is by far the easiest way to figure out what you owe the IRS.

CAUTION: You don't have complete control over when your shares are sold. Check with the company regarding this. Some require written notification. Some sell only at certain times. You could wind up selling on a day when the market is down, even though it might have been up on the day you placed your sell order.

Solution: When you start thinking about selling, ask the company to send you your stock certificates. Deposit them with a discount broker and place a limit order with the broker, stating at what price you want to sell. This way, you control the exact sale date.

Reinvest Your Dividends

Yet another way to reduce your cost of buying stocks is to have your dividends automatically rein-vested in additional shares. (**See:** Dividend Rein-vestment Plans on page 257 for full details.)

INVESTMENT CLUBS

If you're skittish about picking your own stocks or nervous about working with a stockbroker, you can circumvent these problems by pur-chasing stocks through an investment club, a team approach that is used by thousands of Americans.

An investment club is a group of individuals, often neighbors, coworkers, or friends, who meet once a month, contribute a set dollar amount, and invest the common pool in stocks. Every member is responsible for doing research on individual stocks on a rotating basis. They then report their findings to the club, and members debate the risks and rewards of each stock and finally take a vote on which ones to buy.

HINT: Join the National Association of Investors Corp (NAIC). Much of the guidance for clubs comes from the NAIC, a nonprofit organization operated by and for the benefit of member clubs. This association, which has been the force behind the investment club movement in the United States since the 1950s, has about 37,000 clubs with 740,000 total members.

Membership is $40 for clubs plus $14 for each club member and $39 for individuals who are not members of a club. The association offers detailed information on how to start a club, how to analyze stocks, and how to keep records.

Another great plus: Clubs and individual members of NAIC can also dispense with broker-age commissions by participating in NAIC's Low-Cost Investment Plan. Under this program, clubs can buy as little as one share directly from about 160 major participating companies, such as Kellogg, PepsiCo, AT&T, Dow Chemical, and Whirlpool, for a small fee.

Most of these corporations do not charge a commission, although some have a nominal fee ($1 to $5) for each transaction to cover their expenses. All of these companies also have dividend reinvestment programs, so instead of taking dividends in cash, the club or individual members automatically reinvest the dividends in additional shares of the company's stocks.

HINT: According to a recent NAIC survey, 40% of the members have earnings that equal or better the S&P 500 for the year.

Join an Investment Club

If you'd like to start building a portfolio of stocks, but feel uncertain about making your own selections, join an investment club in your area. By pooling your money with that of 15 to 20 other people and sharing research, you can comfortably begin to develop investment savvy.

Kenneth S. Janke, president of the National Association of Investors Corporation, says the following four guiding principles followed by clubs enable them to frequently outperform the S&P 500:

1. Invest a fixed amount regularly to eliminate the guesswork of trying to time the market.
2. Reinvest earnings to take advantage of the magic of compounding.
3. Invest in stocks growing faster than the economy.
4. Diversify among several industries.

For details on joining a club, contact:
National Association of Investors Corp.
P.O. Box 220
Royal Oak, MI 48068
248–583–6242; 877-275-6242
website: www.better-investing.org

KEEPING GOOD RECORDS: IT PAYS TO BE A PACK RAT

You don't need to turn into the Collier brothers, but tossing out papers you need can lead to lots of trouble and hours trying to re-create lost records.

Here's a look at the documents you need to keep:

Tax Records

The IRS has three basic rules you must keep in mind:

1. It has three years from your filing date to audit your return if it suspects "good faith" errors. The three-year deadline also applies if YOU discover a mistake in your return and decide to file an amended return to claim a refund.
2. It has six years to challenge your return—but only if it thinks you underreported your gross income by 25% or more.
3. It can come after you forever if you failed to file your return or filed a fraudulent return. . . . Keep tax-related canceled checks and receipts for six years; including your W–2

forms and 1099s as well as canceled checks or receipts for:

- Alimony
- Charitable contributions
- Child care
- Medical expenses
- Mortgage interest
- Professional dues
- Retirement plan contributions

If you made a nondeductible contribution to an IRA (for which you must use IRS Form #8606), keep the records forever. When it comes time for you to start withdrawing, you will be able to prove that you've already paid taxes on this money.

NOTE: If your IRA contributions are all deductible, you don't need to file Form #8606.

Brokerage Statements

- *Stocks.* Keep the purchase/sales slips from your brokerage or mutual fund until you sell these securities; you need them to prove whether you have a capital gain or loss when you file your taxes.

NOTE: Some brokerage firms give you all the needed documentation on the monthly statement, but some show only the settlement date and total dollar amount of the transaction. Check to see how specific your monthly statements are before tossing any sales slips.

- *Bonds.* The same record-keeping rules that apply to stocks also apply to bonds. In other words, keep the confirmation slips if you are buying a bond for which you have to pay some accrued interest to the seller at the time of purchase. For example, if the last interest payment was two months ago and the next one is four months in the future, you must pay the seller the two months' interest due him or her, because you will be receiving the full payment. This amount returned to the seller can be subtracted from your taxable income. This amount should be noted on your confirmation slip.

- *Dividend notices.* Save these until you receive your annual 1099-DIV form from each issuer. Save dividend reinvestment slips until the end of the year when you receive a summary of all purchases and reinvestments.

- *Stock & bond certificates.* Save until you sell them.

☑ *HINT: Photocopy your certificates and store in a separate location from the originals; copies will help you prove ownership if the originals are lost or stolen.*

Mutual Funds

With mutual funds, as with stocks and bonds, you must pay taxes on any price appreciation when you sell your shares. Therefore, when you buy shares in a mutual fund, save the confirmation slip indicating the number of shares you bought and what you paid for them.

Certain funds pay interest or dividends. In addition, you may get distributions of capital gains from the sale of investments held in the fund's portfolio. Taxes are due on these payouts in the year in which you receive them. Should you reinvest this money in more fund shares, save the statements recording this reinvestment transaction. Otherwise you may forget to include these distributions as part of your cost basis when you sell. Some firms send out cumulative statements, in which case you need to save only the December one, which lists all transactions for the year.

If you decide to sell only some of your shares, your records will help you decide which ones to unload. The IRS assumes that you are selling the first shares you purchased unless you specify to the contrary. This is called first in, first out (FIFO) and can be unnecessarily costly if you have regularly purchased shares in a fund that has continually increased in value.

There are two other options besides FIFO: the identifiable-cost and average-cost approaches. With the identifiable-cost approach, you specify to the fund that you are selling a certain number of shares purchased on a particular date or dates. With a rising fund, this approach enables you to sell the most costly shares—those purchased most recently—and postpone taxes on the cheaper shares purchased earlier. If you sell by phone, send the mutual fund a letter confirming this fact. Keep a copy of your letter plus the transaction statements for six years.

With the average-cost method, you find the total cost of all shares ever purchased, including reinvestments, and divide by the number of shares you own to arrive at the cost per share. Then, multiply this by the number of shares you plan to sell to find your total tax cost. This method must be entered on tax Schedule D when you report the sale, and you must use the same method for future sales.

Ways to Earn Steady Interest

PART OF YOUR MONEY SHOULD BE PUT TO WORK EARNING MORE MONEY. HERE ARE WAYS TO DO JUST THAT.

Investment	Risk Level	Yield
Bank money market account	Low	2.15%
Money market mutual fund	Low	4.53
Certificate of deposit (6 months)	Low	4.30
Certificate of deposit (1 year)	Low	4.66
Certificate of deposit (5 years)	Low	5.11
Treasury bill (3 months)	Low	4.78
Treasury bill (1 year)	Low	5.12
Savings bonds	Low	4.31
Treasury bond (10 years)	Low	5.76
Ginnie Mae certificate	Low to medium	6.99
Utility stocks	Medium	6.72
Utility bonds (A-rated)	Medium	6.80
Corporate bonds (A-rated)	Medium	6.57
Preferred stocks (Utility)	Medium	7.12
Preferred stocks	High	7.15

(As of Fall 1999.)

Banking Records

Go through your checks each year, keeping those relating to your taxes, business expenses, housing and mortgage payments. You can toss out those that have no long-term importance, such as those written for minor purchases and cash.

Housing Records

If you own a house, co-op, or condominium, keep all records documenting the purchase price and the cost of all permanent improvements—remodeling, additions, installations. Also keep records of expenses incurred in selling and buying the property (real estate agent's commission, legal fees, etc.). Even though it's a pain, keep all of these papers for as long as you own your house plus another six years after you sell it.

☑ *HINT: Co-op owners often get an annual tax information letter from the building's accountant indicating additions to your cost basis from amortization payments on the building's mortgage— keep these as well.*

Also keep IRS Form 2119 ("Sale of Your Home") on which you report the sale or exchange of your house and purchase of a new one.

Paycheck Stubs

Keep these until you receive your annual W–2 form from your employer. Make certain the information matches; if it does, toss the stubs. If it doesn't, get in touch with your employer's accounting department and ask for a corrected form, known as a W–2c. You should also save your final paycheck stub for the year, because it records deductions for pension contributions and possibly for deductible medical insurance premiums, charitable contributions, and union dues.

Bills

Once a year, when you go through your checks, also sort out your bills. Basically, once you've paid a bill and the canceled check has been returned, you can throw out the bill. However, bills for big ticket items—jewelry, rugs, appliances, antiques, cars, collectibles, computers, furniture, etc.—should be kept to use as proof of their value in event of loss or damage.

Credit Card Receipts and Statements

Keep your original receipts until you get your monthly statement; if there are no errors, discard the receipts. Keep the actual monthly statements for six years if tax-related expenses, charitable contributions, and other documentation are involved.

NOTE: If your credit card gives you buyer protection or an extended warranty plan, keep related receipts until these perks expire.

Expired CDs and Bankbooks

Save these until January of the following year after they've expired—that's when you will get Form 1099 from the bank showing the amount of interest you earned. Compare this figure with the amount of interested entered in your bankbook or on your CD form. If everything matches, toss the expired certificates and bankbooks.

Retirement/Saving Plan Statements

Keep your quarterly statements from your 401(k) or other plan until the end of the year when you receive the annual summary; if everything matches, toss the quarterlies but keep the annual summaries until you either retire or close your account.

FOR FURTHER INFORMATION

Books

Richard J. Maturi, *The Hometown Investor: How to Find Investment Treasures in Your Own Backyard* (New York: McGraw-Hill, 1995).

Peter Lynch, *Learn to Earn: A Beginner's Guide to the Basics of Business & Finance* (New York: Fireside, 1996).

Newsletters

Call or write for sample issues if you are interested in receiving continual data on the funds.

Income & Fund Outlook
Institute for Econometric Research
2200 SW Tenth Street
Deerfield Beach, FL 33442
800–327–6720; 954–421–1000
website: www.mfmag.com

Monthly; $95 per year. Covers money market funds, Ginnie Maes, and tax-free bonds.

100 Highest Yields
11811 US Hwy One
North Palm Beach, FL 33408
800–327–7717; 561–627–7330
website: www.bankrate.com

Record Keeping

The Standard Homefile
Financial Advantage
37 Constantine Drive
Tyngsboro, MA 01879
800–695–3453

$19.95, plus $4.25 shipping. Includes plastic-coated file dividers and a helpful 48-page handbook.

Recordkeeping for Individuals
IRS Publication 552
800–829–3676
Free.

Direct Purchase of Stocks

Direct Purchase Plan Clearing House
800–774–4117
website: www.enrolldirect.com

Has general information as well as enrollment applications for companies that sell stock directly to the public. You can also enter the name of a company on-line to see if it has a DRIP plan.

DirectInvestor
website: www.netstocdirect.com

Updates a list of companies on a daily basis. Also has a basic primer with useful information for beginners.

6

Investing with Mutual Funds

Although there's no one ideal investment for everyone, mutual funds come closest for many of us.

THE NITTY GRITTY

A mutual fund is an investment company in which your investment dollars are pooled with those of thousands of others; the combined total is invested by a professional portfolio manager in various securities—stocks, bonds, government securities, foreign currencies, and options.

Because you can buy shares in a fund for minimums ranging from several hundred to several thousand dollars, funds give all investors, even those without deep pockets, access to the entire market. And once you buy shares you can add to your account with as little as $100 or $500.

Funds have a wide variety of investment objectives and philosophies, from conservative to middle-of-the-road to extremely aggressive. That means there's a fund to match every conceivable investment goal.

THE 11 ADVANTAGES OF MUTUAL FUNDS

Funds have a number of key advantages over owning individual stocks or bonds, especially for those with less than $30,000.

1. *Diversification.* Unless you have at least $30,000, it is almost impossible to have a properly diversified portfolio. Mutual funds, on the other hand, with 30, 40, even 100 securities in their portfolios, provide excellent diversification.

2. *Professional management.* Mutual fund managers are professionals with experience and a wealth of research to assist them in managing their portfolios. If their fund's performance falters in comparison with those of its peers, the fund manager may be replaced.

3. *Switching privileges.* When a management company, such as T. Rowe Price, Fidelity, or Vanguard, sponsors more than one type of fund (and most do), you may switch from one fund to another within this so-called family, as the market changes or as your goals change. Most funds offer free switching, although some impose nominal fees.

☑ *HINT: Select a fund that permits the portfolio manager to shift out of stocks and into U.S. Treasury bills, jumbo CDs, and other higher-yielding cash instruments if it looks like the stock market may decline. This gives you added protection when the market or interest rates change direction.*

4. *Paperwork.* Mutual funds handle the details of all transactions efficiently, mail dividend checks promptly, provide accurate year-end summaries for income tax purposes, and are always ready to answer questions, politely, on their toll-free lines.

5. *Savings and checking.* Many funds will set up an automatic monthly savings plan, wiring money from your bank into the fund. If your employer has a direct deposit payroll program, you can have part or all of your payroll check automatically invested in certain funds. U.S. government checks, federal salary, and veterans benefits can also be automatically invested.

   Money market funds and some bond funds have check-writing privileges. However, unlike bank checking accounts, there's usually a $250 or $500 per check minimum, and you may be allowed only to write a limited number of checks per month, but the checks are free.

6. *Dollar cost averaging.* This involves regularly investing a set dollar amount in a fund—say, $150 to $500 per month. Many funds will automatically transfer money from your bank account into the fund every month.

   For example, you put $100 into a mutual fund every month: The shares fluctuate in price between $5 and $10. The first month you buy ten shares at $10 each for a total of $100. The second month, because the market dropped, the shares are selling at $5 each, so you buy 20 shares at $5, and so on. At the end of four months you have acquired 60 shares for your $400 at an average cost of $6.67 per share (400 ÷ 60). *NOTE:* During this same period, the average price per share was $7.50.

   HINT: *For a free brochure on dollar cost averaging, contact: T. Rowe Price, 800–638–5660.*

7. *IRAs.* Most funds permit investors to open IRAs with considerably smaller dollar amounts than they require for their regular funds. This is a smart way to invest in a fund whose minimum otherwise is too high.

8. *Telephone trading.* Most funds sold directly to the public allow you to buy, sell, or switch fund shares over the telephone.

9. *Distribution or reinvestment of income.* You earn money from a fund in one of two ways, other than selling your shares at a profit: dividend income and capital gains distributions. Income dividends represent the interest and/or dividends earned by the fund's portfolio holdings, minus the fund's expenses.

   Capital gains distributions represent a fund's net realized capital gains—when there are profits in excess of losses on the sale of any of the portfolio securities. Both income dividends and capital gains distributions can usually be reinvested in the fund automatically, usually at no cost.

   A summary of the distributions made to each shareholder annually, called a Form 1099, is sent to the shareholder and to the IRS.

   CAUTION: *Automatic reinvestment may not always be in your best interest. Mutual funds pay their largest distributions when the stock market is relatively high. Instead of reinvesting at the high level, you may do better to take the cash and wait for the market to decline. Then your cash will buy more shares.*

10. *Beneficiary designation.* You can name your beneficiary by means of a trust agreement so that your investment goes directly to your designated heir when you die, with none of the delays and expenses of probate. Consult your lawyer, because some states prohibit this transfer.

11. *Regular income checks.* You can set up monthly or quarterly income in several ways: (a) by buying shares in several funds, each with different dividend payout months; (b) by arranging for regular quarterly dividends to be paid out; or (c) by arranging to redeem automatically the dollar value of the number of shares you specify. There's usually a $50 or

> ### Uses for Systematic Withdrawal Plans
> - To pay your mortgage
> - As a monthly living allowance for college students
> - As income while on maternity leave
> - For retirement
> - To provide care for someone in a nursing home
> - To meet insurance premiums
> - As income while on sabbatical
> - For alimony or child support payments

$100 minimum per month. The fund will mail a check to you monthly, quarterly, or annually.

Systematic Withdrawal Plans

SWPs, long a favorite with retired people, are also ideal for making mortgage payments, paying insurance premiums, or meeting other regular commitments. SWPs are an alternative to traditional written or telephone requests for withdrawal of your money from a mutual fund. Under an SWP, the fund periodically redeems the dollar value or percentage you request. Payment is made by check to you, to a third party, or to your bank account.

The amount required to maintain an SWP varies with each fund, but typical SWPs require a $5,000 or $10,000 minimum opening balance and a minimum $50 per month withdrawal. You can withdraw money monthly, bimonthly, or quarterly. Some funds permit you to withdraw only on the same day each month; others are more flexible.

Advantages

- Steady stream of controlled income prevents overspending.
- Paperwork is reduced.
- Eliminates telephoned withdrawal requests.

Disadvantages

- You may draw out more money than you need or than you earn on the principal.
- May lead to an apathetic attitude about saving.

Funds offer one or more of four types of withdrawals: (1) straight dollar amounts, (2) a fixed number of shares, (3) a fixed percentage, and (4) a declining balance based on your life expectancy.

✓ HINT: *If you don't wish to tap your principal, remove your money at a lower rate than the fund's increase in net asset value.*

Keep in mind that withdrawing a regular dollar amount is in effect reverse dollar cost averaging. In dollar cost averaging (**see:** page 258) you invest an equal dollar amount every month and in this way buy more fund shares for the same amount when the market is down and fewer shares when it's up. In a fixed-amount withdrawal plan, you are forced to redeem more shares when the market is down to meet the set dollar amount and to sell fewer shares when the market is up.

 CAUTION: *Withdrawals are reportable as sales for tax purposes, whether the result is a gain, loss, or break-even. Keep records of your withdrawals to simplify year-end tax calculations.*

HOW FUNDS WORK

All mutual funds operate along the same lines: They sell shares to the public at net asset value (NAV) price. (NAV per share equals the total assets of the fund divided by the outstanding shares minus liabilities.) The money received is then pooled and used to buy various types of securities. So when you buy into a fund, you are really buying shares in an investment company, but the assets of this company consist not of a plant or equipment, but of stocks, bonds, and cash instruments. The price of your shares rises and falls every day with the total value of the securities in the fund's portfolio.

As the owner of mutual fund shares, you receive periodic payments, provided your fund does well. Of course, if the fund has a poor year, you stand to lose money; that is, your NAV will fall. Most funds pay dividends every quarter and capital gains distributions annually. Capital gains distributions result when a fund sells some of its securities at a profit. You may elect to have your earnings reinvested automatically in additional fund shares, usually at no cost.

Open versus Closed Funds

Funds are either open- or closed-ended. In an open-end fund, shares are continually available to the public at NAV. The fund's shares are always increasing or decreasing in number, depending on sales to the public.

A closed-end fund has fixed capitalization and makes one initial issue of shares. After that it trades as a stock on the major stock exchanges or over-the-counter. In other words, it closes its doors to new investors, and shares can be purchased only by buying the stock.

Prices are determined by supply and demand: When buyers are plentiful, the price of the stock rises, and vice versa. Depending on market conditions, the price will be above or below NAV. When a closed-end fund is selling at a discount from NAV, the investor has an opportunity to see profits from price appreciation. (**See:** Chapter 7 for more on closed-end funds.)

HOW TO SELECT THE RIGHT FUND

There are thousands of mutual funds available, so how do you go about finding those that are right for you?

Know Why You're Investing and Pick a Fund to Meet That Purpose

Your basis choices are: income, growth, and/or a tax-free return.

Has the Fund Made Money?

There are three ways to judge this:

- Follow the price of its shares, officially known as its Net Asset Value, or NAV.
- Track its yield—the amount of income it's paying out to shareholders.
- Look at its total return.

The total return figure takes into consideration changes in the price of shares and then adds in the results of reinvesting income or dividends, plus any capital gains or losses after expenses. (Capital gains and losses result from the sale of securities by the fund's portfolio manager.)

Although all three figures are important, the third—the total return figure—is the only overall indicator of how well a fund is doing, because it shows the total profit generated by the fund.

(*NOTE:* A capital gains payment serves to reduce the fund's NAV, because the fund pays out money that prior to payout counted toward the value of the entire portfolio.) The total return figure is also the best one to use when comparing one fund with another, or one type of fund with another type of fund.

The total return figure over one, three, and five years, as well as from the beginning of the year to date, is given in financial publications and from the funds directly.

HINT: Keep in mind that in a growth fund, the yield figure is not terribly important, because the stocks in the fund were selected for their potential price appreciation, not for their dividends income. In fact, the stocks may not even pay dividends. What is important in a growth fund is whether the share price has been rising steadily for several years. On the other hand, in an income or bond fund, the yield is important, because you selected the fund for income.

Study the total return figures for several years, in both up and down markets. Many fine funds have never been first in any one year, but have done better than the market in good periods and have lost less in bear markets. All of the major financial publications do annual and semiannual roundups of the performances of the major funds. You should also check in *Morningstar,* a weekly reference service that updates mutual funds and their performance; it is absolutely the most thorough coverage of funds. (**See:** For Further Information at the end of this chapter for details.)

Take a Close Look at the Fund's Fees

The more of your money that goes into fees, the less you have actually invested.

EXAMPLE: If you put $1,000 into a fund with an 8.5% commission or sales load, you will be purchasing only $915 worth of shares.

The law requires all funds to list their fees at the beginning of the prospectus, and it must give an easy-to-understand illustration in actual dollars of how much the fees are.

- *No-load funds.* These funds do not charge a sales fee, known as a load (or burden). Most are sold directly by the fund through advertising. Money market mutual funds, even those sold by stockbrokers and banks, are virtually all no-load.
- *Low-load funds.* There are some funds that have loads of 2% to 3%.
- *Load funds.* These are sold by stockbrokers, financial planners, or brokerage divisions of banks, who charge a commission every time you buy new shares. The legal limit is 9.3% of the amount invested. This amount is deducted from the amount of your initial investment. Thus, on a $10,000 purchase, the dollars that

go to work for you are reduced by the 9.3% load to $9,070 ($10,000 − $930).

NOTE: There is no evidence that load funds perform better than no-loads, so if you don't need help in selecting a fund, go with a no-load and save the fee. And if you plan to invest for one year or less, always select a no-load. One year is seldom long enough to make up a 9.3% sales fee.

- *Back-end loads* (also called redemption fees). Some funds charge this fee when you sell your shares, thus reducing your profit or making your loss even greater. They are levied against the net asset value.
- *Deferred loads* (also called contingent deferred sales fees). These are deducted from your original investment if you sell shares before a specified time passes after buying them. They may be based on a sliding scale, often 6% the first year, moving down to 0% in year six.
- *12b-1 fees.* These are named after the SEC regulation that authorized them in 1980. It allows the fund to deduct the costs of advertising and marketing directly from the fund's assets. The deductions typically range from .25% to .30%, but can be as high as 1.25%.
- *Reinvestment loads.* These take a small amount out of the interest, dividends, and capital gains that are reinvested in your account. The maximum is 7.25% of the total investment. For example, if you receive a capital gains distribution of $100 and you automatically reinvest these gains, the fund can retain $7.25 as a selling fee and reinvest only $92.75 in new fund shares.
- *Management fee.* Every fund, load and no-load, charges a management fee to pay the adviser who manages the portfolio. The typical management fee is $1/2$% to 1% of the fund's assets. It may be a flat rate or a sliding scale that gets smaller as the fund's portfolio gets larger.

Yield versus Total Return

It is important to know the difference between yield and total return when evaluating a fund.

- *Yield.* Measures the income (dividends or interest) per share paid out to shareholders by a bond or money market fund for a specified time. It is expressed as a percentage of the current offering price per share.

To calculate yield:

$$\frac{\text{distribution per share}}{\text{price per share}} \quad \frac{\$00.47}{\$10.00} = \text{Yield} = 4.7\%$$

- *Total return.* This measures the per-share change in the total value of a fund, from the beginning of the year to any given date. Total return is derived from dividend and interest income, capital gains distributions, any unrealized capital gains or losses, plus the effect of any reinvested dividends and capital gains.

To calculate total return:

current value	$22,000
– cost of initial investment	$20,000
difference	$2,000

$$\frac{\text{difference}}{\text{cost of initial investment}} \quad \frac{\$2,000}{\$20,000} = \text{Total Return} = 10\%$$

☑ *HINT: Avoid funds with an expense ratio above 1.25%. The highest fees tend to be tied to funds with the highest risks—those with options, futures, short-selling, etc.*

Number Crunching

So, how much do operating expenses, sales loads, and other costs really matter? How can you find out? The SEC now has a "Mutual Fund Cost Calculator" that eliminates much of the mystery surrounding mutual fund mathematics. You put in a dollar investment amount, how long you expect to hold your shares, the fund's total expense ratio, other fees and sales charges, and the anticipated rate of return.

The software then gives the total cost of holding your fund shares for the amount of time you indicated. It also tells what you've lost. Let's

say you paid $300 in loads (or fees). You'll find out what you could have made had that amount been invested.

For information, click on: www.sec.gov

Find Out the Turnover Rate

This shows the dollar amount of stocks or other holdings sold in relation to total assets. Thus, if a fund had assets of $100 million and sold $75 million in stocks in one year, the turnover would be 75%. This is considered high for a blue-chip stock fund and may indicate the manager is either speculating for short-term profits or not making successful choices.

A high turnover rate also means the fund will be paying high commission costs and that you'll have higher capital gains distributions, which are taxed in the year distributed.

EXAMPLE: T. Rowe Price Growth Fund, which contains primarily high-quality stocks, has had a turnover rate that fluctuated from 30% to 51% over the last five years, while its Intermediate U.S. Treasury fund, which holds Treasuries of three- to seven-year maturities, had a turnover ranging from 175% to 195%.

☑ *HINT: Two excellent sources for studying turnover rates are* Morningstar *and* The Individual Investor's Guide to No-Load Mutual Funds. *(See: For Further Information at the end of this chapter.)*

Size Is Also Important

The larger the assets of a mutual fund, the smaller the amount each investor pays for administration. However, stay away from funds whose assets have been under $50 million for over five years. If a fund hasn't grown, its performance must have been so poor that new shares could not be widely sold.

Study Volatility, aka Beta

This is measured by a component called "beta." You can use this figure to compare the fund's volatility with that of the stock market as a whole. (The market's beta is always 1.0 and a money market fund's beta is always 0.) If your mutual fund has a beta of 1.0, it will move with the market. In other words, if the market is up 5%, the fund will be up on average 5%. A mutual fund with a beta of 1.5 is 50% more volatile than the market, so if the market is up 10%, the fund will be up on average 50% more, or 15%.

The beta essentially compares the risk of the fund with the risk of the overall market. It is helpful in selecting a stock fund; less so for a bond fund. Bond funds respond to changes in interest rates, not the market. If you are selecting a bond fund, you should check the ratings given the bonds by Standard & Poor's and Moody's as well as the maturity of the portfolio, rather than its beta.

Look for Adequate Diversification

Although the 5% rule, which limits investments in any one issue to 5% of a fund's assets, provides some protection, bear in mind that the rule applies to just 75% of a fund's assets. That means it could have 25% of its assets into one security and still be within the law. Check the fund's prospectus carefully.

Look at the Portfolio Manager

The person or persons managing the fund are largely responsible for its success or failure. *Morningstar* provides continally updated information on the top three managers.

HOW TO BUY FUND SHARES

You can buy shares in no-load funds directly from the funds themselves. You'll find toll-free numbers for many, as well as performance figures, listed in several financial magazines, including *Money, Your Money,* and *Kiplinger's Personal Finance Magazine.* Simply call the number and request the prospectus of the fund in which you're interested.

☑ *HINT: Whenever you see a mutual fund with a telephone number listed in this book, it is a no-load (or low-load) fund and can be purchased by calling the fund.*

To buy shares in a load fund, you must contact a stockbroker or other commissioned salesperson. Banks and an increasing number of discount brokerage firms also sell load funds. (**See:** the Top Four listed on p. 61.)

The June/July issue of *Your Money* magazine, published in Skokie, Illinois, has one of the easiest-to-read listings—covering the Top 400 Funds for the year. It gives the one-, three-, and five-year re-

The Prospectus

You must read the prospectus before investing in a fund. Although it may appear formidable at first glance, a half-hour with this step-by-step guide will crystallize the entire process and enlighten you about the fund. Here's what to look for:

- What the fund's investment objectives are. These will be spelled out at the beginning.
- A risk factor statement
- What strategies will be used to meet the fund's stated goals
- The degree of diversification. How many issues does it hold?
- What is the portfolio turnover? A low rate, below 75%, reflects a long-term holding philosophy, whereas a high rate indicates an aggressive strategy.
- Fees and expenses. Check in particular the cost of redeeming shares, which should not exceed 1% per year.
- Rules for switching within a family of funds and fees, if any.
- Restrictions. Will the fund sell securities short, act as an underwriter, engage in selling commodities or real estate? What percentage of total assets is invested in any one security? Be wary of a fund that is not adequately diversified. Does it use derivatives?
- How much the fund has gained or lost over one, five, and ten years

turn figures, *Morningstar* rating, sales charges, minimum investment, and toll-free number. The magazine also keeps tabs on funds with low expenses and low portfolio turnover.

Closed-end funds, which trade as stocks and have a limited number of shares available, are sold by stockbrokers. The next chapter is devoted exclusively to closed-end funds.

BUYING MUTUAL FUNDS THROUGH A DISCOUNT BROKER

An easy and inexpensive way to buy a wide variety of funds is by opening a mutual fund account with a discount stockbroker. You can invest in some 300+ funds from more than 25 fund families with absolutely no transaction fees. Or you can pick from several hundred other funds that have transaction fees based upon the amount you invest.

The Top Four:

- *Waterhouse Securities* (800–934–4410). Offers over 6,000 mutual funds, including 1,000 with no transaction fees. For those that do have a fee, it's a flat rate of $25 no matter how many shares of a given fund you purchase.

- *Charles Schwab Onesource* (800–435–4000). Offers more than 600 funds with no transaction fees. If you want to purchase funds outside these 600, you can do so if you pay a transaction fee. With an investment of $15,000 or less, the commission is 0.7% of the principal. The minimum transaction fee is $39.

- *Fidelity Funds Network* (800–544–9697). Has some 900 funds with no transaction fees. For funds with transaction fees, Fidelity charges are based upon the dollar amount of the investment, with a $35 minimum for a $5,000 investment.

- *Jack White & Co.* (800–323–3263). Has 1,200 no-transaction fee funds within 100 fund families plus another 4,000 funds for which there is a transaction fee. The minimum fee is $27, and the maximum, $50.

☑ HINT: *Pick a fund that has an experienced manager. According to a recent* Morningstar *study, stock funds with managers who've been with the fund a number of years have higher returns. Why? Poor fund managers obviously lose their jobs.*

GETTING INTO FAT CAT MUTUAL FUNDS

Until recently one group of mutual funds was open only to insurance companies, pension funds, and other institutions. But this is changing, and about 100 of the 700 institutional choices will accept individual investors. (In the past you couldn't get in because the minimum investment was at least $1 million.)

Now, however, you can purchase shares through discount brokers, sometimes for as little as $1,000. Among the brokers who will sell you shares: Charles Schwab, Jack White, and Waterhouse Securities.

The average expense ratio of U.S. equity funds is 1.2% of assets versus 0.93% for the average institutional fund.

☑ *HINT: Getting the performance figures for institutional funds is not easy, but call Schwab at 800–435–4000 or click on their website (www.schwab.com) for their free guide to mutual funds.*

Among those so-called fat cat or institutional funds with minimums between $1,000 and $5,000 are:

- Quantitative Group Numeric
- MAS Funds Value Portfolio
- PIMCO Equity Adv. Cadence Capital
- UAM Sirach Specialty Equity Portfolio

SHOULD YOU BUY MUTUAL FUNDS FROM YOUR BANK?

Many U.S. banks now sell mutual funds, marketing them very aggressively. Some sell funds from an independent mutual fund company, such as Fidelity, Franklin, or others, while others sell their own line of funds.

According to a study done by *Consumer Reports,* the investment advice about mutual funds given by bank personnel to an investigative reporter was often inappropriate, sometimes wildly so. Only 16 of the 40 bank salespeople asked the potential investor the necessary questions about income, risk level, what other investments he owned. The magazine's conclusion: The odds of getting good advice at a bank selling funds are worse than one in six.

After you've read this chapter you should be able to judge a bank's funds on your own, but keep these points in mind:

- The phrase "a government-guaranteed fund" doesn't mean your money is 100% safe—the fund's shares could drop in value.
- SIPC insurance does not insure the performance of your investment in a bank's mutual fund. SIPC insures bank brokerage accounts for up to $500,000 each, but pays off only if the brokerage firm goes bankrupt.
- FDIC insurance does not cover annuities, mutual funds, insurance policies, stocks, bonds, or money market funds purchased from a bank.
- Banks charge commissions on their funds.

HOW TO READ FUND QUOTES

You will find a listing of mutual funds in the financial pages of the newspaper (**See:** the table on page 63). Funds are listed under the sponsor's name, such as Vanguard or Fidelity. The first column is the name of the fund, then the NAV, or Bid as it may be called. (The NAV is the price at which fund shareholders sold their shares the previous day.) The next column, Offer Price, is the price paid by new investors the previous day.

When the offer price is higher than the NAV, there is a load: The difference between the NAV and the offer price is the sales commission. Funds with "NL" in the offer column are no-loads. A small *r* next to a fund's name indicates that a redemption charge may apply. Funds do not always

Types of Mutual Funds

Fund	Objective
Aggressive growth funds	Seek maximum capital gains, not current income. May invest in new companies, troubled firms. Use techniques such as option writing to boost returns. Highly risky.
Balanced funds	Aim to conserve principal, generate current income, and provide long-term growth. Have portfolio mix of bonds, preferred stocks, and common stocks.
Corporate bond funds	Seek high level of income. Buy corporate bonds, some U.S. Treasury bonds or bonds issued by federal agencies.
Flexible portfolio funds	May be 100% in stocks or bonds or money market instruments. Have the greatest portfolio flexibility of all funds.
Ginnie Mae funds (GNMAs)	Invest in mortgage-backed securities. Must keep majority of portfolio in these securities.
Global bond funds	Invest in debt of companies and countries throughout the world, including the United States.
Global equity funds	Invest in securities traded worldwide, including the United States.
Growth funds	Invest in common stock of well-established companies. Capital gains, not income, is primary objective.
Growth and income funds	Invest in common stock of dividend-paying companies. Combine long-term capital gains and steady stream of income.
High-yield bond funds	Keep two-thirds of portfolio in lower-rated corporate bonds (junk bonds) to achieve high income.
Income bond funds	Invest at all times in corporate and government bonds for income.
Income equity funds	Invest in companies with good dividend-paying records.
Income mixed funds	Seek high current income by investing in equities and debt instruments.
Index funds	Buy stocks to match an index such as the S&P 500.
International funds	Invest in equity securities of companies located outside the United States.
Long-term municipal bond funds	Invest in bonds issued by states and municipalities. In most cases, income earned is not taxed by the federal government.
Money market mutual funds	Invest in short-term securities sold in the money market. Safe, relatively high yields.
Option/income funds	Seek high current return by investing in dividend-paying stocks on which call options are traded.
Precious metals/gold funds	Keep two-thirds of portfolio in securities associated with gold, silver, platinum, and other precious metals.
Sector funds	Concentrate holdings in a single industry or country.
Short-term municipal bonds	Invest in municipals with short maturities—two- to five-year maturities.
Single-state municipal bond funds	Portfolios contain issues of only one state so that income is free of both federal and state taxes.
Socially conscious funds	Avoid investments in corporations that are known to pollute, have poor records in hiring minorities, or are involved in the military, tobacco, and liquor industries.
U.S. government income funds	Invest in a variety of government securities, including U.S. Treasury bonds, mortgage-backed securities, and government notes.

How Mutual Fund Shares Are Quoted

	NAV	OFFER PRICE	NAV CHANGE
Dreyfus Funds			
Cap V p	12.35	12.93	+.12
Index	17.21	NL	−.14
Interm	13.93	NL	−.02
Levge	17.63	18.46	−.14
p—distribution costs apply			
NAV—net asset value			
NL—no-load			

have an *r* when they should, according to a study done recently by the American Association of Individual Investors. (Redemption fees are also called back-end loads.) The *p* denotes that a fund charges a fee from assets for marketing and distribution costs, also known as a 12b-1 plan.

 HINT: *When a distribution is made to shareholders, the NAV is reduced by the amount of the distribution per share. So, buy shares just after a distribution to save paying tax on the distributed amount. Call the fund to get exact dates.*

Don't panic if a fund's quoted price doesn't change much over the year. You may buy shares at $10 per share and find them the same a year later. That's because 90% of income and capital gains have been distributed to shareholders. Instead, judge the fund's total performance (capital appreciation plus dividend income) as a percentage gain or loss. The figure is available by calling the fund.

Team-Managed Funds That Do Well

According to a recent study, mutual funds managed by teams outperform those managed by a single individual and without taking extra risk. The reasons, according to fund expert Sheldon Jacobs, editor and publisher of *The No Load Fund Investor* newsletter, are:

1. There are fewer rushed decisions and fewer mistakes since the decision-making process takes longer with a team
2. When one manager leaves, the fund continues on smoothly
3. The different members of the team contribute their own strengths to the fund

Among those with strong team-management styles are:

■   Brandywine Fund, 800–656–3017
    Total five-year return: 122.14%
    Minimum investment: $25,000

■   Value Line Asset Allocation Fund, 800–223–0818
    Total five-year return: 190.75%
    Minimum investment: $1,000

■   American Century Value Fund, 800–345–2021
    Total five-year return: 139.52%
    Minimum investment: $2,500

How Many Funds Should You Own?

DOLLARS TO INVEST	NUMBER OF FUNDS	TYPE
$4,000 or less	1	A money market fund
$4,000 to $5,000	2	and a government income fund
$5,000 to $10,000	3	and a balanced fund
$10,000 to $20,000	4	and a growth and income fund
$20,000 to $30,000	5	and a high-quality corporate bond fund
$30,000 to $40,000	6	and a tax-exempt municipal bond fund
$40,000 to $50,000	7	and an aggressive growth fund
$50,000 to $60,000	8	and an index fund
$60,000 to $70,000	9	and a small cap stock fund
$70,000 to $80,000	10	and a sector fund
$80,000 to $100,000	11	and an international stock or bond fund

HOW MANY FUNDS SHOULD YOU OWN?

With thousands of funds out there, it's not easy to decide which ones to own or how many. Although there's no magical "right" number, common sense suggests somewhere between three and seven, not including a money market fund—seven being the maximum most people can track on a regular basis. Of course, it also depends upon how much money you have to invest. If you have $5,000 saved in addition to your emergency nest egg, then one or two is appropriate. In the long run, your goal is to cover different aspects of the market and thus protect your investments from wide economic and industry swings. Aim to pick funds that will do well at different points in the economic cycle.

 HINT: *Begin by picking a fund that is already diversified, such as Vanguard Star or T. Rowe Price Spectrum Growth. Both hold a mix of other funds within their own mutual fund family.*

SECTOR FUNDS

If you're confident about what industry or industries will do well during 2000 and 2001, consider a sector fund, one that invests in a single industry. Keep in mind, however, that although such funds offer greater profit potential than broader-based funds, they're also far riskier. This risk factor is reflected in their great price volatility.

Types of Sector Funds

Agriculture
Biotech
Chemicals
Computers
Defense/aerospace
Energy
Environment
Financial services
Foreign countries

Health care
International
Leisure
Precious metals/gold
Real estate
Socially responsible
Technology
Transportation
Utilities

Socially Responsible Equity Funds

FUND	TELEPHONE	TOTAL RETURN/JAN–AUG 1999
Calvert Social Investment; Equity	800–368–2748	14.57%
Domini Social Equity	800–762–6814	8.20
Dreyfus Third Century	800–645–6561	23.07
Parnassus Fund	800–999–3505	19.23
Pax World Fund	800–767–1729	8.00
Pioneer Fund (stocks)		9.08
Pioneer II (stocks)	800–225–6292	3.750
Pioneer Bond Fund A		-2.74
Pioneer American Income		-2.47

Socially Responsible Money Market Funds

FUND	TELEPHONE	YIELD AS OF OCTOBER 1999
Calvert Money Market Fund	800–368–2748	4.58
Pioneer Cash Reserves		3.97
Pioneer Tax-Free Income Fund	800–225–6292	-3.40
Working Assets Money Fund	800–533–3863	3.96

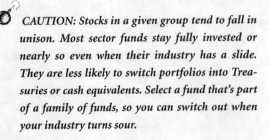 *CAUTION: Stocks in a given group tend to fall in unison. Most sector funds stay fully invested or nearly so even when their industry has a slide. They are less likely to switch portfolios into Treasuries or cash equivalents. Select a fund that's part of a family of funds, so you can switch out when your industry turns sour.*

It's difficult to use past performance to predict future performance in this particular group of funds.

Read one or two of the newsletters listed at the end of this chapter, plus *Value Line Investment Survey* and Standard & Poor's *Outlook* to keep up-to-date on industry developments.

☑ *HINT: Limit your investment in sector funds to 10%. Because they focus on one economic area,* *you'll reduce your chances for loss if that particular sector experiences a downturn.*

INVESTING IN GOOD CAUSES: SOCIALLY RESPONSIBLE MUTUAL FUNDS

If you're concerned about our environment, clean air, women's rights, fair hiring practices, and other such issues, Wall Street offers a way to investing in companies promoting the same.

These funds share fairly similar goals, ranging from avoiding firms that deal in liquor, tobacco, or military weapons, to seeking those that champion the environment. Others look for companies that are involved in community development and low-income housing projects.

Index Funds

FUND	INDEX TRACKED	TELEPHONE
Dean Witter Value-Added Equity	S&P 500	800–869–6397
Fidelity Market Index	S&P 500	800–544–8888
Dreyfus S&P 500 Index	S&P 500	800–645–6561
Dreyfus MidCap Index	S&P MidCap	800–645–6561
Schwab–1000*	Schwab–1000	800–435–4000
Vanguard Index Trust 500	S&P 500	800–662–7447
Vanguard Index Trust Extended Mkt	Wilshire 4500	800–662–7447

*Index of 1,000 largest publicly traded U.S. companies.

The Key Players

1. The granddaddy of socially responsible investing, *The Pax World Fund* of Portsmouth, New Hampshire, is a balanced stock and bond fund that was started in 1971. The fund, which has over $600 million in assets, will not buy companies in the liquor, tobacco, or gambling industries, and it emphasizes health care and education stocks.

2. *The Dreyfus Third Century,* started a year later in 1972, is a large fund with $630+ million in assets. It invests in companies that protect or improve the environment, that make careful use of our natural resources, and that are involved in occupational health and safety and consumer protection. All companies must be equal opportunity employers. Dreyfus will, however, invest in firms with military sales. For the ten-year period through June 30, 1999, the fund chalked up an annual return rate of 17.21%. The one-year return was 23.07%.

3. *The Parnassus Fund* in San Francisco was named for a sacred Greek mountain overlooking the oracle at Delphi. It follows a contrarian philosophy, investing only in stocks that are out of favor with the investment community. Among the factors used in building its portfolio: Companies must produce a product or service of high quality, be sensitive to the communities where it operates, and treat its employees fairly and well.

4. *The Calvert Social Investment Fund* invests in companies that make quality products and environmentally responsible goods. They must be equal opportunity employers, promote women and minorities, and provide safe workplaces. The fund will not buy companies primarily engaged in the production of nuclear energy or weapons systems.

Funds-of-Funds

Here are the best performers; call for one- and five-year total returns:

API Growth	800–544–6060
Fidelity Freedom Funds	800–544–8888
T. Rowe Price	800–638–5660
Vanguard	800–662–7447

5. The 25 funds operated by *The Pioneer Group* rule out investments in liquor, tobacco, gambling, or firearms.

6. *The Domini Social Equity Fund* was launched in 1991. This no-load index fund consists of 400 companies, all screened on social and ethical factors, such as positive records in community involvement. The fund avoids companies that derive a significant portion of their earnings from alcohol, tobacco, gambling, nuclear power, and weapons. The fund's total return since inception: 19.07%.

Socially Responsible Money Market Funds

In addition to these stock funds, there are several socially responsible money market funds for those who want a parking place for their cash. The largest, Working Assets Money Fund, was started in 1983 with $100,000 by a group of eight Bay Area people interested in educating the public on social issues. It invests in money market instruments that help finance housing, small businesses, family farms, higher education, and certain types of energy.

INDEX FUNDS

These funds are designed to keep pace with the market. That's what they do—don't expect more or less.

With an index fund you are the index.

These funds buy the same securities that make up an index, and therefore their performance mirrors that of the index, such as the S&P 500, the Small Cap Index, or the S&P 100. They offer an easy way for you to participate in the long-term growth of the overall stock market, at a relatively low cost. (Index funds are pretty inexpensive, because they don't need a hot-shot portfolio manager to buy and sell stocks.)

There are more than 70 index-linked funds. Because they are designed to closely match the performance of major market yardsticks, they have several unique advantages:

1. During bull markets they provide full market participation.

2. They're relatively cheap. Because their portfolio turnover is low and they don't require large research staffs, most have low operating costs, thereby boosting your returns. (These funds sell shares only when a stock is deleted from an index or when net redemptions force stock sales.) The average equity fund has an expense ratio of about 1.4% versus a little under 1% for index funds. The Vanguard 500 Index, which tracks the S&P 500, has an annual expense of only 0.19%.

3. Taxes are not a big factor. These funds rarely sell stock, so their capital gains distributions are far less than for actively managed funds. Therefore, taxes on such gains are deferred for the most part until you sell your shares.

4. These funds provide excellent diversification, and you know exactly what stocks you're invested in at all times.

Buying on Margin

If you're an aggressive trader, you can buy mutual funds on margin. You must pay 50% of the total cost of your transaction up front. The rest you borrow from your broker. Before doing so, **see** pages 259–262 on how a margin account works, and beware of the pitfalls.

Two brokerage firms offering mutual fund shares on margin are:
• Charles Schwab & Co. (800–435–4000)
• Jack White & Co. (800–233–3411)

INDEX FUNDS VERSUS DIAMONDS

DIAMONDS are a unit investment trust, dreamed up by the folks at the American Stock Exchange, through which you can trade the Dow Jones Industrial Average as a single stock. The DIAMOND trust (ASE: DIA) represents a basket of the 30 stocks that make up the large-cap Dow. You can buy and sell them just like any other stock. You can even short the market if you think the Dow is dropping. Dividends are paid out monthly.

Why consider DIAMONDS over an index fund? There's no minimum investment and they trade throughout the day, so you can buy and sell at any time, getting the current price. (Most index funds have a $2,500 minimum and the share price is not determined until the end of the trading day.) When the market is volatile, the ability to continually trade DIAMONDS can make the difference between a huge profit or loss.

Disadvantages: You can't reinvest your dividends and you'll have to pay a broker's fee.

FUNDS-OF-FUNDS

If you don't have the time, energy, or expertise to put together your own portfolio of funds, you can get into what's known as a funds-of-funds. As the name implies, these are funds that invest in other funds. They give you instant diversification.

The largest are the Vanguard Star Portfolio and the two T. Rowe Price Spectrum funds. One point to take into consideration is that the funds-of-funds pay expenses on each investment in the portfolio. The fund then adds on its own costs, creating a hefty layer of expenses. Both T. Rowe Price and Vanguard cut the expenses by investing within their own family of funds, but then that also cuts diversification.

ASSET ALLOCATION FUNDS

Asset allocation simply means determining where to invest your money among the very broad classes of investments: stocks, bonds, money market securities, and cash.

Asset allocation funds distribute their money among a variety of investments, such as domestic stocks, foreign stocks, bonds, cash, sometimes even precious metals. They may keep their portfolios in permanent fixed percentages—say 30% in domestic stocks, 20% in international stocks, 30% in bonds, 10% in precious metals, 10% in cash—or change the mix in an effort to time the market and improve returns.

Comparing Your Fund with Others

In your fund's annual report you will find the index that the fund manager uses as a benchmark for measuring the fund's performance. You can use that figure, or you can compare your fund with other similar funds. Stick to a single time period for both your fund and the benchmark.

Your Fund Average Annual Total Return	**Index's Annual Total Return**	**Other Fund Average Annual Total Return**

Year
19__ _____
19__ _____
19__ _____
20__ _____

$TIP: Keep in mind that each time a fund sells assets, it's a tax event for you.

With rare exceptions, these funds fall behind the average stock fund during a bull market—that's because the different sectors don't move in tandem and one sector is likely to pull down the overall return, if only temporarily.

Two no-load asset allocation funds:

- Value Line Asset Allocation   800–223–0818
- Vanguard Asset Allocation   800–662–7447

TAXES AND MUTUAL FUNDS

Each time you touch your mutual fund shares, there are tax implications that must be reported to the IRS, including these:

- When you switch from one fund to another within a family, the IRS considers this a sale in one fund and a purchase in another. You must report your profit or loss.
- When your fund earns dividends and taxable interest and passes them on to you, you must pay taxes on this distribution.
- When your dividends are automatically reinvested in more shares, you must report this as dividend income.
- When there are capital gains distributions, these must so be reported.
- For further information, read IRS booklet 564, *Mutual Fund Distributions,* and call T. Rowe Price for a free copy of *Tax Considerations for Investors,* 800–638–5660.

☑   *HINT: If you buy shares in a fund just prior to its annual earnings distribution, you will be taxed on this distribution even though the value of your new shares drops to reflect this distribution. Buy just after distribution. So, before buying a fund toward the end of the year, make certain the fund has already made its capital gains distribution for that year—call the fund and ask or check with your*

stockbroker. After the distribution is made, the price of a fund's shares (its Net Asset Value or NAV) is generally less than it would be had the distribution not been made. This also makes buying after the distribution more attractive.

For example, you buy 1,000 shares of a fund at $10/share. The fund then declares a $1/share capital gains distribution and a 50 cents/share dividend distribution. Your 1,000 shares are now worth just $8.50/share, plus you have a $1,000 capital gains distribution taxable at 20%, and a $500 dividend distribution taxable at your ordinary tax rate, say 28%.

Even if you reinvest your gains, you'll still owe $340 extra in taxes: $200 in capital gains and $140 in ordinary income.

$TIP: You can minimize taxes by picking tax-managed funds. Here are four:

- *Dreyfus Premier Tax-Managed Growth: 800–554–4611*
- *JP Morgan Tax-Aware US Equity Fund: 800–521–5411*
- *State Street Research Legacy: 800–562–0032*
- *Vanguard Tax-Managed G & I: 800–662–7447*

TAX-FREE FUNDS

Should you be in a tax-free mutual fund? To compute how much you need to earn on a taxable investment to equal a tax-free one, use the following formula:

$$\frac{\text{tax-exempt yield}}{1 \text{ minus your tax bracket}} = \frac{\text{equivalent of}}{\text{a taxable investment}}$$

For example, if you're in the 28% tax bracket and a tax-exempt bond is yielding 10%, you would have to receive a yield of 13.88% on a taxable investment to be equivalent:

$$\frac{.10}{1 - .28} = .1389 = 13.89\%$$

In the 31% bracket, a tax-exempt bond yielding 7% is the equivalent of a 10.14% yield on a taxable investment:

$$\frac{.07}{1 - .31} \quad = \quad .1014 = 10.14\%$$

☑ *HINT: In all states, dividends from U.S. Treasury money funds or bond funds are also tax-free, even though you have to pay federal tax on them. And you may be eligible for a foreign tax credit if you own a mutual fund that invests in stocks or securities of foreign corporations. Watch for an indication on your 1099-DIV form of foreign tax paid on your behalf.*

SMART WAYS TO BULLETPROOF YOUR FUNDS

The key to making money in mutual funds is knowing what type of funds to buy and when. Two such times are when the market is having a sharp correction and when interest rates move up or down substantially. Here's how to reallocate your funds under those situations.

When the market drops:
- *Buy a bear fund,* one that is specifically managed to perform well when stock prices are declining by selling short some of its holdings. Selling short means betting that stock prices will decline. *Suggestion:* Robertson Stephens Contrarian Fund, 800–766–3863.
- *Buy a low-volatility stock fund* that invests in a mixture of dividend-paying companies, bonds, and out-of-favor stocks. *Suggestions:* Fidelity Puritan Fund, 800–544–8888, and Mutual Beacon Fund, 800–553–3014.

When interest rates rise:
- *Buy short-term bond funds.* Rising rates depress bond fund shares, especially funds with long-term holdings. *Suggestion:* Van-

guard Short-Term Corporate Portfolio, 800–662–7447.
- *Buy high-yield junk bond funds,* which are less sensitive to changing rates. *Suggestion:* Fidelity Capital & Income Fund, 800–544–8888.

At any time:
- *Buy foreign stock funds.* Other economies do not have economic cycles parallel to ours, so a foreign fund may be a hedge against a declining U.S. market.

WHEN TO SELL YOUR MUTUAL FUND

A fund is not forever. Just as you revise your stock portfolio, you should do the same with mutual funds. They should be evaluated periodically and weeded out, for no fund is perfect for your needs forever. Unquestionably the toughest decision you will face is knowing when to sell. Here are some objective signals for selling and/or switching funds:

- If the portfolio manager quits
- If the fund's performance ranks in the bottom third of funds of its type for over a year
- If the fund lags the market averages, such as the S&P 500
- If the stock market shifts dramatically. Equity funds generally suffer during bear markets. Switch from stock to money market funds at the beginning of a bear market. As a bull market begins, move into conservative blue-chip funds. As the bull begins to roar, put more dollars into aggressive growth funds.
- If interest rates rise. Bond funds tend to be hurt when interest rates move up. Sell bond fund shares when rates start to decline, but buy bond funds with longer maturities when rates seem to be at or near their peak in order to lock in the new higher yields.

IF YOU RUN INTO TROUBLE

If you believe your mutual fund mishandled your account or did not follow your buy or sell instructions, first call the fund and get the name of the general counsel or head of compliance. Write a letter outlining what happened; keep a copy in your file. If the matter is not resolved, then write to:

Office of Investor Education & Assistance
Securities & Exchange Commission
450 Fifth Street, NW
Washington, DC 20549–0213
You may also e-mail your letter to: help@sec.gov

This division was recently created specifically to serve individual investors.

WHEN A MUTUAL FUND MANAGER LEAVES

Just when you've found a fund that's making money, the portfolio manager suddenly leaves to run another fund. Do you stay or follow him to his new home? Generally you're all right to stay put, at least for six months, during which time you can see how the new manager is performing. This is particularly true if switching means paying high redemption fees. If it's a money market fund or an index fund, the manager has relatively little to do with performance, so there's no need to change.

Consider following the manager to his or her new fund after 6 to 12 months if:

1. Its investment goals match yours.
2. Your current fund, under the new manager, is underperforming in its category 6 to 12 months after the changeover.
3. The new manager revises the fund's strategies so that it no longer fits your needs—it becomes too conservative or too aggressive, for example.

HEDGE FUNDS

These popped onto the front page of the news last year when several got into deep trouble, most notably Long-Term Capital Management of Greenwich, Connecticut.

Hedge funds and traditional mutual funds should not be confused. Mutual funds in this country are strictly regulated by the SEC. Hedge funds, on the other hand, are private investment pools and subject to far less regulatory oversight. Hedge funds are unregistered and bound only by the investment agreement or the contract that investors sign with the sponsors of the hedge fund. With the exception of antifraud standards, they are exempt from SEC regulation.

Nor are hedge funds generally subject to any limitations regarding how they are managed—they are not required to disclose information about their holdings or performance—beyond what the sponsor voluntarily agrees to provide investors in the fund's original documents.

The typical hedge fund is structured as a limited partnership and as such can sidestep tough SEC regulations. To participate, investors must have a net worth of at least $1 million in investable assets. Minimum investments range from $100,000 to $20 million, with $1 million being the average.

Fees and Strategies

There are no limits on the fees hedge funds can charge. So, they are high—typically 1% to 2% of net assets plus 20% of profits. Some have front-end sales charges as well. You can withdraw your money, but not overnight. Many require at least 30 days' notice. Some insist you keep your money in the fund for one year.

There are no specific rules governing how hedge fund shares are priced. In fact, it's not unusual for investors to be unable to determine the value of their investment at any given time.

Hedge funds have varying strategies, but all speculate, finding assets whose prices are out of line with their underlying values. Some buy stocks and sell them short, betting on falling prices. Others, known as "macro" funds, have large positions in stocks, bonds, currencies, and derivatives around the world. They take the side of a trade that the majority of investors don't want—for example, that a foreign currency will go up in value against the U.S. dollar.

Hedge funds run the gamut when it comes to risk. LTCM was far more aggressive than most, borrowing $50 for each $1 of equity invested in the fund. According to the Henessee Group, a hedge fund advisory firm, about 60% of hedge funds borrow no more than twice their equity.

If you're looking for a hedge fund, you can contact one directly or go through a brokerage firm that offers them. There are also consultants that charge about 1% of invested assets as a fee for assembling a personalized portfolio.

- Hedge Fund Research in Chicago:
  312–658–0955
- Hennessee Group in New York:
  212–857–4400
- Van Hedge Fund Advisors in Nashville:
  615–377–2949

NOTE: If you're conservative, stick with old-fashioned mutual funds, which are regulated by the SEC.

Load Funds

If you buy a mutual fund through a broker or advisor, you will most likely have a choice of three or more classes of shares. It's important to know what they are.

- *A Shares* come with an upfront or initial sales charge and often with a 12b–1 fee, typically 0.25% a year. (The 12b–1 fee is used to cover advertising, sales, and marketing expenses.)

- *B Shares* have no upfront sales charge, but they do have a deferred sales charge. A deferred sales charge, also known as a back-end redemption fee, typically starts at 5% and then declines annually to 0% at the end of five of six years. You pay the back-end fee only when you sell your shares. It's based only on the principal invested, not on reinvested dividends or capital gains or on appreciation in the value of the shares.
  B Shares may also have a 12b–1 fee.
  In most cases, after a certain number of years, B shares convert to A shares.

- *C Shares* rarely have a front-end sales charge but have a small deferred redemption fee, imposed only if you sell during the first year. They usually have a 12b–1 fee, and because C shares rarely convert to A shares, you wind up paying the 12b–1 fee for as long as you own shares.

☑ *BOTTOM LINE: A shares are best for long-term investors while C shares work better for those who trade frequently. B and C shares are best for those who don't have too much to invest and don't want to pay upfront sales charges. But if you have a sizable amount to invest, most A shares offer reduced sales charges for large purchases. B and C shares don't reduce commissions on large orders. The broker gets a flat commission, usually 4%, for all orders. You probably won't be aware of it because the commission is paid from the fund's annual fees.*

FOR FURTHER INFORMATION

General Directories

Individual Investor's Guide to Low-Load
Mutual Funds
American Association of Individual Investors
625 North Michigan Avenue
Chicago, IL 60611
312–280–0170
An annual guide evaluating 800+ no-load and
low-load funds; $24.95.

The Handbook for No-Load Fund Investors
P.O. Box 318
Irvington, NY 10533
800–252–2042
An annual directory with useful ideas on how
to pick a no-load fund; performance data on
2,000 funds; $45.

The Complete Mutual Fund Kit
Mutual Fund Education Alliance
Box 419263
Kansas City, MO 64193
816–454–9422
website: www.mfea.com

Mutual Fund Fact Book
Publications Division
Investment Company Institute
1401 H Street NW
Washington, DC 20005
202–326–5800
$25

Books

Warren Boroson, *Keys to Investing in Mutual
Funds* (Hauppauge, NY: Barron's Educational Publishing, Inc., 1997).

John C. Bogle, *The Common Sense of Mutual
Funds* (New York: Wiley, 1999).

Steven T. Goldberg, *But Which Mutual Funds?
How To Pick the Right Ones* (NY: Kiplinger Books,
1998).

Sheldon Jacobs, *The Handbook for No-Load
Fund Investors 1997* (Homewood, Ill.: Business
One Irwin, 1997), $40.

Andrew Leckey, *The Morningstar Approach to
Investing: Wiring into the Mutual Fund Revolution*
(New York: Warner Books, 1997), $24.

Joseph Nicholas, *Investing in Hedge Funds*
(New York: Bloomberg Press, 1999).

Pamphlets

Publications Division
Investment Company Institute
1401 H Street NW
Washington, DC 20005
202–326–5800
A Guide to Mutual Funds, $0.35
A Guide to Closed-End Funds, $0.35
A Guide to Unit Investment Trusts, $0.35
A Guide to Bond Funds, $0.35

Newsletters

Morningstar Mutual Funds
Morningstar Inc.
225 West Wacker Drive
Chicago, IL. 60606
800–735–0700
Like *Value Line;* covers 1,500 funds in detail;
updated every other week; $495/year; three-
month trial, $55.

The No-Load Fund Investor
P.O. Box 318
Irvington, NY 10533
800–252–2042
A monthly analysis of the no-load funds;
$129.

No-Load Fund X
DAL Investment Co.
235 Montgomery Street, Suite 662
San Francisco, CA 94104
415–986–7979; 800–323–1510
Monthly; lists top performers by investment goals; $129.

Mutual Fund Forecaster
2200 SW Tenth Street
Deerfield Beach, FL 33442
954–421–1000
Monthly; ranks funds by risk and profit potential; $49.

In order to sample a variety of newsletters, contact:
Select Information Exchange
244 West 54th Street
New York, NY 10019
212–247–7123; 800-743-9346
website: www.siesite.com
SIE is a financial publications subscription agency. Pick 4 newslettters from 100; five months costs $69.

The Social Investment Forum
1612 K Street NW
Suite #650
Washington, DC 20006
202–872–5319
National trade association for socially responsible professionals in the financial field. Their

Membership Directory ($2) lists professionals who specialize in socially responsible investment services.

Check their website for updated information on the performance of socially responsible mutual funds at: www.socialinvest.org

On-line Information

Morningstar
website: www.morningstar.net
Has free market data on 460 closed-end funds. Pay $9.95/month and get analysis and more details.

Site-By-Site!
website: www.site-by-site.com
A free clearinghouse of news, weekly updates, reviews and commentaries, plus rankings and profiles of the majority of closed-end funds.

Internet Closed-End Fund Investor
website: www.icefi.com
Subscription starts at $20/month and covers some 500+ funds.

Many of the no-load fund families provide a wealth of material on their websites. Best bets:
www.fidelity.com
www.troweprice.com
www.vanguard.com
www.monetta.com
www.strongfunds.com
www.roypapp.com
www.federated.com

7

Using Closed-End Funds

Many investors shy away from closed-end funds because they simply don't understand how they work. Yet overlooking these hybrid creatures—part mutual fund, part stock—can mean missing a good investment opportunity. Many offer investors the opportunity to buy their portfolio assets at a discount.

THE NITTY GRITTY

Closed-end funds, also called Publicly Traded Investment Companies, are similar in some ways to open-end mutual funds, described in Chapter 6. Both are investment companies that take money from thousands of investors and assemble portfolios of stocks, bonds, convertibles, and other securities to meet the fund's stated investment goal, and then issue shares to the public. Both use professionals to manage their portfolios.

However, the similarities end there. There are key differences:

- Open-end mutual funds continually issue new shares as people invest their money, and they buy back their shares when investors sell.

- Not so with a *closed-end* fund—these funds raise their initial capital by issuing a fixed number of shares in a process similar to selling a new stock issue. After this initial offering the fund is closed, hence its name. It does not issue new shares (unless it has a secondary offering later), nor does it redeem shares.

From this point on, the fund's shares trade in the secondary market on one of the stock exchanges or over-the-counter as regular stocks. That is why they are sometimes called publicly traded funds. Shares cannot be purchased directly from the fund itself. Instead, you must buy and sell them through a stockbroker, and you pay a commission, just as you do when trading common and preferred stocks.

TAKING ADVANTAGE OF DISCOUNTS AND PREMIUMS

The relationship between a closed-end fund's market value and its *net asset value (NAV)* is quite different from that of an open-end mutual fund.

Each closed-end fund has a NAV, and, like a mutual fund, it changes daily depending on the market value of the stocks and bonds in its portfolio. When you sell shares in an open-end mutual fund, you receive the net asset value per share, minus any redemption fees. But the NAV is not used to determine the market price of a closed-end fund's shares: i.e., its price on an exchange or over-the-counter.

Because they are traded on the exchanges, their shares fluctuate in price based upon demand, just as with any stock. And this price moves independently of the portfolio value. When buyers of the fund outnumber sellers, the price rises, and when sellers outnumber buyers, the price declines.

The result: The price of a closed-end fund's shares may sell *at a premium to* (above) or *at a discount from* (below) its NAV, depending upon investor interest in the fund. The NAV is the market value of the fund's portfolio divided by the total number of shares outstanding, minus any liabilities.

EXAMPLE: If a fund has a NAV per share of $15, based on the current market value of its portfolio, but is priced at $12, it is selling at a 20% discount. Or to look at it another way, when a share of a closed-end fund is selling at a 20% discount, every $12 invested in a share puts $15 in assets to work for you.

The NAV for each closed-end fund and its stock price plus whether it is selling at a premium or a discount from NAV (expressed as a percentage) are listed in the financial press (**see:** box on page 79).

You'll find that most newly issued closed-end funds trade at a premium to NAV, reflecting the start-up costs of the fund. That's because a portion of your investment, often 7% to 8%, goes toward paying underwriting expenses and commissions to brokers who sold the fund at the initial offering.

EXAMPLE: If you pay $10 per share to buy at the initial offering, approximately $9.30 would go toward actual investments.

☑ *HINT: Generally avoid buying shares at the initial offering. Wait until the share price drops below NAV in the secondary market.*

TYPES OF CLOSED-END FUNDS

There are several types of closed-end funds:

- *Closed-end stock funds.* These invest in common and preferred stocks. Some specialize in a given sector, such as health care or energy. (*EXAMPLES:* Gabelli Equity, Blue Chip Value, Cypress.)

- *Closed-end bond funds.* These invest in a range of bonds, including high-quality corporates, low-rated, or junk bonds. Some invest only in U.S. government bonds, municipal bonds, or bonds of foreign governments. As with any fixed-income investment, the price of closed-end bond funds moves in the opposite direction from interest rates. (*EXAMPLES:* ACM Government Opportunity, Nuveen NY Muni, First Australian Prime Income.)

- *Closed-end convertible bond funds.* These have portfolios consisting of bonds that can be converted into common stock. Convertibles offer relatively high yields in comparison to some other investments, and they also have a potential for capital gains. (*EXAMPLE:* Lincoln National Convertible. **See:** Chapter 11 for more on convertibles.)

- *Closed-end single country funds.* These specialize in stocks of a given country or geographical area. (*EXAMPLES:* the New Germany Fund, or the Irish Investment Fund.)

- *Closed-end dual purpose funds.* These funds have two classes of shares. The income shares are entitled to all of the dividends paid out or interest earned. The capital shares receive all the capital gains. Dual-purpose funds usually end 10 to 15 years after being launched. When they are terminated, income shares are redeemed at a specific price. Owners of capital shares divide up the fund's remaining assets, either by liquidating the fund or by converting it to an open-end status and permitting investors to sell their shares at NAV. The closer the ending date, the more likely the fund's discount will disappear. If you are a long-term investor and buy at a discount and hold your shares until the termination date, you will make a nice profit. (*EXAMPLES:* Quest for Value Capital Shares, Quest for Value Income Shares, Hampton Utilities Capital Shares.)

Government Closed-End Bond Funds

ACM Government Income Fund (NYSE:ACG) Price: $8½ Yield: 10.5%
Portfolio consists primarily of U.S. government and agency debt and some foreign government debt.
Managed by Alliance Capital of New York.

Putnam Premier Income Trust (NYSE:PPT) Price: $8¼ Yield: 9.3%
Has assets in U.S. government securities, cash, bonds, and some foreign government debt.

(Prices as of Fall 1999.)

BUYING THE RIGHT CLOSED-END FUND

You should go about selecting a closed-end fund just as you would any other investment: Determine your investment goal and the amount of risk you wish to take, and then find a fund that meets your requirements.

Unlike open-end mutual funds, most closed-end funds issue a prospectus only when they are launched, or on the rare occasion when they issue new shares. You can learn about a closed-end fund's investment objectives, services, extent of portfolio turnover, the proportion of a fund's shares owned by officers and directors, and other facts from the fund's reports to shareholders. Funds will supply copies upon request. As a shareholder, you will receive an annual report.

Be certain to study the fund's performance record and its expense ratio. The average expense ratio for open-end stock funds is 1.3%, so avoid funds with ratios much higher than this, with the exception of single country funds, whose expenses run higher than average.

Closed-end bond funds can use their capital to maintain their dividends (and investor interest), even when it's not earning enough to cover the payouts. The dividend will probably be cut, eventually.

CAUTION: When buying a fund you should also be aware of the discounts and premiums to NAV. The rule of thumb is, all other things being equal, avoid selling at a premium to NAV and aim to buy when the fund's price is at a discount to NAV. Funds tend to trade at a premium when the portfolio contains issues of foreign companies located in countries that have a promising outlook for growth. (See: Chapter 20 for more on single-country closed-end funds.)

It's important to keep in mind that the discount or premium is primarily a function of investor sentiment, rather than changes in the fund's underlying portfolio value.

Value Line investment survey reports on about 40 closed-end funds among the many stocks it follows. For extra protection, you may wish to confine your purchases to those given high rankings for safety and timeliness by its expert analysts. Value line is available at most libraries and brokerage firms.

HOW TO MAKE MONEY IN CLOSED-END FUNDS

There are three basic kinds of return for investors in closed-end funds:

- *Dividend income.* Funds receive interest and dividend income from the securities in their portfolios. This income, minus fund operating costs, is distributed to shareholders as dividends.
- *Capital gains distributions.* Most funds buy and sell portfolio securities throughout the year. If a net gain is realized from these sales,

---

Checking Closed-End Fund Prices

Each week the financial newspapers list closed-end fund prices and net asset values per share. The listings vary depending upon the paper but are typically divided into various categories, such as:

- General Equity Funds
- World Equity Funds
- U.S. Government Bond Funds
- National Muni Bond Funds
- Single State Muni Bond Funds

For each you will find: the fund name; the symbol for the exchange on which it trades, such as NYSE; the NAV or net asset value (given in dollars and cents); the stock price and the percentage difference—a plus or minus figure that indicates how much above or below the fund's net asset value per share the shares are trading.

For example:

| Kemper High Income | NYSE | $9.06 | $8¾ | −3.42% |

---

most funds pay all or most of this money to shareholders as a capital gains distribution.

- *Capital gains.* If you sell shares in the fund for more than you paid for them, you then make your own capital gain through the sale.

WHEN TO SELL YOUR SHARES

As with all your investments, you should determine a selling point when you make your initial purchase. But before you achieve that profit, two conditions may appear, indicating that you should sell your shares:

- If the market is at a high. Traditionally, closed-end fund premiums and discounts reach their best levels when the market tops, not when it bottoms.
- If new, similar funds are brought to market. For example, in November 1989, the Berlin Wall fell and the existing Germany Fund, which had been around a long time, catapulted to an 80% premium in two months. Then, during the first quarter of 1990, three new Germany funds were launched and by the

end of April, all four funds were selling at discounts and their underlying NAVs had also declined.

FOR FURTHER INFORMATION

Investor's Guide to Closed-End Funds
Thomas J. Herzfeld Advisors
Box 161465
Miami, FL 33116
305–271–1900
Monthly; $475/year or $85 for two-month trial.
website: www.herzfeld.com

Wiesenberger's Investment Companies Yearbook
CDA/Wiesenberger
40 West 57 Street
New York, NY 10019
800–232–2285
website: www.wiesenberger.com
An annual directory of open-end and closed-end funds, and variable annuities; $295, plus $19.95 shipping.

8

The Investor's Almanac
for 2000

"Buy old masters. They fetch a much better price than old mistresses."

Lord Beaverbrook

Lord Beaverbrook obviously hadn't run into Gloria Steinem and the woman's movement. Had he, he certainly would have rephrased his advice. Even though his remark was politically incorrect, he was financially correct about investing in works of art. Well-chosen pieces often rise dramatically in price, commanding huge sums—a Monet painting brought $33 million at a Sotheby's auction last year.

So, if you love to rummage through flea markets and antique shops, or attend auctions, read on. You may not find a Monet, but you'll definitely have a good time and, if you pick well, you too may make money.

There are endless numbers of offbeat investment choices if you're willing to be experimental. In this special section we highlight three of the most timely of such choices. These do not come with a guarantee that you'll make a huge killing, but they do come with a guarantee that you'll have fun learning about a new field.

Before you invest in any one of the three Investor's Almanac picks, do a little background research. A reading list is provided for each choice. If you know experts in the area, call and ask for advice.

When considering a collectible:

- Buy only what you like. If later on the value should fall or if you should decide to sell only part of your collection and keep the rest, you will still be left with something you cherish.
- Focus on something. Random collecting tends to be considerably less valuable over the years. Decide on an art form category and then specialize in an artist, period, craftsman, or country. Unrelated individual pieces have less marketability than a cohesive collection.
- Set aside a limited dollar amount. You can revise this amount annually. Don't take all the money in your CDs or Cysco stock and move it into exotic investments. If you should suddenly need cash and everything's tied up in prints by old masters or baseball cards, you'll be forced to sell, perhaps at a low price.
- Buy in your price range. Begin small if the amount of extra money you have is limited. As circumstances and your financial situation improve, you can always go after more elaborate and expensive items. So don't take out a second mortgage to get started in the world of collectibles.

Leading U.S. Auction Houses

C. G. Sloan & Co.
4920 Wyaconda Rd.
North Bethesda, MD 20852
301–468–4911
website: www.sloanauction.com

Christie's
20 Rockefeller Plaza
New York, NY 10020
212–636–2000
website: www.christies.com

DuMouchelle's
409 East Jefferson Avenue
Detroit, MI 48226
313–963–6255
website: www.dumouchelles.com

Guernsey's
108 East 73rd Street
New York, NY 10021
212–794–2280
website: www.guernseys.com

Phillips
406 East 79 Street
New York, NY 10021
212–570–4830
website: www.phillips-auctions.com

Skinner, Inc.
63 Park Plaza
Boston, MA 02116
617–350–5400
website: www.skinnerinc.com

Sotheby's
1334 York Avenue
New York, NY 10021
212–606–7000
website: www.sothebys.com

HOW TO PROTECT YOURSELF AT AN AUCTION

Many collectibles, including the three described on the following pages, are found in antique shops and galleries and through dealers, as well as at shows and flea markets. When you buy from these sources, you have enough time to study each object. But when making a bid at an auction, the gavel swings fast and decisions must be made almost instantly. In this pressurized atmosphere, keep these points in mind to protect yourself from "auction fever" and buy the right piece at the right price.

■ DO YOUR HOMEWORK. Study up on the item. Know the price range.
■ READ THE CATALOG. Purchase the catalog well in advance of the auction. It will give dollar estimates as well as a description of the items for sale. During the auction, write down what each item sold for and use these figures as price guidelines in the future.
■ ATTEND THE PREVIEW. Study the lots on display and make notes in the catalog regarding their size, age, condition, etc. Take a pen, notebook, small flashlight, magnifying glass, and a tape measure with you. At the preview, open drawers, look for cracks, plug in lamps, search for identifying marks, signatures, initials; and turn everything over and/or upside down.
■ MAKE A LIST OF THE ITEMS YOU REALLY WANT. This will help you avoid auction fever and going home with a trunkload of stuff you didn't want.

Then, at the auction:

- After registering, you will be given a number and something to bid with, most likely a paddle.
- Next, find out what the incremental dollar amounts are. Some auctioneers move up by $10, others by $100. Ask or check in the catalog.
- If you don't want your bidding noticed, sit either near the front, a little to the side so you can see the others bidding, or in the back rows.
- Listen to the bidding terminology. "Silver looking" is not the same as "sterling silver."
- Wait to place a bid until after you've become at ease with the auctioneer's patter. Know if you are bidding by the piece or by the lot.
- Get a feel for the timing of the auction. The most important items are generally brought out toward the middle of the sale, when the crowd has been "warmed up." After the major items are sold, the audience may thin out, leaving less competition for the remaining items. This is an excellent time to bid if you're interested in the remaining items.
- Never be the first to bid on an item you want. Auctioneers often set an arbitrary opening price, which may turn out to be artificially high. If so, it will drop if there are no bidders. Watch who else is bidding. You certainly want to avoid bidding against yourself. Bid as you sense the prices rising, or when they are near the top.

DECIPHERING AUCTION CATALOGS

Auction catalogs are excellent resources and should be read carefully. Often they are available well in advance, giving you time to comparison shop and study various subject areas. Catalogs spell out:

1. *Terms of the sale,* including deposit requirements, methods of payment, how to place absentee bids, buyer's fees or premiums, and when and how purchased items should be picked up and paid for.
2. *Policy on reserves.* Although all items are sold to the highest bidder, in practice it may be somewhat different. Certain lots have a "reserve" or minimum price. If a lot does not actually bring this price, it can be withdrawn. Some auction houses use an "R" to designate that a lot has a reserve price.
3. *Descriptive statements.* These are usually given to help the bidder if the piece is by a well-known artist, craftsman, or designer. Beware of such phrases as "attributed to" and "in the school of," which indicate that the experts are not 100% sure that the work is indeed by a certain person.
4. *Descriptive information.* Catalogs often tell the style, patterns, colors, ounces, measurements. The term "style" may signal a reproduction. For example, a Queen Anne table means the table is from the chronological period of Queen Anne; on the other hand, a Queen Anne–style chair means it is a reproduction of that style and may have been made yesterday.

5. *Guarantees or warrantees.* Catalogs are not perfect. Neither are the experts and appraisers. If you buy an item described as silver and it turns out to be silver plate, or mahogany that is really walnut, you may have a claim against the auction house.

6. *Presale estimates.* Estimates represent the auctioneer's opinion based on the current market. If an item seems way above your price limit, don't despair. The estimate may be too high, or interested people may not show up at the auction—any number of circumstances can reduce the sale price.

GETTING AN APPRAISAL

To get an official evaluation or appraisal of your collectible or artwork, you need to hire an appraiser. An appraisal, which is a statement of an accurate and realistic value of a possession made by a knowledgeable person, can be used for establishing an item's worth, either for insurance coverage or to arrive at a price when selling. Appraisals are also required by the IRS when something of value is donated to a charity and you wish to declare a tax deduction.

An official appraisal must be written, dated, and signed. It should also indicate whether the appraisal is the fair market value (used for selling the item, dividing an estate, or donating it to charity), or replacement value (for insurance reimbursement). The object appraised should be described in as much detail as possible and the number of pieces being appraised should be made very clear. For example, if the value given is for a pair of vases, a set of 12 water goblets, etc., these numbers should be given.

Before hiring an appraiser, ask what he or she charges and approximately how long the appraisal will take. Some appraisers charge a flat fee, others an hourly rate.

☑ *HINT: Never hire an appraiser who asks to be paid a percentage of the dollar value of the items appraised.*

FOR FURTHER INFORMATION

Although there are no federal licensing or educational requirements for becoming an appraiser, you can find a reliable one through these sources:

The American Society of Appraisers
Box 17265
Washington, DC 20041
703–478–2228
website: www.appraisers.org
Ask about their free/inexpensive brochures on a number of topics.

The Appraisers Association of America
386 Park Avenue South
New York, NY 10016
212–889–5404
Publishes *Elements of a Correctly Prepared Appraisal.*

Jewelers of America
1185 Avenue of the Americas (30th floor)
New York, NY 10036
212–768–8777
website: www.jewelers.org

Specialized Auction Houses

Hake's Americana & Collectibles
P.O. Box 1444
York, PA 17405
717–848–1333
website: www.hakes.com
Mail auction; with focus on popular Americana items. Call about current catalogs and auction dates.

GOING ON-LINE

The major art houses now have websites, as do major museums. You'll find much useful information and ways to view art. You can peruse world-class collections without leaving your desk.

Other key websites are:

- ArtNet (800–4–ARTNET) at: www.artnetweb.com: Here you'll get access to auction results from 500 houses in about 30 countries as well as from some 50 international galleries.
- World Wide Arts Resources at: www.ar.com: Use it to check current museum exhibits in various cities.

CYBERSPACE COLLECTING

Thanks to the rapid growth of the Internet, bidding online has become easy to do; in fact, there's a gigantic yard sale out there, filled with terrific treasures and terrible trash. As we head for press, there are an estimated 350 various auction sites where you can find everything from Barbie dolls and baseball cards to rare books and prints.

How It Works

The Sellers

Those who want to sell an item must register first with the auction site, providing the starting price and often a "reserve price"—the dollar amount below which they can refuse to sell. They must also list how long they want the auction to last; seven to 14 days is typical.

The Buyers

Buyers also must register and, depending upon the site, give information proving who they are. When the deal is done, the item is shipped, usually at the buyer's expense. It is sent either at once if it was paid for by a credit card, or upon clearance of a personal check.

Protecting Your Wallet

There's no guarantee that you won't get stung when bidding and buying collectibles online, but you can take certain steps to protect yourself.

1. *Know the Return Policy.* Always ask about the site's return policy. They vary widely, with some requiring sellers to accept returns regardless of the reason; others leaving it up to the individual or firm.

   $TIP: Legitimate sellers give buyers at least three days after receipt of an item to send in a notice that it's being returned.

2. *Skip Money Orders.* Do not deal with a seller who insists upon money orders only. You have absolutely no recourse whereas with a credit card and personal check you do.

   If you pay by credit card and your item never arrives or it does but it's not what you ordered or bid on, you can invoke your rights under the Federal Truth in Lending Act and refuse to pay until the situation is resolved.

   Make sure you deal with a site where account information is "secured" or "encrypted" which means it cannot be intercepted during transmission. Better yet: use a site that allows you to pay "off-line" by mail or phone.

3. *Know the Site.* Check for a mailing address and phone number on the homepage. Do not do business with a company that is provides only online contact. And, read the "About Us" section. Honest merchants and entrepreneurs don't hesitate to say who they are.

   $TIP: Check with the Better Business Bureau at: www.bbb.org to see if any negative reports have been filed about a given site. This non-profit organization maintains an impressive list.

4. *Use a Site with Five-Minute Delays.* Snipers, who bid on items just seconds before the session ends, thus outbidding you by a small amount, create havoc. Use an auction site that has instituted a five-minute delay to prevent sniping.

5. *Place Automated Bids to Stay in the Game.* The best sites allow you to place an initial bid and then, in private, indicate a maximum bid. If someone outbids your initial offer, the system automatically raises your bid incrementally until it reaches your maximum.

6. *Read Descriptions.* Don't bid on an item unless the description includes all critical information, such as: date made, history, condition, flaws, and repairs. If you need more information, e-mail the seller.

$TIP: Always print out a copy of the description and use it if, when the item arrives, it does not match the description. And, keep the description in your file in case you decide to sell the item later on.

⊘ CAUTION: *Auction sites do not guarantee the quality of an item or the seller's reputation.*

General On-line Sites

Beginning collectors can get a feel for the action and prices at these general sites:

- *www.collectoronline.com.* Covers collectors club announcements and classified ads for collectibles.

- *www.collectit.net.* Run by Krause Publications, publishers of a number of antiques and collectible magazines, this in-depth site is a good place to start.

- *www.ebay.com.* Said to be the largest and most popular online auction site, with 80,000 new items added daily. It's said it sells more than half of what's offered. You'll find antiques, books, collectibles, stamps, trading cards and more. You list an item for auction by filling out an easy-to-use form on the homepage, paying a small fee, and then paying a percentage of the amount you receive if the item is sold. Auctions tend to run three to seven days. At the end, both the seller and highest bidder are notified by e-mail.

- *www.classifieds2000.com.* This is the address for Excite Auctions which is filled with collectibles, musical instruments, and audio/video equipment.

- *auctions.yahoo.com.* The address for Yahoo! Auctions which offers toys, sports memorabilia, cameras, and video games.

Top Collector-Specific Sites

- *www.autographcollector.com.* This is the official site of "Autograph Collector" magazine. It also posts some of the publication's articles and has an "Ask the Experts" feature.

- *www.rarebooks.org.* Run by the International Book Collectors Association, it offers many titles and also has links to dealers specializing in first editions, collectibles, and specific types of books.

- *www.abebooks.com.* On this Advanced Book Exchange site, you can search for a specific book or browse by subject with over 2,500 booksellers.

- *www.mastercollector.com.* The Master Collector Online has more than 8,000 dolls and toys listed. It also posts doll shows across the country.

- *www.matchcover.com.* Here you'll find over 50,000 matchcovers, ranging from famous restaurants to historical events.

- *www.matchboxtoys.com.* Run by Mattel, this site lists hundreds of available matchbox toys, some starting below $25.

- *www.bjminis.com.* B.J. Miniatures has miniature furniture and accessories for dollhouses plus links to other sites.

- *www.miniworld.com/house.* Run by the House of Miniatures, this site has a wide selection of furniture, books, and catalogs.

- *www.artrock.com.* The place for memorabilia related to the Beatles, the Grateful Dead, Jimi Hendrix, the Doors, Janis Joplin, and others.

- *www.collector-link.com/cards.* The Collector Link site helps you find baseball, basketball, hockey, and even phone cards.

When the Bears Are Out of the Cave

"Gentlemen prefer bonds."

Andrew Mellon

And so do women and children . . . when they're looking for safe, income-producing investments. In fact, most people initially feel more at ease with bonds than stocks, perhaps because they know bonds provide fixed income, during any kind of market, any kind of economy.

Yet bond prices can be almost as volatile as stocks. So even if you have always looked upon bonds as your safe investment, take time to read Part Two and update your position. You'll learn about the safest bonds (those issued by the government) as well as the riskiest (junk or high-yield bonds).

In between, there is information on how to evaluate bonds, use the rating services, read the quotes in the newspaper, and get call protection.

Part Two covers these broad categories:

- Corporate bonds
- Bond mutual funds
- U.S. Treasury issues
- Treasury Inflation-Indexed Securities
- Savings bonds
- Convertibles
- Municipal bonds
- Junk bonds
- Ginnie Maes and Ginnie Mae funds
- Zero coupon bonds
- CMOs

9

Bond Basics: How to Make Money with Corporate Bonds

*I*f you want to protect your principal and also set up a steady stream of income, bonds, rather than stocks, are the answer. Bonds not only generate higher returns than CDs, money market funds, and dividend-paying stocks, but they also have another key advantage: As long as you hold your bonds until maturity, you know exactly how much money you will get back—typically $1,000 per bond—and precisely when you will get it.

Bonds also offer greater security than most common stocks, since the issuer must pay interest on its bonds before it pays dividends on its common or preferred stock. On the other hand, a corporation can and often does cut back or eliminate the dividend on its common stock.

Bonds are issued by corporations, by the U.S. government and its agencies, and by states, municipalities, and their agencies. The latter group, also called "munis," are discussed in Chapter 12; high-yield or junk bonds appear in Chapter 13; and Treasuries, or government issues, in Chapter 10. This chapter is devoted to corporate bonds and corporate bond funds.

THE NITTY GRITTY

Bonds, unlike stocks, are debt. They can best be described as IOUs, or as contracts to pay back money. In other words, when you buy a bond, you become a lender, loaning money to the issuer. In return the issuer owes you the dollar amount shown on the face of the bond plus interest. (You may actually get a bond certificate to put in your safe-deposit box, although increasingly bond ownership is recorded in the form of book entry. This means the issuer maintains a record of bond buyers' names but does not send them certificates.)

The interest rate, officially called the *coupon rate,* is fixed—that means the issuer pays no more and no less for the entire life of the bond. Bondholders receive their interest payments on a regular schedule, generally every six months.

The amount you get back when the bond matures is called the *face value* or *par*—typically $1,000, although sometimes $5,000.

Bonds mature anywhere up to 40 years, although those that mature in 1 to 10 years are known as *notes*. Those issued for over 10 years are officially called bonds.

HOW AND WHY BONDS CHANGE VALUE

Many investors mistakenly think of bonds as being stable in price, almost stodgy. This is simply not true. When bonds are first issued by a corporation or the government, they are sold at face value or par, but immediately afterward they move up and down in price, trading in what is called the secondary market. If they are selling at above par—above $1,000—they are said to be at a *premium;* if they are trading below par, at a *discount*.

The reason they move in price is in response

to changes in interest rates, as explained in greater detail below. The formula is easy to remember:

- When interest rates move down, bond prices move up.
- When interest rates move up, bond prices move down.
- The farther away the bond's maturity date, the more volatile its price.

This price fluctuation actually offers you another way to make money with bonds in addition to earning a fixed rate of interest, and that is by selling your bonds at a higher price than you paid.

NOTE: You'll find that in the financial pages of newspapers, the prices for bonds are quoted on the basis of $100, so always add a zero to the price—a bond quoted at $108 is really selling at $1,080.

FIVE KEY REASONS WHY YOU SHOULD OWN BONDS

1. *Diversification.* When stock prices are depressed, bonds tend to be more sought after and therefore are a viable alternative to stocks.
2. *Current income.* Annual interest payments must be made to bondholders at the stated rate unless the company files for bankruptcy or undergoes a restructuring of its debt. Therefore, your steady stream of income is guaranteed in all but the worst situations. And if the company restructures its debt, it will issue new securities in exchange for existing bonds.
3. *Capital gains.* If you buy a bond at a discount (below $1,000 or par) and sell it for more than you paid, you'll have a profit.
4. *Seniority.* Interest on corporate bonds must be paid before dividends on common and preferred stocks of the same company, again protecting your income.
5. *Safety ratings.* These are available on corporate bonds that help determine how safe they are

as an investment. Both Moody's and Standard & Poor's, independent rating services, rate the financial solidness of corporations and their bonds on a continuing basis.

UNDERSTANDING BOND YIELDS

In order to be successful with bonds, it's necessary to understand how bond yields and price fluctuations work. Like stocks, bonds move up and down in price, and their market value changes due to supply and demand and changes in interest rates.

Because bonds have a fixed rate of interest, the only way the market can accommodate the changes in overall interest rates is by changing the price of bonds.

EXAMPLE: If you buy a bond at par ($1,000) and it has a coupon rate (the annual rate paid to bondholders) of 10%, you will receive $100 each year in interest payments. Now let's say that interest rates move up and the corporation that issued your bond needs to raise more money. The new bonds it issues must pay a higher interest rate in order to attract investors, otherwise no one will buy them. The new rate may be 10.5%. Now, the corporation's older bonds—the ones you own— will fall in price, perhaps to $960, in order to compensate for the fact that their yield of 10% is less appealing than the new 10.5% rate. The older bonds are now selling at a discount.

But, what if interest rates fall?

Exactly the opposite occurs: The corporation will be able to issue new bonds paying a lower rate of interest, and the older bonds, the ones you own, will rise in price, immediately becoming more desirable, due to their higher coupon rate. They now will sell at a premium.

Here's an example of how bond prices move with interest rate changes, supplied by the Vanguard Group. If you own a 30-year bond that yields 8%:

If the yield . . .	The price will . . .
rises to 9%	fall 10%
rises to 10%	fall 19%
falls to 7%	rise 12%
falls to 6%	rise 28%

When dealing with bonds, you'll come upon five different types of yields:

- *Coupon yield.* This is the interest rate stated on the face of the bond: 6.75%, 7%, etc. It is determined by the issuing corporation, and it depends on the prevailing cost of money at the time the bond is issued.

- *Current yield on the purchase price.* This is the annual interest payment based on the bond's current market price. It is higher than the coupon yield if you buy the bond below par, and lower if you buy the bond above par. For example, an 8% coupon bond selling below par at $900 has a current yield of 8.9%. (Take the annual interest payment, which is $80, divide it by the current bond price [$900] and multiply by 100.)

- *Yield to maturity.* This is the current yield and the gain or loss you will get if you hold the bond to maturity.

  Because maturities vary and the current yield measures only today's return, the bond market relies on the yield to maturity (YTM). This is the total return, comprising both interest and gain in price. Put another way, it is the rate of return on a bond when held to maturity. It includes the appreciation to par from the current market price when bought at a discount or depreciation when bought at a premium.

  To approximate the YTM for a discount bond:

1. Subtract the current bond price from its face value.
2. Divide the resulting figure by the number of years to maturity.
3. Add the total annual interest payments.
4. Add the current price to the face amount and divide by 2.
5. Divide the result of step 3 by the result of step 4.

    EXAMPLE: A $1,000 7% coupon bond due in ten years is selling at 72 ($720). The current yield is 9.7% ($70 ÷ $720). The YTM is about 11.4%.

$$1,000 - 720 = 280$$
$$280 \div 10 = 28$$
$$28 + 70 = 98$$
$$720 + 1,000 = 1,720 \div 2 = 860$$
$$98 \div 860 = 11.4\%$$

The YTM is the yardstick used by professionals, because it sets the market value of the debt security. But to amateurs, the spread—between the current and redemption prices—is what counts, because this appreciation will be added to your income. You get a competitive return while you wait—usually over eight years, because with shorter lives, the current yield is modest.

- *Discount yield.* This is the percentage from par or face value, adjusted to an annual basis, at which a discount bond sells. It is used for short-term obligations maturing in less than one year, primarily Treasury bills.

  It is roughly the opposite of YTM. If a one-year T-bill sells at a 6% yield, its cost is 94 ($940). The discount yield is 6 divided by 94, or 6.38%.

- *Yield to call.* This is the same as yield to maturity, except it is based on the assumption that the bond will be redeemed by the issuer at the call date.

☑ *HINT: Yield to maturity and yield to call are not listed in the newspaper. Your broker can give it to you, or you can find it in Standard & Poor's Bond Guide, available at many libraries.*

How Bonds Are Rated: 2000

GENERAL DESCRIPTION	MOODY'S	STANDARD & POOR'S
Best quality	Aaa	AAA
High quality	Aa	AA
Upper medium	A	A
Medium	Baa	BBB
Speculative	Ba	BB
Low grade	B	B
Poor to default	Caa	CCC
Highly speculative	Ca	CC
Lowest grade	C	C
In default	–	D

Ratings may also have a + or – sign to show relative standings in class. Bonds at BBB level and above are considered investment grade.

THE BOND PROSPECTUS

In addition to using the S&P and Moody ratings and your stockbroker's research, you can evaluate bonds on your own by looking at the bond's prospectus. This document details the issue's financial features, the means of payment, what the money raised will be used for, and what analysts think about the issuer's creditworthiness.

The two key points to look for are:

■ *The amount of debt the company has already issued.* Heavy debt means that much of the money raised by this issue could go toward interest payments on the company's debt.

■ *The bondholder's claim on the company's cash flow.* Is it a first claim or subordinated? You want one with first claim. Often the employee pension plan has a higher claim on earnings than bondholders, should there be a default. Note, too, whether the pension plan is funded or unfunded; if a large part is unfunded, discuss the appropriateness of the investment with your broker.

YOUR BOND-BUYING CHECKLIST

There are a number of factors to keep in mind when selecting corporate bonds for your portfolio. A bond's value depends first and foremost on the credit quality of the issuing corporation. Bonds of a solid successful corporation are certainly a better investment than bonds of a weaker firm. Use this checklist to select the right bonds for your portfolio:

■ *The bond's quality rating.* Bond issuers are rated by independent research services, such as Moody's and Standard & Poor's. They analyze the financial strength of the corporation, project future prospects, and determine how well the corporation is prepared to cover both interest and principal payments. These two top services tend to reach the same conclusions about each bond.

Watch, too, for changes in bond ratings. When a bond is upgraded, its market price will probably rise and the yield dip a bit. Downgrading of a bond signals possible trouble, and so the value of the bond may decline.

(Downgraded bonds are called fallen angels on Wall Street.) However, if the rating is not too low, and you are not averse to risk, you can sometimes make money purchasing a fallen angel you believe will be eventually upgraded, either as the economy improves or as the corporation makes changes that puts it on a more solid financial footing.

NOTE: Slight rating shifts are not terribly important as long as the rating is BBB or better.

> ☑ *HINT: Remember, the lower the rating, the higher the yield a bond must pay in order to attract investors. That's why very high-yielding bonds are called high-yield or junk bonds.*

- *The interest rate, or coupon rate.* This is the fixed dollar amount you will be receiving. You obviously want a competitive rate.
- *The maturity date.* This is the date when you will be paid the face value of the bond. Pick maturity dates that meet your needs, say, to pay college tuition or fund your retirement. Remember that by staggering your maturity dates, you will have a stream of income coming due that can be reinvested if interest rates go up. On the other hand, if rates fall, you will have locked in the higher yields.
- *The current yield.* This is the coupon rate divided by the current market price of the bond.
- *The yield to maturity.* This combines the current yield with the price you paid for the bond if that price was more or less than the face value.
- *The yield to call.* This gives you the yield, assuming the bond will be called in or redeemed before maturity date. (Calls are explained on page 97.)
- *The bond's backing or collateral.* Bonds are categorized as either secured bonds or debentures. *Secured bonds* are backed by the corporation's plant, equipment, or other assets. If the collateral is real estate, the bonds are called mortgage bonds; if the collateral is

---

Picking the Right Bond or Note

If you want to invest $10,000 in bonds for ten years, you have these choices:

- A 6-month T-bill that will be rolled over at each maturity.
- A 2- to 3-year Treasury note that at maturity will be turned into a 7- to 8-year note at a somewhat more rewarding yield if interest rates go up.
- A 10-year bond to be held to redemption. This would be best if you expect interest rates to decline or stay about the same.
- A 15- to 20-year bond to be sold at the end of 10 years, best if you expect rates to fall, but the longer the maturity, the greater the risk if rates climb.

---

equipment, they are called equipment certificates. If the corporation defaults on its bond payments, these assets can be sold to pay off the bondholders.

Debenture bonds are riskier in that they are unsecured, backed only by the overall ability of the corporation to meet its bills and other obligations. If the company declares bankruptcy, debentures cannot be paid off until secured bondholders are paid.

- *Poison put provisions.* These guarantee that bondholders in a company that is taken over can redeem their bonds at par. Poison puts accomplish two things: They protect investors and discourage unwanted takeovers. (This was more important during the 1980s when there were a rash of corporate takeovers.)
- *Special terms.* Most bonds issued by the federal government and corporations carry a fixed coupon as well as a fixed date of maturity. But there are occasionally serial bonds in which a portion of the issue will be paid off periodically. Usually, the earlier the redemption date, the lower the interest rate, by 1/4% to 1/2% or so. These bonds are excellent if you have a specific date by which you need money.

SHORT-TERM VERSUS LONG-TERM BONDS

When deciding what maturity of bond to buy, keep in mind that:

- The shorter the maturity rate, generally the lower the yield, but:
- The shorter the maturity, the less the bond is affected by interest rate changes and inflation.
- The longer the maturity, the higher the yield.
- The longer the maturity, the more likely the bond will be redeemed or called early; then you will be paid off, but will be forced to reinvest this money at lower rates.
- To get the highest yields, invest for the shortest time possible while rates are rising. When rates have peaked, sell and buy longer-term bonds to lock in those high yields.
- You can protect yourself against price declines to some extent by purchasing high-grade bonds at a discount—that is, below face value. This is especially true if their maturity is not far away.
- Rather than having all your bonds come due at the same time, own a spread of bonds to come due every year or so. That way you'll periodically receive cash, which you can reinvest to keep the cycle going. Spreading out maturities also tends to average out the effects of price changes.
- If you have less than $50,000 to invest, diversify through a bond mutual fund or unit investment trust, which will also help reduce your risk.

Changes in Bond Ratings

UP:	AOL
	BB- to BB+
DOWN:	Nike
	A+ to A

SOURCE: Standard & Poor's, Summer 1999.

THE NEWSPAPER LISTINGS

When reading a bond listing in the newspaper, keep in mind that:

- Bonds are issued at par ($1,000), but in the financial pages they're quoted on the basis of $100, so always add a zero to the price; for example, a bond quoted at $108 is really selling at $1,080.
- Current yield is the annual yield you will receive if you buy the bond at that day's price. If it's selling at a discount from par (the issue price), the price given in the "Last" column will be under 100. If the bond is selling at a premium or above par, the price will be above 100.
- Sales stands for the number of $1,000 bonds traded that day. (Bonds are usually priced at issue time at $1,000 each.)
- The small "s" that sometimes follows the interest rate means "space" and is used to separate the interest rate from the next group of numbers—the year in which the bond matures.
- The letters "cv" indicate that the issue is a convertible bond and can be exchanged for a fixed number of shares of common stock of the issuer.
- The letters "zr" before the maturity date indicate that the issue is a zero coupon bond.

Debt for Equity

A variation on the sinking fund is a debt-for-equity exchange, which is used by corporations to discharge debts without actually paying them off prior to maturity. The company arranges for a broker to buy a portion of the outstanding bond issues for a fee. The broker then (1) exchanges the bonds for a new issue of corporate stock with a market value equal to that of the bonds and (2) sells the shares at a profit. The corporate balance sheet is improved without harming operations or prospects.

How to Read Corporate Bond Listings

The table below shows a listing in *Barron's* for an A+-rated NY Telephone bond with a coupon of 7⅞% and a 2017 maturity date. The high price was 100, and the low 98⅞, with the last sale at 99½, up 1⅞ from the last sale of the previous week. Altogether 93 $1,000 bonds changed hands.

Standard & Poor's Standard Rating*	Issue	Current Yield	Sales	High	Low	Close	Change**
A+	NYT 7⅞, 2017	7.9%	93	100	98⅞	99½	+1⅞

Each bond pays $78.75 in annual interest, so the current yield is 7.9%. In the year 2017 each bond will be redeemed at 100 ($1,000) for a gain of ½ a point, or $5 per bond.

*The rating is not shown in the press.
**From previous week.

HOW TO GET CALL PROTECTION

To attract investors for long-term commitments, corporations usually include call protection when they issue new bonds.

When a bond is called, the issuer exercises a right (which will appear in the prospectus) to retire the bond, or call it in, before the date of maturity. This right to call gives the issuing corporation the ability to respond to changing interest rates.

If, for example, a corporation issued bonds with an 11½% rate when rates were high and then rates dropped to 7%, it would be to the issuer's advantage to call in the old bonds and issue new ones at the lower prevailing rate. In fact, it is often so advantageous that a corporation is willing to pay a premium over par to call its bonds.

There are three types of call provisions you should know about:

- *Freely callable:* Issuer can retire the bond at any time; therefore, it has no call protection.
- *Noncallable:* Bond cannot be called until date of maturity.
- *Deferred call:* Bond cannot be called until after a stated number of years, usually five to ten.

The *call price* is the price the issuer must pay to retire the bond. It's based on the par value plus a premium, which in theory often works out to be equal to one year's interest at the earliest call date.

For example, an 8% bond would theoretically have an initial call of $1,080—the $80 being the premium. However, there are many variations. For example, the call price can be specified, or it can be based on a declining scale, with greater premiums given for calling in during the earlier years.

 CAUTION: A call on a bond is nearly always bad news for the investor. That's because issuers sel-

Call Alert

Your broker should advise you about the call status of any bond; otherwise, be certain to ask. Calls are also listed in the bond's prospectus and in Standard & Poor's and Moody's bond guides, available from your broker or at your library. Here's how it looks in the bond dealer's guides or on quote sheets:

Corporate bond: "NC" means noncallable for life.

Government bond: "8½ May 1998–01" means the bond matures in May 2001, but is callable in 1998.

dom call a bond when interest rates are rising and when getting your money out would enable you to reinvest at the higher rates. On the contrary, bonds are generally called when rates are declining and you would prefer to lock in your higher yield by keeping the bond. So try to purchase bonds with call protection. Check the prospectus or ask your broker.

EXAMPLE: Safeway Inc., 9.65% debentures, due 2004, are noncallable to maturity. This means that an investor who buys these bonds in 2000 can look forward to almost four years of receiving a 9.65% coupon.

SINKING FUND PROVISIONS

Often a corporation borrows millions of dollars in any one bond issue, so quite obviously that amount of money must be available when the bond matures and the bondholders are paid back the full face value.

In order to retire a portion of that enormous debt, some issuers buy back part of it early—before the maturity date, leaving less to be paid off (to the bondholders) at one time in a lump sum. In this process, the issuer shrinks the corporation's debt. The money used to do this repurchasing is called a *sinking fund.*

When a corporation sets up a sinking fund, it must make periodic predetermined cash payments to a special custodial account set up for this purpose.

Advantages

■ By setting up this process and establishing a sinking fund, the corporation winds up paying less total interest. For example, with a 25-year issue set up to buy back 3.75% of the debt annually, 75% of the bonds will be retired before maturity. This means that the average life of the bonds will be about 17 years, not the 25 years anticipated by the investor.

■ A sinking fund also adds a margin of safety for investors: The periodic purchases provide price support and enhance the probability of repayment when the bond matures.

Disadvantages

■ It actually narrows the time span or length of the bond, so there will be less total income for the long-term investor. The bottom line: Sinking funds benefit the corporation more than the bondholder.

BOND MUTUAL FUNDS

If you have a small amount to invest or simply don't wish to select your own bonds, you can buy bonds through a mutual fund or closed-end fund. (**See:** Chapter 6 on mutual funds.)

Although funds are extremely popular with investors, it's important that you understand that your return in a fund is not as assured as with an individual bond—in other words, with a bond you know what your annual income will be and how much you will get back when your bond matures.

On the other hand, with a bond mutual fund, your return fluctuates, depending upon the hold-

---

The Sinking Fund

A sinking fund specifies how certain bonds will be paid off over time. If a bond has a sinking fund, the company must redeem a certain number of bonds annually before maturity to reduce its debt.

■ *Advantage:* Bondholders get their principal back earlier than the maturity date.
■ *Disadvantage:* If the coupon rate is high, bondholders will not want to retire the bond early.

If your bond is called, your broker should let you know if it is part of your brokerage account; notices also appear in the newspaper. You must take your money, because interest will cease at the specified time.

ings in the portfolio, and when you go to sell your shares, it is possible that your shares will be worth less than what you paid for them—on the other hand, they could be worth more. Make certain before you purchase shares in a bond mutual fund that you understand this concept—that a bond mutual fund's return is in continual flux.

Then,

■ *Check the performance.* Follow performance over at least five years, long enough to include both bad and good years for debt securities.

■ *Consider closed-end bond funds.* They do not issue new shares or units after their initial offering. Instead, they trade on one of the exchanges or over-the-counter. The capitalization of this type of fund is fixed at the outset, and investors must buy shares either at the initial offering or later in the secondary market or aftermarket.

This means that the price of a closed-end fund is determined by two variables: (1) the public's demand for its shares and (2) the

Closed-End Bond Funds

FUND	YIELD	PRICE	SYMBOL
CNA Income Shares	8.9%	$10	CNN
Transam Income	7.4	25	TAI
Dreyfus Strategic Income	8.4	9	GVT
John Hancock Inc. Sec.	7.4	15	JHS
Duff & Phelps Util. & Corp	7.8	15	DUC
New America High Yield	11.3	4	HYB

SOURCE: S&P Stock Guide, Summer 1999.

value of its portfolio. Therefore, such funds sell either at a premium or at a discount from the portfolio's net asset value. Like their open-end cousins, closed-end funds are professionally managed, contain a wide variety of bonds, and make monthly distributions. (**See:** Chapter 7 for more on closed-end bond funds.)

FOR FURTHER INFORMATION

Books

Robert Zipf, *How the Bond Market Works* (New York: Prentice-Hall, 1997).

Hildy Richelson, *Straight Talk About Bonds and Bond Funds* (New York: McGraw-Hill, 1996).

Frank Fabozzi, *Corporate Bonds: Structure and Analysis* (Burr Ridge, IL: Irwin, 1996).

Pamphlets

How to Select a Bond Fund, free pamphlet from The Vanguard Group, 800–523–8809.

A Guide To Closed-End Funds, pamphlet from Investment Company Institute, 1401 H Street NW, Suite #1200, Washington, DC 20005; 202–326–5800; website: www.ici.org; 35 cents.

Closed-End Bond Funds

PROS

↑ Closed-end funds do not have to sell off their portfolios when the market declines as open-end funds must do in order to meet redemption demand by investors.

↑ The managers tend to have greater flexibility in portfolio composition. A fund selling at a deep discount from its NAV is sometimes a takeover candidate.

CONS

↓ Funds react very quickly to interest rate changes: When rates rise, bond prices fall, and vice versa.

↓ Many funds buy lower-quality bonds to boost yields and to compete with older funds that sell at a discount.

Newsletters and Newspapers

The Bond Buyer
One State Street Plaza
New York, NY 10004
212–803–8200
Published daily; $1,897/year; $15 per copy; three-week trial, free.

Investor's Guide to Closed End Funds
Thomas J. Herzfeld Advisors
P.O. Box 161465
Miami, FL 33116
305–271–1900
website: www.herzfeld.com
Monthly; $85 for two-month trial; $475/year.

10

U.S. Treasuries and Savings Bonds

You've heard it over and over—there are no safer securities than U.S. Treasury obligations, which are backed by the full faith and credit of the U.S. government. And it's basically true—if you're looking for a risk-free investment, invest in the federal government. Uncle Sam is continually borrowing money, and thus far has an excellent reputation for paying back his debts.

ADVANTAGES

In addition to safety and affordability, Treasuries provide interest that is exempt from state and local income taxes—a plus for anyone, but especially those who live in high-tax states. And if interest rates fall, you can sell your Treasury for more than you paid.

Treasuries are also easy to unload because of the enormous size of the government bond market. In fact, the Treasury market is the world's largest securities field, with average trading volume in excess of $100 billion annually.

DISADVANTAGES

So, are there any disadvantages? Yes. If interest rates rise after your purchase, the value of that Treasury will fall, because new issues will pay a higher annual interest; to make up for that, buyers will pay only a discounted price for the older issues. Of course, if you hold your Treasuries until maturity, this won't affect you as you're guaranteed to get the full face value.

U.S. Treasury bonds and notes are noncallable unless they have an alternate earlier maturity date. These dates are given in their newspaper lists, for example: 2000–2005. Or ask your broker if specific Treasuries are callable.

Another disadvantage: The rates are lower than on corporate bonds with comparable maturities—but then, corporates are also not as safe as Treasuries.

BUYING NEW TREASURIES

Buying Treasuries is easier today than ever before. You can still buy them from a broker, but you'll pay a minimum commission ranging from $25 to $100, which lowers your yield. Because fees vary, check with several full-service, discount, and on-line brokers if you choose this route.

You can sidestep the commission by buying them yourself over the Internet or phone or by mail. By doing business on the Internet or phone, you also eliminate cumbersome paperwork. Still, the mail remains a popular method of purchase as well.

NOTE: One option no longer exists. You can't walk into a Federal Reserve Bank and buy a Treasury security anymore. Window service ended in August 1999.

Buying by Mail

■ **Step 1.** If you choose to buy by mail rather than by phone or the Internet, the first thing you must do is obtain a TreasuryDirect tender—Form PD F 5381. You can download or order the form on the Internet. Go to: www.treasurydirect.gov and click on "Ordering/Downloading Forms." You can also get the form by calling or writing your Federal Reserve bank. The phone numbers and addresses are on pages 103–104.

■ **Step 2.** Fill out the tender. Be sure to provide your checking or savings account number so that payments may be made directly to your account. This number appears on your checks. You will be asked whether you wish to submit a competitive or noncompetitive bid. Most investors choose the noncompetitive option.

Although the Treasury prefers that you submit the official tender form, you may actually submit a tender by letter. If you do, be sure to type or print the following information and then sign the letter in dark ink: (a) the face amount of the securities you wish to purchase; (b) the maturity; (c) whether you are submitting a noncompetitive or competitive bid (specify yield when making a competitive bid); (d) your name and mailing address; (e) your Social Security number (if the securities are being purchased in two names, you must supply the Social Security number of the first-named purchaser); (f) your telephone number during business hours; and (g) your Treasury Direct Account number, if you have one.

If you do not yet have a Treasury Direct Account, then include: (h) your Direct Deposit information—the name of the financial institution and its routing number, your account name, number, and type (checking or savings account).

■ **Step 3.** Mail the tender and payment to your Federal Reserve Bank or its branch. Print or type in large letters on the front of the envelope: TENDER FOR TREASURY SECURITIES.

■ **Step 4.** To be accepted for a particular auction, your noncompetitive tender must be postmarked by midnight the day before the auction and received by the Federal Reserve bank or branch by the issue date.

You have several payment options. If you choose a convenient new service called Pay Direct, the government will simply debit the bank account you designated for TreasuryDirect. If you don't choose Pay Direct, the following guidelines apply:

■ For T-bills: You may use a cashier's check, certified personal check, or matured Treasury securities.

■ For T-notes and bonds: You may use any of the above methods or a personal check.

■ Checks must be made payable to the Federal Reserve Bank of _____(city)_____ . Each check must have the name and Social Security number of the purchaser on its face. (Endorsed checks are not accepted.)

■ **Step 5.** Auction results are announced by the Treasury in the afternoon of the auction day. The results are also available via e-mail. Sign up for them (as well as for notice of upcoming auctions) at: www.treasurydirect.gov; click on "Mailing Lists." Many Federal Reserve banks provide auction results on recorded phone messages, available 24 hours a day.

■ **Step 6.** The government will set up a TreasuryDirect account, called a Master Record, when you submit your first tender form. You may then request that a Statement of Account be mailed to you at any time; phone: 800–943–6864, or click on: www.treasurydirect.gov and go to "Accessing TreasuryDirect Electronic Services."

This statement shows your name, address, phone number, TreasuryDirect account number, tax information, and payment instructions as well as details on all Treasury securities in the account. When you receive interest payments or when a security matures and you receive money, you will get a copy of the updated record. (T-notes and bonds pay interest twice a year. T-bill interest, which is more complicated, is described below.)

- **Step 7.** Payment of interest, discounts, and principal are deposited electronically into the account at the bank you designated to receive TreasuryDirect payments. Or, you can request automatic reinvestments of a Treasury bill when you purchase it. For example, on the tender form, you can specify that the bill be automatically reinvested (noncompetitively) for up to two years after its first maturity date. Unlike a mutual fund investment in which all interest, dividends, and capital gains can be reinvested in more fund shares, the Treasury rollover involves only your original investment, e.g., the principal.

NOTE: If you already hold Treasury securities in a bank or brokerage account and wish to

A Potpourri of Rates for Savers

INVESTMENT	YIELD/RATE
Passbook savings	2.05%
Bank money market account	2.15
6-month CD	4.30
1-year CD	4.66
5-year CD	5.16
Taxable money market fund	4.53
Tax-free money market fund	3.26
3-month Treasury bill	4.78
6-month Treasury bill	5.01
1-year Treasury bill	5.12
I-bond	5.05
10-year Treasury bond	5.76
30-year U.S. Treasury bond	5.90

(As of September 1999.)

transfer them to the TreasuryDirect system, submit Form PD F 5182, "New Account Request." You can download or order the form on the Internet by going to: www.treasurydirect.gov and clicking on "Ordering/Downloading Forms." You can also request the form from a Federal Reserve Bank.

USING TREASURYDIRECT ELECTRONIC SERVICES

Once you have an account in TreasuryDirect, you can use the Internet or an automated, toll-free phone system to reinvest your securities, make new purchases, check your account balances, and order statements and other items.

To purchase by phone or Internet, you must be an existing account holder who buys noncompetitively and pays for securities by automatic withdrawal from a bank account. If you meet those qualifications, the process is simple. Call: 800–943–6864 on a Touch-Tone phone or log on to: www.treasurydirect.gov and click on "Accessing TreasuryDirect Electronic Services." After you give your TreasuryDirect account number and taxpayer ID number, select the amount of your purchase, its term (or maturity), and you're all set.

THE FEDERAL RESERVE BANKS AND BRANCHES

- ATLANTA. Securities Service Division, 104 Marietta St. NW, Atlanta, GA 30303; 404–521–8653
- BALTIMORE. Box 1378, 502 South Sharp St., Baltimore, MD 21203; 410–576–3300
- BIRMINGHAM. Box 830447, 1801 Fifth Ave. North, Birmingham, AL 35283; 205–731–8708
- BOSTON. Box 2076, 600 Atlantic Ave., Boston, MA 02106; 617–973–3000
- BUFFALO. Box 961, 160 Delaware Ave., Buffalo, NY 14240; 716–849–5000

- CHARLOTTE. Box 30248, 530 East Trade St., Charlotte, NC 28230; 704–358–2100
- CHICAGO. Box 834, 230 South LaSalle St., Chicago, IL 60690; 312–322–5369
- CINCINNATI. Box 999, 150 East Fourth St., Cincinnati, OH 45201; 513–721–4787
- CLEVELAND. Box 6387, 1455 East Sixth St., Cleveland, OH 44101; 216–579–2490
- DALLAS. Securities Dept., Box 655906, 2200 North Pearl St., Dallas, TX 75265; 214–922–6770
- DENVER. Box 5228, 1020 16th St., Denver, CO 80217; 303–572–2473
- DETROIT. Box 1059, 160 West Fort St., Detroit, MI 48231; 313–964–6157
- EL PASO. Box 100, 301 East Main St., El Paso, TX 79901; 915–544–4730
- HOUSTON. Box 2578, 1701 San Jacinto St., Houston, TX 77252; 713–659–4433
- JACKSONVILLE. Box 929, 800 West Water St., Jacksonville, FL 32231; 904–632–1190
- KANSAS CITY. 925 Grand Blvd., Kansas City, MO 64198; 816–881–2000
- LITTLE ROCK. Box 1261, 325 West Capital Ave., Little Rock, AK 72203; 501–324–8272
- LOS ANGELES. Box 512077, Terminal Annex, 950 South Grand Ave., Los Angeles, CA 90051; 213–624–7398
- LOUISVILLE. Box 32710, 410 South Fifth St., Louisville, KY 40232; 502–568–9236
- MEMPHIS. Box 407, 200 North Main, Memphis, TN 38101; 901–523–7171
- MIAMI. Box 520847, 9100 NW 36th St., Miami, FL 33152; 305–471–6497
- MINNEAPOLIS. Box 291, 90 Henrietta Ave., Minneapolis, MN 55480; 612–204–5000
- NASHVILLE. 301 Eighth Ave. North, Nashville, TN 37203; 615–251–7100
- NEW ORLEANS. Box 61630, 525 St. Charles Ave., New Orleans, LA 70161; 504–593–3200
- NEW YORK. Federal Reserve P.O. Station, 33 Liberty St., New York, NY 10045; 212–720–6619

- OKLAHOMA CITY. Box 25129, 226 Dean A. McGee Ave., Oklahoma City, OK 73125; 405–270–8652
- OMAHA. Box 3958, 2201 Farnam St., Omaha, NE 68103; 402–221–5636
- PHILADELPHIA. Box 90, 10 Independence Mall, Philadelphia, PA 19106; 215–574–6680
- PITTSBURGH. Box 867, 717 Grant St., Pittsburgh, PA 15230; 412–261–7802
- PORTLAND. Box 3436, 915 SW Stark St., Portland, OR 97208; 503–221–5932
- RICHMOND. Box 27622, 701 East Byrd St., Richmond, VA 23261; 804–697–8000
- SALT LAKE CITY. Box 30780, 120 South State St., Salt Lake City, UT 84111; 801–322–7900
- SAN ANTONIO. Box 1471, 126 East Nueva St., San Antonio, TX 78295; 210–978–1303
- SAN FRANCISCO. Box 7702, 101 Market St., San Francisco, CA 94120; 415–974–2330
- SEATTLE. Securities Services Dept. Box 3567, 1015 Second Ave., Seattle, WA 98124; 206–343–3605
- ST. LOUIS. Box 14915, 411 Locust St., St. Louis, MO 63178; 314–444–8703

TREASURY BILLS

Treasury bills mature in three months, six months, or one year. T-bills, as they are often called, are issued in minimum denominations of $1,000. New issues are sold at a discount from face value and are redeemed at full face value upon maturity. If, for example, you buy a T-bill through the TreasuryDirect System, you write a check for $1,000.

If you buy via the Internet, the actual purchase price is deducted on auction day from your designated bank. Shortly after the auction, the discount is refunded by mail or electronic deposit into your account.

Let's say the discount or interest rate is 4%: You'll get a check for $40. When the T-bill matures, the Treasury will pay you $1,000, the full face value. Because they are guaranteed by the full faith and credit of the U.S. government, investors have no risk of default. In fact, if the federal government goes into bankruptcy, it won't matter what types of investments you have!

T-bills constitute the largest part of the government's financing. They are sold by the Treasury at regular auctions where competitive bidding by major institutions and bond dealers takes place. Auctions are held weekly for 3- and 6-month maturities, monthly for 1-year bills. (Occasionally the government issues a 9-month T-bill.) The yields at these auctions are watched very carefully as indications of interest rate trends. Floating-rate loans, mortgages, and numerous other investments tie their rates to T-bills.

- *Figuring yields.* Because T-bills are sold at auction at a discount from face value, there is no stated interest rate.
- *To defer income with T-bills.* Because Treasury bills are sold at a discount price—that is, at less than face value—and are redeemed at maturity at full face value, they do not pay an annual interest. Therefore, in the following example, you would not have to pay taxes until your T-bill matured in 2000. This is to your advantage if you expect your income to be lower in 2000.

EXAMPLE: You buy $10,000 worth of 1-year bills in February 1999, for $9,380. Your real yield is 6.6% ($10,000 − $9,380 ÷ $9,380). When you cash in the bills in February 2000, you will receive $620 on a cash investment of $9,380.

☑ *HINT: Use T-bills as a short-term parking place for money received in a lump sum, say, from the sale of a house or yacht, as a bonus, or from a royalty check. Think of them as interest-bearing cash.*

TREASURY NOTES

These intermediate-term securities typically mature in 2, 3, 5, and 10 years. They are issued in $1,000 increments. The interest rate is fixed and de-termined by the coupon rate as specified on the note. It is calculated on the basis of a 365-day year. Interest earned is paid semiannually and is exempt from state and local taxes. Two-year notes are issued monthly; and 5- to 10-year notes, quarterly.

☑ *HINT: In May 1998, the government stopped offering 3-year Treasury notes due to the huge budget surplus. They had been around for some 22 years.*

T-notes are growing in popularity with investors, because their longer maturities usually give investors a higher yield. Another plus is the fact that they are not callable, so you are guaranteed a steady stream of income until maturity.

TREASURY BONDS

These long-term debt obligations are also issued in $1,000 minimums. They range in maturity from 10 to 30 years.

NOTE: As we go to press, only 30-year bonds are being sold.

A fixed rate of interest is paid semiannually. The interest earned is exempt from state and local taxes.

💣 *CAUTION: Unlike T-notes, these bonds are sometimes subject to a special type of call. If a specific bond is callable, its maturity date and call date are both listed in hyphenated form in the newspaper. In the example described on page 106 the 12% bond due to mature in 2013 could be called in at any time starting in 2008.*

☑ *HINT: Because government bonds come in so many maturities, stagger your portfolio to meet future needs and to take advantage of any rise in interest rates.*

INFLATION-INDEXED TREASURY SECURITIES (TIPS)

In 1997, the government introduced the Inflation-Indexed Treasury Security. Its principal is adjusted, based on changes in the Consumer Price Index.

You are paid interest on the principal. At maturity, you redeem these securities either at their inflation-adjusted principal or the original par (or face value) amount, whichever is greater.

So, if inflation occurs, the value of this particular security keeps pace with it. But if deflation prevails over the life of the security, you are guaranteed that your securities value will not drop below its original par amount.

These securities, usually issued quarterly, are sold in increments of $1000, and can be purchased through the TreasuryDirect program at: www.public debt.treas.gov, by phone at: 800–943–6864, or for a fee, through a broker.

Advantages

■   These securities will outperform conventional Treasuries if inflation rises even slightly and they are much less volatile in price than conventional Treasuries.

Disadvantages

■   You have to pay federal taxes on the annual interest and the amount by which the principal is increased for inflation—even though you won't see this money until the bonds mature or are sold.

BUYING ON THE SECONDARY OR AFTERMARKET

After a Treasury issue is first sold, it then trades in the secondary or aftermarket—not on the major exchanges, but over-the-counter. This type of trading is subject to the same market forces that affect corporate bonds (See: Chapter 9) and stocks (See: Chapter 14).

And you will need a broker to handle your trades—all previously issued Treasuries must be purchased through securities dealers, commercial banks, or a stockbroker, not from the Federal Reserve Banks. Very often you will wind up buying directly from the broker's own portfolio of Treasuries,

and you may not have to pay a direct commission or transaction fee. Instead, the extra cost of the securities covers the broker's costs and gives him a profit.

You may wish to buy in the secondary market if you want to have money come due on a certain date. In this case, check the Treasury listings in the newspaper to find a maturity date that meets your goals. You'll note that there's a bid and an asked figure. The bid price is what you're offered if you sell, while the asked is what it will cost you to buy. The figures in the paper, however, are for trades of $1 million. Since you'll most likely be buying less than a million, you'll wind up paying slightly more than the price listed in the newspaper and your yield will be slightly less. (**See:** table on page 107.)

☑️   *HINT: Be certain you check with several brokers, including a discount broker. Charles Schwab, for example, charges $49 per transaction up to $150,000 on all Treasuries; above that amount there is no fee. Fidelity charges $50 to start, but if you are already a Fidelity customer and have an active account, there is no charge.*

HOW TO READ THE QUOTES

All Treasury issues are quoted daily in dollars plus units of $1/_{32}$ of a dollar (0.03125), with the bid, asked change in price, and yield given in the newspaper. The quotations for each note or bond are per $1,000 face value.

The first line in the table at right shows notes due in 2004 with a coupon of $7^1/_8$%, a bid price of 102–12 ($1,023.75), and an asked price of 102–18 ($1,025.63) with a yield of 6.48%. An investor who holds these notes for four years until maturity will get $71.25 per year less the premium of $25.63, for a yield to maturity of 6.48% when redeemed in October of 2004.

The 12% bond due to mature in 2008–2013 has what is known as a double maturity, sometimes referred to as a call date. Its yield is calculated on the earlier maturity, 2008; however, at the Treasury's choice, the maturity may be continued to 2013. Notification appears in the newspaper, and in some cases by letter. All Treasury issues with this modified call feature can be identified in the paper by the hyphenated listing. A small *n* indicates that the issue is a note rather than a bond.

How Government Notes and Bonds Are Quoted

ISSUE	BID	ASKED	CHANGE	YIELD
Oct. 04, 7 1/8	102–12	102–18	–6	6.48%
Aug. 08–13, 12	141	141–04	–24	7.30
May 16, 7 1/4	97–27	97–29	–22	7.44
May 18, 9 1/8	118–09	118–11	–30	7.47

SOURCE: Barron's, Summer 1999.

SELLING YOUR TREASURY SECURITIES

Just as buying T-bills, notes, and bonds is easier than ever, selling them is simpler, too. In the past, if you held Treasury securities in a TreasuryDirect account, you had to transfer them to a brokerage or bank account and, in turn, they were sold for a fee. You can still do that, but a new program, Sell Direct, eliminates the need to deal with a broker or middle person.

With Sell Direct, the government sells your securities for you. It obtains quotes from several different brokers, sells the securities at the highest price, and deposits the money directly into your bank account. You pay a competitive fee—$34 per security as we went to press.

To use Sell Direct, you must complete Form PD F 5179-1, "Security Transfer & Sale Request," and mail it to: Federal Reserve Bank of Chicago, P.O. Box 834, Chicago, IL 60690–0834. When your securities are sold, you'll receive a confirmation notice as well as a Statement of Account reflecting your new balance.

To sell your securities in the traditional manner—where you transfer them to a bank or broker—you must complete Form PD F 5179, "Security Transfer Request." You must include the routing number of your financial institution.

Both of these forms can be ordered from your Federal Reserve bank or on the Internet at www.treasurydirect.gov, clicking on "Ordering/Downloading Forms."

USING THE YIELD CURVE

A yield curve is a diagram that illustrates the relation between bond yields and maturities on a particular day. Use it to decide which type of bond to buy at a certain period. It is published daily in the *Wall Street Journal.*

To draw a yield curve, professionals set out the maturities of like bonds—all Treasuries or all AA-rated corporates—on graph paper on a horizontal line, from left to right, starting with the shortest maturities (30 days) and continuing over days or years to the longest (30 years). Then they plot the yields on the vertical axis and connect the dots with a line that becomes the yield curve.

HINT: When short-term rates are more than a percentage point above long-term rates, the yield curve is inverted. A recession typically follows, usually within six months.

NOTE: The curve is used to tell whether short-term rates are higher or lower than long-term rates. When short-term rates are lower, it is called a positive yield curve. When short-term rates are higher, it's a negative or inverted yield curve. If there is only a modest difference between the two, it's known as a flat yield curve.

Generally, when the yield curve is positive, investors who are willing to tie up their money long term are rewarded for their risk by getting a higher yield.

Although any fixed-income securities can be plotted on a yield curve, the most common one illustrates Treasuries, from a 3-month T-bill to a 30-year bond.

SAVINGS BONDS

Savings bonds are an ultrasafe and extremely easy way to put aside money. They're not just for timid investors or grandparents who are at a loss over what to give their grandchildren. Today, these bonds offer special tax breaks, some of which make them a good deal for families within certain income brackets who are facing hefty college tuition bills.

The Treasury now offers two kinds of savings bonds: Series EE Bonds and the newer Series I or Inflation-Indexed Savings Bonds.

Series EE Bonds

Series EE bonds are sold at one-half their face value and in denominations of $50, $75, $100, $200, $500, $1,000, $5,000 and $10,000. In other words, you actually pay $25 for a $50 bond, $250 for a $500 bond, and so on. The maximum annual investment in EE bonds is $30,000 face value per calendar year per person—that's $15,000 in cash.

EE bonds are an accrual-type security. That means interest is added to the purchase price. EE bonds earn 90% of the market yield on five-year Treasuries. The rate on EE bonds changes every six months—on May 1 and November 1.

Earnings are exempt from state and local income tax and federal income tax can be deferred until the bonds are cashed in or they stop earning interest—which occurs after 30 years. Cash them in before five years and there's a 3-month earnings penalty.

$TIP: **No Probate.** *If, upon the death of an owner, there is a surviving co-owner or beneficiary named on the bonds, the bonds are not a part of the decedent's estate for probate purposes. Subject to applicable estate or inheritance taxes, if any, they become the sole property of the survivor.*

Inflation-Indexed Savings Bonds

These bonds, referred to as I-bonds, were launched a year ago. Their interest, which rises and falls with the inflation rate, is based on two factors:

- On May 1 and November 1, the Treasury announces a fixed rate of return that applies to all I-bonds issued during the forthcoming 6-month period. This rate is based on a fraction of the rate paid on 5-year Treasury notes. The fixed rate, which remains the same for the life of the bond (30 years), currently is 3.30%

- On top of this fixed rate, also changed every May 1 and November 1, the Treasury announces a semiannual inflation rate based on the Consumer Price Index. The semiannual inflation rate is then combined with the fixed rate to determine the bond's rate for the next six months.

The current rate on I-bonds is 5.05%. They start to earn interest from the first day of the month in which they are purchased.

Earnings are exempt from state and local taxes and you can elect to have federal income taxes deferred until you cash in your bonds or they reach their 30-year final maturity. If used to pay for qualified college expenses and provided your income falls within government guidelines, the interest escapes federal taxes, too.

I-Bonds are intended as a long-term investment. In fact, if you redeem them within the first five years, there's a 3-month interest penalty. For example, if you redeem them after 20 months, you'll only get 17 months of earnings.

Unlike their cousin, the EE Savings Bond, they are sold at their full face value. They come in eight denominations ranging from $50 to $10,000. The maximum purchase is $30,000 per Social Security number, per year.

$TIP: Because inflation is low as we go to press, these bonds don't seem terribly exciting. But should inflation rear up again they will immediately have more appeal.

Easy to Buy

EE and I bonds are available through most banks and thrift institutions, employer-sponsored payroll savings plans, and Public Debt's new EasySaver plan. The U.S. Savings Bond EasySaver plan enables you to buy bonds regularly by preauthorized debits to your bank account. EE and I bonds can be redeemed anytime after six months.

$TIP: To find out more about EasySaver, click on: www.easysaver.gov. You can get an EasySaver application by calling 877–811–7283.

EE Savings Bonds

PROS

↑ Safe; principal and interest guaranteed
↑ No fees or commissions
↑ If lost, replaced free of charge
↑ Get a floating rate of interest tied to Treasury yields
↑ Federal taxes can be deferred
↑ No state or local taxes
↑ Market value does not drop when interest rates rise as with other bonds

CONS

↓ Cannot be used as collateral
↓ Limited purchase: $30,000 face value in one year per person
↓ Other vehicles often pay higher rates
↓ Cannot redeem during the first six months
↓ Bonds issued after May 1, 1995, do not have a guaranteed minimum rate
↓ Series E, EE, and bonds issued after November 1995 stop earning interest after 30 years
↓ Series HH bonds and bonds issued before December 1995 mature 40 years from the date of issue and then no longer earn interest

---

For more info and current rates, call: 800–4–US–BOND or click on: www.savingsbonds.gov.

The Savings Bond Wizard

This is a free Windows program that helps you keep inventories of your savings bonds. The Wizard keeps track of bond values, yield to date, the next accrual date, and more. You can download the Wizard for free at www.savingsbonds.gov.

☑ *HINT: To keep a record and track the value of your Savings Bonds, you can download the Savings Bond Wizard program from the Bureau of Public Debt's website: www.publicdebt.treas.gov.*

Older Bonds

E and EE bonds issued before 1997 have different interest rates. To review, to go the Public Debt's Savings Bonds Earnings Report at www.savings-bonds.gov.

HH Bonds

Series HH bonds are income bonds available only by exchanging Series E or EE bonds for them. In other words, you cannot buy them. Series HH bonds are issued in denominations ranging from $500 to $10,000. The minimum exchange must be at least $500 in Series E or EE bonds. When you exchange your EEs for HH bonds, you can continue delaying taxes on the amount you roll over until you cash in the HH bonds or they mature. The amount of deferred interest is printed on the face of the HH bonds. HH bonds pay interest semiannually by direct deposit for 20 years. The rate since May 1, 1993, has been 4%. (Older H and HH bonds may be paying different rates.) The interest on HH bonds is taxed in the year received.

To make this swap, you must fill out Form PDF 3523.

Using EE Bonds to Pay for College: A Great Tax Benefit

For generations Americans have used savings bonds as a way to pay for their children's college degrees, putting them in their child's name. Before doing so, you should be aware of the tax rulings:

1. The first $700 of investment income (also called unearned income) a child receives is tax free. This dollar amount is adjusted to reflect inflation, so check for annual changes.
2. If the child is under age 14, the next $700 of unearned income is taxed at the child's rate, which is probably 15%. Investment or unearned income over $1,400 is taxed at the parent's rate, which is usually higher than the child's rate—most likely 28%, 31%, or 36%.
3. Once your child is 14, all his income—earned and unearned—is taxed at his rate, again usually 15%.
4. Because tax is deferred on EE bonds until they are redeemed, you can purchase them in a child's name and, assuming they are not cashed in before the child is 14, the interest will be taxed at the child's rate, which is presumably lower than the parent's.
5. If a parent is a co-owner of the bonds with the child, the parent is required to pay any tax due.
6. Under certain circumstances, however, it may make sense to report the interest income each year as it is earned; for instance, if the child has little or no other income, then, depending upon how many bonds the child owns and the amount of interest earned, there might be very little or no tax due at all.
7. Fairly complicated rules apply when it comes to using EE bonds to pay for college. True, interest earned on EE bonds can be totally taxfree, that is, free from state, local, and federal income tax if the bonds are used to pay a child's college tuition. In order to qualify for this tax break, the bonds must be purchased in the parent's name, not the child's, and the parent must be at least 24 years old when the bonds are purchased. Bonds purchased before 1990 do not qualify.

CAUTION: There are also income requirements: Single parents who make less than $53,100 and married couples earning less than $79,650 can completely avoid federal taxes on the interest EE bonds earn if they sell the bonds to pay tuition. NOTE: The income requirements are not set in stone and change with inflation; you cannot predict what the figures will be in advance.

HINT: What if you've purchased EE bonds in your child's name? There's an out, but not a well-publicized one. If you purchased the bonds after 1990 and mistakenly put them in your child's name, you can file a reissue form PDF 4000 with the Bureau of Public Debt, Parkersburg, WV 26106–1328, and try to get them changed. Call: 304–480–6112 to speak with a live person.

EE Bonds and Qualifying for Financial Aid

As mentioned above in point 7, the interest earned on EE Savings Bonds will be tax free at the federal level, but only if it's used to pay for qualifying educational expenses, which means tuition and fees (not room and board) at a college, university, technical institute, or vocational school.

EXAMPLE: if parents redeem bonds worth $20,000 and pay $20,000 in tuition and fees, then all interest earned will be tax free; if only $10,000 is paid in education expenses, then just 50% of the interest will be tax exempt.

CAUTION: Keep college savings bonds separated from others you may own. Record the serial numbers, face amounts, and issue and redemption dates. When you redeem them, record the total dollar amount received (interest plus principal) and the name of the school to which you paid tuition.

☑ *HINT: Although grandparents cannot buy the bonds and meet the requirements for this tax break, they can, of course, give the money to the child's parents and let them buy the bonds.*

FOR FURTHER INFORMATION

Books

Daniel Pederson, *Savings Bonds: When to Hold, When to Fold* (Sage Creek Press, 1999).

Pamphlets

U.S. Savings Bonds Buyer's Guide
Department of the Treasury
U.S. Savings Bond Marketing Office
Washington, DC 20226
202–377–7715
Free.

Basic information on Treasury bills is free from your nearest Federal Reserve Bank or:

Federal Reserve Bank of New York
Issues Division, 1st floor
33 Liberty Street
New York, NY 10045
212–720–5000

For material on the TreasuryDirect program, call or write your area Federal Reserve Bank or write:

Bureau of Public Debt
200 Third Street
Petersburg, VA 26106
202–874–4000 (recorded message)
304–480–6122 (live person)
website: www.publicdebt.treas.gov

Determining Bond Values

Two sources of information and reports on the value of your savings bonds:

Dan Pederson, President
Savings Bond Informer
800–927–1901

This is a national fee-based service located in Detroit. Cost is $12 for one to ten bonds.

The Savings Bond Consultant
1540 Route 138
Suite #307
Wall, NJ 07719
732–280–1440; 800–717-BOND
website: www.savingsbonds.com

Has a software program that answers questions on savings bonds and determines value of individual EEs.

11

Convertibles: Income Plus Appreciation

*I*f you're interested in a stock but its price is too high, you might still be able to participate in its growth—check whether there's a convertible available. Convertibles (CVs), which are usually bonds but occasionally are stocks, can be converted or exchanged for a set number of common shares, and their prices tend to track the stocks on their way up.

THE NITTY GRITTY

A convertible is a bond that pays a fixed rate of interest with a unique feature—it can be exchanged for a specified number of the issuing company's common shares, if those shares move up to a certain price. In other words, you can have your cake and eat it, too: You collect the high interest rate from the bond and, if the common shares rise sufficiently in price, make a profit by converting into the shares of the company's common.

What if the common shares do not rise in price? Then you can simply keep collecting your bond's interest payments. (Unlike common stock dividends, which can be cut, postponed, or eliminated, a convertible's interest income is secure.)

NOTE: There are also some convertible preferred stocks, but they are not nearly as common as convertible bonds.

HOW MUCH DOES IT COST TO CONVERT?

This conversion feature does not come cheap. Conversion prices are set at 15% to 20% above the price of the common stock when the convertible is issued, and some premium continues to exist. In fact, convertibles tend to trade at prices that are 5% to 20% above that of the common stock into which they can be converted. The reason behind this premium over the conversion price is that convertibles tend to yield 3% to 5% more than common stock dividends, but less than what you would collect on the same company's straight bonds or preferred stock.

Before considering convertibles, you must know that:

1. If the issuing company's common stock rises above the conversion price, you can exchange your convertibles for the common shares and make a profit.
2. If the issuing company's common stock goes down in price, your convertible will usually hold its value better than the common stock, and you will still be collecting your regular income.

So, this hybrid investment combines the security and fixed income of bonds with the potential price appreciation of common stock. Convertibles pay higher income than common stocks and have greater price appreciation than regular bonds. Their convertibility factor links their price movement with that of the underlying stock, so even though a convertible bond has the low-risk characteristics associated with straight bonds (safety of

---

Tips for Investing in CVs

- Buy a CV only if you like the common stock.
- Avoid CVs of potential takeover companies; you may be forced to convert early.
- Buy only high-rated issues—BB or above as rated by Standard & Poor's or Ba by Moody's.
- Know the call provisions; if a CV is called too early, you may not recover your premium.
- Select a CV whose common stock is expected to rise considerably in price.

---

principal and regular interest payments), they usually fluctuate in price more than straight bonds.

☑ *THE BOTTOM LINE: You give up some safety in exchange for potential capital gains.*

Sometimes the issuing company calls the convertible bonds, forcing a conversion—but never below their conversion value. Bonds are sometimes called when the corporation can replace the convertible debt with new common stock.

If the CV is called when the market value of the stock is greater than the conversion price of the bond, you should opt to convert.

HOW CONVERTIBLES WORK

Company ABC needs to raise capital for expansion but does not want to dilute the value of its common stock by issuing new shares at this time. It also rejects selling a straight bond, because it would be forced to pay the going interest rate, which for this example is 12%. Instead, management offers a bond that can be converted into its own common stock.

Because of this desirable conversion feature, investors are willing to buy the CV bond at a lower rate of only 10%. Bonds are quoted as a percentage of par, or face value, which is $1,000, so this bond is listed as 100. This is the market price, the price at which the CV can be bought and sold to investors.

When Company ABC issues the CV bonds, its common stock is selling at $32 per share. Management decides its offering will be attractive to the public if each $1,000 bond can be converted into 25 shares of common. This is the conversion ratio—the number of shares of common stock you receive by converting one bond. The conversion price of the ABC bond is $40 (divide 25 into $1,000). The current value of the total shares of ABC Corp. to which a bond can be converted is the conversion value. With ABC stock trading at $32 and a CV ratio of 25, the conversion value is $800.

On the day of issue, the difference between $40 (the conversion price) and $32 (the current market price) is $8. To determine the conversion premium, $8 is divided by $32 to yield 0.25, or a 25% CV premium. Another way to figure the conversion premium is to take the price of the bond ($1,000), subtract the CV value ($800), and divide the remainder ($200) by the CV value.

The investment value of ABC's CV is an estimated price, usually set by an investment advisory service, at which the bond would be selling if there were no conversion feature. For ABC it is 75.

The premium-over-investment value is the percentage difference between the estimated investment value and the market price of the bond. Here the investment value is 75 and the market price is 100, so the difference is 25, or 33% of 75. The premium-over-investment value is therefore 33.

HOW YOU CAN MAKE A PROFIT WITH CONVERTIBLES

If the Stock Goes Up . . .

In general, a CV's price will accompany the rise in price of the company's common stock, although it never rises as much. For example, let's say the underlying stock rises by 50%, from $32 to $48. To find the value of the CV bond, multiply the higher price by the conversion ratio: $48 x 25 = $1,200 (or 120, as bond prices are expressed). During the time in which this rise has taken place, the investor has received 10% interest on the bond and has participated in the appreciation of the common stock by seeing the value of the CV bond appreciate by 20%, from $100 to $120.

If the Stock Goes Down . . .

If the underlying stock falls in price, the CV may also fall in price, but less so. Let us assume that the price of ABC, instead of appreciating by 50% to $48, drops by 50% to $16 per share. Its conversion value is now only $400 ($16 x the CV ratio of 25). What happens to the price of the CV? The senior position of the bond as well as the 10% interest rate payable to bondholders serve as a brake on its decline in price. Somewhere between $100 and $40 the safety features inherent in a CV bond become operative, usually at the investment value, which in this case is 75. At 75 the bond's yield will rise to 13.33%.

> ☑ HINT: When you want to make an investment but you fear that the company's common stock is too volatile and therefore risky, check whether there are any convertible bonds or preferreds outstanding.

To Convert or Not to Convert—That Is the Question

By and large, holders of CVs should stay with the security of the CV and not convert. Stock markets are uncertain, and prices of individual stocks have

been known to fall 50% or even more. Therefore, the holder of a CV, which is senior to the common stock, should surrender or convert only under certain circumstances such as these:

- The company, in a restructuring, makes a tender offer for a large percentage of its outstanding common stock at a price well above the market price. The CV bondholder must convert to common stock in order to participate in this tender offer.
- In another type of restructuring, the company pays stockholders a special dividend equal to most of the price of the common stock. Here again, the CV bondholder must convert in order to receive this special dividend.
- Corporations in cyclical businesses pay oversized year-end dividends. General Motors, for instance, did this for many years. To receive a special dividend, CV bondholders must convert prior to the ex-dividend date.

HEDGING WITH CVS

For experienced investors, CVs offer excellent vehicles for hedging—buying one security and simultaneously selling short its related security. The hedge is set up so that if the market goes up, one can make more money on the purchase than one can lose on the sale, or vice versa if the market goes down. Such trading is best in volatile markets (of which there have been plenty in recent years).

Convertible Bonds to Consider

COMPANY/BOND	CV PRICE OF BOND	PRICE OF COMMON	PRICE OF BOND	S&P RATING
Adaptec 4³/₄, 2004	$51.66	$24	$85	BB–
Alza Corp 5, 2006	$38.19	$34	$109	BBB–
Hilton 5, 2006	$32	$31	$110	BBB–
SiliconGraphics 5¹/₄, 2004	$36	$13	$83	BBB–
Systems & Computer Tech. 5, 2015	$26	$16	$86	NR

SOURCE: Standard & Poor's *Bond Guide*, Summer 1999.

Here's an example cited by expert John Calamos, president of Calamos Asset Management in Naperville, Illinois:

EXAMPLE: The CV debenture carries a 10% coupon and is convertible into 40 shares of common stock. The CV trades at 90; the common at 20. Buy 10 CVs at 90 at a cost of $9,000; sell short 150 common at 20—$3,000. Since the short sale requires no investment, the cost is $9,000 (not counting commissions).

- If the price of the stock falls to 10, the CV's estimated price will be 72, so there will be a loss of $1,800 ($9,000 – $7,200). But 150 shares of stock can be acquired for $1,500, for a profit of $1,500. Add $500 interest (10% for six months), and the net profit is $200.

- If the price of the stock dips to 15, the CV will sell at 80 for a $1,000 loss, but this will be offset by the $750 profit on the stock plus $500 interest, for a return of $250.

- If the price of the stock holds at 20, the CV will stay at 90. There will be no profit on either, but the $500 interest will represent an annualized rate of return of 11%.

- If the stock rises to 25, the CV will be worth 104, for a $1,400 profit, but there will be a $750 loss on the shorted stock. With the $500 interest, there'll still be a $1,150 profit.

- And if the stock soars to 40, the CV will trade at 160, for a whopping $7,000 gain, which will be offset by a $3,000 loss on the stock but enhanced by the $500 income, for a total of $4,500 on that $9,000 investment—all in six months!

Says Calamos: Selling short stock against undervalued CVs can eliminate risk while offering unlimited gains if the stock advances.

☑ *YOUR BEST BET: Try out the if projections on paper until you are sure that you understand what can happen. By and large, the actual transactions will follow these patterns. At worst, the losses will be small; at best, the profits will be welcome.*

WRITING CALLS WITH CVS

Writing calls is a conservative way to boost income and, when properly executed, involves minimal risks and fair-to-good gains. Because the CVs represent a call on the stock, they provide a viable

---

Convertibles

PROS

↑ When the stock market falls, CVs do not fall as much as the underlying stock.

↑ You can keep collecting regular income no matter what happens to the stock.

↑ When a takeover bid is made, the common stock usually soars in price.

CONS

↓ You do not receive the full price gain when the stock goes up in price.

↓ You do not earn as much interest as you would had you bought a bond that is not convertible.

↓ CVs are often issued by companies with poor credit ratings.

CV Mutual Funds

If you have limited capital or prefer to let someone else make the selections, there are mutual funds that use a substantial portion of their assets to buy CVs and, in some cases, to write options.

When considering CV mutual funds, keep these tips in mind:

- Usual minimum investment is $1,000.
- Shares can be purchased directly from the fund or from a stockbroker.
- Read the fund's prospectus before investing.
- Check the quality of the fund's underlying stocks.
- Convertibles offer a hedge against volatile changes in the stock market.
- Automatic reinvestment of distribution into additional fund shares is available.
- If you invest in a family of funds and your yield declines, you can switch to higher-yielding funds within the family.

base. Let's say that a $1,000 par value CV debenture can be swapped for 40 shares of common; the CV is at 90, the stock at 20; the calls, exercisable at 20, are due in six months and carry a premium of 2 ($200) each.

Buy 10 CVs for $9,000 and sell 3 calls. (Because the CVs represent 400 shares of stock, this is no problem.) The $600 premium will reduce the net investment to $8,400. If the stock jumps to 40, the CV will sell at 160, for a $7,000 gain. Add $500 interest to get $7,500 income. But there will be a $5,400 loss, because the calls will have to be repurchased with a (tax-advantageous) deficit of $1,800 each. The net profit will thus be $2,100.

 CAUTION: Writing calls on CVs is not for amateurs. To be worthwhile, this technique should (1) involve a substantial number of shares (at least 300), (2) be done with the aid of a knowledgeable broker who watches for sudden aberrations in price spreads, (3) be initiated with adequate cash or margin reserves that may be needed to buy back calls early, and (4) be undertaken only by individuals in a high enough tax bracket to benefit from the short-term losses.

FOR FURTHER INFORMATION

Books

Thomas C. Noddings, *Superhedging* (Chicago: Probus Publishing Co., 1995).

Newsletters

Value Line Convertibles Survey
220 East 42 Street
New York, NY 10017
800–643–3583
48 times per year; $625.

Leading Convertible Bond Mutual Funds

FUND	TOTAL RETURN, JANUARY 1 TO SEPTEMBER 30, 1999
American Capital Harbor Fund (800–421–5666)	14.40%
Putman Convertible Income (800–354–4000)	8.90
Value Line Convertible Fund (800–223–0818)	5.40
Phoenix Convertible Fund (800–243–1574)	1.85

12

Municipal Bonds:
The Last of the Tax Shelters

*I*f you're looking for a way to cut taxes, you don't have too many options. Municipal bonds, munis as they are called, and muni bond funds are about it. If you're in the 28% tax bracket, or aspire to be, read on.

THE NITTY GRITTY

Municipals are tax-exempt debt obligations or IOUs issued by states, counties, cities, and other public agencies, such as school districts, sewer and water districts, airport, bridge and tunnel authorities, and highway authorities.

ADVANTAGES OF MUNIS

Their great advantage is that the interest you earn is exempt from federal income tax, and if the bonds are issued in the investor's state of residence, they are also exempt from state and local income taxes.

    EXAMPLE: If you live in Minnesota, interest on munis issued by the state of Minnesota is exempt from federal and state income taxes. These are known as double tax-free bonds. (Exceptions: Illinois, Iowa, Oklahoma, and Wisconsin impose some limitations on tax exemptions.)

☑ *HINT: Munis issued by the U.S. Territories—Puerto Rico, Guam, and the Virgin Islands—are tax exempt in all states.*

DISADVANTAGES OF MUNIS

Because of their tax-exempt status, munis pay a lower interest rate than taxable corporate bonds. They are issued in units of $5,000 or, occasionally, $10,000. Most stockbrokers are reluctant, to put it mildly, to sell just one bond, and many have $20,000 minimums. Some discount and on-line brokers, however, will accept small-sized orders. But to have an adequately diversified portfolio, you need $40,000 to $60,000. Certainly if you have only $20,000, you may want to invest through a mutual fund or unit investment trust, described at the end of this chapter.

SHOULD YOU BUY MUNIS?

You don't have to be a millionaire to benefit from tax-exempt investments. On the other hand, municipal bonds make sense only if the interest earned is more than the after-tax yield of a taxable investment. For most people, that means being in the 28% tax bracket or higher. Tax brackets are adjusted for inflation each year, but generally if your taxable income is about $26,000 for a single return or $43,000 for a joint return, you will be in the 28% bracket.

To really determine whether to buy a municipal or not, use this formula:

1. Subtract your tax bracket from the number 100. For example:

    $1 - .28$ (tax bracket) $= .72$

2. Then divide the tax-free yield the fund is paying by .72 to find the taxable equivalent:

    $6\% \div .72 = 8.33\%$

3. The result—in this case, 8.33%—is the yield you need on a taxable investment to match the tax-free yield of 6%.

☑ *THE BOTTOM LINE: As you can see, even though a taxable corporate bond might pay 7% or even 7.5%, a muni paying only 6% is actually a better investment in this case. If you live in a high-tax state, such as New York, California, or Minnesota, a municipal bond issued by your state would have even greater benefit.*

Let's look at another example:

EXAMPLE: If you're in the 31% tax bracket, a muni yielding 5.5% is equivalent to a taxable bond yielding about 8%.

$1 - .31 = .69$

$5.5\% \div .69 = 7.97\%$

Again, you would need a taxable bond yielding at least 8% to equal your tax-free muni with only a 5.5% yield.

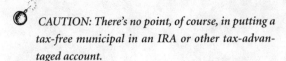 *CAUTION: There's no point, of course, in putting a tax-free municipal in an IRA or other tax-advantaged account.*

Use the table below for additional comparisons.

TYPES OF MUNICIPAL BONDS

If you decide to buy individual bonds, you'll find a number of choices:

General Obligation Bonds (GOs)

Also known as public purpose bonds, these are sold to finance roads, schools, and government buildings. They are the most conservative of the municipals and are backed by the full taxing power of the state or local government that issues them. The interest and principal are repaid to bondholders out of a government's general revenue, primarily its taxes. Therefore, they generally have the highest safety ratings. Most are voter approved.

Revenue Bonds

These are issued to finance public works projects; their interest and principal are repaid only from the revenues generated by the project that bonds were issued to build—an airport, highway, tunnel,

Your Tax Bracket	28%	31%	36%	39.6%
TAX-EXEMPT YIELD		TAXABLE EQUIVALENT YIELDS		
3%	4.17%	4.35%	4.69%	4.97%
4	5.56	5.80	6.25	6.62
5	6.94	7.25	7.81	8.28
6	8.33	8.70	9.38	9.93
7	9.72	10.14	10.94	11.59
8	11.11	11.59	12.50	13.25

SOURCE: Federated Mutual Funds, Pittsburgh.

toll bridge, or a sewage treatment plant, for example. Because of this limited source of income, they are generally regarded as less safe than GOs.

Taxable Municipals

For many years, all munis were tax free, but that's no longer the case. Bonds issued to finance private business activities and ventures, such as shopping malls, sports stadiums, convention and trade shows, industrial parks, and parking facilities, are exempt often from state and local taxes where issued, but subject to federal income taxes. Yet income from certain kinds of private activity bonds, such as those to build a hospital, is still fully exempt. These taxable municipals, or private activity bonds as they're also called, generally yield 2 to 3 percentage points more than fully tax-exempt municipals.

💣 CAUTION: *For investors in high tax brackets who have a sizable amount of tax-sheltered income, interest from such bonds issued after August 7, 1986, may be subject to the alternative minimum tax (AMT). The AMT taxes so-called preference income above a certain level at a flat rate.*

Zero Coupon Munis

These bonds provide no interest income to the owner until they mature. Instead they are sold at a discount (below par) and you receive the full face value at maturity. Because they are sold far below face value, zero coupon munis are an inexpensive way for small investors to participate in the municipal bond market.

Stripped munis, as one part of this investment is called, literally have their semiannual interest rate coupons stripped off. Both parts then are sold separately—the principal and the series of coupon interest payments. By dividing the bond into two pieces, maturities are created that otherwise would not exist.

Prior to the existence of stripped munis, bondholders had to wait 20 to 40 years for a mu-

---

Stripped Munis

PROS

↑ Can time your balloon payment
↑ No problem of where to reinvest income
↑ Noncallable
↑ Know exactly how much you will receive
↑ Shorter maturity dates than regular munis

CONS

↓ Interest is locked in; yields could rise
↓ Should be held to maturity
↓ Slim secondary market

---

nicipal bond to mature; zeros, on the other hand, mature in less than half that time. So when you buy a stripped muni, you are in essence buying a couponless bond with zero interest, hence the name zero coupon.

Tax Advantages

Zero coupon munis provide a real tax break. If, for example, you buy a zero at $800, when it matures you'll receive the face value of $1,000, but there will be no federal income tax due on the $200 profit made during the holding period.

Another advantage: Bonds used for stripping are noncallable, so you know they can be held to maturity. (The call feature of bonds is explained in Chapter 9, beginning on page 101.) Strips are sold by bond dealers.

☑ HINT: *Zero coupon bonds are an excellent way to pay for college or set money aside for retirement or other distant goals. Whoever owns the bonds does not have to pay federal income tax on them.*

Zero Coupon Convertible Munis

Like other zeros, these sell at a deep discount to face value. They have a unique feature, however: At a certain time they convert into regular interest bonds.

EXAMPLE: A 25-year zero coupon convertible muni bond pays no interest during its first 10 years. Then in the 10th year, it converts into a regular municipal bond. At that point the investor starts to receive the stated interest rate in cash and continues to receive it for the remaining 15 years. At maturity, the bond returns its full face value of $1,000 to the investor. Both appreciation and interest income are free of federal income taxes.

 CAUTION: *Some zero coupon convertible munis can be called early.*

Pre-refunded or Escrowed-to-Maturity Bonds

Sometimes a municipality floats a new bond issue when interest rates have dropped, in order to pay off the first bond. The proceeds from the sale of the second bond are invested in U.S. Treasury securities that are held in escrow until the old bonds can be redeemed—at their next call date in the case of pre-refunded bonds, or at their maturity date in the case of escrowed-to-maturity bonds.

Because the money to repay the bonds is set aside and safely invested in Treasuries, these bonds are considered very safe.

Variable-Rate Option Munis

These are long-term municipals whose interest rates are adjusted, up or down, each year based on current market rates. You can usually cash in a variable-rate option muni on a daily, weekly, monthly, or yearly basis and get back what you paid for it. They are best if you know you might need your money within a year, or at least before the bond matures.

Single-State Bonds

If you live in a high-tax state, look for munis issued by your own state and, if possible, local governments. By avoiding state and local taxes you can improve your after-tax return, often adding as much as 1½ percentage points to your yield.

Among the highest-taxed states are California, Massachusetts, Minnesota, and New York.

Funds that specialize in single-state bonds are forced to purchase bonds from a smaller pool than regular bond funds, and consequently have less choice when it comes to bond grade, type, and maturity. This adds a small element of risk to these funds. Single-state municipal bond funds are listed in the table on page 120.

Serial Maturities

Unlike most corporate bonds, which usually have the same redemption date, municipals often mature serially: A portion of the debt comes due each year until the final redemption. Select maturities to fit future needs: college tuition, retirement, house, etc.

PICKING THE RIGHT MUNI BONDS

These are the key points to keep in mind when building a portfolio of individual municipal bonds:

- *Safety.* Like corporate bonds, municipals are also rated for safety—or how likely they are to default—by Standard & Poor's and Moody's. The safest are rated AAA or Aaa. And, of course, the higher the rating, the less interest the bond issuer needs to pay to attract investors. The opposite is also true: The highest interest rates are paid on the riskiest bonds. (**See:** page 94 for rating information.)

  Before purchasing municipals, ask your stockbroker for a research report and bond ratings. Muni prices are rarely listed in the newspaper, so you must use an experienced, reliable broker. Stick with those rated A or above.

- *Maturity date.* For bonds with the same rating, the shorter the maturity, the lower the yield and the greater the price stability. Unless you plan to buy municipals regularly, it is usually prudent to stick to those with maturities of less than ten years. In many cases, these will be older bonds selling at a discount.

$TIP: Select maturities to match your financial goals.

- *Type of bond.* Start with general obligation bonds, which typically yield less than other municipals, or an insured bond. Then consider revenue bonds backed by high, steady streams of income, such as utility bills. Suggested water revenue bonds and electric revenue bonds are given on page 122.

☑ *HINT: Keep in mind bonds of the commonwealth of Puerto Rico. Their income is free from state, local, and federal taxes no matter where you live in the United States. To date, Puerto Rico has never defaulted on a bond issue.*

- *Unrated bonds.* You may run across bonds that are not rated. An unrated bond is not necessarily high in risk. It is often unrated because the municipality is so small or has such modest debt that its bonds have never been rated. If you personally know the community and if it is run well, by all means, add them to your portfolio. But plan to hold them to maturity as there probably is very little demand for them, which translates into a tiny secondary market.
- *Marketability.* If you have to sell bonds before maturity, you want there to be an active secondary market. The most salable municipals are general obligation bonds of state governments and revenue bonds of large, well-known authorities. Smaller issues can be tough to sell.
- *Call provision.* Larger issues usually permit the bonds to be called, that is, redeemed before maturity. In fact, many municipals are issued with a ten-year noncallable provision. If your bond is called, you will have to reinvest that money, probably at lower rates. Try to buy bonds that cannot be called or have call protection. (**See:** Chapter 9.)
- *Insured bonds.* It's very rare for a municipal bond issuer to default. A recent study shows that between 1980 and 1991, only 1.9% of the $155 billion of nonrated bonds sold during that period defaulted. Of the $1.24 trillion of rated bonds sold, only 0.27% defaulted.

  Nevertheless, you can boost your safety level by purchasing insured bonds. With these bonds, the insurance company agrees to pay the principal and interest to bondholders if the issuer defaults. The insurance policy lasts for the life of the bond.

  NOTE: Once a bond is insured, it is given an AAA rating by Standard & Poor's even if the bond originally had a BBB rating. So remember that if you are purchasing an AAA in-

Puerto Rico Municipal Bonds

ISSUER	MOODY'S RATING	APPROXIMATE YIELDS
Puerto Rico Electric Power	Baa 1	5.0%
Puerto Rico Housing/Finance	Baa 1	4.3
Commonwealth of Puerto Rico	Baa 1	5.1
Puerto Rico Public Building Authority	Baa 1	4.3
Puerto Rico Hwy & Bridge	Baa 1	5.0

(As of Summer 1999.)

Electric Revenue Bonds

ISSUER	MOODY'S RATING	APPROXIMATE YIELDS
South Carolina Public Service Authority	AAA (ins)	4.80%
Intermountain Power Agency (Utah)	AA	5.00
New York State Power Authority	AA	4.35
Orlando Utilities Commission (FL)	AAA	5.20

(As of Summer 1999.)

sured bond, it may really be a BBB bond with insurance.

Insured municipal bonds pay lower yields, usually 1 to 1½ percentage points less than comparable uninsured bonds.

To insure its bonds, the issuer pays an insurance premium ranging between 0.1% and 2% of total principal and interest. In return, the insurance company will pay the principal and interest to the bondholders should the issuer default. Policies for new issues cannot be canceled, and the insurance remains active over the lifetime of the bond. With a bond fund or unit trust, the insurance is generally purchased for the entire portfolio.

The oldest insurers are the American Municipal Bond Assurance Corp. (AMBAC) and the Municipal Bond Insurance Association

Five Water Revenue Bonds

ISSUER	MOODY'S RANKING	COUPON
Dallas Water & Sewer	AA 2	5.05%
Los Angeles Dept. Water/Power	AA	4.35
NY City Municipal Water	A	3.90
MA Water Resources	AAA	3.60
CA Dept. Water	AA 2	4.60

(As of Summer 1999.)

(MBIA). Both are rated Aaa by Moody's and AAA by Standard & Poor's.

 CAUTION: Insurance does not protect you against market risks: If interest rates go up, the value of bonds still goes down.

Understanding the Risks Involved

There are two primary risks: interest rate risk and default.

1. As with any bond, the interest rate it pays is fixed. If interest rates rise, the value of a municipal bond will fall. This presents a problem if you sell before the bond's maturity. It's not a problem, of course, if you hold until maturity, because you will receive the bond's full face value.

    In fact, interest rate risk is a greater problem than defaults for municipal bonds.

2. The second risk is that of default—if the issuer cannot make the interest and principal payments. To protect against default, purchase insured bonds.

 CAUTION: Munis rated below A are regarded by many bond experts as risky. (The ratings are behind the true credit risk—they're a lagging indicator.) But because there is a shortage of municipals, many fund managers and others buy them anyway. Certain housing and health care bonds fall into this risk

Eight Tax-Exempt Bond Funds

FUND	YIELD (SEPTEMBER 1999)
Calvert Tax-Free Long Term (800–368–2748)	4.38%
Dreyfus Intermediate Tax-Exempt (800–645–6561)	4.31
Fidelity Municipal Bond (800–544–8888)	4.36
New York Muni Fund (800–225–6864)	4.27
T. Rowe Price Tax-Free Intermediate (800–638–5660)	4.38
Scudder Managed Municipal (800–225–2470)	4.33
SteinRoe Intermediate Municipal (800–338–2550)	4.52
Vanguard Long-Term Municipal (800–662–7447)	4.55

category. When buying a muni fund, trust, or individual bond, check the exact ratings.

MUNICIPAL BOND MUTUAL FUNDS

For small investors, one of the best ways to buy municipals is through a mutual fund. Mutual funds provide diversification (by type, grade, coupon, and maturity), continuous professional management, the opportunity to add to your portfolio with relatively small dollar amounts, the ability to switch to other funds under the same sponsorship, and most important, prompt reinvestment of interest to buy new shares and benefit from compounding.

A fund contains bonds with varying maturities. The manager continually buys and sells bonds in order to improve returns, switching from short- to long-term maturities when yields are high and doing the opposite when yields decline. When interest rates shift quickly, some funds do extremely well; some do not. Keep in mind that your income from the fund will fluctuate, unlike that from an individual bond or a unit trust, where the yield is locked in.

Types of Municipal Bond Mutual Funds

There are five types of mutual funds to consider:

- *Nationally diversified tax-exempt funds.* These hold bonds issued by states and municipalities throughout the country. Income is usually free from federal income tax.
- *Single-state funds.* These invest in bonds of a single state, so investors who are residents of that state can have income that is free from federal and state income tax.
- *Triple-exempt funds.* These invest in municipal bonds of a given municipality, and income earned is free from federal, state, and local income tax.
- *Tax-free money market funds.* These were discussed in Chapter 3. Income is free of federal taxes and, if it's a single-state tax-free money market fund, from state income tax as well.
- *High-yield bond funds.* These invest in lower-rated tax-exempt bonds. Although they are higher in risk than top higher-quality bonds, they also have higher yields. They are suitable only for investors who knowingly wish to assume a high risk for a high return.

☑ *HINT: Before investing in your state's bonds or bond fund, check on the financial health of your particular state's economy. If you have any reservations, limit your holdings, perhaps to a 50-50 division between single-state and multistate funds.*

MUNICIPAL BOND UNIT TRUSTS

These trusts have fixed portfolios of municipal bonds that remain in the trust until maturity, un-

Leading Single-State Municipal Bond Funds

STATE	MUTUAL FUND	YIELD (FALL 1999)
Minnesota	Franklin Minnesota Insured (800–632–2180)	4.84%
New York	Putnam New York (800–225–1581)	4.66
West Virginia	MFS Managed West Virginia (800–225–2606)	4.71
California	MFS Managed California (800–225–2606)	4.82
Oregon	Oregon Municipal Bond Fund (800–541–9732)	4.65

Insured Municipal Bond Mutual Funds

FUND	YIELD (FALL 1999)
Vanguard Muni Bond Insured Long Term (800–662–7447)	4.34%
Merrill Lynch Muni Insured Portfolio (609–282–2800)	4.51
American Capital Tax-Exempt Insured (800–421–5666)	4.29
Dreyfus Insured Tax-Exempt Bond Fund (800–645–6561)	4.43
Fidelity Insured Tax-Free (800–544–8888)	4.60

less, of course, they are called. (An open-ended mutual fund, the type we've just been discussing, has a continually changing portfolio.)

The trust aims to lock in the highest yield possible with good-quality issues at the time of the initial offering. Each trust has a limited number of shares for sale, but new trusts are continually being brought to the market. Sponsors, such as Merrill Lynch, etc., also buy back existing units from investors who want to sell before the trust matures—so you could also buy one in the secondary market.

Trusts are mostly sold through brokers and carry up-front sales charges of 3.5% to 4.9%. A typical national trust issued by Nuveen or Van Kampen Merritt will have about 20 bonds, held typically until maturity unless one is called.

If you purchase a UIT (unit investment trust) it will be registered in your name, and monthly, quarterly, or semiannual checks will be mailed to you, although some unit investment trusts have reinvestment privileges.

☑ *HINT: The monthly payouts from a UIT are more stable than those of a long-term bond fund, giving*

you a more predictable stream of income. Most are long-term, with average maturities of 25 to 30 years, but trusts running 5 to 15 years are not uncommon.

The New Laddered Trusts

The newest type of trust is laddered with various maturities. It returns 20% of your principal each year for five years.

In either the old-fashioned or the newer laddered trusts, when the bonds mature, are sold (rarely), or are called, the principal is returned to the investor as a return of capital. If the sponsor

Mutual Fund versus Unit Trust

- A managed mutual fund is generally a better investment for people who expect to sell in less than ten years. Check the one-, five-, and ten-year performance records of several before investing.
- Unit trusts are best for long-term holdings, especially when the initial yield is high enough that you want to lock it in.

A Freebie for Readers

The Franklin fund family has a free slide rule that lets you figure out your combined state and federal marginal income tax rate. The data are available for every state and for the 28%, 31%, 36%, and 39.6% tax brackets. Call 800–342–5236.

feels a bond is endangering the trust's interest, it can be sold and proceeds paid out.

If you need to sell your trust before maturity date, you can do so in the secondary market, but doing so entails a commission. If interest rates have fallen, you could make a profit, but if they've gone up, you may not get back your original investment. Unit trust prices are based on the price of the securities in the portfolio and are determined either by the sponsor or by an independent evaluator.

Nuveen, for instance, which has a number of trusts, sets the price on a daily basis. Although unit prices are not given in the newspaper, you can call the sponsor for up-to-date quotes.

General and State Trusts

General trusts include bonds from various states and territories, while state trusts have bonds only from a single state, hence the name single-state unit trusts. Income is generally free from state and local taxes in the issuing state, as well as from federal taxes.

Unit trusts are usually sold in $1,000 units, but with a $5,000 minimum. The sales charge plus the annual fee or trust expenses, which both run about 0.2%, are factored into the yield. Mutual funds, by contrast, may be subject to a sales charge (load) or not (no-load).

YOUR TAXES AND MUNICIPALS

Believe it or not, unfortunately interest on some municipal bonds is now subject to taxation. You'll want to be aware of this before investing in a muni. Here are the facts:

Private activity bonds. Interest on these bonds, issued after August 7, 1986, to finance private business activities, such as shopping malls, is generally taxable at the federal level for individuals subject to the alternative minimum tax (AMT). The AMT affects investors in high tax brackets who also have a sizable amount of tax-sheltered income.

Interest on these private activity bonds may be subject to the AMT. The AMT taxes so-called preference income above a certain level at a rate of 26% or 28%. Check with your accountant before investing in private activity bonds.

☑ *HINT: Because of their tax disadvantage, private activity bonds usually have higher yields than public purpose munis. That makes them appealing to those who remain below the AMT threshold.*

An exception: Bonds issued by private, nonprofit hospitals and universities, called 501(c) bonds, are not subject to taxation.

Social Security and munis—tax consequences. Municipal bond income is added to other income to determine whether a retiree must pay taxes on his/her social security benefits. Up to 85% of a retiree's Social Security benefits can be taxed if municipal bond interest income plus adjusted gross income plus half of Social Security payments is more than $32,000 for couples or $25,000 for singles. Again, check with your accountant, as these dollar amounts are subject to change.

FOR FURTHER INFORMATION

David L. Scott, *Municipal Bonds: The Basics and Beyond* (Chicago: Probus Publishing Co., 1995).

Gary M. Strumeyer, *Keys to Investing in Municipal Bonds* (New York: Barron's Business Books, 1996).

13

Nontraditional Bonds:
Zeros, Junks, and the Mae Family

Welcome to the Mae family, various mortgage-backed securities that offer high yields, safety, and convenience. These securities, which actually are shares in pools of secured mortgages, are often called pass-throughs, because the sponsor who packages the mortgages passes through the income (minus a modest fee) directly to you, the investor.

You'll receive payments on a monthly basis, and you can expect the yields to be 1.5+ points higher than those on comparable Treasury bonds. This higher yield is partly because Maes are slightly more risky than Treasuries and also because your monthly payments include principal as well as interest.

CAUTION: This is an important concept that many investors don't fully understand. To state it another way: Mortgage-backed securities do not behave like regular bonds, which provide a return of principal upon maturity. Instead, with members of the Mae family, your monthly check includes both interest and principal. It is important to understand this distinction. Many investors mistakenly believe that these monthly checks are interest only. They are both interest and part payment of principal.

The pass-through technique allows individual investors to share the income derived from monthly mortgage payments and prepayments. They are similar to mutual funds in that investors do not own one particular mortgage but pieces of many mortgages.

HINT: Ginnie Maes are the only securities, other than U.S. Treasury issues, that carry the direct full faith and credit guarantee of the U.S. government. Others in the Mae group, described below, carry an indirect guarantee.

GINNIE MAES

Ginnie Mae stands for the Government National Mortgage Association (GNMA), a wholly owned corporation of the U.S. government that functions as part of the Department of Housing and Urban Development.

The objective of Ginnie Mae is to stimulate housing by attracting capital and guaranteeing mortgages. A GNMA certificate represents a portion of a pool of 30-year FHA- or VA-insured mortgages. It provides payment of interest and principal on a monthly basis.

The Nitty Gritty: How They Work

When a home buyer takes out a mortgage, the house is pledged as collateral. The bank or savings and loan pools this loan with others of similar terms and rates, thus creating a package of mortgages worth $1 million or more. Ginnie Mae reviews the mortgages to make certain they meet certain standards and then assigns a pool number. Stockbrokers and others sell pieces of this pool, called certificates, to the public.

Home buyers then make their payments (interest and principal) to the bank, which deducts a handling fee as well as a Ginnie Mae insurance fee. The rest of the money is passed on to the investors from the mortgage bankers.

Because GNMA certificates carry the guarantee of the U.S. government, they have made mortgage investments especially safe. And because certificates can be traded in the secondary market, they also offer liquidity.

Where and How to Buy Ginnie Maes

You have two choices: to buy a Ginnie Mae Certificate or shares in a Ginnie Mae Mutual Fund.

- *Choice #1.* The minimum investment for a GNMA certificate is $25,000, with $5,000 increments thereafter. Monthly interest in considered ordinary income and is taxed, whereas monthly principal payments are considered a return of capital and are exempt from taxes. Monthly payments are not uniform—they are based on the remaining principal in the pool. As home owners make their mortgage payments, the mortgage pool gets paid down, and although you receive the stated coupon interest, it is on a declining amount of debt.

    In other words, each month the proportion of interest received is slightly less and the proportion of principal slightly more. Over the long term, GNMAs are therefore self-liquidating. When the pool of mortgages is paid in full by home owners, that's it. You don't receive a lump payment or a return of face value as you do with a zero or straight bond.

CAUTION: When interest rates fall, home owners pay off their mortgages and refinance at lower rates. This means your Ginnie Mae is paid off quickly.

- *Choice #2.* You can purchase Ginnie Maes for less than $25,000 through mutual funds (discussion follows), or you can buy older Ginnie Maes in the secondary market. Older Ginnie Maes have been partially paid down and are usually bid down in value to compensate for the declining stream of income.

CAUTION: Ads for Ginnie Maes and their mutual funds often claim they are totally safe and 100% government guaranteed. This is not true. Ginnie Maes are not completely risk free:

The government does not guarantee the yield.

The government does not protect investors against declines in either the value of the fund's shares or the yield.

The government, however, does indeed protect investors against late mortgage payments as well as foreclosures. If home owners default, you will still receive payments on time.

HINT: If you're considering Ginnie Maes, bear in mind that the average 30-year Ginnie Mae is repaid in about 12 years.

GINNIE MAE MUTUAL FUNDS

If you don't want to invest $25,000, Ginnie Maes are available through unit investment trusts and mutual funds for as little as $1,000. In a unit trust, once the trust's portfolio is assembled, it's set. The

---

Hidden Risks in Ginnie Maes for Retirees

- If you spend each monthly check, you are using up both interest and principal.
- You may want to reinvest your monthly payments. Finding a better rate with equal safety is often difficult.
- Monthly checks are not all the same, which is worrisome if you need a set dollar amount to live on.

portfolio manager cannot make adjustments, so if interest rates drop, you face exactly the same dilemma you do in owning a GNMA certificate. Unit investment trusts are explained in greater detail on page 124.

Here are the points you need to understand about these funds:

1. A Ginnie Mae mutual fund is not a pass-through security like the certificates. The fund itself receives interest and principal payments from the certificates in its portfolio. You then own shares in the fund, which in turn pays you dividends. The market value of your shares fluctuates daily, and the interest rate does, too.

   CAUTION: The fund's yield is not fixed, nor is it guaranteed. If interest rates fall, as mortgages are paid off, principal payments are received by the mutual fund. The manager then must reinvest this money, usually in lower-yielding certificates. So if interest rates are declining, your fund yield will fall also.

   HINT: Because of this volatility, Morningstar Mutual Funds says investors should hold fund shares at least three to five years.

2. An advantage of a fund over a unit trust is that portfolio managers can shift the maturities of the certificates in the fund to reflect changing economic conditions. For example, if it appears that inflation is returning, they will move to shorter maturities to protect the return. And in certain types of funds, part of the portfolio can be shifted into other types of investments. The Kemper U.S. Government securities fund, for instance, also invests in intermediate Treasury bonds.

3. An advantage the funds have over straight Ginnie Mae certificates is that they will reinvest the principal payments received from

home owners in more fund shares if you so request.

4. Funds are best for investors who want high current income rather than capital appreciation. Plan on a long-term play, because these funds are volatile and subject to market risks.

5. In seeking high yields, many GNMA funds use almost speculative strategies, investing in put and call options, interest rate futures contracts, etc. Others invest in mortgage-related securities that do not carry the full government guarantee. Check the prospectus, and remember that a fund's shares may go down in value as well as its yield.

6. For every 1% change in interest rates, the value of the average Ginnie Mae fund will move in the opposite direction almost 6%. Therefore, Ginnie Maes are well suited to tax-deferred portfolios, where regular contributions over a period of time cushion any negative effects of price swings.

FREDDIE MACS

The Federal Home Loan Mortgage Corp., known as Freddie Mac, issues its own mortgage-backed securities, which are called participation certificates, or PCs. Freddie deals primarily in conventional single-family mortgages, which are backed by the Veterans Administration, but it also resells non-government-backed mortgages.

If home owners do not make their mortgage payments on time, you will receive your monthly payment on time, but you may have to wait several months to a year to receive your share of the principal.

HINT: A key difference between Freddie and Ginnie is that Ginnie Maes are backed by the U.S. government; Freddies are guaranteed by private mortgage insurance. Even though they're not quite as secure as GNMAs, they are considered very safe. Because of

GNMA Issues

RATE	ASK	CHG.	YIELD
6.00	86:02	86:10	8:07
6.50	89:18	89:26	8:07
7.00	93:00	93:08	8:12
7.50	96:05	96:13	8:18
8.00	99:01	99:09	8:24
8.50	101:16	101:24	8:33
9.00	103:27	104:03	8:34
9.50	106:00	106:08	8:28
10.00	107:20	107:28	8:30
10.50	109:12	109:20	8:31
11.00	111:08	111:16	8:38
11.50	112:24	113:00	8:46
12.00	113:24	114:00	8.26

SOURCE: *Barron's*, Fall 1999.

the discrepancy in safety, Freddie often pays slightly higher yields.

Freddie Macs are sold for $25,000. Because the market is dominated by institutional investors, there are fewer mutual funds: Vanguard and Federated Investors are two. The U.S. AA Income Fund divides its assets between Ginnie and Freddie.

FANNIE MAES

The Federal National Mortgage Association (FNMA, or Fannie Mae) is a private shareholder-owned corporation that buys conventional mortgages, pools them in $1 million lots, and sells them in $25,000 units. Although not backed by the full faith and credit of the U.S. government, Fannies are AAA-rated by both Standard & Poor's and Moody's. Fannie Mae shares also trade on the NYSE.

FREDDIE AND FANNIE TOGETHER

Both Freddie Mac and Fannie Mae are corporations chartered by Congress and are not officially part of the federal government. Therefore, they do not carry the unconditional guarantee of Ginnie Mae. One advantage of this discrepancy in safety is a slightly higher yield. Another is that the mortgage pools are larger than the Ginnie Mae pools. The more mortgages, the more accurately you can predict how fast the principal will be returned.

After their initial offering, both Freddie and Fannie PCs trade in the secondary market.

CMOs

Collateralized Mortgage Obligations (CMOs) were introduced in 1983 by the Federal Home Loan Mortgage Corp. Their advantage is a more predictable payout of interest and principal than with Ginnie Maes. Instead of buying mortgage securities directly, you buy an AAA-rated bond. These bonds are sold against mortgage collateral comprised of GNMA- or FNMA-guaranteed mortgages.

Each bond is divided into four classes, or tranches, having different dates of maturity ranging from 3 to 20 years. Each CMO has a fixed coupon and pays interest like a traditional bond—monthly or quarterly—but, and here's the difference, principal payments are initially passed through only to investors in the shortest maturity class, class A. Once that group has been paid in full, principal payments go to the next class. In the fourth and final class, investors get all interest and all principal in one lump sum.

These certificates generally have slightly lower yields than the regular pass-throughs, because the size and length of payments can be more accurately determined and you have some protection against prepayments. CMOs are available from larger brokerage firms in $5,000 units.

 CAUTION: Although CMOs improve on traditional mortgage securities by smoothing the rate of early principal payments, they are less liquid, more expensive to trade, and harder to track. They also

entail record keeping and reinvestment problems that most individuals want to avoid.

SALLIE MAEs

Created by Congress in 1972 to provide a nation-wide secondary market for government guaranteed student loans, Sallie Mae (the Student Loan Corporation) is to students what Ginnie Mae is to home owners. It issues bonds, rather than certificates, based on a pool of loans.

Each bond is backed by Sallie Mae, and because its assets are made up of loans that have a government guarantee, these bonds are regarded as almost as safe as Treasuries. However, and this is key, this federal backing is only implied, not explicit. They yield about $3\frac{1}{2}\%$ more than equivalent Treasury bonds.

Student Loan Corporation is a publicly owned company chartered by the government. Its stock trades on the New York Stock Exchange. Originally issued at $20 per share, it split a 2.5 for 1 in 1988; as of September 1999, it was selling at $44/share. It also issues floating-rate notes and convertible bonds. The need for student loans is expected to continue, seemingly forever.

GOVERNMENT AGENCY BONDS

These bonds, although they have slightly lower interest rates than those of the Mae family, are almost as safe as U.S. Treasuries. They are either affiliated with or owned by the government and so are mostly insured against default by some type of federal guarantee. No agency has defaulted on its debt. The distinguishing feature of Government Agency Bonds is whether they are guaranteed by the government.

Here's a guide to who's who in agency bonds:

■ *Fully guaranteed agencies.* These bonds are guaranteed against default by the U.S. government and include:

1. Federal Housing Administration (FHA). Insures mortgages made by private lending firms to individual home buyers, thus lowering the costs.
2. Government National Mortgage Association (GNMA). Ginnie Mae improves liquidity of the mortgage trading market by guaranteeing securities backed by pools of federally insured mortgages, for example, by the FHA.
3. Tennessee Valley Authority (TVA). U.S. government–owned utility providing electricity to the Tennessee River Valley and area. Created in 1933 to promote regional growth.

■ *Nonguaranteed agencies.* These do not carry an unconditional guarantee. They are stockholder-owned:

1. Federal Home Loan Mortgage Corporation (Freddie Mac). Increases liquidity of mortgage market by buying mortgages from lending institutions and selling them to individual investors.
2. Federal National Mortgage Association (Fannie Mae). Performs same function as Freddie Mac.
3. Student Loan Marketing Association (Sallie Mae). Improves liquidity of student loan market by providing financing to state student loan agencies and buying loans made by private sources.

■ *Partially guaranteed agencies.* The United States and most other industrialized nations are obligated to contribute funds to these agencies:

1. Asian Development Bank. Makes loans to developing countries in Asia.
2. Inter-American Development Bank. Makes loans to developing nations in Latin America.
3. World Bank. Makes loans to developing countries throughout the world.

JUNK BONDS

If you're looking for very high yields, a solution is to buy some carefully screened high-yield or junk bond, where the rates are substantially more than with higher-quality, safer bonds.

Junk bonds are those rated BB or lower by Standard & Poor's and Ba or lower by Moody's. Some have no ratings at all.

The world of junk bonds is not entirely comprised of junk at all. It is made up of companies with uncertain earnings coverage of their fixed obligations (bond interest payments), along with blue-chip companies that have been forced into heavy debt in order to fend off a takeover or to finance an acquisition or a buyback of their own stock.

When these situations occur in a blue-chip company, a new set of circumstances comes into being:

- Low-earning or unprofitable assets are sold off.
- Costs are cut, reflecting corporate efforts to become lean and mean.

The credit rating gradually improves as these changes are implemented. Thus, a good junk bond is always one in which the coverage of fixed charges increases with time.

Default is not out of the question, however, which is why, unless you have sufficient money with which to speculate, you should invest in junk bonds only with a broker with knowledge of the field or through a mutual fund, where the element of risk is diversified.

Tips on Picking the Best

Let's take a look at how so-called "junk" bonds can improve themselves. In 1994, Eckert (Jack) Corp., the drug company, sold a 9¼ bond due in 2004 at par. It continued to trade around 100 until it was taken over by J. C. Penney, and as we go to press

these bonds are trading around 107 and have an rating. Not bad!

Two other illustrations of good junk:

In 1990, Safeway Inc. issued a 10% note due in the year 2001. These notes are noncallable until maturity and as we go to press are trading on the NYSE around $105, or $1,050 per bond. When issued, they could be purchased around 101 to 102.

In 1995, HealthSouth Corp. sold a 9.5% note due in 2001; these notes traded on the NYSE at 100 to 102 for several years and as we go to press are trading around $97

So, how can you pick the safest of the high-yield/junk bonds? Some tips:

- *Learn about EBITDA.* Earnings Before Interest, Taxes, Depreciation & Amortization can be found in the public financial statement of the company issuing the bonds. (Ask your broker for it if you can't locate it easily.)
- *Figure the coverage.* Find the total amount of interest, including the interest on the new bonds, that the company will be required to pay. Divide EBITDA by the annual interest requirement and you'll come up with the expected bond interest coverage. Coverage as low as two or three times is sufficient if . . .

You and your broker think the business is stable and growing and not just a cyclical company. For example, truck manufacturing, railroad equipment, automotive equipment, and paper and pulp are examples of highly cyclical businesses which are risky for bondholders.

On the other hand, health care, oil and gas production, food and beverages, drugs, TV and radio broadcasting, and gaming and lodging are more stable as well as asset-backed businesses.

- *Select a bond that has common stock trading on the NYSE or ASE.* If financial trouble is brewing within the company, it will show up in the price of its common stock sooner than in its bonds. A drop in stock price is an immediate red warning to recheck the fundamentals and make certain the bond's payments remain adequately covered.

 CAUTION: Mutual funds are not always a suitably safe alternative. High-yield bond funds are so large that they are often forced to include risky bonds in their portfolios. Check by calling the fund directly or reading its most current write-up in Morningstar.

■ *In all cases, stick to the safest of the high-yield bonds.* During times of panic, such as in 1995, when redemptions forced mutual funds to raise cash, mutual fund shareholders lost money in a big way.

Junk Bonds: A Two-Tier System

During 2000, expect high-yield junk bonds to vary widely in quality, ranging from speculative (risky) to those with improving creditworthiness and therefore less speculative. In fact, some junk bonds will continue to rise from junk to investment grade—BBB. Here are four to watch in both categories:

High Risk

TWA	11.50%
Stone Container	10.75
Trump Casino	11.75
Amresco	10.00

Lower Risk

Hollinger	8.70%
Webb (Del)	10.00
Health South	9.50
Beverly Enterprises	9.00

(As of Summer 1999.)

JUNK BOND MUTUAL FUNDS

High-yield junk bond mutual funds offer professional management plus portfolio supervision. As with other mutual funds, track records vary, so care must be exercised. The publicity attached to the Drexel Burnham/Ivan Boesky insider-trading scandals sent shock waves through the junk bond markets, but junk bonds have fared well since, despite the past adverse publicity provoked by these and other notorious cases.

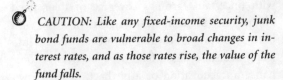 *CAUTION: Like any fixed-income security, junk bond funds are vulnerable to broad changes in interest rates, and as those rates rise, the value of the fund falls.*

Some of the top-yielding junk bond funds are listed in the table below. If one bond in a fund defaults, it means a decrease in the overall fund yield, certainly less of an impact than if you owned the bond directly. However, if several bonds default, the fund share price will suffer.

Junk Bonds to Consider in 2000

Company	S&P Rating	Price
Genesis Health 9¾, 2005	CCC+	$90
Hollinger 9¼, 2006	BB–	104
Rio Hotel 10⅝, 2004	BB+	110
Webb (Del) 9¾, 2008	B–	99

(As of Summer 1999.)

JUNK BOND UNIT INVESTMENT TRUSTS

Unit investment trusts have fixed portfolios. Their yields are more predictable than those of a mutual fund. They have far less flexibility, however, in terms of adjusting the portfolio and getting rid of poor bonds.

 CAUTION: Because they are not actively managed, investors may suffer losses should there be a default.

High-Yielding Junk Bond Mutual Funds

Fund	Yield (September 1999)
Oppenheimer High Yield (800–525–7048)	9.75%
T. Rowe Price High Yield (800–638–5660)	9.56
American Capital High Yield (800–421–5666)	9.61
Prudential Securities High Yield Corp. Fund (800–648–7637)	9.72
Fidelity High Income (800–544–8888)	10.76
Seligman High Yield (800–221–2738)	9.59

The unit investment trust is fine for quality bonds but should be avoided for junk issues.

ADVICE FOR 2000

Junk bonds can be a minefield for the unsophisticated investor. Yet it's hard to say no to an 8% to 11% yield. Here are nine ways to protect yourself if you decide to take the risk.

1. Put no more than 10% of your portfolio in junk bonds.
2. If you want to buy individual bonds, use a broker who knows the area well.
3. Watch the market closely, and be prepared to sell quickly and swallow losses.
4. If you buy individual bonds, diversify among types: fallen angels (companies facing difficulties), emerging growth (companies that have yet to achieve quality ratings), and bonds of companies emerging from a leveraged buyout or takeover.
5. Buy only publicly listed bonds—they are quoted daily and are much easier to buy and sell.
6. Avoid bond issues under $85 million; they tend to be illiquid.
7. Watch the price of the common stock that underlies your bonds. If it suddenly drops in price, it often forecasts trouble for the company's bond.
8. Use a mutual fund for diversification unless you can afford to buy 10 to 15 bonds.
9. If you buy a mutual fund, select it based upon total return, not just yield. A solid fund should generate capital gains along with income. Also, pick a well-diversified fund with no more than 2% to 3% of its assets in any one company's bonds. This broad base helps the fund to weather any adverse economic conditions.

ZERO COUPON BONDS

Zero coupon bonds (zeros) are an excellent choice if you know you will be needing a lump sum of money at a certain date in the future. These bonds, offered by corporations, municipalities, and the U.S. government, are sold at a deep discount from face value ($1,000) and pay no interest. Worthwhile? Yes, as long as you understand the facts.

These bonds are stripped of their interest coupons, and instead of being paid out to you, you get this interest in a balloon payment when the zeros mature. In this respect they are much like EE savings bonds. In other words, they are fully redeemed at par or face value. The difference between the fractional price paid initially and the value at maturity is the return on your investment, that is, the yield to maturity.

EXAMPLE: A zero coupon the Treasury is cur-

High-Yielding Municipal Bond Funds

Fund	Yield (September 1999)
Franklin High Yield Tax-Free Income (800–342–5236)	5.64%
Fidelity Spartan Municipal Income (800–544–8888)	4.74
SteinRoe High Yield Muni (800–338–2550)	5.26
T. Rowe Price Tax-Free High Yield (800–638–5660)	5.53

rently selling at $521 will be worth $1,000 at maturity in 2010. That is a yield to maturity of 6.18%.

Taxes and Zeros

The way zeros are taxed is one of their few drawbacks: The annual appreciation (or undistributed interest) is subject to tax. You must pay taxes annually all along the way, just as if you had actually received the interest payments. Zeros tend to be volatile in price because of this compounding effect; in fact, because there are no interest payments to cushion market swings, zeros can fall dramatically in price when interest rates rise. Therefore, if you buy zeros, plan to hold them to maturity.

Ways to Use Zeros

Zeros are tailor-made for retirement accounts, such as IRAs and Keoghs, because inside these accounts you are able to avoid paying taxes every year on interest you don't actually receive. For example, take an Allied Corp. zero due 2007 selling at 56 ($560 per bond) with a yield of 7.5%. In December 2007, bondholders will receive $1,000 per bond.

☑ *HINT: Zeros are also ideal for saving for a specific goal, such as college tuition payments or a vacation home. If you use zeros to finance a child's college edu-*

cation, have your broker select ones that come due in the years your child will be in school. Better yet, put them in your child's name; when they mature, they'll be taxed at the child's lower rate after age 14.

How to Avoid the Negatives

Locking in your yield can turn out to be a disadvantage if interest rates rise over the life of your zero—in which case other investments will be paying higher yields.

Solutions: To tackle the dual problem of rising interest rates and increasing inflation:

- Select zeros with medium-term maturities—two to five years, possibly ten—and avoid being committed to an interest rate over the long term.
- Purchase zeros continually—say, every year—as part of your IRA, to take advantage of changing rates.
- Purchase zeros with varying maturities to cover yourself in case interest rates rise.

☑ *HINT: Zero coupon Treasuries are backed by the full faith and credit of the U.S. government and are one of the safest and simplest ways to invest for your retirement. You lock in a fixed rate of return, thus eliminating uncertainty.*

The Power of Compounding

HOW MUCH $1,000 IN ZEROS WILL GROW, BEFORE TAXES, AT VARIOUS COMPOUNDING RATES

| Maturity | Semiannual Compounding Rate | | | | |
	6%	7%	8%	9%	10%
5 Years	$1,343	$1,410	$1,480	$1,553	$1,629
10 Years	1,806	1,990	2,191	2,412	2,653
15 Years	2,427	2,807	3,243	3,745	4,322
20 Years	3,262	3,959	4,801	5,816	7,040
30 Years	5,892	7,878	10,520	14,027	18,679

SOURCE: Merrill Lynch.

Types of Zeros

- *Government zeros.* In 1982 Merrill Lynch devised the idea of Treasury zeros by purchasing long-term government bonds, placing them in an irrevocable trust, and issuing receipts against the coupon payments. This created a series of zero coupon Treasuries, one for every coupon date. In other words, Merrill stripped the interest coupons from the principal of the Treasury bond and sold each portion separately. Merrill called these TIGRs (Treasury Investment Growth Receipts). Then along came Salomon Brothers with their version—CATs (Certificates of Accrual on Treasury Securities). All are certificates held in irrevocable trust in a custodial bank.

- *Treasury strips.* In 1985 the government entered the act, introducing its own coupon-stripping program called STRIPs (separate trading of registered interest and principal securities). Because they are issued directly by the Treasury, they are safer than all other types of zeros. Yields are slightly less than those of TIGRs, LYONs, and CATs, because of the greater degree of safety. Treasury strips must be purchased from a stockbroker.

  EXAMPLE: A 20-year bond with a face value of $20,000 and a 10% interest rate could be stripped into 41 zero coupon instruments: the 40 semiannual interest coupons plus the principal. The body upon maturity is worth the $20,000 face value. The other coupon zeros would be worth $1,000 each, or half the annual interest of $2,000 (10% of $20,000) on the payment date.

- *Municipal zeros.* Issued by state and local governments, these are exempt from federal taxes and also from state taxes in the state where issued. They are suggested for investors in high tax brackets.

  EXAMPLE: An A-rated muni zero issued by New York City, due 2011, with a yield of 4.8%, recently sold for $590. That means that in the year 2002 you would receive $1,000 for each $590 invested.

CAUTION: Zeros issued with call features should be shunned.

- *Mortgage-backed zeros.* These are backed by securities issued by Ginnie Mae, Fannie Mae, and Freddie Mac. The securities are secured by AAA-rated mortgages. You'll see some of them referred to as ABCs (agency-backed compounders).

- *Zero coupon convertibles.* This hybrid vehicle allows you to convert the bond into stock of the issuing company. Merrill Lynch, the leading marketer of zero convertibles, calls them LYONs (Liquid Yield Option Notes). Conversion premiums on LYONs are generally lower than on traditional coupon issues; therefore, they offer potential appreciation if the underlying stock moves up in price. LYONs are sold at a substantial discount from par. They give the holder the right, after a certain date, to sell the issue back to the issuer at the original issue price plus accrued interest. This so-called put feature can reduce some of the market risk that accompanies convertibles. (**See:** Chapter 11 on convertibles.)

  EXAMPLE: An Alza Corp. zero due in 2014 sold recently for $510 for a yield of 4.92%. It converts into 12.987 shares.

- *College zeros.* A number of states issue tax-exempt zero coupon bonds as a way to help parents pay for their children's college education. They often have good yields and their interest is exempt from state taxes for the state's residents. The first state to sell these bonds was Illinois—it sold a zero coupon general obligation bond. Some states sell these bonds on an annual or semiannual basis. Check with your stockbroker or state department of education.

  The bonds vary in maturities and interest

rates, but are united by the fact that they are low in risk. Most are general obligation bonds, which are high in safety, because they are backed by the taxing power of the state itself. Most are also noncallable, so if interest rates fall the state cannot call in your bond.

Although you can use the money you earn with these bonds for any purpose, the states often give added incentives if you use the proceeds to pay for college expenses at one of the state's own schools. Illinois, for example, pays an added yield if you use the money to pay for an education in Illinois. Others do not count the income in their formulas for determining whether you or your child is eligible for state financial aid.

These special education bonds, like other municipals, are sold through brokers, not by the states directly. Many states advertise their bonds when they are about to be issued. Some, such as Iowa, give announcements to public school students to take home to their parents. You must move quickly, however. These bonds tend to sell out quickly—often within a week or so.

☑ *HINT: These bonds are sometimes available in the secondary market. Tell your broker if you're interested; it may take him some time to locate the maturity you want.*

A Zero Coupon Bond Mutual Fund

Zeros, like straight bonds, rise in price when interest rates fall and fall when rates rise. And since they are even more sensitive to interest rates, they should be held until maturity. If this is not your plan, use a mutual fund. You'll avoid both being forced to sell early and paying a broker's commission.

■ Benham Target Maturities Trust (800–4 SAFETY)

ZERO COUPON FICO STRIPS

These zero coupon obligations, derived from bonds issued by the federally sponsored agency FICO, The Financing Corp., first appeared on the scene in May 1988. They were the first zeros created from the bonds of a federally sponsored agency.

FICO was created by Congress to raise money for the ailing Federal Savings & Loan Insurance Corp. (FSLIC).

The principal of these bonds is secured by U.S. Treasury securities that match the maturities on FICO bonds. Interest on the bonds is paid from assessments made on the savings and loan industry.

FICO zeros have higher yields than Treasury bonds. The longest-maturing FICOs pay the highest returns.

Although Standard & Poor does not assign credit ratings to FICOs, it has stated that it believes these bonds are very high quality, the equivalent of

---

Zero Coupon Treasury Bonds

PROS

↑ Lock in fixed yield
↑ Maturity dates can be tailored to meet future needs
↑ Call protection available
↑ Predictable cash payment
↑ Guaranteed by U.S. government
↑ Tax-deferred in retirement accounts
↑ No reinvestment decisions
↑ Less expensive than most bonds

CONS

↓ If interest rates rise, you're locked in at a lower yield
↓ Inflation erodes purchasing power of the bond's face value
↓ Commissions and/or sales markups not always made clear
↓ Many zeros have call provisions permitting issuer to redeem them prior to maturity

AAA issues, based on a commitment of Congress to FICO.

FICO strips trade over-the-counter and can be purchased through a stockbroker. Like other bonds, when interest rates rise, their value drops, and vice versa. The minimum face value of a FICO coupon strip is $1,000; of a principal strip, $20,000.

FOR FURTHER INFORMATION

Books

Frank Fabozzi, *Handbook of Mortgage Backed Securities* (New York: Irwin, 1995).

Annette Thau, *The Bond Book: Everything You Need To Know* (Probus, 1994).

Pamphlets

Gabriele, Hueglin & Cashman, 800-422-7435

Freddie Mac

Shareholder Relations Department
Federal Home Loan Mortgage Corp.
Mail Stop #485
8200 Jones Branch Drive
McLean, VA 22102
800–424–5401

Sallie Mae

Investor Relations
Student Loan Marketing Association
1160 Sallie Mae Drive
Reston, VA 20193
703–810–7743

PART THREE

When the Bulls Are Running

"A billion here, a billion there, and pretty soon you're talking real money."

Everett Dirksen

Senator Dirksen, of course, was referring to our federal budget. But you can benefit from his wisdom too—and that is to think big. With the right stocks, it's quite possible to make a billion—maybe closer to, say, a million. In fact, over time stocks outperform all other types of investments. So, whether you have only dreamed about owning a stock or whether you and your broker are trading hundreds of shares every morning and afternoon, we suggest you read this entire section. The basic information is essential to the beginner, and the lists of suggested stocks and the tips on trading options, getting in on new issues, and making money with rights and warrants can help even the most wizened investor.

In Part Three you will learn about:

- Common and preferred stocks
- How to pick stocks that go up in price
- When to buy and when to sell
- Over-the-counter stocks
- Electric utilities and water company stocks
- High-dividend stocks
- Low-debt companies
- Options
- Stock rights and warrants
- IPOs and new issues

14

Stocks: Common and Preferred

WHY OWN STOCKS?

The two basic tools of investing are stocks and bonds, or equity and debt, to use a little Wall Streetese. We discussed the various types of bonds and their pros and cons in Part Two. Now we're going to look into common and preferred stocks—the backbone of every portfolio, including yours.

The ongoing bull market is certainly the most compelling reason for investing in stocks. Yet even in a less impressive market, there are two other equally impressive reasons to be in stocks:

1. *Over the long run, stocks outperform bonds.*
2. *Stocks tend to keep pace with inflation.* With stocks, at least you have a fighting chance of staying even. Not so with bonds: Once you buy a bond, the interest rate is locked in. If, for example, oil prices go up, it doesn't matter—your bond will pay exactly the same whether crude is at $18 or $35 a barrel. On the other hand, if you own shares in Exxon or Occidental Petroleum, you'll participate in the increase in oil prices through higher dividends *and* a rising price for your shares. Stocks, in fact, respond directly to inflation while, at the same time, inflation will eat away at interest earned on fixed-income securities.

THE NITTY GRITTY

A stock is a security that represents ownership in a corporation. That is the one thing all stocks have in common. There are many different types of stocks and despite the bull market, it's important to remember that (1) there's no such thing as a stock that's forever, and (2) it's a big mistake to expect all things from any one stock.

Stocks, in fact, are *not* all designed to do the same thing. There are two distinct types of stocks: those that generate income and those that appreciate in price, a.k.a. growth stocks.

- Income stocks, such as utility stocks, real estate investment trusts (REITs), and closed-end funds that trade on the exchanges, should be held primarily for income; you definitely should not also expect them to appreciate much in price.
- Growth stocks, those selected for price appreciation, are an entirely different matter. Within this growth category you must narrow your selection even further, to low-risk growth stocks or to riskier, speculative stocks.

Throughout this book you will find various lists of stocks suggested for growth, income, or total return.

Success with Stocks

Over the past 20 years, stocks, as measured by the S&P 500 Stock Index, provided an annualized return of 11.9% compared to 9% on 10-year Treasury bonds and 7.7% for 90-day Treasury bills. Inflation averaged 6.3% during this period.

KNOWING THE LINGO

To help sort out the who, what, where, when, and how of making money in stocks, you'll need to be familiar with the following terms, used not only by financial wizards and pundits, but also by your broker, the business newsperson, and writers of investment newsletters, articles, and books.

- *Blue-chip stocks* represent ownership in a major company that has a long history of profitability and continual or increasing dividends with sufficient financial strength to withstand economic or industrial downturns.

  EXAMPLES: General Electric, Exxon, Du Pont, Procter & Gamble.

- *Growth stocks* represent ownership in a company that has had relatively rapid growth in the past (when compared with the economy as a whole) and is expected to continue to grow.

  These companies typically reinvest a large part of their earnings in the company to finance their expansion and growth. Consequently, dividends are small in comparison with earnings.

  EXAMPLES: Yahoo!, Harley-Davidson, Cisco.

- *Cyclical stocks* are common stocks of companies whose earnings move with the economy or business cycles. They generally post lower earnings when the country is in a slump and higher earnings when the economy is in a recovery phase or booming along.

  EXAMPLES of cyclical industries: aluminum, steel, automobiles, machinery, housing, paper, airlines, and travel and leisure.

- *Income stocks* have continually stable earnings and high-dividend yields in comparison with other stocks. Income stocks generally retain only a small portion of earnings for expansion and growth, which they are able to do because there is a relatively stable market for their products.

  EXAMPLES: public utility companies, international oil companies, closed-end bond funds, and REITs.

Now you're ready to start selecting stocks for your own personal portfolio, keeping the following

---

Fifty-Nine Low-Risk Stocks

These stocks were ranked #1 (highest) for safety by *Value Line Investment Survey* in late 1999. Utility stocks, which also have high yields, are not included in this list.

Abbott Labs.	Int'l. Flavors & Frag.
Allied Signal	Interpublic Group
Amer. Home Products	Jefferson Pilot
Amoco Corp.	Johnson & Johnson
Anheuser-Busch	Kimberly-Clark
Atlantic Richfield	Lee Enterprises
Automatic Data	Longs Drug Stores
Processing	McDonald's Corp.
Bemis Co.	McGraw-Hill
Bestfoods Inc.	Merck & Co.
Bristol-Myers Squibb	Minnesota Mining &
British Telecom	Mfg.
Brown-Forman	Mobil Corp.
Chevron Corp.	Morgan, J.P.
Clorox Co.	Nalco Chemical
Coca-Cola	PPG Industries
Colgate-Palmolive	Procter & Gamble
Deluxe Corp.	Royal Dutch Petroleum
Donnelley (RR)	Sara Lee Corp.
& Sons	Schering-Plough
Du Pont	Shell Transport
Emerson Electric	Sysco Corp.
Exxon Corp.	Texaco, Inc.
First Virginia Banks	Tootsie Roll
Gannett Co.	Unilever
General Electric	United Technologies
Genuine Parts	UST Inc.
Grainger Co.	Vulcan Materials
Hancock, J.	Washington Post
Heinz (H.J.)	Weis Markets
Hubbell Inc.	Wrigley (Wm.) Jr.

Cyclical Stocks for 2000	
Canadian National Railway	NYSE: CNI
Commercial Metals	NYSE: CMC
Roper Industries	NYSE: ROP
Solutia	NYSE: SOI
Texas Instruments	NYSE: TX

key consideration in mind: *Every investment involves some degree of risk.*

☑ HINT: *The general rule is that return is correlated to risk: The greater the risk, the greater the expected return.*

HOW STOCKS WORK

When you buy shares in a company, you become part owner of that company, and you can make money in one of two ways: through dividends or through price appreciation when you sell your shares at a profit.

Dividends, a distribution of earnings, are generally declared when the company is comfortably profitable. The actual dollar amount is decided by the board of directors and is traditionally paid to shareholders quarterly.

A stock may *appreciate in price* for a variety of reasons, not all of which are completely rational:

- The company is profitable.
- It has an exciting new product.
- It is part of an industry that is performing well.
- It is the subject of takeover rumors or actual attempts.
- Wall Street likes it.
- It has received a favorable write-up by analysts.
- It has new management.

☑ HINT: *Do not buy a stock, even a solid blue chip, and then never look at it again. While your back is turned the company could be taken over, enter bankruptcy, or just have a bad year. In each case,*

you should be ready to take some form of action— buy more shares, sell all your shares, or sell some of your shares.

COMMON STOCKS VERSUS BONDS

Stocks are *live* investments. The market value of a common stock grows as the corporation prospers, whereas the face value of bonds remains the same, so that over the years, their real value, in terms of purchasing power, decreases.

The prices of bonds are almost completely controlled by interest rates and change almost immediately when rates do. When the cost of money rises, bond values drop to maintain competitive returns; when interest rates decline, bond prices rise. Bonds, therefore, are traded by yields; stocks, by what investors believe to be future corporate prospects.

Stocks also offer the potential of increased dividends; a bond, however, has a set interest rate—your payout will remain the same as long as you own the bond.

RISKS OF OWNING COMMON STOCK

There are, of course, risks associated with ownership of common stocks. The risks are far less with quality corporations and, to a large degree, can be controlled by setting strict rules for selling and by using commonsense. As long as the company continues to make more money, its stock price is likely to rise.

Six Income Stocks with Yields Above 6%		
Stock	Symbol	Yield
Alliance Cap Mgmt	AC	6.50%
British Steel	BST	8.60
Buckeye Partners	BPL	7.9
Constellation Energy	CEG	6.15
New Plan Realty	NPR	8.60
Weingarten Realty	WRI	7.31

(As of Summer 1999.)

Dividends Every Month in 2000

You can receive a dividend check every month of the year by purchasing a group of stocks with different dividend-payment dates. The following is a list of issues broken down by payout dates. By purchasing stocks from each of the groups, you will have a portfolio of stocks producing dividend checks every month of the year.

January, April, July, October

Burlington Northern	Kimberly-Clark
CIGNA	McKesson
Dexter	Morgan (J.P.) & Co.
Dow Chemical	Northern States Power
Eastman Kodak	Ogden
General Electric	Philip Morris
Genuine Parts	Companies
Hanson plc	SCEcorp
Heinz (H.J.)	Thomas & Betts

February, May, August, November

American Tel. & Tel.	Lincoln National
BellSouth	Orange & Rockland
Betz Laboratories	Utilities
Bristol-Myers Squibb	Penney (J.C.) Co.
Brooklyn Union Gas	Procter & Gamble
Clorox	Rochester Telephone
Colgate-Palmolive	Southwestern Bell
Consolidated Natural	TECO Energy
Gas	WPL Holdings

March, June, September, December

American Brands	Kmart
American Home	Minnesota Mining
Products	& Mfg.
Amoco	Norfolk Southern
Atlantic Richfield	Potomac Electric Power
Chevron	South Jersey Industries
Du Pont (E.I.)	Southern Indiana Gas
Dun & Bradstreet	& Electric
Exxon	Tambrands
Indiana Energy	Times Mirror

SOURCE: Dow Theory Forecasts, 7412 Calumet Avenue, Hammond, IN 46324; 219–931–6480.

To reduce your risk with common stocks, follow these four guidelines:

1. Buy stocks with low betas (see page 147 for a full explanation of how beta works).
2. Diversify by both type of stock and type of industry.
3. Spread out your risk over a number of stocks and a number of industry groups.
4. Be defensive by moving in and out of the market when appropriate.

You Should Also Understand Interest Rate Risk

Certain stocks are interest-sensitive, which means they are directly affected by changes in interest rates. These stocks include utilities, banks, financial and brokerage companies, housing and construction, REITs, and closed-end bond funds. You can cut your risk in these stocks by moving to other investments when interest rates are high or on the way up.

The reason these industries suffer during high-interest-rate seasons is because:

1. Utility companies have to pay more on monies borrowed for expansion or upgrading of facilities.
2. Banks and finance companies are forced to pay more on money deposited in their institutions as well as for money they borrow.
3. Building falls off because of higher interest rates.

EIGHT WAYS ANYONE CAN ANALYZE STOCKS LIKE THE PROS

Use these Wall Street analytical tools—they are the most reliable and proven ways to judge a stock:

■ *Earnings per share.* For the average investor, this figure distills the company's financial picture into one simple number. Earnings per share is the company's net income (after taxes

---

Four Stocks with Longest Record of Dividends

Bank of Boston	1784
Fleet/Norstar Financial	1791
Midlantic	1805
First Maryland Bancorp	1806

SOURCE: Standard & Poor's Corp.

Companies with Twenty Straight Quarters of Increased Profits

Stock	S&P Ranking
Abbott Labs	A+
Automatic Data Proc	A+
Avery Dennison	B+
Bank of New York	B+
Coca-Cola	A+
Cracker Barrel	A
Green Tree Fin'l	A-
Int'l Dairy Queen	B+
Johnson & Johnson	A+
Meditrust	nr
Norwest Corp.	A
Sealed Air	A-
SunAmerica Inc.	A-
Sysco Corp.	A+
Textron Inc.	A

---

and preferred stock dividends) divided by the number of common shares outstanding. When a company is described as growing at a certain rate, the growth is then usually stated in terms of earnings per share.

Look for a company whose earnings per share have increased over the past five years; one down year is acceptable if the other four have been up. You will find earnings per share in Moody's, Value Line, Standard & Poor's, or the company's annual report.

■ *Price-earnings ratio (P/E)*. This is one of the most common analytical tools of the trade and reflects investor enthusiasm about a stock in comparison with the market as a whole. Divide the current price of a stock by its earnings per share for the last 12 months: That's the P/E ratio, also sometimes called the multiple.

You will also find the P/E listed in the daily stock quotations of the newspaper. A P/E of 12, for example, means that the buying public is willing to pay 12 times earnings for the stock, whereas there is much less interest and confidence in a stock with a P/E of 4 or 5. A company's P/E is, of course, constantly changing and must be compared with its own previous P/Es and with the P/Es of others in its industry or category.

It is important to realize that the P/E listed in the paper is based on the last 12 months' earnings; Wall Street professionals, however, refer to the earnings of the current year. So

when considering a stock to buy or sell, remember to focus on its future, not its past.

Although brokers and analysts hold varying views on what constitutes the ideal P/E, a P/E under 10 is regarded as conservative. As the P/E moves above 10, you start to pay a premium. If the P/E moves below 5 or 6, it tends to signal uncertainty about the company's prospects and balance sheet.

■ *Book value*. This figure, also known as stockholders' equity, is the difference between a company's assets and its liabilities, in other words, what the stockholders own after all debts are paid. That number is then divided by the number of shares outstanding to arrive at book value per share. The book value becomes especially important in takeover situations. If book value is understated—that is, if the assets of the company are worth substantially more than the financial statements say they are—you may have found a real bargain that the marketplace has not yet recognized. (This

Ten Stocks for Long-Term Appreciation

Company	S&P Rating	Price Summer 1999	P/E Ratio
Abbott Laboratories	A+	$73	23.9
Berkshire Hathaway	NR	714	62.1
Cisco Systems	B+	65	76.5
Federal Home Loan	A+	45	20.0
General Electric	A+	84	30.0
Intel Corp.	A-	83	23.0
MCI World	B	90	45.0
Merck & Co.	A+	119	27.2
Safeway Inc.	B+	52	28.6
Wal-Mart Stores	A+	48	38.4

(As of Fall 1999.)

is often true with in-the-ground assets such as oil, minerals, gas, and timber.)

- *Return on equity (ROE)*. This number measures how much the company earns on the stockholders' equity. It is a company's total net income expressed as a percentage of total book value and is especially useful when comparing several companies within one industry or when studying a given company's profitability trends.

    To calculate a simple ROE, divide earnings per share by book value. A return under 10% is usually considered poor.

- *Dividends*. Check the current and projected dividend of a stock, especially if you are building an income portfolio. Study the payouts over the past five years as well as the current dividend. There are times when a corporation reinvests most of its earnings to ensure its future growth, in which case the dividend will be small.

☑ *RULE OF THUMB: Typically, the greater the current yield, the less likelihood there is of stock price appreciation. It's best, however, if a company earns $5 for every $4 it pays out.*

- *Volatility*. Some stocks go up and down in price like a yo-yo; others trade within a relatively narrow range. Those that dance about

Calculating Growth Rates

ANNUAL RATE OF EARNINGS INCREASE PER SHARE	JUSTIFIED P/E RATIOS			
	5 YEARS	7 YEARS	10 YEARS	15 YEARS
2%	15	15	13	12
4	17	17	16	16
5	18	18	18	18
6	19	19	20	21
8	21	22	24	28
10	23	25	28	35
12	25	28	33	48

Note that there should be only a small premium when a low growth rate remains static over the years. A 5% annual gain in EPS justifies the same P/E no matter how many years it has been attained. But when a company can maintain a high rate of earnings growth, 10% or more, the value of the stock is enhanced substantially.

SOURCE: Graham and Dodd, *Security Analysis*, 4th ed. (New York: McGraw-Hill, 1962).

obviously carry a greater degree of risk than their more pedestrian cousins.

The measurement tool for price volatility, called *beta*, tells how much a stock tends to move in relation to changes in the Standard & Poor's 500 Stock Index. The index is fixed at 1.00, so a stock with a beta of 1.5 moves up and down 1½ times as much as the Standard & Poor's index, whereas a stock with a beta of 0.5 is less volatile than the index. To put it another way, a stock with a 1.5 beta is expected to rise in price by 15% if the Standard & Poor's Index rises 10%, or fall by 15% if the index falls by 10%. You will find the beta for stocks given by the investment services as well as by good stockbrokers.

Four Low Beta Stocks for 1999

Stock	Beta	Business
Canandaigua Wine	0.3	Wine
Proffitts, Inc.	0.21	Retail stores
Quaker State	0.42	Motor oils
Roper Industries	0.40	Industrial mfg.

■ *Total return.* Most investors in stocks tend to think about their gains and losses in terms of price changes, not dividends, whereas those who own bonds pay attention to interest yields and seldom focus on price changes. *Both approaches are mistakes.*

Although dividend yields are obviously more important if you are seeking income, and changes in price play a greater role in growth stocks, the total return on a stock is extremely important. It makes it possible for you to compare your investment in stocks with a similar investment in corporate bonds, municipals, Treasuries, mutual funds, and unit investment trusts.

☑ *HINT: To calculate the total return, add (or subtract) the stock's price change and dividends for 12 months and then divide by the price at the beginning of the 12-month period. For example, suppose you buy a stock at $42 a share and receive $2.50 in dividends for the next 12-month period. At the end of the period, you sell the stock at $45.00. The total return is 13%.*

| Dividend | $2.50 |
| Price appreciation | + 3.00 |

$$\$5.50 \div \$42 = 13\%$$

■ *Number of shares outstanding.* If you are a beginning investor or working with a small portfolio, look for companies with at least 5 million shares outstanding. You will then be ensured of both marketability and liquidity, because the major mutual funds, institutions, and the public will be trading in these stocks. You are unlikely to have trouble buying or selling when you want to. In a smaller company, your exposure to sharp price fluctuations is greater.

DUNNAN'S TECHNIQUES FOR PICKING WINNERS

In addition to the eight analytical tools just described, you can boost your ability to build a winning portfolio by using these guidelines. Look for:

■ *Continual dividend payers.* For investors who place safety first, look for common stocks of companies that have paid dividends for 20 years or more. Many have familiar names: Abbott Labs, Bristol-Myers, H.J. Heinz, Tootsie Roll Industries, Smuckers, and Wrigley.

Always check a company's annual report to see (1) if the dividends have increased fairly consistently as the result of higher earnings, and (2) that the company has been profitable in recent years and appears likely to remain so in the near future. It's great to do business with an old store, but only if the merchandise is up-to-date and priced fairly.

■ *Institutional ownership.* Pick stocks chosen by the

experts—managers of mutual funds, pension plans, insurance portfolios, endowments, etc.

Institutional ownership is no guarantee of quality, but it does indicate that professionals have carefully studied the company and have recommended buying its shares. And institutional ownership tends to boost a stock's price.

☑ *HINT: Every investment portfolio should contain at least three stocks whose shares are owned by at least 175 institutions.*

■ *The most profitable companies.* You obviously want to own shares in a profitable company.

A list of companies that are expected to achieve high total returns because of increasing profits appears on page 146.

■ *Industry leaders.* Companies that capture the business within their particular industry are creative and well managed.

■ *Companies likely to split their stock.* With many stocks at or near new highs, stock splits are on the rise. In a purely technical way, a stock split provides no obvious advantage to shareholders, but the history of splits shows that more often than not a stock will rise in price at about the time the directors vote a split. And

often an increase in the cash dividend accompanies a split.

A stock split also calls the public's attention to the company, to its earnings progress, and this often results in increased buying and eventually a higher price for the company's shares. And, with the new reduced price per share, small investors are attracted to the stock.

To find stock split candidates, look for a sharply higher market price, a history of stock splits, or large stock dividends.

☑ *HINT: Standard & Poor's* The Outlook *generally publishes a list of stock-split candidates once or twice a year.*

Guidelines for Selecting Growth Stocks

■ *Read the annual report backward.* Look at the footnotes to discover whether there are significant problems, unfavorable long-term commitments, lawsuits, etc.

■ *Find a current ratio of assets to liabilities of 2:1 or higher.* This indicates that the company can withstand difficulties and will probably be able to obtain money to expand.

■ *Look for a low debt ratio with long-term debt no more than 35% of total capital.* This means that the company has staying power and the ability to resist cyclical downturns.

■ *Compare a stock's price-earnings ratio* to those of other companies in the same industry. If their ratios are higher, this may be a sleeper.

■ *Look for stocks with strong management and little debt.*

What Stocks to Avoid

It's just as important to know which stocks are losers as winners. And so, to spot the nonachievers among the many companies out there, look for these two danger signals:

Getting Current Info on Stocks

Call Standard & Poor's Research Reports ($9.00; 800–642–2858) or Schwab's Investment Reports Service ($9.00; 800–626–9580) to get five or more pages on each of about 4,000 publicly traded companies. Reports generally tell you how many analysts like the company and how many don't, plus earnings estimates, news about the company, future outlook for the industry, along with Standard & Poor's grade, ranging from one star (sell) to five stars (strong buy).

(As of Fall 1999.)

<table>
<tr><td colspan="2">

Fifteen Companies with Zero Debt

Bob Evans
Dollar General
Dun & Bradstreet
Edwards (AG)
Family Dollar Stores
Kelly Services
Kimball Int'l.
Sigma-Aldrich
Smuckers (JM)
Stride Rite
Tootsie Roll
Walgreen Co.
Washington Post
Weis Markets
Wm. Wrigley Jr.

SOURCE: Value Line, Fall 1999.

</td></tr>
</table>

Ten Stocks With P/Es Below Ten

Company	P/E Ratio
KLM Royal Dutch	9.9
National Bank of Canada	9.8
Smithfield Foods	9.8
Delta Air Lines	9.5
Owens Corning	9.1
Oxford Industries	8.9
Old Republic	8.7
Loews Corp.	7.7
Universal Corp.	7.3
Ryland Group	7.2

SOURCE: Value Line, Summer 1999.

- *Substantial stock dilution.* This means that a company repeatedly and/or exclusively is raising funds through the sale of additional common stock, either directly or through convertibles. There's no harm in small dilution, especially when it appears that earnings growth will continue. But beware of any company with heavy future obligations. Too much dilution merely enlarges the size of the company, leaving stockholders with diluted earnings.
- *Vast overvaluation as shown by price-earnings ratios of 30 or higher.* This is a steep price to pay for potential growth. Take your profits, or at least set stop-loss prices. When any stock sells at a multiple that is double that of the overall market (usually around 14.56), be cautious.

Finding Bargains in Stocks

Benjamin Graham, the grandfather of "security analysis," in his book by the same title, looked for bargains in stocks, which he defined as the time when they trade at:

- A multiple of no more than twice that of the prevailing interest rate: that is, a P/E ratio of 16 versus an interest rate of 8%
- A discount of 20% or more from book value
- A point where current assets exceed current liabilities and long-term debt combined
- A P/E ratio of 40% less than that of the S&P index P/E. For some examples of stocks with low P/Es as of Fall 1998, see box above.

Thirteen Stocks Under $29 for 2000

COMPANY	PRICE
Advest Group	$19
Toll Brothers	19
Arrow Electronics	19
Blair Corp.	18
Kimball Int'l.	17
Volt Info Sciences	17
Dress Barn	15
Micro Warehouse	16
Justin Industries	14
Standard Pacific Corp.	13
United Industrial Corp.	11
Barry (RG)	9
Jackpot Enterprises	8

CAUTION: Above average risk.
SOURCE: Value Line, Fall 1999.

What Are Earnings Worth?

ANNUAL GROWTH RATE	WHAT $1.00 EARNINGS WILL BECOME IN 3 YEARS AT GIVEN GROWTH RATE	THE P/E RATIO YOU CAN PAY TODAY TO MAKE 10% ANNUAL CAPITAL GAIN AND EXPECT P/E RATIO IN 3 YEARS TO BE	
		15x	30x
4%	$1.12	12.6	25.3
5	1.16	13.1	26.2
6	1.19	13.4	26.8
7	1.23	13.9	27.7
8	1.26	14.2	28.4
9	1.30	14.7	29.3
10	1.33	15.0	30.0
12	1.40	15.8	31.6
15	1.52	17.1	34.3
20	1.73	19.5	39.0
25	1.95	22.0	44.0

SOURCE: Knowlton and Furth, *Shaking the Money Tree* (New York: Harper & Row, 1979).

Earnings Growth Rate

Year 1 $1.00 x 20% = 0.20 = $1.20
Year 2 $1.20 x 20% = 0.24 = $1.44
Year 3 $1.44 x 20% = 0.29 = $1.73
Year 4 $1.73 x 20% = 0.35 = $2.08

GUIDELINES FOR SELECTING THE TOP INCOME STOCKS

Dividend-paying stocks are not just for retirees and ultraconservative investors. They are important to everyone, because they both boost the value of a stock and generally indicate that the company is a mature one, no longer in the throes of expensive expansion. A company that can afford to pay high dividends is no longer reinvesting all its profits in the company.

Another reason that high-dividend stocks are looked upon with such favor is that the dividend is likely to increase if the company's earnings grow—unlike a bond, whose coupon rate remains the same throughout its life.

☑ HINT: *Dividend-paying stocks fall less in price when the market falls. A study by Avner Arbel, professor of finance at Cornell University, shows that high-dividend stocks fell only 21% in the 1987 crash, while nondividend payers dropped 32%.*

Twenty-nine Stocks with Ten Years or More of Consecutive Dividend Increases

Company	Symbol
Abbott Laboratories	ABT
Avery Dennison	AVY
Becton, Dickinson	BDX
Campbell Soup	CPB
Clorox Co.	CLX
Con Agra Inc.	CAG
Eaton Vance	EV
Federal National Mortgage	FNM
First of America Bank	FOA
First Security	FSCO
First Tennessee Nat'l	FTEN
First Union	FTU
Gillette Co.	G
Humana	H
Interpublic Group	IPG
Johnson & Johnson	JNJ
Kelly Services	KELYA
Marsh & McLennan	MMC
Marshall & Ilsley	MRIS
Merck & Co.	MRK
Nationsbank	NB
Norwest Corp.	NOB
Old Kent Financial	OKEN
Pentair, Inc.	PNR
Pfizer, Inc.	PFE
Schering-Plough	SGP
South Trust Corp.	SOTR
Superior Industries	SUP
Warner-Lambert	WLA

SOURCE: Standard & Poor's, *The Outlook,* 1999.

Eight Stocks with High Dividends

Stocks with comparatively high dividends give income plus some protection against a falling stock market. But remember, the higher the yield, the higher the risk. This list does not include utility stocks, which traditionally have high yields.

COMPANY	PRICE	FALL 1999 YIELD
Alliance Capital Management	$26	8.0%
BRE Properties	25	6.2
Health and Retirement Prop.	14	9.8
Dryfus Gov't Income	9	8.1
New Plan Realty	19	8.5
Putnam Premier Income Trust	8	9.3
Royce Value	13	11.5
Weingarten Realty	39	7.2

(As of October 1999.)

To determine if a company is likely to continue making dividend payouts:

- Check the dividend-payout history for the past ten years in *Standard & Poor's Stock Guide* or *Value Line Investment Survey*. Those with uninterrupted payouts are your best bet.
- Check the company's payout ratio: total dividends paid divided by net operating income. If the payout ratio is less than 50%, the company will probably continue to pay dividends.
- Check the company's cash flow per share. If cash flow is three times the dividend payout, dividends will probably continue to be paid.
- Avoid or invest very carefully in stocks that have extraordinarily high yields within the industry group. Extremely high yields may signal trouble.
- Don't buy a high-yield stock near the ex-dividend date. That is the beginning of the time period during which purchasers of the stock cannot receive the next quarterly dividend, generally paid three to four weeks later. Usually stock prices are inflated just before the ex-dividend date, and on that date they tend to fall. If you buy the stock at an inflated price in order to receive the dividend, you may not break even, because you'll be paying tax on the dividend income.

TWO WINNING STRATEGIES FOR SMALL INVESTORS

Dollar Cost Averaging

One of the most difficult aspects of investing is timing—should you put money into stocks or mutual funds, this week, next week, or months from now? There's a simple formula to get around this age-old dilemma—dollar cost averaging.

It involves investing the same amount of money in a stock or mutual fund at fixed intervals, monthly or quarterly, for instance. It may seem dull, but it actually requires personal discipline in down markets when the overwhelming temptation is *not* to invest.

Basically, what it does is force you to buy more of a stock or fund when its price is low and less when it is high. Over the long haul, your average cost will be lower than the average price of the security.

CAUTION: Although this is a fine technique, it will not turn a poor investment choice into a winner. If a stock keeps falling in price forever, you wind up buying more losses. To avoid this, select stocks and funds that have a record of long-term upward trends.

Most mutual funds require an initial investment of $1,000 or more, but subsequent investments may be as little as $100. You may be able to dollar cost average with a fund that automatically transfers a preset amount from your bank checking account into the fund's portfolio.

Dividend Reinvestment

You can also dollar cost average with individual stocks. And if the shares are in your name (rather than held by your broker in street name), you may be able to participate in a dividend reinvestment plan. Over 750 companies have such plans in which your dividends are automatically reinvested in additional shares of stock rather than paying you the cash. Many of these companies also allow shareholders to make additional cash investments. This means you can dollar cost average without using a broker.

☑ *HINT: Call the investor relations division of any company you own shares in to see if it has a dividend reinvestment plan or check in:* The Directory of Dividend Reinvestment Plans. *If it's not at your library, order ($39.95) from: Standard & Poor's Corp., Direct Marketing, 25 Broadway, New York, NY 10004; 800–221–5277.*

This annually updated guide lists 700+ companies that offer such programs with telephone numbers, S&P rankings, and other details.

WHEN TO SELL A STOCK

Financial whiz kids and Wall Street gurus are always weaving complex theories about when to buy a stock. That's the easy part. They shy away from explaining when to sell, which is a much trickier business.

Although there's no foolproof system for making certain you always buy low and sell high, you can make an educated decision.

The first basic rule to follow in mastering the art of selling is to know precisely whether you bought the stock for growth or income.

1. *Growth.* If you purchased the stock for growth and price appreciation, hold it as long as the company's earnings keep rising at a steady pace. If profits slow down, find out why. Sell unless you discover a truly viable reason why profits will increase within the year.

2. *Income.* Keep the stock as long as the company is financially solid and its earnings per share exceed the dividend by at least 10% and they (i.e., earnings) are rising more than 5% a year. If earnings stagnate for several quarters, or if an independent rating agency (Standard & Poor's or Moody's) downgrades the firm's creditworthiness, seriously consider selling.

Other when-to-sell guidelines that work:

■ You should also consider selling if you think the company is in serious trouble and its earnings prospects are poor and not likely to recover quickly.

Stocks with Dividend Reinvestment Plans That Permit Cash Investments

STOCK	MINIMUM/MAXIMUM CASH PURCHASE
American Brands	$100/$10,000 quarterly
AT&T	$100/$50,000 annually
Block (H&R)	$25/$2,000 monthly
Bristol-Meyers Squibb	$100/$10,025 monthly
Browning-Ferris	$25/$60,000 annually
Exxon	$50/$100,000 annually
McDonald's	$100/$250,000 annually
Motorola	$25/$5,000 quarterly
PepsiCo	$10/$5,000 monthly
Walgreen	$10/$5,000 quarterly

Five Stocks for the Long Haul

Abbott Labs
Campbell Soup
General Electric
Home Depot
Johnson & Johnson

Dividends Paid for Fifty-Plus Years and Increased Each Year for Last Ten

Abbott Laboratories	Household Int'l.
AmSouth Bancorp	Johnson & Johnson
Bank One	Johnson Controls
Becton, Dickinson	Kimberly-Clark
Bestfoods	Marshall & Ilsley
Bristol-Myers Squibb	Merck & Co.
Campbell Soup	Old Kent Financial
Carolina Power & Light	Pfizer, Inc.
Chubb Corp.	PPG Industries
Coca-Cola	Questar Corp.
Commerce Bancshares	Rubbermaid, Inc.
Duke Energy	SouthTrust Corp.
First Tennessee	State Street Corp.
National	Universal Foods
First Union	Walgreen Co.
Gillette Co.	Warner-Lambert

SOURCE: Standard & Poor's *The Outlook*

■ If your stock suddenly drops in price by 20% or more within a short period—a month or less—you need to find out why and then consider selling.

FOUR SMART WAYS TO KEEP YOUR PROFITS

"No one ever went broke taking a profit." Remind yourself of this old Wall Street expression on a regular basis. It sounds so simple, and of course, the most obvious way to keep your gains is to sell when you've made a profit.

Here are four ways to protect your position on the downside and profit on the upswings.

■ *Enter stop orders.* Have your broker sell your stock if it drops to a particular price. This protects you against major declines.

■ *Sell into strength.* Each time the market makes a major move on the up side, sell a portion of your holdings. For example, if you own 500 shares of Clorox and you have big gains, sell 100 shares each time it appreciates 10%. You reduce your risk, and at the same time you're selling your stock at higher prices.

■ *Buy put options.* This gives you the right to sell 100 shares of a stock at a particular price within a certain time period, up to nine months. These options set a selling floor. For example, if you own a $50 stock, you buy a put allowing you to sell 100 shares for $45 at any time within the next six months. The put costs about 75¢ per share and it limits your loss to $5 per share.

■ *Switch to convertibles.* Move out of common stock into convertibles to lower your risk and still profit from a rise in the market (**see:** Chapter 11 for details).

PREFERRED STOCK

Individual investors usually gravitate toward preferred stocks because of their high, secure dividends. Many are issued by utilities.

The Nitty Gritty

A preferred stock is one that pays a fixed dividend—it does not rise or fall with the company's profits. And, as the name implies, a preferred stock enjoys preferred status over common stocks. Preferred shareholders receive their dividend payments after all bondholders are paid and before dividends are paid on common shares.

The dividend, set at a fixed dollar amount, is secure for the life of the stock. If a payment is skipped because of corporate losses, it will be paid later when earnings recover. That's why preferreds are sometimes called *cumulative,* because the dividends accumulate and must be paid out before common. Most preferreds are cumulative and are indicated by the initials *cm* in the stock guides.

There are also *noncumulative preferreds:* If a dividend is skipped, it is not recovered. It's best to avoid this type of preferred.

- *Pros.* Although there have been a few incidents of corporations skipping preferred dividends, on the whole these securities have an excellent safety record. And if the yield is high, it remains permanently high.
- *Cons.* Inflation and high interest rates can have a large negative impact on preferreds.

That's because the dividend is fixed, and when rates rise, holders are locked in at the old lower rate. Not only are they shut out of rising interest rates, but the opportunity for substantial price appreciation of their shares is limited.

Although preferreds trade like bonds on the basis of their yields, unlike bonds they have no maturity date. With a bond you know that at a specified time you will get back your initial investment, the face value. There is no such assurance with a preferred. Market conditions are the sole determinant of the price you will receive when you sell.

How to Pick Preferreds

The three criteria for selecting preferreds are *quality* of the issuing corporation, as shown by financial strength and profitability; *value,* as indicated by the yield; and *timing,* taking into account the probable trend of interest rates. Then:

- *Deal with a brokerage firm that has a research department that follows this group of securities.* Not every broker is familiar with preferreds, and many will not be able to provide enough pertinent information.
- *Recognize the inherent volatility because of limited marketability.* Preferreds listed on a major

Five Preferred Stocks

COMPANY	PRICE	YIELD
Federal Home Laon Mtg.	$45	4.9%
Fleet Capital Trust	26	7.9
Jersey Central P&L	103	7.6
Kansas City Southern	14	7.3
Ohio Edison	25	7.7

SOURCE: Quotron as of Summer 1999.

stock exchange may drop (when you want to sell) or rise (when you plan to buy) 2 or 3 points the day after the last quoted sale. Preferreds sold over-the-counter (OTC) may fluctuate even more because of their thin markets. As a rule, place your orders at a set price or within narrow limits.

☑ *HINT: Ask your broker about adjustable-rate preferreds. The quarterly dividend fluctuates with interest rates and is tied to a formula based on Treasury bills or other money market rates.*

☑ *HINT: Participating preferreds entitle shareholders to a portion of the company's profits. In nonparticipating preferreds, shareholders are limited to the stipulated dividend.*

Quality

Choose preferred stocks rated BBB or higher by Standard & Poor's or Baa or higher by Moody's if you are conservative. But if you are willing to take greater risks, you can boost your income by buying BB-rated preferreds.

Usually, but not always, the higher rating will be given to companies with modest debt. Since bond interest must be paid before dividends, the lower the debt ratio, the safer the preferred stock. For example, look for utilities with balanced debt and then check the preferred stocks. Buy several different preferreds, so you can benefit from diversification.

Call Provision

This provision allows the company to redeem or call in the shares of a preferred, usually at a few points above par (face value). When the original issue carries a high yield—say, over 10%—the company may find it worthwhile to retire some shares (1) when it can float new debt or issue preferred stock at a lower rate, say, 8%, or (2) when corporate surplus becomes substantial. In both cases, such a prospect may boost the price of the preferred by a point or two.

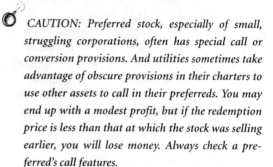 *CAUTION: Preferred stock, especially of small, struggling corporations, often has special call or conversion provisions. And utilities sometimes take advantage of obscure provisions in their charters to use other assets to call in their preferreds. You may end up with a modest profit, but if the redemption price is less than that at which the stock was selling earlier, you will lose money. Always check a preferred's call features.*

Sinking Fund

Corporations use sinking funds to accumulate money on a regular basis in order to redeem the corporation's bonds or preferred stocks from time to time so that the entire issue is retired before the stated maturity date. For example, starting five years after the original sale, a company might buy back 5% of the stock annually for 20 years. The yields of such preferreds will usually be slightly less than those for which there is no such provision.

Preferred Stock

PROS

↑ Generally pays higher dividends than common

↑ Receive your dividend before common stockholders

↑ Dividends generally cumulative; if dividend skipped, made up in future

↑ Know what your dividend income is

↑ Possibility of capital gain in price of stock

CONS

↓ If company's earnings rise, you don't share in increases unless it is a participating preferred

↓ Dividend fixed, with few exceptions

↓ Call provisions allow company to redeem your stock at stated price

↓ No protection against inflation

Stocks the Analysts Don't Follow

Small cap issues that are not big on Wall Street and not widely held by institutions—i.e., neglected stocks—sometimes turn out to be big winners. Stocks are overlooked because they are small, don't promote themselves, don't fit into a simple category . . . or they could be just plain poor investments.

Here are ten that are followed by five or fewer analysts that also are ranked B or above for quality by Standard & Poor's.

- Aaron Rents
- American Precision Ind.
- Catalina Marketing
- Deckers Outdoor
- Eaton Vance
- First Empire State
- Jones Apparel
- Trimble Navigation
- Vulcan Materials
- Watkins-Johnson

(As of Summer 1999.)

☑ *IF YOU DARE: Look for a company that has omitted dividend payouts for several years. It will probably be selling at a discount. Should earnings recover, it will pay off all accumulated dividends, and the price of the stock is likely to rise.*

☑ *HINT: Buy participating preferreds to ensure receiving a percentage of any exceptional profit gain as, for example, if the corporation sells a subsidiary and has excess profits for the year.*

Continual Dividends

Smart investors may get as many as 12 dividends a year by rolling over preferred stocks. By buying shares just before the dividend date, they get the full payout. They sell the next day and buy another preferred with an upcoming dividend payment date. Because of the commission costs and need for constant checking, this technique is difficult for amateurs. Yet it can work well when it involves 500 shares or more and you work with a discount broker.

Timing is the key. After the payout date, the price of the preferred may drop almost as much as the value of the dividend. A 12% preferred thus might trade at $100 before the dividend date and drop back to just over $97 the next day. If you sell, you take a small loss. If you wait a week or so and are lucky in a strong market, you may be able to sell at 100. If you have the time, money, and a feel for this type of trading, you could make substantial profits.

☑ *HINT: You can also own preferreds through the Lindner Dividend Fund (800–995–7777), which has a mixture of preferreds and utilities. This no-load fund had a total return for the first nine months of 1999 of 3.84%, but the yield alone was 6.42%.*

FOR FURTHER INFORMATION

General Guides

Louis Engel and Brendon Boyd, *How to Buy Stocks* (Boston: Little, Brown & Co., 1982; paperback 1994).

Lawrence J. Gitman and Michael D. Joehnk, *Fundamentals of Investing* (New York: HarperCollins, 1990).

Benjamin Graham and David L. Dodd, *Security Analysis*, 5th ed. (New York: McGraw-Hill, 1988)(updated by S. Cotile).

Thomas O'Hara, *Taking Control of Your Financial Future: Making Smart Investment Decisions with Stocks and Bonds* (Homewood, IL.: Dow Jones–Irwin, 1995).

Peter Lynch, *Beating the Street* (New York: Fireside, 1994).

Andrew Tobias, *The Only Investment Guide You'll Ever Need* (New York: Harvest Books, 1999).

Mary Buffett, *Buffettology: The Previously Unexplained Techniques That Have Made Warren Buffett the World's Most Famous Investor* (New York: Scribner, 1997).

Michael B. Lehman, *The Dow Jones–Irwin Guide to Using the Wall Street Journal* (Homewood, IL.: Dow Jones–Irwin, 1990).

Peter Lynch, *Learn to Earn: A Beginners Guide to the Basics of Investing and Business* (New York: Fireside, 1996).

Dividend Reinvestment Guides

Directory of Companies Offering Dividend Reinvestment Plans (Evergreen Enterprises, Box 763, Laurel, MD 20725; $34.95 +$3 shipping; 301–549–3939).

The Drip Investor (newsletter) (NorthStar Financial, Inc.; 7412 Calumet Avenue; Hammond, IN 46324; 219–931–6480; Charles Carlson, editor; monthly; $79/year).

15

Nasdaq, Over-the-Counter, and Penny Stocks

A good investment is not always an obvious one, dancing in the limelight of the New York or American stock exchanges or highly touted by Wall Streeters.

Even the venerable Benjamin Graham, father of security analysis, subscribed to the look-for-hidden-companies strategy. He advised investors to consider making one out of three securities in their portfolios a stock trading elsewhere—in the Nasdaq market, over-the-counter, or on regional exchanges.

And he was right. Nasdaq, which stands for National Association of Securities Dealers Automated Quotations, is the fastest-growing stock market in the United States. Stocks that trade on Nasdaq are listed separately in the financial pages under the heading Nasdaq National Market Issues.

THE NASDAQ STOCK MARKET

Nasdaq is operated by the Nasdaq Stock Market, Inc., a wholly owned subsidiary of the National Association of Securities Dealers, Inc. This nonprofit association, known as NASD, was created in 1939 by amendments to the Securities Exchange Act of 1934. This market is distinctly separate from the over-the-counter (OTC) market, described below, although both are regulated by the NASD.

Unlike the New York and American stock exchanges, Nasdaq does not have a centralized trading floor. Instead it is an electronic market, and in fact was the world's first electronic stock market when it was created in 1971.

Today, with millions of investors around the world, Nasdaq has more companies listed than any other market—nearly 5,500. Of these, many are leaders in the fields of computers, data processing, biotechnology, and financial services.

Interestingly, approximately 725 of the companies that trade on Nasdaq (See: box on page 160) meet the more stringent financial requirements for listing on the New York Stock Exchange. Yet they have chosen Nasdaq, largely because of its competitive market-maker system—a system of multiple trading by many dealers rather than the centralized approach of the New York Stock Exchange, where all trading in a stock must go through the exchange specialist in that stock.

Another important role Nasdaq plays is that of listing many new public companies. Consistently, many of the fastest growing companies in the United States are listed on Nasdaq.

Nasdaq lists more:

- Companies than any other U.S. stock market
- Foreign-based issues than the New York and American stock exchanges combined
- Initial public offerings (IPOs) than any other U.S. stock market

How Nasdaq Is Different

There are two ways in which Nasdaq differs from the traditional stock exchanges: (1) its use of competing market makers; and (2) its advanced technology.

Each company that lists its shares on Nasdaq has several competing securities firms that make the market in its stock. In fact, a minimum of two market makers is required for a company to be listed on Nasdaq. There are some 530 of these multiple dealers, including such firms as Merrill Lynch, Morgan Stanley, Goldman Sachs, PaineWebber, etc., all aggressively competing with one another for investor orders by buying and selling for their own accounts. The typical Nasdaq stock has 11 market makers, although some of the most popular stocks have 40 or more.

These market makers are required to quote a firm bid and ask price. (The bid is the price at which a market maker is willing to buy; the ask is the price at which he/she is willing to sell.)

These trades take place over Nasdaq's electronic network of terminals or screen-based workstations. If, for example, you place an order with your broker to buy 100 shares of Biogen, your broker will route that order to the firm's trading room. If your brokerage firm makes a market in Biogen, it will execute the order internally at a price equal to or better than the best price being quoted in Nasdaq by all of the competing market makers.

If your firm is not a maker in Biogen, it will buy shares from a market maker at another firm. (A market maker is to Nasdaq what a specialist is on the exchanges; a specialist is a member of a stock exchange who maintains a fair and orderly market in one or more securities.)

Your trade and all other Nasdaq trades can be viewed by brokers and investors around the world—there are some 250,000 terminals receiving Nasdaq trading information in 55 countries.

QUALIFYING FOR A NASDAQ LISTING

Every company listing its shares on a U.S. stock market must register them with the SEC and then must provide the SEC with periodic reports on its financial condition. U.S. companies file these reports quarterly, while foreign companies file twice a year. These reports are available to the public.

Nasdaq has two tiers: the Nasdaq National Market and the Nasdaq Small-Cap Market. Listing standards are different for each. The Nasdaq National lists more than 4,400 securities while the Nasdaq Small-Cap lists approximately 1,800.

Nasdaq's requirements are less difficult to meet than those of the NYSE and AMEX, and therefore, it encourages smaller companies to go public.

☑ HINT: *For specific listing requirements, get a copy of the free brochure,* **Nasdaq Backgrounder.**

THE NASDAQ COMPOSITE INDEX

This measures the market value of all domestic and foreign common stocks listed on the Nasdaq, more than 5,500 companies.

THE NASDAQ–100 INDEX

This index, which is market-value weighted, measures the price performance of 100 of the largest nonfinancial companies listed on the Nasdaq National Market. Launched in 1985 with a base value of 250.

THE NASDAQ FINANCIAL 100 INDEX

Consists of 100 of the largest financial organizations listed on the Nasdaq national market.

THE NASDAQ–100 SHARES

In March, the Nasdaq-Amex market introduced a new product that trades on the American Stock Exchange and is very similar to Spiders (**see:** Chapter 24). It is called Nasdaq–100 Shares and is an index-tracking stock designed to replicate the performance of the Nasdaq–100 Index, which includes 100 of the largest nonfinancial U.S. and non-U.S. companies listed on the National Market tier of the Nasdaq Stock Market.

The symbol is QQQ. It reflects the collective performance of all the big tech stocks traded on Nasdaq: Microsoft, Intel, Cisco Systems, MCI WorldCom, Dell, Oracle, etc. Some 75% of the index's weighting is in technology; other components include Starbucks, Northwest Airlines, Costco, and Staples.

The Nasdaq–100 Shares has a very low expense ratio: 0.18%.

THE OTC MARKET

The term over-the-counter stems from the days when securities were sold over the counter in banks and stores, right along with money orders and dry goods. Today it refers to a security not listed and traded on an organized exchange. Over-the-counter companies tend to be smaller, newer, and less well known than those trading on Nasdaq or on the New York and American exchanges.

Over-the-counter (OTC) stocks are listed in a publication known as the Pink Sheets (named for its color) and on the OTC Bulletin Board, an electronic version of the Pink Sheets. The Pink Sheets, which is published daily by the National Quotation Bureau, gives the bid and asked prices for 13,000 OTC stocks as well as listing who makes a market in the stock. (The National Quotation Bureau is a subsidiary of the Commerce Clearing House, a financial publishing company.) For the most part, these stocks are thinly traded and not carried in the newspaper's daily OTC listing. Corporate bonds are listed separately on the Yellow Sheets.

☑ *HINT: For information about the OTC Bulletin Board call: 202–728–8477.*

💣 *CAUTION: Keep in mind the two key problems with pink-sheet stocks: (1) The spreads between the bid and asked can be significant on thinly traded shares, and (2) illiquidity is common.*

Actively Traded Nasdaq Stocks for 2000

■ **United States**
Amazon.com
Bed Bath & Beyond
Cisco Systems
Costco
Dell Computer
Intuit Inc.
McCormick & Co.
Microsoft
Nordstrom
Northwest Airlines
Paychex, Inc.
Rexaall Sundown
USA Networks
Yahoo! Inc.

■ **Foreign**
Akzo (Netherlands)
Cadbury Schweppes (UK)
ECI Telecom (Sweden)
Fuji (Japan)
Newbridge Networks (Canada)
Pacific Dunlop (Australia)
Reuters (UK)
Scitex (Isreal)
Teva Pharnaceutical (Israel)
Toyota (Japan)
Waterford Wedgwood (Ireland)

DUNNAN'S SIX GUIDELINES FOR PICKING TOP NASDAQ & OTC STOCKS

■ Start in your own backyard. Do research on companies in your region. Check with a local stockbroker for ideas. Read annual reports, and visit the company personally.

■ Buy only companies with established earnings growth and, if possible, low debt. Ideally the assets-to-current liabilities ratio should be 2:1.

> ## Over-the-Counter Stocks
>
> ### PROS
> ↑ In an OTC mutual fund, professional management, diversification, liquidity, possibility of switching into other funds within the same family
> ↑ Prices often low
> ↑ Potential capital appreciation
>
> ### CONS
> ↓ May be thinly traded
> ↓ Can be difficult to sell when negative news appears
> ↓ Research difficult to find, sometimes nonexistent
> ↓ Losses can be large
> ↓ Value of fund shares can decline

- Study wide economic and industrial trends, and select companies that have a timely product or service.
- Find companies that have a market niche.
- Allow two to ten months for price and/or earnings movement.
- Avoid penny stocks (stocks that sell for less than 50¢); the bid/asked price spread is often over 25%.

USING THE KEY INDICATORS TO PICK THE BEST STOCKS

If and when you believe the big stocks are overpriced, it's time to move some of your portfolio into smaller issues. To help you time your move, watch these key indicators:

- *Nasdaq Composite Index.* Listed in the major newspapers, its direction and progress can be compared with those of other major indexes. If its trend is up, the environment is favorable.
- *OTC volume.* Tends to verify the direction, up or down, of a market or individual issue. If the market rises on low volume, for example, generally the rise will be short.

- *New highs and lows.* A number of new highs over new lows is a positive buy sign.
- *Block trading.* When trades of 10,000 shares or more take place, it probably signals institutional participation and future interest in the stock.
- *S&P OTC 250 index.* Like the Nasdaq index, Standard & Poor's indicates the overall direction of secondary issues. It is especially valuable to compare it to the S&P 500.
- *Shadow stock index.* In January 1986, the American Association of Individual Investors, a nonprofit educational organization, introduced this index, which covers less well-known stocks. The market value of a company's outstanding stock must fall between $20 million and $100 million to qualify for inclusion. This means that all companies in the shadow stock index have some sort of track record.

SPECIAL NASDAQ TERMS

The National Association of Securities Dealers and Nasdaq use several unique terms in daily trading. Here are some you should know if you trade Nasdaq-listed securities.

- *Affirmative obligations.* Requirements imposed on Nasdaq market makers by the NASD, including quoting firm prices and making two-sided markets on a continuous basis.
- *Aftermarket.* Trading activity in a security immediately following its initial offering to the public.
- *Best-execution requirement.* An NASD rule requiring member firms to execute customer orders at the best prices available.
- *Broker/dealer.* A firm that buys and sells securities as an agent for public customers (brokers) and as a principal for its own account and risk.

- *Capital commitment.* The monies invested by market makers in carrying inventories of the stocks in which they make markets. More than 470 Nasdaq market makers carry inventories valued at some $1 billion.
- *Firm quotation.* The NASD requirement that a market maker receiving an order from another broker/dealer execute it at its displayed Nasdaq price.
- *Last-sale reporting.* Notification by a market maker to the Nasdaq Stock Market of the price and number of shares involved in a transaction in a Nasdaq security. The notification must be made within 90 seconds of the execution of an order.
- *Market makers.* Dealers that buy and sell securities at publicly quoted prices for their own account and risk. Market makers are subject to NASD and SEC rules.
- *Nasdaq Composite Index.* The market-value, weighted measure of the price performance of Nasdaq National Market securities, except warrants, and all Nasdaq Small-Cap Market domestic common stock. The Index is one of the broadest-based and among the most widely followed major market indexes.
- *Nasdaq Small-Cap Market Securities.* The smaller capitalization tier of the Nasdaq Stock Market. Requirements for listing in this market are significantly lower than those for Nasdaq National Market companies.
- *NASD.* The National Association of Securities Dealers, Inc., is the largest self-regulatory organization for the securities industry in the United States. It is responsible for the operation and regulation of Nasdaq and the over-the-counter securities markets. It operates under the 1938 Maloney Act Amendment to the Securities and Exchange Act of 1934.
- *OTC Bulletin Board.* An electronic, screen-based market for small, developing companies that are not eligible for listing on Nasdaq. Operated and regulated by the NASD, this market also includes the American Depository Receipts (ADRs) of foreign companies, some of which are of considerable size.
- *Over-the-counter securities.* OTC securities are those not listed on Nasdaq or any of the other exchanges, including the New York, American, and regional exchanges.
- *Self-regulatory organization.* An entity, such as the NASD, responsible for regulating its members through enforcement of rules and relations governing its members.
- *Small-order execution system.* The SOES is an automatic trade/execution system for customer agency orders of up to 1,000 shares. It guarantees the best bid or asked price available in Nasdaq at the time the order is entered. SOES participation is mandatory for market makers in Nasdaq National Market securities.
- *Third market.* The buying and selling of exchange-listed securities in a dealer market. The Nasdaq system facilities are used by third-market firms to quote and execute trades in this market.
- *Two-sided market.* The obligation imposed by NASD regulations that Nasdaq market makers quote both a bid and ask price for each security in which they make a market and to execute orders at those prices.

PENNY STOCKS

Penny stocks may sound like a nice, inexpensive way to play the market. Not so. They are one of the riskiest areas of investing despite the fact that the word "penny" implies cheap.

The Skinny on Pennies

The official definition of a penny stock is a "low-priced speculative stock." Originally, they were stocks that sold for less than $1 per share, but inflation has left its mark and the phrase now refers to speculative stocks selling for up to $5 or $10 a share.

The Securities Division of the State of Missouri, which has been vigilant about providing updated information in order to protect the average investor from the high risk and fraud found in this type of investment, defines a penny stock as one that trades at or under $5/share and trades over-the-counter in the Pink Sheets.

It also defines penny stocks as those issued by companies that have less than $4 million in net tangible assets and do not have a "significant operating history." That means if a company has real assets (equipment and inventory) and is engaged in a real business, such as manufacturing, it is not considered a penny stock even though its shares are low in price.

The Pink Sheets

These long, narrow sheets of pink paper, updated regularly, list the over-the-counter stocks not routinely traded. They contain bid and asked prices as well as the names of market makers for these stocks.

That means you will have to trade penny stocks through a stockbroker who has access to the Pink Sheets (most do) and who in turn is willing to do business with one of the market makers listed for your stock.

This is where a second problem can emerge— the first being the highly speculative nature of penny stocks. If there are only one or two market makers for a stock, there can be wide markups and even price manipulation.

The Good and the Bad Penny

Yet, despite all the negative press, the real problems, and the millions of dollars lost in penny stocks year after year, there are real honest companies trading in the Pink Sheets at low prices. Struggling young companies, for example.

Richard Maturi, an expert on penny stocks, says that natural resource firms, such as gold mining and oil exploration companies, have traditionally used penny stocks to raise capital. High-tech and biotech companies occasionally are first issued as penny stocks.

If you decide to go ahead with this type of investment, you absolutely must read about the company first and you must use a broker who knows the business and will get written information on the company for you.

The Securities and Exchange Commission has issued these warning signs of penny stock fraud:

1. An unsolicited phone call, promising quick profits with little or no risk; and
2. High-pressure sales tactics, referring to such things as "insider information" or a "unique opportunity."

If you come upon a penny stock you think is legit, get written information and find out how long the company has been in business. If you cannot get both, don't invest.

FOR FURTHER INFORMATION

Books

The 1999 Nasdaq Company Fact Book & Directory
NASD
Media Source
Box 9403
Gaithersburg, MD 20898
202–728–8000
Lists all Nasdaq stocks with their symbols, addresses, and telephone numbers; $24.95.

Magazines

Equities
160 Madison Avenue
New York, NY 10016
212–213–1300

Contains studies of individual stocks; monthly; $21 for seven issues/year.

Newsletters

Growth Stock Outlook
4405 East-West Highway
Bethesda, MD 20814
301–654–5205
Published by Charles Allmon; covers stocks with potential appreciation; twice monthly; $235 per year; three-month trial, $75.

Value Line OTC Special Situations
220 East 42 Street
New York, NY 10017
800–634–3583

Very reliable coverage of OTC and small-cap stocks; bimonthly; $495 per year; trial: $39 (6 issues).

On-Line Information

Securities & Exchange Commission
website: www.sec.gov
For free copies of:
Invest Wisely, which covers picking a broker, picking investments, and avoiding fraud.

16

Utilities

*I*nvestors have always been attracted to utility stocks for their traditionally high yields. And with good reason—you can get an idea of just how high the yields are by checking the boxes on the following pages. Yet high yields come with a downside: Utility stocks are extremely sensitive to interest rates and behave like bonds. When interest rates rise, share prices head down. It could happen again.

Nevertheless, every portfolio should hold some stocks with dependable dividend yields. As we go to press, the composite yield on utility stocks is 5.92% versus 1.25% for the S&P 500.

COMPETITION FUELS THE SCENE

The National Energy Policy Act passed in October 1992 requires power companies to give independent power producers access to their transmission lines. This means that industrial customers can shop around for the best price on power and then have the local utility company deliver it to their factories and office buildings.

The act has also given large industrial customers the right to bypass their local utility company and purchase power directly from remote, lower-cost utilities. Within the industry, this is known as "retail wheeling."

Competition and deregulation have made selecting utility stocks more complicated.

DIVERSIFICATION

A key way utilities are reacting to the end of their monopolistic way of life is with diversification—into cogeneration projects, in this country as well as into utility operations in foreign countries. Successful moves have been made into the U.K., Latin America, Asia, and the Pacific Rim.

As foreign countries gain economic strength, especially the third world economies, demand for power will increase at a rapid rate. U.S. utility companies with an overseas presence will certainly stand to benefit. *NOTE:* Utility earnings derived from foreign countries are not subject to a regulatory cap.

INVESTING TIPS

Before automatically buying a utility stock, here's what you need to know:

- The utility business continues to face competition.
- Only companies that run efficient operations will remain successful in terms of investments.
- Companies that invest in rapidly growing foreign economies are likely to be among the most profitable.
- Utility stocks can no longer be held forever; the scene is continually changing, and utilities,

Nine Utilities with Secure Dividends

COMPANY	SYMBOL	YIELD
Rochester G&E	RGS	6.7%
American Electric Power	AEP	6.5
Kansas City P&L	KLT	6.4
TECO Energy	TE	6.3
New Century Energies	NEE	6.2
Wisconsin Energy	WEC	6.0
Dominion Resources	D	5.9
Minnesota Power	MPL	5.8
PacificCorp	PPW	5.7

SOURCE: Quotron, Fall 1999.

like any other stock, must be watched on a regular basis.

■ Pick utility companies with strong, savvy management that own a large number of shares and are able to make decisions in this increasingly complicated environment.

GUIDELINES FOR PICKING UTILITY STOCKS

For decades, utility stocks moved pretty much as a group, but today the difference between the best and the poorest has widened, and skepticism should be your guiding principle. When making a utility selection you should ask:

■ How good is management?
■ Is the dividend well covered by earnings?
■ How is management addressing deregulation?
■ Is the company planning to make a move overseas?
■ What is the reserve margin? (Reserve margin is power capacity above peak-load usage; if it is especially high, the company may have unused plants and high costs. The industry-wide average is around 25%.)

Moreover:

■ Don't select a utility stock solely on the basis

of its yield. (A high return often reflects Wall Street uncertainty about the safety of the dividend.)

■ Do select stocks that have expectations for higher earnings and growth rates. (Check write-ups in *Value Line Investment Survey* for up-to-date analysis of this.)

■ If all other things are equal, select a utility that has a dividend reinvestment plan. You will save on commissions.

■ Diversify. Buy utilities from several states, to avoid any one state's unfavorable regulatory policies.

You should also study a utility's:

■ *Bond rating,* as determined by Standard & Poor's or Moody's. A company's bond rating is a realistic measure of the company's financial strength.

■ *Regulatory climate.* The attitude of state authorities toward permitting the utility to earn an adequate rate of return is an important factor.

■ *Return on equity.* This is that basic standard of quality—the ability of management to make money with your money. It is often a reflection of the state authorities, who may or may not permit an adequate rate of return.

■ *Main fuel.* This is a key criterion for many an-

Utilities for Long-Term Holding

STOCK	SYMBOL	YIELD
Florida Progress	FPC	6.7%
Cinergy Corp.	CIN	5.7
Eastern Utilities	EUA	5.5
Public Service	PEG	5.3
Allegheny Energy	AYE	5.2
Southern Co.	SO	5.2
DPL, Inc.	DPL	4.9
Con Edison	ED	4.8

(As of Fall 1999.)

Four High-Quality Preferred Utility Stocks	
Arizona Public Service	6.9%
Carolina Power	5.8
PECO Energy	8.6
So Carolina E&G	5.8

(As of Fall 1999.)

alysts. Utilities that use water (hydroelectric plants) have no cost worries.

■ *Percentage of stock owned by management.*

■ *The P/E ratio.* As we go to press the price-earnings multiple is appealing: about 30% below the market.

And finally . . .

■ *Consider high quality* preferred utility stocks (**see:** Chapter 14 for information on preferred stocks). But bear in mind that preferred have no possibility of increased dividends, although they do offer high yields, though generally not as high as public utility bonds. Preferreds are a no-brainer way to lock in a high yield when you prefer not to add bonds to your portfolio.

UTILITY MUTUAL FUNDS

If you prefer not to select individual utilities, there are mutual funds that invest in these stocks. The

The Bell Companies

SYMBOL	COMPANY	PRICE	YIELD
T	ATT Corp.	$50	1.7%
AIT	Ameritech	68	1.8
BEL	Bell Atlantic	65	2.3
BLS	BellSouth	48	1.5
SBC	SBC Communications	52	1.8
USW	U.S. West	54	3.9

(As of Fall 1999.)

funds, however, are not all alike. It is imperative that you read each prospectus before investing. Some have a portion of their assets in utility bonds, while others own natural gas and telephone stocks, whose growth potential is greater than that of electric utilities. Some funds invest in foreign utilities and high-yielding equities. Some focus on electric utilities in a certain area.

☑ *HINT: The more diversified the fund's portfolio, the lower its interest rate sensitivity.*

EXAMPLE: The Pittsburgh-based Federated's Utility Fund (800–245–4770) (created by a merger of two of the company's funds in 1996) owns these utility sectors, as of the fall of 1999:

50%	Electrics & Natural gas
34	Telecommunications
12.6	Nonutility
4.2	Cash

Federated has taken the precaution of holding nonutility convertibles that have high yields as a means of cushioning the fund against changing interest rates.

NOTE: You should also be aware that some mutual funds have two types of shares: Class A and Class B. Class A has a front-end load, while Class B usually has a 1% per annum 12b-1 fee to defray marketing expenses and levy a deferred sales charge if you redeem your shares within a certain number of years, often five or six. If you know you're going to hold your shares five or six years, you're better off with the Class A shares, so you can avoid the ongoing 12b-1 charges.

☑ *HINT: If you are retired, you may want a fund that pays out dividends on a monthly basis, or set up your own automatic payout with individual utility stocks. For example, according to the Dow Theory*

Five Utility Mutual Funds

FUND	YIELD OCTOBER 1999	TELEPHONE
Fidelity Utilities Income	4.52%	800–544-8888
Federated Utility Fund	2.52	800–245–4770
Franklin Templeton Fund	4.87	800–342–5236
Vanguard Utilities Income	3.06	800–662–7447

(As of Fall 1999.)

Forecasts, these six, high-quality utility stocks pay out dividends as follows:

Jan, Apr, Jul, Oct:	*Ipalco Enterprises*
	Northern States Power
Feb, May, Aug, Nov:	*TECO Energy*
	WPL Holdings
Mar, Jun, Sept, Dec:	*SIGCPORP*
	Southern Co.

BUYING UTILITY STOCKS DIRECTLY FROM THE COMPANY

A number of utility companies allow customers to buy stock directly in the company, without a broker.

Among those that do are:

- Central Hudson Gas & Electric
- Central Maine Power
- Central Vermont Public Service
- Dominion Resources
- Hawaiian Electric Industries
- Idaho Power
- Minnesota Power
- Nevada Power
- Philadelphia Electric
- San Diego Gas & Electric
- Union Electric

NOTE: Call the investor relations department of your local utility company to see if you can purchase shares directly.

WATER COMPANIES

Telephone and electric companies have always been in the spotlight, hogging center stage in the utilities industry. Yet stocks of public water companies are a good way to tap into the group. These stocks have low institutional ownership and are still reasonably priced.

Consider water companies because they:

- Provide a commodity everyone needs
- Have no competition; there is no alternative to water—except Handiwipes, which pose no great threat
- Have no nuclear exposure

Although there are over 50,000 water companies in the United States serving 240+ million people, most are municipally owned and regulated by city governments. However, about 23,000 systems are investor-owned, and of these, 18 are publicly traded. American Water Works, the largest, serves 1.5 million customers in 21 states; its largest customer is Monsanto. It has one of the best dividend records in the industry—with increases over the past 12 years.

If you decide to invest in a water company, keep in mind that rate increases are determined by area regulatory bodies and that various local situations, including the weather and the economy, have a major effect on earnings. Residential customers dominate the industry, and companies therefore

Leading Water Companies

COMPANY	EXCHANGE: SYMBOL	PRICE	YIELD
American Water Works	NYSE: AWK	$29	2.90%
Connecticut Water	OTC: CTWS	34	3.4
E'Town Corp.	NYSE: ETW	50	4.0
Middlesex Water Corp.	OTC: MSEX	30	4.0
Philadelphia Suburban	NYSE: PSC	25	2.9
American States Water	NYSE: AWR	34	3.7
United Water Resources	NYSE: UWR	33	2.8

(As of Fall 1999.)

tend to benefit from hot weather spells when Americans use more water. Companies must continually meet the water standards set by the Environmental Protection Agency.

The larger, better-known water firms are listed in the table above. You may also want to investigate your local water company—find out if it is publicly traded—but read the last two annual reports and the current quarterlies before purchasing shares.

UTILITY BONDS

Utility bonds are no longer the well-protected investment they were just a few years ago. Mergers and takeovers have come to the utility industry, and only those bonds with AA ratings should be considered during the next couple of years—or at least until the industry settles down and adjusts to deregulation. Check the list below and/or ask your broker for a list of high-rated issues. As we go to press, yields on new bond issues ranged from 4.5% to 6.9%.

Four High-Quality Utility Bonds

- Dayton Power & Light   Aa3
- Duke Power   Aa2
- Florida Power Corp.   Aa3
- Southern Indiana G & E   Aa2

☑ *HINT: Buy only bonds rated A or above, and check the call feature. Most utilities have only five-year call protection, whereas Treasuries are essentially noncallable. Avoid bonds of companies with nuclear or regulatory problems, or that have not cut costs as a way of addressing deregulation.*

CAUTION: Many high-yielding utility bonds have special, early redemption clauses built into their issues. These call provisions permit a utility to buy back its bonds at face value or even a bit higher, but more often than not at prices below the current market. Utility companies are allowed to use these special calls to cut expenses by retiring high-yield or high-coupon bonds.

17

Options

You know by now that over the long term, stocks are one of the best ways to achieve long-term total returns. But, as in life, it's always nice to have options or fall-back positions. So too it is in the market . . . thus, enter financial options.

They can be extremely effective, provided you understand how to use them. In fact, when used correctly, they can actually increase the profit on stocks you already own and/or reduce the potential for losses in a declining market. They also enable you to take advantage of the concept of leverage, for, with a small amount of money, you can control a large investment. You must be disciplined and adept, however, to make options work.

CAUTION: You should also realize that options are derivatives, which means they derive their value from an underlying asset. Those assets can be common stocks or indexes of common stocks.

If the idea of trading in derivatives is nerve-wracking, think of it this way: A novelist sells an option on his book to a Hollywood movie producer. The option gives the producer the right to buy the story for a movie within a specified time, but it does not actually force or oblige the producer to do so.

In exchange for giving Hollywood a crack at his novel, or an option on it, the novelist receives a payment. If the producer likes the story and decides to make a movie before the option expires, the novelist then must sell the screen rights to the producer, at the agreed-upon price. If the producer decides not to go ahead with the project, the novelist keeps the option payment and his novel, and the producer's rights end or expire when the option's time is up.

So, too, it is with Wall Street options.

HINT: Before actually allocating money to trading options, test several hypothetical examples on paper—follow them in the newspaper to see how options really work. Once you have done this learning exercise, you are ready to take the plunge and spend real money. Or, click on: www.cboe.com and go to "The Toolbox" to simulate trades.

Then, talk to your broker. Depending upon the brokerage firm, you may be asked for your net worth statement, or perhaps to open a margin account (**see:** Chapter 26). And remember, to be successful with options, you must be prepared to devote time to watching the calendar.

THE NITTY GRITTY

Options are the contractual right, but not the obligation, to buy or to sell something. A put is the right to sell, whereas a call is the right to buy. In a way, options are a cross between trading in stocks and trading in commodities. They enable you to control a relatively large amount of stock with a relatively small amount of capital for a fixed period of time. To be more specific: An option represents the right, but not the obligation, to buy or sell a specific stock at a specific price, called the strike price for a specified time. You do not need to own the stock to buy an option on it.

If, for example, you believe a stock will go up in price in the future, you can buy a call on it. This enables you to purchase 100 shares near its current price. On the other hand, if you have reason to believe the stock will fall in price, you can buy a put on that stock, which gives you the right to sell 100 shares near its current price. (You may also sell puts and calls.)

How long a time do options run? Most options are available for three-, six-, or nine-month periods, or remaining fractions thereof. (As their expiration date approaches, they may have as little as one or two weeks or days.)

In a small number of stocks, however, there are options that last a year or two years. These long-term options are known as LEAPS, which stands for Long-Term Equity Appreciation Security. All the same rules apply to LEAPS as to regular options, but the premiums you must pay for such extended times are higher. LEAPS are quoted in a separate section of the *Wall Street Journal* and financial press.

HOW OPTIONS WORK

Now let's look at a very simple example of how options work. You bought a three-month call on IBM at $100 when the stock was selling at $90. The option's selling price or premium was $300 (or $3 per share). One month later, IBM's shares move up to $110. You now have two choices (or options, hence the name of this vehicle): (1) You can exercise your option and buy the IBM shares at $100/share; or (2) you can sell your call, which is now worth approximately $1,000, based on the price of IBM plus whatever the option is now worth. (When a stock rises in price,

as in this example, the premium [$3] tends to diminish.)

You may wonder, Why not buy the 100 shares of IBM to begin with? It would have moved from $90 to $110, and you would have had a nice profit. First of all, you would have had to invest much more money—$9,000 rather than just $300. Had the stock dropped in price, you would have lost much more than you would with the option.

Options trade on the Chicago Board of Options Exchange (CBOE), the American Stock Exchange, the Philadelphia Stock Exchange, the Pacific Stock Exchange, and the New York Stock Exchange. You may also buy and sell puts and calls on the major stock market indexes and on foreign currencies.

LEAPS IN DEPTH

This is a leap you may or may not want to take. Here's what it will be like if you do.

Long-Term Equity Anticipation Securities are put and call options that expire in two or three years instead of the conventional eight months for equity options. They are offered on about 100 large-cap stocks and on the S&P 500 and the S&P 100 indexes. About half of them trade on the CBOE; the rest on the AMEX and Pacific stock exchanges.

Since they were introduced in October 1990 by the Chicago Board of Options Exchange, they've been gaining in popularity. Why? Because regular options expire or disappear so fast, yet LEAPS are longer running, with some that expire up to two to three years away. Their long life is an advantage for most traders.

Each LEAPS has puts and calls on the underlying stock with at least three strike prices: in-the-money, at-the-money, and out-of-the money. At their start, the out-of-the-money strikes are approximately 20% to 25% away from the stock's market value. Initial prices tend to be under $10.

Terms Used in Option Trading

Before moving on to some more sophisticated examples and techniques, let's review the terms involved.

- *At-the-money:* when a strike price is exactly the same as the price of the underlying stock
- *Call:* the right, but not the obligation, to buy a stock at a specified price
- *Closing transaction:* buying or selling an option to close a previously held position
- *Covered option:* an option written against shares of a stock you already own. This is the most popular and a fairly conservative option strategy, letting you get a little more value out of your stock. It involves selling a call option on a stock that is already in your portfolio. The investor who buys the call then has the right to buy your shares (called the "underlying stock") at a predetermined strike price. In other words, the investor can "call" the stock away from you at a certain price. The investor will not exercise the call (that is, take possession of the shares), however, unless the stock rises above the option strike price.

  When you sell a covered call option, you collect some income—the premium. If the price of the stock rises a lot, the investor will exercise the option and you then lose your stock and the ability to benefit from any further appreciation above the strike price.

 CAUTION: This strategy works well if the stock price remains unchanged or stays under the strike price, because then the option expires worthless and you've collected the premium plus any dividends

- *Diagonal spread:* buying and selling options at the same time on the same stock, but with different expiration dates and different strike prices
- *Dividends and rights:* as long as you own the stock, you continue to receive the dividends. That's why calls for stocks with high yields sell at lower premiums than those for companies with small payouts.

  A stock dividend or stock split automatically increases the number of shares covered by the option in an exact proportion. If a right is involved (**see:** Chapter 18), its value will be set by the first sale of rights on the day the stock sells ex-rights.
- *Expiration date:* options last three, six, or nine months, then they expire. The expiration date is the third Friday of the month in which it can be exercised.
- *Horizontal spread:* buying and selling options at the same time on a stock with the same strike price, but with differing expiration dates
- *In-the-money:* an option that will make a profit if exercised
- *Married put:* a put on shares that you already own
- *Naked option:* opposite of a covered option; an option written (sold) against shares you do not already own
- *Out-of-the-money option:* an option that will not be profitable to exercise
- *Premium:* an option's selling price. Premiums vary with the price of the underlying stock and its volatility.
- *Put:* the right to sell a stock at a specified price for a specified time
- *Restricted option:* This may occur when the previous day's price closed at less than 50¢ per option and the underlying stock price closed at more than 5 points below its strike price for calls, or more than 5 points above its strike price for puts. Opening transactions (buying or writing calls) are prohibited unless they are covered. Closing transactions (liquidations) are permitted. There are various exceptions, so check with your broker.
- *Spread:* buying and selling options on a stock at the same time in order to lock in a closing transaction and limit the risk involved
- *Strike price:* the price a stock must reach in order for the owner of the option to exercise the option
- *Vertical spread:* buying and selling options on the same security with the same expiration dates, but different strike prices

Let's look at how they work. This example is supplied by Standard & Poor's:

EXAMPLE: You have a gain in stock ABC, selling at $84. You write a LEAPS call expiring in January with a strike price of $95. That means the option is 11 points out of the money or selling above the current market price. The call represents 100 shares, so you wind up with $1,300 for each. The buyer now can buy ABC shares from you at $95/share by January.

Writing this call merely provides a cushion; it does not guarantee a profit. If the stock rises above $95 by the expiration date, the buyer will exercise the option and take your stock. At any price between $95 and $71, you will have a paper gain, because of the $1,300 received for the call. If the stock falls, it can reach $71 before you have a paper loss.

Putting Your Money in Puts

Or you can buy a LEAPS put.

EXAMPLE: Let's say you bought AT&T stock at $38 3/4. It's now March, and the stock is at $58 3/4. You could buy a January put with a price strike of 60 for 5. Owning the put gives you the right to sell the stock at 60, which guarantees you an out price of at least $55. If AT&T goes to $61, the put goes to zero, but you can then sell your shares for a put price of $56. In any case, you will always get at least $55, which in this example would lock in 16 1/4 points or 81% of your $20 paper profit.

See: For Further Information at the end of this chapter for useful sources of material on LEAPS.

HOW PREMIUMS WORK

The cost of the option is quoted in multiples of 1/16 for options priced below $3, 1/8 for those priced higher. To determine the percentage of premium, divide the current value of the stock into the quoted price of the option. When there's a difference between the exercise price of the option and the quoted price of the stock, add or subtract the spread.

Relative Premiums

As a Percent of Price of Underlying Common Stock When Common Is at Exercise Price

MONTHS TO EXPIRATION	LOW	AVERAGE	HIGH
1	1.8\–2.6	3.5\–4.4	5.2\–6.1
2	2.6\–3.9	5.2\–6.6	7.8\–9.2
3	3.3\–5.0	6.7\–8.3	10.0\–11.7
4	3.9\–5.9	7.9\–9.8	11.8\–13.8
5	4.5\–6.8	9.0\–11.2	13.5\–15.8
6	5.0\–7.5	10.0\–12.5	15.0\–17.5
7	5.5\–8.2	10.9\–13.7	16.4\–19.2
8	5.9\–8.9	11.8\–14.8	17.7\–20.6
9	6.4\–9.5	12.7\–15.9	19.0\–22.2

Here's how options were quoted in the financial pages when EFG stock was at 32 3/8 (see the table on page 175):

EXAMPLE: The April 30 call prices ranged from a high of 4 3/4 ($475) to a low of 2 3/4 ($275), and a closing price of 3 1/8 ($312.50) for a net change from the previous week of 1/8 ($12.50). There were 1,317 sales of contracts for 100 shares each.

The second line lists the action with April 30 puts: a high of 9/16 ($56.25), a low of 1/4 ($25), and a closing price of 3/8 ($37.50). For the week, the net change was 1/16 ($6.25). There were 996 contracts traded.

Traders looking for quick profits were pessimistic, as shown by the heavy volume in puts: 1,422 contracts for the April 35s and 2,219 for the April 40s. But there were fairly sharp differences of opinion, as the April 35 puts were up 5/16 and the April 40s up 3/8.

Investors were more optimistic and appeared to believe that EFG stock was ready for an upswing: April 40 calls, due in a few weeks, were quoted at 1/8, whereas the farther-out October 40s were quoted at 1 5/8. Much of the spread, of course, was due to the time factor.

The prices of the options reflect temporary hopes and fears, but over a month or two they will tend to move with the underlying stock. But do not rely solely on this type of projection: Near the expiration date, the prices of options move sharply.

One key factor to keep in mind is that the premium at the outset reflects the time factor. This will fall rapidly as the expiration date nears. In the last three months of a call, the premium can be cut in half because of the dwindling time.

WRITING CALLS

When you write or sell calls, you start off with an immediate, sure, limited profit rather than an uncertain, potentially greater gain, which is the case for puts. The most you can make is the premium you receive, even if the price of the stock soars. If you write calls on stock you own, any loss of the value of the stock will be reduced by the amount of the premium. Writing covered calls (on stock you own) is a conservative use of options. You have these choices:

On-the-Money Calls

These are written at an exercise price that is at or close to the current price of the stock.

EXAMPLE: In December, Investor One buys 100 shares of Company A at 40 and sells a July call, at the strike price of 40, for 3 ($300). He realizes that A's stock may move above 43 in the next seven months, but is willing to accept the $3 per share income.

Investor Two is the purchaser of the call. He acquires the right to buy the stock at 40 at any time before the expiration date at the end of July. He anticipates that A's stock will move up well above 43.

Investor One will not sustain a dollar loss until the price of A goes below 37. He will probably keep the stock until its price goes above 43. At this price, the profit meter starts ticking for Investor Two, so let's see what happens if company A's stock jumps to 50. At any time before late July, Investor Two can exercise his option and pay $4,000 for stock now

worth $5,000. After deducting about $400 (the $300 premium plus commissions), he will have a net profit of about $600, thus doubling his risk capital.

Investor Two will sell the call at $2 and lose $1 per call. Investor One will end up with about $375: the $300 premium plus two dividends of $50 each minus the $25 commission for the sale of the call.

In-the-Money Calls

In-the-money calls are those where the exercise price is below the price of the underlying stock. This is a more aggressive technique that requires close attention but can result in excellent profits.

EXAMPLE: In January, Investor A buys 300 shares of Glamor Electronics Co. (GEC) at 105 ($31,500) and sells three June 100 calls at 8 each ($2,400). If GEC stock drops below 100, she keeps the premiums and the stock. If it goes to 110, she can buy back the calls at, say, 11, $1,100 ($3,300 total), to set up a loss of $900.

Deep-in-the-Money Calls

These are calls that are sold at strike prices far below the current quotation of the stock—8 to 20 points below. Writing them is best when the investor is dealing in large blocks of stock because of the almost certain commissions that have to be paid when the underlying stock is called. With this approach, the best selection is a stable, high-dividend stock. Your returns may be limited, but they are likely to be sure.

The technique used by professionals is called using leverage: When the exercise price of the call is below that of the current value of the stock, both securities tend to move in unison. Because the options involve a smaller investment, there's a higher percentage of return and, in a down market, more protection against loss.

EXAMPLE: Company XYZ is selling at $97\frac{5}{8}$. The call price at 70 two months hence is 28, so the

How Options Are Quoted

NAME, EXPIRATION DATE, AND PRICE	SALES	HIGH	WEEK'S LOW	LAST	NET CHG.
EFG Apr30	1,317	$4^3/_4$	$2^3/_4$	$3^1/_8$	$-^1/_8$
EFG Apr30 p	996	$^9/_{16}$	$^1/_4$	$^3/_8$	$-^1/_{16}$
EFG Apr35	3,872	$1^1/_4$	$^3/_8$	$^1/_2$	$-^3/_{16}$
EFG Apr35 p	1,422	$3^1/_8$	$1^5/_8$	$2^{15}/_{16}$	$+^5/_{16}$
EFG Apr40	1,526	$^3/_{16}$	$^1/_{16}$	$^1/_8$	$-^1/_{16}$
EFG Apr40 p	2,219	$7^7/_8$	$5^7/_8$	$7^7/_8$	$+^3/_8$
EFG Jul30	426	6	$4^1/_2$	$4^1/_2$	$-^1/_2$
EFG Jul30 p	805	$1^3/_8$	$^7/_8$	$1^3/_8$	$+^1/_8$
EFG Jul35	1,084	3	2	$3^1/_{16}$	$-^3/_{16}$
EFG Jul35 p	870	$3^7/_8$	$2^3/_4$	$3^7/_8$	$+^1/_4$
EFG Jul40	1,145	$1^1/_8$	$^3/_4$	$^3/_4$	$-^1/_8$
EFG Jul40 p	523	$7^3/_4$	$6^1/_8$	$7^3/_4$	$+^3/_8$
EFG Oct35	346	$4^3/_8$	$3^1/_8$	$3^1/_4$	$-^1/_4$
EFG Oct35 p	261	$4^3/_8$	$3^1/_2$	$4^3/_8$	$+^3/_8$
EFG Oct40	137	$2^1/_4$	$1^5/_8$	$1^5/_8$	$-^1/_4$
EFG Oct40 p	326	$7^7/_8$	$6^1/_2$	$7^3/_4$	$+^1/_4$

Stock price: $32^3/_8$. Table does not show open interest because of space limitations.

equivalent price is 98. If XYZ goes to 105, the call will keep pace and be worth 35.

If you bought 100 shares of the stock, the total cost would be about $9,800. Your ultimate profit would be about $700, close to a 7.1% return. If you bought one option, your cost would be $2,800 and you would have the same $700 profit. Your return would be about 25%.

NOTE: All too often, this is more theory than practice. When an option is popular, it may trade on its own and not move up or down with the price of the stock. This separate value will shift only when the expiration date is near.

A variation of this use of deep-in-the-money calls is to create cost by basing the return on the total income received from premiums plus dividends.

EXAMPLE: In January, one professional money manager seeking extra income for his fund bought 1,000 shares of Wellknown Chemical at $39^1/_2$. He then sold April 35 options for $6^7/_8$ each, thereby reducing the price per share to $32^5/_8$. He could count on a 45¢-per-share dividend before the exercise date.

When the call is exercised at $35 per share, the profit on the $32.625 investment will be $2.375 plus the 45¢ dividend, or $2.825 for a return of 8.66% in a four-month period.

Out-of-the-Money Calls

This is when the strike price is above the market price of the underlying stock for a call or the strike price is below the market price of the underlying stock of a put.

WRITING NAKED CALLS

Some calls are sold by speculators or investors who do not own the underlying stock. This is referred to as writing a naked call. The writer is betting that the stock will either remain at its current price or decline. He receives a premium, which he pockets if the stock does not rise above the call price. But if it does, he then must buy back his call at a loss.

☑ *HINT: Don't get involved unless you maintain a substantial margin account, have considerable experience, and feel confident that the price of a stock will stay flat or decline. It's risky, because if the stock hits the strike price before or at the exercise date, you are obligated to deliver the shares you do not own.*

You can, of course, cover your position by buying calls, but if the stock price soars, the loss can be substantial. At best, your premium income will be reduced.

One technique that works well is to write two out-of-the-money calls for every 100 shares you own. This gives you double premiums. Do not go too far out, because a lot can happen in a few months.

EXAMPLE: You own 300 shares of Company XYZ at 32. The 35 call, due in four months, is 3, but you are not convinced that the market, or the stock, will rise soon. You sell six calls, pocket $1,800 (less commissions), and hope that the stock stays under 35. If it moves to 36, you can buy back three calls for, say, 1½ ($450) and let the stock go. But if the stock jumps to 40, you're in deep trouble.

BUYING CALLS

Investors buy calls in anticipation of an increase in the price of the underlying stock. If that happens, the call may also rise in price, and you can sell at a profit. Buying calls means you can invest a fraction of the cost of the stock and obtain greater leverage. You also limit your risk, because the most you can lose is the cost of the option.

The basic problem with buying options is that calls are wasting assets. At expiration date, their values can decline to zero if the stock price

---

Rules for Writing Options

- Define your goal.
- Work on a programmed basis.
- Concentrate on stocks that you would like to own.
- Set a target rate of return.
- Buy the stock first.
- Write long-term calls.
- Calculate your net return.
- Keep your capital fully employed.
- Be persistent.
- Watch the timing.
- Protect your capital.
- Use margin to boost profits.
- Watch the record date of high-dividend stocks.
- Keep a separate bookkeeping system.

---

moves opposite to your expectations or stays fairly stable.

EXAMPLE: On February 15, ABC's common is selling at $40 per share. An October 40 call can be purchased for $500 (100 shares at $5 per share). On April 15, ABC is selling at $46 per share and the October 40 call is trading at a value of $750. The investor, anticipating an increase in the value of ABC, had purchased the call for $500 and sold it for $750, realizing a $250 profit.

Here are the ways leverage works in this situation:

In this example, the call buyer can lose no more than the $500 he paid for the October 40 call, regardless of any decline in the stock, but he can lose the entire $500 if he is wrong. He may be able to resell his option, however, in time to recover some of his cost. Keep in mind that if he had purchased the stock itself for $4,000 and it had gone down in price, he would have lost more than $500 if he had sold. If he decided to hold the stock and it appreciated, he would have another opportunity to make a profit.

A put buyer does not have to resell a profitable call, but can instead exercise it and take delivery of the underlying stock. He can then sell the stock for a gain or hold it for long-term appreciation.

☑ *IF YOU DARE: In an up market, buy calls on up stocks on either of these terms:*

- *Long-term, out-of-the-money options at a low premium, typically 1 or less. By diversifying with four or five promising situations, you may be lucky enough to hit it big with one and make enough to offset the small losses on the others.*
- *Short- or intermediate-term in-the-money or close-to-the-money options of volatile stocks: two months to expiration date, a stock within 5% of the strike price, and a low time premium. If the price of the premium doubles, sell half your holdings.*

Advice from the experts: Never pay a premium of more than 3 for a call on a stock selling under 50, or more than 5 for one trading over 60. Both prices should include commissions.

☑ *HINT: The strike price of the option and the market price of the stock should change by about half as many points as the change in the stock price: For example, if a 30 option is worth 5 when the stock is at 30, it should be worth $2^1/_2$ when the stock falls to 25 and worth 8 when the stock moves up to 36.*

	STOCK	CALL
Bought—February 15	$4,000	$500
Sold—April 15	4,600	750
Profit	600	250
Return on investment	15%	50%

PUTS FOR PROFIT AND PROTECTION

In a broad sense, a put is the opposite of a call: It is an option to sell a specified number of shares (usually 100) of a specified stock at a specified price before a specified date. Puts have the same expiration months and price intervals as listed calls. The put buyer profits when the price of the underlying stock declines significantly. Then he sells the put at a profit, with the holder buying the stock at the lower current market price and selling it at the higher exercise or striking price.

The value of a put moves counter to that of the related stock: up when the price of the stock falls, down when it rises. You buy a put when you are bearish and anticipate that the market or stock will decline. Vice versa with selling puts. As with all options, a put is a wasting asset, and its value will diminish with the approach of the expiration date.

Here again, the attraction of puts is leverage. A few hundred dollars can acquire temporary control of thousands of dollars' worth of stock. The premiums are generally smaller than those of calls on the same stock because of lower demand, reflecting the small number of people who are pessimistic. Sharp traders take advantage of this situation, because they realize that most people tend to be optimistic about the stock market.

Selling (Writing) Puts

This provides instant income but involves your responsibility to buy the stock if it sells, before the expiration date, at or below the exercise price.

EXAMPLE: Ed owns Xanadu stock, now selling at 53, well above the purchase price. He's hopeful that the market will keep rising, but decides to write a put at 50 for 2 ($200).

As long as the stock stays above 50, the put will not be exercised and Ed keeps the $200 per contract. But once the stock falls below 50, Ed must buy the shares or buy back the put, thus cutting or eliminating the opening profit.

Buying Puts

These can be used to protect positions and, of course, to score a quick gain. The profits come when the price of the stock falls.

EXAMPLE: In March, Ann becomes skittish about the stock now trading at 47. She buys a July put at the strike price of 50 for 4 ($400). This put has an intrinsic cash value of 3, because the stock is selling 3 points below the exercise price. In effect, she is paying 1 ($100) to protect her position against a sharp market or stock decline.

If Ann's prediction is right and the price of the stock drops, the value of the put will rise to over 7 when the stock falls to 43.

In late July, the stock price is 45, so Ann sells the put for 5 for a $100 gross profit. If the price of the stock goes below 43, her profit will be greater.

As with calls, the important factor in profitable puts is the related stock. The best candidates for both writing and buying puts are stocks that:

- *Pay small or no dividends.* You are hoping that the value of the stock will decline. Dividends tend to set a floor because of their yields.
- *Sell at high price-earnings ratios.* These are more susceptible to sharp downswings than stocks with lower multiples. A stock with a P/E of 25 runs a greater risk of a quick decline than one with a P/E of 10.
- *Are historically volatile,* with patterns of sharp, wide swings in price. Stable stocks move slowly even in an active market.
- *Are unpopular with institutions.* At the outset, when selling starts, the price drops can be welcome. Later, however, when panic selling is over, there's likely to be minimal action, because there will be few buyers.

TECHNIQUES FOR HIGH ROLLERS

Spreads

A spread is the dollar difference between the buy and sell premiums. Spreads involve buying one option and selling another short, both on the same stock. If the cost of the option is greater than the proceeds of the option sold, it is a debit. If the reverse is true, it's called a credit. If the costs and proceeds are the same, the spread is even money. Your goal: to capture at least the difference in premiums—at least $1/2$ point between the cost of options exercisable at different dates and/or at different prices.

Make your calculations on paper first, and make no commitments until you are sure you understand the possibilities or probabilities.

EXAMPLE: Here's an example involving POP stock priced at 50 in April. The premiums for 50 calls are $3^1/2$ for July, 4 for October.

If POP is below 50 in July, you keep $350 and still own an option worth $250 to $300.

Sell July 50 for $3^1/2$	+$350
Buy October 50 for 4	− 400
Cash outlay	− 50
Commission	− 25
Total cost	−$ 75

If POP goes up by October, the option will be worth $500 or more, so you have a profit of $850.

If POP is at 60 at the end of July, that month's option will be worth 10, so you have to buy it back at a loss of about $650 plus in-and-out costs. But the October call might be at 14, so you could sell that for a gross profit of $1,000 to offset the July loss.

If the stock falls below $46^1/2$, you will lose money unless there's a recovery by October. But with such a stable stock in a rising market, this is not likely. The key factor is the small spread, which keeps the maximum loss low.

Perpendicular Spread

Also called a price or vertical spread, it is based on buying and selling options with the same exercise date but different strike prices.

EXAMPLE: Easy Rider (ER) is at $101^3/4$. The market is moving up and you are bullish. Sell 10 ER October 100s at $12^1/4$ and buy October 90s at $16^7/8$. This requires an outlay of $4,625. Your maximum loss will occur if ER plunges below 90.

If it goes to 95, you will still make $375. At 100 or higher, your profit will be a welcome $5,375, a 120% return on your investment.

If the market is declining, set up a bearish spread. Psychologically, the risk is greater, so it is best to deal with lower-priced stocks, selling at, say, 24⅝.

Buy 10 October 25s at 2⅛ and sell 10 October 20s at 5⅜. This brings in $3,250 cash. Because the October 20 calls are naked, you'll need $5,000 margin (but the premiums cut this to $1,750) to control nearly $50,000 worth of stock.

If the stock goes to 22, you will make $1,250. At 20 or below, your profit is $3,250 for a 180% return.

NOTE: With perpendicular spreads, you know results at any one time. With horizontal spreads, there's the added risk of time.

Straddle

A straddle is a double option, combining a call and a put on the same stock, both at the same price and for the same length of time. Either or both sides of a straddle may be exercised at any time during the life of the option—for a high premium. Straddles are profitable when you are convinced that a stock will make a dramatic move but are uncertain whether the trend will be up or down.

Traditionally, most speculators use straddles in a bull market against a long position. If the stock moves up, the call side will be exercised and the put will expire unexercised. This is more profitable than writing calls, because the straddle premiums are substantially higher than those of straight calls.

But this can be costly in a down market. If the underlying stock goes down, there's a double loss: in the call and in the put. Therefore, when a straddle is sold against a long position, the straddle premium received must, in effect, protect 200 shares.

In a bear market, it is often wise to sell straddles against a short position. The odds are better.

EXAMPLE: In January, QRS stock was at 100.

This was close to the last year's high, and because the stock had bounced as low as 65. The investor felt the best straddle was short term, so she picked a February expiration date. Simultaneously, she bought a call and a put, both at 100: 5 ($500) for the call and 4 ($400) for the put. With commissions (for buying and selling) of about $100, her exposure was $1,000.

To make money, QRS had to rise above 110 or fall below 90. She guessed right. The stock's uptrend continued to 112. She sold the call for $1,300 and was lucky to get rid of the put at $50: $350 profit—in one month.

She would do OK if the stock fell to 88. Then the call would be worth ½, but the put would

---

Making Your Own Put

Options are flexible and can be combined so that the stock purchases, sales, or short sales protect positions and make profits. Here's an example, by Max Ansbacher, of how to create your own put.

Assume that in late summer, your stock is at 69⅞ and the January 65 call is 9¼. You sell short 100 shares of the stock and buy the call. Here are the possibilities:

- If the stock falls to 55 by the end of January, the call will be worthless, so you lose $925. But your profit from the short sale is $1,487.50 ($6,987.50 sale; $5,500 buyback cost) for a net profit of $562.50 (not counting commissions and fees).

- The option limits your risk of loss on the short sale even if the stock price should rise. Thus, if the stock jumps to 100, an unprotected short sale would mean a loss of $3,012.50 ($10,000 purchase price minus $6,987.50 received from the short sale).

- But with a short sale of the stock and a purchase of a call, the loss will be only $437: the purchase price of 9¼ ($925) minus $488 (the spread between the stock price of 69⅞ and the exercise price of 65)—again not counting costs.

bring at least $1,200, so she ended up with about $250.

Strip

A strip is a triple option: two puts and one call on the same stock with a single option period and striking price. A strip writer expects the stock to fall in the short term and rise over the long term. He offers to sell 100 shares that he owns above the market price or take 200 shares below the market. The premium is higher than for a straddle.

Strap

This is also a triple option: two calls and one put on the same stock. The writer gets top premium—bullish over the long term but more negative than the strip seller on short-term prospects.

TWO WAYS TO PROTECT YOUR PROFITS

Buy a Put on Stock You Own

EXAMPLE: Your stock has soared from 30 to 60, so you expect a setback. You buy a short-term put, at 60, for $400. If the stock dips to 50, the put will be worth 10 ($1,000), so you sell for a profit of $600 and still own the stock. If the stock keeps moving up to 70, the put expires worthless. You lose $400, but you have a paper profit of $1,000 on the stock, so you are $600 ahead.

Lock in Capital Gains

The same technique can be used to lock in a capital gain.

EXAMPLE: By buying the put at 60 for $400, you reduce the stock value to 56. If it falls to 50, you sell the stock at the exercise price of 60 for $6,000. Deduct the $400 premium from the $3,000

Option Index Contracts

Contract & Symbol	Exchange	Details
S&P 100 (OEX)	CBOE	Capitalization-weighted index of 100 major stocks in the S&P 500
S&P 100 LEAPS (OAX)	CBOE	Same as above
S&P 500 (SPX)	CBOE	Capitalization-weighted index of 500 stocks representing 70% of the value of U.S. equities
S&P 500 LEAPS (LSW)	CBOE	Same as above
Major Market (XMI)	AMEX	Price-weighted index of 20 stocks that represent the DJIA
NYSE Index (NYA)	NYSE	Capitalization-weighted index of all common stocks on NYSE
S&P Midcap (MID)	AMEX	Capitalization-weighted index of 400 stocks with a median market value of about $1 billion
NASDAQ-100 (NDX)	CBOE	Capitalization-weighted index of the 100 largest financial stocks on Nasdaq
Russell 2000 (RUT)	CBOE	Capitalization-weighted index of the 2,000 smallest firms in the Russell universe
Russell 2000 LEAPS (ZRU)	CBOE	Same as above

profit (from cost of 30), and you still have $2,600. That's $600 more than if you had held the stock until its price fell to 50.

MAKING MONEY WITH OPTIONS ON INDEXES

When the market is at an all-time high, as it was when we went to press, it's a good time to consider using options. This way you can hold onto your profits without selling your stocks.

Index options settle in cash—most of them for $100 x the index value. One exception: LEAPS (discussed above), which settle at $100 x 10% of the index value.

When protecting your stock portfolio with index options, bear in mind that the price-weighted indexes, such as the Major Market Index, are most influenced by the movements of the highest-priced stocks within their index, while capitalization-weighted indexes are most influenced by movements in price of their largest stocks.

FOR FURTHER INFORMATION

Books

The Options Institute, *Options: Essential Concepts and Trading Strategies* (The Options Institute, 1998), 400-page book, $55 plus shipping from 800-OPTIONS.

Harrison Roth, *LEAPS: What They Are and How to Use Them for Profit and Protection* (Irwin Publishing, 1997), $60.

Brokers

Two on-line brokers specializing in options: Discover Brokerage Direct at: www.lombard.com Trade Options at: www.tradeoptions.com

Video

The Options Industry Council, made up of the five exchanges that trade options, has a free, 20-minute video plus a printed guide. Call 800–952–TOOL, or go to their website: www.option central.com

Pamphlets

Characteristics and Risks of Standardized Options
You are required to obtain a copy of this brochure if you want to trade options. Copies are available from the options exchanges and from brokerage offices.

Options Clearing Corporation
440 South LaSalle Street
Chicago, IL 60605
800–537–4258; 312-322-6200
Has a number of inexpensive brochures for the public.

American Stock Exchange
Derivative Securities Dept.
86 Trinity Place
New York, NY 10006
212–306–1000
Has general information brochures and strategy sheets describing in fairly easy, but detailed terms, how to make money with options.

LEAPS Investing Kit
The Chicago Board Options Exchange
400 South LaSalle Street
Chicago, IL 60605
800–OPTIONS; 312-786-5600

18

Stock Rights and Warrants

STOCK RIGHTS

Stock rights are a special type of option that permits current shareholders in a corporation to buy more of that corporation's securities, usually common stock, ahead of the public, without commissions or fees, and typically at a discount of 5% to 10%. All of these factors make certain rights a very good deal.

In most rights offerings, stockholders are allowed to purchase only a fractional share of the new common stock, based on the number of shares of common they already own. That means two or more rights are often required to buy one new share. The price, given in the rights offering or prospectus, is called the exercise or subscription price, and as already stated, it is below the current market price of the stock.

Rights offerings have a short market life, frequently running only for several weeks. If they are not used by their expiration date, they expire and lose all their value.

Why Do Rights Exist?

Rights are a convenient way for corporations to raise additional capital at a modest cost. They are often used by utilities eager to issue more common stock to balance their heavy debt obligations. The fact that they are offered at a discount from the regular market price of the stock makes it pos-

sible for investors (who obviously have confidence in the company) to acquire additional shares at a bargain price or to pick up a few extra dollars by selling the rights in the open market. In this sense, they are a type of reward to existing shareholders.

CAUTION: Keep in mind that rights are worthwhile only when the additional money raised by the company is expected to generate more corporate profits, eventually leading to increased dividends on the additional shares. This is an important aspect of judging rights, because essentially they represent a dilution of your ownership in the company.

How to Find Stock Rights

It's not much of a search—first, you must already own the common stock as of a stated date. If you do, you will be notified in writing of the offering. Because most offerings must be exercised within a short time, usually less than 30 days, read your mail. Or, if your common shares are held in street name—in other words, held not by you but by your broker—ask him or her to keep you informed. You will then exercise your rights through your broker, or in some cases through the company itself. Failure to take advantage of a rights offering could turn out to be a financial mistake.

The Nitty Gritty

The obvious advantages of a stock right is that it allows the holder to purchase stock at a reduced price and to do so without paying a broker's commission.

In addition, however, rights may have a speculative value because of the high leverage they offer: A 10% rise in the price of the stock can mean as much as a 30% jump in the value of the right, or vice versa on the loss side.

EXAMPLE: Let's assume that the stock is trading at $28 per share, that shareholders get one right for every five shares, and that each right entitles the holder to buy one new share at $25 each.

$$VR = \frac{MP - EP}{NR + 1}$$

Where: VR = value of right
          MP = stock's market price
          EP = exercise price
          NR = number of rights needed to buy one share

To calculate the value of one right before the ex-date, add 1 to the number of rights:

$$VR = \frac{28 - 25}{5 + 1} = \frac{3}{6} = 0.50$$

Thus, each right is worth 50¢, and the stock at this time is worth that much more to investors who exercise their rights.

After the stock has gone ex-right, there'll be no built-in bonus for the stock, and the right will sell at its own value, or possibly higher, if the price of the stock advances, lower if it declines.

The Advantages of Rights to You, the Shareholder

Don't overlook stock rights, even if you've never encountered them before. They have some real plusses.

■ *Maintenance of ownership position.* If you like a company well enough to continue as a shareholder, pick up the rights. Historically, 80% of stocks bought with rights have outperformed the market in the year following the issue. That's logical; management was optimistic.

■ *Bargain price.* For example, when Southwestern Public Service issued 29.2 million rights, the offer permitted shareholders to buy one additional common share at $10.95 for each ten shares already held. At the time, the stock was trading at $11.50, so the new shares were available at a 4.8% discount. If you owned 1,000 shares, you could save about $55 on the deal, because there were no transaction costs.

■ *Profits from rights themselves.* If you do not want to acquire more stock, you can sell the rights in the open market, through your broker or through a bank designated by the company. With Southwestern, each right was worth $4\frac{5}{8}$¢ ($4.625 for each 100 rights).

■ *Trading rights.* You can buy rights either to exercise them or as a speculation. Trading in rights starts as soon as the offer is announced.

How Rights Are Quoted

| 52 WEEKS | | | | | WEEK'S | |
HIGH	LOW	STOCK	SALES 100s	YIELD	HIGH	LOW
68	42	XYZ Corp.	132	3.7	64	62$\frac{1}{4}$
1	$\frac{3}{8}$	XYZ Corp. rts.	27		$\frac{7}{8}$	$\frac{1}{2}$

For a while, the prices of both the basic stock and the rights are quoted—the latter on a "when issued" (wi) basis, as shown with XYZ Corp. in the table on page 183.

As a rule, it's best to buy rights soon after they are listed in the financial press; it's best to sell a day or two before the lapse date.

Special Benefits

There are several other investment advantages to owning rights:

1. *You can purchase the shares* offered with a very low margin requirement in a special subscription account (SSA). An SSA is a margin account set up for this purpose. Your broker will explain what is required to open this type of account.

   The key advantage is that the margin requirement for rights is only 25%, compared with 50% for regular stocks. You also have a year to pay, provided you come up with 25% of the balance due each quarter.

   EXAMPLE: You have rights to buy ABC common, selling at 63, for 56 on the basis of one new share for ten old shares. You acquire 100 rights, so you need $5,600 to complete the purchase. You can borrow up to 75% ($4,200), so you can make the deal with only $1,400 in cash or collateral. Every three months you must reduce the outstanding balance by 25%.

   CAUTION: The SSA has two critical disadvantages, however: (1) The price of the stock may decline and you will have to come up with more margin, and (2) you cannot draw cash dividends or use the securities for collateral as long as they are in this special account.

2. *Another advantage:* Neither the receipt nor the exercise of the right results in taxable income to the stockholder, but you will have to pay taxes on ultimate profits when the stock is sold.

3. *Oversubscription privileges.* Some shareholders will not exercise their rights, so after the expiration date, you can buy these rights, usually on the basis of your original allotment. You must indicate your wish to participate in the oversubscription early, preferably when you send in your check for the new shares.

WARRANTS

Warrants, unlike options, are issued by the corporation typically with new issues, bonds, or preferred stock. They are traded on the exchanges.

The Nitty Gritty

A warrant is an option to buy a stated number of shares of a related security (usually common stock) at a stipulated price during a specified period (5, 10, 20 years, or, occasionally, perpetually). The price at which the warrant can be exercised is fixed above the current market price of the stock at the time the warrant is issued. Thus, when the common stock is at 10, the warrant might entitle the holder to buy one share at 15. (This differs from a right, where the subscription price is usually lower than the current market value of the stock and the time period is typically several weeks.)

Because the two securities tend to move somewhat in parallel, an advance in the price creates a higher percentage gain for the warrant than for the stock.

EXAMPLE: Let's say that the warrant to buy one share at 15 sells at 1 when the stock is at 10. If the stock soars to 20 (100% gain), the price of the warrant will go up to at least 5 (400% gain).

But the downside risk of the warrant can be greater than that of the stock. If the stock drops to 5, that's a 50% loss. The warrant, depending on its life span, might fall to $1/8$, an 88% decline.

Characteristics of Warrants

A warrant is basically a call on a stock. It has no voting rights, pays no dividends, and has no claim on the assets of the corporation. Warrants trade on the exchanges and are usually registered in the owner's name. Some warrants are issued in certificate form, although most are not. On expiration date, a warrant loses all its trading value.

The value of a warrant reflects hope that the price of the stock will rise above the exercise price. When the stock trades below that call price, the warrant has only speculative value: With the stock at 19 and the exercise price at 20, the warrant is theoretically worthless. But it will actually trade at a price that reflects the prospectus of the company and the life of the warrant.

When the price of the stock rises above the specified exercise price, the warrant acquires a tangible value, which is usually inflated by speculation plus a premium, because it is a lower-priced way of playing the common stock.

The closer a warrant gets to its expiration date, however, the smaller the premium it commands. Conversely, the longer life of the warrant, the higher the premium if there is real hope that the price of the stock will rise. After expiration, the warrant is worthless.

☑ *HINT: The main advantage warrants have over options is that they run for much longer. The longest an option lasts is nine months. Warrants, however, run for years and some in perpetuity, which gives the investor a chance to speculate on a company over the long term at a relatively low cost. This time frame makes warrants less risky than options.*

Calculating the Value of a Warrant

The speculative value of a warrant is greatest when the warrant price is below the exercise price. If the stock moves up, the price of the warrant can jump fast. The table at right shows guidelines set by warrant experts for the maximum premium to pay. For example, when the stock price is at the exercise price (100%), pay at most 41% of the exercise price. Thus, with a stock at the exercise price of 30, the maximum price to pay for a warrant (on a one-for-one basis) would be about 12. In most cases, better profits will come when the warrant is bought at a lower price.

EXAMPLE: This warrant is perpetual—that is, it does not expire. It trades on the ASE at $3, with an exercise price of $15.625. The market price of the stock here is $1³/₄.

$$3 \div 15.625 = 19\%$$

These percentages fall outside the acceptable buying range using the table below.

Maximum Premium to Pay

STOCK PRICE AS PERCENT OF EXERCISE PRICE	WARRANT PRICE AS PERCENT OF EXERCISE PRICE
80	28
90	34
100	41
110	46

How to Pick Profitable Warrants

Warrants are generally best in bull markets, especially during periods of great enthusiasm. Their low prices attract speculators who trade for quick gains. At all times, however, use these checkpoints:

■ *Buy only warrants of a common stock that you would buy anyway.* If the common stock does not go up, there's little chance that the warrant's price will advance.

The best profits come from warrants associated with companies that have potential for strong upward swings due to sharp earnings improvement, a prospective takeover, news-making products or services, etc. It also helps if they are temporarily popular.

In most cases, the warrants for fast-rising stocks, even at a high premium, will outperform seemingly cheap warrants for issues that are falling.

At the outset, stick with warrants of fair-to-good corporations whose stocks are listed on major exchanges. They have broad markets.

When you feel more confident, seek out special situations, especially warrants of small, growing firms. Many of these new companies rely on warrants in their financing. Their actual or anticipated growth can boost the price of their warrants rapidly.

CAUTION: *But be wary of warrants where the related stock is limited or closely controlled. If someone decides to dump a block of stock, the values can fall fast.*

- *Buy warrants when they are selling at low prices.* The percentages are with you when there's an upward move, and with minimal costs the downside risks are small. But watch out for super-bargains, because commissions will eat up most of the gains.

  Also watch their values, and be cautious when their prices move to more than 20% of their exercise figure.

- *Watch the expiration or change date.* After ex-

piration, the warrant has no value. If you're conservative, stay away from warrants with a life span of less than four years. When you know what you are doing, short-life warrants can bring quick profits if you are smart and lucky. But be careful. You could end up with worthless paper.

- *Spread your risks.* If you have sufficient capital, buy warrants in five different companies. The odds are that you may hit big on one, break even on two, and lose on the others. Your total gains may be less than if you had gambled on one warrant that proved a winner, but your losses will probably be less if you're wrong.

- *Look for special opportunities such as usable bonds with warrants attached.* Some bonds are sold along with detachable warrants. In many cases the bonds can be used at par ($1,000) in paying the exercise price. In other words, they can be used in lieu of cash to pay for the stock at the specified warrant price.

  Should the bond trade at 90, a discount to par, the discounted price of the bond also discounts the exercise price of the warrant.

  Except in unusual situations, all warrants should be bought to trade or sell and not to exercise. With no income, usually a long wait for appreciation, and rapid price changes, warrants almost always yield quick gains to speculators who have adequate capital and time to watch the market.

Some Popular Warrants

COMPANY	EXERCISE PRICE	PRICE OF COMMON	PRICE OF WARRANT
Asia Pulp & Paper	$9.63	$6.00	$1.50
Careside	9.00	5.50	1.75
Total Fina	46.94	64.00	23.00
TransWorld Airways	14.40	4.50	1.00

SOURCE: Standard & Poor's *Stock Guide*, Fall 1999.

Ten Points for Evaluating Warrants

1. *Underlying stock price.* The higher the stock price, all other things being equal, the higher the value of the warrant.
2. *Stock volatility.* The higher the volatility of the underlying stock, the higher the value of the warrant. Volatile stocks are more likely to appreciate or depreciate substantially. A warrant, too, will benefit from appreciation.
3. *Dividend.* The higher the dividend on the underlying stock, the lower the value of the warrant. Warrant holders are not entitled to receive dividends paid to stockholders.
4. *Strike price.* The lower the exercise price, all other things being equal, the higher the value of the warrant.
5. *Time to expiration.* The longer the warrant's life, the higher the value of the warrant.
6. *Interest rates.* Higher rates tend to increase the value of warrants.
7. *Call features.* Call features shorten the life of the warrant and detract from its value.
8. *Usable bonds.* A usable bond can be used at par to pay the exercise price of a warrant. This gives a warrant added value.
9. *Ability to borrow the underlying stock.* This tends to depress the warrant's value.
10. *Takeovers.* If the company is taken over at a high price, warrants will appreciate.

Selling Warrants Short

Selling short means selling a security you do not own, borrowing it from your broker to make deliv-

---

Where to Find Warrants

Warrants Are Issued:

- With bonds as a sweetener to buy them
- As part of initial public offering packages consisting of shares of common as warrants
- In conjunction with mergers and acquisitions

Where to Find Warrants:

- Brokerage firm research lists
- Newspaper securities listings, where they are identified by the letters "wt"

---

ery. This is done in anticipation of a decline in price. Later you expect to buy it at a lower price and make the profit between that lower price and your original short sale.

But short selling is always tricky, and with warrants there can be other problems: (1) limited markets because of lack of speculator interest; (2) exchange regulations—e.g., the American Stock Exchange prohibits short selling of its listed warrants several months before expiration date; (3) the possibility of a short squeeze—the inability to buy warrants to cover your short sales as the expiration date approaches; and (4) the possibility that the life of the warrants may be extended beyond the stated expiration date, advancing the date when the warrants become worthless, so a short seller may not be able to cover a position at as low a price as was anticipated.

19

New Issues

New issues are one of the liveliest and most appealing areas of investment—perhaps because they represent part of our American dream, that start-up companies can succeed in this country. If you're one of those who find the idea of investing in start-ups tempting, it's essential that you follow my guidelines for selecting such companies and make your decision based on the facts, not your emotions.

THE NITTY GRITTY

It is indeed possible to make money in Initial Public Offerings (IPOs), but it requires far more research than most investments, as well as an understanding of the market. Norman G. Fosback, editor of *New Issues,* favors companies that have reported profits for at least five years and whose earnings are trending upwards.

If you don't buy an IPO when it's first issued, you can buy shares in the aftermarket when they trade OTC. If it's a weak market, chances are you won't pay much more, if anything; but in a hot market, expect a 20% to 25% increase in the aftermarket. If you are enamored of the issue but cannot buy at a reasonable price, follow the stock's progress carefully. Wait for the first blush to fade, and move in when it takes a tumble. Often a new company will lose its initial luster or report lower earnings, thus pushing the price down temporarily.

☑ HINT: *Learning about new issues is less difficult than you might think. A number of the larger brokerage firms publish a list of them on a regular basis, but unless you're a major client, you won't hear about them. Your broker or library may subscribe to the bible in the field,* Investment Dealer's Digest, *which lists all IPOs as they are registered with the SEC.*

THE UNDERWRITER

Your chances for success will be increased if you select IPOs from reputable investment bankers. First-class underwriters will not allow themselves to manage new issues that are of poor quality or highly speculative. Moreover, if a fledgling company runs into a need for additional financing, a first-rate banker will be ready to raise more capital. Thus, the prime consideration is the reputation of the underwriters. This guideline is not written in stone, however.

THE PROSPECTUS

Once you learn about a new issue, your first investigative step is to read a copy of the prospectus, generally available when an offering is registered with the SEC. (It's also called a red herring because of the red-inked warning that the contents of the report are not final.) Despite its many caveats, the prospectus will help you form a rough opinion about the company and what it may be worth. Look for:

Details About Management

The success of a company is often determined by the quality of the management team. The officers and directors should have successful experience in the company and/or similar organizations; they should be fully involved in the firm and should not treat it as a part-time activity.

Type of Business

New ventures have the best chance of success in growth areas, such as electronics, specialty retailing, and biotechnology. Software companies, environmental cleanup, waste disposal stocks, and health care are expected to do well. The risks are greatest with companies in exciting but partially proven fields such as biotechnology, genetic engineering, and AIDS research. These companies are tempting but pay off only after heavy capital investments and successful R&D. Try to invest in an area you know something about or a business located near you. A good prospectus will also list some of the company's customers.

Financial Strength and Profitability

Apply the following criteria to the current balance sheet. Glance at the previous year's report to catch any major changes.

- Modest short-term debt and long-term obligations of less than 40% of total capital. With $40 million in assets, the debt should not be more than $16 million.
- Current ratio (of assets to liabilities) a minimum of 2:1 except under unusual, temporary conditions.
- Sales of at least $30 million to be sure that there's a market for products or services.

- High profitability. A return on equity of 20% annually for the past three years—with modest modifications if recent gains have been strong. This will assure similar progress in the future.

Earnings

The company should be able to service its debt. Look for the most recent P/E, and compare it with P/Es of competitors, listed in the newspaper. If a P/E is significantly higher than the industry average of a similar-size company, shares are overpriced.

☑ *HINT: Because a young company has not had sufficient time to build up profits and earnings, you should also study the ratio of total offering price to annual sales. On the whole, this market-capitalization-to-sales ratio should not be greater than 2:7.*

Six Mutual Funds That Invest in Small, Emerging Companies

FUND	TELEPHONE
Govett Smaller Companies	800–643–6838
PBGH Growth	800–809–8008
Goldman Sachs Small Cap	800–526–7384
Seligman Frontier	800–221–2783
Putnam OTC Emerging Growth	800–225–1581
Franklin Small Cap Growth	800–324–5236

(As of September 1999.)

Use of Proceeds

Check out what the company plans to do with the newly raised capital. It should not be devoted to repaying the debt or bailing out the founders, management, or promoters. Most of it should be used to expand the business. If 25% or more is going toward nonproductive purposes, move on.

Avoid firms whose management or a founding shareholder is selling a large percentage of the shares (30% or more).

☑ *HINT: Whenever the public is chasing after new issues, beware of telephone solicitations from high-pressure salesmen who guarantee that you'll double your money once the company goes public. Careful: You're skating on very thin ice.*

FINDING OUT ABOUT IPOS

Many brokers will let their clients know about new issues that their firm either knows about or is underwriting. Make certain to tell your broker if you're interested. In addition, check the publications listed in For Further Information. Several, such as *Barron's* and *Investment Dealer's Digest*, cover IPOs along with all types of financial news. They will give you the following information:

- Name of stock and symbol
- Expected date
- Use of proceeds
- Name of underwriter
- Financial data and balance sheet
- Write-up of what the company has done and plans to do, plus evaluation of the IPO as an investment

☑ *HINT: See Chapter 27 for on-line sources.*

FOR FURTHER INFORMATION

To help you spot the winners and avoid the losers when firms go public, you may want to read one of the following advisory newsletters for background data:

Newsletters

Emerging and Special Situations
Standard & Poor's Corp.
25 Broadway
New York, NY 10004
800–221–5277; 212–208–8000
Monthly; $199 per year; three-month trial: $65.

Barron's
200 Burnett Road
Chicopee, MA 01020
800–568–7625
Weekly; $145 per year.

Books

Norman Brown, *Profiting from IPOs and Small Cap Stocks* (New York: New York Institute of Finance/Prentice-Hall, 1998).

PART FOUR

High Risk
for High Returns

"Why not go out on a limb? Isn't that where the fruit is?"

Frank Scully

Now that you've learned all about banks, mutual funds, stocks, and bonds, you're ready to think about being a little more aggressive, going out a little bit further on the money tree limb. In fact, at a certain point in your investment life, a portion of your portfolio should be earmarked for more speculative plays. You know, of course, that you could lose money, so limit your commitment to no more than 15% of your funds. If you are smart—and lucky—enough to make a killing, immediately put half of your winnings into a money market fund, certificate of deposit, or Treasuries in order to earn interest and wait for the next investment opportunity.

Speculations are not entirely investments. This statement sounds simple-minded, but most people fail to make the distinction. Investments are designed to preserve capital and to provide income. The decisions are made on the basis of fundamentals: the quality and the value of the investment.

Speculations involve risks and are profitable primarily because of market fluctuations. They should not be part of your retirement portfolio. They should be entered into only when you understand what you are doing and with money that you can afford to lose. To be on the safe side, keep in mind that with any speculative choice:

- There is usually a sound reason why a security is selling at a low price or paying a very low yield. Find out just exactly why.
- In making projections, cut in half the anticipated upward move and double the potential downswing.
- Speculate only in a rising market unless you are selling short. Worthwhile gains will come when more people buy more shares—not likely in a down market.
- Be willing to take quick, small losses, and never hold on in blind hope of a recovery.
- When you pick a winner, sell half your shares (or set a protective stop-loss order) when you have doubled your money.

On the next few pages you will read about:

- Foreign stocks, bonds, currencies, and CDs
- Commodities
- Precious metals
- Financial futures and market indexes
- Splits, spin-offs, small-caps, Spiders, and stock buybacks

20

Foreign Stocks, Bonds, CDs, and Currencies

Americans have always been enchanted by products from abroad—French champagne, Swiss chocolate, Japanese cars, German beer, and more recently Australian wine, Italian designer clothes, and Irish woolens. During the last few years we've also become aware of the importance and, at the same time, the riskiness of investing abroad.

The electronic age has made the flow of money and information almost instantaneous, so whatever happens on the Hong Kong stock exchange or to the price of gold in London has a direct impact on investors in Des Moines, Duluth, and Davenport. As we draw closer and closer to one global market, it is essential to widen your investment horizons.

If you're not convinced, consider these awesome statistics:

1. Two-thirds of the total value of the world's stock markets is outside the U.S.
2. Ten of the largest steel companies are outside the U.S.
3. Nine of the ten largest banks are outside the U.S.
4. Eight of the ten largest automobile companies are outside the U.S.
5. Eight of the ten largest electronic companies are outside the U.S.

Therefore, if you invest only in the U.S., you're missing a major portion of the world's investment opportunities and, at various times, some of the best-managed and fastest-growing companies.

THE RIPPLE EFFECT

A key positive for going global is the so-called international ripple effect: At various times and in certain economic cycles, you can make money, because each country's economic cycle is a separate one. When one nation is in the midst of a recession, others are inevitably thriving. Timing overseas investments, however, is tricky.

HEADS UP FOR BEGINNERS

- Be very careful about where you invest. Over the past few years, over 500 new foreign mutual funds have been launched, largely to meet demand from U.S. investors. Not all are successful.
- International investing is quite different from investing in the United States. Stock markets in other countries have less stringent listing requirements for issues, often requesting fewer financial disclosures and having much looser accounting standards.
- When you invest in a foreign stock, you invest also in foreign currency. Changes in the value of the dollar can reduce your profits or, on the other hand, boost your gains.
  EXAMPLE: If you buy a French stock for 42

French francs and the dollar is worth 4 francs, your cost is $10.50/share. If a year later the stock has risen to 50 francs, you may want to sell and take your profit. In the meantime, if the dollar has gotten stronger and is now worth 5 francs, if you sell you will actually get only $10/share and you wind up with a loss of 50¢.

☑ *RULE OF THUMB: Foreign stocks tend to do well if the dollar drops against that foreign currency. Even if the stock doesn't actually rise in price but the dollar declines against the currency of that country, you will make a profit when you sell.*

Why? Because the foreign currency you receive from the stock sale, when converted into dollars, converts into more dollars than it cost you to buy the stock. If the stock should also independently rise in price, you will pocket even more profits.

On the other hand, a decline in the foreign currency will eat into potential profits.

In other words, an investment in a foreign stock offers at least two ways to make a profit or loss:

1. The price of the stock can go up (or down) in its local currency.

2. The value of the foreign country's currency can rise (or drop) relative to the U.S. dollar, thereby increasing or decreasing the value of your stock.

The best situation obviously exists when the price of the stock rises and the value of the country's currency likewise rises against the dollar.

It's not easy for anyone, however, even the professional managers of mutual funds that invest abroad, to call the shots right all of the time. Despite the compelling reasons for international investing, many otherwise clever investors still remain unschooled in the mechanics involved. The necessary guidelines, given here, can be mastered by anyone with the time and inclination to do so.

We'll discuss the major ways to invest in foreign countries, with the exception of real estate; they are, in order of coverage within this chapter:

■ U.S. multinational companies
■ American Depository Receipts (ADRs)
■ Mutual funds
■ Closed-end foreign country funds
■ Foreign CDs
■ Currencies and futures

THE HOWS AND WHYS OF FOREIGN EXCHANGE

Many factors affect global currency markets, but the driving force, of course, is supply and demand. Keep these points in mind as you read on in this chapter:

When the Dollar Is Cheap

The positives are:

■ U.S. goods are less expensive abroad, thus encouraging exports. This can cut the trade deficit and further boost demand for U.S. products and create jobs in this country.
■ It is also cheaper for foreign-owned corporations to produce goods in the U.S., again creating more jobs.
■ Along with the cheaper cost of doing business in the U.S., foreign companies tend to invest more money in factories, spurring on economic growth and creating jobs.
■ Tourism is up in the U.S. when the dollar is cheap.
■ Americans tend to vacation within the U.S., because the dollar doesn't buy as much in foreign countries.

The negatives are:

■ The higher cost of foreign-made goods sold in the U.S. can encourage American companies to raise prices, which can be followed by a rise in inflation.

In the Know: Ten Terms to Impress Your Broker

- *ADR* American Depository Receipt; document indicating you own shares in a foreign stock held by a U.S. bank. ADRs trade on the exchanges or over-the-counter
- *Big Bang* October 27, 1986, when the London Stock Exchange ended fixed brokerage commissions
- *Bourse* French word for stock exchange (from purse). Also used by exchanges in Switzerland and Belgium
- *Denationalization* When a corporation is turned over to private ownership
- *ECU* European currency unit; developed by nations of the European Common Market
- *Eurobond* Bond issued in one European country's currency but sold outside that country
- *Gilts* Government bonds and money market securities in Britain
- *Outsourcing* Shopping the world for the least-expensive suppliers of parts or products and services
- *SDRs* Special drawing rights; credits issued by the International Monetary Fund to its member countries; can be traded on the open market to stabilize the value of a currency in the foreign exchange market
- *Supranationals* Agencies formed by groups of countries to help their economies; International Monetary Fund, World Bank

---

- It is expensive for Americans to travel abroad, to buy foreign products, to do business abroad.
- U.S. products are cheap to buy in foreign countries, which encourages U.S. multinationals to sell even more abroad.

When the Dollar Is Expensive

The positives are:
- It's cheaper for Americans to travel abroad.
- Foreign-made products cost less for Americans to buy.

The negatives are:

- Fewer U.S. exports can result in fewer U.S. jobs.
- Loss of foreign investment may translate into less capital for U.S. businesses and less expansion.

☑ *HINT: For a free copy of "Currency: Making Sense of Exchange Rates," call the Founders Funds at 800–525–2440. This brochure explains how fluctuating exchanges rates affect your investments, including mutual funds.*

U.S. MULTINATIONAL COMPANIES

American multinationals—companies with at least 30% of earnings and profits derived from foreign business—make it possible to invest globally while sitting at home. Among the large number of U.S. blue-chip corporations that fall into this multinational category are:

- Abbott Labs
- Avery Dennison
- Avon Products
- Coca-Cola
- Colgate-Palmolive
- Compaq
- CPC International
- Exxon
- General Electric
- Gillette
- Hewlett-Packard
- IBM
- McDonald's
- Microsoft
- Mobil Oil
- Motorola
- PepsiCo
- Procter & Gamble
- Westinghouse
- Wrigley

You'll find it's simple to find solid research on any of these companies, get copies of their annual and quarterly reports, and know what products and services they offer and how good they are.

Among those with less well-known names are:

- AMP Inc.
- Arwin Ind.
- Donaldson Co.
- Dresser Ind.
- Kennametal
- Mallinckrodt
- Medtronic
- Nucor
- Perkin-Elmer
- Praxair Inc.
- Premark Int'l
- Witco Corp.

SPECIAL ADVICE FOR 2000

Because of the ongoing concern about various economies worldwide, especially in South America and Russia, you will want to limit your exposure in those areas. When adding multinationals to your portfolio in 2000, stick to companies who have a significant portion of revenues generated in the U.S., the U.K., and mainland Europe. It is almost impossible to find a multinational that does not do business in developing countries, but know how much before buying its shares.

INVESTING GUIDELINES

When selecting a multinational stock, keep in mind that:

- When foreign currencies rise relative to the dollar, earnings from an American company's foreign operations are instantly worth more.
- A strong dollar tends to hurt these stocks; it makes U.S. products expensive for foreign buyers and foreign products cheaper for American consumers.
- A strong dollar also creates an exchange loss— that is, if the money an American earns abroad loses value against the dollar, the earn-

---

Foreign Investment

PROS

↑ Provides diversification

↑ Provides additional investment opportunities not available in U.S. markets

↑ Provides hedge against U.S. monetary or economic troubles such as inflation, dollar depreciation, slump in stock market

↑ As vitality shifts from one country to another, foreign firms may represent attractive alternatives

CONS

↓ Currency fluctuations

↓ Local political situations

↓ Less information available on foreign companies than on U.S. firms

↓ Foreign firms not required to provide the same detailed type of information as U.S. firms

↓ Different accounting procedures, which can make accurate evaluation complex

↓ Foreign brokers and foreign exchanges seldom bound by regulations as strict as those imposed by the SEC (every country has its own set of regulations)

↓ Quotes sometimes difficult to obtain

---

ings for the company and its stockholders are reduced.

- The more a U.S. multinational depends on exports for sales, the more it will benefit from a weaker dollar. That means multinationals are a good hedge against a declining dollar.

Select a multinational that:

1. Has a sound, sophisticated management team
2. Is not burdened by too much debt
3. Has products and/or services that are unique or better than their foreign counterparts
4. Has sizable U.S.-generated earnings as a cushion against a decline in foreign revenues
5. Has rising earnings
6. Is ranked #1 or #2 in timeliness and in safety in *Value Line Investment Survey*

FOUR FOREIGN STOCKS TO CONSIDER IN 2000

- **Siemens,** the German electrical giant, is selling weak divisions and cutting costs; a long-term turnaround situation.
- **Royal Sun & Alliance,** a growing U.K. insurance company with substantial business in asset management.
- **Canadian National Railroad,** accounts for over 40% of Canada's total rail shipments; cross-border traffic is expanding rapidly.
- **YPF,** a leading Argentine oil company with growing business; it is also a possible takeover candidate.

USING BASKETS AND WEBS

Two interesting financial projects launched in March of 1996, CountryBaskets and WEBS (World Equity Benchmark Shares), are designed to make overseas investing simpler. Both offer stocks that represent holdings in individual countries—the CountryBaskets has 9, and there are 17 in WEBS.

CountryBaskets is managed by Deutsche Morgan Grenfell/C.J. Lawrence, a U.S. arm of Germany's Deutsche Bank, and WEBS is managed by BZW Barclays Global Fund Advisors, a British outfit.

Prices for these investments will change continually. With mutual funds, the prices for purchases and redemptions are determined only at the end of the trading day, and investors don't know what price they'll pay when they place their order. With these new stocks you'll trade shares just as with any other stock, knowing the price at trading time.

Both CountryBaskets and WEBS are built around a single-country index fund that mirrors the fluctuations of the nation's market:

- COUNTRYBASKETS, on the NYSE, has stocks of Australia, France, Germany, Hong Kong, Italy, Japan, South Africa, United Kingdom, and the United States.
- WEBS, on the AMEX, has stocks of Australia, Austria, Belgium, Canada, France, Germany, Hong Kong, Italy, Japan, Malaysia, Mexico, the Netherlands, Singapore, Spain, Sweden, Switzerland, and the United Kingdom.

A MULTINATIONAL DIRECTORY

These corporations derive at least 30% of sales from international operations. Read their current write-ups in *Value Line,* or get your broker's research.

Auto Industry

Cummins Engine
Echlin Inc.
Goodyear Tire & Rubber

Chemicals

Dow Chemical
Lubrizol Corp.
Monsanto Co.
PPG Industries

Computer/Software

Apple Computer
Hewlett-Packard
Microsoft Corp.
Sun Microsystems

Food and Beverages

Coca-Cola
Heinz (H.J.)
McDonald's Corp.
Ralston Purina
Sara Lee

Ten Foreign Stocks and ADRs for 2000

COMPANY	COUNTRY	BUSINESS	PRICE/OCTOBER 1999
Banco Santander	Spain	Banking	$10
Cable & Wireless	UK	Telecom	35
Elan	Ireland	Pharmaceutical	34
Ericcson	Sweden	Telecom	33
Fletcher Challenge	New Zealand	Paper	14
National Westminster Bank	UK	Banking	124
News Corp.	Australia	Media	30
Norsk Hydro	Norway	Energy	42
Repsol	Spain	Oil & Gas	21
Sony Corp.	Japan	Consumer electronics	129

Drugs

  Abbott Labs
  American Home Products
  Bausch & Lomb
  Bristol-Myers Squibb

Household Products

  Avon
  Black & Decker
  Procter & Gamble

Other

  Eastman Kodak
  Emerson Electric
  Millipore Corp.
  Minnesota Mining & Mfg.
  Polaroid Corp.
  United Technologies
  Xerox Corp.

AMERICAN DEPOSITORY RECEIPTS (ADRS)

ADRs are negotiable receipts representing ownership of shares of a foreign corporation that is traded in an American securities market.

They are issued by an American bank, but the actual shares are held by the American bank's foreign depository bank or agent. This custodian bank is usually, but not always, an office of the American bank (if there is one in the country involved). If not, the bank selected to be custodian is generally a foreign bank with a close relationship to the foreign company for which the ADRs are being issued.

ADRs allow you to buy, sell, or hold the foreign stocks without actually taking physical possession of them. They are registered by the SEC and are sold by stockbrokers.

Each ADR is a contract between the holder and the bank, certifying that a stated number of shares of the overseas-based company have been deposited with the American bank's foreign office or custodian and will be kept there as long as the ADR remains outstanding. The U.S. purchaser pays for the stock in dollars and receives dividends in dollars.

When the foreign corporation has a large capitalization so that its shares sell for the equivalent of a few dollars, each ADR may represent more than 1 share: 10, 50, or even 100 shares in the case

Perennial ADRs

ADR	SYMBOL	BUSINESS
Amway Japan	AJL	Distributor
Barclays plc	BCS	British bank
British Airways	BAB	Airline
British Gas	BRG	Gas
British Petroleum	BP	Oil
British Telecom	BTY	Telephone
Cable & Wireless	CWP	UK phone co
Elf Aquitaine	ELF	French oil co
Glaxco Holding plc	GLX	Pharmaceuticals
Honda Motor	HMC	Japanese cars
Hong Kong Telecom	HKT	Telephone
Imperial Chemical	ICI	Chemicals
Korea Electric Power	KEP	Utility
National Westminster	NW	British bank
News Corp., Ltd.	NWS	Publishing
Shell Transport	SC	Refining
SmithKline Beecham plc	SBH	Drug/Tagament
Stet	STEI	Italian telecom
Tele Danmark	TLD	Danish telecom
Unilever	UN	Consumer goods
Vodafone	VOD	UK cellular phone

of some Japanese companies, where there are millions of shares of common stock.

ADRs are generally initiated when an American bank learns that there is a great deal of interest in the shares of a foreign firm, or when a foreign corporation wants to enter the American market. In either case, the bank then purchases a large block of shares and issues the ADRs, leaving the stock certificates overseas in its custodian bank.

☑ *HINT: If you decide to buy ADRs, select those actively traded in the United States—i.e., listed on one of the exchanges. (Those that are not listed trade over-the-counter. Their prices are not given in the newspaper but are available from brokers.)*

IMPORTANCE OF DIVERSIFICATION

As with any investment, diversification greatly reduces the level of risk involved. With foreign ADRs, stocks, or funds, it is especially important to avoid reliance on the performance of any one ADR or stock, any one industry, or even one country. Risk reduction is best achieved by spreading your investment dollars in at least one of the following ways:

■ *By country.* When some foreign stock markets fall, it is inevitable that others will rise. Diversification by country offers a hedge against a poor economic climate in any one area. Keep in mind that the U.S. market tends to be an anticipatory one, reflecting what the American investor thinks will happen in the forthcoming months.

- *By type of industry.* Buying shares in more than one industry—high tech, computers, oil, automobiles, etc.—likewise provides protection.
- *By company within the industry.* For example, an energy portfolio could include stocks from a number of companies located in the North Sea area, Southeast Asia, Canada, and the United States.
- *By region.* Diversify among the regions of the world. Never become too dependent on any one area.

PURCHASING ADRS DIRECTLY

A growing number of foreign companies are offering direct purchase plans for their ADRs, enabling you to buy them just as you would a U.S. common stock. This new approach is being led by two of the largest administrators of ADR programs: Bank of New York and J. P. Morgan. Both offer relatively inexpensive ways to purchase ADRs. For information on:

- The Bank of New York's program, "Global BuyDirect," call 800–345–1612 or click on: www.bankofny.com/adr
- J.P. Morgan's "ADR's Shareholder Services Program," call 800–749–1687 or click on: www.adr.com.

Among the ADRs available through these direct programs:

- Amway Japan
- Bank of Ireland
- Barclays Bank
- British Airways
- British Petroleum
- Cadbury Schweppes
- Durban Roodeport Deep
- Fila
- General Cable

- Grupo Industrial Durango
- Harmony Gold
- Imperial Chemical
- National Westminster Bank
- NetCom Systems
- Pacific Dunlop
- Randgold
- Rank Group
- Royal Dutch
- SmithKline Beecham
- Sony
- TDK

MUTUAL FUNDS

Another way to go global with relative ease and little paperwork, especially if you do not have the time or inclination to do your own research, is to purchase shares in one of the funds specializing in foreign investments. In this way, you can participate in a diversified portfolio and, as with domestic funds, reap the advantages of professional management—in this case, with foreign expertise.

Although most of these funds are American-owned and -operated, they have foreign consultants (and offices) providing up-to-the-minute research on specific stocks as well as on the country's political situation and outlook.

There are two basic types of foreign funds: international funds, which invest exclusively abroad, and global funds, which mix U.S. and foreign equities.

Recommended Funds

Among those recommended in late 1998 by Sheldon Jacobs, the preeminent expert on no-load funds (and winner of the *New York Times* mutual fund performance contest for the last several years), are:

- *For global funds:* Fidelity Worldwide, Scudder Global Small Company, and Lexington Global Fund

- *For international funds:* T. Rowe Price International Stock Fund, Scudder International Fund, Oakmark International, Warburg, Pincus International Equity Fund, and Twentieth Century International Equity
- *For emerging markets:* Montgomery Emerging Markets, Robertson Stephens Developing Country, T. Rowe Price Emerging Markets, Vanguard International Equity Emerging Market, and VonTobel Eastern European Equity
- *For Europe:* Invesco European Fund, Scudder Greater Europe Growth, T. Rowe Price European, and Vanguard International Equity European Fund
- *For Latin America:* Scudder Latin American Fund
- *For Asia:* Montgomery Emerging Asia, and Strong Asia Pacific

FOREIGN BOND FUNDS

Most of these funds are global and include some U.S. bonds in their portfolios. The individual funds have different requirements that determine what they can invest in. Some, such as the T. Rowe Price Global Government Bond Fund, invest primarily in high-quality U.S. and foreign government bonds.

A more aggressive philosophy allows the GT Global High Income to buy debt of emerging countries.

GLOBAL INCOME FUNDS

High yields in short-term global funds are enticing, but take care. This type of fund has risk and volatility. These funds invest primarily in high-grade foreign debt with maturities of three years or less, and usually have some portion of their assets in dollar-denominated securities.

For example, Global Balanced Fund had a total return of 4.27% in late 1999, and is primarily invested in the United States, Canada, Sweden,

Mutual Funds That Invest in Foreign Bonds

FUND	YIELD	TELEPHONE
Fidelity International Bond	5.97%	800–544–8888
GT Global Government Income (AIM)	5.10	800–824–1850
PaineWeber Global	5.30	800–457–0849
Schdder International Bond	3.87	800–225–2470
T. Rowe Price International Bond	4.03	800–638–5660
Franklin?Templeton Global	6.49	800–237–0738

(As of Fall 1999.)

France, Mexico, and Italy. Its aim is to purchase A-rated securities, yet up to 35% of its assets may be in BBB- or BB-rated securities, and within that 35%, 10% in BB debt.

The oldest of the short-term global funds, the Alliance Short-Term Multi-Market Trust, has had remarkably stable share prices—$7.51 when first sold in 1989 and, as of Fall 1999, $8.09.

CAUTION: Although these funds are often marketed as relatively low-risk alternatives to money market funds or CDs, don't be misled. They are not a substitute for either. Their share price, unlike that of a money market fund, fluctuates with interest and currency swings, making them considerably higher in risk.

CLOSED-END COUNTRY FUNDS

These funds are an excellent way for investors to participate in foreign bull markets without having to select individual stocks. They are not risk-free, however, and should not be confused with international mutual funds.

Unlike open-end funds, which continually issue new shares to the public, closed-end funds sell their shares just once, when they begin operating. After that, shares can be bought or sold only

Closed-End Country Funds for 2000

NAME	SYMBOL
Asia Pacific	APB
Austria	OST
Chile	CH
First Australia	IAF
First Iberian	IBF
First Philippine	FPF
India Growth	IGF
Irish Investment Fund	IRL
Italy	ITA
Korea	KF
Malaysia	MF
Mexico	MXF
New Germany	GF
ROC Taiwan	ROC
Scudder New Asia	SAF
Singapore Fund	SGF
Spain	SNF
Swiss Helvetia	SWZ
Taiwan	TWN
Thai	TTF
Turkish Inv. Fund	TFK
United Kingdom	UKM

on stock exchanges or over-the-counter through a broker. Their prices then move up and down with investor demand just like any stock. Consequently, their price is often above or below net asset value (NAV), the value of the holdings in the portfolio divided by the number of shares. When the price of a fund is above NAV, it is being sold at a premium; when it falls below NAV, it's at a discount. **See:** Chapter 7 for full details on closed-end funds.

☑ *HINT: Buy at a discount. Closed-end funds provide investors with the possibility of buying a dollar's worth of common stock for less than $1. This occurs if you buy shares at a discount, and thereafter the shares move up to or above NAV.*

Foreign Country Sector Funds

PROS

↑ Professionally managed

↑ Offer diversifications within a country, which reduces risk

↑ Provide a hedge against U.S. market

↑ Way to maintain position in overseas markets

↑ High liquidity

↑ May be able to buy shares at a discount

CONS

↓ If foreign currency declines, value of your investment drops

↓ Value of stocks in fund can fall

↓ May be special taxes for Americans

↓ Political uncertainty

↓ Price of funds subject to fluctuations, like any stock

↓ Foreign markets less well regulated than U.S. market

This can work negatively in reverse: If you're forced to sell your shares at the same or a larger discount, you'll lose money.

Most closed-end shares trade at a premium to NAV for a spell just after their initial public offering. Then, if they continue to sell at premium, it's often because they've cornered the market. Generally, however, closed-end funds trade at a discount to NAV, partly because there are no salespeople keeping them in the public eye.

☑ *IF YOU DARE: Purchase closed-end shares at a discount and hold until they are selling at or above NAV. When funds reach NAV, they may become takeover targets or be converted into a regular mutual fund.*

FOREIGN CDS

You may have heard about CDs with yields as high as 13% to 18%—and they're out there, but not at your local bank.

Yet another path to foreign investing is through foreign-currency CDs. They're available at large U.S. branches of overseas banks, through some currency traders, and at the four U.S. banks listed below.

Your investment is tied to the value of the currency in the foreign country, relative to the U.S. dollar. And, as with any CD, higher yield equals higher risk. You must not underestimate the currency risk: To actually pocket the higher yield a foreign CD offers, when it matures and you convert it back to U.S. dollars, if the currency is down against the dollar, you could wind up with a loss.

On the other hand, a foreign CD could be a good investment if the dollar is weak and/or the foreign interest rate is higher than you can get at home.

Citibank, for example, has accounts available in a number of different currencies. The minimum deposit requirement is the equivalent of $25,000. At the Mercantile Bank, it's $10,000 on many currencies. Although these accounts are protected by FDIC insurance up to $100,000, they are not protected from losses due to currency swings. And at the First Union National Bank the minimum is a hefty $100,000.

For specific details on buying foreign CDs, these three banks will help you out; ask about FDIC insurance and one-time administration fees.

- Citibank, Tarrytown, New York, 800–755–5654
- First Union National Bank, Charlotte, North Carolina, 800–736–5636
- Mercantile Bank, St. Louis, Missouri, 800–926–4922; website: www.mercantile.com

TRAVELER'S CHECKS

A low-cost way to play the game is to purchase traveler's checks in the currency you feel will rise

---

Four Ways to Make a Profit Overseas

- When the price of a stock rises
- When a foreign currency rises against the U.S. dollar
- When you buy shares in a closed-end investment company at a discount to NAV, and the discount narrows because of increased demand
- When both the stock and the foreign currency advance, creating a compounding effect

---

against the dollar. Cash them in when that currency rises to pocket your gains.

The key disadvantage with traveler's checks is that you do not earn interest on your money.

FOREIGN CURRENCY TRADING

Currency Options

Before investing in currency options, see Chapter 17 on Options. Then, if you think a given currency will rise against the U.S. dollar, you can buy a call. If you think it will fall, then purchase a put.

Let's say, for example, you believe that the dollar will fall against the Japanese yen. By purchasing a call option on the yen, you gain the right to purchase a stated number of yen at a predetermined strike price in dollars. You have that right until the expiration date—usually at three-month intervals.

CAUTION: If the option exercise date comes up and the yen is below your strike price, your entire investment is lost.

Options of seven countries are traded on the Philadelphia Exchange. They are for the deutsche mark (DM), pound sterling, Canadian dollar, Japanese yen, Australian dollar, French franc, and Swiss franc. The premiums run from $25 for a short-life out-of-the-money option to $2,000 for a long-term deep-in-the-money call or put. These options expire at three-month intervals.

The quotations are in U.S. cents per unit of the underlying currency (with the exception of the yen, where it's 1/100¢): Thus, the quote 1.00 DM means 1¢ per mark, and because the contract covers 62,500 DM, the total premium would be $625.

Futures Contracts

Futures contracts on various foreign currencies are traded on the International Monetary Market Division (IMM) of the Chicago Mercantile Exchange.

For the most part, positions are taken by importers and exporters who want to protect their profits from sudden swings in the relation between the dollar and a specific foreign currency. A profit on the futures contract will be offset by a loss in the cash market, or vice versa. Either way, the businessperson or banker guarantees a set cost.

The speculation performs an essential function by taking opposite sides of contracts, but unlike other types of commodities trading, currency futures reflect reactions to what has already happened more than anticipation of what's ahead.

For small margins of 1.5% to 4.2%, roughly $1,500 to $2,500, you can control large sums of money: 100,000 Canadian dollars, 125,000 German marks, 12.5 million Japanese yen, etc.

The attraction is leverage. You can speculate that, at a fixed date in the future, the value of your contract will be greater (if you buy long) or less (if you sell short).

The daily fluctuations of each currency futures contract are limited by IMM rules. A rise of $750 per day provides a 37.5% profit on a $2,000 investment. That's a net gain of $705 ($750 less $45 in commissions). If the value declines, you are faced with a wipeout or, if you set a stop order, the loss of part of your security deposit, and vice versa when you sell short.

Why Exchange Rates Fluctuate

Exchange rates among currencies fluctuate for a number of reasons. Here are the key factors to watch.

- *Inflation.* Rates move to reflect changes in the currencies' purchasing power.
- *Trade deficits.* Countries with large trade deficits usually have a depreciating currency. Inflation is often a cause of this deficit, making country's goods more expensive and less competitive, which in turn reduces demand for its currency abroad.
- *Productivity.* If a country produces superior products, foreigners will pay more for them. Those products and the country's currency will tend to rise in value.
- *Interest rates.* High rates usually boost currency values in the short term by making these currencies appealing to investors. If high rates are the result of high inflation, in the long run the currency will fall in value.
- *Political instability.* Upheaval makes a country a hazardous place in which to invest.

Crosses

One of the favorite deals is playing crosses, taking advantage of the spread between different currencies: buying francs and selling liras short, etc. For example, when the German mark was falling faster than the Swiss franc relative to the U.S. dollar, an investor set up this spread:

April 15—He buys a June contract for 125,000 francs and sells short a June contract for 125,000 marks. The franc is valued at .6664¢, the mark at .5536¢. Cost, not including commissions, is the margin: $2,000.

May 27—The franc has fallen to .6461, the mark to .5120. He reverses his trades, selling the June contract for francs and buying the mark contract to cover his short position.

The result: The speculator loses 2.03¢ per

franc, or $2,537.50, but he makes 4.16¢ per mark, or $5,200.00. The overall gain, before commissions, is $2,662.50, a return of 133% on the $2,000 investment—in about six weeks.

CAUTION: Trading in foreign currencies can be exciting and profitable. It can also be hazardous to your financial health. Small margins tempt novices overlooking the fact that they are financially liable for the full extent of any losses. So:

- *Don't* trade currencies or futures on currencies unless you know the full extent of your potential loss. Write it down.
- *Don't* get involved at all unless you have a reliable and trustworthy stockbroker or adviser.

FOR FURTHER INFORMATION

Books

You can add to your list of multinationals by studying one of the standard reference books such as Moody's *Handbook* and Standard & Poor's *Stock Market Guide* or *Value Line*. All three give the percentage of a company's earnings and sales derived from foreign operations. You should also read various company annual reports to learn what areas their sales come from. Earnings from Western Europe and Japan are currently more stable than those from Latin America.

Moody's International Manual and News Reports
Moody's Investors Service
60 Madison Avenue
New York, NY 10010
800–342–5647; 212–413–7601
website: www.moodys.com
Contains financial information on 9,000 stocks and institutions in 100 countries. Three-volume annual; $1,825.

Periodicals

The following periodicals cover foreign markets as well as individual stocks:

Wall Street Journal, 800–568–7625
Financial Times (London), 800–628–8088
Asian Wall Street Journal, 800–622–2742
The Economist, 800–456–6086
International Herald-Tribune, 800–882–2884

Newsletters

These newsletters regularly cover foreign stocks:

Capital International Perspective
Morgan Stanley
1221 Sixth Avenue
New York, NY 10020
212–761–7353
website: www.msci,com
Monthly; $3,000 per year.

Dessauer's Journal
7811 Montrose Road
Potomac, MD 20854
800–804–0493
Monthly; $99 per year.

International Economic Trends
Federal Reserve Bank of St. Louis
P.O. Box 442
St. Louis, MO 63166
314–444–8809
Quarterly; free.

International Living
105 West Monument Street
Baltimore, MD 21201
800–851–7100
Monthly; $34 per year.

21

Commodities

The concept of buying and selling agricultural goods at a price agreed upon today, but with actual delivery of the goods sometime in the future, is a time-honored practice dating back to the early 19th century. But don't allow the long history of commodities trading lull you into thinking it's an easy way to make money.

Trading commodities is one of the riskiest games on Wall Street—some studies indicate that well over half the people who invest in commodities lose their money. In fact, commodities futures are almost always 100% speculation, because you must try to guess, months in advance, what will happen to the prices of food products, natural resources, metals, and foreign currencies.

The greatest appeal of trading commodities lies in the impressive amount of leverage they provide. Your broker will require you to meet certain net worth requirements and make a margin deposit. Nevertheless, there are low cash requirements: 5% to 10% of a contract's actual value, depending on the commodity and the broker's standards. That means $2,000 could actually buy, say, $29,000 worth of soybeans. So if you're good at it, you can make sizable profits with very little money.

CAUTION: Don't get involved unless you have some money you can afford to lose, an ability to follow trends, and a lot of emotional stability and calmness. If prices move against you, your broker will require more money, and unless you have the cash readily available, he will sell out your position and you could suffer huge losses.

HINT: To help reduce the risks involved, you can give your broker a stop-order loss on each futures contract, thus establishing a price at which you will automatically sell your position rather than suffer greater losses. (See: Chapter 26 for details on stop-order sales.)

WHICH COMMODITIES ARE TRADED WHERE

- *Chicago Board of Trade (CBOT)*
  Corn, Ginnie Mae mortgages, gold, oats, paper, plywood, silver, soybeans, soybean meal, soybean oil, Treasury bonds, wheat
- *Chicago Mercantile Exchange (CME)*
  Broiler chickens, cattle, certificates of deposit, currencies, eggs, Eurodollars, gold, hogs, lumber, pork bellies, potatoes, silver coins, S&P 500 Index futures, Treasury bills
- *Coffee, Sugar & Cocoa Exchange (New York City)*
  Aluminum, copper, gold, silver
- *Kansas City Board of Trade*
  Wheat, Value Line Stock Index futures
- *Mid America Commodity Exchange (Chicago)*
  Corn, gold, oats, soybeans, wheat

- *Minneapolis Grain Exchange*
  Sunflower seeds, wheat
- *New York Cotton Exchange*
  Cotton, orange juice, propane gas
- *New York Futures Exchange (part of the NYSE)*
  New York Stock Exchange Composite Index, options on futures
- *New York Mercantile Exchange*
  Beef (imported), gasoline, gold, heating oil, palladium, platinum, potatoes, silver coins

Commodity Futures Options

COMMODITY	SYMBOLS	ONE CONTRACT EQUALS
Options on T-bond futures	CG, PG	One T-bond futures contract
Options on soybean futures	CZ, PZ	One soybean futures contract
Options on corn futures	CY, PY	One corn futures contract
Options on silver futures	AC, AP	One 1,000-ounce silver futures contract
Options on 10-year Treasury futures	TC, TP	One 10-year Treasury futures contract

SOURCE: Chicago Board of Trade.

WHAT ARE COMMODITIES FUTURES?

A futures contract is an agreement to buy or sell a certain amount of a commodity at a particular price within a given period of time. The price of the contract is established on the floor of a commodities exchange.

Futures are traded in many areas: grain, meat, poultry, lumber, meats, gold, foreign currencies, petroleum, Treasury bonds and notes, and even stock indexes.

You can make money in one of two ways: by going long, which means buying a contract to take ownership of a product to be delivered on a certain date at a predetermined price; or by going short, which means agreeing to hand over a product on a certain date at a predetermined price. To take your profits or to cut your losses, you cancel your contract by offsetting it with a contract for the opposite trade.

In other words, a futures contract obligates the buyer to buy and the seller to sell unless the contract is closed out by an offsetting sale or purchase to another investor before the so-called settlement date.

EXAMPLE: If you had purchased a May 1998 wheat contract and you wanted to get out of the market, you would sell a May 1998 contract, thus closing out the position. The two positions cancel each other out. If you don't offset, you are obliged to take physical delivery. It would be cumbersome and costly to have wheat unloaded into your living room.

The theory or rationale behind futures trading is twofold:

1. Futures are supposed to transfer risk from one party to another; and
2. They are designed to even out price fluctuations. Although this theory tends to be true in agricultural markets, the proliferation of financial and stock index futures has led to increased volatility and speculation.

Farmers use futures as a hedge against changes in prices for agricultural prices; manufacturers use them to lock in the price of raw materials they need, such as orange juice, oil, rubber, corn, wheat, and sugar. International traders lock in values for currencies. Others, especially institutional investors, use futures to protect against stock market drops, using futures on indexes, such as S&P's 500 Stock Index.

HOW THE MARKET OPERATES

Commodity trading is different from investing in stocks. When you buy a common stock, you own a

Agricultural Commodities Contracts

COMMODITY	SYMBOL	ONE CONTRACT EQUALS
Soybeans	S	5,000 bushels
Soybean oil	BO	60,000 pounds
Soybean meal	SM	100 tons
Oats	O	5,000 bushels
Wheat	W	5,000 bushels
Corn	C	5,000 bushels
Silver	AG	1,000 troy ounces
Gold	K	1 kilogram

SOURCE: Chicago Board of Trade.

part of the corporation and share in its profits, if any. If you pick a profitable company, the price of your stock will eventually rise.

With commodities, there is no equity. You basically buy hope. Once the futures contract has expired, there's no tomorrow. If your trade turned out badly, you must take the full loss. And it's a zero sum game: For every $1 won, $1 is lost by someone else.

Hedging

Let's say a hog farmer has animals that will be ready for market in six months. He wants to assure himself of today's market price for these hogs. He does this by selling a contract of today's market price for these hogs, that is, selling a contract for future delivery. When the hogs are ready for market, if the price has dropped, he will be forced to take a lower price on the actual hogs, but he will have an offsetting gain, because the contract he sold six months ago was at a higher price. In other words, he closes that contract with a profit.

■ *The advantage to the sellers:* They have themselves locked in a price, thereby protecting themselves from any future fall in the price of hogs. In effect, they have transferred this price risk to the buyers.

■ *The advantage to the buyers:* They also have locked in a price, thereby protecting themselves from any future rise in the price of hogs. The buyer in this hypothetical case might be a speculator, a meat packer, or a meat processor.

Margin

Because payment is not received until the delivery date, a type of binder or good faith deposit is required. It is called margin. The margin in the world of commodities is only a small percentage of the total amount due, but it serves as a guarantee for both buyer and seller.

Unlike margin for stocks, which is an interest-bearing cost, margin for commodities is a security balance. You are not charged interest, but if the price of your futures drops by a certain percentage, more money must be deposited in the margin account or your position will be closed out by your broker.

In reality, most futures trading is not this simple. More often than not, the opposite side of each transaction is picked up by speculators who believe they can make money through favorable price changes during the months prior to delivery.

Trading Limitations

The commodity exchanges set day limits, based on the previous day's closing prices, specifying how widely a contract's trading price can move. The purpose of these limits is to prevent excessive short-term volatility and therefore also to keep margin requirements low. But trading limits can also lock traders into positions they cannot trade out of, because the contract held is either up or down to the daily limit.

EXAMPLE: An investor buys one gold contract (100 ounces) at $500 per ounce on June 30. On July 1 gold falls to $470 an ounce. The trading limit on gold is $20 per day, which means that on that day gold can be traded anywhere from $480 to

---

Special Terms in Commodities Trading

- *Arbitrage.* Simultaneous purchase and sale of the same or an equivalent security in order to make a profit from the price discrepancy
- *Basis.* The difference between the cash price of a hedged money market instrument and a futures contract
- *Contract month.* Month in which a futures contract may be fulfilled by making or taking delivery
- *Cross hedge.* Hedging a cash market risk in one financial instrument by taking a position in a futures contract for a different but similar instrument
- *Forward contract.* An agreement to buy or sell goods at a set price and date, when those involved plan to take delivery of the instrument
- *Hedge.* Strategy used to offset an investment risk that involves buying and selling simultaneously in the futures market
- *Index.* Statistical composite that measures the ups and downs of stocks, bonds, and commodities; reflects market prices and the number of shares outstanding for the companies in the index
- *Long position.* Futures contract purchased to protect the investor against a rise in cost of a future commitment or against a drop in interest rates
- *Mark to the market.* Debits and credits in each account at the close of the trading day
- *Open interest.* Contracts that have not been offset by opposite transactions or by delivery
- *Physical.* The underlying physical commodity
- *Selling short.* A popular hedging technique involving sale of a futures contract that the seller does not own. A commodity sold short equals a promise to deliver at a future date.
- *Spot market.* Also known as the actual or physical market, in which commodities are sold for immediate delivery
- *Spread.* Holding opposite positions in two futures contracts with the intent of profit through changes in prices

---

$520 per ounce. Because the price has dropped below $480, trading is halted, and the investor is locked into his position, unable to sell on that day. On the next day, July 2, the trading limits change to $460 to $500.

Price Quotations

Commodity prices are printed in the papers in various ways. In general you'll find the "high" (highest price of the day), the "low," and the "close." "Net change" refers to the change from the prior day's settlement price. The final column gives the high-low range for the year. Grain prices are given in cents per bushel; for example, wheat for December may be listed at a closing price of 3.71 per bushel.

Important Protective Steps to Take

Choose an Experienced Broker

Deal only with a reputable firm that (1) has extensive commodities trading services and (2) includes a broker who knows speculations and can guide you. Never buy or sell as the result of a phone recommendation until it has been confirmed in written or printed form.

Zero in on a Few Commodities

Preferably those in the news. For instance, during the drought in the Midwest in the spring of 1988, soybeans and grains experienced wild price gyrations. Watch for such movements and remember that in commodities the trend is your friend.

Avoid Thin Markets

You can score when such a commodity takes off, but the swings can be too fast and may send prices soaring or plummeting, and the amateur can get caught with no chance of closing a position.

Look for a Ratio of Net Profit to Net Loss of 2:1

Because the percentage of losses will always be greater than that of profits, choose commodities where the potential gains (based on confirmed trends) can be more than double the possible losses.

Prepare an Operational Plan

Before you risk any money, test your hypothesis on paper until you feel confident that you understand what can happen. Do this for several weeks to get the feel of different types of contracts in different types of markets.

With an active commodity, buy contracts at several delivery dates and calculate the potential profits if the price rises moderately.

Never Meet a Margin Call

When your original margin is impaired, your broker will call for more money. Except in most unusual circumstances, do not put in more money. Liquidate your position and accept your loss. This is a form of stop-loss safeguard. When a declining trend has been established, further losses can be expected.

Be Alert to Special Situations

Information is the key to profitable speculation. As you become more knowledgeable, you will pick up many points, such as these:

- If there's heavy spring and summer rain in Maine, buy long on potatoes. They need ideal weather.
- If there's a bad tornado over large portions of the Great Plains, buy wheat contracts. Chances are the wheat crop will be damaged, thus changing the supply and demand.

Trade with the Major Trend, against the Minor Trend

With copper, for example, if you project a worldwide shortage of the metal and the market is in an uptrend, buy futures when the market suffers temporary weak spells. As long as prices keep moving up, you want to accumulate a meaningful position.

The corollary to this is never to average down. Adding to your loss position increases the number of contracts that are returning a loss. By buying more, you put yourself in a stance where you can lose on more contracts if the price continues to drop.

Generally, if the trend is down, either sell short or stay out of the market.

Watch the Spreads between Different Delivery Dates

In the strong summer market, the premium for January soybeans is 8¢ per bushel above the November contract. Buy November and sell January.

If the bull market persists, the premium should disappear and you will have a pleasant limited profit. Carrying charges on soybeans run about 6½¢ per month, so it is not likely that the spread will widen to more than 13¢ per bushel. Thus, with that 8¢ spread, the real risk is not more than 5¢ per bushel.

Commodities

PROS

↑ Large potential capital gains

↑ High amount of leverage available

↑ Small initial investment

↑ High liquidity

CONS

↓ Extremely risky

↓ Requires expertise

↓ Highly volatile

↓ Must continually monitor position

↓ Could lose total investment

Never Spread a Loss

Turning a long or short position into a spread by buying or selling another contract month will seldom help you and, in most cases, will guarantee a locked-in loss. When you make a mistake, get out.

Watch the Price Peaks and Lows

Never sell at a price that is near the natural or government-imposed floor, and never buy at a price that is near its high.

Similarly, do not buy after the price of any commodity has passed its seasonal high or sell after it has dropped under its seasonal low.

Risk No More Than 10% of Your Trading Capital in Any One Position

And risk no more than 30% of all capital in all positions at any one time—except when you have caught a strong upswing and can move with the trend. These limits will ease the effect of a bad decision. Few professionals count on being right more than half the time.

COMMODITY ADVISERS

One avenue for help is the trading adviser. These professionals must be registered with the Commodity Futures Trading Commission. They charge in one of two ways: a percentage, usually 6%, of the funds turned over to them, or an incentive fee, typically 15% of any profits generated by the adviser.

☑ *HINT: Select an adviser who has an annual rate of return of at least 25% for a minimum of three years.*

FOR FURTHER INFORMATION

Software

Burlington Hall Asset Management, in Hackettstown, New Jersey, offers a software program, called LaPorte Asset Allocation System, which evaluates trading advisers. For details, call 908–813–0077; or click on: www.laportesoft. com.

Performance records of major advisers are also tracked by several of the publications listed below.

Periodicals

Commodity Traders Consumer Report
Box 7603
New York, NY 10150
800–832–6065
Tracks commodities advisers and provides useful information on how to trade. Monthly; $225 per year.

Managed Account Reports
220 Fifth Avenue
New York, NY 10001
212–213–6202

Tracks commodity funds and futures funds. Monthly; $425 per year; one free sample copy.

Books

The CRB Commodity Yearbook, 1999 (New York: Wiley, 1999).

Nick Battley, *Introduction to Commodity Futures & Options* (New York: McGraw-Hill, 1998).

Richard E. Waldron, *Futures 101: An Introduction to Commodity Trading* (Boston: Squantrum Publishing Co., 1999).

22

Precious Metals

Some say it's a hedge against inflation; doom-sayers swear it's our only protection against the inevitable downfall of our entire economic system. And in between are those who believe in diversification. Precious metals have a place, albeit a small place, in every portfolio as long as one realizes they are volatile—you have to know when to sell or else be willing to hold long term.

If you decide to invest, here are your choices:

- *Bullion.* You can buy actual bars of the metal itself, called ingots, through larger banks, brokerage firms, and major dealers. It must be assayed (certified for weight and purity) before reselling. Bullion requires storage and does not pay dividends or benefit from compounding.

- *Bullion certificates.* Unless you want to fill up your living room with bars or coins, buy certificates. The minimum is typically $1,000, and they are sold at roughly 3% over the price of the metal.

- *Bullion coins.* Not to be confused with rare coins, these have very little or no value as a collectible. Bullion coins, issued by the United States and a handful of other countries (**see:** box on page 214), also must be stored. Their price is based on their gold content, whereas rare coins purchased at auctions or from dealers have a numismatic value, which is based upon their age, rarity, and popularity.

- *Mining stocks.* Another route is to purchase the individual stocks of mining companies. Stocks offer potential price appreciation and dividend income, yet leave you subject to political upheavals, mining strikes, and the overall trend of the stock market. Mining stocks tend to rise faster in price than the gold itself when the market is up, and they usually drop faster than the metal when its price drops.

- *Mutual funds.* Funds specializing in precious metals are one of the easier ways to invest. This is not a pure play, however, because you are buying partial shares of stocks of companies that mine metals. Your profit will depend on how well the fund is managed.

- *Options.* Options on metals and mining stocks are listed in the newspaper. (**See:** Chapter 17 for more on options.)

- *Futures contracts.* These are available on precious and industrial metals and are the riskiest choice, because they involve betting on the future direction of prices. With a gold, silver, or platinum futures contract, you agree to buy or sell a certain quantity at a specified price. You are required to put up 5% to 10% of the value of the contract as margin. Although you control a large amount of metal for a relatively small amount of money, you can lose your entire investment if your bet is wrong. (**See:** Chapter 23 for more on futures.)

Before Buying a Precious Metal

Follow these guidelines and heed these warnings:

- Paper trade for at least one month. Make decisions, calculate margins, set stop-loss prices, and monitor how well you are doing in theory.
- Never commit more than 5% of your risk capital to metals. If you are trading contracts, keep the balance in a money market account to meet any margin calls.
- Read the commodity columns in the *Wall Street Journal* and *Barron's*. Ask several dealers to send you their research reports.
- Track the direction of interest rates, inflation, and the spot prices of the metals. (Spot price is the cash price for metals that are delivered at once.)
- Never give discretionary powers to anyone in the business.
- Never place an order over the phone with someone who has called you cold.

A PURIST'S VIEW

The true gold buffs shun mutual funds, stocks, and certificates, maintaining that if the world caves in, only the real tangible metals will be valuable. If you're less of a purist, then you may be content with a certificate or shares of a stock or a fund. After all, gold, silver, and platinum do not pay dividends and can never benefit from compounding.

 CAUTION: Put no more than 5% to 8% of your portfolio in precious metals.

GUIDELINES FOR BUYING PRECIOUS METALS

Here are the key facts to keep in mind:

Gold

To enhance your potential profits in gold, watch for changes in these leading indicators:

- Political situation in South Africa
- The trend of inflation and the Consumer Price Index
- Movement of interest rates
- Direction of the dollar
- Third-world debt and related banking problems
- Changes in gold production

Remember, gold vies with the dollar as the world's safest currency. When the dollar is strong, gold tends to be low in price, and vice versa.

In 1980, gold was $612 per ounce; in 1990, $383 per ounce; and as we go to press, it is $253 per ounce, proving its volatility.

Silver

Silver is primarily an industrial metal; its price is directly related to supply and demand and less (as is the case with gold) to inflation, interest rates, and politics. Silver is used in coins, jewelry, and silverware, but its greatest demand is in the photographic, electronic, dental, and medical fields. Its industrial uses are so great, in fact, that the world consumes as much silver as is mined.

In 1980 the Hunt brothers tried to corner the market in silver, and at that time the price soared to $48 an ounce, only to fall rapidly. As we go to press it's $5.11 an ounce. The American silver bullion coin is called the Silver Eagle.

Leading Gold Coins

- American Gold Eagle
- Austrian 100 Corona
- Canadian Maple Leaf
- Australian Nugget
- Mexican 50 Peso
- Hungarian Corona
- Mexican Onza
- Chinese Panda

Platinum

Although platinum has generally been considered more valuable than gold or silver because of its limited availability, it has never been as popular with investors. Its primary uses are in the electronics, chemical, and automobile industries. It is an essential ingredient in the production of catalytic converters for pollution control in cars.

Its use as an antipollutant is expected to create more demand as emission control regulations become increasingly strict in both the United States and Europe. Platinum coins include the Noble, Canadian Maple Leaf, and Australian Koala.

As we go to press, it is selling at $3.47 per ounce.

No-Load Gold Funds

FUND	TELEPHONE
Bull & Bear Gold Investors	800–847–4200
U.S. World Gold	800–873–8637
Lexington Gold Fund	800–526–0056
Vanguard Spec Portfolio-Gold	800–662–7447

BUYING METALS BY PHONE

Although you should never succumb to a high-pressure salesman, you can buy bullion bars and coins by phone from reliable dealers; however, check and compare the prices and fees of those listed below before purchasing.

■ *Fidelitrade Trust Refined Investments* allows clients to use their Visa or MasterCard to buy precious metals, provided you store the metals with them. Call 800–223–1080. Their 24-hour Quoteline gives the latest spot prices.

■ *Merrill Lynch's Blueprint* program has a minimum purchase of only $100, with $50 thereafter. Call 800–637–3766.

■ *Benham Certified Metals* has a discount brokerage division. The minimum for silver is 100 ounces and for gold and platinum, 1 ounce. Call 800–447–4653.

■ *Bank of Providence* has an accumulation account. Call 800–343–8419.

FOR FURTHER INFORMATION

Newsletters

Dow Theory Letters
P.O. Box 1759
La Jolla, CA 92038
619–454–0481
$250 per year.

Pamphlets

Your Introduction to Investing in Gold ($5)
Your Introduction to Investing in Silver ($4)
The Gold and Silver Institute
1112 16th Street NW
Washington, DC 20036
202–835–0185

Books

Michael J. Kosares, *The ABCs of Gold Investing* (Omaha, NB: Addicus Books, 1997).

23

Financial Futures and Market Indexes

FINANCIAL FUTURES

If trading corn and pork bellies is too tame for you, you can move along to another type of commodity: futures on interest-bearing securities, such as Treasury bonds and notes, CDs, and Ginnie Maes. For amateurs, financial futures and stock indexes are just about the riskiest areas of Wall Street. Yet professional money managers use them as investment tools, as a way to hedge their portfolios. Just as agribusinesses rely on commodities futures, so money managers and others use financial futures to protect their profits.

Financial futures trading requires an ability to predict correctly the short-term or intermediate movements of interest rates, because futures involve debt issues whose values move with the cost of money—that is, with interest rates. With tiny margins (as small as $800 to control $1 million), a shift of ¹/₂% in the interest rate can double your money—or lose most of your capital.

☑ *HINT: If you are a modest investor, skip this chapter. If you have over $100,000 in a portfolio, read it rapidly. If you are a speculator who can afford to lose half your stake, study the explanations and then deal with an experienced broker.*

THE NITTY GRITTY

Basically, financial futures are contracts that involve money. They are used by major investors, such as banks, insurance companies, and pension fund managers, to protect positions by hedging: What they gain (lose) in the cash market will be offset by the loss (profit) in the futures market.

The terms and rules of trading are set by the exchanges.

A financial futures contract is in essence a contract on an interest rate. The most popular are Treasury bills, bonds, and notes; Ginnie Maes; and CDs. They are sold through brokers or firms specializing in commodities. Contract sizes vary with the underlying security and the exchange, but they range from approximately $20,000 to $1 million. However, because margin requirements are low, sometimes only 5% to 10% of total value, your actual outlay is surprisingly little, relatively speaking.

The value of a financial futures contract is determined by interest rates:

- When rates rise, the price of fixed-income securities and the futures based on them fall.
- When rates decline, these investments rise in value.

☑ *HINT: Place stop orders with your broker. These provide instructions to close out your position when the price falls to a certain level, which will help limit any potential losses.*

U.S. TREASURY BOND FUTURES

Since their introduction in 1977, U.S. T-bond futures have become the most actively traded futures contract worldwide. Although there are various other financial futures traded, we will illustrate the principle with T-bonds and T-notes. (For Further Information at the end of this chapter lists more in-depth studies of trading financial futures.)

Like all futures contracts, T-bond futures contracts are standardized (see box on page 218). Their only variable is the price, which is established on the floor of the Chicago Board of Trade. Bond prices, of course, move in inverse relationship to interest rates: When rates rise, bond prices fall. Speculators and others use T-bonds to take advantage of anticipated interest rate changes; hedgers focus more on reducing and managing risk for their portfolios.

If You Expect Interest Rates to Fall

Such an expectation implies that bond futures will rise. This means you'll want to take a long position in order to take advantage of the potentially rising bond market (to be long on a contract is to buy it; to short a contract is to sell).

EXAMPLE: If bond futures are now trading at 72% of par, you go long one $100,000-face-value bond contract. If bond prices then rise to 74% of par, you offset your original long position by going short for a profit of 2 points, or $2,000.

> Long one contract @ 72 or $72,000
> Short one contract @ 74 or $74,000
> Profit: $2,000

If You Expect Interest Rates to Rise

You then take a short position. Then when bond prices fall to 69, you can offset your original position by going long for a $3,000 profit.
EXAMPLE:

> Short one contract @ 72 or $72,000
> Long one contract @ 69 or $69,000
> Profit: $3,000

Spreads

Speculators usually trade financial futures by going long on one position and short on another with both contracts due in the same month. But you can also use spreads: buying one contract month and selling another. This technique is used when there's an abnormal relation between the yields and thus the prices of two contracts with different maturities. These situations don't come often, but when they do, they can be mighty rewarding, because the gains will come from a restoration of the normal spread.

EXAMPLE: An investor notes that June T-bonds are selling at 80–11 (each $1/_{32}$% equals $3.125 of a standard $100,000 contract) and that September's are at 81–05. The basis for quotations is an 8% coupon and 15-year maturity.

Based on experience, he decides that this $^{26}/_{32}$ difference ($81^{5}/_{32} - 80^{11}/_{32} = {}^{26}/_{32}$) is out of line with normal pricing. He sells the September contract and buys the June one. In a couple of weeks, prices begin to normalize: The September contract edges up to 81–08, and the June one surges to 80–24. Now he starts to cash in: He loses $^{3}/_{32}$ ($93.75) on the September contract but gains $^{13}/_{32}$ ($406.25) on the June one: $312.50 profit minus commission.

FOUR SMART RULES TO FOLLOW

If you have money you can afford to lose, time enough to keep abreast of developments in the financial world, strong nerves, and a trustworthy, knowledgeable broker, trading in financial futures may be rewarding and surely will be exciting. Of course, if you're involved with substantial holdings, you probably are already familiar with hedging, so you can stick to protective contracts. Otherwise, follow these rules:

1. Make dry runs on paper for several months. Interest rates change slowly. Pick different types of financial futures each week, and keep

---

U.S. Treasury Bond Futures

- *Trading unit:* $100,000 face value of U.S. T-bonds
- *Deliverable:* U.S. Treasury bonds with a nominal 8% coupon maturing at least 15 years from delivery date if not callable; if callable, not for at least 15 years from delivery date
- *Delivery method:* Federal Reserve book entry wire transfer system
- *Par:* $1,000
- *Price quote:* Percentage of par in minimum increments of $1/32$ point, or $3.125 per "tick," e.g., 74–01 means $74^1/_{32}$% of par
- *Daily price limit:* $6^4/_{32}$ or $2,000 per contract above or below the previous day's settlement price
- *Delivery months:* March, June, September, or December
- *Ticker symbol:* US
- *Traded on:* The Chicago Board of Trade

---

practicing until you get a feel for the market and risks and, over at least a week, chalk up more winners than losers.

2. Buy long when you look for a drop in interest rates. With lower yields, the prices of all contracts will rise.

3. Sell short when you expect a higher cost of money. This will force down the value of the contracts, and you can cover your position at a profit.

4. Set a strategy and stick to it. Don't try to mix contracts until you are comfortable and making money.

☑ *HINT: Set stop and limit orders, not market orders. A market order is executed immediately at the best possible price. A stop order, to buy or to sell at a given price, becomes a market order when that price is touched. A limit order is the maximum price at which to buy and the minimum at which to sell.*

OPTIONS ON FUTURES

Another way to participate in the futures market is through options (**see**: Chapter 17). A futures option is a contract that gives you the right to buy (call) or sell (put) a certain futures contract within a specified period of time for a specified price (called the premium).

Options on Commodities Futures

Options are traded on futures for agricultural commodities, oil, livestock, metals, etc. Quotes are listed in the newspaper under Futures Options. These involve far less money than contracts do: roughly $100 for an option compared to $1,800 for a futures contract. There are no margin calls, and the risk is limited to the premium, but these are for professionals and gamblers. If you ride a strong market trend, you can make a lot of money with a small outlay and rapid fluctuations, or you can make a modest profit by successful hedging.

 CAUTION: Be careful, and always limit your commitment. It's easy to con yourself into thinking you're a genius when you hit a couple of big winners fast, but unless you bank half of those profits, you will lose money over a period of time if only because of the commissions.

Options on Financial Futures

Options are also traded on some interest-bearing securities, such as Treasury bills and notes. T-bond options, for example, are traded on the Chicago Board of Trade. The T-bond futures contract underlying the option is for $100,000 of Treasury bonds, bearing an 8% or equivalent coupon, which do not mature and are noncallable for at least 15 years. When long-term interest rates fall, the value of the futures contract and the call option increases, while the value of a put option decreases. The opposite is true when long-term rates rise.

Contract Specifications of Futures

	U.S. TREASURY BONDS	10-YEAR U.S. TREASURY NOTES	GNMA-CDR	GNMA II
Basic trading unit	$100,000 face value	$100,000 face value	$100,000 principal balance	$100,000 principal balance
Price quotation	Full points (one point equals $1,000) and 32nds of a full point			
Minimum price fluctuation	$^{1}/_{32}$ of a full point ($3.125 per contract)			
Daily price limit	$^{64}/_{32}$ (2 points or $2,000) above or below the previous day's settlement price			
Date introduced	Aug. 22, 1977	May 3, 1982	Oct. 20, 1975	1984
Ticker symbol	US	TY	M	CT

SOURCE: Chicago Board of Trade.

Premiums for T-bond futures options are quoted in $^{1}/_{64}$ths of 1% (1 point). Thus $^{1}/_{64}$ point equals $15.63 ($100,000 x 0.01 x $^{1}/_{64}$). A premium quote of 2–16 means $2^{16}/_{64}$, or (2 x 64) + 16 x $15.63, or $2,250.72 per option.

The profit is the premium you receive when the option is sold minus the premium paid when you purchased the option.

Setting Up Hedges

Options provide excellent opportunities to set up hedges if you plan your strategy and understand the risks and rewards. Here's an example cited in *Forbes*:

EXAMPLE: In March, the June T-bond contract is selling at 72–05 ($72^{5}/_{32}$). Calls at 72, 74, and 76 are quoted at premiums of 2–06, 1–20, and 0–46, respectively; puts at 68, 70, and 72 are available at 0–30, 0–61, and 1–54. You think that the market will remain stable, so you make these paper projections of hedges with a margin of $3,000:

Sell June 72 call	$2,093.75
Sell June 72 put	$1,843.75
Total income	$3,937.50

If the T-bond is still worth 72 on the June strike date, both options will expire worthless, so you have an extra $3,937.50 minus commissions.

Sell June 74 call	$1,312.50
Sell June 70 put	$1,953.13
Total income	$3,265.63

This is less risky, and profitable, because both options will expire worthless if the last-day price is between 70 and 74.

Sell June 76 call	$ 718.75
Sell June 68 put	$ 468.75
Total income	$1,187.50

If the final price is between 68 and 76, you will do OK. You swap a lower income for a broader price range.

STOCK INDEXES

You can also trade stock index options and stock index futures options.

These are the fastest-growing area of speculations and make it possible to play the market without owning a single share of stock. They combine the growth potential of equities with the speculative hopes of commodities.

With a stock index, you are betting on the future price of the composite of a group of stocks: buying if you anticipate a rise soon, selling if you look for a decline. You put up cash or collateral equal to about 7% of the contract value versus 50% for stocks. All you need is a little capital and a lot of nerve. A minor jiggle can produce sizable losses or gains. There are also options that require even less money.

 CAUTION: To emphasize the speculative nature of indexes, some brokerage firms advise their brokers to limit trading to individuals with a net worth of $100,000 (exclusive of home and life insurance).

Government Instrument Futures Contracts

COMMODITY	SYMBOL	ONE CONTRACT EQUALS
U.S. Treasury bonds	US	Face value at maturity: $100,000
10-year T-notes	TY	Face value at maturity: $100,000
GNMA	M	$100,000 principal balance
30-day Treasury repo	—	$2.5 million face value
90-day Treasury repo	—	$1 million face value
Zero coupon T-bonds	—	Discounted
Zero coupon T-notes	—	Discounted

SOURCE: Chicago Board of Trade.

SIX GUIDELINES FOR SUCCESS

■ *Follow the trend.* If the price of the index is higher than it was the day before, which in turn is higher than it was the previous day, go long. If the reverse, sell short.

■ *Set stop-loss prices at 3 points below cost.* If they are too close, one erratic move can stop you out at a loss even though the market may resume its uptrend soon.

■ *Recognize the role of the professionals.* To date, most contracts have been traded by brokerage houses active in arbitrage and spreads and in hedging large block positions. That means you are competing against top professionals who have plenty of capital and no commissions to pay and who are in positions to get the latest information and make quick decisions.

■ *Study the price spreads.* Contracts for distant months are more volatile. In a strong market, buy far-out contracts and short nearby months; in a weak market, buy the closer months and short the distant ones.

■ *Be mindful that dividends can distort prices.* In heavy payout months, these discrepancies can be significant.

■ *Use a hedge only when your portfolio approximates that of the index:* roughly a minimum of $250,000 (very rarely does a major investor buy only 100 shares of a stock). In most cases, any single portfolio has little resemblance to that of the index.

WHY OPTIONS FOR 2000

As we go to press the stock market is extremely jumpy, with the yield on the S&P 500 at 1.60%. One way a sophisticated investor can address this scenario is to use index options.

FOR FURTHER INFORMATION

Books

Mark J. Powers, *Inside the Financial Futures Markets* (New York: John Wiley & Sons, 1991).

Stock Indexes

These stock indexes currently have futures contracts and/or options on futures available:

- **Standard & Poor's 500 (SPX).** Stocks of 500 industrials, financial companies, utilities, and transportation issues, all listed on the NYSE. They are weighted by market value. This means each stock is weighted so that changes in the stock's price influence the index in proportion to the stock's representative market value. Contracts are valued at 500 times the index. They are traded on the Chicago Mercantile Exchange. Generally this is the index favored by big hitters, as contracts are extremely liquid, and it's widely used to measure institutional performance. Options on the SPX trade only on the Chicago Board of Options Exchange (CBOE).
- **Standard & Poor's 100 (OEX).** A condensed version of the S&P 500 index. It is weighted by capitalization of the 100 component corporations, all of which have options traded on the CBOE. The value is 100 times the worth of the stocks.
- **Standard & Poor's 100 LEAPS (OAX).** Capitalization-weighted index of 100 major stocks in the S&P 500. Options trade on the CBOE.
- **Standard & Poor's 500 LEAPS (LSW).** Capitalization-weighted index of 500 stocks. Options trade on the CBOE.
- **Value Line Composite (XVL).** An equally weighted geometric index of about 1,700 stocks actively traded on the NYSE, AMEX, and OTC. Contracts are quoted at 500 times the index. This tends to be difficult to trade because of a thin market on the small Kansas City Board of Trade. Options trade on the Philadelphia Exchange.
- **AMEX Market Value Index (XAM).** Measures the changes in the aggregate market of over 800 AMEX issues. The weighting is by industry groups: 32% natural resources, 19% high technology, 13% service, 11% consumer goods. No one company accounts for more than 7% of the total.
- **Major Market Index (XMI).** Based on 20 blue-chip NYSE stocks and price-weighted so that higher-priced shares have a greater effect on the average than lower-priced ones. Options trade on the American Exchange.
- **AMEX Oil & Gas Index (XOI).** Made up of the stocks of 30 oil and gas companies, with Exxon representing about 17%. Options trade on the AMEX.
- **Computer Technology Index (XCI).** Stocks of 30 major computer companies, with IBM accounting for about half, and Hewlett-Packard, Digital Equipment, and Motorola another 16%. Options trade on the American Exchange.
- **NYSE Composite Index (NYA).** A capitalization-weighted average of about 1,500 Big Board stocks. Options trade on the New York Stock Exchange.
- **Standard & Poor's Computer & Business Equipment Index (OBR).** A capitalization-weighted average of a dozen major office and business equipment companies, with IBM about 75%, Digital Equipment, Wang, and NCR about 18%.
- **Technology Index (PTI).** A price-weighted index of 100 stocks of which 45 are traded OTC. Very volatile. Options trade on the Philadelphia Stock Exchange.
- **Gold & Silver Index (XAU).** Options trade on the Philadelphia Stock Exchange.
- **National OTC Index (NCMP).** Options trade on the Philadelphia Stock Exchange.
- **NYSE Beta Index (NHB).** Options trade on the New York Stock Exchange.
- **NYSE INDEX (NYA).** Capitalization-weighted index of all common stocks on the New York Stock Exchange; options trade on the NYSE.

Stock Indexes *(continued)*
- **Standard & Poor's Midcap (MID).** Capitalization-weighted index of 400 stocks with a median market value of about $1 billion. Options trade on the AMEX.
- **NASDAQ-100 (MDX).** Capitalization-weighted index of the 100 largest nonfinancial stocks traded on Nasdaq. Options trade on the CBOE.
- **Russell 2000 (RUT).** Capitalization-weighted index of the 2,000 smallest companies in the Russell universe of 3,000 stocks. Options trade on the CBOE.
- **Russell 2000 LEAPS (ZRU).** Capitalization-weighted index of the 2,000 smallest companies in the Russell universe of 3,000 stocks. Options trade on the CBOE.

Richard E. Waldron, *Futures 101: An Introduction to Commodity Trading* (Boston: Squantum Publishing Co., 1998).

Pamphlets

Contact the following exchanges for pamphlets on futures trading:

The Chicago Options Exchange
400 South LaSalle
Chicago, IL 60605

312–786–5600; 800-OPTIONS
website: wwwcboe.com

Chicago Board of Trade
Literature Services Department
141 West Jackson Blvd.
Chicago, IL 60604
312–435–3500

Chicago Mercantile Exchange
30 South Wacker Drive
Chicago, IL 60606
312–930–1000

24

Splits, Spin-Offs, Small-Caps, Spiders, and Stock Buybacks

*T*his catchall chapter is simultaneously geared to experienced investors and those with money set aside to try their hand at some speculation in the market. Even if you decide against participating in any of these *S*-word opportunities, you'll find them interesting to read about.

Here's what you'll find in the next few pages:

- *Splits.* Companies that split their stocks can be excellent investments when these splits are justified by profitable growth. The techniques used in buying and selling, however, can be speculative: That is, when it appears that a company may split its stock, the price of its shares will usually rise rapidly and, after the split, fall sharply. The long-term investor who bought the shares when undervalued will probably benefit automatically. The speculative investor, however, buys as the prospects of a split catch Wall Street's fancy and sells at a quick profit right after the announcement.
- *Spin-offs.* When a company divests itself of a subsidiary, the investor in the parent company automatically owns stock in the new company as well. This provides possible price appreciation.
- *Small-caps.* Companies with a small number of shares can be profitable when you know, and have confidence in, management and/or the owners. But many are extremely risky, because they have limited capital, no ability to expand, and declining sales.

- *Spiders.* A unit investment trust that tracks the performance of the Standard & Poor's 500 Stock Index. It trades on the American Stock Exchange.
- *Stocks of bankrupt companies.* Bankrupt stocks offer speculative investors an opportunity to make money if the company pulls itself together or restructures successfully.
- *Stock buybacks.* Companies often buy back their own shares to maintain control. This procedure often boosts the stock's price.

COMPANIES THAT SPLIT THEIR STOCKS FREQUENTLY

One of the most rewarding and exciting investments can be a corporation that increases the number of its shares of common stock: issuing one or more shares for each outstanding share.

Such splits usually occur when:

- The price of such a stock has moved to an historic high, so high, in fact, that many investors are simply unwilling or unable to buy shares. Psychologically, a stock trading at 50 will attract far more investors than one trading at 100.
- A small, growing company, whose shares are traded OTC, wants to list its stock on an exchange where the rules for listing are far tougher. Such a listing broadens investment acceptance, as many institutions prefer the liq-

uidity of an established market, and more individuals can use the shares as collateral for margin loans.

■ A corporation seeks to make an acquisition with minimal cash or debt.

■ The price of the stock reaches $75 per share. The most attractive range for most investors is $20 to $45 a share, so few splits are declared when the stock price is that low.

■ Management becomes fearful of an unfriendly takeover. When the top officials hold only a small percentage of the outstanding shares, a stock split will make more shares available at a lower price and thus, it is hoped, lessen the likelihood of a raid.

■ Earnings are likely to continue to grow, which means that the price of the shares will keep rising. With more stock, the per-share profits will appear smaller—for a while.

■ The company has a record of stock splits. This indicates that the directors recognize, and are familiar with, the advantages of adding shares to keep old stockholders and attract new ones.

SPIN-OFFS

What was perhaps the most famous of all spin-offs—AT&T's decision to split into three companies (telecom services, equipment, and computers) made 1995 a record year for corporate divestitures. The trend has continued, because U.S. corporations are under tremendous pressure to downsize, to increase shareholder values. And for the most part, spin-offs wind up boosting the parent company's stocks.

Spin-offs take place when the parent company divests itself of a division, which may be unrelated to the rest of the business or may not fit into the parent company's future plans. It's also a way for a company to get rid of a unit that's underperforming. The new division becomes an independent company, and often, once loosed from its parent, blossoms.

The parent company then issues shares in this new corporation to shareholders of the parent company in proportion to their original investment. Now they hold shares in two companies instead of one.

The theory behind a spin-off is that the division will be better off operating independently and that the parent company will be better off without this particular division. A prime example: General Mills's spin-off of its restaurant division, Darden Restaurants, several years ago. The deal was one share of Darden for every one share held of General Mills. Thus, shareholder value was maintained and the parent company's objectives were met.

☑ *HINT: If you have a good sense of timing, you may be able to cash in on spin-offs. Most follow a fairly similar pattern:*

■ *When a new stock is spun off, it tends to be sold by the shareholder recipients.*

■ *Afterwards, the spun-off stock tends to rise in price as its true value is realized.*

If you own shares in a company that has announced a spin-off, you might want to wait until you sell them, or even consider buying some of the spun-off shares. Why?

The fact that corporate spin-offs create shareholder wealth has been verified by several studies. The Pennsylvania State University's Department of Finance found that performance of parent companies' shares outpaced the benchmark indexes, and in one out of seven cases, the spin-offs eventually attracted premium-priced takeover bids. A University of Texas Graduate School of Business study found that shares of spin-offs fell 4% to 10% during the first days of trading and then moved up. That time period is obviously optimum buying time.

☑ *IF YOU DARE: Buy spin-off shares after they decline, if you have faith in the company, and hold for the long term or until they have rebounded close to their initial price.*

☑ *HINT: Two publications that periodically track potential spin-offs are:*

1. Dow Theory Forecasts
2. S & P's The Outlook

In a pure spin-off, each shareholder receives a pro-rata distribution of the entire spun-off unit. This is a tax-free transaction, because the shareholder technically owned both companies before the spin-off.

A more common type of spin-off is the partial or equity carve-out in which the parent sells a stake in an initial public offering, while at the same time remaining effectively in control. Generally, the stake sold is 20% or less—in order to keep the tax-free status of any subsequent spin-off.

In either case, the spin-off is likely to result in shareholder value as management of the new spin-off has independence and freedom to cut overhead, get mean and lean, or even pursue new ventures.

☑ *HINT: Studies show that within three years, spin-offs outperform the overall market by as much as 6%. Once disconnected from the parent company, the new team is likely to increase research and improve productivity. Lucent Technologies is a good example. Between April 3, 1996, and April 3, 1999, it went up 640%. Its parent company, AT&T, was up 87% during the same time period. When Allstate and Sears split up, Allstate moved up 188% and Sears 96%.*

SMALL-CAP STOCKS

Small-cap companies typically have a capitalization of $150 million or less. With blue chips up in price, small-caps offer a defensive position against market corrections as well as a pleasant alternative to paying high premiums for quality stocks.

Small-caps have outperformed larger stocks in the early stages of the last eight bull markets. Sta-

tistics compiled by Ibbotson Associates show that since 1954, in every 12-month period following a recession, small-company stocks have outperformed large-company stocks.

Small-cap stocks are not without their problems, however. Many are not heavily followed (if at all) by analysts, which means little readily available research. The other side of that coin: They're often undiscovered and still low in price.

Because small-caps have performed well as a group and have gained a large following, Standard & Poor's introduced a new SmallCap 600 Index in late 1994. It consists of 600 U.S. issues that range in market value from roughly $46 million to $940 million. It complements the MidCap 400 and the larger-capitalization S&P 500. As a group, the 1,500 stocks in the three S&P indexes represent about 82% of the total market capitalization of stocks traded in the United States.

This index, like all the S&P indexes, is market-weighted (stock price times shares outstanding), which means the performance of one stock affects the index only in proportion to its market value. New York Stock Exchange–listed companies make up 43% of the issues in the index.

If you prefer to have a professional select small-cap stocks, then call for the prospectuses of the mutual funds listed on page 226. If you want to do your own research, the list of 12 fast-growing small-cap stocks for 2000 will give you some ideas with which to begin. All trade on Nasdaq.

Small-Cap Mutual Funds

Although their returns continually gyrate, and usually more than with other types of equity funds, they're an excellent way to immediately have a diversified, albeit risky, portfolio of small-cap companies.

☑ *HINT: To cushion the uncertainty related to small-cap companies: (1) Only put up to 25% of your equity money in these funds; (2) plan to stay invested*

Twelve Fast-Growing Small/Mid-Cap Stocks for 2000

Aaron Rents	RNT
American Freightways	AFWY
Buckle Inc.	BKE
Kellwood Co.	KWD
Media Arts Group	MDA
RehabCare Group	RHB
Roper Industries	ROP
Texas Industries	TXI
Toll Brothers	TOL
Veterinary Centers of Amer	VCA
Vishay Intertechnology	VSH
Waste Industries	WWIN

SOURCE: Standard & Poor's *The Outlook,* Summer 1999.

a minimum of three years; and (3) select small-cap funds that aim to preserve capital, such as those listed below.

SPIDERS

Leave it to Wall Street to come up with another animal product (**see:** Chapter 13 on LYONs). The Spiders crawled out of the financial web on January 29, 1993, when they became available on the American Stock Exchange.

SPDRs (Standard & Poor's Depository Receipts) are shares in a unit investment trust that tracks the performance of the Standard & Poor's 500 Index.

Their key advantage is that they enable you to buy the Standard and Poor's 500 just as if it were a single share of stock. They actually provide all the diversity and market-tracking ability of an index fund, and they have the plus of being liquid, since they are a widely held and actively traded stock.

NOTE: Index funds are designed to give you an opportunity to earn market returns by buying all or a portion of the securities in a market index. **See:** Chapter 6 for a discussion of index funds, including those that mimic the Standard & Poor's 500.

 CAUTION: Because Spiders trade like stocks, they are subject to price fluctuations. The Standard & Poor's 500 as of summer 1995 was around 559.05. Spiders at the same time were priced at approximately one-tenth of the index valuation, at $56. As we go to press, they are selling at: $138. The symbol for Spiders, which trade on the American, is SPY.

How do you decide whether to buy a Standard & Poor's index fund or this Spider? It depends upon the amount of your investment and how long you plan to hold it. Keep these factors in mind:

Seven Small-Cap Stock Funds

FUND	TOTAL RETURN JAN–SEPT 1999	TELEPHONE
Baron Small Cap	28.4	800–992–2766
LKCM Small Cap Equity	9.1	800–688–5526
Nicholas Limited Ed.	−7.2	800–227–5987
SAFECO Growth	−10.4	800–624–5711
Strong Small Cap	15.65	800–368–1030
T. Rowe Price Small Cap	3.9	800–225–5132
Vanguard Small Cap	6.4	800–635–1511

Twelve Stocks Selling Well Below Book Value

Book value can be seen as what shareholders would receive theoretically after all of a company's debts were paid. Stocks with low price-to-book value ratios are often overlooked bargains. On the other hand, stocks with high book values may be overpriced and due for a fall.

Percent Price to Book Value

STOCK	PERCENT PRICE BOOK VALUE
Gibson Greetings	34%
Johnson Worldwide	54
Sunrise Medical	57
Lonestar Steakhouse	60
Hudson Bay Co.	65
Burlington Ind.	68
Olsen Corp.	78
Laidlaw Inc.	79
Loews Corp.	79
Cleveland Cliffs	85
Wellman, Inc.	87
Int'l. Aluminum	94

(*SOURCE:* Value Line Investment Survey, 1999)

- You buy shares in an index fund directly from the sponsor at the net asset value (the total of the fund's holdings divided by the number of shares outstanding).
- Spiders must be bought through stockbrokers, which entails a commission. They are also sold with a bid/asked spread.
- Index funds may have a load or sales fee or may be of the no-load variety.
- Spider management expenses are deducted from the quarterly cash distribution and are capped at $1/20$ of 1%.
- Index funds often have an annual account

maintenance fee—Vanguard's, for example, is $10.
- Most people who invest in funds have their dividends reinvested.
- Spiders distribute all dividends on a quarterly basis, so you do not have the benefit of increasing your holdings through accrual.
- The Spider dividend rate, as of fall 1999, was only about 1.10%—about the same as bank savings rates.
- With an index fund, you pay taxes on capital gains distributions once a year.
- With Spiders, you pay tax on any capital gains only when you sell your position.

☑ *HINT: If you are a frequent trader, Spiders seem to be a better bet, even taking brokerage commissions into consideration. You can trade them all day long, while with index funds (or any funds, for that matter) purchases and redemptions are based only on end-of-the-day prices.*

Index funds, however, are more cost-efficient over time. Of the nearly 30 funds that track the Standard & Poor's 500, the largest in which individuals can invest is the Vanguard Index Trust 500. Although it has no load, it takes 19 basis points off dividends for operating expenses, and you must pay a $10 annual maintenance fee. With a Spider, you pay a brokerage commission, and a management fee of 20 basis points is taken out of dividends.

Vanguard limits its investors' trades, however, to two purchases and sales a year. Buy and sell requests are mailed only, not relayed by telephone or fax. This creates a time lag between when transactions are ordered and executed. Most other index funds allow more frequent trades, but they have made these transactions very expensive in order to discourage them. This does not make them an appropriate choice for those who like to trade on a daily or even weekly basis.

By way of contrast, Spiders trade continually, so if you're the type who carefully tracks market movements, you can make profits during the day in a Spider.

SELECT SECTOR SPDRS

In late December 1998, nine new sector index funds began trading on the American Stock Exchange. Called Select Sector SPDRs, they are in essence an unbundling of the S&P 500 Index. In other words, all 500 stocks now fall into one of nine groups, outlined below.

Who For?

Select Sector SPDRs are useful if you want to make a commitment to a particular market sector—think of each SPDR fund as a sort of unit trust or sector fund. With annual expenses of just 0.65%, they are far cheaper than the average sector fund.

These Select Sector SPDRs can also save you money on taxes. They rarely record capital gains because they adjust their portfolios only when an index component leaves the S&P 500 and they are never hit by shareholder redemptions which compel a sell-off of holdings. Investors simply liquidate their holdings by selling shares on an exchange rather than asking for their money back from the fund manager. Select Sector SPDRs can also be used for hedging and selling short.

The nine Select Sector SPDRs are:

- *Technology Index (XLK).* There are 82 companies in the index, including Microsoft, Intel, IBM, Cisco Systems, Lucent Technology, Apple Computer, Polaroid, and Data General.
- *Consumer Staples Index (XLP).* Includes Merck, Coca-Cola, Pfizer, Bristol-Myers Squibb, Philip Morris, and Procter & Gamble.
- *Energy Index (XLE).* Top three holdings are Exxon, Royan Dutch, and Mobil.
- *Cyclical/Transportation Index (XLY).* Holdings include The Gap, Loew's, Sears, Ford, GM,

Wal-Mart, Home Depot, Burlington Northern Santa Fe, FDX, Norfolk Southern, and AMR Corp.

- *Industrial Index (XLI).* Holdings include GE, Tyco International, 3M, Emerson Electric, Allied Signal, Waste Management, and Caterpillar.
- *Basic Industries Index (XLB).* Dominated by DuPont, Monsanto, Dow Chemical, International Paper, Alcoa, PPG Industries, and Barrick Gold.
- *Utilities Index (XLU).* BellSouth, Bell Atlantic, SBC Communications, GTE, Ameritech, and US West account for over 55% of this index.
- *Financial Index (XLF).* There are 71 companies in this index. The top 6 are: AIG, Citigroup, First Union, Chase Manhattan, American Express, and Freddie Mac. Others: Merrill Lynch, Allstate, PNC, Bank Corp, and BankAmerica.
- *Consumer Services Index (XLV).* The top three are Time Warner, Walt Disney, and McDonald's; others include Aetna, Gannett, CBS, Marriott, and Viacom.

$TIP: For a complete list of all stocks in each of the nine sectors, check out the Nasdaq-AMEX website at: www.nasdaq-amex.com

STOCKS SELLING BELOW BOOK VALUE

Book value is the net worth per share of common stock: all assets minus all liabilities. When the stock price is below book value, it is at a bargain level in that (1) the corporation may be worth more dead than alive: If it were liquidated, shareholders would get more from the sale of assets than the current value of the stock; and (2) the company may be a candidate for a takeover.

The usefulness of book value as a criterion depends on the type of corporation. Steel firms and manufacturers of heavy machinery have huge investments in plants and equipment, so they usually have a high book value. But they rarely make much money. By contrast, a drug manufacturer or re-tailer will have a low book value but will often have excellent earnings.

☑ *HINT: The trick in using book value effectively is to find a company whose stock is trading below that figure and is making a comeback that has not yet been recognized in the marketplace.*

In such a situation, you will get a double plus: buying assets at a discount, and a higher stock price due to better profits. Just make sure that the assets are real and that the earnings are the result of management's skill, not accounting legerde-main.

STOCKS OF BANKRUPT COMPANIES

When corporations fall upon hard times, their misfortunes can signal investment opportunities for the strong-willed. Before these companies re-vive, their stocks and bonds are often available at bargain prices. What are your chances for success? About fifty-fifty.

If you'd like to select your own stocks, begin by looking at management. If a company has gone through restructuring and the new team is compe-tent, the value of the stock will rise. It takes time for the improved performance to be recognized.

- *Look for corporations that have resources and a strong position in their field.* The broader the customer base, the greater the chance of suc-cess.
- *Diversify with at least three holdings.* If you're lucky, one will prove to be a winner, the sec-ond will stay about even, and the loss on the third will be small. Hopefully, that right choice will pay off well enough to make all the risks worthwhile.
- *Buy soon after emergence from Chapter 11.* At that point, there's the greatest uncertainty and maximum risk, but also a low base for future gains.

According to the National Institute of Busi-ness Management, investors can identify a com-pany preparing for a strong comeback by looking for these traits:

- A large tax loss carryforward that can be writ-ten off against future earnings, thus sharply boosting after-tax profits
- Substantial salable assets relative to debt, indi-cating that the securities will appreciate even if the company is partially or completely liqui-dated
- A new management team, especially one with turnaround experience
- Selling off of unprofitable divisions or buying of profitable new ones
- Restructuring of debt to improve cash flow
- Reduced leverage

☑ *IF YOU DARE: Because many institutions shy away from stocks of troubled companies, individual investors willing to assume the high degree of risk involved can sometimes make large profits in turn-around situations. To be on the safe side of an un-safe situation, wait until the company has announced a reorganization plan, or buy secured debt of the company.*

STOCK BUYBACKS

A corporate action that remains amazingly popular is the stock buyback. And as a shareholder you gen-erally benefit when a company repurchases some of its shares. That's because buybacks are very often a sign that the company's cash flow is improving and that management views its company's stock as un-dervalued by the overall market. It also sees it as a way of creating shareholder value rather than in-creasing dividends or paying down debt.

If the shares of repurchased stock are returned to the status of treasury shares, then the number of the company's outstanding shares is reduced. This should eventually raise per-share profits and boost the price of the remaining outstanding shares.

Companies buy back their shares primarily for one of three reasons:

1. To have stock available for employee stock-ownership programs
2. For executive stock options
3. For making acquisitions

By purchasing its shares in the open market, the company avoids diluting shareholder equity, which would be the case if it issued new stock.

Various studies show that the best price impact comes from what is called a Dutch auction. This is a type of self-tender in which the shareholder is asked to specify the lowest per-share price he will accept within a range set by the seller. A study at the University of Rochester's Graduate School of Business found that Dutch auctions generally provide returns of about 8% versus the Standard & Poor's 500, while open-market repurchases, which can take many months to complete, give excess returns of about 2%.

CAUTION: Not all corporate buybacks are a positive sign. If the company borrows money to reac- quire its shares, it is taking on additional interest expenses, which may offset the benefit of increased per-share earnings.

HINT: Standard & Poor's weekly publication, The Outlook, *occasionally runs a list of stock repurchase programs, indicating which stocks they favor for investor's portfolios.*

FOR FURTHER INFORMATION

Books

David Alger, *The Raging Bull: How to Invest in the Growth Stocks of the 90s* (Homewood, IL.: Business One Irwin, 1992).

Newsletters

Dow Theory Forecasts
Dow Theory Forecasts, Inc.
7412 Calumet Avenue
Hammond, IN 46324
Weekly; $233/year
213-931-6480

PART FIVE

You and Your Account

"Where large sums of money are concerned, it is advisable to trust nobody."

Agatha Christie

I don't fully agree with Agatha, but she was absolutely right to be concerned. It is essential that you find totally trustworthy people to take care of your money, to advise you about insurance, taxes, estate planning, stocks, bonds, and real estate.

The financial planner, broker, or accountant you select, the firm you use, and the type of account you have make the difference between success and failure, between being in charge of your money or merely letting someone else, often a stranger, pull the strings. So, before you start trading securities, read this section carefully, or if, unfortunately, you are in the midst of a situation you're displeased with, study the suggestions for changing brokers and arbitrating disputes.

In this section you will learn:

- How to find, interview, and select the best professionals
- How to settle discord with your broker
- Whether to use a full-service, discount, or on-line broker
- The advantages of regional stockbrokers
- How to change brokers
- The type of brokerage account that's best for you
- What types of orders to use and when
- Easy ways to build a profitable portfolio
- Whether or not to have a margin account
- How to do your own research
- Dividend reinvestment plans
- Dollar cost averaging
- How to invest on-line

25

Finding the Best Professional Help

*E*ven if you are willing to spend time doing research and follow the investment principles I've outlined in this book, you're still going to need some professional help—to execute your trades, if nothing else.

And there are other times when a pro is useful, even essential: for direction when you are starting out; for confirmation when you become more experienced; and for management when you have sizable assets and no time to oversee them.

Nevertheless, I urge you to be cautious, very cautious about letting anyone else manage your money without first understanding your goals. It's your money, you worked hard to earn it, and in most cases, you know your risk tolerance and future needs better than anyone else.

There are three general categories of people whose job it is to help you with your investments: financial planners, stockbrokers, and investment advisers. Below are guidelines for selecting the best in each category, but a word of general advice first:

☑ *HINT: Don't use a financial planner, broker, or investment adviser who:*

- Has a criminal record or a history of securities-related complaints. Check with your state Securities Agency, or contact The National Association of Securities Dealers, 800–289–9999. This info is also available on-line at: www.nasdr.com
- Has no staff or operates from a post office box

or telephone answering service. Insist on visiting the office, and then check out the person's ties with other professionals. No one planner can master the U.S. Tax Code, pension laws, stocks, bonds, real estate, and insurance.

FINANCIAL PLANNERS—GETTING EXACTLY THE RIGHT ONE

If you feel you need help with your overall financial decision making, you may want to turn to a generalist, known as a financial planner. Planners, unlike stockbrokers, become involved with all your assets—stocks, bonds, mutual funds, real estate, insurance, trusts, tax plans, even collectibles. Most planners work independently or in a group practice, although many are on the staffs of accounting firms, brokerage houses, banks, insurance companies, or mutual funds.

A good financial planner will begin by looking at your net worth, reviewing key documents relating to your assets and debts. He should have a checklist to be certain everything is covered: bank and brokerage firm statements, insurance records, mortgage papers, titles and deeds, tax returns, pension plans, a list of valuable objects, estimates of monthly living expenses, and so forth.

Next he should review your goals. You need to be forthcoming about your investments, your job and possible promotions, what you might inherit, your retirement plans, as well as any major expenses you will be incurring. He should draw up, along with your help, a workable budget to help you meet your goals.

By putting all of this together, the planner can then advise you on appropriate investments, what insurance you do or do not need (health, disability, property, and damage), if you need to rewrite your will, set up trusts, or make other plans for passing your wealth to others.

He should also discuss whether you should invest in real estate, and if you are saving enough toward retirement. He should spot errors in how you've been handling your finances: if you have the wrong kinds of insurance, too risky a portfolio, a poorly executed will or estate plan, or sloppy tax returns.

This analysis should be presented to you in writing, with specific suggestions on ways to improve your financial picture. Some planners then put into motion all aspects of the plan; others turn to professionals, such as an accountant for tax purposes, an attorney for trust plans, stockbrokers, insurance experts, and others.

CAUTION: These generalists, who help you develop an overall financial plan and then implement it with you, are not licensed or regulated by the government.

At least 200,000 people call themselves financial planners, according to the Consumer Federation of America, but only 15% to 20% have ever completed a course in the field. With no federal regulations and no nationwide accreditation requirements, it's not easy to weed through the crop.

Categories of Planners

There are three types of planners.

■ *Fee-only financial planners.* A few years ago, advisers who charged only fees instead of commissions were difficult to find, but in the last couple of years their ranks have increased. Today there are an estimated 5,500 of them, up from 2,700 in 1992. Of this group, about

500 belong to the National Association of Personal Financial Advisors.

One reason for their increased popularity is that many people feel more comfortable turning to someone for advice who does not have a potential conflict of interest. Conflict can arise when an adviser earns a commission on the sale of investments, such as stocks, bonds, or insurance.

Costs: These planners charge either an annual fee, based on your assets and investment activity, or an hourly fee, ranging from $50 to $250. Annual reviews may be another 25% to 50% of the initial fee. Although fee-only planners do not sell you products, they will recommend them and, of course, eventually you will have to pay for any securities you purchase. You'll also be charged for the fee-only planner's plan, whether you choose to follow it or not.

■ *Commission-only planners.* Some planners do not charge a fee but receive a commission on the investments they sell—for example, on a mutual fund or insurance product. With a commission-only planner, you benefit from one-stop shopping. Because any financial plan entails investments with a commission, you can do it all with the same person.

The commission-only planner, however, may have a vested interest in selling particular commission products. If you have a good relationship with your planner, this need not be a problem.

■ *Fee plus commission planners.* Many planners charge a fee for their overall plan and a commission on investments you purchase. In many cases the commission is lower than with a commission-only planner, simply because under this arrangement the adviser also receives a fee. In addition, the fee is almost always lower than with a fee-only planner.

Unless you have a complicated situation, don't pay more than 1% of the assets involved for a financial plan.

☑ *HINT: Always get a written estimate of what services you can expect for what price before making a commitment to any type of planner or stockbroker.*

Associations That Will Help You in Your Search for a Planner

Unless you know an exceptional financial planner personally, confine your search to those who have demonstrated their seriousness by obtaining one of the several designations offered in the field. Although meeting the requirements is not a guarantee of brilliance, it does represent dedication to the field.

☑ *HINT: Begin by reading "Who's Who in the Financial Planner & Investment Field" at: www.nasaa.org*

Most of these groups will provide a list of members in your area.

PFS (Personal Financial Specialists)

For CPAs who concentrate on financial planning, contact:

American Institute of CPAs
Personal Financial Planning Division
1211 Avenue of Americas
New York, NY 10036
888–777-7077

CFP (Certified Financial Planners)

For the more than 33,800 planners licensed by the Certified Financial Planner Board of Standards. To stay licensed, CFPs must participate in continuing education. Over 93 educational institutions offer courses to prepare students for the CFP exam—a comprehensive ten-hour, two-day-long exam. The group does not provide referrals, but you can call them to determine if a planner is licensed and to lodge a complaint about a planner. Contact:

Certified Financial Planner Board of
Standards
1700 Broadway
Denver, CO 80290

303–830–7500; 888–CFP–MARK
website: www.cfp-board.org

Institute of Certified Financial Planners

For the over 15,000 CFPs, and those working toward their degree, who make up the membership in the Institute of Certified Financial Planners. Contact at:

3801 East Florida Avenue
Denver, CO 80210
800–282–PLAN
website: www.icfp.org

IAFP (International Association for Financial Planning)

For some 17,000 members who must abide by a strict code of professional ethics. Contact at:

5775 Glenridge Drive NE
Atlanta, GA 30328
800–945–4237
NOTE: If you call 800–945–IAFP, you can get the names of planners in your area, drawn from a selected list of highly recommended professionals.

NAPFA (National Association of Personal Financial Advisors)

For fee-only planners, contact at:

355 West Dundee Road
Buffalo Grove, IL 60089
888-FEE-ONLY
website: www.napfa.org

Checking Up on an Adviser's Reputation

A Financial Planner

If you have any reservations about a planner, you can contact these groups to see whether any lawsuits or complaints have been filed:

1. The North American Securities Administrators Association, 202–737–0900; www.nasaa.org
2. Your state attorney general's office
3. Your local Better Business Bureau

A Stockbroker

To check up on a broker, call the National Association of Securities Dealers (NASD) hotline at 800–289–9999; website: www.nasdr.com. This group maintains a huge database known as the Central Registration Depository, or CRD. It contains a broker's employment history for the past ten years, certain felonies and misdemeanors, bankruptcies or outstanding liens, investment-related disciplinary actions, consumer complaints alleging fraud or losses of $10,000 or more, and consumer complaints that were settled for at least $5,000.

You'll get an expurgated or abbreviated report from NASD. For the full report, you must contact your state securities commission. For the correct phone number, call the NASAA at 202–737–0900.

Although the financial planning field is not nationally regulated nor does it require a special license, more and more advisers are electing to register with the Securities and Exchange Commission, which, in turn, keeps background information as well as a record of customer complaints.

Anyone who registers with the SEC must provide customers with a fee schedule and a list of services.

☑ *HINT: You can request a copy of the filing, which includes information on the planner's education and work history. You must supply the name of the adviser and his/her address and company name, if there is one. The cost is $0.24 per page.*

Contact:
SEC
Public Reference Department
450 Fifth Street NW
Washington, DC 20549
(Although requests must be made by mail, here's the telephone number: 202–942–8090.)

NOTE: For general information on your rights as a customer to file complaints against an adviser, write the SEC's Freedom of Information Act Officer at the above address, adding Room 2115.

STOCKBROKERS

These are representatives or agents who act as an intermediary between a buyer and a seller of securities. Brokers, who receive commissions for their services, are sometimes partners in a brokerage firm, but if not, they are called registered representatives (reps) and are regular employees. Brokers and registered reps must first be employed by a member firm of the National Association of Security Dealers (NASD) and then pass a comprehensive exam. Only upon successful completion of the exam is the broker registered and allowed to buy and sell securities for customers.

REGISTERED INVESTMENT ADVISERS

This professional may be a financial planner, but not all financial planners are investment advisers. An investment adviser actually can be anyone who has paid the fee (under $200) to register with the Securities and Exchange Commission so that they can give advice about securities. The SEC has the authority to disqualify someone if they suspect or know of fraud. Many states also require financial advisers to register; some have an exam and a test.

NOTE: Those who write investment newsletters must register with the SEC and, thus, are technically also known as investment advisers.

An investment adviser can recommend stocks, bonds, or mutual funds that are appropriate to your goals and risk level. If you give the adviser a discretionary account, he or she will buy and sell securities without first consulting you. Or you may require that he consult with you regarding trades.

Many investment advisers require high minimums—at least $100,000. Annual fees start at 1½% to 2% of the assets up to $500,000, with a sliding scale of lower fees on heftier accounts. You also pay brokerage costs.

Beware of the Ponzi Scheme: 2000

Every year, as I revise this guide, I consider removing this warning; but then I meet someone who has been bamboozled by a fast-talking, usually good-looking, con artist. So, I leave in the following, hoping you'll read it and remember it when you next meet a Ponzi type at a dinner party, fund-raiser, auction, or your club. *And remember,* as you're thinking, "Hmm, this sounds good," that con artists come in male and female versions!

An amazing number of intelligent people are taken in by seemingly attractive, smart embezzlers through the Ponzi scheme—a swindle in which the first few investors are paid interest out of the proceeds of later investors. The latter end up with zero when the balloon breaks and the swindler pockets the remaining money. Ponzi schemes masquerade as tax shelters, deals in precious metals, gold and diamonds, real estate, and collectibles, as well as in putting together unique, tailor-made portfolios.

A sure sign: a guarantee of far higher interest rates or returns than the prevailing market is paying.

☑ *HINT: Ask your lawyer, accountant, or stockbroker for names of reliable investment advisers.*

You can also get a list by writing to:
Investment Counsel Association of America
1050 17th Street NW
Washington, DC 20036
202–293–4222
website: www.icaa.org

HOW TO INTERVIEW A STOCKBROKER OR FINANCIAL ADVISER

Select a stockbroker or financial adviser the same way you do your doctor: with great care and caution. Your financial well-being is second only to your physical health. Don't be tempted by tips you hear at cocktail parties or Little League baseball games. By following these steps, you will find the person best suited to guide your financial future.

Step 1. Ask for names from friends and colleagues whose business judgment you respect.
Step 2. Ask your lawyer and accountant for referrals.
Step 3. If you have a contact at a particular firm, ask the manager or president for the names of the best two or three brokers.

The number one consideration in choosing any type of investment adviser is comfort: Select someone you respect and whose advice you are willing to follow, who operates in a professional manner (with integrity, intelligence, and information), answers your questions, and eases your doubts and fears.

These criteria eliminate those brokers who are hustling for commissions, as well as salespeople who make quick recommendations without considering your assets, income obligations, and goals; and everyone who promises large, fast returns.

☑ *HINT: Look for someone who:*

Has been around for some time.
Select someone with at least five years' experience in order to cover both bull and bear markets. Anyone can be lucky with a few stocks for a few years, but concentrate on an individual or firm whose recommendations have outpaced market averages by at least 2 percentage points: higher in up markets, lower in down periods. A minimum expectation of return on investment from an investment adviser should range between 12% and 18%, including income and appreciation.

Has a really good record.
Superior performance should be a continuing criterion. Every six months, compare the returns on your investments with those of a standard indicator: for bonds, the Dow Jones Bond Average, or for tax-frees, the Dow Municipal Bond Average; for stocks, Standard & Poor's 500 (which is broader and more representative than the Dow Jones Industrial Average).

Then subtract the commissions you paid to see whether you're getting your money's worth.

Has a really good reputation.
Comments from old customers are most valuable for helping you learn how you are likely to be treated, including promptness and efficiency of service and reports. Is extra cash moved quickly into a money market fund? Are orders executed promptly and correctly? Are dividends posted immediately? Are monthly reports issued on time?

Is compatible with you.
Choose advisers whose overall investment philosophy matches your objectives of income or growth. If you're conservative, stay away from a swinger who constantly comes up with new issues, wants you to trade frequently, suggests speculative situations, and scoffs at interest and dividends.

If you're aggressive, look for someone who keeps up on growth opportunities and is smart enough to recognize that no one should always be fully invested in equities and not recommend bonds or liquid assets under unfavorable stock market conditions.

Will tell you about his/her strategies.
Find out by asking questions such as these:

■ *Where do you get investment ideas? From in-house research or from brokerage firms?*

■ *What are your favorite stock-picking strategies? Out-of-favor stocks with low price-earnings ratios? Small company growth stocks? Larger corporations whose shares are now undervalued according to predictable earnings expectations?*

■ *How diversified are the portfolios? Do you shoot for big gains from a few stocks or seek modest profits from a broader list?*

■ *When do you sell?*

☑ *HINT: Successful investing relies on two factors: how much you make and how little you lose. Check the composition of several portfolios the broker has*

managed—look at the past five years. If the accounts are still holding glamour stocks bought at peaks and now near lows, move on! Don't use a professional who ignores losses or who is too busy (or stubborn) not to take profits.

More Interviewing Tips

Whatever you do, don't select someone to help you with your investments by walking into a firm cold, off the street. And never sign on with the first person you talk with. Set up interviews with several candidates. Go to the interview prepared with a series of questions, and compare how each of your potential advisers answers them.

Jay J. Pack, a broker and author of *How to Talk to a Broker,* suggests the following six basic questions:

1. What do you suggest that I do with my $25,000 (or whatever amount you have)? Beware of the person who suggests you put it all in one product.

2. How long have you been in business? With this firm?

3. Will you give me several references so that I may check on your record?

4. What will it cost me to use your help? Get specifics about fees and commissions, in writing.

5. What sort of return can I expect from my investment?

6. What research materials do you rely on?

And keep in mind that any good planner, adviser, or broker should:

■ Be willing to meet with you in person for a free consultation

■ Provide you with references or sample portfolios

■ Ask you about your net worth, financial goals, and tolerance for risk

■ Offer you several alternatives and explain them

■ Be able to refer you to other professionals for specific help

■ Set up a schedule for reviewing your securities, assets, and overall financial picture

■ Answer your phone calls promptly

> ☑ *HINT: The NASD will tell you if a broker or his or her firm has been slapped with a disciplinary action or convicted of a crime. Unresolved complaints are not disclosed. Call 800–289–9999; or click on www.nasd.com.*

DISCOUNT STOCKBROKERS

If you like to make your own buy-and-sell decisions, do your own research, and can operate independently of a full-service brokerage firm, it is possible to save between 30% and 80% on your commissions by using a discount broker.

These no-frills operations are able to offer lower rates because they do not provide research, they hire salaried order clerks and not commissioned brokers, and they maintain low overheads. Yet many have a surprisingly complete line of investment choices available: In addition to stocks and bonds, many handle Treasury issues, municipals, options, and mortgage-backed securities and will set up self-directed IRAs or Keoghs. The country's largest discounter, Charles Schwab & Co., also handles mutual funds.

Discounters are also moving into the world of computerized investing: Quick & Reilly, Charles Schwab, and Fidelity Brokerage Services market soft-

ware programs enabling customers to place trades from their home computers, to receive stock quotes, and even to evaluate their portfolios. (**See:** Chapter 27 for information on how to trade on-line.)

As a general rule, you will be able to save $25 to $75 when doing a 300-share trade. But discounters set up varying schedules, so it definitely pays to shop around when selecting a firm.

With some—called value brokers—the rates escalate with both the number of shares and their price. With others—called share brokers—rates are tied solely to the number of shares traded. You will save more with lower-priced shares if you use a value broker, and with higher-priced stocks if you use a share broker.

You should use a discount broker only if you:

■ Like to select your own stocks

■ Belong to an investment club

■ Have inherited a few shares that you want to sell

■ Have a portfolio of $100,000

■ Trade at least twice a month in units of 300 shares or more

■ Feel so confident of your stock market skill that you do not want someone else to monitor or question your decisions

■ Are not involved with special securities such as convertibles, options, or warrants, where accurate information is difficult to obtain

Don't assume that all discount firms are alike. Always ask what services are offered in addition to buying and selling stocks at a discount. For example, Charles Schwab & Co., headquartered in San Francisco, makes it possible for clients to:

■ Purchase any of hundreds of no-load and low-load mutual funds through any of its branch offices

■ Place buy and sell orders 24 hours a day

■ Purchase fixed-income securities, including Treasuries, municipals, and corporate bonds

■ Purchase hundreds of no-load funds available without transaction fees

Commissions: Full-Rate versus Discount Brokers

Broker	200 SHS. @ $25	500 SHS. @ $18	1000 SHS. @ $14	Annual Fee
Merrill Lynch	$129.50	$225.23	$308.28	$35†
Schwab	89.00	106.60	123.60	$29†
Fidelity	113.00	155.00	165.00	$24†
Waterhouse Securites	35.00	57.62	90.33	$0

Should You Use a Discount Broker?

YES, if:

- You have investment savvy
- You enjoy following the stock market and have time to do so
- You have clear ideas about what to buy and sell, and when
- You subscribe to an investment service or to serious professional periodicals
- You follow technical indicators
- You read market news on a regular basis
- You trade often
- You are not afraid to make mistakes

NO, if:

- You cannot decide what to buy and sell
- You require investment advice
- You are too busy to follow the market
- You are nervous about things financial
- You are inexperienced

SOURCE: Jay J. Pack, *How to Talk to a Broker* (New York: Harper & Row, 1985).

- Receive independent research reports by fax, phone, and mail
- Trade your account by modem and access stock market research through its software package
- Get a no-fee CMA-type account, called the Schwab One Account, free checking, and a Visa debit card
- Trade stocks and mutual funds, get price quotes, and check on your account through TeleBroker, an automated service available to customers with Touch-Tone phones
- Trade on-line.

REGIONAL STOCKBROKERS

Regional brokerage firms, those with home bases outside New York, are recognized for their personal touch, local knowledge, and independent nature. Many are excellent in picking stocks. That's because regional brokers are in positions to spot promising unnoticed stocks and bonds of local companies, ones Wall Street firms either ignore or do not follow closely. For you, this means a chance to buy a stock before the rest of the investment world becomes bullish.

Leading Discount Stockbrokers

Baker & Co., Cleveland, Ohio
   800–321–1640
   $40 minimum fee for trading
Fidelity, Boston, Massachusetts
   800–544–3939
   $59 minimum
Dreyfus Brokerage Services, Los Angeles, California
   800–421–8395
   $25 + $4 service fee minimum
Quick & Reilly, New York, New York
   800–672–7220
   $37.50 minimum
Charles Schwab & Co., San Francisco, California
   800–435–4000
   $35 minimum
Shearman Ralston, Inc., New York, New York
   800–221–4242; 212–248–1160 in New York City
   $40 minimum
Securities Research, Inc., Vero Beach, Florida
   800–327–3156
   $35 minimum
Muriel Siebert & Co., New York, New York
   800–872–0711
   $37.50 minimum
StockCross, Inc., Boston, Massachusetts
   800–225–6196
   $25 + 8.5¢ minimum per share
Jack White & Co., San Diego, California
   800–233–3411; 619–587–2000
   $33 + 3¢ minimum
Wilmington Brokerage Services, Wilmington, Delaware
   800–345–7550; 302–651–1011
   $39 minimum

The regionals also pride themselves on better service. Brokers tend to stay longer at these firms, which lessens the chances of a rookie or broker-of-the-day handling your account. They also have the freedom to sell products of other firms—mutual funds, unit investment trusts, limited partnerships, and so forth.

To check out a regional firm:

1. Read the annual report to see whether it's been profitable during bull and bear cycles.
2. Call and ask for some sample research; read and compare with other firms.
3. Talk to smart investors in the area who are either customers of the firm or can tell you why they are not.

GETTING YOUR BROKER'S RESEARCH

The advantage of a full-service broker is access to excellent investment research. Reports on individual companies as well as industry groups are prepared by security analysts. Assigned to follow a particular industry, these analysts interview corporate executives, study financial reports, and identify trends, potential problems, and new developments. Their reports are the basis of many of the investment decisions your broker makes.

Reports produced by analysts are a mixed bag—some are financial tables of little use to individuals, while others contain useful comments on a company's stock. Some are brilliant; some are ordinary. Many analysts tend to run with the pack. To overcome this tendency, interpret the advice to "hold" a stock as really meaning it's "OK to sell."

If your broker recommends a stock, always ask for the most recent report on the company. Or, if you hear about a potentially interesting buy, find out whether the firm has taken a position on it. If you are a regular customer, your broker should send you the firm's weekly or monthly roundup reports, which cover a number of stocks. If your bro-ker resists sending these to you, maybe you should look for another broker. (Don't, however, expect the firm's best reports if you make only a handful of trades a year.)

TOP RESEARCH SOURCES YOU CAN TAP INTO

If you decide to do your own research or supplement what's offered by your stockbroker or adviser, three publication services will be enormously helpful. They are expensive, so you may want to use them at your library or broker's office before buying your own copies.

Moody's

Moody's Investors Service
60 Madison Avenue
New York, NY 10010
212–413–7601; 800–634–3583
website: www.moodys.com/fis

A leading research and information service aimed primarily at the business community, Moody's (a Dun & Bradstreet Corporation company) is known throughout the world for its bond ratings and factual publications. It is not an investment advisory service.

Here's what it publishes:

Moody's Manuals

The company publishes eight manuals annually. Each is continually updated, some as often as twice a week. The manuals cover 25,000 U.S. and foreign corporations and 14,000 municipal and government entities. Each one gives financial and operating data, company histories, product descriptions, plant and property locations, and lists of officers. The eight are:

■ *Bank and Finance.* Covers 20,000 financial institutions, including insurance companies, mutual funds, banks, and brokerage firms.

Regional Brokerage Firms

Firm	Telephone	Firm	Telephone
Advest Inc. 90 State House Square Hartford, CT 06103	860–509–1000 800–243–8115	Janney Montgomery Scott Inc. 1801 Market Street Philadelphia, PA 19103	215–665–6000 800–526–6397
J.C. Bradford & Co. 330 Commerce Street Nashville, TN 37201	615–748–9000 800–251–1060	Legg Mason Wood Walker 100 Light Street Baltimore, MD 21202	410–539–0000 800–368–2558
B.T. Alex Brown Inc. 1 South Street Baltimore, MD 21202	410–727–1700 800–638–2596	McDonald & Co. 800 Superior Avenue Cleveland, OH 44114	216–443–2300 800–553–2240
Crowell, Weedon & Co. 624 South Grand Avenue Suite 2600 Los Angeles, CA 90017	213–620–1850 800–227–0319	US Bancorp/Piper, Jaffray Inc. 222 South 9th Street Minneapolis, MN 55402	612–342–6000 800–333–6000
Dain Bosworth Inc. Dain Bosworth Plaza 60 South 6th Street Minneapolis, MN 55402	612–371–2711	Raymond James Financial 880 Carillon Parkway St. Petersburg, FL 33716	727–573–3800 800–248–8863
D.A. Davidson & Co. P.O. Box 5015 Great Falls, MT 59403	406–727–4200 800–332–5915	Dain Rauscher, Inc. 2711 North Haskell Dallas, TX 75204	214–989–1000 800–777–0289
Edward D. Jones & Co. 201 Progress Parkway Maryland Heights, MO 63043	314–515–2000	Sutro & Co. 201 California Street San Francisco, CA 94111	415–445–8500 800–652–1030
A.G. Edwards & Sons, Inc. One North Jefferson Avenue St. Louis, MO 63103	314–955–3000	First Security/Van Kasper & Co. 600 California Street San Francisco, CA 94108	415–391–5600 800–652–1747
ILJ Wakovia 201 North Trion Street Charlotte, NC 28202	704–379–9000 800–929–0724	Wheat First Union 901 East Byrd Street Richmond, VA 23219	804–649–2311 800–627–8625

- ■ *Industrial.* Covers 2,000 industrial corporations on the NYSE and AMEX, plus others on regional exchanges.

- ■ *OTC Industrial.* Covers 2,500 industrial companies.
- ■ *OTC Unlisted.* Covers 2,200 hard-to-find com-

panies not listed on Nasdaq's National Market System or on regional exchanges.

- *Public Utility.* Covers every publicly held U.S. gas and electric utility, gas transmission, telephone, and water company and many privately held ones.

- *Transportation.* Covers airlines, railroads, oil pipelines, bridge and tunnel operators, bus and truck companies, and auto and truck rental and leasing firms.

- *International.* Covers 9,000 international corporations in 100 countries.

- *Municipal and Government.* Covers 11,600 bond-issuing municipalities and government agencies; includes bond ratings.

Moody's Handbooks

These softcover books, published quarterly, give concise overviews of 2,700 corporations. Useful for instant facts and financial summaries. They are *Handbook of Common Stocks* and *Handbook of NASDAQ Stocks.*

Other Publications

- *Moody's Dividend Record.* Detailed reports on current dividend data of 22,000 stocks; updated twice weekly.

- *Moody's Industry Review.* Ranks 3,000 leading companies in 137 industry groups.

- *Moody's Bond Record.* Monthly guide to 68,000 fixed-income issues including ratings, yield to maturity, and prices.

- *Moody's Handbook of Dividend Achievers.* Lists high-yielding stocks and records of dividend payouts.

☑ HINT: *A word about Moody's bond ratings. Their purpose is to grade the relative quality of investments by using nine symbols ranging from Aaa (the highest) to C (the lowest). In addition, each classification from Aa to B (for corporate bonds) sometimes has a numerical modifier: The number 1*

indicates that the security ranks at the highest end of the category; the number 2, in the middle; and the number 3, at the lower end.

Standard & Poor's

Standard & Poor's Corp.
25 Broadway
New York, NY 10004
212–208–8000; 800–221–5277
website: www.standardandpoors.com

For over 120 years Standard & Poor's has been providing financial information, stock and bond analysis, and bond rating and investment guidance. Its materials are used by investors as well as the professional and business community.

Major Publications

- *Corporation Records.* Seven volumes covering financial details, history, and products of 12,000 corporations. One volume, *Daily News,* provides continually updated information five days a week about these publicly held corporations.

- *Stock Reports.* Analytical data on over 4,400 corporations. Includes every company traded on the NYSE and AMEX plus 1,500 over-the-counters. There are two-page reports on each company.

- *Industry Surveys.* This four-volume loose-leaf is continually updated and covers 52 leading U.S. industries. Surveys cover all aspects of an industry, including market trends, earnings, and government regulations.

- *Stock Guide.* A small paperback containing 46 columns of statistical material on 5,900 stocks. A broker's bible.

- *The Outlook.* A weekly advisory newsletter covering the economic climate, stock forecasts, industry predictions, buy-and-sell recommendations, etc. Presents a "master list of recommended issues" with various portfolios.

Other Publications

Securities Week, Bond Guide, Standard & Poor's *Register of Corporations, Directors and Executives, and Security Dealers of North America.*

Standard & Poor's Bond Ratings

S&P rates bonds from AAA (the highest) to D (bonds in default). Those with ratings between AAA and BBB are considered of investment quality. Those below BBB fall into the speculative category. Ratings between AA and CCC often have a + or – to indicate relative strength within the larger categories.

The company also rates stocks from A+ (highest) to A (high), A– (above average), B+ (average), B (below average), B– (lower), C (lowest), to D (reorganization). With the exception of banks and financial institutions, which are rated NR (no ranking), most publicly owned corporations are listed. Never invest in any company rated below B+.

Value Line, Inc.

220 East 42nd Street
New York, NY 10017
800–535–8760
website: www.valueline.com

An independent investment advisory, Value Line, Inc., publishes one of the country's leading investment advisory and research services, the *Value Line Investment Survey,* as well as several other publications and the Value Line index.

Value Line Investment Survey

Begun in 1935, it's a weekly advisory service published in a two-volume loose-leaf binder. It analyzes 1,700 common stocks divided into 100 industry groups.

A report on each industry precedes the individual stock reports. Each stock is given two rankings: one for "timeliness" (the probable relative price performance of the stock within the next 12 months) and one for "safety" (the stock's future price stability and its company's current financial strength). Within these two categories each stock is assigned a rank from 1 (the highest) to 5 (the lowest).

Other Publications

- *The Value Line OTC Special Situations Service.* Covers fast-growing smaller companies. Published 24 times a year.
- *Value Line Options.* Evaluates and ranks nearly all options listed on the U.S. exchanges. Published 48 times a year.
- *Value Line Convertibles.* Evaluates and ranks for future market performance nearly 600 companies and 60 warrants. Published 48 times a year.

SETTLING DISPUTES WITH YOUR BROKER

As with all businesses, there are individuals who either deliberately or carelessly give poor advice. In the brokerage business, integrity is paramount— all the exchanges have strict rules, and most firms have compliance officers whose responsibility it is to monitor trading, make sure that full information is provided to all clients, and act promptly when there are deviations.

Generally, trouble develops when the customer does not understand an investment or when the broker is not clear about all the facts or has not made them clear to the client. When the price of the securities goes down, recriminations start.

If you take a flier, you can't blame the broker for your mistake. But brokers may be at fault if they cross the line between optimism and misrepresentation or, of course, if they churn your account or are intentionally dishonest.

☑ HINT: *The areas most prone to problems are options, commodities, and margin accounts, or what are called other, esoteric investments.*

How to Protect Yourself

- Keep track of all your trades, including monthly statements.
- Note all important conversations with your broker in a diary.
- Contact your firm's manager if there's a problem—the company wants to keep, not lose, customers.
- If you're not satisfied, contact an experienced lawyer; ask about fee structure.
- Figure out your brokerage losses plus the lawyer's fee. Is it worth taking the next step?

Every broker is required to know each customer and not put any customer in an inappropriate, high-risk investment. A client's net worth, income, investment objectives, and experience help determine what is suitable.

If you have a problem with your broker, begin by trying to settle it informally with him or her. If the problem remains unresolved, take the following action:

- *Step 1.* Talk to the broker's supervisor or branch manager. Brokerage firms do not want to earn bad reputations with the public or have a number of vociferous, complaining clients.
- *Step 2.* Write a letter of complaint to the broker and the firm's compliance officer, with a copy to the branch manager. Request a written response from the compliance officer.
- *Step 3.* Send a copy of the letter to the state securities administrator. The North American Securities Administrators Association is the national organization for all 50 state securities officials. Call NASAA for the person in your state: 202–737–0900.
- *Step 4.* Contact the SEC, Office of Consumer Affairs, 450 5th Street NW, Washington, DC 20549. If your problem involves a commodities or futures contract, a copy of the com-

plaint letter should go to the Commodity Futures Trading Commission, Office of Public Information, 1155 21st Street NW, Washington, DC 20581, or call 202–418–5000.

- *Step 5.* Send a copy to the exchange involved (**see:** Appendix D for addresses).
- *Step 6.* If you are unable to resolve your complaint through phone calls and letters—and if it involves a great deal of money—the next step is arbitration.

$TIP: If you think your broker made a mistake or "done you wrong," the SEC has a new division to help you resolve the situation called Investor Assistance & Complaints. You can reach it by e-mail at: help@sec.gov or write to:

Office of Investor Assistance & Complaints
SEC
450 Fifth Street, NW
Washington, DC 20549

Their website has a great deal of useful material on how to handle such matters on your own. Click on: www.sec.gov. You can go even further to: www.sec.gov/consumer/jcompla.htm

GOING TO ARBITRATION

CAUTION: When you opened your brokerage account, you signed a customer's agreement form of some sort. Many forms specify which arbitration body will hear a case if there is a dispute. Contact that body. It will probably be one of these three.

1. *Arbitration panels sponsored by the brokerage industry's self-regulatory bodies. These consist of three people, but only one can be affiliated with the securities industry. These industry-sponsored panels, which have awarded punitive damages of as much as $1 million, often also award attorneys' fees.*

2. *Another mediation source is The American*

Arbitration Association, which has absolutely no connection to the brokerage industry. Although it seemingly may be more impartial, filing with the AAA is also more costly—from $500 for a dispute involving $10,000 or less to $7,000 for disputes of $1 million or more.

3. *The National Association of Security Dealers charges fees of $225 for $1,000 or less and $2,450 for amounts over $500,000.*

☑ *HINT: The U.S. Supreme Court has upheld a ruling that allows securities dealers to refuse to open accounts for clients who do not agree in advance to settle disputes through arbitration rather than by suing. Arbitration is generally quicker and less costly than a long court battle. (See: For Further Information at the end of this chapter.)*

Before You Undertake Arbitration . . .

Arbitration is a long and often unpleasant procedure and should never be entered into casually.

According to Jay J. Pack, author of *How to Talk to a Broker:*

- The odds for an arbitration settlement in your favor are typically fifty-fifty.
- You will improve your chances if you are prepared ahead of time. Gather proper documentation and other evidence to support your case.
- In 1987, the SEC ruled that arbitration results are binding. Therefore, if you decide to go to arbitration and the case is not decided in your favor, you cannot turn around and sue your broker.
- Act immediately if you are planning to go to arbitration. Arbitrators won't look favorably upon your complaint if you wait to see whether the investment in question goes up in price.

See: For Further Information at the end of this chapter.

AN OUNCE OF PREVENTION

It's nice to know arbitration is available for resolving disputes, but it's nicer still to avoid them in the first place. Here's how to reduce the possibility of the need for arbitration:

Put in writing (not e-mail) to your broker:

- Your financial objectives
- Your income, assets, liabilities
- Your financial obligations to others
- Directions for trading your account
- Where you can be reached during trading hours to confirm buy or sell positions
- Where you can be reached weekends, vacations, holidays, or if you're in the hospital.

And always:

- Read your monthly statement, trade slips
- Call quickly if there's a problem
- Know whether your account is up or down in value over the previous month, over a year ago at the same time

Once a year, review with him or her:

- Changes in your financial situation
- The performance record of your account
- Your net worth and income tax bracket

And . . .

- Ask your broker and accountant to communicate with one another about your tax situation

FOR FURTHER INFORMATION

Arbitration

Director of Arbitration
New York Stock Exchange
20 Broad Street
New York, NY 10005
212–656–3000

Director of Arbitration
National Association of Security Dealers
125 Broad Street
New York, NY 10004
212–858–4400

Office of Investor Education
Securities & Exchange Commission
450 Fifth Street NW
Washington, DC 20549
202–942–7040

American Arbitration Association
140 West 51st Street
New York, NY 10020
212–484–4000

The NASAA Directory
North American Securities Administrators
 Association
Ten G Street NE
Washington, DC 20006
202–737–0900

Lists telephone numbers and addresses of state administrators and federal agencies; $5.

Financial Planners

Financial Planning: Secure Your Financial Future
International Association for Financial
 Planning
5775 Glenridge Drive NE
Atlanta, GA 30328
800–945–5237
Free

Selecting a Qualified Financial Planning Professional
Institute of Certified Financial Planners
3801 East Florida Avenue

Denver, CO 80210
800–282–PLAN
Free

Tips on Financial Planners
Council of Better Business Bureaus, Inc.
Publications Dept.
4200 Wilson Boulevard, 8th floor
Arlington, VA 22203
703–276–0100
$2; send a self-addressed stamped envelope

Why Select a Fee Only Financial Planner
National Association of Personal Financial
 Advisors
355 West Dundee Road
Buffalo Grove, IL 60089
888-FEE-ONLY
website: www.napfa.org
Free

Investment Swindles: How They Work and How to Avoid Them
National Futures Association
Public Affairs Dept.
200 West Madison Street
Chicago, IL 60606
312–781–1300
Free

Ten Questions to Ask When Choosing a Financial Planner
Certified Financial Planners
888-CFP-MARK
website: www.cfp-board.org

26

Managing Your Brokerage Account

*I*n the previous chapter you learned how to select a top-notch pro to help you buy and sell securities and manage your overall portfolio. Once you've lined up this adviser, you're not off the hook. You still have some decisions to make—such as what type of account to use, what types of orders to place, and the degree to which you want to be involved in running your account, all topics covered in this chapter.

Please read this chapter carefully—whether you are opening your first account or already have an established relationship with a broker.

YOUR ACCOUNT—WHAT TYPE IS BEST?

First, you must decide between a *margin account* and a *cash account*. Most investors should and do use a cash account. In a cash account you pay for your securities within three business days after the transaction.

A margin account is not only more risky, because it involves borrowing, but it can lead to actual dollar losses if you do not monitor your position on a regular basis. Margin accounts are discussed in detail later in this chapter.

Discretionary or Nondiscretionary Accounts

If you are just beginning to work with your broker, do not, repeat, *do not* sign a discretionary account agreement. This type of account gives the broker the power to buy and sell securities without consulting you first.

Discretionary accounts should be used only with brokers you have worked with for a number of years and you trust more than your own mother.

Not surprisingly, discretionary accounts often cause problems—customers think the broker is churning their accounts (executing too many trades merely to rack up commissions) or not buying the right types of securities. The customer may or may not be right. Mismanagement of an account is hard to pinpoint, but it does indeed happen. So don't let it become a possibility—stick with a regular or what's known as a "cash" account instead.

In Street Name

Your broker will also ask you if you want your securities held in "street name"—that is, held with the firm—or if you want them registered in your own name with the certificates sent directly to you. If you decide to take physical possession of your securities, you will have to wait several weeks for them to arrive. If they are in street name, they become simply a computerized book entry at your firm, and your dividends and any stock splits are automatically collected and recorded for you.

☑ *HINT: If securities are in the broker's custody, transfer of shares when you sell them is easier than if you hold the certificates. You have to get the certificates out of your safe deposit box and deliver them to the broker's office—tricky if you're on vacation, not feeling well, in a hurry, etc.*

CAUTION: *If you travel or trade often, you certainly should not hold your own certificates—it makes selling shares quickly to take advantage of the market almost an impossibility.*

Joint Accounts

Before you open your account, check with your lawyer, especially if you are married, have children, and/or are involved in estate planning. You may want to establish a joint account.

- *In a joint tenancy with the rights of survivorship,* if one person dies, the other receives all the securities and cash in the account. The assets bypass probate and go directly to the survivor, although estate taxes may have to be paid.
- *In a tenancy-in-common account,* the deceased's share of the account goes to the deceased's heirs, not to the joint account holder. The survivor must then open a new account.
- *If you have children,* you may want to open a Uniform Gifts to Minors account. Whoever establishes the account names a "custodian" for the minor—very often they name themselves. All trading activity is then done by the custodian for the child's benefit. When the child reaches majority (age 18 or 21) he or she can legally take control of the account.

Wrap Accounts

A product of the nineties, the Wrap Account is designed to put your money decisions in the hands of a professional. Wrap accounts are offered by many brokerage firms, financial planners, and some banks. They manage your money for a fixed annual fee—instead of charging you commissions whenever you buy or sell something.

All your expenses, including the expense of hiring an outside, professional manager to pick your investments, are "wrapped" into that one, single fee.

Sounds good—but before you leap in, consider that doing so will cost you about 3% of your assets per year.

In a way, wrap accounts wrap you up in several layers of money management. First of all, your money is invested by private money managers in individual stocks and bonds and/or in a mixture of mutual funds.

Second, you're also paying part of your fee to the stockbroker or financial planner who referred you to the professional manager. Some brokerage firms try to talk customers into hiring an in-house manager; but a good wrap program should offer several outside managers who are not part of the firm.

CAUTION: *You may wind up paying the fee, year after year, for services that you need only now and then.*

Wrap programs make sense sometimes:

1. If there's a private money manager you like and this is the only way you can get access to him/her. (Managers often require a minimum of $1 million, but in a wrap program that minimum might be dropped to $100,000, or in the case of a wrap program that uses mutual fund managers, to $25,000.)
2. To avoid transaction charges if you do lots of trading.
3. To have someone else pick and monitor your mutual funds.

HINT: *Before opening a wrap account, check out an asset-allocation fund with T. Rowe Price, Fidelity, or one of the other large investment companies. In this type of fund your money is allocated among the company's various mutual funds; fees are significantly less than in a wrap account.*

HOW TO SWITCH BROKERS

One of the most time-consuming and sometimes awkward tasks investors face is switching brokers. Transferring assets from one firm to another ought to be easy, but it often occurs at a tortoiselike pace. Delays sometimes last weeks or months, and occasionally investors lose money, because securities dropped in value during the transit process.

Here's how to head off delays and trouble:

■ Your new broker will ask for a list of what's held in your old account. Have that ready. Give him a copy of your last monthly statement, or fax it to him.

   Under the rules of the National Association of Securities Dealers and the New York Stock Exchange, the old broker must deliver the holdings in five to ten days.

■ If that deadline cannot be met, the old brokerage firm must send the new one cash equaling the market value of the securities under what is called a "fail-to-deliver contract." This money enables the customer to trade. When the securities arrive, the money is returned.

   (Fail-to-deliver contracts are required by the NASD under a 1986 ruling adopted because of the number of customer complaints about transfers.)

Handling Snags

Problems, of course, do arise. The key reasons are that:

1. There are assets that cannot be moved quickly, such as an IRA that requires a change of custodians or proprietary investments, or a mutual fund run by the transferring brokerage firm.
2. The account has assets with virtually no value—bankrupt companies or companies with other technical problems.
3. The old broker stalls—he or she may be annoyed that you're leaving, on vacation, or no longer with the firm.

Talk first with the old broker, then with the supervisor. Ask why there is a hang-up. Prod gently, then firmly. You'll find most firms are accustomed to making this type of transaction within two weeks.

Serious Solutions

■ For serious delays, you can bring the matter to the attention of both the NASD and the SEC. Complaints to the NASD should be filed with the district office nearest the receiving broker. Contact the NASD in Gaithersburg, Maryland (800–289–9999), for the address of its nearest office.

   The SEC will contact the brokers and ask for an update. Contact the Office of Consumer Affairs, SEC, 450 Fifth Street NW, Washington, DC 20549 (202–942–7040).

■ If you lose money because of a delay and your former broker won't help out, your only recourse is to use the NASD's arbitration service. For the proper forms, write to the NASD's Arbitration Office, 125 Broad Street, New York, NY 10004 (212–858–4400). Expect to spend between $30 and $1,250, depending on the amount involved. Cases take about six to ten months to complete, and the decision is binding.

TYPES OF STOCK MARKET ORDERS

Once you have opened your account you're ready to trade. Although both dividend reinvestment plans and dollar cost averaging, discussed later on, are sensible ways to buy shares of stocks or mutual funds without using a broker, they only work for securities you already own. When adding to your holdings or selling stocks, you need to know what type of order to place.

Most investors simply call their broker and place an order, called a market order. However, there are several other ways to go about it. Armed with a little more information, you can place a specific type of order and thereby protect your portfolio.

Market Order

This is the most common type of order. It tells your broker to buy or sell at the best price obtainable at the moment, or at the market. If the order is to buy, the broker must keep bidding at advancing prices until a willing seller is found. If the order is to sell, the broker offers it at increasingly lower prices. With a market order, you can be certain that your order will be executed.

Limit Order

Usually a market order is sufficient, but when prices are fluctuating, it is wise to enter a limit order, which tells the broker the maximum price you're willing to pay, or if you're selling, the minimum you'll accept. For example, if you put in a limit order to buy a stock at 20 when the stock is trading at 22, your order will not be filled unless the stock falls to 20 or lower.

Day Order

This is an order to buy or sell that expires unless executed or canceled the same day it is placed. All orders are day orders unless you indicate otherwise. The key exception is a "good-until-canceled order."

Good-Until-Canceled Order

Also known as an open order, this is an order that remains in effect until executed or canceled. If it remains unfilled for long, the broker generally checks to see whether the customer is still interested in the stock should it reach the designated or target price.

Scale Order

An order to buy or sell specified amounts of a security at specified price increments. For example, you might want to buy 5,000 shares but in lots of 500, each in stages of $1/4$ points as the market falls.

Not all brokers will accept scale orders, because they involve so much work.

Stop Order

An order to buy (or sell) if the stock trades at a certain price. If the stock reaches this price your order is automatically triggered and becomes an order to buy (or sell) "at the market." A stop order may also be placed with a price limit to avoid its being executed at a substantially different price than the price of the stop.

Stop-Loss Order

An order that sets the sell price below the current market price. Stop-loss orders protect profits already made or prevent further losses if the stock falls in price.

 CAUTION: Both the New York and American stock exchanges have the power to halt stop orders in individual stocks to prohibit further sell-off in a declining stock. They very rarely use this power, however, and in fact did not do so during the 1987 market crash.

HOW TO USE STOP ORDERS

Stop orders basically provide protection against the unexpected by forcing you to admit your mistakes and thus cut your losses. In effect, they say that you will not participate above or below a certain price. For example, if you bought a stock six months ago at $50 per share and it's now at $75, you can set a stop-loss order to sell at $60. Then, should it fall in price, you know that your broker will sell you out at $60. Stop orders are useful for the following purposes.

To Limit Losses on Stocks You Own

You buy 100 shares of Allied Wingding at 50 in hopes of a quick gain. You are a bit queasy about the market, so at the same time you enter an order to sell the stock at 47⅜ stop. If AW drops to 47⅜, your stop order becomes a market order and you've limited your loss to 2⅝ points per share.

Traders generally set their loss targets at 10% below cost or recent high. Those who are concerned with long-term investments are more cautious and prefer a loss figure of about 15%: say, 42⅜ for a stock bought at 50.

> ☑ HINT: *For best results, set stop prices on the down side and have courage enough to back up your decisions. Once any stock starts to fall, there's no telling how far down it will go. Cut losses short and let your profits run.*

To Ensure a Profit

A year ago you bought 100 shares of a stock at 42, and it is now at 55. You are planning a vacation trip and do not want to lose too much of your paper profit, so you give your broker an order to sell at 51 stop, good until canceled. If the market declines and the sale is made, you will protect most of your 9-point-per-share gain.

Similarly, the stop order can protect a profit on a short sale. This time, you sell short at 55. The price falls to 40, so you have a $15-per-share profit. You look for a further price decline but want protection while you're away. You enter a buy order at 45 stop. If the stock price does jump to 45, you will buy 100 shares, cover your short position, and have a $1,000 profit (assuming that the specialist is able to make the purchase on the nose).

To Touch Off Predetermined Buy, Sell, and Sell-Short Orders

If you rely on technical analysis and buy only when a stock breaks through a trend line on the up side and sell, or sell short when it breaks out on the down side, you can place advance orders to "buy stop," "sell stop," or "sell-short stop." These become market orders when the price of the securities hits the designated figure.

EXAMPLE: Your stock is at 48¾ and appears likely to shoot up. But you want to be sure that the rise is genuine, because over the years there's been resistance at just about 50. You set a buy stop order at 51⅜. This becomes a market order if the stock hits the price 51⅜.

HOW TO SET STOP PRICES

Broadly speaking, there are two techniques to use:

- *Set the order at a price that is a fraction of a point above the round figure.* At 50⅛, for example. Your order will be executed before the stock drops to the round figure (50), which most investors will designate.

> ☌ CAUTION: *There is no guarantee that your stock will be sold at the exact stop price. In a fast-moving market, the stock may drop rapidly and skip the stop price, and thus the sale will be at a lower figure than anticipated.*

- *Relate the stop price to the volatility of the stock.* This is the beta. In making calculations, the trader uses a base of 1, indicating that the stock has historically moved with the market. A stock with a beta of 1.1 would be 10% more volatile than the overall market; one with a beta of 0.8 would be 20% less volatile than the market. If your stop price is too close to the current price of a very volatile stock, your order may be executed prematurely.

Use these guidelines for relating your stop order to the volatility or beta of your stock:

- Under 0.8, the sell price is 8% below the purchase price
- Between 0.8 and 1, the stop loss is set at 10% below the cost or recent high
- 1.1 to 1.3: 12% below

- 1.4 to 1.6: 14% below
- Over 1.6: 16% below

EXAMPLE: XYZ stock is acquired at 50. Its beta is 1.2, so the stop loss is set at 44: 12% below 50. If the market goes up, the stop is raised for every 20% gain in the stock price. At 60, the sell order would be 53: 12% below 60.

The lower the price of the stock, the greater the probable fluctuations; the higher the price of the stock, the smaller the swings are likely to be.

SELLING SHORT

Shorting is the flip side of buying stocks. In shorting, you sell stock you do not own at the market price in anticipation of a drop in price. You borrow the stock from your broker, who either has it in inventory, has shares in the margin account of another client, or borrows the shares from another broker. If the stock drops to a lower price than the price at which you sold it short, you buy it, pocket the profit, and return the stock you borrowed to your broker.

EXAMPLE: The stock of Nifty-Fifty, a high-technology company, has soared from 20 to 48 in a few months. A report from your broker questions whether NF can continue its ever-higher earnings. From your own research—of the company and the industry—you agree and decide that after the next quarter's report, the price of the stock will probably fall sharply. You arrange with your broker to borrow 500 shares and sell these shares at 48.

Two months later, the company announces lower profits, and the stock falls to 40. Now you buy 500 shares and pocket a $4,000 profit (less commissions). Or if you're convinced that the price will continue to go down, you hold out for a lower purchase price.

This technique seems easy, but short selling is one of the most misunderstood of all types of securities transactions and is often considered un-American and dangerous, as indicated by the Wall Street aphorism "He who sells what isn't his'n buys it back or goes to pris'n." Yet when properly executed, selling short can preserve capital, turn losses into gains, defer or minimize taxes, and be profitable.

With few exceptions, the only people who make money with stocks in a bear market are those who sell short.

Short selling is not for the faint of heart or for those who rely on tips instead of research. You may have some nervous moments if your timing is poor and the price of the stock jumps right after you sell short. But if your projections are correct, the price of that stock will fall—eventually. You must have the courage of your convictions and be willing to hang on.

Rules and Conditions for Selling Short

Because it's a special technique, short selling of all securities is subject to strict operational rules:

- *Margin.* All short sales must be made in a margin account, usually with stock borrowed from another customer of the brokerage firm under an agreement signed when the margin account was established.

☑ *HINT: For those who want to feel more comfortable with a short sale, it's best to maintain a margin balance equal to 90% of the short-sale commitment. This will eliminate the necessity for coming up with more cash.*

- *Interest.* There are no interest charges on margin accounts.
- *Premiums.* Once in a while, if the shorted stock is in great demand, your broker may have to pay a premium for borrowing, usually $1 per 100 shares per business day.
- *Dividends.* All dividends on shorted stock must be paid to the owner. That's why it's best to concentrate on warrants and stocks that pay low or no dividends.

■ *Rights and stock dividends.* Because you are borrowing stock, you are not entitled to rights or stock dividends. You must return all stock rights and dividends to the owner.

If you know or suspect that a company is going to pass or decrease its payout, you can get an extra bonus by selling short. The price of the stock is almost sure to drop. But be careful: The decline may be too small to offset the commissions.

■ *Sales price.* Short sales must be made on the uptick or zero tick: That is, the last price of the stock must be higher than that of the previous sale. If the stock is at 70, you cannot sell short when it drops to $69\frac{7}{8}$, but must wait for a higher price: $70\frac{1}{8}$ or more.

☑ EXCEPTION: *The broker may sell at the same price, 70, provided that the previous change in the price was upward. There might have been three or four transactions at 70. A short sale can be made when the last different price was $69\frac{7}{8}$ or lower. This is called selling on an even tick.*

Picking Stocks for Short Sales

Ask your broker for recommendations and then take a look at these fairly simple indicators:

■ *Insider transactions.* If officers and directors of the corporation have sold stock in the previous few months—the assumption is that when the number of insiders selling exceeds the number buying, the stock is at a high level, and these knowledgeable people believe a decline is ahead.

■ *Volatility.* As measured by the beta of the stock. This is the historical relation between the price movement of the stock and the overall market. A stock that moves with the market has a beta of 1.0; a more volatile issue is rated 1.5, because it swings 50% more than the market.

The more volatile the stock, the better it may be for short selling. You can hope to make your profit more quickly.

■ *Relative strength.* Or how the stock stacks up with other companies in the same or similar industries. This calculation takes into account the consistency and growth of earnings and whether the last quarter's profits were lower or higher than anticipated by Wall Street.

These data are available from statistical services such as *Value Line* and Standard & Poor's *Earnings Forecast.*

When corporate earnings are lower than the professional forecasts, the stock will almost always fall sharply. Catching such a situation so that you can sell short early will depend on your own projections, which can be based on news stories or information that you have gleaned from your personal contacts.

What to Sell

As a rule of thumb, the best candidates for short selling are:

1. Stocks that have zoomed up in a relatively short period.
2. One-time glamour stocks that are losing popularity—after reaching a peak, these stocks will be sold rapidly by the institutions, and because these "professionals" follow the leader, the prices can drop far and fast.
3. Stocks that have begun to decline more than the market averages—this may be an indication of fundamental weakness.
4. Warrants of volatile stocks, which are selling at high prices.

Guidelines for Successful Short Selling

■ *Don't buck the trend.* Do not sell short unless both the major and intermediate trends of the market—or, on occasion, those of an industry—are down. Make the market work for you. You may be convinced that an individual stock is overpriced, but do not take risks until there is clear, confirmed evidence of a fall in the market and for the stock you're considering.

■ *Don't sell short at the market when the stock price is heading down.* Place a limit order at the lowest price at which you are willing to sell short.

■ *Do set protective prices, on the up side,* 10% to 15% above the sale price, depending on the volatility of the stock. In most cases, a quick small loss will be wise.

■ *Don't short several stocks at once* until you are experienced. Start with one failing stock; if you make money, you will be ready for another.

■ *Do rely on the odd-lot selling indicator.* This is available from several technical advisory services or can be set up on your own. It is calculated by dividing the total odd-lot sales into the odd-lot short sales and charting a ten-day moving average. When the indicator stays below 1.0 for several months, it's time to consider selling short. When it's down to 0.5, start selling.

On the other hand, when the indicator rises above 1.0, do not sell short and cover your positions. And if you hesitate, cover all shorts when a one-day reading bounces above 3.0.

■ *Do set target prices.* But be ready to cover when there's a probability of an upswing. There will usually be a resistance level. If this is maintained with stronger volume, take your profit. You can't afford to try to outguess the professionals.

BREAKING EVEN

Before you hang on to a stock in hopes that its price will rise so that you can break even, check the table on this page. You'll see that a stock must rise 100% to correct a 50% decline! If your stock de-

clines from 100 to 50, it has dropped 50%. But it will take a doubling in price (a 100% increase) to rise from 50 back to 100.

☑ *MORAL: Take losses early; set stop orders to protect profits; stop dreaming.*

PROGRAM TRADING

An ongoing situation individual stock investors should be aware of is program trading, a complicated strategy used by institutions whereby computers trigger buy and sell orders.

It is less of a problem than in the past, although it does add to market volatility and was blamed for much of the market's drop in October 1987.

Program trading is the result of the introduction of index options, index futures, and computers to Wall Street. It takes advantage of the price gap between index futures and option prices and the market value of the stocks making up the indexes.

The trader uses computers to follow the price differentials and then to sell automatically at a specified point. When a number of big institutions follow the same strategy, the market swings can be large.

IF A STOCK DROPS THE FOLLOWING PERCENTAGE	IT NEEDS TO RISE THIS PERCENTAGE FOR YOU TO BREAK EVEN
5% (100 to 95)	5% (95 to 100)
10% (100 to 90)	11% (90 to 100)
15% (100 to 85)	17% (85 to 100)
20% (100 to 80)	25% (80 to 100)
25% (100 to 75)	33% (75 to 100)
30% (100 to 70)	42% (70 to 100)
40% (100 to 60)	66% (60 to 100)
50% (100 to 50)	100% (50 to 100)
60% (100 to 40)	150% (40 to 100)
75% (100 to 25)	300% (25 to 100)

NAME OF ISSUE	DECLARED	EX-DIV.	RECORD	PAYMENT
Consolidated Edison	1/25	2/10	2/16	3/15/2000

Here are two typical trading situations:

- If the value of the S&P 500 futures contract drops below the market price of the stocks that make up the index and the spread (or price gap) becomes wide enough, computers send out automatic signals to sell stocks. This huge sell order can lead to a drop in the price of the stocks.

- If the prices of the S&P 500 stocks fall behind the futures on the index, the computers will signal to buy these stocks and sell the futures when the spread reaches a certain amount. This can lead to a rise in stock prices.

SPACE YOUR TRADES

If you are making a large investment (500 shares or more) in any one stock, consider spacing out your purchases over a period of several days or even weeks. The commissions will be higher, but you'll gain a time span in which to review your investment decisions without committing all your funds. And if you decide that your choice was wrong, you can cancel the rest of the order.

CHECK THE EX-DIVIDEND DATE

Always check the ex-dividend dates before you sell. This will ensure extra income benefits.

The Triple Witching Hour

Four times a year, three "items" expire on the same day: stock index futures, index options, and stock options. Program traders take offsetting positions, and a burst of buying and selling takes place, sometimes just before the market closes. There's no way to determine if the result will push the market up or down. This occurs on the third Friday of March, June, September, and December.

Ex-dividend means without dividend. On the stock tables, this is shown by the symbol "x" after the name of the company in the "sales" column.

The buyer of a stock selling ex-dividend does not receive the most recently declared dividend. That dividend goes to the seller. With Consolidated Edison, the date is shown in Standard & Poor's *Stock Guide* as in the table on this page.

Once a dividend is ex-dividend, shareholders then look to the next dividend to be declared.

Going ex-dividend is actually a two-step process. The new dividend is payable to those who are "holders of record" as of a certain date. To be a holder of record, one must buy the stock at least five business days before the record date. On the fourth business day prior to the record date, the stock trades ex-dividend; that is, without dividend. Step two involves payment of the dividend by the corporation to the holders of record. This payment occurs two or three weeks after the official record date.

Once you have decided to sell a stable stock, you may want to delay the sale until a few days after the ex-dividend date, so you can earn the dividend. On the ex-dividend date, the stock will usually drop by the amount of the dividend but will tend to make it up in the following few days.

Ex-rights means without rights. As outlined in Chapter 18, rights offer stockholders the opportunity to buy new or additional stock at a discount. The buyer of a stock selling ex-rights is not entitled to this right after the ex-right date.

AUTOMATIC WAYS TO BOOST YOUR PORTFOLIO

The simplest, easiest way to buy shares of a stock—once you own it, that is—is through a dividend reinvestment plan, so we'll discuss that approach first. Dollar cost averaging is another automatic way to add to your portfolio holdings. Neither dividend reinvestment nor dollar cost averaging requires a great deal of work or thought on your part once you've actually purchased the stock or mutual fund for your portfolio.

Dividend Reinvestment Plans (DRIPs)

In this plan, offered by most blue-chip companies, dividends are automatically reinvested in shares of a company's stock without a brokerage fee. A number also offer a 5% price discount on new stock purchases. This service is offered by corporations to strengthen stockholder relations and raise additional capital at low cost; for investors, it is a handy, inexpensive means for regular saving. It avoids the nuisance of small dividend checks and forces regular investments . . . and since you never see the dividend checks, you won't be able to spend them.

Many corporations permit extra cash deposits, ranging from $10 to $3,000 each dividend reinvestment time. There is usually an annual cap ranging anywhere from $10,000 to $100,000 per year.

Under such a plan, all dividends are automatically reinvested in the company's stock. The company then credits the full or fractional shares and pays dividends on the new total holdings.

Because these cash dividends are reinvested automatically at regular quarterly intervals, they resemble dollar cost averaging and turn out to be a way to buy more shares of a stock when its price is low. Full as well as fractional shares are credited to your account.

CAUTION: You must pay income taxes on the dividends reinvested just as though you had received cash. If you buy the stock at a discount from its current market price, the difference is regarded as taxable income.

Dollar Cost Averaging (DCA)

This, the most widely used direct-investment formula plan, eliminates the difficult problem of timing when to buy and sell. You purchase a fixed dollar amount of stocks at specific time intervals: one month, three months, or whatever time span meets your savings schedule. Consequently, your average cost will always be lower than the average market price. This is because lower prices always result in the purchase of more shares.

EXAMPLE: If you invest $100 per month regardless of the price of the shares, the lower the market value, the more shares you buy. The stocks you buy fluctuate in price between 10 and 5 over four months. The first month you buy 10 shares at $10 each for a total of $100. The second month you buy 20 shares at $5 each, and so on. At the end of four months you have acquired 60 shares for your $400 at an average cost of $6.67 per share (400 ÷ 60).

NOTE: During this same period, the average price was $7.50.

Total invested: $400

40 shares @ $5 = $200
20 shares @ $10 = $200
                 $400

Companies with Dividend Reinvestment Plans: 2000

AT&T	Illinois Power
Bell Atlantic	Kroger Co.
BellSouth	McDonald's
Bristol-Myers Squibb	MMM
Citicorp	Morgan (J.P.)
Clorox	PepsiCo
Commonwealth Edison	Piedmont Nat. Gas
Disney (Walt)	Raytheon
Duke Power	Sears, Roebuck
Du Pont	Southwestern Bell
Exxon	Texas Utilities
General Electric	United Water
Green Mountain Power	Resources
Hawaiian Electric	Wells Fargo
Heinz	WPL Holdings
IBM	Xerox Corp.

☑ *HINT: Start your program a week or two before the date you expect to receive a dividend check from the company whose stock you plan to buy.*

☑ *HINT: Shares of mutual funds are excellent vehicles for DCA. They provide diversification, generally stay in step with the stock market as a whole, and usually continue to pay dividends.*

Reverse Dollar Cost Averaging

This is a technique that is best used after retirement when you begin to liquidate shares of a mutual fund. Instead of drawing a fixed dollar amount (as most retirees do), you sell a fixed number of shares. The average selling price will come out higher that way.

As an example only, the illustration below shows the values of fund shares that fluctuate widely over a six-month period. To get $100 income, you must sell 10 shares in the first month, 20 in the second, etc. Over the half-year, you liquidate 75 shares at an average price of $8.

But if you sell a fixed number (10) of shares each month, your income will vary: $100 in month one, $50 in month two, $200 in month four. Overall, you will cash in only 60 shares at an average redemption price of $10.

Reverse dollar cost averaging can be dangerous for two reasons:

1. You won't get the same dollars every month, but over the same period of time you will receive as much and have more shares still invested. Yet when the price of the shares drops,

---

Stocks for Dollar Cost Averaging: 2000	
Abbott Laboratories	Iowa Gas & Electric
American Home	Johnson & Johnson
Products	Longs Drug Stores
Becton Dickinson	McDonald's
Boeing Co.	Merck & Co.
Bristol-Myers Squibb	PepsiCo
British Telecom (ADR)	Pfizer, Inc.
Caterpillar	Procter & Gamble
Clorox Co.	Rockwell Int'l.
Coca-Cola	Rollins, Inc.
Disney (Walt)	Rubbermaid, Inc.
Dominion Resources	Seagram Co.
Emerson Electric	Smucker, J.M.
Exxon Corp.	TECO Energy
Federal Home Loan	Texaco
General Electric	Tootsie Roll Indus.
Goodyear Tire	Upjohn Co.
Health & Retirement	Weingarten Realty
Prop.	Winn Dixie Stores
Heinz	Wrigley (Wm.)
IBM	Xerox Corp.

---

you will have to unload more shares and will have fewer assets invested in the fund.

2. You cannot know in advance the correct number of shares to sell; if you have to change the formula, you may be in trouble.

☑ *HINT: This system is arithmetically correct but may be difficult for people who do not have additional income to live on in months when fund per-share price is low.*

ALL-IN-ONE ACCOUNTS

If you have a brokerage account, a money market fund, and a major credit card, as well as some type of checking account, you may find it useful and economical to wrap it all together and put it into a combo, or asset management account. In this way, all your financial transactions will be handled under one roof—at a bank or brokerage firm—

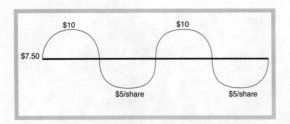

Reverse Dollar Cost Averaging

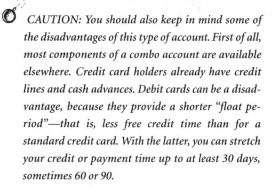

SHARE PRICE	$100 PER MONTH: NO. SHARES SOLD	10 SHARES PER MONTH: INCOME
10	10	$100
5	20	50
10	10	100
20	5	200
10	10	100
5	20	50
Total	75	$600
Average redemption price per share	$8	$10

which saves you time, red tape, and sometimes money, too.

A typical central assets account consists of one versatile package that can include stocks, bonds, your IRA, a money market fund, and credit or debit card transactions. But you must be able to meet the minimum amount set by the brokerage firm or bank, which ranges from $5,000 to $20,000.

For a yearly fee (zero to $200) the sponsoring bank or brokerage firm will provide unlimited check-writing privileges on a money market account; an American Express, Visa, or MasterCard account; a line of credit; a securities brokerage account; and an all-inclusive monthly statement.

An important additional benefit, known as the "sweep" feature, automatically transfers or sweeps any idle cash (from the sale of a security, a CD that matured, or dividends) into a high-paying money market fund.

This system not only relieves you of keeping track of the money but, more importantly, prevents any loss of interest between transactions.

A central asset account comprises seven basic ingredients:

1. A brokerage account in which securities can be bought and sold at regular commissions

2. Automatic investment of idle cash into money market funds

3. A checking account, usually with free checks; minimum amounts vary

4. A debit or credit card that can be used for purchases, loans, or cash

5. A line of credit—that is, the privilege of borrowing against your credit or debit card

6. Quick loans secured by the margin value of the securities held in the account, with interest charged at slightly above the broker call rate

7. Composite monthly statements showing all transactions and balances

CAUTION: You should also keep in mind some of the disadvantages of this type of account. First of all, most components of a combo account are available elsewhere. Credit card holders already have credit lines and cash advances. Debit cards can be a disadvantage, because they provide a shorter "float period"—that is, less free credit time than for a standard credit card. With the latter, you can stretch your credit or payment time up to at least 30 days, sometimes 60 or 90.

Easy access to credit means those without a lot of self-control can zoom through their credit line without even thinking about it. If you fall into this category, steer clear of the central assets account.

The Better Business Bureau in many areas has free material on central asset accounts, banks, and brokerage services. Contact your local office.

MARGIN ACCOUNTS

A margin account enables you to do a couple of things. If you need a loan, you can borrow money against securities that you already own—provided these securities are held in a margin account (as opposed to a cash account). Or you can borrow money from your brokerage firm to make an initial purchase of securities. Your broker, in turn, will ask for securities or cash as collateral.

You can typically borrow up to 50% of the

Directory of Central Assets Accounts, 2000

Citicorp: Citigold Account
  (800–285–1701)

Morgan Stanley Dean, Witter: Active Assets Account
  (800–869–3326)

A. G. Edwards: Total Asset Account
  (800–677–8380)

Fidelity: Ultra Service Account
  (800–343–8721)

Merrill Lynch: Cash Management Account
  (800–262–4636)

Prudential-Bache: Prudential Command Account
  (800–222–4321)

Charles Schwab: One Account
  (800–421–4488)

Solomon Smith Barney: Financial Management Account
  (800–221–3434)

value of common stocks, mutual funds, and corporate bonds, and up to 90% of the value of Treasury securities. To protect themselves, however, most brokers ask for a higher initial margin.

A chief advantage of margin debt, of course, is the interest rate. They average around 7%, a lot lower than the 18% on the average credit card.

Before you open a margin account, read through the following rules. Discuss any points you're not clear about with your broker—this is an area full of detailed and seemingly complicated requirements. If you don't understand them, you could wind up losing money.

The Rules

1. When you open a margin account you will be asked to sign a margin agreement and loan consent.
2. The loan consent feature gives your broker permission to lend the securities in your account.
3. Stocks in your margin account will be held "in

street name," which means in the broker's firm. Therefore, you cannot put your stock certificates in your vault.

4. You will be subject to "margin call" if you use the assets in your account to the point where you have no more credit, or if the value of your portfolio falls below a minimum amount. When either takes place, your broker will "call" to ask you to reduce your loan. If you cannot come up with the cash or additional securities, your broker will sell enough of your remaining stocks to "meet the call."

Margin accounts are governed by the Federal Reserve Board's Regulation T, the New York Stock Exchange, the National Association of Securities Dealers, and individual brokerage house rules.

5. Under the rules set forth by the Federal Reserve Board, the initial requirement for margin on stocks is 50%. So to buy $10,000 worth of securities you must put up at least $5,000. Greater leverage is allowed on government bonds, where you can borrow up to 95%.
6. The New York Stock Exchange, however, has stricter requirements. It asks members to demand that investors deposit a minimum of $2,000 in cash or its equivalent in securities in order to open a margin account. That means that if you want to buy $3,000 in stock, your initial margin requirement is actually $66^2/_3$%, or $2,000, rather than the $1,500, or 50%, that the Federal Reserve Board requires.
7. Some brokers set even higher requirements.
8. The New York Stock Exchange also requires that the equity in the account be maintained at 25% to 30% at all times. This is called a "minimum maintenance margin." When the value of your portfolio drops below this level, your broker will issue a margin call, as described above, and you will have to come up with more cash or the broker will sell enough securities in your account to bring it up to the required level.

Calculating Your Yield When Buying on Margin

To determine exactly what yield you get by buying on margin, you must ascertain the return on your actual investment: the *margin equivalent yield*. You can calculate this from the accompanying formula.

The *cash yield percent* (CY%) is the return on securities bought outright. The same formulas can be used for both pre-tax and after-tax yields.

$$MEY = \left(\frac{100}{\%M} \times CY\%\right) - \left[\left(\frac{100}{\%M} - 1\right) \times DI\%\right]$$

where MEY = margin equivalent yield
%M = % margin
CY% = cash yield %
DI% = debit interest %

EXAMPLE: You are on a 50% margin base, receive 12% cash yield from dividends, and pay 20% in your debit balance.

$$MEY = \left(\frac{100}{50} \times 12\right) - \left[\left(\frac{100}{50} - 1\right) \times 20\right]$$

$$MEY = (2 \times 12 = 24) - [(2 - 1 = 1) \times 20 = 20]$$

$$MEY = 24 - 20 = 4\%$$

Thus the 12% return, with margin, dwindles to 4%.

EXAMPLE: Let's say you want to buy 200 shares of a $50 stock. In a regular cash account, you would put up $10,000 ($50 x 200 = $10,000). But in a margin account, you only have to put up 50% of the purchase price, or $5,000 plus commission. Your broker lends you the other $5,000 and charges you interest on it.

The Loan Rate

Mounting interest charges can take a big chunk out of profits in a margin account, especially if you hold your stocks a long time. You are charged in-terest daily based on the broker call rate, the rate the banks charge brokers for money. The interest the broker then charges you may run from 0.5% to 2.5% above the broker loan rate, which as we went to press ranged from 7% to 8¼%. The more active and the larger your account, the lower the rate is likely to be. Dividends, of course, can help offset some of the interest.

☑ *HINT: The interest you pay on your margin account is tax deductible to the extent that it is offset by investment income—dividends, interest, and capital gains. So to deduct $2,000 in interest, you must report at least $2,000 in investment income. In other words, margin account interest is deductible if used for taxable investments but not for other purposes. So if you take out a $25,000 loan to pay your child's tuition or buy a house, you cannot deduct the interest.*

NOTE: Since 1993, capital gains are no longer classified as investment income for purposes of investment interest deduction—unless the taxpayer elects to have all or part of the gains subject to the 20% maximum tax classified as investment income

Exchange and Federal Margin Requirements

Assuming you put up cash in the amount of $10,000 in each case, you could buy on margin:

- $20,000 worth of marginable stocks
- $20,000 worth of listed corporate convertible bonds

You can invest on margin in nearly every issue on the New York and American stock exchanges and in nearly 2,000 over-the-counter securities. To open an account, you must sign a margin agreement that includes a consent to loan securities. The margin account agreement states that all securities will be held "in street name"; that is, by the broker. The consent to loan means that the broker can lend your securities to others who may want them for the purpose of selling short.

Do Not Have a Margin Account If:

- You lack the temperament
- You are dealing in small amounts of money
- You cannot absorb a loss
- Your portfolio consists primarily of income equities
- You tend to buy and hold stocks

To Minimize Risks:

- Set stop orders above the 30% loss point
- Borrow less than the maximum
- Buy on margin only in a bull market
- Watch for increases in the broker loan rate
- Check the prices of margined stock once a week to avoid a surprise margin call

---

to offset additional investment interest. But, in that case, the gains are subject to ordinary income tax rates, which can be as high as 39.6%.

 CAUTION: The New York Stock Exchange may set special margin requirements calling for more cash or securities or require full cash payments in very volatile stocks.

Special Miscellaneous Account

If you have excess cash or equity in your margin account, this is known as a special miscellaneous account (SMA). It is created by the deposit of more than 50% of the purchase price of stocks or securities bought on margin, by the accumulation of dividends, or by a rise in the value of the margined portfolio. As long as the value of your margined portfolio is at or above the minimum maintenance margin, you may use your SMA to buy additional securities, but if your account is below the minimum margin maintenance requirement, your broker will use your SMA to meet the margin call.

Margin Call

If your firm requires a 30% minimum maintenance rather than 25%, to find out if you're approaching a call, multiply the price of the stock at the time you purchased it by 0.71. If it has reached that price, your phone will ring.

 HINT: If you use margin, don't let your equity fall below 50%. In a volatile market, you can get into trouble very fast; therefore, borrow against blue-chip stocks, government securities, and other conservative investments.

Additional Regulations

- Margin rules have been extended to some mutual funds.
- Individuals are allowed to have more than one margin account at the same brokerage house under certain circumstances, which vary from firm to firm. Check with your broker.
- Not all securities traded over-the-counter are marginable. Stocks under $5 usually cannot be margined.
- The NYSE sets special loan limits for individual issues that show unusual volume, price fluctuations, or rapid turnover, to discourage undue speculation.
- Customers whose accounts show a pattern of "day trading" (purchasing and selling the same marginable issues on the same day) are required to maintain appropriate margin before the transactions are made.
- Each brokerage firm sets its own margin requirements for nonconvertible bonds, municipal bonds, and U.S. government bonds.

FOR FURTHER INFORMATION

Books

Charles B. Carlson, *Buying Stocks Without a Broker* (New York: McGraw-Hill, 1997). $14.95 + $3 shipping, from: Dow Theory Publications, Inc., 7412 Calumet Avenue, Hammond, IN 46324, 219–931–6480.

Services

Direct Purchase Plan
800–774–4117 or:
www.enrolldirect.com

This 24-hour hotline service provides a single source for enrollment information for a number of direct stock purchase plans. Among the companies you can receive information on:

- Amoco
- CSX Corp.
- Central & Southwest
- Duke Energy
- Energen
- Home Depot
- Houston Industries
- Lucent Technologies
- McDonald's
- Merck
- Motorola
- Piedmont Natural Gas
- Quaker Oats
- Walgreen

27

Investing On-line

Just as Alexander Graham Bell changed forever the world of communication back in 1876, so too the Internet is changing the world of investing. Along with other revolutionary techniques wrought by going on-line—book and CD buying, car and equipment shopping, on-line auctions, and dissemination of information on every imaginable topic—the Internet has also taken a bite out of traditional stock and bond trading. . . and the bite is big. *Very big*. Approximately one-third of all equity trades placed by individuals are now placed on-line. And the numbers are multiplying each and every day.

ON-LINE TRADING GOES MAINSTREAM

A landmark event occurred in mid-1999 when Merrill Lynch, bastion of Wall Street tradition, announced it had moved to the Internet, a step that confirmed what everyone suspected—that on-line investing was part of the mainstream.

As more brokerages set up shop on-line—there were 12 in 1995 and today there are over 100—picking the right one becomes increasingly complicated. Comparing costs is an obvious first consideration. Other factors to look into: access to reliable, free research; dividend reinvestment plans; handling of investment club accounts; access to IPOs; and, of course, having a dependable broker who will execute your trades quickly and accurately.

The amount of money you want to invest must also be factored into your decision. Merrill Lynch requires a minimum of $20,000 to open an account, with on-line trades priced at $29.95 each. If you want Merrill's unlimited trading program, there's no minimum balance, but there is a minimum annual fee of $1,500. That makes the unlimited trading plan appropriate only for very active investors. In other words, stick with the firm's standard plan unless you make more than 52 trades per year.

With Charles Schwab, who also offers free research and likewise charges $29.95 per trade, you need an opening balance of $2,500. Other companies are even cheaper: E*Trade, a major player, has a $1,000 minimum and trades are $14.95. Datek has no minimum (if you get preapproval) and trades are just $9.99. Suretrade charges $7.95.

RATING THE ON-LINE BROKERS

No one on-line firm excels at everything. However, as the business grows, so does the information and research about it—Gomez Advisors and Forrester Research, for example, rate on-line brokers on a regular basis. According to Forrester, about 3.5 million households are expected to invest on-line this year, compared to about 2.5 million a year ago.

Rapid growth has also caused trading delays and system failures—no fun when your money is at stake. In fast markets, with thousands of investors wanting to trade at the same time, prices change instantly and delays develop. Executions and confirmations slow down and reports of prices actually lag behind real prices. The bottom line: On-line brokers are facing greater scrutiny by the SEC as customers suffer serious service problems and file class-action lawsuits.

Here's where you can find in-depth ratings of the leading on-line brokers, based on service, price, accuracy of trades, research, and extra help.

- Expert Online Investment Advocates: www.xolia.com
- Forrester Research: 617–497–7090
- Gomez Advisors: www.gomez.com
- KeyNote Systems' Online Brokerage Index: www.keynote.com
- PC World: www.pcworld.com
- TheStreet.com: www.thestreet.com

SEVEN THINGS TO KNOW BEFORE OPENING AN ON-LINE ACCOUNT

Although with a click of a mouse you can buy and sell stocks within minutes, on-line investing is not a license to give up doing your homework. In fact, it's just the opposite.

Because there is no one to advise you, no one to talk with, no one to hold your hand, you need to be extremely savvy before trading on-line. Otherwise you can easily lose your nest egg in a day—not only because the pace is so fast but because it also comes with a free-for-all atmosphere. At a minimum, you must understand the following seven trading concepts.

1. *Limit order.* An order to buy or sell at a specific price. A buy limit order can be executed only at the limit price or lower. A sell limit order can be executed only at the limit price or higher. Limit orders enable you to avoid buying or selling a stock at a price higher or lower than you want.

CAUTION: It's possible that your limit order may never be executed if the price quickly surpasses your limit before your order can be filled.

2. *Market order.* An order to buy or sell at the best available price. Most orders are market orders.

CAUTION: With a market order you cannot control the price of the trade as you can with a limit order.

3. *Day order.* An order to buy or sell that expires unless executed or canceled the day it is placed. All orders are day orders unless otherwise specified. The main exception: a "good 'til canceled order."

4. *All or none order.* Also known as an AON, this buy or sell order tells the specialists and market makers on the floors of the exchanges to trade all of your stock and not to make a partial transaction.

CAUTION: An all or none order is not automatically canceled if a complete transaction is not executed unless the order entry is marked FOK, meaning "fill the full number or kill."

5. *The float.* The number of shares outstanding and available for trading by the public. A small float means the stock will be more volatile, since a larger order can influence its price dramatically. A stock with a large float will be less volatile. You don't want to enter a market order unless you know you're buying or selling a stock that is liquid—one with plenty of shares outstanding. If you're working with a thin stock—one that trades only a few thousand shares a day—your order to buy or sell might be the only one out there at the time.

SOLUTION: Instead of a market order, put in a

limit order, stating the price at which you want to trade.

$TIP: CBS MarketWatch (cbsmarketwatch.com) covers floats, price gaps, and volume for NYSE, AMEX, and Nasdaq stocks that have moved more than 5% within the last 20 minutes, or those that have gone up more than 100% in the last 20 minutes.

6. *Rush hours.* Be very careful, even reluctant, about buying or selling at the open or close of the trading day. This is particularly true if you're placing a market order. With hot stocks you're joining a herd of other buyers or sellers, especially at the opening bell when prices are often irrationally high or low. In most cases, a stock's price will bounce back from opening ups and downs and you'll have a chance to trade at a better time.

7. *Margin accounts.* If your margin account falls below the firm's maintenance margin requirement, your broker has the legal right to sell your securities at any time, without consulting you first. "Margin calls" are a courtesy, not a requirement. Brokers are not required to make margin calls to their customers.

   Even when your broker gives you time to put more cash or securities into your account to meet a margin call, the broker can act without waiting for you to meet the call. If the market is falling rapidly, the broker could sell your entire margin account—at a loss—because the securities have dropped in value. (**See:** Chapter 26 for more on margin accounts.)

DUNNAN'S ADVICE FOR ON-LINE INVESTING

■ *Practice first.* If you're a novice when it comes to the Internet investing, practice entering market and limit orders, placing orders for Treasuries, buying mutual fund shares, and

trading options at DLJ's site (www.dljdirect. com). Click on the trading demo program. This way you'll learn the techniques before spending real money.

■ *Follow the price of a stock in real time.* Many on-line sites post delayed prices, which come in 20 minutes after the fact. Instead, check out: Wall Street City at: www.wallstreetcity.com; Free Real Time at: www.freerealtime.com; and Quote.com at: www.quote.com.

■ *Track a stock's highs and lows before making a trade.* Use CBS MarketWatch at: cbs.market-watch.com/newsroom/gap_NYSE_now.htx.

■ *Know how to reach your broker.* Use a broker that offers alternatives to the Internet: Touch-Tone telephone trades, faxed orders, and person-to-person orders. Know which is best and what it costs.

■ *Make sure canceled is canceled.* Find out how the firm will notify you if a canceled order is indeed canceled. Although you may receive an electronic receipt for the cancellation, don't assume that means the order was indeed canceled. You want a backup verification.

■ *Diversify among brokers.* Don't have all your money with one small on-line firm. Regulators point out that if the market has a severe correction, these companies could fall short of capital requirements.

■ *Speak up.* If you have a problem, begin by e-mailing the firm and then notify the SEC (www.sec.gov) and the National Association of Security Dealers (www.nasd.org). Let the companies that rate on-line brokers also know—see the list on page 265.

DAY TRADING

Because of the Internet revolution, extremely low commissions for on-line stock transactions and easy access to real-time quotes (replacing the 20-minute delayed quotes that used to be the norm), day trading has taken the country by storm. In fact, day traders—those who buy and resell stocks within hours, often minutes, in order to scalp a point here and there—are becoming a major factor in the market. Credit Suisse First Boston estimates that day traders, who make up about 5% of the customers trading on-line, are actually responsible for about 25% of on-line trades.

THE FOOD IS BETTER IN VEGAS

But, don't be fooled. Not all day traders make money. Statistics are hard to come by but Yahoo! maintains that at least one-third of day traders "go broke and quit within a year." Those that hang in there "seldom see a profit before 18 months." Philip Feigin, executive director of the North American Securities Administrators Association, cautions, "For the typical retail investor, day trading isn't investing; it's gambling. If you want to gamble, go to Las Vegas. The food is better."

My caution: If you must day trade, despite the obvious and not so obvious risks, first read the chapters in this book about investing. Then, if you're still tempted, here are some lessons to boost your chances of keeping your shirt.

1. *Think small.* Day traders need to have trades confirmed within minutes. That means using a smaller on-line broker with less traffic and fewer system failures is a good bet. As we go to press, according to Keynote Web Brokerage Index (www.keynote.com/measures/brokers), which follows on-line brokers, some of the biggies, such as Schwab and E*Trade, have longer fulfillment times and more problems than smaller brokers. Check out Keynote on a regular basis for updates. Two current recommendations: On-Site Trading (www.onsite trading.com) and MB Trading (www.mb-trading.com). Expert Online Investment Advocates (www.xolia.com) and Gomez Advisors (www.gomez.com) also post recommended brokers for day traders.

2. *Get real time quotes.* Delayed prices won't work. These sites, favorites with day traders, will give you what you need instantly: Thomson Financial Services (www.thomsonrtq. com), StockInvestor, (www.stockinvestor.com), and FreeRealTime.com (www.freerealtime. com). For $35 a month, CBS MarketWatch RT (rt.marketwatch.com) will give you 2,500 snapshots a day. For $75 a month, PC Quote (www.pcquote.com) has streaming quotes, automatically updated.

3. *Talk only to smart traders and rely upon solid research from analysts.* Day traders seem to live on tips and many tipsters are phonies. You should know why and what you are buying or selling, and the risks involved. Continue to do research using traditional sources (see: "Dunnan's On-line Directory" at the end of this chapter). And use common sense when assessing information you gleam from chat rooms or message boards. Much of what you read may be from stock promoters, touting their own positions . . . which brings us to our next point.

INTERNET FRAUD

The Internet is an excellent tool for all of us, enabling us not only to do research but to trade quickly and inexpensively. But it's also an excellent tool for unsavory, no-good types. And, unfortunately, there are plenty of scam artists out there—so many in fact that the SEC now has a special division to deal with them. Its "sweeps" regularly turn up phony promoters who take millions of dollars in cash and shares in exchange for touting their stock on the Internet.

The most common sources of Internet fraud are:

■ *On-line investment newsletters.* There are many reliable newsletters—you'll find them mentioned throughout this book. On the other hand, there are some companies that pay those who write on-line newsletters in cash or securities to recommend their stocks. The SEC points out that this is not in and of itself illegal. The law, however, requires newsletters to disclose who has paid them, the amount, and the type of payment. Obviously fraudsters do not willingly report this information. They skip it all together or they simply lie, claiming the research on stocks mentioned in their newsletter was done independently.

CAUTION: *The SEC sites the following phrases, frequently found in on-line newsletters, as red flags because they do not contain specific information:*

- "From time to time, XYZ Newsletter may receive compensation from companies we write about."
- "From time to time, XYZ Newsletter or its officers, directors, or staff may hold stock in some of the companies we write about."
- "XYZ Newsletter receives fees from the companies we write about."

$TIP: Avoid newsletters that bury disclosures or put them in very tiny typeface. Legitimate on-line newsletters that have been paid to push stocks will clearly say so.

And, check with the SEC to see if the newsletter has ever been in trouble. Whenever the SEC sues a newsletter (or a stock promoter), it issues a "litigation release" and immediately posts it on its website (www.sec.gov).

- *Bulletin boards.* Messages on bulletin boards may be true, or they may be bogus. Phony promoters often pretend to reveal "inside" information about new products, future profits, and special announcements. There's simply no way of knowing who you're dealing with. Take every message with more than a grain of salt. Better yet: ignore them entirely.
- *E-mail spams.* Junk e-mail, known as spam, is cheap and easy to send and a great favorite for

bogus investment schemes. Delete it from your screen.

- *Stock promotion sites.* There are many on-line stock reports under the guise of "research" that are actually paid advertisements. "The Stock Detective" has been monitoring on-line stock promoters and sites for several years. Kevin Lichtman, publisher, found only a dozen such sites when he started his service; today there are well over 50. As we go to press, among those he says have insufficient disclosure are: Internet Stock Market, Investment Hotlines Online, Market Vision, and Stockpickers.

$TIP: Before trading, check out Lichtman's list of suspicious stock sites at: www.stockdetective.com. It covers companies that are targets of SEC actions, those that have made outrageous claims, and on-line stock sites with either insufficient or blanket statements about real or potential company earnings.

- *Pump and dump schemes.* These occur when clever con artists artificially inflate the price of a stock and then sell it at its high. Their messages appear all over the Internet—in chats, on bulletin boards, in e-mails. They claim to have inside information on special developments. Once they sell and make a fortune, they stop hyping the stock and it drops in price. They walk away with a profit, but investors are left with a stock that's tanked. To avoid getting pumped and dumped:

1. **Be suspicious.** If a stock is touted in a chat or on a message board as a sure thing, ask yourself, "Why?" If it's so hot, why is someone telling everyone about it on the Internet? Promises of quick profits based on inside tips should be ignored.

2. **Get SEC filings.** The law requires that the following companies file reports with the SEC:

- All U.S. companies with more than 500 investors and $10 million in net assets
- All companies that list their securities on the Nasdaq Stock Market, or a major national exchange, such as the New York Stock Exchange

$TIP: You can download these reports from the SEC's EDGAR database for free. Or, Free Edgar (www.freeedgar.com) will e-mail you this material.

- Some companies are not required to register with the SEC—those with less than $5 million in a 12-month period may be exempt under a rule known as "Regulation A." However, these companies must file a hard copy of their offering circular. Companies raising less than one million dollars, although they too do not have to register with the SEC, must file a Form D— a brief notice that includes the names and addresses of owners and stock.

$TIP: If you can't find a company on EDGAR, call the SEC at: 202–942–8090 and ask if the company has filed under Regulation A or has filed a Form D. Request a written copy.

3. *Do some legwork.* Never invest in small companies that don't file regular reports with the SEC unless you get financial statements from the company and call suppliers and customers to verify that they're really doing business.

- *The pyramid.* Electronic versions of the classic "pyramid" scheme, in which participants attempt to make money solely by recruiting new participants into the plan are all too common. Be wary of messages such as "Make a killing in stocks from your home computer," and the like.
- *The risk-free deal.* No investment is risk free. No investment can guarantee a profit. Watch out for "exciting, low-risk investment opportunities" in wireless cable projects, land, and eel and peacock farms.

Finally, as you get ready to click on and place your orders, keep in mind that the SEC receives up to 300 complaints a day from investors about alleged Internet fraud, many of them pertaining to illegal promotion of stocks. Often companies that have no products are promoted, or misleading information is given out in order to manipulate the price of a stock.

Buy a stock on the Internet only if you would buy it in your regular brokerage account.

FOR FURTHER INFORMATION

Books

Douglas Gerlach, *The Complete Idiot's Guide To Online Investing* (New York: Macmillan, 1999).

Dunnan's On-line Directory

One of the great attributes of the Internet is that it is giving all investors access to information that was once available only to the pros and insiders. The growing democratization of investing doesn't mean you can know everything an analyst knows, but you have the opportunity to learn almost as much if you have the time and patience. Here are websites that will help you do just that.

MAJOR SITES

- *AltaVista Finance* (www.altavista.wallst.com). Largest and fastest search engine. Offers standard portfolio and quote machines, new market data, and fundamentals of any public company.
- *Financial Center* (www.tfc.com). Best known for its "Market Mavens" section with opinions by Wall Street analysts, it also has columns on biotech, global investing, small-cap stocks, options, utility stocks, and mutual funds. The "Insider Trading" column has updates about what employees are doing with their company stock.
- *FinancialWeb* (www.financialweb.com). A good place to learn about on-line investing and get research, quotes, and financial news. Has info on small-cap stocks, on-line fraud, annual reports, IPOs, etc.
- *Inter@ctive Investor* (www.zdii.com). Ziff-Davis's free resource site, it has late-breaking news, and articles from the Red Herrin and Reuters. "The Day Ahead" is a free, pre–opening bell newsletter full of tips, IPO updates. Also has a portfolio tracker.
- *Invest-O-Rama!* (www.investorama.com). Links to more than 7,000 sites, each well described and divided into thirteen categories. Doug Gerlach includes original articles.
- *Microsoft Investor* (www.investor.msn.com). Has market updates three times a day, daily articles and opinions by financial analysts and journalists, and a wide breath of information.
- *The Motley Fool* (www.fool.com). Has a punchy style; covers stocks, news, and commentary.
- *The Raging Bull* (www.ragingbull.com). Delivers news, analysis, and commentary.
- *Thomson Investor Network* (www.thomsoninvest.com). Enables you to click on any stock symbol and get charts and graphs. Up to 50 real-time stock quotes per day for free.
- *Wall Street Research Net* (www.wsrn.com). For serious and professional investors, it contains entries on 17,000 companies and reports by Wall Street analysts.
- *Yahoo!Finance* (www.quote.yahoo.com). Type in a ticker symbol and get all the financials you need: delayed stock quotes, performance charts, and a company's fundamentals. Also has news, SEC filings, and earnings estimates. Create a personal portfolio. Links to the Web's other finance and investing sites.

PERSONAL FINANCE

- *Bank Rate Monitor* (www.bankrate.com). Has information on many aspects of personal finance, credit cards, auto loans, home equity, banking; daily updates of bank savings rates and mortgages.
- *DT Online* (www.dtonline.com). Has weekly financial tips from the accounting firm Deloitte & Touche; covers 401(k)s, buying a house, tax updates, info for small businesses.
- *FinanceCenter.com* (www.financecenter.com). How to calculate mortgages, study the pros and cons of a Roth IRA, figure out how long to keep a car, determine how exchange rates affect foreign stocks, and more.
- *Quicken* (www.quicken.com). Covers personal and household finances and has tax tips and helpful calculators.
- *The Universal Currency Converter* (www.xe.net/currency). Covers all major currencies, including the new Euro.
- *Women.com* (www.women.com). Covers investing, mutual funds, stocks, credit, budgeting, taxes, paying for college, buying a house; check out the Q&A column written by Cash Flo. Cosponsored by Bloomberg.

OPTIONS AND FUTURES

- *Chicago Board Options Exchange* (www.cboe.com). The website of the world's largest options exchange. Covers derivatives and delayed quotes from the trading pits; has info on interest rates, emerging markets, the currency index, and commodity derivatives traded on the exchange; also has an options calculator.
- *Futures Magazine Online* (www.futuresmag.com). Has analysts' views, educational tools, and current information from the magazine.
- *Netpicks Stock Option Advisory System* (www.netpicks.com). Gives an evening update and three intraday reports plus tips on trading stock options.
- *NumaWeb* (www.numa.com). Designed for the experienced trader; describes advanced strategies, but also has educational materials.
- *Options Industry Association* (www.optionscentral.com). A good place for beginners, it contains excellent information on trading.

STOCK RESEARCH

- *Bridge.com* (www.bridge.com). An excellent source for global charts and quotes.
- *Cents Financial Journal* (Ip-Ilc.com/cents). Has daily market commentary by economists and analysts at Moody's, Morgan Stanley, S&P, etc.
- *Companies Online* (www.companies.online.com). Combines Lycos and Dun & Bradstreet and has links to 100,000+ public and private corporations. Look for specific companies or browse by industry.
- *FinanceCenter* (www.financecenter.com). Has free on-line calculators for stocks, bonds, and mutual funds.
- *Hoover's Online* (www.hoovers.com). Lets you search for companies by industry, location,

company type, or annual sales. Lists forthcoming IPOs, market data, corporate news, proprietary profiles on 3,300 companies; links to other sites.

- *JustQuotes* (www.justquotes.com). Lets you enter a ticker or a company name and will come up with links to research reports and SEC documents; easy to use.
- *Public Register's Annual Report Service* (www.prars.com). Don't be misled by the unsophisticated design—this service mails out free copies of annual reports for companies listed on NYSE, AMEX, and Nasdaq as well as for over-the-counter firms. Has surveys of best stocks, investment strategies, and brokers. Links to brokerage websites.
- *Value Line* (www.valueline.com). Has free research on the economy, sectors, stocks, and mutual funds.
- *World Mergers & Acquisitions Network* (www.worldm-anetwork.com). Has information on how to profit from mergers and acquisitions around the world; lists potential takeover targets by industry.
- *Zacks Investment Research* (www.ultra.zacks.com). Helps individual investors get some of the same research that the pros get—free and paid stock evaluations, analyst watch, stock screening tools, brokerage firm research. Has daily market commentary and links to other sites.

ANALYSTS' CALLS

These on-line sites provide access to analysts' conference calls:

- *BestCalls.com* (www.bestcalls.com)
- *Broadcast.com* (www.broadcast.com)
- *StreetFusion* (www.streetfusion.com)
- *V Call* (www.vca.com)

BOND RESEARCH

- *Bonds Online* (www.bondsonline.com). Has a database of recent and current offerings.
- *Bond Market Association* (www.investinginbonds.com). Lists the previous day's prices for 1,000 municipals.
- *Discover* (www.discoverbrokerage.com). Has real-time prices of municipals and Treasuries.
- *E*Trade* (www.etrade.com). Maintains the largest inventory of all types of bonds that you can buy on-line; gives real-time prices.
- *U.S. Treasury* (www.publicdebt.treas.gov). Lets TreasuryDirect account holders buy and sell government securities on-line.

IPOS

- *Direct Stock Market* (www.dsm.com). Has short write-ups and corporate documents on companies making public and private offerings; chat forums.
- *Direct IPO* (www.webipo.com). Has direct-to-the-public offerings via the Internet. Free e-mail updates about upcoming IPOs; articles, analysis.
- *IPO Maven* (www.ipomaven.com). Has regular updates on new offerings, market and IPO news, and research tools for evaluating companies.

■   *Wit Capital* (www.witcapital.com). The site of a New York discount on-line broker specializing in IPOs. Members can buy new issues directly. Has explanations of rules, updates, bulletin boards for members.

COMMODITIES

The exchanges each have helpful sites:

■   *Chicago Board of Trade* (www.cme.com)
■   *Kansas City Board of Trade* (www.cbot.com)
■   *Chicago Mercantile Exchange* (www.kcbt.com)
■   *MidAmerica Commodity Exchange* (www.midam.com)
■   *New York Mercantile Exchange* (www.nymex.com)

Other sites:

■   *Commodity Trader* (www.commoditytrader.net)
■   *Stockscape* (www.stockscape.com)

MARKET DATA

■   *Big Charts* (www.bigcharts.com). The best site for free financial charts and graphing tools for overviews of NYSE, AMEX, and Nasdaq.
■   *Briefing.com* (www.briefing.com). Has frequently updated market commentaries, stock analysis, info on security analysts' upgrades/downgrades, stock splits, and earnings; commentaries on currencies, bonds, and overall indicators.
■   *Free Real Time* (www.freerealtime.com). Will send you immediate quotes followed by links to on-line brokers (DLJdirect, Ameritrade, Datek).
■   *NASDAQ* (www.nasdaq.com). Provides free delayed quotes and bid-ask spreads on Nasdaq.
■   *Quote.com* (www.quote.com). Has delayed and real-time quotes on stocks, options, futures, mutual funds and indices, news, earnings forecasts, market analysis, annual reports, company profiles, and more.
■   *Standard & Poor's Equity Investor Service* (www.stockinfo.standardpoor.com). Covers daily market commentaries, S&P indices, company descriptions, feature stories, portfolio tracking.

MUTUAL FUNDS

The major mutual fund companies have their own websites. Here are some recommended independent sources.

■   *Find-a-Fund* (www.findafund.com). Reports weekly on top performing funds, has analysts' coverage, and helps you decide if you're adequately diversified. Its Directory of Funds is all-inclusive.
■   *FundAlarm* (www.fundalarm.com). Tells you when to sell a particular fund. Also has performance data, general information, and tracking.

- *ICI Mutual Fund Connection* (www.ici.org). This is the mutual fund industry's free education site, known as the Investment Company Institute. A good place to begin.
- *Micropal* (www.micropal.com). An excellent source of information on mutual funds around the world.
- *Morningstar* (www.morningstar.net). This is the research publication for mutual funds. Daily updates, analysis on 15,000 stocks and funds, fund ratings, and more.

BUSINESS NEWS

- *Bloomberg Online* (www.bloomberg.com). News, the markets, financial analysis, and what's happening around the world, continually updated.
- *CBS MarketWatch* (cbs.marketwatch.com). Loaded with solid news, much of it originally written, plus interviews with analysts, continually updated market coverage, and quotes. Good place to check in with throughout the day.
- *The Daily Rocket* (www.dailyrocket.com). One of the liveliest on-line financial publications, this has original news coverage, features, daily market commentary (with hypertext links to companies mentioned). Portfolio management software with news, stock data, and tips about so-called insider trading.
- *Investor's Business Daily* (www.investors.com). Has content from this daily printed financial newspaper; covers business, financial and economic news, national events, international economies; and has technology updates.
- *News Alert* (www.newsalert.com). Enables you to get the latest company news from a wide variety of wire sources. Search by company name, ticker symbol, or industry.
- *The Street.com* (www.street.com). A sometimes outrageous, always interesting source of news. Well-written daily articles covering stocks, mutual funds, companies. Founder James Cramer writes a feisty, scathing column.
- *Wall Street Journal Interactive* (www.interactive.wsj.com). Costs $49 a year (versus $175 for print subscription) and includes some material from the Asia edition, Barron's Online and Smart Money, plus search tools.

Two media sites:

- *www.cnnfn.com*
- *www.cnbc.com*

GOVERNMENT DOCUMENTS

To access SEC filings, IPOs, insider-trading filings, you have several choices:

- *FreeEdgar* (www.freeedgar.com)
- *Federal Filings Online* (www.fedfil.com)
- *SEC-Live* (www.seclive.com)

WATCHDOGS

- *Internet Fraud Watch* (www.fraud.org/ifw.htm). Covers all types of financial/money scams and explains how to avoid them.
- *National Association of Securities Dealers* (www.nasd.com). This is the place to check out a broker's history; good primers for beginning investors.
- *Stock Detective* (www.stockdetective.com). Covers investment scams, stocks to avoid, and ways to protect yourself when investing on-line. Very frank coverage. Lists "No Gooders" that are targets of SEC action; its "Stinky Stocks" column makes for interesting and important reading.

Financing Your Lifestyle

"Money can't buy friends, but you can get a better class of enemy."

Spike Milligan

Now that you've come this far, it's time to think about using some of your money to finance the lifestyle you'd like—for yourself, for your family. Your investments and savings will enable you to buy a better college education for your kids, a better house in a better school district, and eventually a better class of retirement. Whether you're a baby boomer, new parent, empty nester, or member of the senior-something crowd, or whether you're single or living together, you need to arrange your finances to suit your lifestyle. In this section we look at the most important areas of financial planning as they relate to your particular needs:

- Housing: residential, rental, second homes
- Mortgages: how to get the best rate
- Paying for college: for your kids and yourself
- Adjusting to adult children returning home
- Helping aging parents
- Retirement plans, IRAs, Keoghs, 401(k)s, SEPs
- Getting the most out of Social Security
- Understanding GICs
- Insurance and annuities
- Retirement living: adult communities, nursing homes, reverse mortgages
- Financial gifts for children, brides, grooms, and grads
- Stock options

28

Housing: Buying, Financing, Renting

The purpose of this book is to advise you on investing and managing your money—not on what house to buy. The various bits of information and advice given below, however, will help you make a wise real estate investment and, as a result, have more money with which to invest and fund the other aspects of your life. Besides, buying a house is often the biggest investment most of us ever make—and you want it to be the right one, aesthetically, emotionally, and financially.

WAYS TO DEAL IN REAL ESTATE IN 2000 WITHOUT PAYING TOP DOLLAR

Check out the following:

1. *Distress sales and auctions.* There are always "distress sales," no matter whether we're in a bull or bear market. Of course, you won't find as many troubled properties for sale as in the previous years, but this is still fertile territory for savvy buyers. Public notices of default sales are generally announced in local newspapers and, in some places, posted at the city hall. You can also find out about such sale properties from local real estate dealers—take time to let several know of your interest. Realize, however, that you can seldom find a house in a hurry using this approach.

   ☑ HINT: *For a list of foreclosed properties offered by Fannie Mae (Federal National Mortgage Association), call 800–732–6643.*

   ☑ HINT: *For information on property seized by the government that's going up on auction, click on: www.usaweb.com/auction.html*

2. *Rental property.* If you're investing for rental income, pick a location within a day's drive; it's easiest to be a landlord if your property is nearby.

3. *Refinancing.* With lower interest rates, the question of refinancing your mortgage pops up. The rule of thumb is, do not refinance unless the new rate is at least 2 percentage points lower than the old one. This guideline, however, overlooks a critical factor: how long you plan to stay in your home. The sooner you intend to move, the greater the rate differential between the two loans must be for refinancing to pay off.

   Why? You will probably pay 3% to 4% of the total loan in points and closing fees on a new loan, and it will take two to four years to recoup the up-front charges (**see:** box on page 283).

4. *Consider a lease option.* If you own a house you would like to sell but haven't been able to, or if you want to buy but can't quite afford the down payment, a "lease-option" plan may solve the problem.

   Under this arrangement, the potential buyer moves into the house as a tenant, paying monthly rent. The rent, however, is considerably higher than normal, sometimes even double. The extra is credited toward the down payment. Some landlords also require an up-front cash payment. At the end of a specified time, typically one to four years, the tenant finds a mortgage and buys the house. If he cannot, the owner keeps the extra payments. Most of these arrangements are made through ads in local newspapers.

CAUTION: Make certain the lease includes an exclusive contract that the property will be sold to the tenant for a set price when the lease expires and states whether or not the deposit is refundable. An option to buy could prove worthless unless a sales contract is attached to the lease and the contract has been signed in advance by the seller.

5. *Buying in an unknown area.* Whether it's rental property or a home for yourself, get a "destination appraisal" before buying in unfamiliar territory. Otherwise you might move in and find out six months later that an office building is going to be built nearby. Prepurchase appraisals range in price from $200 to $400. They let buyers know about hidden problems as well as give them an idea of the going prices.

HINT: To find a qualified appraiser, contact the Appraisal Institute, 875 North Michigan, Suite 2400, Chicago, IL 60611. Call 312–335–4100 and request the Directory of Designated Members.

6. *Investing in vacant lots.* In areas where the price of land is relatively low, this is a good time to consider land as a long-term investment. You can avoid a lot of problems if you know what your legal rights are—so take time to read the Department of Housing and Urban Development's brochure, *Buying Lots from Developers,* available from:

HUD
Program Information
451 7th Street SW, 8th floor
Washington, DC 20410
202–708–1420
Free

Where to Find Bargains in Rental Real Estate

- Someone desperate to sell, who has already moved, is being transferred, or has purchased another piece of property
- An REO (real estate owned), also known as a foreclosure. Local bankers maintain listings. Prices are often well below market.
- Estate liquidations and family breakups
- Distressed properties sold through sheriff's sales, IRS seizures for back taxes, and other forced sales
- Discounted mortgages. These are existing loans sold by the lender for less than the balance owed. Check with real-estate brokers, or place an ad in the newspaper. Review state foreclosure laws carefully.

SORTING OUT THE MORTGAGE MAZE

One thing that has not changed over the years is the fact that getting a mortgage is one of the largest financial commitments most people make. To help get through the mortgage maze, review these most popular types. It helps to understand the lingo when applying for a loan and negotiating terms.

Fixed-Rate Mortgage

The old standby, the 30-year fixed-rate mortgage, remains the most popular type of real estate loan. Interest rate and monthly payments are fixed for the life of the loan, which protects buyers from increased monthly payments when interest rates rise. On the other hand, when rates drop, it often pays to refinance this type of mortgage in order to get lower monthly payments.

☑ *HINT: Shop carefully for a fixed-rate mortgage, because even a small rate difference affects your monthly payments.*

This mortgage is generally considered a good choice for those planning to remain in their houses a number of years. The borrower knows what the payments will be, and equity builds up steadily over time.

A variation on this theme is the 15-year fixed-rate mortgage. The good news here is that the debt is paid off in half the time it would be with a 30-year mortgage, and the total interest cost of the loan is lower.

The bad news: Monthly payments are higher. On a $100,000 loan, for instance, the monthly payment would be $1,106 on a 15-year mortgage at 10.5% versus $953 on an 11%, 30-year loan. The major advantage of a 15-year mortgage is that you build equity faster and save on interest costs. This makes it a logical choice for those near retirement who want to be free of mortgage payments and/or those with sufficient disposable income to handle higher monthly payments.

Biweekly Mortgage

This is another way to build equity more quickly and reduce interest costs. Instead of paying down your mortgage on a monthly basis, you do so every two weeks. The biweekly payments are half of what a monthly payment would be, but there's the equivalent of one more monthly payment per year. In other words, 26 biweekly payments equal 13 monthly payments. Most lenders require that biweekly payments be automatically deducted from your bank account.

Adjustable-Rate Mortgages

Called ARMs for short, this mortgage generally offers lower initial rates than fixed-rate home loans, but the interest rate and the monthly payment are adjusted periodically according to terms specified by the lender. Most peg the rate to an index based on short-term Treasury bill rates. Many ARMs are adjusted annually, semiannually, or once every three years over a five-year period, and thereafter remain fixed. With others, the rate remains fixed for one or more years and then is adjusted annually. In most cases, the increase in interest is capped and cannot be adjusted by more than 2 points over the life of the loan. Some ARMs have a conversion feature allowing borrowers to convert (for a fee) to a fixed-rate mortgage, usually between the second and fifth year.

☑ *HINT: ARMs are particularly well suited to young people who anticipate growth in income and those who do not plan to stay in the same home for more than a few years.*

Seven-Year Two-Step

It may sound like a dance, but it's a mortgage with fixed monthly payments for the first seven years at a rate ¼ to ½ a percentage point less than those on a 30-year fixed. After seven years, the rate is adjusted to market level.

GRADUATED PAYMENT MORTGAGES (GPMS)

With this type of mortgage, monthly payments start out low and gradually increase at a set rate for the first five to ten years and then level off toward the end. They are designed for buyers who have good jobs and who expect their income to rise over time.

ALL ABOUT POINTS

Regardless of what type of mortgage you wind up with, make certain that any "points" you pay in connection with your mortgage are for interest (1 point equals 1% of the loan amount). As long as you pay points up front with a separate check or if the seller pays the points, they are tax deductible in the year you buy the property.

The rules regarding points that are really origination fees are confusing and subject to change, so check with your accountant. As we go to press, "origination fees" are deductible if based on a percentage of the loan in exchange for a lower interest rate. If not, then they are additions to the cost of the home.

On the "Uniform Settlement Statement," they may be called "points," "loan origination fees," "loan discount," or "discount points." Points paid for refinancing a mortgage are not deductible in full in the year they were paid. They must be deducted over the term of the mortgage. This is particularly important because lenders send reports to the IRS.

ESCROW PAYMENTS

In late May of 1995, a new Department of Housing and Urban Development ruling went into effect, specifying how escrow payments must be calculated and how much surplus a lender may collect.

Under the guidelines, monthly escrow payments may not be more than one-twelfth of the total due annually for taxes and insurance premiums, plus enough for a two-month surplus. (Previously, some lenders kept a surplus of up to eight months.)

☑ *HINT: If your lender overcharged you (HUD says this may be the case with 5 million home owners), you should get a refund or an adjustment made on future payments. Check with your lender, and if you have problems, contact your area HUD office.*

UNNECESSARY MORTGAGE INSURANCE

💣 *CAUTION: In 1998, Congress passed a law that requires lenders to automatically cancel Private Mortgage Insurance (PMI) when a home owner's equity reaches 22% of the original value of the property. It only applies to loans originated on or after July 29, 1999.*

How to Avoid Drowning in a Mortgage

1. *Shop around.* Call several banks and mortgage companies and find out what they are offering. Compare details carefully. Don't rely only on your real estate broker's recommendation.

2. *Do your math.* You must figure out the exact amount you will pay each month for each type of mortgage. When doing the numbers for ARMs, assume interest rates will rise to the maximum.

3. *Look for hidden traps.* Read the mortgage document before signing on. Among the traps to look for in the fine print: a bank that requires permission for borrowers to obtain a second mortgage or a home-equity line of credit; a clause requiring you to sell your old house before the bank will let you close on a new one; any add-on charges and fees.

4. *Make extra payments.* Assume a mortgage only if it lets you make payments above the stated required amount. This reduces the length of your mortgage and will save you thousands of dollars in interest, since the prepaid amount is applied to the principal.

PMI is required by most lenders when the down payment on a house is less than 20% of the purchase price. It protects the lender if the borrower defaults—a situation more likely to happen when the buyer has less equity. PMI allows people to buy homes who otherwise might not be eligible to do so. The problem has been that many home owners keep paying for this insurance after they equity reaches 20%. PMI can cost anywhere from $300 to $950 a year.

Recently, Fannie Mae, the nation's largest source of home mortgage money, started requiring lenders to automatically cancel PMI on loans when they reach midterm. This will apply retroactively. That means when a loan reaches its 15th year of a 30-year loan, PMI would end. Fannie Mae gave mortgage companies until January 2001 to implement the change.

$TIP: Check with your lender to see if you can cancel your PMI.

MORTAGES—BEYOND YOUR NEIGHBORHOOD BANK

Government agencies and mortgage lenders also often list with local brokers; many accept smaller-than-usual down payments.

- *FDA-insured loans.* Require down payments of only 5%; check with your lender to see if you qualify.
- *VA (Veterans Administration) loans.* Now available not only to vets, but also members of the National Guard and military reservists with six or more years of service. Low or no down payments required. Check your regional VA office.
- *Fannie Mae loans.* The Federal National Mortgage Association, the nation's largest source of mortgage money, has some loans that require interest-only payments in the first year, plus a variety of other loans. For info and list of lenders, call 800–732–6643, or: click on www.homepath.com.
- *Farm Service Agency.* Helps low- and moderate-income people who live in rural areas with loans.

☑ *HINT: For information, contact your area's Farm Service Agency Office, listed under "Department of Agriculture" in your phone book, or write: Farmer Service Agency, 14th & Independence Avenue SW, Washington, DC 20250, 202–720–5237, or click on: www.fsa.usda.gov*

- *Mortgage brokers.* These intermediaries match you with a mortgage banker or commercial bank; they will save you time and are helpful for those having difficulty getting a mortgage. You usually pay a flat fee or an additional point or two for the service.

☑ *HINT: For information, call the National Association of Mortgage Brokers at 703–610–9009, or: click on www.namb.org*

- *Public agencies.* Local real estate brokers and lenders can tell you about state-run programs, such as the Community Homebuyers Program, that make below market-rate financing available to low- and moderate-income buyers.

   Also, contact The National Council of State Housing Agencies for more info at 202–624–7710.

GREAT SOURCES FOR HARD-TO-GET INFORMATION

Comparing Mortgage Rates

A key part of successful investing is leverage—that is, your mortgage. For current rates and information, keep up-to-date by reading the popular press and talking to bank loan officers. To help you make informed decisions, consult the following:

HSH Associates
1200 Route 23
Butler, NJ 07405
800–873–2837

   This group operates a mortgage hotline (973–838–8197), which lists the national average rates on a variety of mortgages. For $20 plus $3 shipping, HSH will send you a listing of mortgage rates in your area plus a 56-page planning kit. HSH covers 50 metropolitan areas. Also available at: www.hsh.com. The website has links to lenders plus a refinancing calculator.

Refinancing

Tables to determine whether you should refinance or pay off your mortgage early appear in *Consumer's Guide to Refinancing Your Mortgage*, available from:

The Benefits of Refinancing Your Mortgage

Follow these basic points to determine how refinancing pays off. You can also order a software package called The Banker's Secret Loan that will run the calculations for your particular situation; it's $42.93, available from Good Advice Press, 800–255–0899.

- *Point #1.* If you have a $150,000 mortgage, payable over 30 years at 9.5%, your monthly payments are $1,261. If after four years you refinance the balance, about $145,712, at 7.5% (for a new 30-year term), your monthly payment will drop to $1,019, for a savings of $242 each month.
- *Point #2.* You must take into account, however, administrative fees and other expenses: Refinancing your $145,712 balance will cost $2,686 ($500 in fees and $2,186 for your 1.5% points, a percentage of the loan amount).
- *Point #3.* Then, balance that against what you save in monthly payments: Your refinancing costs will be recovered in just 11.1 months ($2,686 divided by $242 = 11.1 months).
- *Point #4.* After that, your gross monthly cash flow is boosted by $242.

☑ *HINT: Put that $242 into prepaying your mortgage each month and you'll actually wind up saving over $107,000 in interest expenses—and reducing your loan term by 12 years and 10 months. And that's in addition to nearly $27,000 in interest expenses saved by refinancing.*

SOURCE: The Banker's Secret; 800–255–0899.

Consumer Information Catalog
888–8–PUEBLO
or: www.pueblo.gsa.gov

Prepaying Your Mortgage

Design your own mortgage prepayment plan with *The Banker's Secret.* The book ($17.95) or book-and-software package ($42.95) is available from:

Good Advice Press
P.O. Box 78
Elizaville, NY 12523
914–758–1400; 800–255–0899

Adjustable-Rate Mortgages

For a copy of *Consumer Handbook on Adjustable Rate Mortgages,* contact:

Consumer Information Catalog
888–8–PUEBLO
or: www.pueblo.gsa.gov
50¢

ON-LINE SOURCES OF MORTGAGE INFORMATION

- www.bankrate.com
- www.eloan.com
- www.getsmart.com
- www.hsh.com
- www.homeshark.com
- www.mortgage-net.com
- www.quicken.mortgage.com

YOUR HOME AS A TAX SHELTER

The 1997 Tax Relief Act changed some of the rules pertaining to home ownership. Now you can exclude from your taxable income the profits from the sale of your principal residence—up to a certain limit. This new tax break applies to houses sold after May 6, 1997.

- Singles can exclude up to $250,000 in profits; married couples filing jointly can exclude up to $500,000 in profits.

- In order to get this new break, you must have owned and actually lived in the house as your principal residence for two out of the last five years before the sale.
- The tax exclusion applies only to sales taking place every two years or longer. That means you can claim a new and different $500,000 or $250,000 exemption every two years.
- Some nice exceptions: if you are unable to live in your house long enough to meet the two-year ruling because your job required you to move, there's still hope. You will most likely be able to exclude a fraction of the $250,000 or the $500,000 . . . check with your accountant.

Five Tips to Keep in Mind

The new ruling makes selling the old family home-stead and moving to a smaller one much more appealing tax-wise. So, in general, it now makes sense to:

1. Sell if you've been laid off and move to a less expensive home. Use the gains you make to live on until you find a new job.
2. Take early retirement if you wish and, again, live on (or invest) the gains from the sale of your house.
3. Sell if you kept the house in a divorce settlement. Up until now if you didn't sell because you couldn't meet the onerous capital gains bill, now you can.
4. If you move into what was formerly your vacation home, and if you are there two out of the last years before you sell, it then becomes your "principal" residence.

CAUTION: You may have read in some of the more popular financial publications that you no longer need to keep track of home improvements in order to reduce taxes when you sell your house, that documentation of a new furnace or a swimming pool is required only if you think you'll exceed the $500,000 capital gains exclusion.

Don't be foolish. Keep everything. No one knows what the real estate market will do in the future or what changes may be made in the next tax act.

So, save another shoe box or spring for a filing cabinet and keep all relevant receipts and canceled checks.

5. To make certain you whittle down the size of any eventual tax bill, keep good records. When your home is sold at a profit, the difference between the net sale price and the seller's "basis" in the property is the amount that is subject to tax.

The basis is calculated as the price paid for the property plus closing costs, such as title insurance, incurred in making the purchase. Add to this expenses for capital improvements made over the years, but subtract any depreciation or casualty losses claimed. A capital improvement is anything that adds to the value of the property—for example, a roof that has been replaced, fences, gates, central air-conditioning, or a burglar alarm. Painting and repairs are maintenance expenses, however, and do not increase the owner's basis in the property. So keep canceled checks, copies of invoices relating to capital improvements, and notices of co-op apartment assessments.

HINT: Call the IRS at 800–TAX–FORM (829–3676) to get a copy of Publication 523, **Selling Your Home.**

HOME-EQUITY LOANS

Interest on up to $100,000 of a home-equity loan or a home-equity line of credit is fully deductible as long as the loan is secured by your principal home or a second home that you own.

The elimination several years ago of the deductibility of personal interest (on credit card loans, for example) has added to the appeal of home-equity loans. And because this type of loan

> **Deductions You May Take on Rental Property**
> - Maintenance
> - Depreciation
> - Repairs
> - Utility bills
> - Insurance
> - Advertising

is secured by your home, interest rates are often lower than those charged on other borrowing.

☑ HINT: *Call the IRS at 800–TAX–FORM (829–3676) to get a copy of Publication 936,* **Home Mortgage Interest Deduction.**

Banks often promote these "credit line" types of loans to pay for big-ticket items such as cars, college education, and vacations.

💣 CAUTION: *Use a home-equity line of credit only if necessary. Your home could be repossessed if you fail to make payments.*

With a home-equity line of credit, the bank allows borrowers to apply for a loan, pay closing costs just once, and then borrow money as needed. You can usually borrow up to 80% of the home's appraised value minus any existing mortgages. Interest is higher than on first loans, but it is assessed only on money you actually draw. Fees and closing costs tend to be low because of lender competition.

☑ HINT: *Because interest rates are usually tied to prime, look for a loan with an interest rate cap.*

THE JOYS OF RENTAL INCOME

If you're renting your condo in Florida, ski house in Montana, or center-hall colonial in the suburbs, you should discuss the tax implications with your accountant. But a few general tips:

1. Depreciation can only be taken on the cost of the buildings, not on the underlying land.
2. If your property produces rent, the income or losses generated are considered "passive," which means you cannot offset salary or investment income with your rental losses, with one exception:
3. If your adjusted gross income is under $100,000 ($50,000 for married couples filing separately), the tax law allows you to write off up to $25,000 a year in rental property tax losses against other income, including your salary—provided you actively manage the property.
4. This special $25,000 allowance is phased out as you become wealthier; if your adjusted gross income exceeds $150,000 ($75,000 for married couples filing separately), there is no such break.

💣 CAUTION: *If at least one-half of your personal services are performed in rental real-estate business and you materially participate for at least 750 hours, the $25,000 limit does not apply.*

☑ HINT: *Recalculate the return you receive on any property. If your property generates a loss and your income is less than $150,000, make certain you satisfy the IRS requirement of being an "active" participant in order to get the loss allowance.*

5. To be considered an active manager, you must own 10% of the property involved as well as make decisions on repairs, rents, and tenants. If you hire a manager but provide guidance, you will still be considered active provided you can document your involvement to the IRS.
6. If you make more than $150,000 annually, you can still reap some benefits, because the changes pertain to tax reporting, not to your cash flow. This means that if your rental income covers mortgage payments, the only plus you've lost is the tax shelter aspect. In the meantime, keep a running account of your

losses and apply them when you eventually sell the property or to offset passive income from limited partnerships or other rental income.

VACATION HOMES—FOR PROFIT AND PLAY

If you have a ski condo, beach cottage, or fishing shack, or something much grander, read on so you'll be certain to take all the tax breaks possible on your property. Find the category that applies to your particular situation regarding renting or not renting.

- *If you do not rent out* your vacation home, you can deduct interest on your mortgage, in the principal amount, up to the original purchase price plus the cost of improvements.
- *If you use your vacation property personally* for more than 14 days a year or more than 10% of the time you rent it out (at a fair market rate), whichever is greater, then the IRS considers it a "residence." In that case, any time that you spend on repairs and upkeep does not count toward personal or rental use. Deductions for rental expenses on a "residence" are for the most part limited to the income received. The IRS formula is precise; check with your accountant.
- *If you rent out for no more than 14 days a year,* the income is tax free and you are not even required to report it, but the expenses, other than property taxes and interest, are not deductible.
- *If you use the vacation home less than 14 days or 10% of the time,* the house is classified as rental (not residential) property. Deductions are allocated in proportion to the time used as a rental. If the property was placed in service prior to January 1, 1987, you can still use the 19-year accelerated depreciation schedule, which allows larger deductions in early years. Otherwise, you must use the 27½-year depreciation schedule.

Rental expenses, under these circumstances, cannot be used to offset regular income, because they are considered passive losses. Under the 1986 law, these expenses can be deducted only from pas-

sive income from other rental properties or from limited partnerships and not from your wages, salary, or portfolio income.

NOTE: There is an exception for those whose adjusted gross income is $150,000 or less, as explained earlier.

☑ *HINT: If your income is too high to benefit from the $25,000 active rental allowance, you may be better off converting a "rental" vacation home into a "residential" property and writing off the full amount of the mortgage interest.*

SWAPPING PROPERTY

The IRS allows you to sell one piece of investment property and buy another, while deferring capital gains taxes. In fact, you can swap any number of times and not pay taxes until you actually sell for cash. The exchange must be completed within 180 days and it must be with "like kinds" of property— rental property for rental property. Rulings are fairly detailed, so talk it over with your accountant.

☑ *HINT: Discipline yourself to invest the money that would have gone to pay the capital gains tax.*

To qualify for this tax deferral you must:

- Exchange like pieces of property
- Use the property for business or hold it as an investment; your home does not qualify, nor does an interest in a real estate limited partnership

If the two pieces of property involved in a swap are not of equal monetary value, cash or an additional piece of property is used to make up the difference.

NOTE: The cash or extra property is a taxable transaction.

HOW TO REDUCE YOUR PROPERTY TAXES

Experts estimate that 60% of all home owners pay too much property tax. Take time to study your taxes, and if you suspect you're being overcharged, file a challenge.

The Most Common Mistakes

Errors in paperwork and/or math are amazingly widespread. So go in person to the tax assessor's office and ask to see the worksheet used when your property was evaluated. You have a legal right to examine this document. Check for:

1. *Typographical errors.* The assessment amount on the worksheet should match the assessment on the tax bill.
2. *Measurements.* Dimensions and square footage should be accurate.
3. *Evaluation.* After checking out the figures, look at how your property was evaluated. The assessed value of property, adjusted by the local tax assessment office, is almost always lower than the market value.

To find out whether you are being over-assessed, ask what the *adjusted* assessment value is plus what *multiplier* was used to make the adjustment.

For instance, if your tax bill shows an assessed value of $100,000 and the multiplier is 2, then your home is really assessed at $200,000.

Using this example, if you believe your home is worth less than $200,000, you would want to challenge the assessment by following these steps:

1. *Find out the assessed values* of comparable property in your neighborhood. This is public information.
2. *Get the actual selling prices* of similar homes in the "Recorder of Public Deeds" office at your town hall.
3. *Locate copies* of any existing professional appraisals of your property. (Your bank is likely to have this document.)
4. *Arrange a new appraisal* to document the fact that the value of your home is lower than its appraised value.

The Seafaring Loophole

Although tax reform eliminated interest deductions on most consumer credit loans, yacht owners and houseboat dwellers got a break. If your boat qualifies as a personal residence by having a head, galley, and sleeping facilities, you can probably deduct interest on any loan you take out to buy the floating home. Have your accountant check Code section 163(h)(3) and (4)(a)(i)(ii), which governs interest deductions for qualified residences.

Then present these facts to the assessor. If your appeal is denied, you can present your case to a board of review for an impartial opinion. Ask the assessor for an appeal form and the filing deadline.

☑ HINT: *About half the home owners who question their assessments through official appeals win reductions of 10% or more. Prepare for your appeal by reading* How to Fight Property Taxes, *from:*

National Taxpayers Union
108 North Alfred Street
Alexandria, VA 22314
703–683–5700
$6.95

INVESTING IN REAL ESTATE STOCKS AND MUTUAL FUNDS IN 2000

Investing in real estate stocks and mutual funds, like any other market industry, has a degree of risk—and in this particular case, the degree of risk is substantial. There are some interesting opportunities, however, provided you can keep a close watch on the condition of real estate—both residential and commercial. One of the easier ways to own a diversified, hence less risky, real estate portfolio is through REITs—Real Estate Investment Trusts.

REITs are like mutual funds—they own a variety of properties or mortgages on properties. Their shares trade on the stock exchanges. While some are high in risk, many are considered relatively sound investments, offering an easier way to participate in commercial real estate than direct ownership—say, of an office building.

REITs, created by Congress in 1960 to give individuals a way to invest in commercial real estate, are like mutual funds. They own a variety of properties or mortgages on properties. Their shares trade on the stock exchanges. While some are high in risk, others are quite sound investments.

REITs have a unique tax structure. They avoid corporate taxation as long as they pay out 95% of their income to shareholders—which they do in the form of dividends. This means they tend to have high dividend yields. As we went to press, the average REIT yielded roughly 7.2%, versus the 1.25% yield on the S&P 500.

REITs frequently focus on specific geographical areas and/or on particular property types—shopping centers, commercial buildings, health care facilities.

Among those to consider:

Boston Properties	5.2%
Chelsea GCA Realty	8.5
Equity Residential	7.0
New Plan Realty Trust	8.6
Vornado Realty	5.2
Washington REIT	7.2
Weingarten Realty	7.1

ARMs

Adjustable rate mortgage mutual funds are a relatively new and fast-growing type of investment vehicle that invests primarily in adjustable rate mortgage securities issued by Ginnie Mae, Fannie Mae, and Freddie Mac (**see:** Chapter 13). Because the rates on ARM securities are adjusted periodically, prices are less volatile than fixed-income securities. Some investment uncertainty, however, is created by the varying patterns of mortgage prepayment by property owners.

The yield on ARM securities generally tracks the ebb and flow of short-term interest rates, but is typically 1.5% to 2% higher.

29

Family Finances: Children, College, Parents, Financial Gifts

THE HIGH COST OF CHILDREN

For many people, nothing is ever as exciting as having a baby—or as expensive. It's certainly one of life's most costly endeavors. Depending on where you live and how extravagant you want to be, raising a child from birth to age 18 can set you back anywhere from $40,000 to $160,000 . . . and that's before college bills. So there's no question that having a baby will drastically change your financial life.

The best way to enjoy parenthood is to have enough money to care for your child, maintain the lifestyle you and your spouse had before baby made three, and minimize as many financial sacrifices as possible. The biggest sacrifice for most couples is the loss of the mother's income, because the majority of women take three to six months off for the first child. Yet, armed with a sensible financial plan, you can minimize the dollar drain and fully enjoy the newest member of your family.

Prenatal to Age 2

As soon as you know you'll be having a baby, both you and your spouse should find out what your respective firms offer in terms of maternity leave, including possible benefits for the father. Then check your health coverage. Whether you have a private policy or one sponsored by your firm, determine precisely what medical costs for the first two years are covered.

☑ *HINT: Borrow maternity and baby clothes as well as equipment from friends, or buy from secondhand shops, discount stores, and outlets. And don't be shy: encourage baby showers. Your family and friends may pitch in and purchase some of the big-ticket items for you. Use family members to baby-sit, or join a baby-sitting cooperative and share the task with other parents.*

Build up your savings as soon as you know you'll be having a baby. Stash all or part of one salary in a money market fund and practice living on one salary, which will be the case when the baby arrives.

If you already have a nest egg, divide it into two categories: Put half into a money market fund, so you can draw on it to pay immediate bills when the baby is born, and put the remainder into a revolving certificate of deposit program, purchasing CDs with staggered maturity dates. Save all cash gifts the baby receives. You'll need to get the baby a Social Security number to put them in his or her name; a number is now required in order to claim a dependency exemption for any child—that's a relatively new ruling.

Ages 2 to 5

Now that the start-up costs of having a baby have been absorbed, use these years to replace or add to your savings, especially if you plan to move to a larger home. If you have not done so, you and your spouse should try to put at least 3% to 5% of your take-home pay in safe investments, such as Treasuries. You'll also need this money if you have a second child. Make certain you have adequate life and disability insurance to provide for your child, up to and through college. Finally, make out your wills and name guardians and backup guardians for the baby.

Elementary School Years

When your child reaches age six, you have approximately 12 years left in which to save money for college. Begin immediately adding to the college fund established when he or she was born. An early start will pay off. For example, a zero coupon Treasury that matures in 18 years can be purchased for approximately $150. When it comes due you will receive $1,000.

Junior and Senior High School

Encourage your child to earn his or her own money. Do not pay for everything. Instead, teach your child how to save and pay for certain items. And remember, children learn by what they see regularly—make sure you are not living off credit and neglecting to save while encouraging your child to do so.

☑ *HINT: Start to investigate financial aid for college by ordering a free copy of* The College Planning Kit *from T. Rowe Price, 800–368–5660.*

Tax Tip for Parents

The 1997 Tax Relief gives you a small break—if you and your spouse have an adjusted gross income of $110,000 or less (or if you're a single parent with an AGI of $75,000 or less), you can claim a $500 credit on your 2000 tax return for each child in your family age 16 and under.

The more money you have, however, the less

you get. The credit actually disappears entirely when your AGI reaches $120,000 for marrieds or $85,000 for singles.

In order to get the new credit, your child must qualify as your dependent—that means you must provide more than half of the child's support. If you're divorced, you and your ex will have to work this out.

Savings Bonds Pay for College

The earlier you start saving, the more you will have when your child is ready for college.

CHILD'S AGE	VALUE AT AGE 18, BASED ON MONTHLY ALLOTMENTS OF:	
	$50	$100
1	$14,579.32	$29,158.64
6	9,233.20	18,466.40
10	5,656.16	11,312.32
12	4,069.28	8,138.56

The values in this table are based on the guaranteed interest rate of 4% per annum, compounded semiannually.

SOURCE: The Treasury, U.S. Savings Bond Division, 1999.

PAYING FOR YOUR KID'S COLLEGE

Most children have plenty of toys, clothes, bikes, and even cars, but very few have a nest egg to pay for one of life's biggest expenses: a college degree. It takes more than good grades to get through school: It takes a lot of cash. According to the College Board, tuition, room, and board at state schools hovers around $10,000; at the average private school, $22,000.

Early planning certainly eases the pain, as the time value of money works to everyone's advantage. For instance, if you want to accumulate $35,000 by the time your child reaches age 18, based on a fixed interest rate of 9%, compounded monthly, you must save $73.08 per month, if your child is now one year old. If you wait until the child is 14, that figure jumps to $608.48 a month.

Yet the picture's not all that hopeless. There are a number of ways to stockpile money and find financial aid. Here's what parents and grandparents can do to meet college costs.

Step 1. Know who should own the nest egg. Money earmarked for college can be held in an adult's name, in the child's name, or in trust with the child named as beneficiary. Putting the money in the adult's name is, of course, the easiest, and it gives the adult complete control over the money and how it is used. It's also advantageous when it comes to seeking financial help: Most financial aid formulas require the student to contribute 35% of his or her assets to college costs annually, while parents are expected to contribute far less, typically around 5%.

Money can be put in the child's name through the Uniform Gifts to Minors Act (UGMA), adopted in almost all states, and the Uniform Transfers to Minors Act (UTMA), available in over 30 states. The key difference between them is the type of property an adult can transfer to a child. UTMA allows any kind of property—real estate, personal property, securities, cash—to be given as a custodial gift, whereas UGMA restricts custodial gifts to bank deposits, securities (including mutual funds), and insurance policies.

Both are simple to set up and administer. Almost any bank, mutual fund company, stockbroker, or attorney can do so. The custodian, who can be a parent or someone else named by the person funding the trust, controls the money until the child becomes of legal age (18 or 21, depending on the state). The custodian can invest, manage, or even dispose of the gifted property on the minor's behalf.

CAUTION: At age 18 or 21, the money must be turned over to the child, who can then use it any way at all—to buy a BMW, join the circus, or, ideally, pay for college.

Each UGMA and UTMA is always in the child's name and under his or her Social Security number; the account includes the name of one child and one custodian.

There are other types of tax-advantaged trusts for sizable amounts of money that an accountant or attorney can explain.

Step 2. Understand the tax law. The so-called kiddie tax seriously affects college nest eggs. Study the box on page 293 and talk to an accountant or tax lawyer before deciding who should hold the assets for college.

The current ruling is: If your child is under age 14 and receives more than $700 a year in unearned income (from investments and savings), the next $700 will be taxed at the child's rate, usually 15%. But, be aware: All unearned income above $1,400 per year will be taxed at the parent's top marginal rate, which could be as high as 39.6%.

Then when your child turns 14, all income he or she receives will be taxed at his or her rate, again typically 15%.

HINT: As the rules stand now, if your child is under age 14, it's advantageous to put the money in the child's name, only as long as the income it earns does not exceed the annual income cap.

Step 3. Go for gifts. A parent, grandparent, or anyone else can give a child up to $10,000 a year without paying gift taxes. If parents or grandparents have sizable estates that they plan to leave to the family, such a gift reduces future estate taxes.

Grandparents can also make cash gifts in any amount and pay no gift tax as long as the gift goes for tuition and is paid directly to the college. And a grandparent can give an additional $10,000 free of gift tax to pay for room and board directly to the college or university.

Step 4. Set up a savings plan. Save a certain amount every month. Parents who find this difficult or who lack the discipline to do so on their own can establish an automatic payroll-deduction plan at work so that a set amount is taken out of paychecks on a regular basis and is used to purchase EE savings bonds or is transferred to a high-yielding money market fund. Both are low in risk.

The current yield on money market funds is between 5% and 6%.

For the current yield on EE Savings Bonds, call your bank or 800–US–BONDS.

Although the interest on these bonds has always been exempt from state and local taxes, it's now exempt from federal taxes if the bonds are purchased after January 1, 1990, and are used to pay college tuition. The parents' total income, however, must fall below a certain dollar amount when the bonds are cashed in. This income cap is adjusted annually for inflation.

CAUTION: EE Savings Bonds purchased in this tax-free college education plan cannot be held in the child's name.

HINT: What if you've already purchased Series EE Bonds in your child's name—is there any way you can get this tax break? Perhaps. Try filing a Reissue Form PD F4000 with the Bureau of the Public Debt. This is a request to reissue the bond in the name of a different owner. Send the form, along with a letter stating that you initially purchased the bonds for education and you didn't know they had to be in your name.

Skip the whole process, however, if you have high adjusted gross income. For 1999, the phase-out starts at $78,350 for couples and $52,250 for single taxpayers; it's completely eliminated at $108,350 for couples and $67,250 for singles. And, of course, don't bother if you purchased bonds before 1990, which is when this education tax break was launched.

Your request will be considered on a case-by-case basis.

Step 5. Pick smart investments. Certain investments are particularly suited for a college nest egg because they grow in value over time. One of the most popular is zero coupon bonds (see Chapter 13). Growth stocks and mutual funds are suitable for long-term investments. Conservative choices include certificates of deposit and Treasury bonds and notes. Deferred annuities can be purchased so that they start paying out income when tuition bills come due. An added advantage: Earnings inside an annuity grow tax deferred until the money is paid out.

Step 6. Look into Baccalaureate Bonds. A growing number of states offer special municipal zero coupon bonds to help parents. They are sold at a discount from face value and do not pay interest until they mature. At that time, the bondholders receive the principal plus earned interest in one lump sum. Their great advantage: Parents know exactly how much money is coming due on a certain date. Some states even pay a cash bonus when the bonds mature if the child attends a state college. These bonds are exempt from federal taxes and, for state residents, from state and local taxes. Call your stockbroker or your state's treasury department for current details.

Step 7. Study prepaid tuition plans. A growing number of states now offer plans in which you can pay your child's college tuition in advance. The key advantage—you lock in the cost long before your child is ready for freshman year. Depending upon the plan, you can do so either in a lump sum or in installments. For example, if tuition at your state

How a Child's Money Is Taxed

IF THE CHILD IS:	THEN:
Under age 14	The first $700 of income is tax free; $701 to $1,400 of income is taxed at the child's rate, usually 15%
Age 14 or older	All income is taxed at the child's rate

college is $3,000 a year and your child is three years old, pay $12,000 now and the state guarantees that your investment will cover four years of tuition some 15 years from now when your child is 18—regardless of what the tuition is at that time.

In all state plans, the money earns interest at a rate that is guaranteed to keep up with tuition increases. Then, when the parents need money for tuition, they cash in the investment.

You can defer paying federal taxes on the money until you take it out. State taxes on investment gains in most programs are also deferred. More good news: Withdrawals from state prepaid plans are taxed at the child's rate, which is almost always lower than that of the parents.

CAUTION: If your child decides to go to a private college or a college in another state, some plans return only your original investment. If your child does not go to college, you might lose a portion of your money. There are other hitches. So before signing up, ask these eight questions:

1. *What if my child wants to attend a school not covered by the plan, or doesn't go at all?*
2. *What if we move out of state?*
3. *Can the credits be transferred to other children in our family?*
4. *For what reasons can the money be refunded? If so, do I lose the interest earned?*
5. *Are there any fees involved?*
6. *How will this plan affect eligibility for financial aid?*
7. *Does the plan cover room, board, and books or only tuition?*
8. *What happens to my investment if my child drops out of school or transfers?*

Most state plans will accept your money only if you live in the state. However, a handful are open to everyone:

Connecticut	Colorado
Delaware	Indiana
Iowa	Massachusetts
Missouri	Montana
New Hampshire	New York
Rhode Island	Utah

$TIP: For a continually updated list of prepaid tuition plans, contact: College Savings Organization at: 877–277–6496 or click on: www.collegesavings.org

Step 8. Study special college deals. Tuition prepayment plans allow parents to pay a flat one-time dollar amount that is guaranteed to cover the cost of schooling later on. These plans eliminate the risk that inflation will boost tuition bills out of sight.

HINT: Before signing up, ask the following questions. Can the money be transferred to another member of the family? What does the plan cover—tuition only, or other costs? Is the plan insured or guaranteed? Is there an on-campus residency requirement? Is the money available in an emergency? What if the child elects to go to another school?

Many schools will also arrange for bills to be paid on an installment basis, typically with monthly payments over a ten-month period, for a nominal fee.

Step 9. Always apply for financial aid. Although it's tough to get, financial aid is available, even to middle-income families. When visiting college campuses or writing for catalogs, ask each school about its financial aid packages. A statement of the family's financial resources must be submitted along with the application. Be sure to mention if more than one person in the family is attending college.

CAUTION: Keep in mind that shifting money into a child's name may jeopardize aid, as explained above.

Many people assume incorrectly that they won't qualify for financial aid. The three most common misconceptions about aid are:

1. The money I've saved in my retirement account will count against my child's chances of getting aid. Wrong: Money in 401(k)s, IRAs, and Keoghs is not counted in the formula for determining aid.
2. If one child was rejected, the other will be too. Wrong: Families with more than one child in school often have a better chance than those with just one in college.
3. Older people returning to college or those who are going for the first time aren't financial aid candidates. Wrong: Older students are just as eligible as traditionally aged students.

Step 10. Borrow if you must. Meeting the staggering costs may mean borrowing. Check these relatively low-cost sources first:

1. Many companies allow employees to borrow from their 401(k) retirement plans to pay college bills. The major advantage: Interest payments are made into the account, not to a bank.
2. Borrow against a universal life insurance policy. Policyholders pay premiums to the company, which are then invested in an account where they grow tax deferred. When it's time to pay tuition, policyholders can withdraw the cash balance or borrow against it. Loan rates are almost always lower than bank rates.
3. Home-equity loans offer a tax break in that the interest is tax deductible.

☑ *HINT: Most state schools exclude the value of your house when calculating eligibility for financial aid, but many private schools count the equity as an asset. When you borrow against your home, you reduce your equity and boost your chances for school aid.*

4. PLUS (Parent Loan for Undergraduate Students) loans do not require parents to show financial need, although they must have a good credit history. These loans are made by private financial institutions, not the government. Generally the parents can borrow up to the full cost of education minus any other estimated financial aid received by the student. Other similar loans are available. The college financial aid office will give you information on them.

☑ *HINT: Using life insurance for college lets you take advantage of the current formula used by colleges to calculate financial aid. The equity in your home, your retirement plans, annuities, and life insurance policies are currently excluded from being counted as assets or toward the amount you are expected to contribute to tuition. To put it another way, life insurance and annuities help you avoid being penalized for saving for your kid's college.*

Crunching the Numbers for Tuition

According to the College Board, the average private college in the United States costs almost $22,000 a year, while for public schools, it's nearly $10,000.

Assuming an 8% after-tax return, here's approximately how much you'll need to invest per month to pay for your son's or daughter's college. (Assumes a 6% increase in college costs.)

AGE	PUBLIC	PRIVATE
Newborn	$188	$392
5 years old	248	517
10 years old	381	794
15 years old	974	2,030

Step 11. Insist your child help out. Encourage children to shoulder some of the expenses by saving money from jobs or working part time. Another cost-cutting choice: Attend a school that offers a work-study program in which students alternate working and attending classes, so they earn money as they go along. Among the leading such

schools are Drexel in Philadelphia, the University of Detroit, and Northeastern University in Boston.

Students can also commute and eliminate the cost of room and board, or attend a community college for the first two years, where the tuition is much lower than at a four-year school. Military schools supported by the government, such as West Point, Annapolis, or the Air Force Academy, provide free education if, in return, the student pledges a certain number of years of military service. These schools are difficult to get into, but most other colleges and universities offer ROTC, which is open to all and covers most school expenses.

Step 12. Use software. The program Scholarships 101, by Pinnacle Peak Solutions of Scottsdale, Arizona, lists thousands of scholarships and grants. You punch in your child's interests, family income, hobbies, academic record, etc., and out comes a list of potential scholarships with addresses for getting more material. The program is $69.95 for the DOS, Windows, and Macintosh versions. Call 800–762–7101.

Step 13. Make moves in high school. By the time your kids are freshmen or sophomores you need to make some smart moves. Get financial aid forms—the two most popular are the FAF (Financial Aid Form) from the College Board in Princeton, New Jersey, and the FAFSA (Free Application for Federal Student Aid), available from the Education Department's Federal Student Aid Information Center, 800–433–3243. Obtain copies when your child is a junior, so you'll know how to answer the questions when he or she is a senior.

Also, by the junior year you want to reduce the income held in your child's name, as financial aid formulas count 35% of a student's assets as being available for tuition, but only 5.6% of yours.

Step 14. Take advantage of new tax rulings. The 1997 Tax Relief Act provides some important aid for parents of college kids. Here's what you need to know, even if your child is a newborn:

■ *The Education IRA.* Couples with Adjusted Gross Incomes (AGIs) of $150,000 or less ($95,000 for single parents) can put up to $500 a year for each of their children (up to age 18) in a special "Educational Savings Account," also referred to as an ESA, to help pay for future education. This break phases out at $160,000 for marrieds and $110,000 for singles.

Although the contribution is not tax deductible, the money will grow on a tax-deferred basis. You can take it out, tax free, provided you use the money for undergraduate or graduate school tuition, room, board, and books.

☑ *TIP: If you put away $500 a year, starting when your child is born, and if it earns 8% annually, by the time he or she is 18, there'll be over $22,000 in the account.*

■ If you open an ESA, keep in mind that the person you want to have the money must be named as the beneficiary. When that person turns 30, any money left in the account will be included in the gross income of the beneficiary and must be distributed. At that point, the earnings will be subject to a 10% penalty.

■ However, if the child does not use the money in the account, it can be transferred to a new educational IRA for a different member of your family. That transfer will be tax free and penalty free if it is done before the initial beneficiary turns 30.

■ The amount you invest in an Education IRA does not count against the maximum you may invest in your other IRAs.

■ *If you have a friendly employer.* Washington has extended an old provision, allowing taxpayers to receive up to $5,250 annually from their employers to use for education—without having to pay tax on the money. This particular tax

Financial Aid Primer

Take this list of key programs with you when visiting colleges; discuss with the school's financial aid officer.

■ *Pell Grant.* A federal award of up to $3,125 to help needy undergraduates. More than 4 million recipients annually; does not have to be repaid.

■ *Federal Supplemental Educational Opportunity grants.* A college-administered program that awards up to $4,000 to needy students.

■ *Federal College Work Study.* Colleges provide 10 to 15 hours of work per week, on/off campus to some students.

■ *Federal Stafford loans.* These low-interest loans are backed by the federal government and available regardless of need. Needy students may also qualify for a subsidized loan—on which the government pays the interest while the student is in school plus six months after graduation. On the unsubsidized version, repayment begins six months after the student graduates or leaves school. And you must pay interest while in school. First-year dependent students can borrow up to $2,625.

■ *Federal Perkins loan.* Low-interest loans of up to $3,000 for needy students.

break runs through May 2000 and is only for undergraduate education. It can, however, be used for education not directly connected to or related to your job.

■ *Student loans.* As you know, the interest you pay on personal debts, with the exception of mortgages and home-equity loans, is not tax deductible. It hasn't been since about 1990. But there is a special deduction for interest payments incurred in repaying loans for a college or vocational school education—for your own loans or those of a dependent.

You can deduct up to $2,000 in 2000 and $2,500 in 2001. You don't have to itemize your deductions to get this new break but the deduction phases out the more you earn. Right now the income levels for phasing out are between $60,000 and $75,000 for marrieds and $40,000 and $55,000 for singles. The deduction applies to the first 60 months of interest payments, regardless of when they began.

CAUTION: The deduction cannot be taken by a person claimed as a dependent by someone else.

■ *The Hope Scholarship credit.* If your kids are in college, or you are, you'll be able to claim what's known as the Hope Scholarship credit. This tax credit reimburses parents up to $1,500 a year for tuition paid during the first two years of college or vocational school—all of the first $1,000 in expenses and half of the next $1,000. This applies to college for you, your spouse, or your child.

■ *The Lifetime Learning credit.* After the first two years of college, you can claim a Lifetime Learning credit of up to $1,000 a year for each year of college—that includes third and fourth year of undergraduate schooling, graduate school, and schooling to improve your job skills. The credit is up to $1,000. This credit will rise slowly, reaching a maximum of $2,000 in the year 2003.

The Lifetime Learning credit begins to phase out for couples with Adjusted Gross Incomes between $80,000 and $100,000 and for singles, the figures are between $40,000 and $50,000. In other words, at $100,000 for marrieds and $50,000 for singles, the credit drops to zero.

FOR FURTHER INFORMATION

■ *Paying for College: A Guide for Parents*, $14, plus $4 shipping, along with other publications on financial planning, from: The College Board, 800–323–7155.

■ *Don't Miss Out: The Ambitious Student's Guide to Financial Aid*, Octameron Press, Box 2748,

Alexandria, Virginia 22301; 703–836–5480; $8, plus $3 shipping.

- *The College Planning Kit: A Step by Step College Planning Guide*, free from T. Rowe Price, 800–638–5660.
- *Funding Your Education*, free from Federal Student Financial Aid Information Center, 800–433–3243. Explains eligibility requirements on government loans and grants.

BOOMERANG KIDS: THOSE ADULT KIDS WHO COME BACK HOME

Your child may wend his or her way back home after college, bringing the stereo, posters, and a pile of dirty clothes. He or she may plan to stay just for the summer or longer—until landing an apartment, a job, a spouse, or all three. Or your child may have no plan at all. You face a philosophical decision about money at this point: Should you be an indulgent parent and provide free housing, a car, spending money, a lavish wardrobe? Even though you say it's because you're a loving parent, such moves actually encourage dependence and continue to keep your son or daughter in the role of child.

Alternatively, you can treat the stay as you would that of any other adult boarder: charging room and board, drawing up a simple contract, and encouraging adult behavior and self-reliance.

Check insurance coverage for adult children living at home:

- *Medical.* If the plan where you work does not include grown dependents, then your child will need individual coverage, unless he or she is working and is covered there.
- *Automobile.* Drivers under age 25 typically add to the premium costs of family vehicles.
- *Personal liability.* You may want to take out an umbrella policy that will supplement your

> **Scholarships & Financial Aid on the Web**
> Check out these five web addresses for reliable, continually updated information:
>
> www.collegeboard.com
> www.fastweb.com
> www.finaid.org
> www.salliemae.com
> www.nelliemae.com
> www.fafsa.ed.gov
> www.finaid.com
> www.ed.gov

coverage for accidents around the house as well as in the family car.

From time to time, even when the nest is empty, you may receive requests for additional financial help—for graduate school, a down payment on a car or house, or a wedding. If your child has a trust fund or a secure job, encourage the child to use his or her own money, perhaps with some help from you.

If you're in a quandary about how much to help, set dollar and time limits and divide the responsibility. You may want to make a no- or low-interest loan. At this point, you must also think about your own financial needs, about saving for retirement or to help your elderly parents if they need it. Although you want to be supportive, emotionally and financially, you also want to encourage self-reliance—what you set out to do when you taught your toddler how to cross the street and tie shoelaces.

These judgment calls are not easy to make: They are filled with emotion. It's particularly hard to say no to your own children. But keep in mind that setting limits is sensible and reasonable, for both of you. Regardless of the choice you make, when you make a loan you should get a written IOU spelling out the amount of the loan, interest, and terms of repayment.

TRADING PLACES: HELPING YOUR PARENTS

When age or a serious illness hits one's parents, adult children must step in and come to their rescue. Yet, as in anything financial, the results will be far superior if some planning takes place before a crisis hits. Your parents have three sources of support: their own assets, help from their children or other relatives, and the government. Here's what you can do to make certain all three are fully used.

First, talk. While your parents are still fit, discuss their plans for the future.

REVIEW PERSONAL FINANCES

Take time to discuss these important and sometimes emotional topics with your parents, but in a helpful not intruding fashion. Let them know you care and want to make certain that if and when they need your help you'll be armed with the information you need to step in and protect them, both financially and medically.

Among the topics to cover:

- *Assets and liabilities.* Ask parents to make a complete list of bank accounts, stocks, bonds, mutual funds, CDs, life insurance policies, safe-deposit boxes, real estate, and other holdings. Debts should be listed as well.

☑ *HINT: If they are reluctant to share this information with you, honor that wish, but ask them to make the list anyway and simply let you know where it's kept in case of an emergency.*

- *Income.* Review sources of income: Social Security, investments, pensions.
- *Wills.* Each parent should have a separate will, and all wills should have been updated since the 1997 Tax Act; following relocation to a new state; a death, divorce, or birth in the family; retirement; disability; a change in income.

- *Important papers.* Where are documents stored? Who has the key to the safe-deposit box? Get names and telephone numbers of attorney, accountant, stockbroker, insurance agent, financial planner, and clergy. Is there a burial plot? Where is the deed?
- *Insurance.* Determine whether parents are adequately insured or overinsured. Parents 65 or older are eligible to enroll in Medicare, a federal health insurance program. Still, supplemental insurance may be required to fill in the gaps.

☑ HINT: **For an explanation of benefits and exclusions under the Medicare program, ask your doctor for a copy of** Medicare: What It Will and Will Not Pay For, **published by the American Society of Internal Medicine.**

- *Housing.* Be prepared to help your parents move to a new, smaller home, a retirement community, or perhaps even a nursing home.
- *Incapacity.* If no provisions are made for physical or mental incapacity, the court can declare parents incompetent and appoint a guardian or conservator. So get a lawyer to draw up one or more durable powers of attorney to ensure that a person the parents trust will manage their financial welfare and make other decisions if they cannot. Parents can confer the power on each other and also name, as successor, one of their children. The powers can be broad or narrow: The appointed individual can manage all finances, for instance, or merely have check-writing privileges. A medical or health care durable power of attorney enables an appointed trustee to make health care decisions on the parents' behalf.

Three additional, important tips:

- A joint checking account, usually with a spouse or child, can provide funds for an incapacitated individual.

■ Discuss drawing up a living will that specifies medical measures to be taken or not taken in case of terminal illness, and whether to use artificial or heroic measures to prolong life.

■ Consult a knowledgeable attorney regarding joint ownership of property and various types of trusts. A revocable living trust, for example, in which a parent is the trustee but makes provisions for a successor trustee, provides money management in case the parent becomes mentally or physically disabled.

Providing Financial Help to Parents

Review these suggestions with a lawyer familiar with estate planning.

■ *Hire parents.* Children who own a business can hire parents to work on a part- or full-time basis. This is a good way to provide fit parents with income while receiving tax benefits.

■ *Make tax-free gifts.* Anyone can give as much as $10,000 ($20,000 if given jointly with a spouse) without incurring a gift tax. If parents don't want to accept a gift, try making a loan instead. The money can eventually be repaid from the estate or sale of their home.

 CAUTION: Beware: there may be income tax consequences of below-market interest loans of over $10,000.

■ *Increase investment income.* Money in low-yielding bank accounts or CDs should be transferred to higher-yielding money market funds.

■ *Tap equity in their home.* See Chapter 28.

 HINT: One final note—you are not alone. Thousands of children face similar situations. Children of Aging Parents, Woodbourne Office Campus, 1609 Woodbourne Rd., Suite 302A, Levittown, PA 19057, will put you in touch with a support group in your area. Membership is $20 a year, or send an SASE. Call 215–945–6900.

Sources of Help

■ *ElderCare Locator, 800–677–1116.* This helpline, sponsored by the National Association of Area Agencies on Aging, will refer you to appropriate AAA offices near your parents' home. The AAA has information on topics ranging from adult day care centers to legal assistance.

■ *The Administration on Aging, 800–677–1116.* This federal group maintains a Directory for Older People.

■ *Elder Web, www.elderweb.com.* Has articles on finances, housing, and other topics with links to regional and national sources.

■ *AARP, www.aarp.org.* Updates legislation involving long-term care and related topics.

■ *Children of Aging Parents, 800–227–7294.* Advice on all subjects with connections to others in the same situation.

■ *Long-Term Care Insurance Organization, www.longtermcareinsurance.org.* Has helpful information on the topic. Call 800–945–1953 for a free pamphlet.

■ *National Association of Professional Geriatric Care Managers, 520–881–8008.* This group will provide you with the names of people who evaluate a parent's situation and then advise on the appropriate type of care. They also locate professionals who help the elderly.

■ *National Academy of Elder Law Attorneys, 520–881–4005, www.narl.org.* Free information on how to choose an estate planner or elder law attorney, and find one in your area.

AVOIDING PROBATE

Probate is the legal process that kicks in when someone dies. It includes:

■ Proving in court that the person's will is valid
■ Taking an inventory of the person's property
■ Having the property appraised
■ Paying taxes and any debts
■ Distributing the property according to the will

Property left in a will generally cannot be distributed to beneficiaries until this process is complete. (Interim distributions sometimes can be made and if so may allow for some favorable tax treatment since an estate can have a fiscal year. This could allow the beneficiaries to postpone income.) Probate seldom benefits beneficiaries and always costs them time and money—a lawyer usually must be hired and his/her fee is paid from estate property that would otherwise go to the deceased's beneficiaries. It often takes a year or more to complete.

This is why you should discuss with an estate lawyer the advantages of avoiding probate. Many states, in fact, allow a certain amount of property to pass free of probate. And property that passes outside your will is not subject to probate. If you own a sizable amount of property, if you're over 55, or if you're in poor health, you'll want to take some steps to avoid probate. Here are several ways to do just that.

- *Joint tenancy.* In this form of shared ownership, the surviving owner(s) automatically inherits the share of the owner who dies. It's often used by couples who purchase property together. In some states, it's known as "tenancy by the entirety" and is designed just for married couples.
- *Living trusts.* This revocable type of trust enables you to transfer property to it without giving up control over the property. When you die, the trust property is distributed directly to the beneficiaries named in the trust document, without having to go through probate.

A living trust is a private document, unlike a simple will, which may be open to public inspection and may expose the surviving partner to legal attacks by the deceased partner's relatives.

Up to $650,000 in assets (rising to $675,000 in 2000 and $1 million by 2006) are exempt from federal estate taxes. These taxes range from 37% to 55% and must be paid within nine months of the date of death.

- *Insurance.* You can designate a beneficiary in your life insurance policy. The proceeds will not go through probate unless you name your own estate as the beneficiary.
- *Pay-on-death accounts (PODs).* This is a way to avoid probate for bank accounts, government Treasuries, EE Savings bonds, IRAs, and, in all but 14 states, stocks and other securities. In a handful of states, you can even transfer your car through a POD account.

You simply fill out a form, naming the person to inherit the property upon your death. You keep complete control of the property while you are alive, and you can change the beneficiary any time you like.

New FDIC rules now insure POD accounts up to $100,000 for each qualified beneficiary. Upon your death, the beneficiary presents the bank or brokerage firm with a certified copy of the death certificate.

 CAUTION: Estate taxes can be collected from POD accounts if you don't make a provision in your will for how these taxes should be paid.

GOING BACK TO SCHOOL AS AN ADULT

Some say that youth is wasted on the young. The same might be said about a college education, which is one reason so many adults return to school with enthusiasm, absorbing new information and skills. If you're planning to return to college or professional school, be prepared for the fact that tuition is probably higher than when you last sat in a classroom. Keep in mind that raising money takes time; start as early as possible.

Here are some tips for funding your schooling:

- *Ask the school* you're applying to about special tuition deals. Many state institutions reduce tuition for nontraditional and/or adult students.

- *Contact the school's financial aid officer* as soon as you're accepted. This person typically knows the most about sources of money.
- *Look into state loan programs* for students pursuing careers as teachers, with "forgiveness" features for those who wind up in the classroom, as well as incentives for professionals the state needs—usually medicine, nursing, and special and bilingual education.

☑ *HINT: Write to the appropriate state department of higher education. For addresses, see* **Need a Lift? Educational Opportunities, Careers, Loans, Scholarships, Employment,** *$4.95, from the American Legion, Box 1050, Indianapolis, IN 46206; 317–630–1200.*

- *Perkins loans* are available for both undergraduates and graduate students. They are distributed by the school's financial aid office.
- *Stafford Student loans* are federally guaranteed student loans made by banks, S&Ls, and credit unions. Interest rate is 1.7% while in school and 2.3% after school above the 91-day T-bill rate, with an 8.25% cap. Get a loan application from a lender and send it to the college.

☑ *HINT: For quick information about loans and procedures, call 800–4–FEDAID; for information about other public student loans, call College Credit at 800–831–5626.*

- *Private loans,* unlike public funds, do not carry income limits or have needs tests provisions. Approval is based on the creditworthiness of the applicant or, if necessary, on the participation of a reliable cosigner. The three leading sources are:

  - Nellie Mae loans: 800–634–9308
  - CONCERN/PLATO loans: 800–767–5626
  - TERI loans: 800–255–8374

- *Part-time, Internet, and long-distance courses.* If you're going back to school part-time, say to acquire a new skill, update your computer knowledge, or get an MBA, check out SLM Financial, a subsidiary of Sallie Mae. It offers loans for part-time students, those who are taking courses long distance or via the Internet, or who are studying as part of job-training courses. Ask about the Education Capital Professional Loan. Interest rates start at prime plus 1%. And, while you're in school, you pay only the interest due. For information call: 800–559–3220.

PARENT AND STUDENT AT THE SAME TIME

If you're working or home with children, check out various "Weekend Colleges" designed to meet your specific needs. Classes are held on Friday evenings, Saturdays, and Sundays, depending upon the school. Some, such as Trinity College in Washington, D.C., provide on-campus baby-sitting and rent dorm rooms for only $15/night. Others, such as The College of St. Catherine in St. Paul, Minnesota, allow adult students to pay tuition using their Visa or MasterCard and spread out the bills over three payment periods—for which there is a small interest charge.

☑ *HINT: Read IRS Publication 508,* **Educational Expenses,** *in order to learn what expenses qualify as income tax deductions.*

INVESTMENTS GIFTS TO GIVE TO OTHERS

Financial gifts are a wonderful, easy way to defray the cost of raising a family, buying a house, paying for college, even funding retirement. The next time you're asked "What do you want for your birthday?" or when you're wondering what to give a recent graduate, a newlywed couple, or a retiree, the answer may be a financial gift—it will last much longer than the silver candelabra or juicer.

Throughout this book we have suggested specific stocks, bonds, and mutual funds—any that fall within the conservative category make sound presents. To simplify matters, here are ten suggestions.

- *Stock in a company the recipient knows.* Suggestions: one's local public utility company, the chewing gum maker William Wrigley & Co., the cereal giant Kellogg Co., Nike, Disney, Microsoft, PepsiCo, Toys R Us, Harley Davidson, and Coca-Cola.

☑ *HINT: Check with several discount brokers to compare the commissions for buying a small number of shares. See list on page 240. Or buy on-line; see Chapter 27 for a list.*

- *EE savings bonds.* Available at your local bank with no commission or fee. These ultrasafe bonds earn a floating interest rate and are available for as little as $25. (**See:** Chapter 10 for more on using savings bonds as a tax-deferred investment.)

- *Mutual fund shares.* Pick a no-load fund with a good track record. The Alger Funds have no minimum (with the exception of their money market fund) and the Monetta Funds require just $250 to open account. The latter has an attractive gift certificate you can give to the recipient. Call: 800–MONETTA. (**See:** Chapter 6 for more fund suggestions.)

  Many well-known no-load funds will reduce their minimum investment requirement (usually $1,000 to $2,500) for Uniform Gift to Minor Accounts. Check with Vanguard and T. Rowe Price.

- *SteinRoe Young Investor.* This mutual fund buys companies children know about, often those who have well-known brand names, such as Apple, McDonald's, and Wrigley. The fund has some excellent literature for kids, aimed at teaching them about saving and investing. For details, call 800–338–2550.

- *Utility stock or bond.* Your local utility company is a known entity. And most utilities are generally recession-proof and have above-average yields. Some utilities sell shares of stock (but not bonds) directly to investors, so you avoid a brokerage commission.

- *Zero coupon bonds.* These sell at a substantial discount from the $1,000 face value, yet the owner will receive the full $1,000 when the bond matures. Treasury zeros are especially safe. (**See:** Chapter 13 for details.)

- *Tuition.* A course in investing or financial planning is always a wise choice. Check local colleges, YMCAs, and other schools in your area. Beware of courses taught by financial products salespeople; some may be prospecting for customers.

- *Session with a financial planner.* Call the International Association for Financial Planning (800–945–IAFP) or the National Association of Personal Financial Advisors (800–366–2732) for referrals to planners in your area.

- *Subscription to a financial publication.* (**See:** page 2 for suggestions.)

- *Financial software.* These programs, such as Quicken, will balance a checkbook, prepare budgets, and track investments. "For the Record" stores your personal history and financial and estate plans, and lists where to find key documents and possessions. (**See:** Appendix A for additional software information.)

30

Stock Options

Stock options, once offered only to corporate executives, have become an attractive employee benefit offered to many of the rank and file. Upstart technology firms have always used stock options to compensate employees, but now mainstream companies, such as PepsiCo and Starbucks, are granting options to just about every full-time employee. Gap, Borders, Brooks, Norwest, and Chase Manhattan are also on the bandwagon.

At CBS, the traditional pension plan is being phased out and starting in the spring of 1999, employees began getting their stock options based on 10% of their salary. Employees hired at CBS after April 1, 1999, get no traditional plan, just options and a 401(k). This move helps companies conserve the cash they would otherwise have to pay in salaries or into a pension plan.

Here's what you need to know about stock options.

FROM THE MAILROOM TO THE CORPORATE OFFICE

- *Definition:* A stock option gives the employee the right to buy a certain number of shares of their company's stock in the future, but at a prestated fixed price, known as the "exercise" price. The exercise price is typically the market price of the stock on the day the option is granted.

- *The "exercise date":* The date on which you're allowed to make the transaction; the date is in the future, the hope being, of course, that the stock will have greatly appreciated in price by that time.

  For example, your company may have given you the option to purchase 250 shares of its stock at $10/share in three years. If, at the end of the three years, the stock is selling for $25/share, you can "exercise" your option to buy it for the $10/share price and make a $15/share profit.

- *Advantages:* Stock options let employees play the market without risking their own money. If, for example, the $10 stock in our example falls to $5/share, the employee doesn't lose any money. The worst scenario: the options expire, worth nothing.

- *Vesting:* Generally, executives and other employees have to wait a certain time period before they can cash in their options. Most stock options "vest" over five years, typically at the rate of 20% per year. In other words, after a year you are 20% vested. That means you can buy up to 20% of the shares in the initial grant. After two years, you are 40% vested, and so on. With most companies, you have a stated number of years—say ten years—in which to exercise your options. If you don't, you lose them.

- *Going Underwater:* Because options do not have to be exercised, they seem to be risk free, and on paper, they are. But if the market falls below the grant price, you're then in a situation known on Wall Street as "underwater" or "out of the money." You haven't actually lost any of your money, but it's no fun feeling as though you had.

- *All in the timing:* One of the most difficult decisions employees have to make is knowing when to exercise their options. When the stock keeps moving up in price, owners of options are often confused or uncertain. If you exercise too soon you wind up kicking yourself for not waiting for a higher price.

☑ *THE BOTTOM LINE: Don't get too greedy.*

- *Tax considerations:* The enthusiasm for stock options sweeping the nation has put the matter of taxes in the backroom. But taxes are an important factor here. Once you own the shares outright, you can sell them whenever you wish, but if you sell them in less than 12 months after exercising your option, you will owe ordinary income tax on your profit. In other words, your capital gains will be taxed at 28%, 31%, 36%, or 39.6%.

On the other hand, if you hold your shares for more than 12 months, you will wind up paying the lower, long-term capital gains rate. This rate is only 20% or, if you are in the 15% tax bracket, just 10%.

In general, it's to your advantage to wait 12 months before selling. Of course, the risk involved in waiting is that the stock could drop in price.

- *More details:* It can however, be somewhat more complicated, depending upon the type of options you own. If you're uncertain, discuss the situation with your accountant. You need to know basically that nonstatutory options are taxed when granted unless the option has no ascertainable value at the time. Statutory or qualified options are taxed when the stock is sold, but the tax treatment depends on the timing of the sale as explained above: taxed as ordinary income if sold within two years of the grant or within one year of exercise. If the option price is less than 100% but at least 85% of the stock's fair market value when granted, the spread is regarded as ordinary income.

☑ *THE BOTTOM LINE: Companies regard stock options as an incentive—to keep employees and to keep them working hard for the firm. And, if the stock goes up and up, it can indeed be a great incentive for staying with the company.*

31

Retirement Life: Where to Live, Where to Work, Reverse Mortgages

As retirement draws near, most people begin to reevaluate their housing needs. So should you, if you haven't already done so. The house you bought 20, 30, or 40 years ago may indeed be your most valuable asset, one that you can put to active use to provide income and security as well as shelter.

TO MOVE OR NOT TO MOVE

That is indeed the question everyone faces as they get older.

Your wonderfully rambling three-story Victorian was perfect for raising the family, but now it seems to be empty most of the time. You're thinking about selling it and moving to smaller quarters, all on one floor, with no driveway to plow and repave. Then some days it seems as though you'd like to stay put but make better use of the space.

Either way, you can certainly profit from the fact that you own a major asset.

Among the investment-related alternatives to consider are:

- Selling and moving to a less expensive, smaller house or apartment
- Renting out part of your house
- Sharing your house with a friend or relative, especially if you live alone
- Remodeling to create a separate, self-contained apartment, either to live in or to rent

- Selling and moving to a retirement or planned community

☑ *HINT: If you're thinking of this last possibility, be certain that you want to live with people all the same age. If so, select a place where you have friends or can easily make new ones, where you are near work if you would like to work part time or as a consultant, and where you have the kinds of activities you enjoy close at hand—golf, swimming, schools, etc. Adequate transportation and health facilities are also important when relocating.*

If you buy into a community, select one that is accredited by the American Association of Homes for the Aging, preferably one that has a waiting list. Both are indications of a well-run establishment. Among the other points to check out before making a financial commitment are:

- Management's experience and reputation
- The corporation's balance sheet
- Potential price increases
- Restrictions on use of the property (pets, children, car space, visitors)
- Any deed restrictions

FREEING UP THE ASSETS IN YOUR HOUSE

Here is a thumbnail sketch of techniques that can turn your house into a source of income. For more on each one, check the source list at the end of this chapter. And regardless of which path you take, consult your accountant or tax lawyer well in advance. Laws change, and state regulations vary widely.

Selling to the Children

You can sell your house to your children and then lease it back, paying them a fair market value. This gives them the tax advantages associated with real estate as well as your rental money with which to meet their costs. You can invest the money from the sale, perhaps in an annuity or other vehicle that provides you with a steady stream of income.

Move to a Rental That May Go Co-Op or to a Condo

Check the local and state laws first. In many areas, when a rental building converts to co-op or condo, tenants over a certain age can stay on forever as renters. This is known as a non-eviction plan. If the rent is modest, this could be to your financial advantage.

Take Out a Mortgage on Your Home

. . . Then invest the proceeds. You can deduct the interest portion of your mortgage payments.

Be cautious about selling your home, especially to someone outside your family, and certainly if it is your only residence. Your house is immune from claims by the government, even if you or your spouse apply for Medicaid, particularly if one of you lives in it. Cash is not!

Get a Reverse Mortgage

A reverse mortgage is a way to get cash out of your house while you're still living in it. It is designed to help older home owners who are house-rich but cash-poor and, if handled correctly, it can be a good solution.

With a reverse mortgage, you receive money in one of three ways: (1) as a lump sum; (2) on a monthly basis; or (3) on an "as needed" line of credit arrangement. Payments are not taxable because they're considered a loan, not income. You can never owe more than the market value of your home. So if you live to 100 and the lender's monthly payments to you have exceeded the home's value, the lender cannot go after your heirs for the balance.

Unlike traditional mortgages, there's no repayment until you are no longer living in the house. In other words, the mortgage is repaid when the home owner moves out—to a retirement community, to live with adult children, or into a nursing home—or, of course, when he or she dies. The home owner's estate pays off the loan, usually by selling the house.

Who Qualifies?

You must be 62 and you must own and occupy the house as your principal residence. It can't be a weekend retreat at the beach. There must be no mortgage on the house, or very little left, such as two or three payments.

Most lenders grant reverse mortgages only for single-family homes, although more are gradually accepting two- and four-unit homes and condos. The Federal Housing Administration has relaxed its rules for these types of loans. However, mobile homes and cooperatives still do not qualify.

How Much Can You Get?

- Short-term reverse mortgages run three to ten years, which can be a problem if you outlive the loan because you must repay it in full, refinance, or sell.

- Long-term reverse mortgages make payments until the owner sells the house or dies. The amount received is based on the value of your home, your age, prevailing interest rates, and the percentage of future increases in the value of the house that you agree to share with the lender.

- The limit set by the U.S. Department of Housing & Urban Development (HUD) is currently $150,000 to $155,250. NOTE: These caps are expected to increase soon. For information call HUD: 888–466–3847.

- The Federal National Mortgage Association (Fannie Mae) has a Home Keeper Mortgage that has an adjustable rate that's tied to the one-month CD rate. You can arrange for equal monthly payments or a line of credit to tap into as needed. You can even change from one type of loan to another at any time, for a fee.

To get this loan, you must attend an education session on reverse mortgages. Fannie Mae encourages potential borrowers to bring along other members of the family.

Fannie Mae also has other types of reverse mortgages enabling home owners to tap up to $214,600 of their equity. For information call: 800–732–6643. Counselors answer telephone inquiries and will refer you to approved lenders.

The Negatives

The downside to reverse mortgages: high costs. Most banks charge at least 1% over the current rate for conventional mortgages. Add onto that a 2% origination fee, a 1% insurance fee, an appraisal, and a credit check. Banks may also hit lenders with a monthly servicing fee.

Even though you don't make monthly payments, there is interest—it's figured into the loan amount. But unlike home equity loans and regular mortgages, the interest on reverse mortgages is not tax deductible.

When you die, the lender, not your children, will get your home.

And then there's the question of your heirs. Unless the borrower has a sizable estate or the borrower's heirs are wealthy, the heirs will probably wind up being forced to sell the house to pay off any remaining loan.

Final word: use an approved lender and have your lawyer review all terms.

CONTINUING CARE RETIREMENT COMMUNITIES (CCRCS)

If you are concerned that your parents, or you, may need health care services in the future and are now independent, consider CCRCs. If you qualify medically and financially, CCRCs offer you the assurance that health care services will be available when and if you should ever need them. You generally will also be able to predict what your future costs will be for accommodations and care. As of 1999, more than 625,000 Americans were living in these communities. CCRCs offer a range of activities as well as residential and nursing services.

In a typical CCRC, you do not purchase your home, but you purchase a contract that assures you a residence and placement in a health care facility should you ever need it. Many facilities require an entry fee that pays for future health care, while others do not require this fee. Entry fees and monthly fees vary widely depending on the contract and type and location of the CCRC. A growing number of CCRCs offer an ownership arrangement, such as a condo, co-op, or membership. Those with entry fees may or may not offer refund options. Refundability usually increases the costs.

If you move to a health care facility, your monthly fees generally do not increase if you've paid an entry fee. Some contracts include a specified number of health care facility days per year or lifetime, without additional costs. After the given number of days, the monthly rate becomes higher.

Predicting your illness or that of your parents is not easy to do. But your decision can be guided by other more "known" factors. For instance: Can you or your parents afford to pay the monthly fees for as long as the CCRC resident lives? Select a

CCRC that's in sound financial shape; ask to see its audited financial statement and review it with a knowledgeable accountant. Know under what circumstances the monthly fees can rise, or if there are any refunds in the event you or your parents move or do not need long-term care. Determine what happens to the fee and the unit if one parent moves to the health center.

CAUTION: *Choose a CCRC that has a seal of approval from the American Association of Homes and Services for the Aging (AAHA). Of the 2,100 CCRCs in the United States, about 265 have been so accredited. For a list, send an SASE to CCRC, 901 E Street NW, Washington, DC 20004, or click on www.ccacon line.com.*

SHARED AND CO-HOUSING

If you don't want to live alone or can't afford to, and yet you're not ready for a nursing home/retirement-type institution, you may want to join with others in a shared nest. A growing number of such communities and housing arrangements exist nationwide.

$TIP: A helpful source of information is:
The American Association of Retired Persons
800–424–3410 (202–434–2277 in the Washington,
D.C., area)
Or go to their website: www.aarp.org

RETIRING ABROAD

If you decide to retire outside the United States, keep in mind that:

- *Medicare* does not cover health services in foreign countries, with the exceptions of Canada and Mexico. Medicare, for example, will pay for emergency care in a qualified Canadian or Mexican hospital for U.S. residents if that facility is closer than an American hospital.
- *U.S. citizens* can receive Social Security benefits outside the country as long as they are eli-

gible. The same is true for eligible dependents and survivors who live abroad—they, too, can collect benefits based on your Social Security record.

- *If you are not a U.S. citizen,* in some countries checks may not be sent to your dependents or survivors unless they have already met specific residency requirements in the United States. In certain countries, your checks will stop after you've been out of the United States six months.

HINT: *Check out the facts in the Social Security pamphlet,* Social Security: Your Payment While You Are Outside the United States; *for updated information call 800–772–1213.*

CLOSING UP YOUR HOUSE FOR THE LAST TIME

If you do decide to move, you'll find cleaning out years of scrapbooks, photo albums, clothes, and furniture will be time consuming and, of course, emotional. It will ease the burden, however, if you also view it as an opportunity to lighten up on possessions and to make some money.

Some downsizing tips:

- *Have an auctioneer* look at your furniture, collections, and jewelry and give you estimates.
- *Get estimates* also from used-furniture dealers.
- *Then hold a garage sale* for items that the auctioneer and furniture dealer do not want.
- *Finally, have a reliable charity* pick up what doesn't sell and you don't want to move. Be certain you get a receipt for tax purposes.

HINT: *Be smart and request the IRS Publication 526,* Charitable Contributions, *well in advance; call 800–829–3676.*

Before you move to another state:

- *Look into state laws.* If you maintain residences in two states—say, one in the south and one up north—you could wind up paying taxes in both. Know how many days spent in each makes you a resident for tax purposes.

■ *Change* your driver's license and voter registration.

■ *Review your municipal bonds.* If you own municipal bonds in your home state you'll have to pay income tax on the interest when you move to a new state, provided the new state has an income tax. That's because bonds are tax free only in the state in which they were issued, with the exception of bonds issued by Puerto Rico.

THE LAW RELATING TO STATE TAXES

In January 1996, President Clinton signed a bill that has taken the sharp bite out of what was known as the "source tax," making it easier for older people to relocate to states with little or no income tax and be free of their tax obligations where they originally lived.

Prior to the law change, residents who moved from one state to another and who had tax-deferred pensions were frequently made to pay taxes to their former state, and if they did not, they were penalized—even though they no longer resided in the old state.

The new law affects retirement income received after December 31, 1995, and covers IRAs, 401(k)s, and other tax-deferred employer-sponsored retirement savings plans.

This means residents of California, New York, Massachusetts, and other high-income-tax states can retire to Florida, Texas, Nevada, Alaska, Washington, Wyoming, and South Dakota, where there's no income tax—New Hampshire and Tennessee tax only dividend and interest income—and no longer worry about filing in their former state every year they receive pension income.

☑ *HINT: You should also be aware of the fact that 25 states and the District of Columbia exclude Social Security benefits from taxation, including:*

Arizona
California
Georgia
Michigan
New Jersey
New York
South Carolina

Some states give 100% pension-income exclusions, among them:

■ Alabama
■ Hawaii
■ Illinois
■ Massachusetts
■ Mississippi
■ Pennsylvania

☑ *HINT: If you're thinking of moving, find out what the income tax rulings are for various states, and ask your accountant to find out where you can keep the most of your pension dollars.*

IF YOU RETIRE EARLY OR ARE FIRED OR LAID OFF

In recent years a great many American corporations have eliminated thousands of blue- and white-collar jobs. No one, not even top executives, are immune to cutbacks. Those who planned to glide into retirement are cast adrift. Those on the fast track are suddenly being derailed.

If you're one of the many Americans who has been "let go," you face a number of important financial decisions. Although it is beyond the scope of this book to guide you through this period in your life, the following financial tips may help make life a bit easier.

1. *Make a realistic budget and stick to it.* Prepare for leaner times. Cut back on luxury items, eating out, taxis, and the like.

2. *Keep any severance pay in a liquid account,* such as a money market fund. If you received

a sizable amount, put half in a fund and half in T-bills.

3. *If you are given the choice* of taking severance in a lump sum or payments, it's generally best to opt for the lump sum and invest it, so it starts earning interest. This way you won't need to worry about your ex-employer's financial condition. If it's near year-end, it may be better to schedule payments so that you can defer income into the next year.

☑ HINT: *Be sure you read* Receiving a Lump Sum Distribution: A Guide for Investors Aged 50 and Older, *prepared by the AARP Investment Program and available from Scudder Mutual Funds; the 30-page booklet is free; call 800–322–2282.*

4. *Do not make the common mistake* of using the severance check to pay off the mortgage. You may need this money, and a mortgage is usually one of the lowest-rate loans around with interest being tax deductible.

5. *If you receive a large sum* from your 401(k) or other retirement plan, try not to touch it. That money has never been taxed. If you take it out now, you will pay income tax on it plus a 10% penalty if you're under age 59$\frac{1}{2}$. In many cases, profit-sharing and stock option plans can be left with the company. If you suspect that your pension might be underfunded, however, provide for a direct transfer to your IRA to avoid the 20% withholding. It will continue to grow on a tax-deferred basis with no penalty. Keep this IRA money separate from any other IRAs; if you take a new job, you can roll it over into the new employer's plan.

6. *Don't be too proud* to take unemployment insurance if you were fired. (You cannot collect if you leave voluntarily.) You and your employer have helped fund this benefit over the years; now you're certainly entitled to use it.

7. *In a true emergency* you may have to use some of your retirement savings.

8. *Keep track of job-hunting expenses.* Some of these may be deducted from your taxable income as "miscellaneous itemized deductions." Check with your accountant for details.

☑ HINT: *Among the expenses to track are recruitment and agency fees, transportation, telephone calls, and résumé preparation.*

9. *Keep your health insurance.* In 1986 a federal law (COBRA) was enacted requiring employers sponsoring group health plans to offer employees and their dependents the opportunity to extend their health coverage at group rates. This is called continuation coverage, and it lasts for 18 months, longer if you are disabled.

    You will have to pay the costs, but they will be far less than taking out your own policy. If you are forced to take out your own policy, look into group rates offered by professional associations, unions, an alumni association, or the Medical Savings Account discussed on page 361.

☑ HINT: *If you are self-employed, look into membership in the National Association for the Self-Employed; call 800–232-NASE.*

10. *Don't panic.* Most problems have solutions and people willing to help you find them. Join a local group composed of others who are out of work. There's much to be gained by sharing your situation with others. The worst thing you can do is to bury your head in the sand and hide from the reality of what has happened.

See: Chapter 32 for suggestions on how to work after official retirement.

FOR FURTHER INFORMATION

Reverse Mortgages

For a list of reverse mortgage programs and a fact sheet, send $1 plus a self-addressed, stamped envelope to:

The National Center for Home Equity
  Conversion
360 North Robert Street
St. Paul, MN 55101
651–222–6775

The Center publishes:

Your New Retirement Nestegg: A New Consumer Guide to Reverse Mortgages, available at libraries or for $24.95 plus $4.50 shipping, from: Bookmasters at: 800–247–6553.

Reverse Mortgages for Beginners, $14.95 if you send a check or money order to NCHEC; add $4.50 if ordering by telephone or credit card from: 800–247–6553. This book answers the most frequently asked questions, tells you where to look, what to consider, and all about the market.

The NCHEC has a new website where you can get reverse mortgage estimates on-line at: www. reverse.org. You just type in your date of birth, value, and location of your home. You then see how much cash you could get either all at once, every month, or whenever you choose. You also see the loan's total annual average cost and how it changes over time.

*HomeMade Money: Consumers' Guide to
Home Equity Conversion*
AARP Home Equity Information Center
601 E Street NW
Washington, DC 20049

General Information on Housing Issues

Free literature and a directory of members from:
    American Association of Homes and Services
      for the Aging
    901 E Street NW
    Washington, DC 20004
    202–783–2242
    website: www.aahsa.org

Selecting Retirement Housing
American Association of Retired Persons
601 E Street NW
Washington, DC 20049
202–434–2277
website: www.aarp.org
Free

Retiring Abroad

International Living
105 West Monument Street
Baltimore, MD 21201
800–851–7100
Monthly; $34/year

Taxes

Older Americans' Tax Guide
IRS Publication 554
800-TAX-FORM
Free

32

Social Security, IRAs, Keoghs, 401(k)s, and Pension Plans

The time to start planning for a financially secure retirement is the day you receive your first paycheck, although few of us ever do. But don't agonize over the fact; just avoid further delays and start now. This chapter is not intended to be a complete retirement guide, but the information here will help you lay the financial groundwork that makes the difference between merely getting along and continuing life at full tilt.

HOW MUCH MONEY WILL YOU NEED?

Lots. Retirees are living much longer now—a person retiring in 2000 at age 60 is expected to live at least another 25 years or more. This means that accumulating enough money to carry you through those years is critical. The combination of a pension and Social Security may equal only 40% to 60% of preretirement income, so the balance must come from personal savings and/or part-time work. In addition, the higher your annual earnings, the less percentage-wise may be replaced by Social Security in the future. Inflation, too, will erode retirement funds: At 4% a year, $1,000 will be worth only $380 in 25 years.

☑ *RULE OF THUMB: To maintain your current standard of living, your pension, investment income, and Social Security must add up to 70% to 80% of your last year's salary.*

☑ *HINT: To retire at your current standard of living:*

1. *Begin saving 10% of your income while you're in your twenties and thirties.*
2. *As soon as possible—and certainly by age 40—begin increasing that by at least 1% each year.*
3. *When your children are out of college, boost savings to 15% per year until retirement.*
4. *Aim to have your mortgage paid off by the time you retire.*

TWO TOOLS THAT HELP

I recommend that you take time out today to fill out these two interactive tools to help determine how much you'll need. Neither is foolproof and neither requires you to be a rocket scientist, but both will point you in the right direction.

- T. Rowe Price has an excellent "Retirement Planning Worksheet." It's free on-line at: www.troweprice.com. Then click on "Tools & Insights." Fill in ten different items about your financial situation and the calculator will determine how much you need to save. An even more thorough planning workbook is available by calling 800–225–5132.

- "The Ballpark Estimate" developed by the American Savings Education Council (ASEC) has 11 blanks to fill in. When completed, you'll have a base figure. You can then save more or

313

less than the suggested dollar amount. Click on: www.asec.org or call the U.S. Department of Labor at: 800–998–7542.

WHAT A DIFFERENCE $1,000 MAKES

You might not think that saving just $1,000 a year could make much difference in your retirement nest egg—it's a little less than $20 a week. Yet if you start saving $1,000 a year each year, beginning on your 45th birthday, and it earns 6% annually, by the time you're 65 you'll have almost $39,000, not taking into consideration income taxes. Obviously your best bet is to save the money in a tax-exempt investment or tax-deferred account such as an IRA, SEP, or Keogh.

ANNUAL INTEREST RATE	20 YEARS	10 YEARS	5 YEARS
5%	$33,775	$13,124	$5,794
6%	38,993	13,972	5,975
7%	44,211	14,810	6,156
8%	49,423	15,645	6,335

SOURCE: Case Western Reserve University.

YOUR SOCIAL SECURITY

How It Works

Although we all spend a lot of time talking and thinking about Social Security, few of us know how the system works. It is a social insurance program that provides old-age benefits for retirees and their survivors, disability insurance for workers, and survivor benefits for dependents.

It is called an entitlement because Congress has set eligibility requirements—age and the number of years worked. The system is financed by matching contributions from employers and employees.

In order to plan your retirement intelligently, start by taking a close look at your Social Security situation. Then build around this basic data. It may seem like a nuisance, but ignoring Social Security records could lead to lower benefits than you're legitimately entitled to, because benefits are based on the Social Security Administration's records of what you have earned. It's up to you, and not the folks in Washington, to find out whether your records are accurate. Serious errors could cost you thousands of dollars in benefits.

Four Simple Steps You Absolutely Must Take

Step 1. Request a written statement of earnings. Call the Social Security Administration, 800–772–1213, or visit your local office to get a copy of Form SSA–7004, "Request for Social Security Earnings and Benefit Estimate Statement." You can also make your request on-line at www.ssa.gov.

Fill it out, sign it, and mail it back. In a few weeks, you will receive a computerized statement showing all earnings credited to your account. It will give a year-by-year listing of earnings, with an estimate of your monthly benefits.

Step 2. Check the information for errors. If you suspect a mistake, contact your Social Security

For Help with Social Security

To reach one of the several thousand Social Security representatives who help the public, call 800–772–1213. The lines are least busy early in the morning, later in the week, and later in the month. Social Security representatives can answer most questions and will also send you helpful publications.

Hundreds of lawyers specialize in resolving Social Security problems related to disability benefits. They are members of the National Organization of Social Security Claimants' Representatives, which operates a nationwide referral service. For a member in your area, call 800–431–2804.

office. Provide them with copies of as much data as possible, including dates of employment, wages received, employer's name and address, copies of W–2 forms, and paycheck stubs. The most common error results from incorrect reporting by your employer, unreported name changes because of marriage, or clerical errors at the Social Security Administration.

☑ HINT: *If for some reason you cannot find your old W–2 forms, try to get copies from the employer you had at the time of the error. If you fail, you can get a certified copy of any tax return from the last six years for $23 by sending Form 4506 to the Internal Revenue Service Center where you filed your return.*

In 1989, Congress virtually eliminated the three-year statute of limitations on errors, so you can now correct mistakes, even those the Administration previously refused to address.

Step 3. Request this statement periodically, especially if you have changed employers, or if you have more than one employer.

Step 4. File an application three months before you want retirement benefits to begin. You should file for disability or survivor benefits as soon as possible after disability or death occurs. Start any application by calling 800–772–1213. Social Security will not start sending your benefits until you file an application. Most applications can be taken by telephone. If you are late in filing an application, it's possible you may be paid only some of your benefits. Social Security seldom goes back more than 12 months, no matter how long ago you could have started receiving benefits had you filed on time.

Facing Reality

Now that you know what you're likely to receive from Social Security, you're undoubtedly shocked or at least impressed with the fact that you will need a great deal more to continue a comfortable lifestyle after age 65! Other ways to build a

retirement nest egg are covered later in this chapter.

When Full Benefits Kick In

If you were born on January 2, 1938, or later, your retirement plans may be affected by a provision that raises the age at which full Social Security benefits are payable. When Congress passed the Social Security Act in 1935, it made age 65 the age at which a worker could be eligible for full benefits. Despite longer life expectancies, this provision didn't change until 1983, when Congress decided an increase was necessary.

The increase will occur in gradual steps over a 27-year period that begins in 2000. Under this schedule, in 2000 the age for full benefits for a person born after January 1, 1938, will be 65 years and 2 months. For someone born January 2, 1939, through January 1, 1940, it will be 65 years and 4 months, and it will continue to increase until it reaches 67 in 2027.

For widow(er)s and divorced widow(er)s applying for survivor's benefits, the provision will affect individuals born on January 2, 1940, or later. Under the new schedule, the retirement age for full benefits will be 65 and 2 months. It will continue to increase in 2-month increments until it reaches age 67 for persons born on January 2, 1962, or later.

Under the 1983 changes, the early retirement option will be available at age 62 for retirees, their spouses, and their divorced spouses. However, they will receive less than individuals currently retiring before age 65.

Your Income Taxes and Social Security

If you have relatively high income, believe it or not, you might have to pay taxes on your Social Security benefits. Up to half of your annual Social Security benefit is subject to federal income tax if your "provisional income" exceeds $25,000 if you're single, or $32,000 for married couples filing jointly.

Provisional income consists of your adjusted gross income plus nontaxable interest income (such as municipal bond income) and half of your Social Security benefits.

CAUTION: Single taxpayers with provisional income above $34,000 and married couples filing joint returns with provisional income above $44,000 can have as much as 85% of their benefits taxed. If you're in the situation, consult with your accountant and/or estate lawyer.

If your benefits are subject to income tax, you can elect to have the tax withheld by the Social Security Administration. That way, you don't have to come up with the cash to pay this particular tax on April 15.

For information, call the IRS at: 800–829–3676 and request Form W–4V. Or, click on: www.irs.ustreas.gov and fill out the form on-line.

WHEN TO RETIRE—EARLY OR LATE?

Should You Retire Early?

There's no easy yes or no answer to this one. It depends on lots of factors . . . and so before making a decision, consider these points:

- Up until now, the usual retirement age has been 65. Social Security calls this "full retirement age" and the benefit amount that is payable is considered the full retirement benefit.
- Because of longer life expectancies, the full retirement age will be increased in gradual steps over a 27-year period that begins this year (2000), until it reaches age 67 in 2027 (see box on page 317).
- You can begin receiving Social Security at age 62, but if you do, your benefits will be permanently reduced. Benefits will be reduced by 5/9 of 1% (or 1/180) of the full retirement benefit

for each month of benefits before your full retirement age.

- Taking early retirement could also affect the amount your spouse receives. The spouse's benefit is always based on the worker's benefits at full retirement age, even if that worker retires before then.
- Assuming you are already collecting benefits, at full retirement age your spouse would get 50% of your retirement benefits. However, if your spouse begins receiving benefits early—at age 62, for example—the spouse's portion would be reduced by 25/36 of 1% (or 1/144) for each month of benefits before your spouse's full retirement age.

Should You Retire Late?

Well, again, it depends. Here are the facts:

- If you retire after your full retirement age, you can receive additional Social Security "delayed retirement credits" for each year you work, up to when you turn 70.
- If you decide to put off collecting Social Security, be certain to apply for Medicare when you turn 65. Medicare coverage does not begin automatically.
- Signing up for Medicare Part A is a no-brainer. That insurance covers hospital and skilled nursing care and is free to anyone over age 65 who is eligible for Social Security.

Should You Work After Retirement?

Many Americans don't want to spend the day on the golf course or playing bridge; others delight in it. We do know that one out of five beneficiaries age 65 and older today has some earned income. Some points to consider:

- If you continue to work, you can contribute up to $2,000 a year in an IRA until the year before you reach age 70½.

Age for Full Social Security Benefits

RETIREES, SPOUSES AND DIVORCED SPOUSES		WIDOW(ER)S AND DIVORCED WIDOW(ER)S	
Full benefit at age:	Date of birth	Full benefit at age:	Date of birth
65	January 1, 1938, or earlier	65	January 1, 1938, or earlier
65 & 2 Months	1938	65 & 2 Months	1940
65 & 4 Months	1939	65 & 4 Months	1941
65 & 6 Months	1940	65 & 6 Months	1942
65 & 8 Months	1941	65 & 8 Months	1943
65 & 10 Months	1942	65 & 10 Months	1944
66	1943 thru January 1, 1955	66	1945 thru January 1, 1957
66 & 2 Months	1955	66 & 2 Months	1957
66 & 4 Months	1956	66 & 4 Months	1958
66 & 6 Months	1957	66 & 6 Months	1959
66 & 8 Months	1958	66 & 8 Months	1960
66 & 10 Months	1959	66 & 10 Months	1961
67	1960 or later	67	1962 or later

SOURCE: Social Security Administration.

- If you are self-employed, you can contribute to a Keogh plan—as much as 25% of your earned income, up to $30,000. Contributions to a Keogh can be made even when you are over age 70½.

- If you do keep working after retirement, it could affect your Social Security benefits and your tax situation, but not your Medicare benefits. That means . . .

- If you are between the ages of 65 and 69 and have more than $15,500 in earned income, your Social Security benefits will be reduced by $1 for every $3 of earned income above this amount.

- If you are under age 65, you will lose $1 in benefits for every $2 of earnings above $9,600.

- The money held back by Social Security is not a total loss. You get a "delayed retirement credit," which pads your benefits slightly after your earnings drop or you turn 70.

- If you are 70 or older, you can earn any amount you like.

- If you're working and you don't need your Social Security, delay your application past your full retirement age. Whether or not you are working, Social Security will adjust your benefit. (**See:** box above).

- The current tax law is in favor of waiting for full benefits if your income, including half of your Social Security benefits, is high enough to trigger a tax on your benefits. If your income is over $32,000 on a joint return or $25,000 on a single return, as much as 85% of your benefits will be taxed.

☑ *HINT: An easy-to-follow guide,* Social Security: Understanding the Benefits, *SSA Publication 05–10024, is free by calling 800–772–1213.*

Seven No-Load Growth Funds for Your 2000 IRA

Unless you're very close to retirement, you can afford to devote 20% to 40% of the total amount of your IRA to low-to-moderate-risk stock or balanced funds; the latter hold both stocks and bonds. The following seven funds charge low IRA custodial fees and have had high average annual returns.

Fund	Total Return January 1–September 1, 1999
Janus Olympus	28.79
Janus Mercury Fund	35.17
Janus Enterprise	37.41
Strong Growth 20 Fund	28.32
T. Rowe Price Value	16.55
Vanguard Index Growth	13.59
Vanguard Capital Opportunity (High Risk)	41.79

How an IRA Can Pay Off

If you invest $2,000 a year and you are in the 28% tax bracket, here's what you'll earn in an IRA versus in a taxable investment. The figures assume that you'll earn 7% annually on the money invested.

	IN AN IRA	IN A TAXABLE INVESTMENT
5 years	$12,306	$11,617
10 years	29,567	26,473
15 years	53,776	45,469
20 years	87,730	69,759
30 years	202,146	140,537

SOURCE: Chase Manhattan Bank.

INDIVIDUAL RETIREMENT ACCOUNTS (IRAs)

Whether you work for yourself or someone else, you should take advantage of an IRA—through it you can build a retirement nest egg on a tax-deferred basis. In fact, if you've been stashing away $2,000 a year (the maximum amount allowed) since 1981, when IRAs were made available to all workers even if they had a pension plan, you have a sizable amount of money on hand. An IRA should not be regarded passively, however, as some sort of savings account that can be ignored or placed in a CD. It is an important investment—one requiring diversification and thoughtful management.

You can have an IRA only if you have earned income; investment income does not count.

What to Put in Your IRA

How best to invest your IRA depends on several factors: the current economic environment, your age, other sources of income, and your appetite for risk. The closer you are to retirement, of course, the less risk you should take. You must also decide whether you are temperamentally suited to manage your account or whether you need a professional.

In general, conservative investments should form the basic core of most IRAs, but there are exceptions and variations. A part of your IRA should be in other vehicles such as growth stocks, which protect your nest egg from reduced returns when interest rates are low and yet take advantage of a rising stock market.

Only a few investments are excluded by law from IRAs: collectibles (such as gems, stamps, art, antiques, and Oriental rugs), commodities, and leveraged investments (those made with borrowed cash). Interestingly, you can include U.S. legal tender gold and silver coins acquired after December

Six No-Load Income Funds for Your 2000 IRA

FUND	YIELD	TELEPHONE
Janus High Yeild (high risk)	9.86%	800–525–8983
Janus Flexible Income	7.28	800–525–8983
T. Rowe Price Corp. Income	7.27	800–638–5660
T. Rowe Price GNMA	6.56	800–638–5660
Vanguard Preferred Stock	5.91	800–662–7447
Wellesley Income (Vanguard)	5.46	800–662–7447

(As of Fall 1999.)

15 Stocks for Your IRA: 2000

An IRA holds plenty of appeal for building retirement funds. These stocks combine good capital gains potential with attractive yields, dividend growth prospects, and above-average safety.

STOCK	REASON
Abbott Laboratories	Growing overseas profits
American Home Products	Top dividend record
Bristol-Myers Squibb	Attractive drug issue
Citizens Utilities B	Impressive dividend and growth
Coca-Cola	Solid overseas sales
Duke Energy	Growth and dividend income
General Electric	Growing revenues
Gibson Greetings	Strong cash flow
H.J. Heinz	Continued earnings growth
IBM	Bluest blue chip
Pfizer	New drug approvals
Royal Dutch Petroleum	Energy play; high yield
J.M. Smucker	Leader in jams and jellies
T. Rowe Price	Impressive balance sheet
Tootsie Roll	Well managed; low debt

31, 1986, but they must be held by a custodian, not the IRA owner.

IRA money must be invested with an IRS-approved custodian, such as a bank, brokerage firm, mutual fund, or insurance company.

☑ *HINT: You may borrow money to put in your IRA, but margined stocks, commodity futures, and mort-*

gaged real estate are out. Among the tax-advantaged investments that make no sense in an IRA are municipal bonds, tax shelters, and deferred annuities.

THE NEW IRA RULINGS

The 1997 Tax Relief Act changed a lot of things, among them IRAs, giving all of us greater flexibility in investing. The changes went into effect on January 1, 1998.

Here's a summary of what you need to know.

The Old-fashioned IRA

The key change is that more people are now able to deduct their annual contribution to regular IRAs.

Under the old law, you could deduct your contribution—up to $2,000 a year—if you did not have an employer-sponsored plan, or if you did have such a plan but your Adjusted Gross Income (AGI) was $40,000 or less for marrieds or $25,000 or less for singles.

Under the new law, the caps for a tax-deductible IRA rise significantly over time, doubling from $40,000 in 1997 to $80,000 in 2007 for marrieds filing jointly; and from $25,000 in 1997 to $50,000 in 2005 for singles.

In addition, individuals who do not participate in an employer plan, but whose spouses do, will be eligible to make a $2,000 deductible contribution to an IRA, provided the couple's AGI is not over $150,000.

A married couple can contribute up to $4,000 a year, even if one spouse does not work.

And under the new rules you may withdraw money, penalty free, but not tax free, before age 59½, for two reasons:

1. to pay for a first home, or
2. to pay for qualified education for you, your spouse, child, or grandchild.

A qualified, first-time home-buyer distribution constitutes a withdrawal of up to $10,000 once during an individual's lifetime. It must be used within 120 days to pay the cost of buying or constructing a principal residence. The home buyer may be the owner of the IRA, that person's spouse, or any child or grandchild of the individual or spouse.

Qualified higher-education expenses include:

tuition, fees, books, supplies, room and board and equipment expenses, but not travel to and from school.

Traditional IRA Distributions

If you have a traditional IRA, pay attention to when you were born. You are not required to take distributions from a Roth IRA while you are living, but you must start taking money from your traditional IRA by April 1 of the year after the year in which you reach age 70½.

For example, if you were born in the first half of 1929, you turned 70½ in 1999, so distributions must begin by April 1, 2000. If you were born in the second half of 1929 (after June 30), you don't have to start taking money out until April 1, 2001.

The New Roth IRA

Named after its proponent and champion, Senator William Roth of Delaware, the chairman of the Senate Finance Committee, this IRA is also called a back-loaded IRA.

Like the regular, old-fashioned IRA, you may contribute up to $2,000 a year into the account. There is, however, a phaseout of the maximum allowable contribution for single taxpayers with AGI between $95,000 and $100,000 and $150,000 and $160,000 for joint filers.

Where the two IRAs differ is in the tax treatment. *The bad news:* regardless of your income and regardless of whether or not you participate in an employer's retirement plan, contributions to the Roth IRA are NOT tax deductible.

The good news is that all of your investments earnings are tax free. And when you begin to take out qualified distributions, they will not be taxed.

Another plus for those who live long lives, as is the case for more and more Americans: you can contribute to the Roth IRA after age 70½ and there's no required minimum distribution until death.

If the account has been open at least five years, you can make penalty-free and tax-free distributions under these circumstances:

1. you are at least age 59½
2. you are disabled
3. you use the money for a qualified first-home purchase

Can You Have a Regular IRA and a Roth IRA?

Yes. You can invest in either or both, each year, but your total contributions cannot exceed $2,000 or 100% of your earned income, whichever is less.

The new rules do not affect how much you invest in your 401(k) or any other employer-sponsored retirement plan.

Which Is Better?

The answer pretty much hinges on whether you think your income tax rate will be higher or lower than it is now when you retire. As long as your rate is the same or higher when you take money out, the Roth is a better choice, even though it's not tax deductible up front.

On the other hand, if you anticipate that your tax rate will be lower when you retire, the traditional IRA will be a better bet.

To Convert or Not to Convert

That is the question. You can transfer your existing IRA to the new Roth, but unless you're good at number crunching, I urge you to get professional advice on this one.

The ruling is that if your Adjusted Gross Income is under $100,000 you can roll over any existing IRAs you have (deductible or nondeductible) into a Roth IRA.

If you elect to roll over, you'll have to pay tax on all those earlier deductible contributions.

So should you pay the tax now in exchange for

a tax-free withdrawal later on? Not if you expect your income tax rate to be lower when you retire.

☑ *HINT: For help in weighing the Roth versus the regular IRA, get in touch with the Strong Funds for a copy of "The Roth IRA Analyzer." You enter your financial and demographic data and the analyzer determines if you're eligible for the new Roth IRA, the older deductible IRA, or the new education IRA. It also compares the results of investing in a regular IRA or a Roth.*

Website: www.strong-funds.com

The Education IRA

For details on how to put aside $500 a year for college in a tax-deferred IRA, **see:** Chapter 29.

Four Painless Ways to Fund Your IRA

By now you've probably figured out that I think you should have an IRA no matter what—whether it's tax deductible or not, whether you earn lots or little. To make it easy:

- You don't have to pay all $2,000 in one lump sum. To make it easy: Divide $2,000 by 12 months and you get $166.66—put that amount in each month.
- Make your IRA contribution as early as possible in the new year—this will boost the value of your account in the long run. Most people wait until April 14 to fund their IRA, because they either feel that they can't spare the $2,000 or they can't decide where to invest the money.
- Use an automatic plan with a mutual fund or your stockbroker. Plan to deposit $167 each month, even if it's into a money market fund. You will have accumulated $2,000 within a year, painlessly. (See page 25 for a list of high-yielding money market funds.)
- If you can only make nondeductible IRA contributions, consider a deferred annuity in which you accumulate interest and dividend earnings tax free. An added plus: With an an-

nuity, there's no limitation on the amount you can invest.

💣 *CAUTION: Avoid investments that are attractive largely for tax advantages, such as tax-exempt municipal bonds. Because IRAs are already sheltered from taxes, the exemption is wasted. In addition, all income, including tax-free yields, will be taxed when withdrawn.*

☑ *HINT: The Cleveland Electric Illuminating Co. was the first company to establish an IRA for those who buy the stock through its dividend reinvestment plan. There are no brokerage commissions, and dividends can be automatically reinvested. Check with the electric utility company in your area.*

Your IRA and Your Heirs

If you're blessed with sufficient income from other sources, you may want to leave IRA funds to your heirs.

In general, the Roth IRA is a better way to leave money to your beneficiary. With a Roth you do not have to take money out, ever, so your account can keep on growing tax free. Compare that with a traditional IRA that requires you to start taking taxable withdrawals each year after you turn 70½. You can also keep contributing to a Roth as long as you have earned income. This, too, helps boost the value of the account.

And with a Roth, your beneficiary receives the assets free of federal income tax, whereas assets in a traditional IRA are subject to federal income taxes. If a traditional IRA is left to an heir under age 14, it is taxed at the parents' rate. And this money cannot be rolled over (see below), so the tax benefit is eliminated.

💣 *CAUTION: Roth assets, just like the assets in a traditional IRA, may be subject to federal estate and/or state income taxes.*

Another plus for the Roth: Your beneficiary can spread out the Roth distributions over his or her lifetime.

IRA Rollovers

If you receive a partial or lump-sum distribution from a qualified retirement plan or tax-sheltered annuity, you may roll it over into an IRA. The amount you roll over may not include your after-tax contributions to the plan, but you may roll over all or only part of the distribution that would otherwise be taxable.

Once in the IRA rollover, the savings continue to accumulate tax free until payouts start—permissible after age 59½, mandatory at 70½. The transfers must be made within 60 days after the distribution.

☑ *HINT: Be extremely careful when rolling over or transferring these funds; in order to not incur a tax penalty, make the transfer from trustee to trustee, rather than accepting it yourself.*

💣 *CAUTION: A rollover from a single IRA can be made only once in a one-year period (one-year waiting period between distributions applies separately to each IRA), but for direct trustee-to-trustee transfers, the one-year waiting period does not apply.*

To Avoid Any Tax Penalties

If for some reason you have inadvertently put too much money into your IRA, take it out immediately. For each year the excess remains in the account, a 6% excise tax is levied on both it and earnings. Earnings on the excess must be reported as income in the year earned. The excess and earnings on the excess may also be subject to a 10% penalty when withdrawn.

YOUR COMPANY PENSION PLAN

The next scheduled stop on your road map for an enjoyable retirement should be your company pension plan. The crash of 1987 and the severe correction of 1996 proved to all of us that the value of even the best-run pension plan can decrease, just as a personal portfolio can. So even if you have little or no control over where your plan is invested, you need the facts. Ask. Find out what you can expect to receive. The answer will help you determine what additional savings you will need to live comfortably in your later years.

Here are 13 questions you should gather the answers to during the course of 1999. (See Chapter 4 for additional information on how to protect your pension plan.)

1. Am I eligible to receive retirement benefits? If not now, when will I be?
2. What type of retirement plan do I have—defined benefit or defined contribution? (A defined-contribution plan gives you some flexibility regarding where the money is invested, but it doesn't guarantee you any set amount when you retire. A defined-benefit plan is less flexible, but it guarantees you a certain amount when you retire.)
3. What choices do I have about where my pension is invested? How many times a year can I move my money from one place (usually a mutual fund) to another?
4. What are the penalties for early withdrawal?
5. Can I borrow money from my plan? How much? At what rate? For what purposes? For how long?
6. Can I make contributions to my plan to build up the dollar amount? How much? How often?
7. Does the company contribute to my plan? If so, how much?
8. How much is my plan worth today?
9. How much do you estimate it will be worth when I retire?
10. How will the benefits be paid out? What are the advantages and disadvantages of taking it in a lump sum?
11. What happens if I become disabled? If I die?
12. What happens to my pension if the firm is bought by another company or if the firm closes down?
13. What is the estimated amount I will receive on a monthly basis when I retire?

☑ *HINT: A relatively new ruling you should know about: It is no longer necessary for you as an employee (other than a 5% owner of the company) to take distributions from a qualified pension plan, even if you're over age 70½, as long as you are still employed. This does not apply, however, to a traditional IRA, where you still must start withdrawing by that age.*

☑ *HINT: If you have no pension plan, you're not alone. According to AARP, thousands of Americans are in this situation. The organization has two booklets that will help you: "Working Options" and "Planning Your Retirement." Order from AARP Fulfillment Office, 601 E Street NW, Washington, DC 20049.*

Types of Retirement Plans

There are several basic types of retirement programs available to employees, described below. Programs for the self-employed—Keoghs and SEPs—are discussed later in this chapter.

■ *Defined-benefit plan.* The most traditional type of pension plan. Pays a fixed retirement benefit, such as 50% of your final salary, determined by a formula. The advantage: You know what your final pension will be.

■ *Defined-contribution plan.* Popularly called a profit-sharing plan. The company decides how much it wants to contribute each year and then specific amounts are contributed to individual employee accounts.

The employee's final benefit is not determined in advance, but depends upon the amount of money accumulated in his or her account prior to leaving the company. In a self-directed plan, you, the employee, assume responsibility for whether the money is invested in stocks, bonds, or money market accounts.

■ *Money-purchase plan.* The company contributes a fixed percentage of your salary into an individual benefit account. You decide how it should be invested.

■ *401(k) plan.* You voluntarily contribute part of your own salary into individual accounts. The tax advantages are explained below. The company often supplements your contribution by matching a percentage of employee contributions.

■ *Combination plan.* Your company may set up more than one plan—say, for example, a pension plan and a profit-sharing plan. The most common combination is a money-purchase plan to which the company makes an annual contribution equal to, say, 10% of salary, combined with a profit-sharing plan to which the company has the option of contributing up to another 15%.

■ *Medical benefit plan.* Some companies pay medical benefits to retirees.

■ *Employee stock ownership plans (ESOPs).* An ESOP is a retirement program that invests contributions in the company's own stock. The ESOP buys company stock with money obtained from a third-party lender, thus giving the company, in effect, the proceeds of a bank loan. The bank loan is repaid through annual contributions to the ESOP.

■ *Cash-balance plan.* In 1999, IBM, long regarded as a leader in employee benefits, dropped its lifetime pension program in favor of a more flexible plan that lets workers take their retirement money with them from job to job. Called a cash-balance plan, it's sweeping across the country, with AT&T, Bell Atlantic, Signa, MCI, Chase Manhattan, Xerox, and others using it. Here's how it works.

Under a traditional defined-benefit pension, retirees generally get monthly payments until they die. The amount is based on the retirees' years with the company and their highest pay in the five years before retirement. Employees have to stay with the company most of their working lives in order for the pension to be worth much.

With a cash-balance plan, money accumulates over time. Employers typically contribute 4% to 7% of a worker's pay each year into an account with a guaranteed rate of return. (The return is often tied to the 30-year Treasury bond or, in some cases, the S&P 500 Index.)

When employees change jobs, they can generally take a lump-sum payment from the plan with them.

According to a study by the Society of Actuaries, these plans are great for young workers who work for a company for five years or so and then move on. However, older workers tend to get hurt by them.

Allocating Pension Money

As more companies offer more investment choices, it becomes more difficult to decide how to allocate your pension money. For 1999, use these guidelines:

Treasuries or Treasury bond fund	10%
Corporate bonds or bond fund	20%
Small-cap stocks or stock fund	15%
Blue-chip/growth stocks or stock fund	30%
Foreign stocks/multinationals fund	10%
Money market fund or GIC	15%

401(K) PLANS

This plan, also known as a "salary-reduction" plan, is offered by nearly four out of five major firms. Employers like it because it reduces the firm's pension costs by encouraging employees to save more themselves. Employees like it because they can set aside untaxed dollars in a special account and their employer will add to their contribution.

How They Work

1. Your employer sets up the plan with a regulated investment company, a bank trust department, or an insurance company.
2. You set aside part of your salary into a special savings and investment account. You have several options, typically a guaranteed fixed-rate income fund, a stock fund, a bond fund, or short-term money market securities. The amount set aside is not counted as income when figuring your federal income tax. For example, if you earn $50,000 and put $5,000 into a 401(k), you report only $45,000 compensation. In addition, earnings that accumulate in the 401(k) plan do so free of tax until withdrawn.
3. Many companies match employee savings, with many chipping in 25¢ to 50¢ for each $1 the employee saves. The total amount of annual contributions, including employer and employee contributions, can be up to 25% of your compensation or $30,000, whichever is less.
4. The maximum you can currently contribute is $10,000. There is a 10% penalty for withdrawing funds before age 59½. The maximum contribution is adjusted annually for inflation, so check it for the existing tax year.

You can withdraw money without paying a penalty under certain circumstances:

- When you reach 59½
- If you separate from service and you are age 55 when the distribution occurs
- If you are disabled
- If you need money for medical expenses that are greater than 7.5% of your adjusted gross income

WHAT TO INVEST YOUR PENSION IN

As with any investment portfolio, make it a point to diversify. If your plan does not offer many choices, you can diversify in your IRA or regular brokerage account.

If you are ten years or more from retirement, a large portion of your 401(k) should be in stocks or stock mutual funds. Over almost any 15-year period, they have outperformed interest-paying investments. So don't shy away from stocks because of the risk involved. (**See:** box of suggested stock funds on page 318.)

As retirement approaches, gradually swing more toward conservative investments, but do

---

ALCOA—A Leading 401(k) Plan

Compare your company's plan with Alcoa's, one of the best in the nation.

- *Matching.* Each division determines how much it will match; it ranges from 50% to 100% of up to 6% of the employee's salary.

- *Investments choices:*
  1. Guaranteed investment contracts (GICs)
  2. American Balanced (a growth and income fund)
  3. Investment Company of America (a growth and income fund)
  4. Amcap (a growth fund)
  5. New Perspective (a global fund)
  6. Alcoa stock

- *Features.* Automated phone system for account balance and for executing transactions. Sales fees on all mutual funds are waived.

not completely abandon stocks. Stocks continue to protect you from inflation. The percentage of your stock portfolio should equal 100 minus your age. (**See:** suggested income funds in Chapter 6.)

CAUTION: Don't overinvest in your company's stock. You've seen what has happened to even the bluest of the blue chips: Stocks of IBM, General Motors, and other major companies at various times have taken nose dives. It's a serious mistake to have more than 40% of your assets in your company's stock, because your job is also dependent upon the company.

Many 401(k) plans offer the same mutual funds that are sold to the public, in which case getting information on their performance is not difficult. But some plans put money into funds run by banks, insurers, or private money managers. In this case you must turn to your benefits director for information. Ask for each vehicle's investment objective, largest holdings, fund manager's name, and long-term and year-to-year performance records. If you can't get adequate answers, don't invest in that particular fund.

HINT: There are several hundred private-label mutual funds sold only through insurance companies and pension plans. Some of them have names that sound like those of banks or other funds, yet you will not find their performance figures listed in most financial publications.

To track their performance records, read Morningstar's "Variable Annuity/Life Performance Report," $450/year, 800–735–0700; or read Barron's.

Taking Money Out of Your 401(k)

It's tough to take money out of your 401(k). However, if you're in a tight spot—a very tight spot—you may possibly qualify for what's known as a "hardship withdrawal," explained later. However, there are several situations in which you can take money out without being hit with the 10% early withdrawal penalty. They are:

■ You've reached age 70½
■ You leave the company
■ You become disabled
■ The plan is terminated
■ The employer (company) that sponsors the plan is sold
■ You die
■ The money is going for medical expenses that exceed 7.5% of your adjusted gross income

Hardship Withdrawals

Most 401(k) plans allow hardship withdrawals, although they are not required to do so. Your Summary Plan Description will clarify this matter. These reasons qualify:

■ Unreimbursed medical expenses for you, your spouse, or your dependents.
■ Down payment on your principal residence.
■ Postsecondary tuition, room, and board for you, your spouse, or dependents.
■ Prevention of eviction from your primary residence or foreclosure on its mortgage.
■ Between 15% and 20% of plans permit hardship withdrawals to pay for funeral expenses for a family member or to pay child support.

If you do qualify for a hardship withdrawal, you cannot take out more than you actually need. You must pay federal (and usually state) income tax on the amount you withdraw. The plan will send a 1099-R to both you and the IRS. And you'll be hit with a 10% early withdrawal penalty if you're under age 59½. And, finally, to add insult to injury, after receiving the money you won't be allowed to make contributions to your plan for one full year.

Borrowing from Your 401(K)

Balances up to half the funding but no more than $50,000 can be borrowed under many plans. You pay interest on the loan to your own account, typically a percentage point more than prime—what banks charge preferred customers, which, as we go to press, was 8.25%.

By law, 50% of your balance must stay in the account as security against the loan. The loan must be repaid at least quarterly and fully within five years, unless the money goes for buying a principal residence.

CAUTION: You lose tax-deferred compounding until you repay the loan, so if you own a home, get up to $100,000 from a tax-deductible home-equity loan instead.

Whatever amount you borrow usually must be paid back within five years, although extensions are usually granted if the loan is helping you purchase your principal residence.

Leaving Your 401(k)

Before you leave your company, find out the exit rules. In general, here's what you'll be faced with:

- If you take the money from your 401(k), you'll owe taxes on everything except any after-tax contributions made.
- If you are under age 59½, there is also a 10% penalty on the taxable amount.
- You may be able to leave your money in the company's plan after you leave.
- You may be able to have it transferred to the 401(k) of your new employer.
- You can shift the money into an IRA through an IRA rollover.

CAUTION: If you decide to do this, make certain the money is transferred directly from the 401(k) to the IRA and not to you. If you personally take the payout and roll it over into an IRA, 20% of your money will be withheld for taxes by the IRS.

Also take care not to add any other money to the special IRA created for your 401(k) rollover funds. If you do, you lose the right to transfer the funds into a new employer's 401(k) later on should you get a new job.

IF YOU HAVE A 403(B) OR 457 PLAN

Over 17 million Americans are eligible for these two plans, which differ slightly from 401(k)s.

- *403(b) plans.* Designed specifically for employees of colleges, universities, hospitals, research institutes, schools, and other nonprofit organizations. In fact, the country's largest retirement plan—the $115-billion Teachers Insurance and Annuity Association and College Retirement Equities Fund (TIAA-CREF)—is a 403(b). Rules for contributions, rollovers, withdrawals before age 59½, and hardship withdrawals are almost identical to those for a 401(k). The maximum annual contribution is $10,000 or up to 20% of your salary, adjusted for inflation.

- *457 plans.* These are sponsored by state and local governments and nonprofit organizations. They are considerably different from 401(k)s in that matching contributions from the employer are rare and the maximum you can contribute annually is the lesser of $8,000 or 33⅓% of includable compensation. The money you contribute remains the property of the employer until you leave your job and thus is subject to the claims of the employer's creditors.

Rules for taking money out under hardship conditions are tougher than with a 401(k)—buying a house or paying for college do not qualify. Nor can you borrow from a 457. When you leave your job, you cannot make a tax-free rollover of your funds to an

IRA. The one advantage: There's no penalty for withdrawing funds if you leave your job before you turn 59½.

☑ *HINT: An excellent resource: The 401Kafé at: www.401kafe.com*

GUARANTEED INVESTMENT CONTRACTS (GICS)

Few people realize that the most popular investment in most 401(k) and company pension funds is a guaranteed investment contract, or GIC. A GIC is a contract between an insurance company and the pension plan that guarantees a specific rate of return on the invested capital over the life of the contract. The life or time period is typically one to five years. They are the life insurance industry's equivalent of bank CDs, although they are not federally insured. They tend to yield ⅔ of a percentage point more than Treasuries.

How GICs Work

The insurance company invests the cash it raises in a number of conservative investments, such as long-term bonds, public utility bonds, real estate, and mortgages, and to some extent, stocks. The rate of return is guaranteed by the issuer—i.e., the insurance company, but no specific pool of funds, backs a GIC, and despite the use of the word "guarantee," they are not backed by federal insurance or government guarantees. Instead, the assets of the insurance carrier back the principal contract, so any default of an underlying issue or drop in interest rates is absorbed by the insurance company.

Most employees who select where to invest their retirement funds select GICs but know little about them, because the contracts are sold to the pension plan and not individuals. You should be aware that they also go by other names, such as "guaranteed fund," "stable return fund," or "benefit accumulation contract."

Check the Quality

As a member of a 401(k) plan you are legally entitled to at least annual reports from your plan manager on how your plan is performing. When you receive yours, check for the name of the insurance company that sold your plan its GICs.

Then contact one of the independent rating companies given in the *HINT* below for a financial evaluation of the soundness of the insurance company. Do not invest in GICs of a parent company ranked below A.

You should also call the state insurance commissioner for the state where the insurer is domiciled to find out whether the state requires the bailout of a failed insurer. Many states, such as New York, do require this type of protection.

☑ *HINT: For information on the financial health of an insurance company, click on A.M. Best,*

Moving Your IRA, SEP, or Keogh

As your account grows or as market conditions change, you may want to invest your dollars elsewhere. The IRS has strict rules to follow.

A TRANSFER

- If you arrange for a direct transfer of funds from one custodian to another, there is no limit on the number of switches you can make.
- Plan on transfers taking at least a month. Banks, brokerage firms, and even some mutual funds are often backlogged with paperwork.
- Get instructions early on, ideally in writing, from both the resigning and accepting sponsor. Pay fees and notarize necessary papers immediately. Keep track of details as well as deadlines; don't depend on the institution to do this for you.

A ROLLOVER

- You may take personal possession of your money once a year for no more than 60 days.
- If you hold the money longer than 60 days, you'll be subject to the 10% penalty.

www.ambest.com; call Weiss Research, 800–289–9222; Moody's, 212–553–0377; or Standard & Poor's, 212–208–1527.

CAUTION: GICs guarantee only the interest rate; the ability to pay is not guaranteed and depends upon the creditworthiness of the insurance company.

And insurance companies can face problems— during 1990, for example, First Executive Corp. of California ran into financial trouble because it had more than 5% of its assets in junk bonds.

PLANS FOR THE SELF-EMPLOYED: KEOGHS & SEPS

If you run an unincorporated business, either full time or part time, you can reduce your income tax by funding a qualified retirement plan with your earnings. The two most popular choices are a Keogh or a simplified employee pension (SEP). The money you contribute grows on a tax-deferred basis and, in fact, is not taxed until you withdraw it.

To qualify for a Keogh plan or a SEP, your earnings must come from your business or from fees for services you provided. The IRS will recognize you as self-employed if the companies that paid you send you Form 1099-MISC, which is used to report nonemployee compensation, instead of the Form W–2.

Keogh Plans

Keoghs work much like IRAs but have several added advantages. You can put away as much as $30,000 a year and, as with an IRA, your Keogh contribution is deductible from income when calculating your taxes. Earnings are not taxed until withdrawn. If you have a Keogh, you may also have an IRA.

NOTE: Because the maximum compensation limit is $160,000, the maximum contribution has

been effectively limited to $24,000, although the IRS still uses the $30,000 figure.

To get your annual deduction, however, you must have the Keogh officially set up by the end of that year, although dollar contributions don't have to be completed until you file your income tax return.

CAUTION: One disadvantage to keep in mind: If you, as a self-employed person, establish a Keogh for yourself, you must extend its benefits to your employees. In fact, employees must get comparable benefits on a percentage basis. For example, if you put in 15% of earned income for yourself, you must match that 15% for each employee.

Withdrawals

You must start taking money out of your Keogh or SEP by April 1 of the year after you turn $70\frac{1}{2}$. (You can keep contributing after that date, however.) If you were born before 1936, you can use the even more advantageous ten-year averaging.

Simplified Employee Pension Plans (SEPs)

There is another type of tax-saving retirement plan for the self-employed that has received far less publicity than either the IRA or Keogh, yet it permits employer contributions greater than $2,000 a year. Called an IRA-Simplified Employee Pension plan, it is suitable for small businesses and sole proprietors. Designed to cut red tape, it's considerably easier to set up and administer than a Keogh.

Although its initial purpose was to encourage small and new firms to establish retirement programs for their employees, a self-employed individual without a Keogh can have a SEP as well.

The deadline for setting up a SEP is April 15, just as it is with a regular IRA or the extension date if you file for one. (With a Keogh, the date is much earlier, December 31.)

Some facts you need to know:

- When an employer—which can be you as a sole proprietor—establishes a SEP, the employee then opens an IRA at a bank, brokerage firm, mutual fund, or other approved institution.
- The employer can put up to 15% of an employee's annual earnings in the SEP, to a maximum of $24,000.
- A self-employed person can put in 13.0435% of the net income from his business, to a maximum of $20,870.
- The amount you can contribute for employees, or for yourself, is limited because the maximum amount of earnings on which the contribution is based is currently $160,000. (This amount is adjusted periodically.)
- The contributions made on your behalf are not included in total wages on your W–2, but there's no tax deduction for the amount contributed in your behalf.
- If your business grows and you hire employees and you already have a SEP in place, then you must establish SEPs for each employee who has worked for you three of the last five years and is 21 years old. You must give them the same benefits you give yourself—if you contribute 10% of your earnings then you basically must contribute 10% for them. As stated above, you can contribute up to 15% of the employee's compensation.

    NOTE: For the self-employed business owner, the SEP formula is not based solely on earnings as it is with employees, but rather on the business's net income (the figure on the bottom line on Schedule C) minus the amount you contribute to the plan, minus half the money paid in self-employment tax. This works out to be 13.045%, not 15%. With employees, the figure is up to 15% of the employee's compensation.

- There is no minimum contribution required.
- You can change how much you contribute based on the income your business generates, so if you have a poor year you can put in less, or nothing at all. When times are good, you can up your contribution.

SIMPLE Plans (Savings Incentive Match Plan for Employees)

This plan is designed to be used by employers with fewer than 100 employees. It enables employers to set up the plan for each employee as IRAs or as 401(k) plans. Employers who set up a SIMPLE must either match employee pay-ins, up to 3% of pay, or put in 2% of pay for all employees.

Employers are required to match the pay-ins only of employees who earn more than $5,000 a year. Employees can defer up to $6,000 of their pay in their SIMPLE account.

The maximum amount for a SIMPLE IRA, combining both employer and employee contributions, is $12,000.

Other factors:

- Employers can't be running other retirement plans.
- Employees are immediately fully vested in the money the employer contributes.
- Early withdrawal penalties are really stiff: 25% on withdrawals in the first two years and thereafter, the same 10% as with other plans if you're under age 59½.
- If you're self-employed, you can have a SIMPLE instead of a Keogh.

MOVING YOUR RETIREMENT MONEY

Every year investors move money from one IRA, 401(k), or other retirement plan to a new retirement plan. If you're among them, here's what you need to know.

- *Direct IRA transfer from one institution to another.* This is also known as an asset transfer. It's usually the simplest to do. You may want to transfer your IRA from, say, Vanguard to T. Rowe Price. You can make this type of asset transfer as often as you like.

- *Roll over money from your 401(k) to your IRA.* If you quit your job you have 60 days in which to roll your 401(k) money into another tax-deferred plan. If you don't, you'll pay federal income tax and, if you're under 59½, a penalty.

   If you like your old 401(k) plan and you don't want to roll it over into your new employer's 401(k), you can ask the plan provider to set up an IRA. If Fidelity was managing the old plan, they could be authorized to set up an IRA for you. Or you could roll it over into an IRA elsewhere, say at Vanguard or T. Rowe Price. You'll need to get forms from your former employer and the new management company.

- *Roll over from your old 401(k) to a new 401(k).* You have 60 days to make this transfer when you change jobs. However, be aware that some companies do not allow new employees into their 401(k) plans at once—you may have to wait a year. If that's the case, you can either leave your money in your old 401(k) plan or set up your own IRA. Then transfer the money from your IRA to the new 401(k) plan later on. You are limited to one IRA rollover per year.

Solving Problems

1. *Fees.* Read the prospectus of your mutual fund manager to find out about redemption fees so you won't be in for a surprise.

2. *Evaluation.* Find out how often the financial institution where your retirement plan is currently being held evaluates holdings. It may be once a day or once a month, or once a quarter. Then, time your transfer accordingly.

3. *Timing.* Check to see when CDs mature. You don't want to be hit with an early withdrawal penalty. And make certain the bank doesn't automatically roll over your old CD into a new one instead of into your new IRA. Put your instructions in writing at least 30 to 60 days in advance.

4. *Forms.* Ask for authorization and transfer forms as well as an IRA application. Keep duplicate copies.

5. *Minimums.* Be sure you have enough money to meet minimum requirements of the new IRA institution. They vary widely.

6. *Signature guarantee.* Once you have the authorization form, get a signature guarantee from your broker or bank. Most companies will not process your transfer without this special type of guarantee.

CAUTION: A guarantee from a notary public will not be accepted.

7. *IRAs.* Don't mix up IRAs. Ask for specific directions. You don't want to transfer a traditional IRA into a Roth IRA. You must first convert the traditional IRA into a Roth at your current company and then transfer it to a Roth at the new company. Alternative: transfer your traditional IRA to a traditional IRA at the new company and later on convert it to a Roth.

CAUTION: Converting a traditional IRA to a Roth means you will have to pay federal income tax on any untaxed contributions and earnings in the old account.

Annuities and Your Pension

If you're close to retirement or changing jobs, you're faced with the issue of how to handle the balance in your pension account. There are four basic choices: (1) cashing it in for a lump-sum distribution, (2) taking it in monthly payments,

(3) rolling it over into an IRA, and (4) buying an annuity. Your accountant should be consulted prior to making a final decision.

To help you have an intelligent conversation with him/her, you should know that:

- *With a lump-sum payment,* you will have control over your investment choices and you may also be able to take advantage of the five- or ten-year-averaging tax formula.
- *If you decide on monthly payments,* your employer uses your pension dollars to buy an annuity. As discussed in the next chapter, annuity returns vary widely. Find out. Of course, you can also buy your own individual annuity.
- *With an IRA rollover,* your money will grow tax free until withdrawn, starting no later than age 70½.
- *If you elect an annuity,* you can specify how your pension savings will be invested: for fixed income, where the holdings will be bonds and mortgages to provide a set sum each month, or variable income, where the investments are split between bonds and stocks and the returns will vary, depending on how well the portfolio performs.

If you have a defined-benefit plan, in which the amount of distribution is guaranteed, you will probably have these four choices:

1. *Straight-life (single-life) annuity.* This is the classic annuity in which you get a fixed monthly payment for the rest of your life, whether you live five days, 50 years, or more. Best for: singles with no dependents and people with dependents who are unlikely to outlive them. It offers the highest monthly payment. Some plans also offer a guaranteed minimum of five years of payment, which are made to your beneficiary if you die within five years of retiring.

2. *Joint and survivor annuity.* You get a fixed monthly payment during your lifetime, and if you predecease your spouse, he or she receives a set percentage of that monthly amount for the rest of his or her life. The younger your spouse and the higher his or her percentage, however, the smaller the current payment you'll receive. Since 1984, this plan is required by law to make a minimum 50% payment to the surviving spouse of married retirees. A married person can select a different option only if the spouse provides written consent within 90 days of the person's retirement date.

3. *Period-certain annuity.* This annuity makes payments for your entire life, but if you die within a certain number of years, your surviving dependent receives your full monthly pension for the remaining years.

☑ *HINT: Best for those who need to provide for a current dependent who will eventually become independent. Also ideal for people with spouses who are expected to live only a few years.*

4. *Lump-sum certain.* Although this is not usually offered in defined-benefit plans, you should know its ramifications. Here you relieve your company of its legal obligation to pay you a lifetime monthly retirement benefit. In exchange, it gives you one large lump sum. This single payment is based on the average life expectancy for someone your age and a given interest rate. Of course, the older you are and the higher the rate, the lower the lump sum.

☑ *HINT: Best for retirees with other resources who are not terribly dependent on their pension, and for those in poor health who will not be receiving annuity payments for very long.*

FINDING WORK AFTER YOU OFFICIALLY RETIRE

By now you may be thinking, "I'll never have enough money to really retire." Or perhaps you're the type that doesn't like to spend the day fishing, golfing, or watching the sitcoms on TV.

According to a study by the Commonwealth Fund, a New York philanthropic group, about 2 million retired Americans over age 50 want to work, but they're not looking for jobs—they think employers will say they're too old.

Wrong! The study points out that certain employers are clamoring for mature workers. The best jobs are found by word of mouth—so talk to everyone about your interest in working.

- *Banks.* Older workers are excellent as tellers and customer service representatives. The Bank of America, Citibank, and others actively seek older workers.
- *Hotels.* Over one-third of Days Inn's employees are 55 and older. Their absentee rate is only 3%. Other chains, including Marriott and Holiday Inns, also hire older people.
- *Home health care.* Demand for home health aides is soaring—physical therapists, companions, preparation and delivery of meals.
- *Travel agencies and tourism.* Because one in four pleasure trips is taken by someone age 55 or older, the gray-haired employee is a plus in this industry. Take a six- to eight-week course at a travel agent school. And you get extra perks: reduced hotel rates and airfares.
- *Hardware stores.* Builders Emporium, Hechinger, and Home Depot all rely heavily on older employees who have fix-up experience.
- *Tax-return preparers.* The IRS hires people during tax time; so do accounting firms.
- *Bookstores.* Older people are from a generation of readers rather than TV watchers. Bookstores (and news/stationery stores) value their expertise about literature.

- *Sewing and knitting stores.* Require expertise and skills that older people often have.
- *Florist/garden shops.* Many hire older people part-time to fill in at peak times: Christmas, Mother's Day, Valentine's Day, and during spring planting time.
- *Child care.* The growing number of working moms has lead to a whole new industry, one in which older people bring experience and ideas.

Use a Temp Agency

According to the National Association of Temporary Services, some 260,000 retirees are working as temps.

☑ *HINT: If you work as a temp you can get around the fact that Social Security benefits are cut when annual wages are over $9,600 for someone under age 65 or $15,500 for someone age 65 to 69—when your income reaches that amount, you simply delay going to work until next year.*

You can find work in an office, on an assembly line, in a lab, restaurant, law firm, or hospital. Depending upon what you do, you can earn anywhere from $8 to $30 an hour. Some agencies even offer free training to those who register. Manpower, for example, teaches computer skills and office organization.

Larger agencies that actively use older people are listed below. Check your local phone book first for a listing; if none, then call the company's headquarters as given here.

Kelly Services	
Troy, MI	248–362–4444
Manpower Inc.	
Milwaukee, WI	414–961–1000
Olsten Corp.	
Melville, NY	516–844–7800
Staff Works	
Denver, CO	303–756–4440

Initial Staffing
    Houston, TX   800–999–1515
AccuStaff
    Phoenix, AZ   602–200–3910
AccuStaff
    San Antonio, TX   210–366–4402

The group's trade association, National Association of Temporary Services, in Alexandria, Virginia, will also refer you to a local agency. Call 703–549–6287.

☑ *$TIP: If you can prepare tax returns, the IRS and accounting firms hire people during tax season. And if your adult children are self-employed or own their own businesses, ask if they need a reliable, trustworthy worker!*

If You're Discriminated Against . . .

You should know that it is unlawful to be turned down for a job because of age, if you're 40 and older. If you feel you've been discriminated against because of age, take action! Write or call:

Equal Employment Opportunity
    Commission (EEOC)
1801 L Street NW
Washington, DC 20507
800–669–4000

Setting Up Your Own Retirement Business

You may also wish to start your own business. Ideally it should be based upon expertise you already have. One of the least expensive routes to take is to become a consultant, working from a home office.

If you like or can do any of the following, you're apt to find plenty of work:

- Appliance, car, computer/printer/fax repair
- House-sitting and housecleaning
- House/apartment repairs
- Lawn and garden care
- Pet care/kennel
- Child and elderly care

- Research and clipping service
- Catering
- Bill paying, letter writing
- Delivery or messenger service

FOR FURTHER INFORMATION

General Retirement Material

Retirement Planning Kit
T. Rowe Price
800–638–5660
Free

Retirement Planning Guide and Retirement Investment Strategies Workbook
Fidelity Investment
800–544–8888
Free

Retirement Plans for Small Businesses
IRS Publication 560
800–TAX–FORM (829–3676)
Free

Tools & Insights: A Retirement Planning Worksheet
website: www.troweprice.com
Fill in ten items and find out how much you need to save.

The Ballpark Estimate
800–998–7542
website: www.asec.org
Fill in 11 questions to get a base savings figure.

Pension Checkups

Your Guaranteed Pension: What You Should Know about Your Pension Rights
Consumer Information Center
Box 100
Pueblo, CO 81002
50¢
Free on-line at: www.pueblo.gsa.gov

Your Pension Plan
A Woman's Guide To Pension Rights
American Association of Retired Persons
Fulfillment Dept.
601 E Street NW
Washington, DC 20049
Both pamphlets are free

How to File a Claims Benefits
What You Should Know About Your Pension
Protect Your Pension
Pension and Welfare Benefits Administration
U.S. Department of Labor
800–998–7542
website: www.dol.gov/pwba

Taxes and Retirement

Older Americans' Tax Guide
IRS Publication 554
800–TAX–FORM (829–3676)
Free

Social Security Benefits
IRS Publication 915
800–TAX–FORM (829–3676)
Free

Working After Retirement

How Work Affects Your Social Security Benefits
Free from your local Social Security office

Working Options—How to Plan Your Job
Search, Your Work Life

American Association of Retired Persons
AARP Fulfillment Center
601 E Street NW
Washington, DC 20049

Lisa Rogak and David Bangs Jr., *100 Best Retirement Businesses* (Dover, NH: Upstart Publishing Co., Inc.), $15.95, plus $5 shipping; 800–235–8866.

Linda Stern, *Money-Smart Secrets for the Self-Employed* (New York: Random House, 1997), $20.

Social Security Benefits

Joseph Matthews, *Social Security, Medicare & Pensions* (Nolo Press), 800–992–6656. A guide to rights and benefits for those 55 and older, $21.95.

The Social Security Book: Crucial Questions
& Straight Answers
AARP
Fulfillment Center
601 E Street, NW
Washington, DC 20049
website: www.ssa.gov
Full of advice on how to get all your benefits.
Free

Social Security: What Every Woman Should
Know (#SSA05–10127)
Social Security Administration:
800–772–1213
Free

33

Insurance and Annuities

*I*n this chapter we will cover life insurance and annuities, and touch briefly on medical and nursing home insurance.

LIFE INSURANCE

What It Is

A life insurance policy is a contract between the insurance company and you, the policyholder, in which the company agrees to pay a specified amount to the beneficiary you name upon your death, provided you die while the policy is in force. The amount paid to your beneficiary when you die, known as the proceeds, is not taxed.

To fund this cash payout to your beneficiary, you must pay the company premiums.

LIFE INSURANCE AS A TAX SHELTER

Life insurance is one way you can turn your life into a tax shelter. Certain types of life insurance not only cover your life, providing money for your heirs, but they can also double as an investment, as a tax-deferred way to save, and as a source of loan money.

Back in 1986, when Congress passed the Tax Reform Act it preserved the tax-free buildup of savings (called cash value) inside both insurance policies and annuities, making them one of the few ways left to defer taxes. (Other ways to defer taxes: IRAs, Keoghs, SEPs, 401(k)s, and other types of

qualified pension plans—all discussed in the previous chapter.)

Other advantages to this type of tax shelter:

- In a crisis you can cash in your policy and get most of your money back.
- With some policies, you can withdraw part of your cash value. (This may trigger a taxable income, up to the amount of any policy dividends and previous loans.)
- With many you can borrow the cash portion at fairly low rates.

☑ *HINT: If you decide to purchase either life insurance or an annuity, deal only with a financially stable company, one rated A or A+ by A. M. Best Co. or Weiss Research, two independent nationwide rating services. (For telephone numbers, see For Further Information at the end of this chapter.)*

💣 *CAUTION: This is not idle advice on my part. In 1991, First Executive Corp., a Los Angeles–based holding company that owns four life insurers with $18 billion in assets, failed and was taken over by the state of California.*

But before you even think of speaking to an insurance agent, you need to protect yourself by knowing what products are out there; otherwise, you could be a sitting duck—buying and paying for something you absolutely don't need.

THE TWO TYPES OF LIFE INSURANCE

There are two basic types of life insurance plans—term and cash (which is also called permanent), as well as a hybrid known as universal life.

Term

Term provides only life insurance—only coverage for your beneficiary. It is also the least expensive type of insurance, giving coverage only for a specified time or "term" as its name indicates, usually 1, 5, 10, or 20 years, or up to age 65. It has absolutely no savings feature. If you die during the term of the policy, then your beneficiary receives the full face value of the policy.

On the other hand, if you die and you have not kept your policy alive, there's no payout at all to your family or other named beneficiary.

There are some variations on term insurance:

- Although your policy must be renewed at the end of every "term," with premiums increasing each time, you can instead purchase what is known as a "level premium" term policy in which your payments are fixed for the entire term—say, five or ten years. Your initial premiums will be higher with a "level premium" policy, but they don't rise during the term and could save you money over a longer period of time.

- Although there is no cash buildup—that is, no savings—inside a term policy, you can buy a "convertible" term policy that can be converted, for a higher premium, into permanent insurance, without a medical exam.

  NOTE: Permanent insurance, discussed below, has a savings element.

- You can also purchase "decreasing term" in which the cost of your premiums will remain the same—a tradeoff for the fact that the death payout will decline.

  Because it has no savings features and no extras, term is less expensive than permanent or cash insurance, at least when you are young. Because the premiums rise significantly with age, a rule of thumb has evolved:

☑ *HINT: Buy term if you need insurance for ten years or less, because the premiums will be lower than those for cash or permanent insurance.*

- Like all rules of thumb, it's not perfect, but generally the older you are the less insurance coverage you will need, and so when that point in your life arrives, you can then end your term policy.

☑ *THE BOTTOM LINE: Term is best for those who need coverage for a certain term or time period—parents of young children or home buyers, for instance, who do not want to spend as much as permanent insurance costs—who need coverage but are not cash rich.*

☑ *HINT: If you select term, make certain you buy a policy that has a "renewable provision," so you do not have to prove you are insurable at the end of each term.*

Also get a "convertible" term policy that gives you the option to convert to permanent insurance, if you wish, also without a physical exam. Both will boost your premium slightly, but it's worth it, especially if you should develop health problems.

Permanent Life (Cash) Insurance

This type of policy is part insurance and part investment. Unlike term, it has a tax-deferred savings feature. It is called permanent because, as long as you pay your premiums, it provides coverage—that is, it does not end at a certain point as does term insurance.

Your premium is based on your age when you purchase the policy; you pay it monthly, annually, or quarterly. During the early years, the premium exceeds the insurance company's estimated cost of insuring your life.

Then after several years the surplus and interest are channeled into a cash or savings-like fund.

Types of Permanent Life Insurance

- *Modified life:* Premium is relatively low in the first several years but escalates in later years. Designed for those who want whole life but need to pay lower premiums when they are young.
- *Limited-payment whole life:* Provides protection for the life of the insured, but the premiums are payable over a shorter period of time. This makes the premiums higher than for traditional whole life.
- *Single-premium whole life:* Provides protection for the insured's life, but the premium is paid in one lump sum when you take out the policy.
- *Combination plans:* Policies are available that combine term and whole life within one contract. Generally premiums for combination plans do not increase as you get older.
- *Universal life:* Can pay premiums at any time in virtually any amount subject to certain minimums.
- *Variable life:* The cash value fluctuates according to the yields earned by the fund in which the premiums are invested.

You do not select where your cash value is invested—the insurance company does it for you, usually in conservative, fixed-rate, long-term bonds and mortgages, and blue-chip stocks. The insurance company uses part of this cash fund to pay administrative costs and any agent's commission. If you cancel your policy, you receive the cash value back in a lump sum.

Because of the cash reserve feature and the fact you are getting permanent, lifelong coverage, premiums for whole life insurance are higher than those for term.

One advantage permanent has over term is that you can borrow from your cash reserve, typically at low rates, currently in the neighborhood of 5% to 8%, and still be insured. You don't have to pay back the loan, but if you don't, the amount due will be subtracted from the death benefit.

☑ *HINT: You should consider permanent insurance only if you need to protect your spouse; if you have small children; if your spouse does not work; if you had children late in life; if you need to cover estate taxes; or if you are wealthy.*

Within this broad category of insurance there are three basic types of coverage: whole life, universal, and variable life.

Whole Life

This is the most traditional type of cash value coverage. The premiums remain the same for the entire life of the policy, which has given rise to the name "straight life." The policy remains in place until you die, at which time the company pays a set or predetermined death benefit. You accumulate a cash reserve within the policy, but the insurance company, not you, decides where it is invested—typically in safe, often low-yielding securities.

Universal Life

Universal life, launched in the late 1970s, is popular because of its unique and flexible features:

- The death benefit—i.e., the face value—can be increased or decreased while the policy is in force.
- The premium payments can vary, subject to a basic minimum. You can elect to pay annually, quarterly, or monthly.
- You can use money from your cash buildup value to meet premium payments.
- You can borrow against the cash value at low interest rates.
- You can cash in the policy at any time and receive most of your savings.

With universal life, part of each premium is used to cover sales commission and administrative fees; this is called a load charge. The rest of your premium is invested in various low-risk vehicles.

With some universal life policies, you can designate how much you want to go for insurance and how much into savings. The company, however, determines the rate of return, which is often tied to an index, such as the Treasury bill rate. Rates generally are guaranteed for one year, but when changed will not fall below the minimum stated in the policy—about 3%.

Some companies now offer a variable universal life plan that lets you switch your investments among several mutual funds sponsored by the insurance company.

💣 CAUTION: *Sales fees and other costs can eat up as much as 50% of your first year's premium and between 2% and 5% annually thereafter. So plan to hold your policy at least ten years.*

No-load universal life is sold by a handful of companies. The premiums are less, because, of course, there are no commissions. No-load, however, does not mean no cost. There are still administrative costs and other fees.

Variable Life

This hybrid type of cash value insurance is designed basically for investment growth. To accom-

plish that aim, the cash portion is invested in mutual funds that you, not the company, select from a menu of funds. Most companies offer several stock, bond, and money market funds as well as the opportunity to switch from one to another. Consequently, the death benefit and the cash value vary based on how successfully your cash reserve is invested.

With this type of insurance, you have the potential of a far greater return than with other types of cash value policies, but there is also substantially more risk in that your cash value is uncertain.

💣 CAUTION: *If your investment choices turn out to be poor, you could conceivably wind up with less cash value in a variable policy than with other types of insurance.*

There are two types of variable: scheduled premium and flexible premium. Premiums in the scheduled premium plans are fixed, both in timing and dollar amount. With a flexible premium plan, you can change both the timing and the amount.

WHICH: TERM OR PERMANENT?

That is the question. And not such an easy one to answer. An even bigger question is whether to buy life insurance at all. Only you can be the final determinant . . . take care not to let an insurance agent talk you into either, and before you meet with him or her, consider the following points:

- Commissions are higher for permanent life. Agents, aware of this fact, may try to steer you away from term, saying it is really only a temporary solution. Term almost always provides the most insurance coverage for the price, however, and is initially cheaper.
- Term premiums become extremely expensive as you get older. If your family is adequately covered by your pension and other sources of income, you could conceivably drop term in your later years.

- Term tends to be best for those who need large amounts of coverage for a given time span: parents of young children, for example, or home owners with a mortgage.
- If you purchase a term policy, make certain it is convertible and renewable. Then switch to whole life as your age and family circumstances change.

ARE YOU TOO OLD FOR TERM?

It's easy to hang on to term insurance long after it's smart. It provides a lump sum upon death, but has no investment value. Unlike investment-type insurance policies, whose premiums tend to remain about the same, term insurance premiums start low and begin to rise rapidly when you hit midlife. For example, State Farm Insurance charges a non-smoking male in good health about $360/year for a $100,000 policy at age 50. When he hits 60, the cost is $940 and at age 70, $2,504.

At some point you may be too old for term. Consider giving up term insurance if:

- You have educated your children
- Your spouse is not dependent solely on your income
- Your mortgage is paid off
- You are independently wealthy
- You have a sizable pension

FIVE INSIDER PROTECTIVE TIPS

A recent study by the Federal Trade Commission concluded that (1) life insurance is so complicated that the public is practically unable to evaluate the true costs of various policies; (2) the savings portions of cash value policies that do not pay dividends offer an extremely low rate of return; (3) prices for similar policies vary widely; and (4) the public loses large amounts of money when they surrender cash value policies within the first ten years.

As a result of these FTC conclusions, the CFA,

an independent consumer advocacy group, devised these guidelines for selecting an insurance policy:

1. Don't buy if you don't need it. If you are without dependents, you probably don't need life insurance, and don't buy a policy to cover your children's lives.
2. If you buy term, buy only an annual renewal policy.
3. Never buy credit life insurance. This is useless insurance, marketed to pay off a particular loan, often a mortgage. It is way, way overpriced in most states, although New York is an exception. Instead, purchase a term policy to cover your loan.
4. Don't buy mail-order life insurance unless you compare its price to annual renewable term and find it less expensive.
5. Don't let an agent talk you into dropping an old policy. If it still pays dividends, you may be better off borrowing out any cash value and reinvesting it elsewhere at higher rates.

SHOPPING FOR THE RIGHT COVERAGE

If you decide you need coverage, shop for it as if you were buying a car or household appliance. Compare features and prices. Your employer may already offer you life insurance as part of your benefits package. This is usually the best deal you can get, even if you have to pay some of the premiums. You may also be able to increase your coverage through your company—*ask.*

☑ *HINT: If you live in Connecticut, New York, or Massachusetts, look into low-cost term and cash value insurance offered through savings banks.*

Low-load policies, sold directly to the public, have lower fees, because there is no sales commission.

Finally, a good insurance agent should be able to show you several policies; of course, make certain you're working with a reliable person.

You can also turn to:

Insurance Quote Firms

They provide four or five of the lowest-cost policies in their computer files. Most deal only with highly rated companies. Some operate in all states; others are licensed only in certain areas. For further information, contact:

- Insurance Information
    Cobblestone Court #2, 23 Rte. 134
    South Dennis, MA 02660
    800–472–5800
- Insurance Quote
    3200 North Dobson Road, Building C
    Chandler, AZ 85224
    800–972–1104
    website: www.iquote.com
- SelectQuote
    595 Market Street
    San Francisco, CA 94105
    800–343–1985
    website: www.selectquote.com

Other Internet Quote Services

- www.accuquote.com
- www.insuremarket.com
- www.insweb.com
- www.quotesmith.com
- www.rightquote.com
- www.term4sale.com

Low-Load Term Insurance

■ American Life of New York	800–872–5963
■ First Ameritas (NY)	800–552–3553
■ Fidelity Investments	800–544–2442
■ John Hancock Variable	888–994–2626
■ Midland Life	800–808–5810
■ USAA	800–531–8000
■ U.S. Financial	800–808–5810
■ Zurich Life Insurance of America	800–542–5433

SWITCHING YOUR LIFE INSURANCE POLICY

Before changing your policy, take time to compare the death benefit, annual premium, initial rate of cash buildup, and most importantly, the net yield—what your money earns after all charges and fees. This is, unfortunately, an area where very aggressive agents try to talk unknowing people into switching policies when there's no need to; the only one who benefits is the agent who earns a commission on issuing the new policy.

For help analyzing the rate of return, write:

Consumer Federation of America's Insurance
  Group
1424 16th Street NW
Washington, DC 20036
202–387–6121

For $40 for the first proposal and $30 for each additional one, CFA will analyze the rate of return on your current cash value policy.

HOW MUCH INSURANCE DO YOU REALLY NEED?

When you decide to buy any kind of insurance, don't automatically rely on an agent's advice. They have an inherent desire to sell you as much coverage as possible. Instead, begin with these general guidelines and then adapt them to your particular situation.

Life

The amount of life insurance you should have is related to other sources of coverage (pension, social security, investments, etc.) and, of course, to how old you are and how many people need your financial help. If you have several small children, you want enough coverage to support them until they are 18 or through college, but if you are single, put your money elsewhere.

☑ *HINT: The rule of thumb is five to six times your annual earnings—but this does not all have to come from life insurance. Factor in other savings, Social Security benefits, pension, property, and investments.*

☑ *HINT: Before you purchase life insurance, read: "What You Should Know About Life Insurance," available free from www.pueblo.gsa.gov or 800–878–3256.*

Health

You need a major medical policy that covers at least 80% of doctor and hospital bills above your deductible. Avoid a policy that has exclusions for expensive diseases such as cancer.

Disability

Get a policy that replaces 60% to 80% of your net income. Select one that will pay out when you cannot work at your own occupation, not when you cannot do any type of work.

Medigap Insurance

This supplemental policy is designed to fill the gaps between your medical bills and what Medicare covers. Before you buy such a policy, be clear about what Medicare now covers:

- Hospital stays after a deductible and copayments; check for limitations
- Up to 100 days in a skilled nursing facility; with some copayments
- Hospice-care benefits for the terminally ill; check for certain limitations
- Home health care
- 80% of approved doctor's charges after a $100 deductible

NOTE: The rulings are continually being revised and may have changed when you read this.

☑ *HINT: The Medicare Handbook has complete explanations of coverage. Call 800–772–1213 for a* *free copy, or stop in at your local Social Security Office.*

Whether or not you need a Medigap policy depends on what other coverage you already have. Review your existing policies carefully, and take full advantage of the "free look" provision recommended by the National Association of Insurance Commissioners (NAIC), which gives you 30 days to change your mind after purchasing a policy. Most states have adopted this provision. Follow these guidelines:

- Buy one comprehensive policy, not several with possible overlapping coverage.
- Buy a policy that is guaranteed renewable for life.
- Find out about exclusions for preexisting conditions and waiting periods.
- Turn down any policy that says it is government-sponsored or guaranteed; it's not.
- Write a check only to the insurance company, not the agent. If your policy does not arrive in 30 days, call your state insurance office.

Auto

At the very least, meet these minimums: $100,000 for one injury; $300,000 total per accident, and $50,000 for property damage.

If your car has lost at least one-third of its initial value, consider canceling collision. Your state may require you to be covered against uninsured motorists. Ask if discounts are available for safe drivers, nonsmokers, honor-roll students, graduates of driver education courses, and owners of cars with airbags.

Home Owners

Be covered for at least 80% of the replacement cost of your home, not including land value, plus a minimum of $100,000 for liability. Ask if discounts are available for those with smoke alarms, deadbolt locks, and fire extinguishers.

If you're renting, don't overlook insurance for your possessions as well. And if you live part or full time in someone else's house or apartment, make sure any valuables you keep there are insured as well—known as off-the-premises coverage.

Umbrella Policy

If your assets are above $100,000, if you have a swimming pool, if you throw lots of parties or race cars, or if you are vulnerable to lawsuits, take out an umbrella policy for $1 million at once.

MEDICARE UPDATE FOR 2000

Dramatic changes are taking place due to the explosion of Medicare costs. In a nutshell, here are the basics. For full details, see For Further Information at the end of this chapter.

People 65 and older now must choose among six forms of health insurance, collectively known as "Medicare + Choice." The six are: traditional Medicare, three versions of managed-care programs, a fee-for-service plan, and medical savings accounts.

With the exception of the traditional Medicare, all the new options are offered by private companies. Until the year 2001, senior citizens can enroll or switch to another plan on a monthly basis. After that both enrollments and switching will be allowed less frequently until the year 2003. Then there will be only one enrollment/switching period per year.

- *Traditional Medicare.* This basic fee-for-service program has been running some 30 years. A major advantage is that there are few restrictions on choice of doctors, specialists, hospitals. Traditional Medicare also limits how much health providers can charge. However, Medicare does not pay for outpatient prescriptions, chiropractic services, hearing aids, eyeglasses, vision exams. And it does allow physicians to charge 15% over fixed costs. To

pay for charges not covered, most people wind up buying Medigap insurance policies.
- *Managed-care plans.* You give up free choice of doctors, hospitals, and procedures here and in turn get more coverage—eyeglasses and prescription drugs, for example. Shop around carefully and hold onto your Medigap policy for several months after switching—just to make sure you're pleased.

  The three types are: health maintenance organizations (HMOs), preferred provider organizations (PPOs), and provider service organizations (PSOs).
- *Private fee-for-service (PFFS).* You can choose from a list of approved insurance companies. Medicare allocates a monthly payment toward the purchase of this plan. You pay an uncapped monthly premium. You can choose your doctor, including those that don't participate in Medicare, but costs may become higher and higher.
- *Medical savings account.* With this option, the government will give you a fixed monthly sum—a minimum of $367. This amount will vary, depending upon where you live. You use it to purchase a private health insurance policy (your pick) with a high deductible—up to $6,000. Any money left over from what the government gives you goes into a tax-free, interest-earning, custodial savings account to be used for future medical expenses.

NURSING HOME/LONG-TERM INSURANCE

As you (or members of your family) approach your late 60s or 70s, part of retirement planning should deal with long-term care. Depending on your financial situation, you may want to consider this type of insurance. According to the Health Insurance Association of America, the national average for nursing home costs are approximately $120/day for basic services. Many senior citizens

Part Six • Financing Your Lifestyle

> **Three Nursing Home Insurance Providers**
>
> CNA
> 100 CNA Drive
> Nashville, TN 37214
> 800–775–1541
>
> GE Capital Assurance Co.
> Box 2080
> San Rafael, CA 94912
> 800–456–7766
>
> John Hancock
> Box 111
> Boston, MA 02117
> 800–543–6415

incorrectly believe that Medicare will pick up the total bill. It does not.

Although an insurance policy may initially seem the logical solution, this particular field is complex and riddled with problems. Read the brochures listed at the end of this chapter before purchasing a policy.

Over 100 companies sell long-term care coverage, according to the Health Insurance Association of America. And although the National Association of Insurance Commissioners has issued guidelines for policies, insurers are not legally forced to abide by them. This means you must do some serious research before purchasing a long-term care policy. The companies listed in the box above may be a good place to begin gathering information, as are the sources listed at the end of this chapter. Before taking out a policy, discuss the matter with your insurance agent or financial planner, and study at least two, preferably three, different plans before making a final decision.

The downside of long-term health care policies is that if you never need this care, the premiums paid are not recoverable. A new type of policy, which uses the structure and guarantees of whole life insurance, however, recently came onto the market. With a single premium of $10,000 or more, you can purchase a death benefit that also doubles as an account for paying for the cost of long-term care. It is available on a single life or joint basis, and if an insured needs nursing home care, the policy will pay up to 2% (4% for both insureds) of the death benefit for these costs.

☑ *HINT: For information, call The Golden Rule Insurance Company in Lawrenceville, Illinois, at 800–950–4474.*

Key Nursing Home Insurance Rulings

Many long-term insurance care policies have flaws. To address them, the National Association of Insurance Commissioners has drawn up some minimum guidelines, which many states have adopted. Be absolutely sure that you purchase a policy that meets the NAIC standards.

One rule requires insurers to let buyers designate up to three people to be notified if a policy is about to lapse because of nonpayment. (The designees would not be liable for payment.) The rules also require an insurer to reinstate a policy for a period of at least five months after termination if

> **General Insurance Tips**
>
> **DO:**
> - Take the maximum deductible you can afford
> - Ask if you qualify for a discount
> - Get coverage through a group when possible; it's cheaper
>
> **DON'T:**
> - Buy narrow policies; they frequently duplicate coverage you may have in other policies
> - Switch from one policy to another without studying the costs; fees and commissions are high
> - Use life insurance only for an investment; your first goal is coverage, then investment

the lapse was due to mental or physical impairment of the insured.

NOTE: AMEX Life Assurance, for example, offers a nine-month reinstatement period, but not all insurers do.

Another rule would bar insurers from describing premiums as "level" unless they are set for life. Many insurers use the term even though they have the right to raise rates.

☑ *HINT: For more information, get a free copy of:* A Shopper's Guide to Long-Term Care Insurance, *by writing to NAIC, 120 West 12th Street, Suite 1100, Kansas City, MO 64105; 816–842–3600; and* Before You Buy *from AARP.*

Tips for Evaluating Nursing Home Insurance Policies

Be certain you select a policy that:

- Covers these three areas: skilled, intermediate, and custodial care.
- Does not require being hospitalized before receiving long-term care. Those with Alzheimer's, for instance, are not usually hospitalized before entering a home.
- Covers long-term care in the home.
- Guarantees renewability for life.
- Covers "organically based mental conditions" (*e.g.,* Alzheimer's).
- Has an inflation clause—you want to have your benefits ride up with the cost of living.
- Covers any type of health-care facility, not just a Medicare-certified nursing home.
- Has a 30-day think-it-over period.

ANNUITIES: A VIABLE ALTERNATIVE FOR TAX-DEFERRED SAVINGS

If you'd like to stockpile tax-deferred savings for your retirement years, then take a close look at an annuity—it's one of the few investment vehicles that has survived IRS rulings.

Annuities have all the benefits of an IRA, but no $2,000 cap on annual contributions, and with most you can continue to invest on an after-tax basis even beyond age 70. The minimums are low, often only $1,000, and with most you can invest as much as you like.

Annuities are complicated, however, riddled with fees, charges, rules, and restrictions, so do your homework first.

The Nitty Gritty

An annuity is simply a contract between you and an insurance company in which you pay a sum of money and in return receive regular payments, for life or for a stated period of time. The money grows on a tax-deferred basis until you begin receiving it, typically after age 59½. At that point you can postpone the tax bite by annuitizing, that is, converting your assets into a monthly stream of in-

---

Questions to Ask an Insurance Company About Annuities

Before purchasing an annuity, read the contract, have your accountant or financial adviser review it as well, and make certain you know the answers to these questions:

- What is the current interest rate?
- What were the rates for the last three to five years?
- How long is the rate guaranteed for?
- How is the rate determined?
- What are the bond ratings in the portfolio? (Select a policy with bonds rated A or above.)
- How long has the insurance company been selling this particular annuity?
- What is the company's A.M. Best rating? (Again, it should be A or above.)

All You Ever Needed to Know About Variable Annuities: A Checklist

- Annuities are insurance contracts
- Contributions are not tax deductible
- Taxes on earnings are deferred until you withdraw the money
- Withdraw money before 59½ and there's a 10% tax penalty, and a surrender fee may be imposed by the insurance company
- There is no limit on how much money you can put into an annuity
- You don't have to withdraw money until age 70½
- You are not guaranteed a rate of return
- You select your own investments from a menu of mutual funds; your return thus varies
- You can switch among mutual funds, with no capital gains tax consequences
- Variable annuities are immune from creditors in some states
- If you die before you start withdrawing money, your beneficiary receives all you put in, or the accumulated value, whichever is larger
- Money withdrawn is taxed as regular income and not as a capital gain
- Variables have various withdrawal choices, including payments for life

come. Then, only that portion of the payout representing growth or interest income is taxed.

Annuities are often confused with life insurance. They are not the same. An annuity provides a steady stream of income while you are alive, while a life insurance policy pays off upon your death and benefits your heirs.

There are two key types of annuities: fixed and variable.

Fixed Annuities

With a fixed annuity the premiums are invested in fixed-rate instruments, usually bonds or mortgages. Your money earns a fixed rate of return that

is guaranteed for a certain time period, anywhere from one to five years, occasionally longer. After the guarantee period is over, your assets are automatically rolled over for a new time period at a new rate. The new rate will have moved up or down, depending upon the general direction of interest rates.

HINT: Fixed annuities are best in times of high interest rates, when you can lock in good yields.

Most fixed annuities have a "floor" or guaranteed rate below which your return will not drop. This floor, often tied to the T-bill rate or other index, lasts the life of the annuity.

CAUTION: Watch out for any plan that entices investors with an initially high teaser rate and then reduces it drastically when the guarantee period is up. And make certain when you roll over that the new rate is equal to that being paid to new customers.

Variable Annuities

This insurance product, still sold through insurance agents or stockbrokers as well as some no-load alternatives, works rather like a tax-deferred mutual fund, but has more pizzazz—as well as more risk.

Your premiums are invested in stocks, bonds, mutual funds, real estate, money market instruments, and managed portfolios, thus offering the potential of a higher return than with a fixed annuity.

With some you can pick from a menu of stock, bond, and money market mutual funds or let the insurance company do so for you. Your return varies, depending upon the portfolio's performance—hence the name, variable annuity.

In other words, unlike regular annuities, variables do not promise a set payoff when you start

Variable Annuities with Their Ratings

COMPANY/INSURER (CONTRACT NAME) TELEPHONE	S&P RATING
MFS/Sun Life (Compass 3-NY-VA) 800–343–2829	AAA
Hartford Life Ins. (The Director-VA) 800–862–6668	AA
Guardian Ins. & Annuity (Retirement Asset Manager) 800–221–3253	AA+
Keyport Life Ins. (Keyport Advisor) 800–437–4466	AA–
Hartford Life Ins. (Putnam Capital Mgr-VA) 800–862–6668	AA
Nationwide Life Ins. (Best of Amer 4) 800–321–6064	AA+

(As of Fall 1999.)

making withdrawals. How much money you have upon retirement depends upon the mutual funds you picked.

If you die, your beneficiaries are guaranteed to receive the principal you've invested, minus any withdrawals—and even more if your account is larger than your contribution.

☑ *HINT: Contribute the maximum amount to your 401(k) plan at work before you invest in a variable annuity. Unlike annuities, 401(k) plans let you defer taxes on the dollar amount you contribute . . . and most employers match some of your contributions.*

You should also contribute the max to your IRA before investing in an annuity—IRAs don't have the high fees that most annuities do.

Ways to Pay for an Annuity

You can select either a *single-premium annuity*, in which case you make a one-time payment, or an *installment* or *flexible premium*, which you pay for in stages over time. You can also purchase an annuity long before you retire, which is known as a *deferred annuity*, or close to retirement, known as an *immediate annuity.*

An immediate annuity, in which payments begin almost at once, is often used by those who receive a lump-sum payment from a company pension plan. In a deferred payment annuity, no payments are made until at least a year or more after you've paid your premium.

Getting Your Money Back

When you reach $59\frac{1}{2}$ your money is returned to you in one of several ways: in a lump sum, in regular monthly payments, or as lifetime income for you and your spouse. Payments vary depending on the amount you have contributed, your age, the length of time your money has been compounding, and the rate of return on the portfolios. Taxes must be paid on all payouts.

Six Variable Annuities with Relatively Low Expenses

These companies sell no-load (no sales fee) variable annuities; call for literature.

COMPANY	800 NUMBER	MINIMUM INVESTMENT
John Hancock MarketPlace	800–824–0335	$5,000
Schwab Select	800–838–0650	$5,000
Scudder Horizon Advantage	800–225–2470	$2,500
T. Rowe Price No-Load	800–469–5304	$10,000
USAA Life Variable	800–531–6390	$1,000
Vanguard Variable	800–523–9954	$5,000

💣 *CAUTION: If you withdraw money before age 59½, there is a 10% IRS tax penalty.*

Here are the basic types of payouts:

- *Lump sum.* Withdrawal of all the annuity's assets upon retirement. You'll have to pay taxes and reinvest your money somewhere else. And you're tossing aside one of the major advantages of an annuity—a guarantee of lifetime income.
- *Systematic withdrawal.* This keeps most of your money invested; you take a fixed amount at regular intervals—let's say $300 a month—until all assets have been withdrawn. How long this takes depends upon how well your investments performed. This method spreads out your tax payments.
- *Annuitization.* With this option you get payments for life, either fixed or variable amounts, depending upon your annuity. Even if your investments perform poorly, insurance companies generally guarantee to pay you at least 3% to 5% annually.
- *Lifetime income, life income, or life only.* You receive payments for life, but payments end when you die.
- *Life with period certain.* If you die before the preset period of payments has ended, the remaining payments continue on to your named beneficiary.
- *Joint and survivor or lifetime income for two.* Designed primarily for married couples, upon death of either, payments continue to the survivor. Payments to the survivor can remain the same, or be greater while both of you are alive.

Cashing in Early

Cashing in your annuity early is expensive. As mentioned above, there's a 10% IRS penalty for money taken out before you reach 59½. In addition, most insurance companies let you take out only up to 10% of your assets before they impose a surrender charge. Go beyond that 10% and you'll be slapped with a fee, typically 6% of the withdrawal during the first year, going down to 0% by the seventh year.

✅ *HINT: One plan, The Golden Select DVA Plus from Golden America in Wilmington, Delaware, lets you cash out up to 15% with no fee. Call 800–243–3706.*

The combination of surrender charges and a 10% penalty means an annuity must be viewed as a long-term investment.

💣 *CAUTION: Look for a plan that has a "bailout" clause, so you can cash out with no surrender charge if the insurer lowers the renewal rate by more than 1% below the initial rate.*

Picking Out the Best Annuity

Annuities are not federally protected or guaranteed. If you need that type of security, you should purchase a bank CD, which is covered by FDIC insurance, or Treasury securities, which are backed by the full faith and credit of the U.S. government. With an annuity, you must depend on the financial strength of the insurance company. It should have an A or A+ A. M. Best rating. (Most large libraries carry this rating book, or you can ask the insurance company what its rating is.)

It's a good idea to check the ratings periodically, because insurance companies can be downgraded. Remember, Baldwin United, which filed for bankruptcy several years ago, once had an A+ rating! (The company had approximately $3.4 billion in annuities. The investors did not lose their principal, but a great many did not have access to it for several years.)

✅ *HINT: If your company's rating drops, you can make a tax-free exchange into another annuity. Called a 1035 exchange, it is similar to a tax-free IRA rollover.*

Additional protection is provided in all 50 states—but not in Washington, D.C. If one insurer goes bankrupt, the state fund assesses charges against other insurance companies in the state to cover investor losses. Call your state insurance commission to determine whether you live in one of these states. Coverage is generally limited to $300,000 per life insurance policy or $100,000 per annuity—find out!

Checking Up on an Annuity's Performance

Before selecting an annuity, gather information on the parent insurance company, consulting one of the sources listed below in For Further Information at the end of this chapter.

After selecting an A-rated company, you should then get its performance figures, using one or more of these services:

- Each month, *Comparative Annuity Reports* monitors 400+ single- and flexible-premium deferred annuities (accumulation phase) and single-premium immediate annuity (payout and income phase) programs. For a special introductory newsletter covering the top 100 programs and detailed reports on others, send $10 to: *Comparative Annuity Reports,* Box 1268, Fair Oaks, CA 95628.
- Returns on variable annuities are tracked by Lipper Analytical Services (New York; 212–393–1300) and then reported weekly in *Barron's.*
- *Morningstar's Variable Annuity/Life Performance Report,* available at libraries; for subscription information, call 800–735–0700.

ⓞ *CAUTION: The tax-deferred advantages of an annuity do not come cheap. Sales charges, surrender fees, management costs, and other expenses can eat away at your return. You can reduce some of these costs by purchasing a no- or low-load annuity.*

FOR FURTHER INFORMATION

Life Insurance

Glenn Daily, *The Individual Investor's Guide to Low-Load Insurance Products* (New York: International Publishing Corp., 1996), $22.95.

What You Should Know About Buying Life Insurance
888–8–PUEBLO
website: www.pueblo.gsa.gov
Free

Term Life Insurance—The Simplified Buyers Guide
Choice Quote
800–778–2001

For a list of publications, as well as "Rate of Return" data, contact:
Consumer Federation of America's Insurance Group
1424 16th Street NW
Washington, DC 20036
202–387–6121

Medicare

A Medicare, Medigap & Managed Care: Consumer Update
United Seniors Health Cooperative
409 Third Avenue
Washington, DC 20024
Or using a Visa or MasterCard: 202–479–6615
$3.50

Insurance Counseling & Assistance Program
Provides free health-care counseling in all states. For the nearest program in your area, call: 800–638–6833 or 800–677–1116.

Long-Term Health Care Insurance

Long Term Care: A Dollar and Sense Guide
United Seniors Health Cooperative
409 Third Avenue
Washington, DC 20024
202–479–6615
$18.00

A Consumer's Guide to Long Term Care Insurance
Health Insurance Association of America
555 13th Street NW
Washington, DC 20004
202–824–1600
website: www.hiaa.org
The Association will also send you a list of private insurers offering long-term health care policies in your state.

Medigap Insurance

Medicare Basics: Selecting Medicare Supplement Insurance
AARP Fulfillment
601 E Street NW
Washington, DC 20049

Guide to Health Insurance for People with Medicare
Guide to Choosing a Nursing Home
Healthcare Financing Administration
800–MEDICARE
website: www.medicare/gov/publications

Insurance Company Ratings

The insolvencies of several companies have highlighted the importance of dealing with an A-rated company. To determine a company's financial soundness you can get reports, for a fee, from:

Best's Insurance Reports
website: www.ambest.com
$4.95 per rating

Standard & Poor's Insurance Rating Service
25 Broadway
New York, NY 10004
212–208–1527

Weiss Research, Inc.
4176 Burns Road
Palm Beach Garden, FL 33410
800–289–9222

Term Insurance

QuickQuote has a term life estimator: you type in your age, income, living expenses and find out how much coverage you need. Helps locate the right policy.

800–867–2404
website: www.quickquote.com

Similar help is available from:
www.instantquote.com
www.quotesmith.com

Annuities

A Consumer's Guide to Annuities
888–8–PUEBLO
website: www. pueblo.gsa.gov
Free

About Annuities
MetLife
800–METLIFE
website: www. metlife.com
Free

PART SEVEN

Taxes and Your Investments

"The income tax has made more liars out of the American people than golf has."

Will Rogers

I'm not recommending that you lie on your tax return, but I definitely want you to give the Internal Revenue Service as little as legitimately possible. There are two ways to do that—one is to have a nodding acquaintance with our tax laws and the second is to hire the right expert to help you out. The U.S. Congress is continually overhauling the tax code. Unless you know the basic current rulings, you could unwittingly lose hundreds of dollars to the IRS. It is particularly crucial that every financial decision you make be made only after reading the following two chapters and consulting with your tax adviser.

These chapters explain the pertinent parts of the law and how it relates to investments, and also show you how to take advantage of the current rules. Among the topics covered are:

- The tax rates
- Margin loans
- AMT
- Taxes on investments
- Ten sources of tax-free income
- Last-minute tax savers
- Shifting income to children
- Deductions for investors
- Choosing the right tax preparer
- The marriage penalty . . .

  and perhaps most importantly,

- Year-end tax moves for 2000

34

Beating the IRS: Deductions, End-of-the-Year Moves, and Other Breaks

*I*n this chapter we cover four aspects of taxes and investments:

- Key points in the tax act
- Smart end-of-the-year tax moves you can make for 2000
- Tax deductions available to investors
- Ten sound sources of tax-free income

KEY POINTS YOU SHOULD KNOW

Here are the points you need to know about the 1997 Tax Relief Act and how they relate to your investments and financial planning for 2000–2001. You will also want to read the sections of personal relevance in the next chapter.

Starting on page 355, you will find a discussion of end-of-the-year moves you can make to keep your taxes to a minimum.

INDIVIDUAL TAX RATES

There are five individual income-tax rates: 15%, 28%, 31%, 36%, and 39.6%. For 1999, the 36% rate applies to taxable income over:

- $158,550 for married couples filing jointly
- $130,250 for single taxpayers
- $144,400 for heads of household
- $79,275 for married individuals filing separate returns

The 39.6% rate results from a 10% surtax imposed on taxable income over $278,450 ($139,225 for married persons filing separate returns). This surtax effectively raises the top individual tax rate to 39.6%.

THE ALTERNATIVE MINIMUM TAX

This tax was designed to make certain that Americans with high incomes and high deductions would still have to pay an appropriate amount of income tax. That means, no matter how rich you are, no matter how many loopholes or tax shelters you participate in, if you have sufficiently high income, you still must pay a minimum amount of federal income tax.

The AMT is actually a separate, parallel tax system under which many of the deductions and credits allowed under the regular tax are modified or eliminated.

The AMT calculation begins with your regular taxable income as reported on Form 1040, to which certain AMT "adjustments" and "tax preference items" are added. You must pay the AMT only if it exceeds your regular income tax.

A two-tier structure exists: A 26% rate applies to the first $175,000 of AMT income above an exemption amount; and on amounts above $175,000 ($87,500 married filing single), the rate is 28%. The level of income exempt from AMT is:

- $45,000 for married filing a joint return
- $33,750 for unmarried individuals

- $22,500 for married individuals filing separate returns

How do you know whether you're subject to AMT? The most common way to incur the AMT is to make investments that take advantage of (or even exploit) tax shelter provisions of the tax code, such as accelerated depreciation methods for real estate or passive losses from passive activities. Other more common situations may make you subject, however. For instance, if you:

- Own private activity municipal bonds (direct ownership or in a mutual fund)
- Exercise incentive stock options granted by your employer
- Own real estate investment trusts (REITs) that use accelerated depreciation on their holdings
- Report substantial itemized deductions for state and local income and property taxes paid or miscellaneous deductions

ALL ABOUT CAPITAL GAINS TAXES

It's a given—you have to pay tax when you make money. But there's good news on this front. The 1997 Tax Relief Act reduced capital gains, basically from 28% to 20%. But the IRS never makes anything quite that simple . . . there are lots of variations on the new 20% rate.

Here's the skinny:

- Treatment of short-term capital gains remains the same. In other words, profits on assets held for 12 months or less are taxed at ordinary income rates, which range from 15% to 39.6%.
- The maximum capital gains tax on profits from the sale of stocks, bonds, or mutual funds held long-term has been dropped, from 28% to 20%. Long-term is still defined as 12 months.

There's really good news for those of you in the 15% tax bracket . . .

- Starting with sales of investments made after May 6, 1997, the capital gains rate is just 10%. The 15% tax bracket encompasses those joint filers with taxable income of $41,200 or less and for singles, about $24,650 or less.

☑ *TIP: Don't forget to include your gross capital gain income in determining your tax bracket . . . it could push you up and into a new bracket.*

- Starting after December 31, 2000, the capital gains tax on stocks held for more than five years will be even lower—taxed at a top rate of 18%. And if you're in the lowest tax bracket of 15%, that rate drops to 8%.

TAXATION OF SOCIAL SECURITY BENEFITS

As dreadful as it may seem, very often Social Security recipients must pay income tax. The maximum percentage of Social Security benefits subject to tax is 85% for "provisional income" in excess of:

- $34,000 for unmarried persons
- $44,000 for married persons filing jointly
- $0 for married persons filing separately

A 50% exclusion rule applies when their income is between:

- $25,000 and $34,000 for singles
- $32,000 and $44,000 for married couples filing jointly

"Provisional income" is essentially adjusted gross income plus all tax-exempt interest income and one-half of Social Security or Railroad Retirement Tier 1 benefits.

- *Salary deferral.* Up to $10,500 can be contributed on a pretax basis to 401(k) plans and SEPs that offer a salary-deferral feature.
- *Retirement limits.* The maximum compensation level to be considered in making qualified retirement plan contributions is $160,000.

- *Estimated taxes.* These rules have been somewhat simplified. You can avoid penalties by basing your estimated tax payments on:

1. 90% of the current year's tax
2. 100% of the prior year's tax if adjusted gross income is $150,000 or less ($75,000 for married filing separately)
3. 106% of the prior year's tax if adjusted gross income is over $150,000 ($75,000 for married filing separately)

YEAR-END TAX MOVES TO MAKE FOR 2000

Despite New Year's resolutions and other good intentions, most of us still wind up putting off organizing our tax return materials until the first week in April. But if you're really serious about reducing your tax bite, you should start at the end of the year. In fact, there are a number of fairly easy steps you can take to improve your tax picture. So, come November and December, review this list carefully and also check the clip-and-save calendar pages at the end of this book for other tax savings ideas.

Use Bond Swaps

Another year-end strategy that can help save on taxes is a bond swap. Under certain circumstances it pays to sell a bond worth less than its initial cost in order to set up a tax loss, and then reinvest that same money in a similar bond. By converting a paper loss into an actual loss, you can offset any taxable gains you earn in other, more profitable investments. In the process of swapping, you may also be able to boost your bond yield.

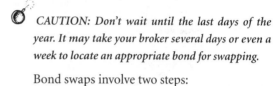 CAUTION: *Don't wait until the last days of the year. It may take your broker several days or even a week to locate an appropriate bond for swapping.*

Bond swaps involve two steps:

1. Selling bonds that have declined in price
2. Replacing these bonds with similar (but not substantially identical) bonds

By immediately purchasing similar bonds for approximately the same price as the ones you sold, you restore your market position and your income.

A bond swap is also useful if you move from a state with no income tax to one that has an income

1999 Tax Rates and Brackets

	SINGLE TAXPAYERS	MARRIED TAXPAYERS FILING JOINTLY
15%	$0–25,750	$0–43,050
28%	$25,751–62,450	$43,051–104,050
31%	$62,451–130,250	$104,051–158,550
36%	$130,251–283,150	$158,551–283,150
39.6%	over $283,150	over $283,150

	HEADS OF HOUSEHOLD	MARRIED FILING SEPARATELY
15%	$0–34,550	$0–21,525
28%	$34,551–89,150	$21,526–52,025
31%	$89,151–144,400	$52,026–79,275
36%	$144,401–283,150	$79,276–141,575
39.6%	over $283,150	over $141,575

tax. Buy municipal bonds issued by the new state that are not subject to state taxes.

Swapping Costs

Unlike stocks and most other securities, where commissions are noted separately from the purchase or sale price, municipal bonds have their commission included in the price of the bond. Commissions range from $5 to $20 per $1,000-face-value bond, which means that a swap involving $50,000 worth of bonds could entail a commission somewhere between $500 and $2,000.

Shift Income to Children

Any unearned (or investment) income of a child aged 14 or less is taxed to the child, but at the parent's rate when this income exceeds $1,400 per year. The first $700, however, is not taxed at all, and the next $700 is taxed at the child's rate. Then when the child is over 14, all income is taxed at his or her rate, which is presumably a lower rate than the parent's.

If you wish to give money to a child under 14 but you don't want it to be taxed at your rate, you are limited to a handful of choices:

1. Tax-free municipal bonds and bond funds
2. Low-dividend-paying stocks
3. EE Savings Bonds.

In the latter case, interest is not taxed until the bonds mature or are cashed in.

When your child turns 14, you can change the portfolio mix to higher-yielding taxable investments and periodically cash in the bonds, because the income will be taxed at the child's rate.

If you are involved in income shifting, keep careful records indicating that you have separate accounts for your children.

Shift Other Income

You have until December 31 to shift money to re-

duce your taxable income for the following year and, at the same time, avoid the gift tax. The law allows you to give anyone up to $10,000 a year ($20,000 for a married couple) tax free. Although there is no gift tax on the transfer, there will be income tax on any earnings the gift generates. (Gifts are not a deduction from income.)

NOTE: The recipient of the gift must have immediate access to the funds transferred. Check with your accountant for exceptions.

It may be advantageous for you, if you are in a high tax bracket, to transfer appreciated property or income-producing property to your children ages 14 and older to take advantage of their lower tax bracket. A child claimed as a dependent can earn up to $700 of investment income without incurring a tax liability.

Set Up a Keogh Plan

If you have income from your business or freelance work, set up a Keogh retirement account at a bank, brokerage firm, or mutual fund. The dollar amount you contribute is tax deductible directly from your taxable income, and the principal grows on a tax-deferred basis. Unlike an IRA, which can be established up until April 15th, a Keogh must be opened before the end of the year to qualify for a tax deduction. You do not need to make a dollar contribution, however, until you actually file your tax return—on April 15 or extension dates.

NOTE: You can have a Keogh even if you have a 401(k) or other retirement plan, if you have self-employment income.

Contribute Early to Your IRA

Fund your IRA, SEP, or Keogh plan as soon as possible. Tax is deferred on the income earned from the day you contribute it up until you withdraw it. If you delay making your contribution until the last minute, you are giving up months of compounded tax-deferred income.

Fund Your 401(k) Plan to the Max

The contribution is not counted in your income.

Add Up Your Deductions

Take time to determine whether you have spent enough on tax-deductible items to qualify for write-offs: (1) Miscellaneous deductible expenses must be greater than 2% of your adjusted gross income in order to be itemized. (2) Unreimbursed medical expenses must add up to more than 7.5% of your AGI to be deductible. If you are still far away from these minimums (known as "floors"), try to postpone these expenses until next year when you may have enough to deduct them. On the other hand, if you are near these thresholds, consider making additional expenditures that will lift you above the floor.

Establish a Charitable Remainder Trust

Feeling philanthropic? Consider a remainder trust in which you give appreciated securities, such as stocks, bonds, or property, to a charity in exchange for a qualified annuity. You can retain the income from the property for life or for a set number of years as well as get a tax deduction. The deduction amount is determined by IRS tables. Another advantage: This type of annuity is not subject to premature withdrawal penalties or to the new pension excise tax. Because rulings are complex, work out this particular tax move with a knowledgeable accountant.

Charitable Donor-Advised Fund

For many years, community foundations have offered donor-advised funds—in Boston, Cleveland, Philadelphia, and San Francisco, for example.

More recently, public charities have been established to offer such funds, one of the best known being the Fidelity Investments Charitable Gift Fund (800–682–4438). This type of fund does not limit the donors' contributions to charities in a specific geographical location.

Here's how it works: You invest in a stable of stock and/or bond funds for growth. Later on, you can direct the Gift Fund to pay out proceeds to your favorite charity.

 CAUTION: Your donations are irrevocable. And you don't receive income from the gift fund.

Since the IRS has approved the fund as a tax-exempt public charity, you can claim a tax deduction for the contribution, based on the fair market value at the time of the donation.

If you're in the 39.6% federal tax bracket, a $10,000 donation could save nearly $4,000 in taxes; in the 31% bracket, you'd save $3,100 in taxes.

The assets grow tax free until you decide to distribute them. The minimum initial and subsequent investments are $10,000 and $1,000 respectively.

There are no sales loads for the Gift Fund but there is a 1% annual administrative charge.

Vanguard Group of Funds in Valley Forge, Pennsylvania, has a similar program with a minimum investment of $25,000 and subsequent investments of at least $5,000. There are no sales charges and the annual administrative fee is just 0.45%.

File Correct Estimates

Figure out whether you withheld enough during 1999, because if you underestimated you will be subject to hefty penalties. Or if you overestimate, you then lose the earning power of that money. So to be safe, estimate 100% or 106% of last year's tax liability, or 90% of what you owe this year. Check with your accountant. It's not too late to get your employer to withhold more.

Deductible Items—23 of Them

If you itemize, check with your accountant to see if you can take these deductions:

- Long distance calls to an out-of-town doctor or hospital
- Lamaze classes for pregnant moms
- Birth control pills
- Mileage to/from a doctor's office
- Alcoholism treatment
- Lead paint removal
- Contact lens insurance
- Home improvement, if required, such as handrails, an elevator if you can't climb stairs, ramps, widened doorways
- Medically prescribed diet—salt-free, fat-free diet
- Cost of cellular phone for someone with a serious situation who needs to reach his/her doctor in an emergency
- Air conditioner, heater, humidifier—if your doctor prescribes them to treat a serious condition
- Hearing aids
- Dentures
- Eyeglasses
- Prescription drugs and insulin
- Cosmetic surgery to correct a deformity or personal injury
- Cost of education to improve your skills in your present occupation or to keep your job
- Alimony—if you're the one doing the paying
- Appraisal fees to determine the value of property donated to a charity
- Job-hunting expenses if you're looking for work in the same field in which you're currently employed. (Take the deduction even if you didn't land the job.) Expenses include: cost of preparing and mailing resumes and travel expenses away from home.
- Penalties. If you withdrew money from a time deposit, such as a CD, before it matured, any penalty you pay is deductible as an adjustment to income.
- Cost of gas, oil, parking, and tolls to drive to your volunteer work. Or bus, subway, or taxi fares.
- Cost and upkeep of uniforms worn doing charitable work, such as a Red Cross or volunteer fire department uniform.

Prepay Property and State and Local Income Taxes by December 31

If you pay 100% of your state tax liability by December 31, you can deduct it on this year's federal income tax return.

Make Charitable Contributions with Appreciated Investments

If you are thinking about making a charitable contribution, do so by December 31 and use appreciated investments, such as stocks, bonds, antiques, paintings, etc., that you've held at least one year. The advantage of doing so: You can deduct the full market value of the gift and your capital gains tax will be forgiven.

☑   *$TIP: To qualify as a deduction, your contribution must be to a tax-exempt organization recognized by the IRS. These organizations are listed in IRS publication 78, "Charitable Contributions: A Cumula-*

tive List of Organizations," which is free by calling 800–829–3676 or click on: www.irs.ustreas.gov/prod/ search/eosearch.htm. You can search by the name of the organization or by city and state. For a contribution under $250, a canceled check is sufficient documentation; over $250, you need a written receipt from the organization.

Defer Income

If it is to your advantage to reduce this year's income; delay receipt of self-employment income or year-end bonuses, or delay billing customers, so payments are made to you after December 31. This is a smart move if you expect to be in the same tax bracket from one year to the next, because you'll have use of money you otherwise would have paid in taxes. And if you drop to a lower bracket in 2001, you'll actually reduce the amount you must pay in taxes.

This move may also keep you from inching up into a higher bracket, something to be avoided at all costs. You can also defer income by transferring money out of investments paying current interest—money market funds, savings accounts, etc.—into Treasury bills or bank CDs that mature within a year or less and that won't pay interest until 2001.

Pay Your Taxes Early

Pay your fourth-quarter estimated state and local taxes by December 31. They are deductible on your next federal income tax return.

Prepay Your Mortgage

Make the January mortgage payment in December. The interest portion is tax deductible. (Although you can't prepay the interest, the January installment actually includes interest for December.)

Tax Deductions for Investors

You can deduct the amount over 2% of adjusted gross income for certain expenses incurred to produce and collect income and to manage or maintain property held to make income. Among these deductible-as-itemized deductions are:

- Subscriptions to investment publications
- Cost of books on investing and taxes
- Clerical expenses
- Insurance on investment property
- Safe-deposit box rent or home safe, if used to hold securities
- Fees for accounting or investment advice and for legal advice if related to tax or investment matters; includes cost of tax preparation, cost of tax preparation software, and fees paid to file electronically
- Expenses directly related to tax (but not investment) seminars, including transportation
- Travel expenses to visit your broker, your safe-deposit box, and your tax accountant or lawyer for investment or income-tax purposes
- The cost of a computer used in managing your investments is sometimes deductible. (If you use your computer for business over 50% of the time, you can depreciate it over five years.)
- IRA, SEP, or Keogh account custodial fees if paid by a separate check
- Appraisal fees for charitable deductions

Clean Out Your Closets

Take all the stuff you'll never use or wear again to a thrift shop run by a charitable organization. Get a written receipt acknowledging your donation and its fair market value.

Hire Your Kids

If you're self-employed, hire your children during the holiday season (or any time) and you can deduct their salaries as a business expense.

Give a Holiday Party

If you're a business owner, you can generally deduct the cost of a party given for your employees as well as up to 50% of the amount you spend on holiday entertainment and business parties for customers and clients. This includes food, beverages, tips, and taxes.

Spend Money

If you own a business or are self-employed and if you need office equipment you can get a deduction for a desk, computer, fax machine, copier, etc. Section 179 of the Tax Code lets you sidestep complicated depreciation rules and immediately deduct up to $20,000 worth of equipment put into use in 2000.

FOUR TAX DEDUCTIONS YOU DON'T WANT TO MISS . . .

1. *State and local taxes.* Except for sales tax, these taxes continue to be fully deductible.
2. *Investment expenses.* These expenses, including tax planning, the cost of this book, tax-return preparation, investment publications, and other miscellaneous items are deductible, but only for amounts in excess of 2% of your adjusted gross income.
3. *Charitable deductions.* Get a receipt, and remember, you must itemize on your tax return in order to deduct your charitable contributions.
4. *Medical expenses.* You can deduct unreimbursed medical expenses, but only if they exceed 7.5% of your adjusted gross income.

TEN SOURCES OF TAX-FREE INCOME

By carefully planning your investment strategies, you can easily increase the amount of tax-free or tax-deferred money you receive every year. Here are ten surefire ways to do just that:

1. *IRAs.* You don't pay any tax on the earnings inside an individual retirement account until you withdraw the money. Interest earned is reinvested and thus continues to compound on a tax-deferred basis.
2. *Life insurance.* As with an IRA, the interest income earned inside a life insurance investment is tax deferred until you cash in the policy. Proceeds paid to your beneficiary upon your death are free of income taxes.
3. *Disability insurance.* If you paid your own disability insurance premium, the benefits from accident or health insurance policies are tax free. (If your employer paid the premiums, however, any income you receive from the policy is taxable.)
4. *Municipal bonds.* Interest earned on muni bonds is free from federal income tax. You may have to pay a state income tax if you purchased bonds issued by a state other than your state of residence—for example, if you live in Minnesota and purchase a bond for New York State, you may have to pay Minnesota tax on the income.

   CAUTION: Some municipal bonds are subject to the AMT; check with your accountant.

5. *Real estate.* Some rental and business real estate investments yield depreciation deductions over the life of the property.
6. *Savings plans, annuities, and pension plans.* Any investment made with after-tax income is tax free when you withdraw it or when you receive a payment that represents the return of your investment. Or to state it another way, the principal is tax free, although the income earned on the principal is generally taxed.
7. *Social Security.* Disability, retirement, or surviving spouse income may be tax free, depending on your other income. Taxpayers with income greater than $32,000 ($25,000 for

singles) have to pay tax on up to half of their Social Security income.

A maximum of half of this income is tax free.

NOTE: Under the 1993 law, up to 85% is taxable if couples have income over $44,000, and for individuals, over $34,000.

8. *Tax-deferred annuities.* (Sometimes called single-premium deferred annuities.) The money invested with an insurance company in this type of annuity and the interest earned is deferred until you cash in and receive that income.

9. *Tax-free money market funds.* Mutual funds whose portfolios consist of municipal notes offer tax-free income.

10. *U.S. Treasury issues.* Treasury bonds, notes, and bills, and savings bonds are exempt from tax at the state and local levels no matter what state you live in. You must, however, pay federal income tax on these investments.

LONG-TERM CARE INSURANCE

Long-term care insurance policies that meet certain provisions qualify as a deductible medical expense. In fact, if your policy meets the requirements promulgated by the National Association of Insurance Commissioners relating to renewal, noncancellability, preexisting conditions, etc., here's what is deductible, depending upon your age:

Age	Deductible
40 or younger	Up to $210
Over 40 to 50	Up to $380
Over 50 to 60	Up to $770
Over 60 to 70	Up to $2,050
Over 70	Up to $2,570

THE MEDICAL SAVINGS ACCOUNT

If you're self-employed or work for a small business with 50 or fewer employees, you should look into opening a Medical Savings Account (MSA) in order to pay health care expenses. They are designed to replace the traditional health plan with its small deductible and copayment arrangement.

This pilot program is available only to the first 750,000 participants who apply each year, through the year 2000.

MSA plans must have high annual deductibles: a minimum deductible of $1,500 and a maximum deductible of $2,250 for individuals; for families: $3,000 minimum deductible and $4,500 maximum. The maximum out-of-pocket limitation is $3,000 for individuals and $5,500 for families.

Employees must pay all expenses up to the deductible amount.

Contributions, which are deductible from your adjusted gross income, may be made up to the due date of your tax return (but not including extensions). The top tax deduction is limited to 65% of up to $2,250 for singles and 75% of up to $4,500 for families. (This refers to the specified percentage of the policy that's deductible.)

Employees are taxed on any additional amount they put into the MSA, but payments to MSAs by an employer are fully deductible for employees who only have MSAs.

Withdrawals to pay for qualified medical expenses are not taxed, but distributions for other purposes, including to pay for medical insurance, are taxed. Withdrawals for nonmedical purposes are taxed at ordinary rates and also subject to a 15% tax penalty unless the distribution is made after age 65 or upon death or disability.

Income in an MSA is not taxable unless taken out for nonmedical purposes.

 CAUTION: Medical expenses paid from the distributions cannot be claimed as an itemized deduction.

MARRIAGE PENALTY

According to *Bride's Magazine*, the average couple spends $19,000 on their wedding. But long after you've paid the photographer and musicians, you'll face another whopper: the marriage penalty. It's particularly rough on working couples who make approximately the same amount.

The penalty kicks in when the two incomes together push a couple into a higher tax bracket, forcing them to pay more in taxes than if they hadn't tied the knot and had filed as singles.

However, if one spouse makes a great deal more than the other, you may not be in trouble. If there's less than a 15% difference in your salaries, you face higher taxes.

Other Marriage Woes

■ *Investment losses.* If you lost money in the stock market, you can deduct up to $3,000 on your return. If you and the person you live with both lose in the market and file separately, you can each deduct $3,000. But if you're married and filing jointly, you are limited to a total of $3,000 per couple, no matter how much you lose.

If you're married and file jointly, each of you can deduct $1,500 and then only for each one's individual losses. So, if one spouse lost $2,000 and the other lost $1,000, filing separately would only allow $1,500 to the first spouse and $1,000 to the second one.

However, there is one plus: if you earn, let's say, $5,000 in capital gains and your spouse loses $5,000, you can offset your gains with your spouse's losses, provided you file jointly.

■ *Roth conversions.* If you're single, you can convert a traditional IRA to a Roth if your adjusted gross income is less than $100,000. But if you're married and your combined adjusted gross income is over $100,000, you cannot convert.

FOR FURTHER INFORMATION

These publications are available free of charge at your local IRS office or by calling 800–TAX–FORM (829–3676). Or, if you're on the Internet, go to www.irs.gov and under "Browse" you'll find links to all IRS material.

78, *Charitable Contributions*
523, *Selling Your Home*
527, *Residential Rental Property*
530, *Tax Information for First-Time Homeowners*
550, *Investment Income and Expenses*
554, *Older Americans' Tax Guide*
560, *Retirement Plans for Small Businesses*
564, *Mutual Fund Distributions*
575, *Pension and Annuity Income*
590, *Individual Retirement Arrangements (IRAs)*
915, *Social Security Benefits*

For a complete list of all IRS brochures, ask for Publication 910, *Guide to Free Tax Services*.

35

An Alphabetical Directory of Your Investments and Their Tax Status

The information that follows is general in scope and intended as an introductory explanation of how taxes affect your investments. To begin with, keep in mind that the IRS recognizes three types of income:

- *Portfolio or investment income:* dividends and interest
- *Active income:* salaries, wages, fees, commissions, and personal services
- *Passive income:* from businesses you don't actively manage and from rental property.

NOTE: Passive losses cannot offset active or portfolio income; they can only offset passive income.

ANNUITIES

- Interest earned can accumulate tax free until withdrawn. When it is withdrawn, only the interest earned is taxed, not your initial investment.
- If you withdraw money prior to age 59½, there is a 10% tax penalty. With qualified employer-sponsored annuities, there is no 10% penalty if you immediately transfer the money to a qualified annuity with another company.
- For other rulings, check your policy.

ANTIQUES, ART, COINS, GEMS, STAMPS, AND OTHER COLLECTIBLES

Profits made upon sale are subject to federal income tax at the regular rate of 15%, 28%, 31%, 36%, or 39.6%. If the asset is held long-term, the maximum capital gains tax is 28%. The purchase price, of course, is subject to state and local sales tax.

BONDS (AGENCY ISSUES)

- Interest income is subject to federal tax.
- Interest income on some agency issues is exempt from state and local taxes. Ask your broker or accountant.

BONDS (CORPORATE)

- Interest income is subject to federal, state, and local taxes.
- Gains made when bonds are sold are taxed at capital gains rate—20%—if held long term, 12 months and a day; 10% if you're in the 15% tax bracket.
- Losses can be used to offset other net gains you may have, plus up to $3,000 of wages, salary, and other "ordinary" income.

BONDS (DISCOUNT)

Gains on disposition of bonds purchased at a discount from face value (also called "market discount") is ordinary interest income to the extent of accrued market discount. You can elect to include market discount in your gross income for years to which it is attributable. This included discount is then added to the original cost.

BONDS (MUNICIPAL)

- Interest earned on most munis is exempt from federal income tax and from state and local taxes for residents of the state where the bonds are issued.
- Most states tax out-of-state bonds.
- Bonds issued by the Commonwealth of Puerto Rico and the District of Columbia are exempt from taxes in all states.
- Interest earned on certain "private activity" bonds that were issued after August 7, 1986, is regarded as a tax preference item and is included in the calculation of the alternative minimum tax. If you are not subject to the AMT, you will not pay taxes on these particular bonds.
- Some municipal bonds are subject to federal tax but remain exempt at the state and local levels. These include bonds to help finance convention centers.
- Illinois, Iowa, Kansas, Oklahoma, and Wisconsin tax any municipal bonds issued in their state.
- Interest earned on fully tax-exempt bonds can be taxed when held by a retiree receiving Social Security. If you are retired and if your adjusted gross income plus half your Social Security plus all your tax-exempt interest income is over $25,000 for a single return or $32,000 for a joint return, interest earned on the tax-exempt bond is effectively taxable.

BONDS (PREMIUM)

If you purchase a bond at a premium, you can only use any amortizable premium to offset your investment income. In other words, you cannot use the premium as a deduction against other types of income. The amortized premium is subtracted directly from the interest you earn on the bond, rather than deducted as a separate expense subject to the investment interest expense limitations.

NOTE: Amortization of premium is not required for taxable bonds, but is required for tax-exempt bonds to prevent deduction of the premium as a loss upon sale or maturity.

BONDS (ZERO)

- Taxes must be paid on the so-called imputed interest that accrues annually, even though, of course, no interest is actually paid to the bondholder.
- Because you must pay tax as though you had received interest, zeros are well suited for IRAs, SEPs, and Keoghs where interest income is deferred from taxes until withdrawn, and for children over age 14 who are no longer subject to the kiddie tax.
- Zero coupon municipals are usually exempt from federal taxes and from state and local taxes when bonds are issued in the investor's state.
- Zero coupon Treasuries are exempt from state and local taxes.

CERTIFICATES OF DEPOSIT (CDs)

- Any interest earned is subject to federal, state, and local taxes. Interest is taxed at one's regular tax rate: 15%, 28%, 31%, 36%, or 39.6%.
- Interest is taxed in the year it is available for withdrawal without substantial penalty, whether or not you withdraw it.

NOTE: Interest can be deferred on a CD with a term of one year or less. For example, if you invest in a CD before July 1, the entire amount of interest is paid six months later and taxable in the year paid out. If you invest in a CD after June 30, however, only the interest actually paid out or made available for withdrawal without penalty is taxable in the year issued. The balance is taxable in the year of maturity—the next year. The interest, however, must specifically be deferred to the year of maturity by the terms of the CD.

CHILDREN'S INVESTMENT INCOME

Unearned income of children under the age of 14 is taxed at the marginal rate of their parents, as if the parents had received the income, rather than at the child's lower rate. This income falls under special rules: The child can use $700 of his/her standard deduction to offset unearned income. The next $700 of unearned income is taxed at the child's tax bracket. Unearned income over $1,400 is taxed as if it were included in the parent's return.

NOTE: Form 8615 is required for this purpose.

See: also Savings Bonds.

COMMERCIAL PAPER

- Any interest earned is subject to federal, state, and local taxes.
- *Exception:* Commercial paper issued by state and local governments is usually, but not always, exempt from federal as well as state and local taxes.

COMMODITIES AND FUTURES CONTRACTS

- Profits and losses are taxed at 60/40 rates, 60% long-term and 40% short-term, and reported at the end of the year. Losses may be carried back to the three prior years to offset any regu-

lated futures contract gains (but not other income) from those years.
- Profits become taxable at the end of the year, even if you have not closed out your position. The IRS, in effect, will tax you on your paper profits.
- In some cases, you can deduct paper losses, even of positions that are still open. These rules may apply to any contract subject to the mark-to-the-market rule. Check with your accountant.

CONVERTIBLE STOCKS AND BONDS

There is no gain or loss when you convert a bond into a stock or preferred stock into common stock of the same corporation, if the conversion privilege was granted by the bond or preferred stock certificate.

CREDIT UNION ACCOUNTS

Even though depositors are actually shareholders of the credit union and the money earned is known as a dividend, your earnings are regarded as interest and subject to federal, state, and local taxes.

DIVIDEND INCOME

Dividends and interest you receive are reported to the IRS by the company on various versions of Form 1099: dividends on Form 1099-DIV; investment interest on Form 1099-INT; and original issue discount on Form 1099-OID. You will receive copies from the company and must report the amounts shown on your tax return. The IRS will use its forms to check the income you report.

Dividend and interest income is taxed at your regular tax rate; it does not receive the more favorable long-term capital gains rate.

- *Cash dividends.* If you receive dividends from IBM, General Electric, or any other corporation, the amount is reported by the company directly to the IRS. You, in turn, receive Form 1099-DIV from each corporation stating precisely how much you received for the year.

- *Stock dividends.* If you own common stock in a company and receive additional shares as a dividend, it is usually not taxable. *Exceptions:* If you can take either stock or cash or if it is a taxable class of stock. The company will notify you if it is taxable.

- *Dividend reinvestment plans.* If you sign up to have your dividends automatically reinvested in the company's stock and if you pay fair market value for these shares, the full cash dividend is taxable. The IRS maintains that because you could have had cash but elected not to, you will be taxed the same year you receive the dividend.

- *Return of capital.* Corporations sometimes give a return of capital distribution. If this is the case, it will be so designated on your 1099 slip. Most return of capital is not taxed; however, your basis of stock must be reduced by whatever the amount is. If a return of capital exceeds basis, the excess is taxable and the basis is reduced to zero.

- *Insurance dividends.* Any dividends you receive on veterans' insurance are not taxed, and dividends received from regular life insurance are generally not taxed. If you are in doubt, check with your accountant or insurance company.

- *Other types of dividends.* Money market mutual funds pay what is called a dividend, and you should include it as such on your tax return.

EQUIPMENT LEASING PARTNERSHIPS

- Income is subject to federal, state, and local taxes.
- Because it is a partnership, items of income and deductions are passed through and are

thus subject to the at-risk rules. Interest expense may be used to the extent of interest, dividend, and other net investment income.

- Deductions generated by the partnership will help shelter some of the income derived from lease payments. The key deduction is depreciation for the cost of equipment. If the partnership borrows to pay for the equipment, interest may also be deductible.

- When deductions are greater than income, resulting losses cannot be used to shelter your salary, wages, interest, and dividend income or profits made in the stock market. The partnership losses can only be used to shelter income from other passive activities.

- If the partnership is publicly traded, income and loss require special treatment; check with your accountant.

FOREIGN INCOME

- If you have a foreign bank account or a foreign securities account, you must indicate this on Form TDF 90–22–1, if the value of the account at any time during the year was over $10,000.

- Foreign dividends may be subject to a withholding tax by the payer. You must also include the gross amount of the dividend on your U.S. income tax return, but you can deduct or receive a tax credit for the taxes paid to the foreign country.

GINNIE MAE, FREDDIE MAC, & FANNIE MAE CERTIFICATES

- The interest portion of the monthly payments you receive is subject to federal, state, and local taxes.
- Profits from the sale of any mortgage-backed security are taxed as well.

GOLD AND SILVER

- If you buy gold or silver coins or bullion, most states impose state and local sales tax. In many cases, you can sidestep this tax if you do not take delivery but leave the metal with the dealer and hold certificates instead.
- Profits from the sale of gold and silver are taxed at regular rates.
- Dividends from precious metals stocks and mutual funds are taxed at regular rates.
- Profits from futures and options: *See* Commodities and Futures Options.
- An exchange of gold for gold coins or silver for silver coins usually qualifies as a tax-free exchange of like-kind property, for example, if you exchange Mexican pesos for Austrian coronas. However, exchanging silver for gold is not tax-free, nor is exchanging collectible coins for bullion coins (*i.e.*, exchanging coins whose value is based on rarity for coins whose value is based on the weight of metal).

HISTORIC REHABILITATION OF PROPERTY

- The credit is 20% or 10% of qualified rehabilitation expenditures, depending on the building—10% for nonresidential buildings put into service prior to 1936 and 20% for all certified historic structures.
- This tax credit is not a deduction: It provides a dollar-for-dollar reduction in the actual amount of tax you owe.
- This tax credit is applicable only to depreciable buildings—those used in a trade or business or held for the production of income, such as a commercial or residential rental property. A nondepreciable building may qualify as a certified historic structure if it is the subject of charitable contributions for conservation purposes.

    NOTE: The amount of the credit reduces the cost basis of the building for depreciation, thus reducing the amount of the deduction for depreciation.

- A certified historic structure is any structure that is listed individually in the National Register of Historic Places, maintained by the Department of the Interior, or located in a registered historic district and certified by the Secretary of the Interior.

HOME-OFFICE DEDUCTIONS

- If you have a home-based business, whether it's your full-time job or a part-time activity, you may be able to deduct a portion of your home mortgage or rent, real estate taxes, insurance, utilities, and equipment costs. The home-office deduction is figured on Form 8829 and then entered on Line 30 of Schedule C.
- Your deduction cannot be more than the income generated from your home-office business. Any excess can be carried forward and used in a future year when there is enough income to offset it.

☑ *Read: Business Use of Your Home, IRS publication 573; free by calling: 800-TAX-FORM.*

INVESTMENT CLUBS

- If the club is considered a corporation, it reports and pays a tax on the club's earnings. As an individual member, you report dividend distributions made to you by the club.
- If the club is a partnership, the club files a partnership return that includes the tax consequences of its transactions and the shares of each member. The club does not pay a tax. You and the other members pay tax on your shares of dividends, interest, capital gains, and any other income earned by the club. You report your share as if you earned it personally.

    NOTE: You may deduct as itemized deductions your share of the club's investment expenses, subject, of course, to the 2% AGI floor.

IRAs, SEPs, and KEOGHs

See: Chapter 32.

LAND

- Any profits made when land is sold are taxable.
- Rental income is subject to regular tax, although it may be partially offset by deductible expenses, property costs, and mortgage interest payments.
- Land does not qualify for depreciation deductions.
- Check with your accountant regarding the status of income-producing land vis-à-vis the current passive loss rules, as these rules are complex.

LIFE INSURANCE

- When you purchase whole life insurance, part of your premium goes toward the purchase of insurance; the rest is an investment. The earned income on the investment portion builds up tax deferred until you cash in the policy. If you die before you cash in, and the benefits are paid to your children or spouse, this buildup becomes completely tax free, not just tax deferred.

CAUTION: Single-premium annuities or life insurance policies, where you pay only one premium, no longer qualify for this tax-deferred treatment.

- If you purchased a single-premium contract after June 30, 1988, and you borrow from the contract, the loan is treated as a distribution of income on which you must pay regular income tax, and in most cases, a 10% penalty on the taxable portion. (There's no 10% penalty

if distributions are made after you reach 59½, or if you are disabled, or if the distribution is part of a life annuity.)

- The same rules apply to a partial surrender of the contract, a cash withdrawal, or the distribution of dividends that are not retained by the insurance company as a premium if received on or after the annuity starting date. If received before the annuity starting date, special rules apply. Check with your accountant.
- These rules generally apply also to any life insurance plans ("modified endowment contract") that you fund with fewer than seven annual payments of equal size.
- You must also pay income tax on distributions from single-premium contracts purchased on or after June 21, 1988, to the extent that the distributions exceed your contract investment. Distributions of less than $25,000 made after your death to cover your burial are not taxed.

LOW-INCOME HOUSING

- Tax credits are available to those who buy, build, or rehabilitate low-income housing.
- The credits can offset regular income tax, subject to certain limits, but are phased out if your adjusted gross income is over $200,000. If your income exceeds $250,000, there are no credits. This income limitation does not apply to property placed in service after 1989.
- The annual credit is adjusted monthly for projects placed in service after 1987.

CAUTION: This can be a high-risk investment and should be examined by a professional. Avoid projects of inexperienced developers.

MARGIN LOANS

- Interest you pay on money borrowed from your broker for investment purposes is deductible only to the extent that it is offset by investment income (from dividends, interest income, and royalties). For example, if you want to deduct $1,500 worth of interest on your margin loan, you must report at least $1,500 of investment income to the IRS.

■ You must use the money borrowed to make an investment in order to deduct the interest. Keep careful records to document this fact.

CAUTION: If you borrow to buy municipal bonds or any other tax-exempt investment, interest (or margin) expense is not deductible.

MONEY MARKET DEPOSIT ACCOUNTS

Interest earned is subject to federal, state, and local income taxes, and at your regular tax rate.

MONEY MARKET MUTUAL FUNDS

■ Interest is subject to federal, state, and local income taxes.

■ With tax-exempt money market funds, interest is exempt from federal tax and possibly from state and local tax if the fund buys tax-exempt securities in the investor's state.

MUTUAL FUNDS

■ Dividend income and capital gains distributions are usually taxed at federal, state, and local levels, except for tax-free or municipal bond funds.

■ Income from municipal bond funds is exempt from federal tax and is also exempt from state and local taxes if the securities in the portfolio are issued in the taxpayer's state.

■ Mutual fund companies must send investors a year-end statement documenting all distributions and their tax states: Form 1099-DIV and/or Form 1099-B.

■ A dividend declared in December by a mutual fund is taxable in the year declared (*i.e.*, that year) if it is paid before February 1 of the following year.

■ All capital gains distributions are considered long-term.

■ When you sell your fund shares at a profit, the gain is taxed at your rate: 15%, 28%, 31%, 36%, or 39.6%, with the maximum rate of 20% for shares held long term.

■ Losses can be used to offset gains and up to $3,000 in salary, wages, and ordinary income.

■ Most funds make their largest distribution at the end of the year; call the toll-free number to verify. Avoid buying fund shares just before major distributions. The fund's NAV or share price immediately drops by the amount of the distribution. By waiting for a fund to go ex-dividend, you can buy in at a lower price and avoid paying some taxes.

☑ *HINT: Consult IRS Publication 564,* Mutual Fund Distributions.

OPTIONS

Rulings are extremely complicated. Consult your accountant.

POINTS

See: Real Estate.

PUBLIC LIMITED PARTNERSHIPS

■ If a limited partnership trades publicly, income earned is not passive but is considered portfolio income, and current losses cannot be used to offset income from other public partnerships.

■ Because a partnership is a pass-through entity, reportable income may be greater than actual cash distributions.

REAL ESTATE

A home can be a house, condo, co-op, mobile

home, even a boat if it provides basic living acco-modations, which the IRS defines as sleeping space, cooking facilities, and a toilet.

■ *Acquisition debt.* This is money used to pur-chase or substantially improve a residence. You may deduct all mortgage interest costs on up to a total of $1 million in acquisition debt for primary and secondary residences pur-chased or refinanced after October 13, 1987.

■ *Home-equity debt.* This is money you borrow using your home as collateral. You may deduct interest on home-equity loans up to $100,000. The proceeds of this loan can be used for any purpose.

■ *Points.* Lenders charge "points" above the regu-lar interest rate to increase their fees and get around state limits. The rules on points seem to be continually changing; check with your accountant and/or lender, and in all cases, al-ways pay points with a separate check. Cur-rently, you may deduct points if the payment is solely for your use of the money and not for services performed by the lender, which are separately charged. Points paid to refinance a loan are deductible in the year paid, but only if you used the money to improve your home. If you used the money for something else—to re-duce the interest on your mortgage or change from an adjustable rate to a fixed rate mort-gage—then you must deduct the points in equal amounts over the term of the mortgage.

■ *Selling.* When you sell your house, you can ex-clude from capital gains taxes up to $250,000 for single taxpayers and up to $500,000 for couples filing jointly. You do not need to be a particular age nor buy a replacement resi-dence to qualify. You can take this exclusion every two years, but you must have lived in the home as your primary residence for two out of five years before the sale. The two years need not be consecutive ones. If you sell before the two years, the exclusion is prorated if you're

moving to take a new job or for medical rea-sons.

$TIP: Keep track of the money you spend over the years improving your house. You can add these costs to your original purchase price. Then, when you sell, if your capital gain is above the excluded amount (stated above), the cost of improvements will help reduce your profit.

To qualify, a home improvement must add to the value of the house or extend its useful life. Putting on a new roof, finishing an attic, replacing a furnace, planting trees, and the like qualify. Fixing a leaky faucet does not.

REAL ESTATE INVESTMENT TRUSTS

■ Most dividends you receive are taxable, even those that represent capital gains distributions from the sale of property held by the REIT.

■ *Exception:* Dividends paid out of the share-holder's equity and treated as a return of your original investment are not taxed.

■ When you sell your REIT stock, any gains made are taxed at the regular rates; at 20% for long-term holdings.

■ Losses from a REIT stock can be used to offset gains, plus up to $3,000 of salary, wages, and ordinary income.

REAL ESTATE LIMITED PARTNERSHIPS

Check with your accountant.

RENTAL REAL ESTATE

(See: Vacation Homes.)

■ Rental income and profits when property is sold are taxed at regular rates.

■ Much rental income can be sheltered by de-ductions and expenses, such as mortgage interest, property taxes, depreciation, mainte-nance, repairs, and travel to and from the property. You can write off the cost of residential rental properties over a period of 27½ years, or 39 years for commercial property placed in service after May 13, 1993.

- Up to $25,000 per year in tax losses can be used to offset your wages, salary, and other income, provided that your adjusted gross income is under $100,000. This $25,000 cap is reduced 50¢ for each dollar by which your adjusted gross income exceeds $100,000. By the time your income hits $150,000, the cap is at zero. You must, however, pass the active participation test to receive this break.

- If your adjusted gross income is over $150,000, you can use tax deductions only up to the amount of rental income received that year. If there are any excess losses, they can be carried over until such time as you have excess income. These losses, however, can be used to offset income from other passive activities.

- To claim losses, you cannot have less than 10% ownership in rental property.

SAVINGS ACCOUNTS

Interest earned is taxable, even though you do not present your passbook to have the interest entered. Interest is taxed at regular tax rates; it does not receive the favorable long-term capital gains rate.

NOTE: Dividends on deposits or accounts in some institutions are reported as interest income: mutual savings banks, cooperative banks, domestic building and loan associations, and savings and loan associations.

SAVINGS BONDS

- Interest is exempt from state and local taxes.
- Federal income tax can be deferred on Series EE bonds until the bonds are redeemed or mature, or you can report the income annually as it accrues.
- If you roll over your Series EEs into Series HHs, federal tax on the accrued EE series in-

terest can again be deferred until the HH bonds either mature or are redeemed.

- Interest on Series HH bonds is taxed each year. HH bonds pay interest semiannually and must be reported in the year in which it is paid.

- If you elect to pay the federal tax due each year on EE bonds, you pay on the annual increase in redemption value of the bond. Once you begin paying, however, you must continue doing so for the bonds you presently own plus any new ones you buy.

- Children's accounts. If a child is under age 14, the first $700 of investment income is not taxed. The next $700 is taxed at the child's rate. Any investment income over $1,400 per year is taxed at the parent's rate, which is presumably higher. Starting at age 14, the income is taxed at the child's lower rate. By timing bonds to come due after the child turns 14, you can save on taxes.

- EE Savings Bonds purchased after January 1, 1990, by a bondholder at least 24 years old, and used to pay college tuition for the bondholder, his or her spouse, or dependent children, are free from federal income tax provided the bondholder falls within certain income guidelines at the time the bonds are used to meet college costs. Since these income guidelines are inflation-indexed, check with your accountant or bank to see if you qualify for this tax break.

  NOTE: This break is not available if you are married and filing separately.

STOCK INDEX OPTIONS AND FUTURES

- Profits are generally taxed the same as commodities: 60/40 rule for gains and losses and a three-year carryback for losses.

- Profits on futures and options become taxable at the end of the year, even if you have not closed out your position. In effect, the IRS will tax you on your paper profits.

- In some cases, you can deduct paper losses, even of positions still open. Check with your accountant.

STOCK RIGHTS

- If you sell your rights, the profit is taxed.
- If you exercise the rights, you will eventually pay tax, but not until you sell the new stock.
- If you receive stock rights (as opposed to purchasing them in the market) and then let them expire, you cannot claim a deduction for the loss.
- If you purchase rights in the market and let them expire as worthless, you can deduct the loss.

STOCK SPLITS

Stock splits are not dividends; they do not represent a distribution of surplus funds as do stock dividends. Therefore, stock splits are not taxable.

STOCKS

- Profits from the sale of stocks and dividends earned are taxed at regular rates, and at a maximum of 20% on long-term gains—those held at least 12 months and one day.
- Losses from sale may be used to offset any gains you have plus up to $3,000 of salary, wages, and other income.
- Interest on margin loans may be claimed as an itemized deduction. (*See also:* Margin Loans.)
- Gain on the exchange of common stock for other common stock (or preferred for other preferred) of the same company is not taxable. An exchange of preferred stock for common, or common for preferred, in the same company, is generally not tax free, unless the exchange is part of a tax-free recapitalization.

- Worthless stock. You may deduct as a capital loss the cost basis of securities that became worthless during the year.

  NOTE: It is deductible only in the year it became completely worthless. To support this deduction, you must show that it had some value the previous year and that it became worthless in the current year—showing that the company went bankrupt, stopped doing business, or is insolvent. Check with both your stockbroker and accountant.

STOCKS (FOREIGN)

- If you have foreign tax withheld from dividends of a foreign stock, you are entitled to a tax credit. To determine how much, divide your taxable foreign income by your total income, then multiply by the amount of U.S. tax. Example: You receive taxable foreign income of $5,000 and your total taxable income is $100,000. Divide $5,000 by $100,000 and multiply that by $28,000 (the estimated U.S. tax on $100,000). The maximum tax credit you could claim in this situation would be $1,400.

  Your credit would be the lesser of the amount withheld and the maximum credit calculated. Any amount disallowed in the current year may be carried forward.
- You can also list foreign taxes as an itemized deduction on line 7 of Schedule A, but you must choose one method or the other.

STUDENT LOANS

Interest paid on a student loan taken out by the student to pay higher education expenses (tuition, fees, room and board, books, and equipment) for the student, his/her spouse, or dependents may be deductible. On-the-job training and correspondence and night schools do not qualify. Nor does money borrowed from a friend or relative.

To be eligible for the deduction you must be going to school at least half time and you can't be making a whole lot of money. The full deduction ($2,000 for 2000) can be claimed only if your modified Adjusted Gross Income (AGI) is below $40,000 if you're single and below $60,000 on a joint return. The interest deduction phases out once modified AGI reaches $55,000 for singles and $75,000 for marrieds filing jointly.

CAUTION: Married couples must file jointly to get the deduction. And you cannot take the deduction if you can be claimed as a dependent on another person's tax return.

If your income is between the dollar amounts given above, there's a formula that determines how much you can deduct. The worksheet is on page 27 of the 1040 instructions.

The deduction is allowed for interest paid on the loan during the first 60 months in which payments are required. Once you've paid interest for 60 months, there is no deduction. You can't get around this by refinancing the loan in order to restart the 60-month period. Any loan and refinancing are treated as one loan by the IRS.

$TIP: Students receive Copy B of Form 1098-E ("Student Loan Interest Statement") from their lenders. Use the figure given on this form. The IRS requires that these forms be sent to borrowers by February 1.

TREASURY BILLS

- Interest income is subject to federal tax, but not state and local taxes. It is taxed at your regular tax rate and does not receive the more favorable long-term capital gains rate.
- The income earned is subject to taxation the year in which the T-bill matures or in which you sell it.
- With T-bills, the dollar difference between the original price and the amount you receive

when you redeem the bill is regarded as the interest income.

- You can defer income from one year to the next by purchasing a T-bill that matures in the next calendar year.

TREASURY BONDS AND NOTES

- Interest is subject to federal tax, but free from state and local tax.
- Any profit made when T-bonds or notes are sold is taxed, with 20% being the maximum on long-term gains.
- Losses from sales can be used to offset any capital gains you have plus up to $3,000 of salary, wages, and other ordinary income.

VACATION HOMES

- If a home is solely for personal use, you can deduct mortgage interest and real estate taxes, as you can with your principal residence. Mortgage interest is not deductible on third or fourth homes unless they are rental properties.
- You can deduct mortgage interest on loans up to the amount of your original purchase price plus improvements. Special rules apply to refinancing.
- If a home is used for pleasure and for rental purposes, your tax liability varies. If you rent it out for no more than 14 days per year, the rental income is not taxed. You do not even have to report it.
- If you use your home more than 14 days a year or 10% of the number of days rented, whichever is greater, your property qualifies as a second home. Mortgage interest and property taxes become deductible. Rental expenses can be deducted, but only up to the amount of rental income. If you have excess expenses, however, they can be carried forward.
- If you use your house 14 days or less a year or 10% of the number of days the house is rented

out, whichever is greater, the house then becomes rental property, not property used as a home, in which case see Rental Real Estate. Although expenses, including mortgage interest and real estate taxes, must be apportioned according to actual days of personal use and rental use, rental expenses in excess of gross rents might be used to offset other income.

    NOTE: This is a fairly complicated situation; check with your accountant.

■ When you sell a vacation home, any profit will be taxed at the new capital gains rates, except that any profits due to depreciation will be taxed at a maximum of 25%.

WARRANTS

■ Profits made when warrants are sold are taxed at regular rates.

■ If your warrant expires worthless, the cost of the warrant can be used to offset capital gains plus up to $3,000 of salary, wages, and other ordinary income.

■ If the warrant is converted to stock shares, no taxes are due on the transaction. Cost of the warrant, if any, is added to the cost of the stock purchased.

PART EIGHT

Your Customized Portfolio for 2000

"Put not your trust in money, but put your money in trust."

Oliver Wendell Holmes

But, of course, it's got to be the right trust. You've now read over 300 pages about investing, provided you started at the beginning and plowed straight through to this point. Yet all reading and no action won't make you rich.

It's now time to actually pick specific investments that will work for you. In this special section you will find suggestions for what to buy—and why. Although I've divided the sample portfolios according to age and lifestyle, you should really read all of them and then mix and match according to your goals and income level.

If you're worried or nervous about making a move, I urge you to resist the temptation to merely sit on the sidelines. It may appear that doing so is safe, that earning 3% in a bank savings account means you're fully protected; but it's not smart, because bank savings accounts barely equal the rate of inflation.

So calm your investment jitters by heeding the advice of our great cowboy-humorist, Will Rogers:

"Even if you're on the right track, you'll get run over if you just sit there."

Individual sample portfolios follow for those of you who are:

- Just out of school
- Newly married or living with a significant other
- Raising a family
- Empty nesters
- Retired or just about to be
- Have, or are starting, a business

Plus, you'll find solid information on how to protect your portfolio during tough economic times.

36

What to Invest In . . .

*O*ften we spend more time thinking about what car or personal computer to purchase than we do about what to buy for our portfolio. We pore over consumer magazines, talk to friends, test-drive endless models, read the ads. Well, you need to spend the same time and enthusiasm researching and finding the right stocks, bonds, and mutual funds.

The investments you should own, like a car, depend upon lots of personal factors—your age, your income, your family situation, your feeling about risk, and what other securities you already own.

Bear in mind that as you grow older your investment needs will change, along with your income and your fiscal responsibility to others. That means, of course, that you must review your portfolio on a regular basis. Your financial goals, too, will change over time. So stocks, bonds, or mutual funds that do not meet your changing goals should be sold and replaced with ones that do.

The following sample portfolios contain ideas that are geared toward the various stages of your life. Many of them, particularly the stocks, should be held at least a year or more; the bonds should be held until maturity or their call date.

I've divided the portfolios into seven lifestyle categories:

- Just out of college
- Newly married or coupled

- Having/raising a family
- Empty nester
- Approaching or in retirement
- Owning your own business
- If you've just been fired or laid off

☑ *HINT: Read all the portfolios even though you may fall into only one category; the investment recommendations are indeed transferable.*

SECTION 1

IF YOU'RE JUST OUT OF SCHOOL

This is a time for new beginnings—you're on your own, perhaps for the first time in your life, and although your income is probably modest, it's likely to increase quite quickly. Your responsibilities are limited, too—perhaps only to you and your cat—so you can focus your financial attention on building up a solid cash base.

Follow these ten steps to achieve financial independence:

Step 1. Set financial goals (see suggestions on page 378).

Step 2. Open a bank account. If you're new in the area, use the same institution your company uses.

Step 3. Get a credit card, and pay all bills on time to establish a good credit rating.

Portfolio for the Recent Grad

INVESTMENT	AMOUNT	DETAILS
• Money market account	3-months' living expenses	Add cash gifts, bonuses, freelance income
• Certificates of deposit	Due in three and six months	Roll over only if rates go up
• Company you work for	100 shares	Use employee stock purchase plan
• *or* . . . stock in:		
Barnes & Noble, AOL, Staples, The Gap, Cisco Systems	100 shares	Monitor carefully and reinvest the dividends
• Electric utility stock	100 shares	Reinvest all dividends
• Roth IRA	$1,000	Stock, CDs, Treasuries

Step 4. Open a money market mutual fund. A list of high-yielding funds appears on page 25.

Step 5. Sign up for the automatic payroll savings plan where you work and have 3% to 5% of your paycheck transferred into your money market fund.

Step 6. After you've accumulated cash enough to cover three months' worth of living expenses, you're ready to invest. (Aim to keep housing costs to 30% or less of your take-home pay.) Begin by purchasing several short-term bank CDs with different maturities, either at a local bank for convenience or with an out-of-the-area bank that has higher rates. Check the financial section of the newspaper for a list of the nation's top-yielding bank CDs.

Step 7. Purchase 100 shares of stock in the company you work for, if you have faith in its future, using the company's stock purchase plan, if one exists. You'll avoid a broker's commission, and you may be able to buy shares at a discount.

Alternatives: Buy 100 shares of a company whose product you use or like, or one that is within the industry where you work. *Suggestions:* Coca-Cola, IBM, Kellogg, Border's, Barnes & Noble, Staples, Procter & Gamble, The Gap, Gillette, Cisco Systems, Lucent Technologies. Use this as a learning experience, as your introduction to the stock market.

Step 8. Study the financial condition of your local electric or gas utility company. Read the annual report and check the rating in *Value Line*. If Value Line rates the utility a #1 or #2 in safety, add 100 shares to your portfolio. If your particular utility is not a smart investment, select one of those listed in Chapter 16.

Step 9. After a year or two you can afford to take greater risks with your money. Consider the sample portfolios that follow and incorporate those choices that you find appealing, keeping in mind that it is essential to diversify—between types of investments as well as types of industries.

Step 10. Open a Roth IRA so that 35 years from now you'll have a sizable retirement fund. Put in $2,000 all at once or in small monthly or quarterly payments.

☑ *HINT: Look into a "Smart Loan" Account, which enables college grads to consolidate their student loans into a single loan. Monthly payments in the first four years (when interest is typically higher) are cut by nearly 40%. Students can stretch repayment terms from 10 to 15 years, although you should realize that doing so may boost the total cost of the loan. For more info, call Sallie Mae, 800–524–9100.*

Portfolio for the Newly Coupled

INVESTMENT	AMOUNT	DETAILS
• Company you work for	100 shares	Use employee stock purchase plan
• Electric utility stock	100 shares	Reinvest all dividends
• U.S. Treasury notes or zeros	$1,000 minimum	Hold until maturity
• Municipal bond fund or UIT	$1,000 minimum	Hold until maturity
• Janus Mercury Fund	$2,500 minimum	Call 800–529–8583
• IRA (Roth or regular)	$2,000/year	Stocks, CDs, Mutual Funds
• General Electric	100 shares	Price: $109 Yield: 1.3%
• Marshall & Ilsley	100 shares	Price: $65 Yield: 1.5%
• Montgomery Street Income Securities	200 shares	Price: $17 Yield: 7.9%
• Alliance Capital Mgmt.	100 shares	Price: $27 Yield: 7.1%

(Prices as of Fall 1999.)

SECTION 2

IF YOU'RE NEWLY MARRIED OR LIVING TOGETHER

Now that you've added someone else to your life, review and revise your financial goals. Decide whether to invest jointly or separately, or do a little of both, keeping in mind that your dual incomes give you doubled investing and saving power.

Step 1. Review the portfolio for the recent grad. All suggestions there should be part of your financial life, too.

Step 2. Focus on the housing issue. You've probably been renting, but now together, by putting aside 3% to 5% of both your salaries, you can save a sizable amount for a down payment on a house or co-op. Begin by purchasing Treasury notes with two- to four-year maturities. Put the semiannual monthly interest payments in your money market fund. Don't spend them! This cash plus your CDs can be combined with your Treasuries when the latter come due, making a nice down payment.

Step 3. Because you have many years left for building assets, the securities you own should be primarily for growth, not income. Check the list of suggested stocks in the box on page 146. Regard them as long-term holdings, but monitor earnings trends twice a year and be prepared to sell.

Step 4. If you are in the 28% tax bracket, put 10% to 15% of your investments in municipal bonds, or in a tax-free unit investment trust.

Step 5. If you and your spouse spend weekends going to flea markets, auctions, or garage sales, consider becoming a knowledgeable collector. Every year, the "Investor's Almanac" section of this book contains ideas for building a savvy collection. Check your library for previous editions.

- *Marshall & Ilsley (MRIS).* A Wisconsin-based holding company, growing steadily with rising profits.
- *Montgomery Street Income Securities, Inc. (MTS).* These shares, with their impressive 7.9% yield, are suitable for conservative investors regardless of age.
- *General Electric (GE).* Owns NBC, GE Financial; a way to invest in the market as a whole.

SECTION 3

IF YOU HAVE A FAMILY

Once you know you're going to have kids:

Step 1. Check your firm's maternity leave policy as well as your health coverage. Make certain you're adequately insured.

Step 2. Put all or part of the mother-to-be's salary in a money market fund and practice living on one salary, which is likely to be the case when the baby arrives, at least at the beginning.

Step 3. Then put half of your money market fund into a series of bank CDs, staggered to come due at various dates—for example, one every two months after the baby is born. This will provide an influx of much-needed cash.

Step 4. Start a college education fund before the baby leaves the hospital nursery. You'll need to get your child a Social Security number for savings bonds and other financial presents. (See Chapter 29 for the tax implications of holding securities in a child's name versus your name.)

Step 5. At this stage, your portfolio should be both income- and growth-oriented: income to cover the extra costs of the family, and growth to make it possible to move into a larger home, add on to your present one, save for college tuition, and finance any expansion of your family. See the suggested stocks and bonds listed below.

- *Dreyfus Strategic Income (DSI).* This closed-end bond fund states its investment objective to be income and conservation of capital. It invests largely in government bonds—U.S. and foreign. Hold for its 9% yield.

- *EarthLink Network. (ELNK).* Leading Internet provider; 20% owned by Sprint. Rapidly growing subscriber base; also a prime takeover candidate.

- *Abbott Labs (ABT).* Leading maker of health care products, drugs, and diagnostic tests, including Similac, Sucaryl, and Murine. Several drugs to help AIDS patients boosting visibility and annual earnings.

- *Wrigley (WWY).* The world's largest manufacturer of chewing gum has no debt and no pension liability, but does have a steady growth rate. The family owns about 27% of the stock. Conservatively managed, it offers a continually popular, cheap, disposable product. Moves into foreign markets have been very successful.

Portfolio for Those with a Family

INVESTMENT	AMOUNT	DETAILS
• Company you work for	100 shares	Use employee stock purchase plan
• Electric utility company	100 shares	Reinvest all dividends
• Municipal bond fund or UIT	$1,000 minimum	Hold until maturity
• Janus Mercury Fund	$2,500 minimum	Sell when you've reached your profit point (800–529–8583)
• U.S. Treasury notes or Treasuries	$1,000 minimum	Time to mature when you buy a house or pay tuition bills
• IRA	$2,000/year	Stocks, CDs, Mutual Funds
• Dreyfus Strategic Income	200 shares	Price: $8 Yield: 9.0%
• EarthLink	100 shares	Price: $65 Yield: 1.3%
• Abbott Labs	100 shares	Price: $43 Yield: 1.6%
• Wrigley (Wm.)	100 shares	Price: $77 Yield: 1.1%

(Prices as of Fall 1999.)

SECTION 4

IF YOU'RE AN EMPTY NESTER

These are the peak payout years of your life, whether you are married or single, with or without children. You can now afford to focus on maintaining a comfortable lifestyle, caring for your own aging parents, or fueling an expanding business or career.

During this period, your income is probably the highest it will ever be, which enables you to make more aggressive investments than when you were footing the bill for college education or just getting started. Look at purchasing a second home or rental property, additional growth-oriented stocks, and even some high-yielding bonds. Be sure to fund your 401(k), Keogh, and/or IRA to the fullest, and take time to set up a tax-deferred annuity.

- *Tootsie Roll Industries (TR).* This low-debt, well-run company, like Wrigley (see page 380) offers a continually popular, relatively low-priced disposable product.
- *Nasdaq 100 Shares (QQQ).* A stock that tracks the Nasdaq 100 Index; an excellent way to participate in Internet and technology stocks.

SECTION 5

IF YOU'RE RETIRED OR ABOUT TO BE RETIRED

Now the emphasis should be primarily on income plus some growth. Safety is critical—so add top-rated bonds, blue-chip stocks, and high-yielding securities to your portfolio. But keep in mind that the average American lives twenty years after retirement, so you will want some growth stocks as well.

In addition to the specific suggestions given in Chapter 32, take a look at the list of high-yield bonds in Chapter 13, and add to your portfolio if you can assume the extra risk.

Also, load up on zero coupon Treasuries, timed to come due at various stages of your retirement years. You can read about zero coupon bonds in Chapter 13.

- *Treasury bonds.* As we go to press, U.S. Treasury bonds due in 30 years are yielding over 6%.
- *High-yield bonds.* If you are willing to assume some risk, put a portion of your portfolio in these bonds. See Chapter 1 for a recommended list.
- *Zero coupon bonds.* Use to mature at or soon after your retirement. Remember, zeros do not pay annual interest, but you must pay annual taxes on the imputed income.

Portfolio for the Empty Nester

INVESTMENT	AMOUNT	DETAILS
Tootsie Roll Ind.	100 shares	Price: $34 Yield: 0.7%
Nasdaq 100 Shares.	50 shares	Price: $120 Yield: 0.2%
AT&T 7s, 2005, 101	5 to 10 bonds	Reinvest income for retirement or to buy real estate
Duke Power 6⅜s, 2008, 96	5 to 10 bonds	Reinvest income
Government zeros	5 to 10 bonds	Pick maturity date to match your retirement

(Prices as of Fall 1999.)

Portfolio for Those Retired or About to Be

INVESTMENT	AMOUNT	DETAILS
• Florida Progress (FPC)	100 shares	Price: $42 Yield: 4.7%
• AT&T 7 1/8s, due 2002, 102	5 to 10 bonds	Use interest income or reinvest; noncallable
• 1838 Bond Debenture Fund	150 shares	Price: $18 Yield: 7.9%
• Merck & Co.	100 shares	Price: $68 Yield: 1.7%
• Hollinger 9¼	5 to 10 bonds	Use interest income or reinvest
	100 shares	Price: $101 Yield: 9.1%
• Royal Dutch Petroleum (RD)	50 shares	Price: $62 Yield: 3.7%
• U.S. Treasury notes	$1,000 minimum	Hold until maturity
• Ginnie Mae certificate	$25,000	Hold until maturity

(Prices as of Fall 1999.)

■ *Ginnie Maes or Fannie Maes.* These pay high yields (7 to 7¹/₂%) through monthly checks. Most pass-throughs are fully paid out in less than 15 years, so time your certificates to coincide with your retirement.

■ *Merck & Co. (MRIF).* Worldwide manufacturer of prescription and over-the-counter drugs; recently acquired Astra.

■ *Royal Dutch Petroleum (RD).* Major player in the international energy field with solid management.

SECTION 6

IF YOU HAVE OR ARE STARTING A SMALL BUSINESS

More and more Americans in 1997 are working at home, freelancing, or running their own incorporated businesses. This has become increasingly common with the advancement of computers, e-mail, and the art of communications. And it has been exacerbated by the general downsizing of corporate America.

Before either starting a business or expanding an existing one, I suggest you follow these steps:

Step 1. Address personal financial needs. No one should be in business for themselves if there's any question about where money for the kids' education or the next mortgage payment is coming from. I have increased my rule of thumb for business owners: You should have enough money set aside in a money market fund or in CDs to cover at least one year's worth of personal living expenses. (Under ordinary circumstances, that time frame is three to six months, depending upon the economy and one's age.)

Step 2. Take care of medical and disability insurance. Under federal law you have the right to continue medical coverage for 18 months after leaving a job, at your expense. Because premiums for a group policy are lower than for individual coverage, it is wise to arrange to continue coverage by paying the premiums yourself.

Bear in mind that various benefits—health, life, and disability insurance, plus paid vacations—make up almost one-third of most employee's annual salaries. So for you to just stay even, your business must generate more than only your salary.

Step 3. Order these free IRS publications by calling 800–829–3676:

Portfolio for Business Owners

INVESTMENT	DETAILS
• Money market account	9-months' living expenses
and/or	
Certificates of deposit	9-months' living expenses
• IRA	$2,000/year
• IRA-SEP, or Keogh Plan	See Chapter 29
• Dreyfus Strategic Govt. Inc. (NYSE: DSI)	Price: $8 Yield: 9.0%
• Florida Progress (NYSE: FLC)	Price: $47 Yield: 4.7%
• AT&T 7 1/8s due 2002 selling at 102	Solid utility bond
1838 Bond Debenture Fund(NYSE: BDF)	Price: $18 Yield: 7.9%
Webb (Del) 9 3/4s due 2008 selling at 95	Hold for income
Hollingen Int'l 9 1/4s due 2006 selling at 101	Hold for income
Montgomery Street Income Securities (NYSE: MTS)	Price: $17 Yield: 8.4%
Weingarten Realty (NYSE: WRI)	Price: $40 Yield: 7.2%
Putnam Premier Income Trust* (NYSE: PPT)	Price: $7 Yield: 10.0%

(Prices as of Fall 1999.)

$TIP: Three sources for small business owners:
   www.inc.com
   www.netscape.com/netcenter/smallbusiness
   www.quicken.com/smallbusiness

Step 4. Gear your portfolio to provide income to weather any downturns in your business and to provide collateral should you wish to use part of it to obtain a loan.

There are two ways to finance a business: debt financing consists of loans that the business must repay; equity financing consists of money given to a business in exchange for an ownership in the business, commonly done through selling shares of stock. In most cases, a balance between the two is ideal. Too much debt necessitates a huge cash flow to pay the interest on the loans, and too much equity means you've given away control.

The suggestions in the box above are aimed primarily at providing income as well as securities that can be used as collateral for a loan, or sold if you should need an infusion of capital. *NOTE:* The first three suggestions should be taken care of before attempting the rest.

IF YOU MAY BE FIRED OR HAVE BEEN FIRED

The ongoing downsizing of corporate America, with layoffs in virtually every industry, has affected all of us. Some of us have lost jobs; others have had to face frozen salaries or a cutback in hours. It's not surprising that many Americans are worried about their finances. Whether or not you're dealing with a personal cash flow struggle, it's smart to know what steps to take to protect your family's money during tough times, now or in the future. Here are some tips for doing just that.

Build Up Your Nest Egg

If you're worried about your job security, start now to build up enough cash to see you through the hard times. Without fail, you should set aside a monthly sum immediately after paying the rent or mortgage. Don't wait to save until later. Useful steps:

1. *Use automatic savings plans.* Sign up for payroll deduction programs. Arrange for automatic transfers from checking to savings or to a money market fund. Purchase EE Savings Bonds this way as well.
2. *Pay cash for purchases.* Avoid using credit cards, which often lead to overspending, debt buildup, and high interest rate charges.
3. *Reduce and/or pay off the loan with the highest interest rate.* Make this a priority. Then tackle the next highest rate loan.
4. *Fund your 401(k) or other retirement plan.* If you're ever really pressed, you can borrow from these plans and pay back yourself rather than a bank. You'll also be reducing your tax bite.
5. *Increase tax withholding.* Get a bigger tax refund by boosting salary withholding. Then save the refund.

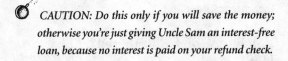 *CAUTION: Do this only if you will save the money; otherwise you're just giving Uncle Sam an interest-free loan, because no interest is paid on your refund check.*

Other Strategies

If you are experiencing financial difficulties:

1. *Go on a crash budget.*
2. *Review avenues of income and fixed and variable expenses.*

For Any Portfolio: The Top-Yielding Stocks in the Dow

At any time when you have accumulated enough cash, use this simple strategy that almost always beats the market: On a given day—say, January 2 or your birthday—buy equal amounts of the ten highest-yielding stocks in the Dow Jones Industrial Average. Then, replace any that have fallen out of the top ten.

STOCK	YIELD (%)
Philip Morris	5.1%
General Motors	3.0
J. P. Morgan & Co.	2.9
Chevron Corp.	2.6
Eastman Kodak	2.4
MMM	2.3
Du Pont, E.I.	2.1
Exxon Corp.	2.0
Merck	1.9
AT&T Corp.	1.8

(As of Fall 1999.)

---

3. *Trim variables,* such as entertaining, travel, eating out, dry cleaning.
4. *Stop outrageous spending.*
5. *Talk to the children.* If you or your spouse has lost a job or has a sudden cutback in income, it's important to let the children know the truth, but without frightening them. After all, they will be affected, too. Reassure them that hard times won't last forever.
6. *Claim benefits.* If you are laid off and entitled to unemployment compensation, do not be embarrassed to collect. After all, you've been paying to fund the system for many years.
7. *Reduce debt.* Paying off high-rate loans, such as credit card debt, is critical. Pay all credit card balances within 30 days to avoid interest charges. Consolidate high-rate debt if you can get a lower interest rate by doing so.

Alternative Portfolio Suggestions for All Ages

- *Buy:* Puerto Rico Electric Power Authority bonds, $5\,^3/_8$, due 2027, selling at $990. Total cost for 10 bonds will be $9,900. Annual income will be approximately $520. Puerto Rican municipals are exempt from local, state, and federal taxes in all 50 states.

- *Buy:* U.S. Government (Treasury) zeros, due September 2005, with a yield of 6.35%. Cost per bond is $630; total cost for $10,000 worth of bonds will be $6,030. In September 2005 your zeros will mature, and you will receive the full $10,000.

- *Buy:* Dreyfus Strategic Gov't. Fund (DSI). This closed-end bond fund trades on the NYSE and invests in U.S. and foreign government debt. Its shares in Fall 1999 were $9, for a yield of 8%.

- *Buy:* Janus Flexible Income Fund. Invests in corporate and convertible bonds; minimum investment $2,500; yield as of Fall 1999 was 7.27% (800–544–8888).

8. *Pinch pennies.* You'll know where to do so. Start by leaving your credit cards at home.

9. *Eat home more.* Or if dining out, have drinks and dessert at home.

Finding Extra Cash

Don't be surprised if you need extra cash to tide yourself over until you get a job, a raise, or your spouse is employed. Here are four tips:

1. *Review your portfolio* and first sell securities that are not performing well. If need be, slowly sell other securities, holding until last the best performers.

2. *Consider a home-equity line of credit.*

   CAUTION: It is virtually impossible to get this type of loan when you are out of work. If you fear losing your job, process the loan now. There's no obligation to use it, although you will incur some expenses in setting it up.

3. *Borrow against the cash value in any life insurance policies.*

4. *As a last resort, borrow from your 401(k) plan.* Hold off tapping this source as long as possible, because it's hard to replace these funds, which you will need when you retire. Most companies let employees borrow up to 50% of the amount vested, or $50,000, whichever is less. Typically you repay the money in installments through payroll deductions. Finance charges are based on current market rates—expect to pay prime plus one or two percentage points. Terms and conditions vary, so check with your benefits officer.

Investment Analysis and Information Sources

"Chance favors only the prepared mind."

Louis Pasteur

Knowing where to get reliable information, how to reach the experts, and how to interpret financial statements improves your chances not only of making it but also of keeping it.

In the Appendixes we help prepare your financial mind by explaining:

- How to read an annual report
- How to use technical analysis
- How to study charts
- How to use software programs
- How to find the various exchanges
- How to use the leading indexes

And finally,

- How to understand Wall Street jargon

NOTE: In Parts Three and Four we explained the various types of stocks and the analytical tools for evaluating securities. You may want to review these points as you now learn precisely how to select top-quality securities on your own, including knowing the stock exchanges, indexes, and averages.

Managing Your Money
with a Computer

If you've got a personal computer you've got access to a world of investment information—stuff on financial planning, investing, and even preparing tax returns. It not only does the obvious—make number-crunching faster and easier—but with the right software you can gain access to a large amount of research that until recently was the private domain of the professionals on Wall Street.

Don't ignore it.

A COMPUTER IS NOT A SUBSTITUTE FOR THINKING

There's all sorts of help available—programs for writing checks, filing taxes, getting current stock and mutual fund data, doing a budget, talking to other investors and experts in chat sessions. No one program, however, does it all, and no combination of programs can replace intelligent, sensible decision making. So look upon your computer as an additional way to improve your financial bottom line, and not as a substitute for thinking. Use it in conjunction with the basic investment guidelines you've learned by reading this book and from other resources.

Following is an overview of some of the best software and on-line programs, starting with the simplest programs first—those that do check writing. Read what we have to say, talk with knowledgeable friends who use financial software programs, check your public library (many have

programs you can practice with), and then call the sources for the promotional literature.

Before purchasing any software you need to consider two things:

1. How complex are your financial affairs?
2. What format do you need—Macintosh or Windows?

CHECKBOOK MANAGEMENT

- *Microsoft Money.* Has a great deal of built-in assistance for keeping track of your checkbook and budget. Its on-screen graphic resembles a checkbook. You fill in the necessary information and the calculations are done automatically. Click on: www.windows.com/hk/product/p_desktop.htm
- *Quicken.* This best-seller is just about the easiest to learn and use. It sorts financial information into budgeting and tax categories for record-keeping purposes. The data can then be transferred to most major tax-preparation software packages. Small businesses can add on a payroll program, QuickPay, for an extra $60. Check it out at: www.intuit.com
- *Quicken for Windows.* This version has an extra feature for the same price called "IntelliCharge": Users can apply for a Visa Gold Card; all charges placed on the card are then electronically sent via modem to your computer and automatically sorted into the two categories.

- *QuickBooks.* Similar to Quicken, but with a simple accounting program that is useful if you have a home office or small business. It uses the same checkbook entry plan as Quicken, but adds on business features such as invoicing, accounts payable, and accounts receivable.

FINANCIAL PLANNING

- *Andrew Tobias's Managing Your Money.* One of the most comprehensive and popular financial planning packages available. In addition to doing checkbook, budget, and portfolio management, it tracks stocks and has an address keeper, calendar, to-do list, simple word processor, and tax planner. The program also calculates mortgage payments and can help you determine whether it's better to buy or lease a car or home. A well-written and enjoyable-to-read manual.

TAXES

You'll have to spend about two hours learning a tax program, but it does make filling out returns easier. The math is almost always correct. Other advantages: You have to enter the data in only one place; information is transferred quite easily to state forms; the good ones do some analysis of your return and help locate errors.

None of the programs answers every question—you may still have to consult IRS publications or even a professional. Don't get too smart for your own good and assume that now that you use a software program you also know all the ins and outs of the tax code.

Among the best:

- *Andrew Tobias's TaxCut.* A question-and-answer format that gets you to the right IRS forms and then leads you through the forms with help screens. Keeps track of important

receipts and tax information throughout the year. Prints out IRS-approved forms on any printer.
- *Kiplinger Taxcut.* This takes the Andrew Tobias's TaxCut program and adds material from the tax editor of *Kiplinger's Personal Finance* magazine. This extra help, written in easy-to-follow language, makes calculations much easier. The package also includes the Kiplinger TaxEstimator program for tax planning and a copy of Kiplinger's 476-page tax guide, *Sure Ways to Cut Your Taxes.*
- *MacInTax.* Has a question-and-answer format and a useful, easy-to-follow help program. For another $19.95, you can file tax returns electronically for faster refunds.
- *TurboTax.* Available from Intuit, easy to use with clear instructions; $9.95/return.
- *Deloitte & Touche.* Has an excellent website with continually updated tips. Click on: www.dtonline.com.

MUTUAL FUND SOFTWARE

With thousands of mutual funds out there, picking the right one is not an easy task. Specialized software and on-line services will help you narrow the choices. Some alert you to the best buys and sells; others will match your risk level and goals with the right funds.

Call and get literature first or a trial subscription.

The best software to date:

- *Mutual Fund Expert (800–237–8400).* Screens 9,000+ funds including money market funds; $35 trial; $95/year for quarterly updates. Windows and Mac.
- *Morningstar Principia (800–735–0700).* Screens more than 10,000 funds with information taken from its weekly publication. $95 for trial; Windows.

- *AAII's Quarterly Low-Load Mutual Fund Update (312–280–0170).* Ideal if you want only no-load and low-load funds; screens 900 of them; $39/year for members and $50 for non-members; Windows.

FOR FURTHER INFORMATION

Books

Ted Allrich, *The On-Line Investor: How to Find the Best Stocks Using Your Computer* (New York: St. Martin's, 1997).

Jim Jubak, *The Worth Guide to Electronic Investing: Everything You Need to Know to Use Your Home Computer to Make More Money in the Stock Market* (New York: HarperBusiness, 1998).

American Association of Individual Investors, *The Individual Investor's Guide to Computerized Investing,* 15th ed. (AAII, 1999).

Douglas Goldstein, *The Online Guide to Personal Finance & Investing: The Best Online Sites, Resources & Services in: Investments, Credit Cards, Home Financing Real Estate, Banking Services, Financial Planning, Taxes* (Irwin Professional Publishing, 1998).

☑ *HINT: If you (or someone you know) feel you're too old to get up and on-line, get in touch with SENIOR NET in San Francisco. They'll give you details about the national network of senior-oriented centers where classes on how to use a computer are held. Classes range from just $25 to $75. Call: 800–747–6848 or 415–495–4990.*

B

Behind the Scenes:
How to Read Annual Reports

Annual reports can be one of the most important tools in analyzing a corporation to determine whether to buy, hold, sell, or skip its securities. In a few minutes you can check the corporation's quality and profitability and learn about the character and ability of management, its methods of operation, its products and services and, most importantly, its future prospects.

If you own securities of a corporation, you will receive a copy of its annual report about three months after the close of the fiscal year. If you don't own securities, you can get a copy from your broker or by writing to the company—get the address from *Standard & Poor's, Value Line,* or *Moody's,* copies of which are in most libraries.

First, skim the text; check the statement of income and earnings to see how much money was made and whether this was more or less than in previous years. Review the list of officers and directors for familiar names.

An annual report's statements will always be factually correct, but the interpretations, especially those in the president's message, will naturally be the most favorable possible, within legal and accounting limits.

If you are considering a stock to buy, look at three years' worth of annual reports. Here are the key points to be aware of:

TRENDS

In sales, earnings, dividends, accounts receivable. If they continue to rise, chances are that you've found

a winner. Buy when they are moving up; review when they plateau; consider selling when they are down.

INFORMATION

From the tables: corporate financial strength and operating success or failure. From the text: explanations of what happened during the year and what management projects for the future. If you don't believe management, do not hold the stock.

POSITIVES

New plants, products, personnel, and programs. Are the total assets greater and liabilities lower than in previous years? If so, why—tighter controls or decreases in allocations for R&D, marketing, etc.?

If the profits were up, was the gain due to fewer outstanding shares (because of repurchase of stock), nonrecurring income from the sale of property, or higher sales and lower costs?

NEGATIVES

Plant closings, sales of subsidiaries, discontinuance of products, and future needs for financing. Not all of these will always be adverse, but they can make a significant difference with respect to what happens in the next few years.

If the profits were down, was this because of the elimination of some products or services? Price wars? Poor managerial decisions?

FOOTNOTES

Read these carefully because they can point out problems. Be cautious if there were heavy markdowns of inventory, adverse governmental regulations, rollovers of debt, and other unusual events.

BALANCE SHEET

To see whether cash or liquid assets are diminishing and whether accounts receivable, inventories, or total debts are rising. Any such trend can serve as a yellow flag, if not a red one.

FINANCIAL SUMMARY

Not only for the past year but for the previous five years. This will provide an overall view of corporate performance and set the stage for an analysis of the most recent data.

In the stock market, past is prologue. Few companies achieve dramatic progress or fall on hard times suddenly. In most cases, the changes have been forecast. The corporation with a long, fairly consistent record of profitable growth can be expected to do as well, or better, in the years ahead and thus prove to be a worthwhile holding. The er-

ratic performer is likely to move from high to low profits (or losses), and the faltering company will have signs of deterioration over a two- or three-year period.

READING THE REPORT

When you review the text, you will get an idea of the kind of people who are managing your money, learn what they did or did not do and why, and be able to draw some conclusions about future prospects.

Begin with the Shareholders' Letter

This message from the chairman outlines the company's past performance and its prospects. Compare last year's letter with this year's facts. Did the company meet its previously stated goals? Beware of the chairman who never mentions any problems or areas of concern. If there were failures, there should be logical explanations. Management is not always right in its decisions, but in financial matters, frankness is the base for confidence. If previous promises were unfulfilled (and that's why you should keep a file of past annual reports), find out

---

To Translate the President's Message

Here are some of the techniques used in writing annual reports to phrase comments in terms that tend to divert the reader's attention away from problems.

WHAT THE PRESIDENT SAYS	WHAT THE PRESIDENT MEANS
"The year was difficult and challenging."	"Sales and profits were off, but expenses (including executive salaries) were up."
"Management has taken steps to strengthen market share."	"We're underselling our competitors to drive them out of the market."
"Integrating the year's highs and lows proved challenging."	"Sales were up; profits went nowhere."
"Management worked diligently to preserve a strong financial position."	"We barely broke even but were able to avoid new debts."
"Your company is indebted to the dedicated service of its employees."	"We don't pay 'em much, but there's not much else to cheer about."

Consolidated Statement: Fred Meyer, Inc.

	FISCAL YEAR ENDED ($ IN THOUSANDS EXCEPT PER-SHARE AMOUNTS)		
	JANUARY 31, 1996	FEBRUARY 1, 1996	FEBRUARY 2, 1996 (53 WEEKS)
Net sales	$1,688,208	$1,583,796	$1,449,108
Cost of merchandise sold	1,200,379	1,135,836	1,053,689
Gross margin	487,829	447,960	395,419
Operating and administrative expenses	430,469	397,841	354,914
Income from operations	57,360	50,119	40,505
Interest expense, net of interest income of $1,679, $2,983, and $3,090	11,945	17,652	19,565
Income before income taxes and extraordinary items	45,415	32,467	20,940
Provision for income taxes	21,350	13,000	8,000
Income before extraordinary items	24,065	19,467	12,940
Extraordinary items	(1,530)		2,649
Net income	$ 22,535	$ 19,467	$ 15,589
Earnings per Common Share			
Income before extraordinary items	$ 1.15	$ 1.06	$ .73
Extraordinary items	(.07)		.15
Net income	$ 1.08	$ 1.06	$ .88
Weighted average number of common shares outstanding	20,870	18,355	17,790

why. If the tone is overly optimistic, be wary. If you are skeptical, do not hold the stock or buy.

Watch for Double-Talk

Clichés are an integral part of business writing, but they should not be substitutes for proper explanations. If you find such meaningless phrases as "a year of transition" or some of the locutions listed in the box on page 393, start getting ready to unload. There are better opportunities elsewhere.

Study the Balance Sheet

This presents an instant picture of the company's assets and liabilities on the very last day of the fiscal year. Divide the current assets by the current liabilities to get the current ratio. A ratio of 2:1 or

better signals that there are enough assets on hand to cover immediate debts.

Look at Long-Term Debt

Divide long-term debt by long-term capital (i.e., long-term debt plus shareholders' equity). If it is below 50%, the company is probably solid, but, of course, the more debt, the less cash to help weather rough times.

Review Accounts Receivable

Listed under current assets, this figure reflects the payments for products or services that the company expects to receive in the near future. If receivables are growing at a faster pace than sales, it may indicate that the company is not collecting its bills fast enough.

Look at Current Inventories

If inventories are rising faster than sales, the company is creating or producing more than it can sell.

Look at Net Income Per Share

Note whether this figure, which reflects earnings, is trending up or down.

Compare Revenues and Expenses

If expenses are greater than revenues over time, management may be having trouble holding down overhead. Discount earnings increases that are due to a nonrecurring event, such as sale of a property or division. Nonrecurring items should be explained in the footnotes. The footnotes also reveal changes in accounting methods, lawsuits, and liabilities.

Study the Quality and Source of Earnings

When profits are entirely from operations, they indicate management's skill; when they are partially from bookkeeping, look again. But do not be hasty in drawing conclusions. Even the best of corporations may use "special" accounting.

EXAMPLE: In valuing inventories using LIFO (last in, first out), current sales are matched against the most recent inventory costs so that earnings can rise sharply when inventories are reduced and their costs get older and thus lower. When oil prices were at a peak, Texaco cut inventories by 16%. The LIFO cushion, built up over several years, was a whopping $454 million and transformed what would have been a drop in net income into a modest gain.

Such "tricks" are one reason that stocks fall or stay flat after annual profits are reported. Analysts are smart enough to discover that earnings are more paper than real.

Read the Auditor's Report

If there are hedging phrases such as "except for" or "subject to," be wary. These phrases can signal the inability to get accurate information and may forecast future write-offs.

Look at Foreign Currency Transactions

These can be tricky and often difficult to understand. Under recent revisions of accounting rules, it's possible to recast them retroactively when, of course, they can be favorable. One major firm whose domestic profits had been lagging went back four years with its overseas reports and boosted its per-share profits to $7.08 from the previously reported $6.67 per share.

Most international corporations have elaborate systems for hedging against fluctuations in foreign currencies. These are relatively expensive, but they tend to even out sharp swings in the value of the dollar.

Check for Future Obligations

You may have to burrow in the footnotes, but with major companies, find out about the pension obligations: the money that the firm must pay to its retirees. One way to boost profits (because this means lower annual contributions) is to raise the assumed rate of return on pension fund investments.

Calculate the Cash Flow

Add after-tax earnings and annual depreciation on fixed assets and subtract preferred dividends, if any. Then compare the result with previous years. Cash flow is indicative of corporate earning power, because it shows the dollars available for profits, new investments, etc.

Beware of Overenthusiasm About New Products, Processes, or Services

Usually it takes three years to translate new operations into sizable sales and profits—and the majority of new projects are losers.

Pay Special Attention to the Return on Equity (Profit Rate)

This is the best measure of management's ability to make money with your money. Any ROE above 15% is good; when below, compare the figure with that of previous years and other firms in the same industry. Some industries seldom show a high rate of return: for example, heavy machinery because of the huge investment in plants and equipment, and utilities because of the ceiling set by public commissions.

Watch Out for Equity Accounting

This means that earnings from other companies, which are more than 20% owned, are included in total profits. There are no cash dividends, so the money cannot be used for expansion or payouts to shareholders. This maneuver can massage the reported earnings, but that's about all. Teledyne, a major conglomerate, reported $19.96 per share profits, but a close examination revealed that $3.49 of this was from equity accounting—phantom, not real, earnings.

FOR FURTHER INFORMATION

How to Read a Financial Report (pamphlet), free from any Merrill-Lynch office, or call 800–MERRILL.

George T. Friedlob and Ralph E. Welton, *Keys to Reading an Annual Report* (Hauppauge, NY: Barron's Educational Series, 1989).

John A. Tracy, *How to Read a Financial Report* (New York: Wiley, 1999).

C

Using Technical Indicators

Technical analysis (TA) is a way of doing securities research using indicators, charts, and computer programs to track price trends of stocks, bonds, commodities, and the market in general. Technical analysts use these indicators to predict price movements.

If you understand the basics of both technical and fundamental analysis, you'll have a great advantage as an investor.

Technical analysis neither as complex nor as esoteric as many people think. It's a tell-it-as-it-is interpretation of stock market activity. The technician glances at the fundamental values of securities but basically concentrates on the behavior of the market, industry groups, and stocks themselves—their price movements, volume, trends, patterns; in sum, their supply and demand.

Basically, TA is concerned with what is and not with what should be. Dyed-in-the-wool technicians pay minimal attention to what the company does and concentrate on what its stock does. They recognize that over the short term, the values of stocks reflect what people think they are worth, not what they are really worth.

Technical analysts operate on the assumption that:

1. The past action of the stock market is the best indicator of its future course.
2. 80% of a stock's price movement is due to factors outside the company's control and 20% to factors unique to that stock.
3. The stock market over a few weeks or months is rooted 85% in psychology and only 15% in economics.

THE DOW THEORY

There are a number of technical theories, but the granddaddy is the Dow theory. It is the oldest and most widely used. As with all technical approaches, it is based on the belief that stock prices cannot be forecast accurately by fundamental analysis, but that trends, indicated by price movements and volume, can be used successfully. These can be recorded, tracked, and interpreted, because the market itself prolongs movements: Investors buy more when the market is rising and sell more when it's dropping.

This follow-the-crowd approach enables the pros to buy when the market is going up and to sell or sell short when the market turns down. For amateurs, such quick trading is costly because of the commissions involved and the need for accurate information. But when properly used, TA can be valuable in correctly timing your buy and sell positions.

The Dow theory is named after Charles H. Dow, one of the founders of Dow Jones & Company, Inc., the financial reporting and publishing organization. The original hypotheses have been changed somewhat by his followers, but broadly interpreted, the Dow theory signals both the beginning and end of bull and bear markets.

Dow believed the stock market to be a barometer of business. The purpose of his theory was not to predict movements of security prices but rather to call the turns of the market and to forecast the business cycle or longer movements of depression or prosperity. It was not concerned with ripples or day-to-day fluctuations.

The Dow theory basically states that once a trend of the Dow Jones Industrial Average (DJIA) has been established, it tends to follow the same direction until definitely canceled by both the Industrial and Railroad (now Transportation) Averages. The market cannot be expected to produce new indications of the trend every day, and unless there is positive evidence to the contrary, the existing trend will continue.

Dow and his disciples saw the stock market as made up of 2 types of "waves": the primary wave, which is a bull or bear market cycle of several years' duration, and the secondary (or intermediary) wave, which lasts from a few weeks to a few months. Any single primary wave may contain within it 20 or more secondary waves, both up and down.

The theory relies on similar action by the two averages (Industry and Transportation), which may vary in strength but not in direction. Robert Rhea, who expanded the original concept, explained it this way:

Successive rallies, penetrating preceding high points with ensuing declines terminating above preceding low points, offer a bullish indication . . . and vice versa for bearish indication. . . . A rally or decline is defined as one or more daily movements resulting in a net reversal of direction exceeding 3% of either average. Such movements have little authority unless confirmed by both Industrial and Transportation Averages . . . but confirmation need not occur in the same day.

Dow did not consider that his theory applied to individual stock selections or analysis. He expected that specific issues would rise or fall with the averages most of the time, but he also recognized that any particular security would be affected by special conditions or situations.

These are the key indicators of the Dow theory:

- *A bull market is signaled as a possibility* when an intermediate decline in the DJIA stops above the bottom of the previous intermediate decline. This action must be confirmed by the action of the Transportation Average (DJTA). A bull market is confirmed after this has happened, and when on the next intermediate rise, both averages rise above the peaks of the last previous intermediate rise.

- *A bull market is in progress* as long as each new intermediate rise goes higher than the peak of the previous intermediate advance and each new intermediate decline stops above the bottom of the previous one.

- *A bear market is signaled as a possibility* when an intermediate rally in the DJIA fails to break through the top of the previous intermediate rise. A bear market is confirmed (1) after this has happened, (2) when the next intermediate decline breaks through the low of the previous one, and (3) when it is confirmed by the DJTA.

- *A bear market is in progress* as long as each new intermediate decline goes lower than the bottom of the previous decline and each new intermediate rally fails to rise as high as the previous rally.

A pure Dow theorist considers the averages to be quite sufficient to use in forecasting and sees no need to supplement them with statistics of commodity prices, volume of production, car loadings, bank debts, exports, imports, etc.

Interpreting the Dow Theory

Interpreting Dow theory leaves no room for sentiment.

- A *primary bear market* does not terminate until stock prices have thoroughly discounted the worst that is apt to occur. This decline requires three steps: (1) the abandonment of hopes upon which stocks were purchased at inflated prices, (2) selling due to decreases in business and earnings, and (3) distress selling of sound securities despite value.
- *Primary bull markets* follow the opposite pattern: (1) a broad movement, interrupted by secondary reactions averaging longer than two years, where successive rallies penetrate high points with ensuing declines terminating above preceding low points; (2) stock prices advancing because of demand created by both investors and speculators who start buying when business conditions improve; and (3) rampant speculation as stocks advance on hopes, expectations, and dreams.

☑ *HINT: A new primary trend is not actually confirmed by the Dow theory until both the DJTA and the DJIA penetrate their previous positions.*

Criticism

There are analysts who scoff at the Dow theory. They point out that the stock market today is vastly different from that in the early 1900s when Dow formulated his theory. The number and value of shares of publicly owned corporations have increased enormously: In 1900, the average number of shares traded annually on the NYSE was 59.5 million. Now that's the volume on a very slow day.

The sharpest criticism is leveled against the breadth, scope, and significance of the averages. The original Industrial index had only 12 stocks, and today's 30 large companies do not provide a true picture of the broad, technologically ori-

ented economy. Critics point out that the Transportation Average is also unrepresentative, because some of the railroads derive a major share of their revenues from natural resources, and the airlines and trucking companies are limited in their impact. Add the geographic dispersal of industry, and Transportation is no longer a reliable guide to the economy.

Finally, the purists argue that government regulations and institutional dominance of trading have so altered the original concept of individual investors that the Dow theory can no longer be considered all-powerful and always correct.

To most investors, the value of the Dow theory is that it represents a sort of think-for-yourself method that will pay worthwhile dividends for those who devote time and effort to gaining a sound understanding of the principles involved.

PSYCHOLOGICAL INDICATORS

Keeping in mind that the stock market is rooted 15% in economics and 85% in psychology, some analysts predict the future by using such technical indicators as these:

Barron's Confidence Index (BCI)

This is published weekly in the financial newsmagazine *Barron's*. It shows the ratio of the yield on 10 highest-grade bonds to the yield on the broader-based Dow Jones 40-bond average. The ratio varies from the middle 80s (bearish) to the middle 90s (bullish).

The theory is that the trend of "smart money" is usually revealed in the bond market before it shows up in the stock market. Thus, Barron's Confidence Index will be high when shrewd investors are confident and buy more lower-grade bonds, thus reducing low-grade bond yields, and low when they are worried and stick to high-grade bonds, thus cutting high-grade yields.

If you see that the BCI simply keeps going back and forth aimlessly for many weeks, you can probably expect the same type of action from the overall stock market.

Overbought–Oversold Index (OOI)

This is a handy measure, designed by *Indicator Digest,* of a short-term trend and its anticipated duration. Minor upswings or downturns have limited lives. As they peter out, experienced traders say that the market is "overbought" or "oversold" and is presumably ready for a near-term reversal.

Glamour Average

Another *Indicator Digest* special, this shows what is happening with the institutional favorites, usually trading at high multiples because of their presumed growth potential and current popularity (in a bull market). By and large, this is a better indicator for speculators than investors.

Speculation Index

This is the ratio of AMEX-to-NYSE volume. When trading in AMEX stocks (generally more speculative) moves up faster than that in NYSE (quality) issues, speculation is growing. It's time for traders to move in and for investors to be cautious.

BROAD-BASED INDICATORS

Odd-Lot Index

This shows how small investors view the market, because it concentrates on trades of fewer than 100 shares. The small investor is presumably "uninformed" (a somewhat debatable assumption) and so tends to follow established patterns: selling as the market rises; jumping in to pick up bargains when it declines. The signal comes when the odd-lotter deviates from this "normal" behavior.

When the small investor distrusts a rally after a long bear market, that investor gives a bullish signal: Initial selling is normal, but when this contin-

ues, it's abnormal and a signal to the pros to start buying.

Moving Average Lines

You can also watch the direction of a stock by comparing its price to a moving average (MA). A moving average is an average that's periodically updated by dropping the first number and adding in the last one. A 30-week moving average, for example, is determined by adding the stock's closing price for the current week to the closing prices of the previous 29 weeks and then dividing by 30. Over time, this moving average indicates the trend of prices.

A long-term moving average tends to smooth out short-term fluctuations and provides a basis against which short-term price movement can be measured.

Moving averages can be calculated for both individual stocks and all stocks in a group—say, all those listed on the NYSE or all in a particular industry. Technical analysts use a variety of time frames: 10 days, 200 days, 30 weeks, etc. In most cases they compare the moving average with a regular market average, usually the Dow Jones Industrial Average. For example:

- As long as the DJIA is *above* the MA, the outlook is bullish.
- As long as the DJIA is *below* the MA, the outlook is bearish.
- A confirmed downward penetration of the MA by the base index is a *sell* signal.
- A confirmed penetration of the MA is a *buy* signal.

Beware of false penetrations, and delay action until there is a substantial penetration (2% to 3%), upward or downward, within a few weeks. In other words, don't be in a hurry to interpret the chart action.

Moving averages are vulnerable to swift market declines, especially from market tops. By the time you get the signal, you may have lost a bundle, because prices tend to fall twice as fast as they rise.

If you enjoy charting, develop a ratio of the stocks selling above their 30-week MA. When the ratio is over 50% and trending upward, the outlook is bullish. When it drops below 50% and/or is trending down, there's trouble ahead.

> ☑ HINT: *The longer the time span of the MA, the greater the significance of a crossover signal. An 18-month chart is more reliable than a 30-day one.*

Buying Power

Buying power basically refers to the amount of money available to buy securities. It is determined by the cash in brokerage accounts plus the dollar amount that would be available if securities were fully margined. The bottom line: The market cannot rise above the available buying power.

The principle here is that at any point investors have only so much money available for investments. If it's in money market funds and cash, their buying power is stored up and readily available, not only to move into stocks but to push up prices. By contrast, if most investor buying power is already in stocks, there's little left for purchasing more stocks. In fact, in this situation investors could actually push the price of stocks down should they begin to sell.

Buying power is shown by these indicators:

- *Rising volume in rallies.* Investors are eager to buy, so the demand is greater than the supply, and prices go up.
- *Shrinking volume on market declines.* Investors are reluctant to sell.

With this technical approach, volume is the key indicator: It rises on rallies when the trend is up and rises on reactions when the trend is down.

> ☑ HINT: *Volume trends are apt to reverse before price trends. Shrinking volume almost always shows*

up before the top of a bull market and before the bottom of a bear market.

One other measure of buying power is the percentage of cash held in mutual funds. The Investment Company Institute in Washington, D.C., publishes this figure every month. In general, the ratio of cash to total assets in mutual funds tends to be low during market peaks, because this is the time when everyone is eager to buy stocks. The ratio is high during bull markets.

> ☑ HINT: *When cash holdings, as compiled by the Investment Company Institute, are above 7%, it's considered favorable; 9% to 10% is out-and-out bullish.*

Most Active Stocks

This list is published at the top of daily or weekly reports of the NYSE, AMEX, and Nasdaq, and it gives the high, low, and last prices and change of 10 to 15 volume leaders. Here's where you can spot popular and unpopular industry groups and stocks.

Forget about the big-name companies, such as Exxon, GE, and IBM. They have so many shares outstanding that trading is always heavy. Watch for repetition: of one industry or of one company. When the same names appear several times in a

---

London's Financial Times Index

The Financial Times Index is a British version of the Dow Jones Industrial Average. It records data on the London Stock Exchange: prices, volume, etc. Because it reflects worldwide business attitudes, it's a fairly reliable indicator of what's ahead, in two weeks to two months, for the NYSE.

There are, of course, temporary aberrations due to local situations, but over many years it has been a valuable technical tool. Since London is five hours ahead of New York, early risers benefit the most.

NYSE Biggest % Movers

WINNERS					LOSERS				
NAME	VOLUME	CLOSE	CHANGE	% CHG.	NAME	VOLUME	CLOSE	CHANGE	% CHG.
BetzDearb	62986	$67^{11}/_{16}$	$+31^{13}/_{16}$	+88.7	AGCO	20157	$13^{11}/_{16}$	$-2^{1}/_{16}$	−13.1
Pediatrx	3046	$39^{7}/_{8}$	+6	+17.7	WellptHlt	53613	64	$-7^{5}/_{8}$	−10.6
GrhmFl	8752	$5^{9}/_{16}$	$+^{13}/_{16}$	+17.1	AMF n	3802	$16^{3}/_{8}$	$-1^{7}/_{8}$	−10.3
MedPart	19025	$5^{7}/_{16}$	$+^{11}/_{16}$	+14.5	Bally TotF	20560	$26^{7}/_{8}$	$-3^{1}/_{16}$	−10.2
GuangRy	1482	$5^{11}/_{16}$	$+^{11}/_{16}$	+13.8	Vestalns	2613	$15^{5}/_{16}$	$-1^{5}/_{8}$	−9.6

SOURCE: Barron's.

AMEX Biggest % Movers

WINNERS					LOSERS				
NAME	VOLUME	CLOSE	CHANGE	% CHG.	NAME	VOLUME	CLOSE	CHANGE	% CHG.
ColLb	5387	$8^{5}/_{8}$	$+1^{3}/_{16}$	+16.0	Hmisph wt	1748	$4^{1}/_{4}$	$-^{3}/_{4}$	−15.0
Comforce	283	$8^{3}/_{4}$	$+^{3}/_{16}$	+10.2	PLC Sys	7277	8	$-1^{3}/_{8}$	−14.7
Westwr wt	64	$23^{1}/_{8}$	$+2^{1}/_{8}$	+10.1	Hemispx	13218	$8^{1}/_{8}$	$-^{7}/_{8}$	−9.7
EngyRsh	188	$18^{7}/_{8}$	$+1^{5}/_{8}$	+9.4	Heico A n	123	$23^{3}/_{4}$	$-1^{7}/_{8}$	−7.3
GetchGld	1748	$14^{1}/_{4}$	$+^{13}/_{16}$	+9.1	PLM	101	$6^{3}/_{8}$	$-^{1}/_{2}$	−7.3

SOURCE: Barron's.

Nasdaq Biggest % Movers

WINNERS					LOSERS				
NAME	VOLUME	CLOSE	CHANGE	% CHG.	NAME	VOLUME	CLOSE	CHANGE	% CHG.
InControl	11662	$5^{13}/_{16}$	$+1^{13}/_{16}$	+45.3	Friendly n	23382	$8^{1}/_{8}$	$-3^{7}/_{8}$	−32.3
ThinkNw	11944	$22^{1}/_{2}$	$+5^{3}/_{16}$	+30.0	Accelr8	8874	$4^{3}/_{8}$	$-1^{5}/_{8}$	−27.1
GilmC wt	27	$9^{5}/_{8}$	+2	+26.2	NewsEdge	11771	$6^{5}/_{8}$	$-2^{1}/_{4}$	−25.4
PSC	4713	$8^{1}/_{8}$	$+1^{5}/_{8}$	+25.0	Marten s	166	$13^{1}/_{2}$	$-3^{1}/_{2}$	−20.6
RuthMoran	1450	14	$+2^{5}/_{8}$	+23.1	Magabio n	209	$5^{1}/_{4}$	$-1^{13}/_{16}$	−18.4

SOURCE: Barron's.

week or two, something is happening. Major investors are involved: buying if the price continues to rise, selling if it falls.

Watch most-actives for:

■ *Newcomers, especially small- or medium-sized corporations.* When the same company pops up again and again, major shareholders are worried (price drop) or optimistic (price rise).

Because volume requires substantial re-sources, the buyers must be big-money orga-nizations. Once they have bought, you can move in, if the other fundamentals are sound.

- *Companies in the same industry.* Stocks tend to move as a group. Activity in computer retail-ers such as IBM and Apple could signal inter-est in this field.

Percentage Leaders

This list is published weekly in several financial journals. It's primarily for those seeking to catch a few points on a continuing trend.

Although the value of the percentage leaders list has diminished recently because of the high gains scored by takeover or buyout candidates, it is still a way to spot some potential winners and to avoid losers. If you're thinking about making a move, check this list first. You may find several yet undiscovered stocks moving up in price.

Advances versus Declines (A/D)

This is a measure of the number of stocks that have advanced in price and the number that have de-clined within a given time span. Expressed as a ratio, the A/D illustrates the general direction of the market: When more stocks advance than de-cline on a single trading day, the market is thought

NYSE Advances and Declines: Highs and Lows

NYSE	WED	TUE	WK AGO
Issues traded	2,267	2,282	2,268
Advances	821	1,010	883
Declines	881	698	829
Unchanged	565	574	556
New highs	72	62	91
New lows	13	19	10

SOURCE: Wall Street Journal.

By Dollar Volume: NYSE

NAME	VOLUME	CLOSE	CHANGE
MicronTch	22834268	$89^7/_8$	$+13^1/_2$
IBM	20353360	$98^7/_8$	$-3^7/_8$
TexInstr	8178621	$78^3/_4$	$+6^1/_4$
Chrysler	7634676	$57^3/_4$	$+3^1/_8$
Motorola	7270874	$79^5/_8$	$+5^1/_8$

SOURCE: Barron's.

to be bullish. The A/D can be an excellent guide to the trend of the overall market and, occasionally, of specific industry or stock groups. The best way to utilize A/D data is with a chart where the lines are plotted to show the cumulative difference between the advances and the declines on the NYSE or, for speculative holdings, on the AMEX. The total can cover one week, 21 days, or whatever period you choose, but because you're looking for developing trends, it should not be too long.

To spot trouble ahead, compare the A/D chart with that of the DJIA. If the Dow is moving up for a month or so but the A/D line is flat or dropping, that's a negative signal. Watch out for new highs and lows on the A/D chart. Near market peaks, the A/D line will almost invariably top out and start declining before the overall market. At market lows, the A/D line seldom gives a far-in-advance warning.

Be cautious about using the A/D line alone. Make sure that it is confirmed by other indicators or, better yet, confirms other signals.

Volume

Trading volume, or the number of shares traded, is an important indicator in interpreting market di-rection and stock price changes. Changes in stock prices are the result of supply and demand; that is, the number of people who want to buy a stock and the number who want to sell. The key point here is that a rise or fall in price on a small volume of shares traded is far less important than a move supported by heavy volume. When there's heavy trading on the up side, buyers control the market, and their enthusiasm for the stock often pushes its price even higher.

☑ HINT: *Volume always precedes the direction of a stock's price.*

Momentum

This indicator measures the speed with which an index (or stock) is moving rather than its direction. Index changes are seldom if ever abrupt, so when an already rising index starts to rise even faster, it is thought likely to have a longer continuing upward run.

To measure momentum effectively you need to compare current figures to an index or previous average such as a 30-week moving average or the S&P 500.

New Highs or Lows

Every day the newspaper prints a list of stocks that hit a new price high or low for the year during the previous day's trading activity. Technical analysts use the ratio between the new highs and the new lows as an indication of the market's direction. They believe that when more stocks are making new highs than new lows, it's a bullish indication. If there are more lows than highs, pessimism abounds.

☑ HINT: *You should not use these figures as an absolute prediction of the future course of the market, because for a while a number of the same stocks will appear again and again. Also, the further into the year it is, the more difficult it is for a stock to continually post new highs.*

These figures are most effective when converted to a chart and compared with a standard av-

erage. As long as the high and low indicators stay more or less in step with the Dow Jones Industrial Average or the S&P 500, they are simply a handy confirmation. But when the high-low line starts to dip while the average moves up, watch out: Internal market conditions are deteriorating.

This index of highs and lows exposes the underlying strength or weakness of the stock market, which is too often masked by the action of the DJIA. In an aging bull market, the DJIA may continue to rise, deceptively showing strength by the upward moves of a handful of major stocks; but closer examination will usually reveal that most stocks are too far below their yearly highs to make new peaks. At such periods, the small number of new highs is one of the most significant manifestations of internal market deterioration. The reverse is the telltale manner in which the total number of new lows appears in bear markets.

USING THE INDICATORS

Never rely on just one technical indicator. Only rarely can a single chart, ratio, average, MA, or index be 100% accurate. When an indicator breaks its pattern, look for confirmation from at least two other guidelines. Then wait a bit: at least two days in an ebullient market, a week or more in a normal one. This won't be easy, but what you are seeking is confirmation. These days a false move can be costly.

This emphasis on consensus applies also to newsletters, advisory services, and recommendations. If you select only one, look for a publication that uses—and explains—several indicators. Better yet, study two or three.

FOR FURTHER INFORMATION

Robert D. Edwards and John Magee, *Technical Analysis of Stock Trends* (New York: AMACON, 1997).

Martin Pring, *Technical Analysis Explained*, 4th ed. (New York: McGraw-Hill, 1997).

D

Where, What, When: Stock Exchanges, Indexes, and Economic Indicators

*I*n keeping with Wall Street jargon and financial reporting, initials are used frequently. Here are some of the most widely used.

EXCHANGES

NYSE: New York Stock Exchange, 11 Wall Street, New York, NY 10005; 212–656–3000, or click on: www.nyse.com. This is the oldest and largest exchange in the United States. To be listed, a corporation must:

■ Demonstrate earning power of $2.5 million before federal income taxes for the most recent year and $2 million pretax for each of the preceding two years

■ Have net tangible assets of $40 million

■ Have market value of publicly held shares of $40 million

■ Report a total of 1.1 million common shares publicly held

■ Have 2,000 holders of 100 shares or more

AMEX: American Stock Exchange, 86 Trinity Place, New York, NY 10026; 212–306–1000, or click on: www.nasdaq-amex.com. These corporations are generally smaller and less financially strong than those on the NYSE. To be listed, a corporation must have:

■ Pretax income of at least $750,000 in its last fiscal year or in two of the last three

■ Market value of public float: $3 million

■ Stockholders' equity of $4 million

■ Minimum price of stock: $3

NOTE: There are alternate financial guidelines: see website.

Nasdaq: This is the market for securities that are not listed on major exchanges. The trading is conducted by dealers who are members of NASD (National Association of Securities Dealers, 1735 K Street NW, Washington, DC 20006; 202–728–8000) and who may or may not be members of other exchanges. Trading is by bid and asked prices. The primary market is Nasdaq (National Association of Securities Dealers Automated Quotations), which consists of about 5,400 of the most actively traded issues. Some 13,000 other stocks are quoted in daily financial summaries. The website is: www.nasd.com.

CBOE: Chicago Board of Options Exchange, 400 South LaSalle at Van Buren, Chicago, IL 60605; 312–786–5600. The major auction market for calls and puts, primarily on NYSE stocks, and recently for special types of options, such as those on Treasury bonds and on the S&P 100 and 500.

ACC: AMEX Options Exchange, 86 Trinity Place, New York, NY 10006; 212–306–1000. The division of AMEX that trades puts and calls, almost entirely on NYSE-listed and OTC stocks.

CBT: Chicago Board of Trade, 141 West Jackson Boulevard, Chicago, IL 60604; 312–435–3500.

A major market for futures contracts: commodities, interest rate securities, commercial paper, etc.

NYCE: New York Cotton Exchange, 4 World Trade Center, New York, NY 10048; 212–742–5800. Trading in futures in cotton and orange juice.

KCBT: Kansas City Board of Trade, 4800 Main Street, Suite 303, Kansas City, MO 64112; 816–753–7500. Trades in futures of commodities and Value Line futures index.

NYFE: New York Futures Exchange, 4 World Trade Center, New York, NY 10048; 212–748–1248. A wholly owned subsidiary of the NYSE that trades in the NYSE Composite Index futures contract.

NYME: New York Mercantile Exchange, 1 North End Avenue, New York, NY 10282; 212–299–2000. Trading in futures of petroleum, platinum, and palladium.

FEDERAL AGENCIES

SEC: Securities and Exchange Commission, 450 Fifth Street NW, Washington, DC 20549; 202–942–7040. A federal agency established to help protect investors. It is responsible for administering congressional acts regarding securities, stock exchanges, corporate reporting, investment companies, investment advisers, and public utility holding companies.

FRB: Federal Reserve Board, 20th and C Streets NW, Washington, DC 20551; 202–452–3000. The federal agency responsible for control of such important investment items as the discount rate, money supply, and margin requirements.

FDIC: Federal Deposit Insurance Corporation, 550 17th Street NW, Washington, DC 20429; 800–934–3342. An agency that insures bank deposits.

SAIF: Savings Association Insurance Fund, 550 17th Street NW, Washington, DC 20429;

Other Stock Exchanges

UNITED STATES

Boston Stock Exchange 1 Boston Place, 38th floor Boston, MA 02108	617–723–9500
Chicago Stock Exchange 440 S. LaSalle Street Chicago, IL 60605	312–663–2222
Pacific Stock Exchange 301 Pine Street San Francisco, CA 94104 or	415–393–4000
233 South Beaudry Avenue Los Angeles, CA 90012	213–977–4500
Philadelphia Stock Exchange 1900 Market Street Philadelphia, PA 19103	215–496–5000

CANADA

Alberta Stock Exchange 300 Fifth Avenue SW Calgary, Alberta T2P 3C4	403–974–7400
Montreal Stock Exchange 800 Victoria Square (4th floor) Montreal, Quebec H4Z 1A9	514–871–2424
Toronto Stock Exchange Exchange Tower 130 King Street West Toronto, Ontario M5X 1J2	416–947–4700
Vancouver Stock Exchange 609 Granville Street/Box 10333 Vancouver, British Columbia V7Y 1H1	604–689–3334
Winnipeg Stock Exchange 620 One Lombard Place Winnipeg, Manitoba R3B 0X3	204–987–7070

800–934–3342. An agency that insures deposits with savings and loan associations.

CFTC: Commodity Futures Trading Commission, 1155 21st Street NW, Washington, DC 20581; 202–481–5025. This is a watchdog for the commodities futures trading industry.

STOCK MARKET AVERAGES

These indicators are used to measure and report value changes in representative stock groupings.

An average is simply the arithmetic mean of a group of prices. An index is an average expressed in relation to an earlier established base market value. Indexes and averages may be broad-based (made up of many stocks) or narrow-based (made up of stocks in a particular sector or industry).

Dow Jones Industrial Average (DJIA). The oldest and most widely used stock market average. It shows the action of 30 actively traded blue-

Stocks in Dow Jones Averages as of October 1999

Industrials (DJIA)

Alcoa*	Du Pont, E.I.	McDonald's Corp.
Allied Signal	Eastman Kodak	Merck & Co.
American Express	Exxon Corporation	Minnesota Mining & Manufacturing
AT&T	General Electric	J.P. Morgan
Boeing	General Motors	Philip Morris Co.
Caterpillar	Goodyear Tire	Procter & Gamble
Chevron	Hewlett-Packard	Sears, Roebuck & Co.
Citigroup	International Business Machines	Union Carbide
Coca-Cola	International Paper	United Technologies
Disney (Walt)	Johnson & Johnson	Wal-Mart Stores

Transportation (DJTA)

Airborne Freight	FedEx	Southwest Airlines
Alexander & Baldwin	GATX Corp.	UAL Corp.
AMR Corp.	Hunt (J.B.)	Union Pacific Corp.
Burlington Northern	Norfolk & Southern	U.S. Airways
CNF Transport	Northwest Airlines	U.S. Freight
CSX Corp.	Roadway Express	Yellow Corp.
Delta Airlines	Ryder Systems	

Utility (DJUA)

American Electric Power	Edison International	Reliant Energy
Columbia Energy	ENRON	Southern Company
Consolidated Edison	Pacific Gas & Electric	Texas Utilities
Consolidated Natural Gas	PECO Energy	Unicom Corp.
Duke Energy	Public Service Enterprises	Williams Companies

*Aluminum Co. of America

chip stocks, representing about 15% of NYSE values.

This popular indicator of the direction of the stock market was devised in 1884 by Charles H. Dow, a founder and first editor of the *Wall Street Journal*. At that time it was simply a list of the average closing prices of 11 railroad and manufacturing stocks, published in *The Customer's Afternoon Letter,* a forerunner of the *Journal*.

The Dow average is determined by adding up the closing prices of the component stocks and using a divisor that is adjusted for splits and stock dividends. The average is quoted in points, not dollars. Initially the divisor was 11; in the 1920s it became 30, when the number of stocks was increased from 11 to 30; today it is .24275214. Each Dow Jones Average—transportation, utility, and industrials (**see:** table on page 401)—measures the stocks' performance during one day. The Dow Jones Composite Index, also called the 65 Stock Average, combines the other three indexes and consists of 30 industrials, 20 transportation, and 15 utility stocks. It is not widely followed.

☑ *HINT: Last year (1998) Waterhouse Securities launched the first no-load, no-transaction-fee index fund to track the total return of the Dow. It invests primarily in the Dow 30. The minimum investment is just $1,000; if you sign up for the free Periodic Investing Program, the monthly minimum is only $100. For information: 800–301–3026, or click on: www.waterhouse.com*

Recent Trends

For many years the Dow Jones Industrial Average hovered around 100, peaking at 386 in 1929 just before the crash. Afterwards it climbed back up slowly, never moving much past 200 until World War II, when it hit 700. In 1966 it reached 1,000. It fell again to 570 in 1974 only to return to 1,000 two years later. In August 1987 the Dow posted an all-time high of 2,722.42, but two months later, on October 19, it plunged a record 508 points to 1,738.74. Since then there have been numerous ups and downs. In early July 1988 the Dow reached 2,158.61, the highest point since the October crash. A year later, in July 1989, it was 2,456.56. As we went to press in the fall, it was 11,326.

The Dow is often criticized for the fact that a high-priced stock has a greater impact on the average than lower-priced issues. In other words, the stocks are not equally weighted, so on any given day, a fluctuation of significance in one or two high-priced stocks can distort the average. The Dow, then, captures absolute price movement without regard to current share price or market capitalization. A $1 change in the price of a lower-priced stock has the same effect as a $1 change in a higher-priced stock.

As a result, the Dow is useful for tracking the direction of the market over the long term, but is often less reliable on a daily or even weekly basis. With only 30 stocks, it is also regarded by many as too small.

Standard & Poor's Composite Index of 500 Stocks. This index addresses some of the criticism of the Dow. Unlike the Dow, the S&P 500 is market-weighted—that is, its component stocks are weighted according to the total market value of their outstanding shares. The result: The impact of any single component's price change is proportional to its overall market value. Devised in 1957, the S&P 500 covers 500 stocks and is computed by multiplying the price of each stock by the number of shares outstanding. This gives larger and more influential corporations more weight and, many think, makes it a better general measure than the Dow.

The 500 stocks consist mainly of NYSE-listed companies, with some AMEX and OTC stocks. There are 400 industrials, 60 transportation and utility companies, and 40 financial issues. Options on this index trade on the Chicago Board of Options Exchange and futures on the Chicago Mercantile Exchange.

Standard & Poor's 400 Midcap Index. Introduced in June 1991, this index is comprised of 400 domestic companies. The median market capitalization of stocks in the index is $610 million versus about $2.2 billion for stocks in the S&P 500. It is a market-weighted index (stock price times shares outstanding).

Standard & Poor's 100 Stock Index. This consists of stocks for which options are listed on the Chicago Board of Options Exchange. Options on the 100 Index are listed on the Chicago Board Options Exchange and futures on the Chicago Mercantile Exchange.

Wilshire 5000 Equity Index. This value-weighted index is derived from the dollar value of 5,000 common stocks, including all those listed on the NYSE and AMEX and the most active OTC issues. It is the broadest index and thus is more representative of the overall market. Unfortunately, it has not received adequate publicity. The Wilshire is prepared by Wilshire Associates in Santa Monica, California. No futures or options are traded on the Wilshire.

NYSE Composite Index. A market-value-weighted index covering the price movements of all common stocks listed on the Big Board. It is based on the prices at the close of trading on December 31, 1965, and is weighted according to the number of shares listed for each issue. The base value is $50. Point changes are converted to dollars and cents to provide a meaningful measure of price action. Futures are traded on the NYFE and options on the NYSE itself.

Nasdaq-Composite Index. This represents all domestic OTC stocks except those having only one market maker. It covers a total of 3,500 stocks and is market-value weighted. No futures or options are traded.

Value Line Composite Index. This is an equally weighted index of 1,700 NYSE, AMEX, and OTC stocks tracked by the *Value Line Investment Survey.* Designed to reflect price changes of typical industrial stocks, it is neither price- nor market-value weighted. Options trade on the Philadelphia Exchange and futures on the Kansas City Board of Trade.

AMEX Major Market Index. Price-weighted, which means that high-priced stocks have a greater influence than low-priced ones, this is an average of 20 blue-chip industrials. It was designed to mirror the Dow Jones Industrial Average and measure representative performance of these kinds of issues. Although produced by the AMEX, it includes stocks listed on the NYSE. Futures are traded on the Chicago Board of Trade.

AMEX Market Value Index. This is a capitalization-weighted index that measures the collective performance of more than 90% of AMEX-listed companies, including ADRs, warrants, and common stocks. Cash dividends are assumed to be reinvested. Options are traded on the AMEX.

Dow Jones Bond Average. This consists of bonds of ten public utilities and ten industrial corporations.

Barron's Confidence Index. Weekly index of corporate bond yields published by *Barron's,* the financial newspaper owned by Dow Jones. It shows the ratio of the average yield of ten high-grade bonds to the Dow Jones average yield on 40 bonds. The premise is that when investors feel confident about the economy they buy lower-rated bonds.

Bond Buyer's Index. Published daily, it measures municipal bonds.

Market Indicators, Indexes, and Averages

Whether you're bullish, bearish, or uncertain, you can get a reading on the direction of the market, interest rates, and the overall economy by following some of the key statistics (or indicators) regularly churned out by Wall Street and Washington. These should be regarded not as gospel but rather as tools to help you make informed and intelligent decisions about your investments and for timing moves between stocks, bonds, and cash equivalents. Make a point of jotting down these numbers on your own chart and track the trends. You will see definite patterns between the market, interest rates, and the money supply. (The indicators are presented in alphabetical order.)

ECONOMIC INDICATOR	COMPOSITION	WHAT IT PREDICTS
Consumer Price Index (CPI)	The average price of consumer goods and services	The direction of inflation and changes in the purchasing power of money
Dollar index	The value of the dollar as measured against major foreign currencies	Domestic corporate profits and multinational earning power
Dow Jones Industrial Average (DJIA)	30 major companies whose stock is held by many institutions and individuals; index is price-weighted so that moves in high-priced stocks exert more influence than those of lower-priced stock	Action of the stock market, which in turn anticipates future business activity
Employment figures and payroll employment	Number of people working or on company payrolls	Potential consumer spending, which in turn affects corporate profits
Gross domestic product (GDP)	Total goods and services produced in United States on an annual basis; inflation can distort the accuracy of this figure, so subtract inflation from GDP to get "real" GDP	General business trends and economic activity
Index of industrial production (IIP)	Shown as a percentage of the average, which has been tracked since 1967; base is 100	Amount of business volume
Money supply: M1	Currency held by the public plus balances in checking accounts, NOW accounts, traveler's checks, and money market funds	Extent of consumer purchasing power and liquidity of public's assets, used by Federal Reserve as a gauge for predicting as well as controlling the pace of the economy; when M1 shows a big increase, the Fed usually reduces the money supply, which sends interest rates up; Fed reduces M1 by selling Treasuries; tightening of M1 serves to curb inflation; an increase in M1 fuels inflation
M2	M1 plus time deposits over $100,000 and repurchase agreements	
M3	M2 plus T-bills, U.S. savings bonds, bankers' acceptances, term Eurodollars, commercial paper	

Market Indicators, Indexes, and Averages *(continued)*

ECONOMIC INDICATOR	COMPOSITION	WHAT IT PREDICTS
Standard & Poor's 500 stock index	Indexed value of 500 stocks from NYSE, AMEX, and OTC; more useful than the Dow Jones Industrial Average, because it's broader; includes 400 industrials, 40 public utilities, 20 transportations, and 40 financials; stocks are market-value weighted; that is, price of each stock is multiplied by the number of shares outstanding	Direction of the economy and the market; good leading indicator, because the market tends to anticipate future economic conditions
3-month Treasury bill rate	Interest rate paid to purchasers of T-bills	General direction of interest rates; gives indication of the Federal Reserve system's fiscal policy; for example, during a recession, the Fed increases the amount of available currency to lower the T-bill rate; during inflation, currency is reduced and the T-bill rate rises; rising interest rates tend to reduce corporate profits because of the increased costs of borrowing; therefore, a continual rise in T-bill rates presages a decline in the stock market; falling rates help stock and bond prices
Wage settlements	Percentage changes in wages that come about because of new labor contracts	Price changes for goods and services; sharply higher wage settlements result in higher inflation rates

E

Glossary
Wall Street Jargon Made Simple

adjustable rate mortgage (ARM): A mortgage whose interest rate shifts, typically twice a year, to reflect general changes in interest rates.

after-tax contributions: Money that you've paid income tax on that is contributed to your savings plan; also called voluntary contributions. Because you have paid taxes on this money when you earned it, it cannot be mingled with the pretax money you or your employer contributed to your savings plan.

all or none order (AON): An order in which the customer wants to execute an entire buy or sell at once price. The order does not have to be executed immediately, but it must be executed in its entirety on the same transaction.

alternative minimum tax: A special income tax for high earners with certain tax-exempt investments.

American Depository Receipts (ADRs): A security, created by a U.S. bank, showing ownership of a certain number of shares of a foreign stock; certificates are held in a depository or bank in the country of the issuing company. ADRs trade on the exchanges.

amortization: Gradual reduction of a debt by a series of periodic payments. Each payment includes interest on the outstanding debt and part of the principal.

annuity: A contract, usually sold by an insurance company, that makes periodic payments to the person who holds it (the annuitant) at a future date, usually beginning at retirement. A fixed annuity pays a guaranteed rate; a variable an-

nuity produces investment returns that are tied to the performance of the market. An immediate income annuity begins income payments right away. A deferred annuity can be fixed or variable and keeps your investment growing, shielded from taxes until you begin withdrawals.

arbitrage: Profiting from price differences when a security, currency, or commodity is traded on different markets. Also, to buy shares in a company that is about to be taken over and sell short the shares of the acquiring company.

asked price: The lowest price at which a security is offered for sale.

asset: A possession that has present and future financial value to its owner.

asset allocation fund: A mutual fund that allocates its assets among stocks, bonds, and money market securities. As the market and economic conditions change, the fund manager shifts assets among the particular industry categories to maximize returns and protect the principal.

ATMs: Automated teller machines, located primarily at banks. Upon insertion of a magnetically coded bank identification card, the computer-controlled machine dispenses cash that you request or deposits money to your account and indicates the status of your account on a viewing screen. No teller is necessary. The majority of ATMs are open 24 hours.

automatic dividend reinvestment (ADR): A plan in which shareholders can elect to have their dividends automatically used to purchase additional shares of stock instead of receiving a cash dividend payment.

back-end load: A commission paid when you sell mutual fund shares; also known as redemption fees. They may be eliminated after you've owned your shares a certain number of years.

balance sheet: A statement showing the financial condition of a company at a given point in time. It includes assets, liabilities, and net worth. The term comes from the fact that assets always equal, or balance, the liabilities plus net worth.

basis point: One hundredth of 1%; used in discussing bond yields. For example, 1% equals 100 basis points, and a yield rise from 5.40% to 5.50% is a 10 basis-point increase.

bearer bond: A bond certificate held by the owner with coupons that are detached and presented in order to collect the interest due. It is not registered to an owner on the books of the issuer; it is owned by the person holding or bearing the certificate.

bear market: A sharp, prolonged decline in the price of stocks, usually brought on by a slowing economy. A bear fights by slapping downward with his paws, thus the phrase for a downward market.

beneficiary: The person(s) named to receive your benefits in the event of your death.

beta: A number that compares the price volatility of a stock with that of the overall market. A beta of less than one indicates less volatility and risk than the market; a beta of over one indicates higher risk than the market. The market's beta is always one.

bid price: The highest price that a buyer is willing to pay for a security.

block trade: A purchase or sale of a large quantity of stock, usually 10,000 shares or more.

blue chip: The common stock of a well-known national company with a history of earnings growth and dividend increases, such as Exxon or General Electric.

blue-sky laws: State laws that require issuers of securities to register their offerings with the state before they can be sold to its residents.

bond: A security that represents debt of the issuing corporation. Usually the issuer is required to pay the bondholder a specified rate of interest for a specified time and then repay the entire debt (also known as face value) upon maturity.

book value: The current net worth of a company—i.e., its assets minus its liabilities divided by the number of shares on the market. If a stock's price is lower than its book value and the company is financially solid, it is considered a bargain.

breakpoint: The dollar amount at which the sales charge or commission is discounted when you make a large mutual fund purchase; breakpoints tend to be at $50,000, $100,000, $250,000, $500,000 and $1 million.

bullion: Gold or silver sold in bars called ingots.

bullion coins: A coin whose value resides only in the precious metal it contains.

bull market: A sharp, prolonged rise in the price of stocks that usually last at least several months, often much longer, and consists of high trading volume. A bull attacks by thrusting upward, thus the term for an upward market.

call: An option for the right to buy a stock.

call date: A feature of many bonds giving the issuer the right to call in or redeem the bonds before their maturity date.

capital: Also called capital assets; property or money from which a person or business receives some monetary gain.

capital gains: Profits from the rising price of an investment.

capitalization: A firm's capital structure, composed of total securities issued by a corporation, including bonds, debentures, preferred and common stock, and all surpluses.

cash equivalents: The generic term for assorted short-term instruments such as U.S. Treasury securities, CDs, and money market fund shares, which can be readily converted into cash.

cash flow: Net income plus other noncash charges, such as depreciation and amortization. Cash flow determines a company's ability to pay its dividends to shareholders.

cash flow multiple: Price of a stock divided by its cash flow per share.

central asset or combo account: Brokerage, money market fund, and checking account combined with a credit card. Offered by both banks and brokerage houses, some central asset accounts include forms of life insurance, mortgages, traveler's checks, and other special features.

certificates of deposit: Also called CDs or "time certificates"; official receipts issued by a bank stating that a given amount of money has been deposited for a certain length of time at a specified rate of interest. CDs are insured by the U.S. government for up to $100,000.

charts: Records of price and volume trends as well as the general movement of stock and bond markets, economic cycles, industries and individual companies, updated continually. Chartists believe that past history as expressed on a chart gives a strong clue to the next price movement. They "read" the lines to determine what a stock has done and may do.

class A & B shares: Some companies issue two or more classes of stock, typically with one having controlling voting rights but both sharing equally in dividends. Reason: to sell one class to the public and keep second class for the company's founders.

closed-end fund: Mutual funds that issue limited numbers of shares and then are traded on stock exchanges as common stocks.

COBRA: Federal law requiring companies with 20 or more employees to offer departing workers the option of continued medical coverage for at least 18 months. Widows can get even longer coverage. You receive the same coverage, but you pay the premiums, which legally can be up to 102% of your employer's cost. You have only 30 days upon leaving a company to file a COBRA request.

commodities: Anything in which contracts for future delivery may be traded, such as precious metals, food, grain, oil, U.S. Treasury securities, foreign currencies, and stock indexes.

common stock: *See* stock, common.

compound interest: The amount earned on the original principal plus the accumulated interest. With interest on interest plus interest on principal, an investment grows more rapidly.

confirmation: A printed acknowledgment of the purchase or sale of a security, sent to the customer by the brokerage firm or mutual fund company.

convertibles: Bonds, debentures, or preferred stock that may be exchanged or converted into common stock.

correction: A reverse downward in the prices of stocks, bonds, or commodities.

cost of living adjustment: A boost in wages, Social Security, or a pension designed to offset the impact of inflation.

credit card: A plastic card issued by a bank or financial institution that gives the holder access to a line of credit to purchase goods or receive cash. Repayment may be required in full in 30 days or in installments. *Compare with* debit card.

current assets: Cash, inventory, accounts receivable, and other assets that can be converted to cash in a relatively short time, usually within a year.

CUSIP number: A nine-character code on the face of each stock certificate that is assigned to a security by Standard & Poor's Corp. It helps expedite the settlement process. It stands for Committee on Uniform Security Identification Procedures.

custodian: The financial institution responsible for the safekeeping of your investment assets.

cyclical stocks: Stocks that tend to rise quickly in price when the economy heats up and fall quickly when it cools. Examples: housing, automobile, and heavy equipment stocks.

day order: A buy or sell order that is valid only until the close of trading on the day it is placed.

debenture: An unsecured bond backed only by the general credit of the company.

debit card: A deposit access card that debits the holder's bank account or money market account immediately upon use in purchasing. There is no grace period in which to pay; payment is transferred immediately and electronically at the moment of purchase.

defensive stock: A stock not subject to changes in the business cycle, such as food stores and manufacturers, and utility companies.

defined-benefit plan: A pension that promises to pay a specified amount to all employees who complete a set number of years of work. In many plans, employers make all the contributions and invest them.

defined-contribution plan: Usually called a 401(k) or salary-reduction plan. It allows employees to contribute up to 10% of their pretax salaries to various investment funds. The account grows tax free, but employees who select funds that perform poorly have no recourse.

depreciation: An accounting method for recovering the cost of fixed assets, such as plant and equipment. The cost is amortized over the depreciable life of the assets and is considered a noncash expense.

derivative: A financial instrument whose value derives from the performance of an underlying asset, such as a stock, bond, currency rate, or market index.

diamonds: A unit investment trust that lets you invest in a basket of the 30 stocks that make up the large-cap Dow Jones Industrial Average. Diamonds (DIA) trade on the American Stock Exchange and are designed to trade at about $1/100$th of the value of the DJIA. Shares can be traded through a broker; you can even "short" the market if you think the Dow is headed down. The trust pays dividends monthly.

discount rate: The interest rate the Federal Reserve charges member banks; it provides a floor for interest rates that banks then charge their customers.

discretionary account: A brokerage firm account in which the customer gives the broker permission to buy and sell securities on the customer's behalf.

disinflation: A reduction in the rate of ongoing inflation.

distribution: The income and capital gains paid by a mutual fund to its shareholders.

dividends: A portion of the company's net profits distributed to its shareholders; usually a fixed amount for each share of stock held and paid quarterly in cash; dividends also may be in the form of property, script, or stock. Dividends must be voted on by the company's directors before each payment.

DJIA (Dow Jones Industrial Average): Price-weighted average of 30 blue-chip stocks, representing overall price movements of all stocks on the New York Stock Exchange.

downtick: A transaction executed at a price lower than the preceding transaction in the same security; opposite of an uptick.

earnings per share: A company's net income divided by the total number of outstanding shares.

effective annual yield: Rate of return earned on your savings if you do not incur service charges or penalties.

emerging markets: Geographical areas with developing economies and markets, such as Asia, Eastern Europe, and parts of Latin America.

employee stock ownership: Called an ESOP plan, it encourages workers to buy their employer's stock, usually at a reduced price.

equity: Stocks or ownership interest held by shareholders in a corporation as opposed to bonds. In a brokerage account, the market value of securities minus the amount borrowed.

ex-dividend date: The date on or after which a security begins trading without the dividend included in the contract price.

face value: Value of a bond or note when issued. Corporate bonds are usually issued with $1,000 face value; municipals with $5,000; T-bills with $10,000. Also called par value.

FDIC (Federal Deposit Insurance Corporation): An independent agency of the U.S. government whose basic purpose is to insure bank deposits.

fiduciary: An individual or organization that exercises discretionary control or authority over management of someone else's money.

financial futures: Contracts to deliver a specified number of financial instruments at a given price by a certain date, such as U.S. Treasury bonds and bills, GNMA certificates, CDs, and foreign currency.

401(k) plan: One that allows an employee to contribute pretax dollars to a company pool, which is invested in stocks, bonds, or money market instruments; also known as a salary reduction plan.

front running: A trader knowing in advance of a block trade that will affect the price of a security and buying to profit from the trade.

fundamental analysis: The study of a company's past record of sales, earnings, assets, management, and other factors to predict its future.

futures: *See* commodities.

general obligation bonds: Municipal bonds backed by the full faith and credit of a municipality; issued to finance schools, libraries, etc.

going public: When a private company first offers shares to the public.

good until canceled: An order to buy or sell a stock at a specific price that is left in force until executed or canceled by the customer.

guaranteed investment contract: Known as a GIC, it

is a contract between an insurance company and a corporate savings or pension plan that offers a fixed rate of return on the capital invested over the life of the contract. It is not federally insured.

index: A statistical yardstick that measures a whole market by using a representative selection of stocks or bonds. Changes are compared to a base year. Futures are sold on stock indexes, such as the S&P 500.

index arbitrage: Profiting from the difference in prices of the same security. In program trading, traders buy and sell to profit from small price discrepancies, using computers that monitor both the S&P 500 stock index and futures contracts on the index. When there is a larger than normal gap, the computers notify the traders to sell.

index future: A contract to buy or sell an index (S&P 500, for example) at a future date. An index is not an average. *See also:* index.

individual retirement account: Called an IRA, this personal fund defers taxes on the money put in and any income it generates until the owners begin withdrawing their money, which they cannot do without penalty before the age of $59\frac{1}{2}$.

inflation: An increase in the average price level of goods and services over time.

institutions: Organizations that trade huge blocks of securities, such as banks, pension funds, mutual funds, and insurance companies.

interest: Money paid for the use of money. *See also:* discount rate; prime rate.

investment banker: The middleman between the public and a corporation issuing new securities. He/she usually buys a new issue of stocks or bonds directly from the issuing corporation and sells them to individuals and institutions. Investment bankers also act as agents to distribute very large blocks of stocks and bonds.

IPO: Initial public offering; a company's offering of

stock, not previously issued, for sale to the public; aka new issue.

IRA rollover: A technique allowing employees to avoid taxes by transferring lump-sum payments from a 401(k) or a profit-sharing plan into an IRA within 60 days.

junk bonds: High-risk, high-yielding bonds, rated BB or lower.

LBO (leveraged buyout): The purchase of a corporation by using a large amount of debt, much of it short-term bank loans secured by the assets of the company being acquired. After the buying is completed, the acquired company issues bonds to pay off a portion of the debt taken on in the takeover.

liability: A debt; something owed by one person or business to another.

limited partnership: Investment organization in which your liability is limited to the dollar amount you invest; a general partner manages the project, which may be in real estate, farming, oil, and gas.

limit order: An order to buy or sell a security at a specific price or better. A buy limit order is placed below the market price while a sell limit is placed above the market price.

liquid: Cash or investments easily convertible into cash, such as money market funds or bank deposits.

lump-sum distribution: Payment of a retirement account's complete holdings at once, usually when one leaves a job.

"Mae" family: Various mortgage-backed securities either sponsored or partially guaranteed by a handful of government agencies or private corporations, such as the Government National Mortgage Association (GNMA, or "Ginnie Mae") and the Federal Home Loan Mortgage Corporation ("Freddie Mac").

margin: The amount a client deposits with a broker in order to borrow from the broker to buy stocks.

margin loan: A loan from a brokerage firm which is collateralized by the securities in this special account.

market capitalization: Total value of a company's securities on the market; calculated by multiplying the number of outstanding shares by current market price. Large-cap companies have $5 billion or more; mid-cap, between $1 and $5 billion; and small-cap, less than $1 billion.

market order: An order to buy or sell a certain number of shares of a stock at the best possible price at the time the order is given.

mark to the market: The value of any portfolio based on the most recent closing price of the securities held.

material news: Information given out by a company that might affect the value of its stocks or bonds or influence investors' decisions; example: tender offers, very poor or good earnings, a stock split, a corporate event.

mature: To come due; to reach the time when the face value of a bond or note must be paid.

money market fund: A mutual fund that invests only in high-yielding, short-term money market instruments, such as U.S. Treasury bills, bank CDs, and commercial paper. Shareholders receive higher interest on their shares than in a bank money market deposit account.

Moody's: A trademark for issuance of ratings on the relative investment quality of corporate and municipal bonds and for the company's financial publications.

multiple: Price-to-earnings ratio.

municipal bonds: Debt obligations of state and local entities. For the most part, the interest earned is free from federal income tax and often from state and local taxes for residents.

mutual fund: An investment company in which investors' dollars are pooled with those of thousands of others. The combined total is invested by a professional manager in a variety of securities; shares are sold to the public.

net asset value (NAV): The price at which you buy

or sell shares of a mutual fund on a given day. To determine NAV, mutual funds compute their assets daily by adding up the market value of all securities owned by the fund, deducting all liabilities, and dividing the balance by the number of shares outstanding. The NAV per share is the figure quoted in the newspaper.

net worth: Total value (of cash, property, investments) after deducting outstanding expenses and amounts owed.

no-load fund: An open-end investment company that sells shares directly to customers without applying a sales charge.

odd lots: A stock transaction that involves less than 100 shares.

open order: An order to buy or sell a stock that remains in effect until it is either canceled by the customer or executed.

option: The right to buy (call) or sell (put) a certain amount of stock at a given price (strike price) for a specified length of time.

over-the-counter (OTC) stock: A security not listed or traded on a major exchange. Transactions take place by telephone and computer network rather than on the floor of an exchange.

point: A measure of a price change. With a stock, a point change means a change of $1; with a bond that has a $1,000 face value, it refers to a $10 change.

points: Up-front fee charge by the lender in a real-estate deal; separate from interest but designed to increase the overall yield to the lender. A point is 1% of the total principal amount of the loan; on a $100,000 mortgage, 2 points would equal $2,000.

preferred stock: *See* stock, preferred.

premium: Amount by which a bond sells above its par or face value.

price/earnings (P/E) ratio: Price of a stock divided by its earnings per share. Also known as the multiple, it gives investors an idea of how much they are paying for a company's earnings power.

prime rate: Interest rate banks charge their largest and most financially solid business clients; lower than rate charged to consumers.

principal: Face amount of a debt or mortgage on which interest is either owed or earned; balance due on an obligation as separate from interest.

profit-sharing plan: An agreement by which a company makes annual contributions out of its profits to an account for each employee. This money is invested in stocks, bonds, or money-market securities. The funds are tax deferred until the employee leaves the company.

proprietary: Products offered and controlled completely by a financial company, usually a brokerage firm.

prospectus: A printed summary of data that is also a registration statement filed with the SEC in conjunction with a public offering of securities, including mutual funds. It contains information about the company and its business that enables investors to evaluate the security and decide whether or not to buy. Among the data included is information about the company's products, services, facilities, management, and the risks involved. SEC regulations determine what must be set forth in every prospectus.

proxy statement: Information required by the SEC to be given to a corporation's stockholders in order to be able to solicit votes.

public float: The portion of a corporation's outstanding shares that are owned by public investors; in other words, shares not held by the company's officers, directors, or investors who hold a controlling interest in the company.

put: An options contract giving the investor the right to sell a specified number of shares by a certain date at a certain price.

quick ratio: Current assets minus inventory divided by liability; measures financial risk of a company, indicating how much cash, securities, and receivables it has on hand to cover short-term needs; it is also a measure of the market's expectation regarding the company's earnings growth and risk.

real rate of return: The inflation-adjusted rate of return on an investment. If an investor earns a 12% return during a year when inflation is 3%, the real return is 9%.

red herring: A preliminary prospectus issued by underwriters to determine interest in a prospective offering. It must contain a warning, printed in red, that the document does not contain all the information and that some of it may be changed before the final prospectus is made public.

regional stock exchange: A national exchange outside New York City that is registered with the SEC. Examples: Boston, Chicago, Philadelphia, Pacific Coast.

registered representative: A stockbroker. All stockbrokers must be registered before they can do business with the public and must pass qualifying exams given by the NASD.

Regulation T: A Federal Reserve Board rule that governs how much credit stockbrokers can give to customers to purchase securities in margin accounts.

revenue bond: Municipal bond paid off with revenues from the project built with the proceeds; for example, from toll roads, airports, and stadiums.

round lot order: An order to buy or sell stock in multiples of 100 shares; the generally accepted unit of trading.

seat: Term for membership on an exchange, such as the New York Stock Exchange or the American Stock Exchange; gives the holder the right to trade securities on the exchange floor.

SEC (Securities and Exchange Commission): A federal agency with power to enforce federal laws pertaining to the sale of securities and mutual fund shares and the governing of the exchanges, stockbrokers, and financial advisers.

SEC Rule 13d: Requires that anyone acquiring 5% or more stock in any one company file certain disclosure papers with the SEC.

secondary: The market in which existing securities are traded after their initial public offering. Also called the aftermarket.

selling short: Sale of a security that must be borrowed to make delivery. Usually involves the sale of securities that are not owned by the seller in anticipation of making a profit from a decline in the price of the security.

series 7: Exam that qualifies a candidate to be a broker and sell securities.

sharedraft: Interest-bearing checking account at a credit union.

shares outstanding: Shares of a corporation that have been issued to common shareholders.

SIPC (Securities Investor Protection Corporation): An independent agency established by Congress to provide customers of most brokerage firms with protection similar to that provided by the FDIC for bank depositors, in the event that a firm is unable to meet its financial obligations.

split: Division of outstanding shares of a corporation into a larger number of shares. Splits can be 2 for 1, 3 for 1, etc.

spread: The difference between the bid and asked prices of a security; the difference in yields between two fixed-income securities.

stockbroker: An agent who handles the public's orders to buy and sell stocks, bonds, commodities, and mutual funds. A broker may be a partner of a brokerage firm or a registered representative, who is an employee of a brokerage firm. Brokers charge a commission for their services.

stock, common: A security that represents ownership in a corporation.

stock, preferred: A stock that pays a fixed dividend and has first claim on profits over common stocks for payment of that dividend. The dividend does not rise or fall with profits.

stock right: A short-term privilege issued by a corporation to its existing stockholders granting them the right to buy new stock at a stated price.

stock symbol: A letter symbol assigned to a security that is used to identify issues on stock tickers and in automated information-retrieval systems.

street: Jargon for Wall Street and the financial services industry.

strike price: The dollar amount per share at which an option buyer can purchase the underlying stock or a put option buyer can sell the stock. Also called the exercise price.

takeover: When the controlling interest of a corporation is taken over by a new company. Takeovers can be friendly or hostile.

tax bracket: The point on the income tax rate schedules where one's taxable income (income subject to tax after exemptions and deductions) falls. It is expressed as a percentage to be applied to each additional dollar earned over the base amount for that bracket. The current tax brackets for individuals are 15%, 28%, 31%, 36%, and 39.6%.

tax-deferred: Taxes postponed until a later date. Pretax money invested in retirement plans is tax deferred but not tax exempt or tax free, which means that no taxes will ever have to be paid.

tax shelter: An investment that allows one to realize tax benefits by reducing or deferring taxable income.

Taylor's rule: Formula developed by Stanford University economist John B. Taylor that predicts the Federal Reserve's moves.

top heavy: A retirement plan in which the assets of executives are more than 60% of the plan's total assets.

total return: Dividend or interest income plus any capital gain; a better measure of an investment's return than just dividends or interest. For a mutual fund it is an historical measure of the fund's overall performance, reflecting dividends and capital gains distributions, if any, and the increase (or decrease) in net asset value over a specific time period.

trading halt: Suspension of trading in a security while certain "material" news about the company is being disseminated, giving all investors an equal chance to evaluate the news and make buy or sell decisions. *See also:* material news.

Treasuries: Bills, notes, and bonds backed by the U.S. government and sold through the Department of the Treasury. The interest they pay investors is exempt from state and local taxes.

triple tax-exempt bonds: Municipal bonds exempt from federal, state, and local taxes for residents of the states and localities that issue the bonds.

underwriter: An investment banker who agrees to purchase shares of a new issue of securities and sell them to investors. The underwriter makes a profit on the spread—the difference between the price paid to the issuer and the public offering price.

value stocks: Securities whose valuations are below the market average or below their own historical average. They are generally cheap in price because they have been overlooked by other investors, having been beaten down in price because of a negative event, poor earnings, or they are in an industry that's in a slump.

vested benefits: The nonforfeitable dollar amount in a pension plan that belongs to the employee even if he/she leaves the job. An employee typically becomes vested after five years with the same firm. Until you're vested, you cannot take your employer's contributions and earnings with you if you leave your job, get fired, or retire. You can keep all *your* prior contributions and earnings, but your company's vesting schedule will determine how much of the company's money you can keep.

warrant: A security, usually issued with a bond or preferred stock, giving the owner the privilege of buying a specified number of shares of a stock at a fixed price, usually for a period of years.

webs: Webs is short for World Equity Benchmark Shares. It tracks the 17 foreign indexes maintained by Morgan Stanley. They offer access to some markets for which they are few similar investments. In 1998, fewer than 100,000 shares traded each day, making it sometimes difficult to find buyers.

yield: The income paid or earned by a security divided by its current price. For example, a $20 stock with an annual dividend of $1.50 has a 7.5% yield.

zero coupon bond: A bond that pays no current interest but is sold at a deep discount from face value. At maturity, all compounded interest is paid and the bondholder collects the full face value of the bond (usually $1,000). EE savings bonds are zeros.

Securities Index

This list includes closed-end funds since they trade as stocks on the exchanges.

MUTUAL FUND INDEX

INDEX

Real estate (*cont.*)
swapping property, 287
taxes and, 360, 367, 368, 369–371
principal residence, sale of, 284–285, 370
property taxes, reducing, 287–288
rental property, 286–287, 370–371, 373–374
2000 suggestions, 279–280
vacant lots, 280
Receivables, 394
Record-keeping, 49–53, 299
home improvements, 285, 370
Refinancing, mortgage, 7–8, 279, 283–284
Regulators, banking, 30
Reinvestment loads, 58
REITs, 288–289, 370
Relationship banking, 19
Remainder trusts, charitable, 357
Rental income, 286–287, 370–371, 373–374
bargains in rental real estate, 280
property location, 279
Repurchase agreements, 35
Restricted options, 172
Retail sales, 43
Retirement, 306–335
abroad, 309, 312
age discrimination, 334
annuities for, 331–332
CDs for, 21
continuing care communities, 306, 308–309
early, 310–311, 316
financial needs during, 313–314
fraud protection, 38–39
Ginnie Maes and, 127
goals, financial, 13
guaranteed investment contracts (GICs), 36, 328–329
housing options. *See* Housing
incapacity, 299
IRAs. *See* Individual retirement accounts (IRAs)
Keogh plans, 134, 328, 329, 356
late, 316
long-term care insurance, 343–345, 349–350, 361
Medicare. *See* Medicare
monthly dividends, 144, 167–168
nursing homes, 299, 343–345
pension plans. *See* Pension plans
portfolios for, 381–382
record-keeping, 52
of self-employed, 329–330
SEPs (simplified employee pension plans), 328, 329–330
SIMPLE plans (Savings Incentive Match Plan for Employees), 330
Social Security. *See* Social Security
taxes and, 310, 312, 335

working after, 233–234, 316–317, 335
zero coupon bonds for, 134
Return on equity (ROE), 146, 396
Revenue bonds, 118–119, 122
Reverse dollar cost averaging, 258, 259
Reverse mortgages, 307–308, 311–312
Revocable testamentary accounts, 29
Risk
derivatives, 34
Ginnie Maes, 127
high, for high returns, 191–192
interest rate, 144
investments ranked by, 51
life insurance, 36–37
maturities and, 33
money market fund, 25–26
municipal bond, 122–123
stock ownership, 143–144
Roth IRAs, 8–9, 320–321, 362
Rush hours, on-line trading, 266
Russell 2000 LEAPS (ZRU), 180, 222
Russell 2000 (RUT), 180, 222

Safe deposit boxes, 32
Salary reduction plans, 325–328
Sallie Maes, 130, 137
Savings
accounts, 9, 20, 41, 370
annuities for. *See* Annuities
budgeting for, 11, 15–16
for college costs. *See* College, paying for
mutual funds and, 55
for retirement, 314
strategies for, 384–385
Savings Association Insurance Fund (SAIF), 28, 29, 31, 406
Savings bonds, 41, 108–111
buying, 109
for college, 110–111, 291, 293
gifts of, 303
inflation-indexed (I-bonds), 108–109
pros and cons, 109
taxes and, 108, 110, 293, 370
Wizard program, 109
Savings & loans (S&Ls), 28, 31–32
Scale order, 251
Scams. *See* Fraud
Secondary markets, 106
Sector funds, 63, 65–66, 202
Sector index funds, 228
Secured bonds, 95
Securities. *See also* Investment(s); Portfolios
individual, mutual funds vs., 40
Treasury. *See* Treasury securities
Securities and Exchange Commission (SEC), 236, 250, 406
information on-line, 164, 274
Internet fraud and, 267–269
Securities index, 423–426
Securities Investor Protection Corporation (SIPC), 35–36

Select Sector SPDRs, 228
Self-employed persons
home-office deductions, 367
medical savings accounts (MSAs), 361
National Association for the Self-Employed (NASE), 311
portfolios for, 382–383
retirement business set-up, 334
retirement of, 329–330
year-end tax moves, 360
Self-regulatory organizations, 162
Selling short, 187, 209, 253–255
Senior citizens. *See* Retirement
Seven-year two-step mortgages, 281
Severance pay, 310–311
Shadow stock index, 161
Shareholders' letters, 393–394
Short positions, 187, 253–255
Short-term municipal bond funds, 63
Silver, 214, 367
SIMPLE plans (Savings Incentive Match Plan for Employees), 330
Simplified employee pension plans (SEPs), 328, 329–330
Single country funds, 77
Single-life annuity, 332
Single-state municipal bond funds, 63, 123, 124
Sinking funds, 98, 155–156
Small-cap stocks, 156, 223, 225–226
Small-order execution systems, 162
Socially responsible funds, 66–68
Social Security, 309, 314–317, 335
essential steps, 314–315
full benefits, age for, 317
late retirement and, 316
municipal bond income and, 125
post-retirement work and, 317, 333
taxes on. *See* Taxes
SPDRs, 223, 226–228
Special drawing rights (SDRs), 195
Special miscellaneous account (SMA), 262
Special subscription account (SSA), 184
Speculation, 191, 203–205
Speculation index, 400
Spiders (SPDRs), 223, 226–228
Spin-offs, 223, 224–225
Splits, 148, 223–224, 372
Spot market, 209
Spreads, 172, 178–179, 209, 210–211, 217
Stafford student loans, 297, 302
Standard & Poor's Corp.
bond ratings, 94, 96, 244
Computer & Business Equipment Index (OBR), 221
Depository Receipts (SPDRs), 223, 226–228
500 Index (SPX), 180, 221, 408, 411
500 LEAPS Index (LSW), 180, 221
400 Midcap Index, 409